AF872198

Dublin University Law Journal

2013 ♦ VOLUME 36

CLARUS
PRESS

Dublin University Law Journal

The *Dublin University Law Journal* follows the Oxford Standard for Citation of Legal Authorities (OSCOLA) and, as adapted for Ireland, OSCOLA Ireland, which is available for download at LegalCitation.ie.

SUBSCRIPTIONS
Subscriptions, individual copies and previous volumes are available from:
Clarus Press Ltd, Griffith Campus, South Circular Road, Dublin 8, Ireland.
Tel: 00353 1 415 0439; Fax: 00353 1 454 9265; e-mail: info@claruspress.ie.

ISSN: 0332-3250
ISBN: 978-1-905536-61-0

Dublin University Law Journal
2013 ♦ VOLUME 36

Table of Contents

Articles

Case Notes and Recent Developments

This Journal may be cited as (2013) 36 DULJ

Book Reviews

Dublin University Law Journal

The *Dublin University Law Journal* is an
anonymously peer-reviewed journal.

Articles and case notes for publication are welcomed and should be sent on an exclusive basis to the editors at dulj@tcd.ie. For further information on submission of manuscripts, see the *Dublin University Law Journal* website at www.dulj.ie.

Irish Consumer Law: Asserting a Domestic Agenda

Mary Donnelly and Fidelma White*

Abstract—This article asserts the importance of developing a distinct Irish consumer law and argues that the matter of consumer protection cannot simply be ceded to Europe. In developing this argument, the article first identifies the hybrid common law and European origins of Irish consumer law. It then traces the development of consumer law in this jurisdiction and focuses on the re-activation of the national consumer protection agenda, both in Ireland and across the European Union, in the last decade. The article also argues that a necessary pre-requisite in setting a domestic agenda is a comprehensive understanding of the nature and distinguishing features of the domestic consumer. Hence, the article undertakes a critical analysis of available data indicating the ways in which Irish consumers understand and use consumer law, drawing on annual surveys commissioned by the National Consumer Agency; an extensive EU wide Eurobarometer study on Consumer Empowerment and a focussed Irish study conducted in Winter 2012.

Introduction

Irish consumer law, as a discipline in its own right, has suffered an identity crisis, from its origins to the modern day. In part, this is because ongoing poverty post-independence[1] led to the late development of an Irish consumer society[2] and meant that issues of consumer protection did not receive the same kind

---

* Senior Lecturers, Faculty of Law, University College Cork. We are grateful to the UCC Law Faculty Strategic Research Fund, which provided research funding; to Dr Darius Whelan for his input; and to Cormac Gilroy, who acted as research assistant.

1. On the interlinkage between increased affluence and the development of a consumer society, see John Benson, *The Rise of Consumer Society in Britain, 1880–1980* (Longman 1994).
2. The limited development is attributed to the absence of an industrial revolution and to the high rates of emigration and poverty, which continued until the 1960s: see John Blackwell, 'Government, Economy and Society', in Frank Litton (ed), *Unequal Achievement, The Irish Experience 1957–1982* (Institute of Public Administration 1982) 43; Kieran A Kennedy, Thomas Giblin and Deirdre McHugh, *The Economic Development of Ireland in the Twentieth Century* (Routledge 1988); Tom Garvin, *Preventing the Future: Why Was Ireland so Poor for so Long* (Gill and Macmillan 2004); *cf* Patrick Atiyah, *The Rise and Fall of Freedom of Contract* (Clarendon Press 1979) 572–81.

of policy attention in Ireland as in more developed economies.[3] Even as Irish society became more affluent, mechanisms to take account of the consumer voice remained relatively underdeveloped and, in 2001, an OECD review of regulation in Ireland noted a poorly developed consumer culture and a policy bias in favour of producer interests.[4]

The establishment of a Consumer Strategy Group by the Minister of Enterprise, Trade and Employment in 2004 marked the beginnings of a policy shift towards greater recognition of consumer interests. The subsequent publication of the policy paper, *Make Consumers Count: a New Direction for Irish Consumers* led, in May 2007, to a new consumer protection body, the National Consumer Agency (NCA), being placed on a statutory footing.[5] Within a short time, in October 2008, the Minister for Finance announced an intention to amalgamate the National Consumer Agency with the Competition Authority to create a single enforcement and protection agency in respect of consumer and competition matters. The impetus for the proposed amalgamation was cost-saving in the context of the emerging economic crisis in the public finances rather than the pursuit of more effective consumer protection. Nevertheless, the proposed institutional architecture does offer potential for better consumer protection. While progress on implementing this proposal has been slow, at the time of writing, the amalgamating legislation is shortly expected to be brought before the Oireachtas.

As might be expected, the lack of policy concern with consumers was largely reflected in an impoverished legal framework. It was not until the late 1970s, with the enactment of the Consumer Information Act 1978 and the Sale of Goods and Supply of Services Act 1980 that the Irish consumer was identified and specifically protected. Shortly thereafter, however, the active legislative role of protecting the Irish consumer shifted to Europe and any possibility of a distinct Irish consumer law agenda was brought to an abrupt end. More recently, there have been moves to reclaim Irish consumer law. For instance, following the final report of the Sales Law Review Group,[6] a political commitment has been

3. See, for example, the United Kingdom, where the Moloney Committee on Consumer Protection was established in 1959 and reported in 1962: Board of Trade, *Final Report of the Committee on Consumer Protection*, Cmnd 1781/1962.
4. See Organisation for Economic Co-operation and Development, *Regulatory Reform in Ireland* (2001) <www.oecd.org/dataoecd/48/35/2475450.pdf> accessed 25 October 2013; see also see also Consumer Strategy Group, *Make Consumers Count: A New Direction for Irish Consumers* (April 2005).
5. Established by the Consumer Protection Act 2007, s 7. The NCA had been established on an interim basis in May 2005.
6. Sales Law Review Group, *Report on the Legislation Governing the Sale of Goods and Supply of Services* (2011) Prn. A11/1576. See Fidelma White, 'Report on the Legislation Governing the Sale of Goods and the Supply of Services: Something Old, Something New' (2012) 19 CLP 23; 'Sale of Goods Law Reform: An Irish Perspective' (2013) 42 CLWR 172.

made to introduce 'comprehensive' consumer rights legislation.[7] However, the scheme of the legislation has yet to be agreed and such legislation is unlikely to be forthcoming before the end of 2014 at the earliest.

This article argues that, in any reform of Irish consumer law, policy-makers and legislators need to understand the hybrid foundations of Irish consumer law and the specific needs and circumstances of the Irish consumer.[8] The matter of consumer protection cannot simply be ceded to Europe. In order to advance this argument, the article begins by identifying those aspects of the legal context that make Irish consumer law distinct. It then explores the reactivation of the domestic consumer protection agenda, both in Ireland and in the European Union, in the last decade. A necessary prerequisite in setting a domestic agenda is a comprehensive understanding of the nature and distinguishing features of the domestic consumer. Hence, the third part of this article undertakes a critical analysis of available data indicating the ways in which Irish consumers understand and use consumer law. In this, we draw on annual surveys commissioned by the National Consumer Agency between 2007 and 2012[9] together with an extensive EU wide Eurobarometer study on Consumer Empowerment conduced in 2010[10] and a focussed Irish study conducted in Winter 2012 ('the UCC study').[11] The data suggests a degree of dissonance between Irish consumers' self-perceptions and their actual levels of knowledge. It also indicates that Irish consumers may have similar levels of difficulty in understanding their rights under European-derived law and under law that is domestic in origin.

Tracing the Mixed Pedigree of Irish Consumer Law

In order to understand Irish consumer law, it is important to appreciate the mixed pedigree of the current legal framework. This may explain why the development of Irish consumer law has been relatively slow. The hybrid

7. See speech of Minister for Jobs, Enterprise and Innovation, 18 October 2011.
8. On the importance of recognising the specifics of individual jurisdictions' consumer cultures, see Thomas Wilhelmsson, 'The Abuse of the "Confident Consumer" as a Justification for EC Consumer Law' (2004) 27 JCP 317, 328.
9. The results of some of these studies are available at the NCA website: see *Consumer Empowerment and Complaining* (August 2009); *Consumer Empowerment and Complaining* (January 2010); *Consumer Empowerment and Complaints* (August 2011); *Consumer Empowerment and Consumer Service* (March 2012) <http://corporate.nca.ie/eng/Research_Zone/Reports/> accessed 25 October 2013.
10. Special Eurobarometer No 342 *Consumer Empowerment* (2011) <http://ec.europa.eu/consumers/consumer_empowerment/docs/report_eurobarometer_342_en.pdf> accessed 25 October 2013.
11. Mary Donnelly and Fidelma White, *Consumer Perception and Knowledge* (UCC 2013) <http://www.ucc.ie/en/media/academic/law/documents/UCCConsumerPerceptionsandKnowledgeReport2013forweb.pdf> accessed 25 October 2013.

common law and European foundations may also impact on the way in which Irish consumers understand their legal rights: a point investigated in the third part of this article.

Consumer Law as Commercial Law

Irish consumer law derives in the first instance from commercial law cases and statutes of the late Victorian period. Cases that we might today identify as early consumer law cases typically involved consumers purchasing goods for their own private use and consumption that turned out to be defective. As a result, this defect caused the consumer some injury or loss. The Cork case of *Wallis v Russell*,[12] which made its way ultimately to the English Court of Appeal, illustrates the point. In that case, the plaintiff sought to purchase two 'nice fresh crabs' for her tea from the defendant fishmonger. The defendant had no live crabs but offered boiled crabs instead. The plaintiff asked whether they were nice and fresh and the defendant assured her that they were. Having purchased the crabs, the plaintiff and others ate some that evening and subsequently became seriously ill. In order to seek redress in these circumstances the plaintiff had to resort to the Sale of Goods Act 1893 (hereinafter the 1893 Act): a commercial law statute.

The 1893 Act was one of a series of statutes that sought to consolidate a number of important areas of commercial law at this time.[13] It is notable that, while the 1893 Act made a distinction between sellers acting in a private capacity and sellers acting in the course of a business (eg s 14, which implied terms as to the quality of goods, only applied in the latter case), no such distinction was made in relation to the status of the buyer. As a result, buyers acting in the course of a business and private (ie consumer) buyers were treated as one, pursuant to this legislation. Mrs Wallis brought an action for breach of the implied term as to quality in s 14(1) of the 1893 Act. The Court of Appeal, affirming the earlier decision, found that the crabs had been bought for a particular purpose made known to the seller (ie for human consumption), and that the buyer had relied on the seller's skill and judgment, and hence there was a breach of s 14(1) because the crabs were not fit for their purpose and damages were awarded to the plaintiff in the sum of £150.[14]

---

12. [1902] 2 IR 585.
13. See also the Bills of Sale (Ireland) Acts 1879 and 1883; the Bills of Exchange Act 1882; the Factories Act 1889; the Partnership Act 1890; and the Marine Insurance Act 1906. See further Michael Bridge, 'The Evolution of Modern Sales Law' [1991] LMCLQ 52; Alan Rodger, 'The Codification of Commercial Law in Victorian Britain' (1992) 108 LQR 570.
14. There are numerous other examples from this period where private purchasers utilised the Sale of Goods Act 1893 to their advantage. In *Priest v Last* [1903] 2 KB 148, the purchaser of a hot-water bottle successfully sued the seller for injuries when the bottle burst, having being filled with hot water. The Court of Appeal had little difficulty in finding that the goods were not reasonably fit for their purpose under s 14(1) of the 1893 Act and damages were awarded. Again, in *Grant v Australian Knitting*

Cases of this nature led to questions about the relationship between commercial law and consumer law: in particular, whether consumer sales law was a separate discipline or merely a subset of commercial law.[15] Under the latter approach the particular needs and features of consumers were largely invisible with the legislative framework treating the parties as if they met on equal terms. The dominance of commercial law clearly influenced the development of consumer law in Ireland until the latter part of the twentieth century and arguably retarded its progress as a distinct discipline.

The Emergence of a Distinct Consumer Agenda

The 1893 Act governed Irish sales law for the majority of the twentieth century. The concept of statutory implied terms was borrowed from the 1893 Act and adapted to hire-purchase transactions in the Hire-Purchase Act 1946, which also made no distinction between commercial and consumer hirers.[16] It was not until the 1970s that the weaker position of consumers was identified and addressed in legislative form. In line with other jurisdictions, such as the UK and various Canadian provinces, concerns were raised about the suitability of the 1893 Act to a modern society and economy and, in particular, it was argued that the interests of consumers were not being protected.[17] In response to these concerns, the Sale of Goods and Supply of Services Act 1980 (hereinafter the 1980 Act) was enacted.[18] It made a number of important changes to the law. First, the 1980 Act recast the implied terms on quality, including by providing

---

Mills Ltd [1936] AC 85 a consumer bought woollen underwear and subsequently suffered severe dermatitis because there were excess sulphites, a chemical irritant, in the underwear, which had not been washed out in the manufacturing process. The Privy Council held, *inter alia,* that the goods were not fit for their purpose and were unmerchantable and hence there was a breach of s 14 of the South Australian Sale of Goods Act 1895 and damages were awarded.

15. See, eg, Francis Reynolds, 'The Applicability of General Rules of Private Law to Consumer Disputes' in Steven Andermann et al (eds), *Law and the Weaker Party* (vol 2, Abingdon 1982) 93–110.
16. In fact, the Bill as introduced was limited to transactions not exceeding £100 (as per the equivalent UK legislation at that time); however, this limitation did not find its way into the legislation as enacted.
17. See National Prices Commission, Occasional Paper No 9, *Consumer Protection Law in America, Canada and Europe* (Stationery Office 1973) (known as the Whincup Report); National Consumer Advisory Council, Submission to the Minister for Industry and Commerce on Proposals for Legislation to Assure the Consumers' Interests (Stationery Office 1974); Dáil Debates 16 November 1978, vol 309, no 7, cols 1100–1106.
18. The 1893 Act remains the principal Act in Ireland today, with Part II of the 1980 Act amending certain provisions of the 1893 Act by substitution and introducing some new provisions: together this legislation is referred to as the Sale of Goods Acts 1893 and 1980: 1980 Act, s 9.

a statutory definition of 'merchantable quality'[19]; adding a few more implied terms to the mix[20]; as well as regulating, for the first time, product guarantees provided by manufacturers and others.[21] Second, the remedies regime was amended[22] and a new consumer right to request 'cure' was introduced to supplement the buyer's primary right to reject goods (and claim a refund of the price) where goods are defective.[23] Third, and perhaps most significantly, rules on the enforceability of exclusion clauses were introduced whereby clauses that sought to exclude or limit the liability of sellers for breach of the statutory implied terms were rendered void against consumers.[24]

The 1980 Act represented a major step forward in the development of Irish consumer law.[25] Moreover, it was part of a package of legislative measures that began to address the position of the Irish consumer at that time. Other such measures included the Consumer Information Act 1978, which amongst other things established the Office of the Director of Consumer Affairs; the Trading Stamps Act 1980 and the Pyramid Selling Act 1980. However, many innovative provisions from the Sale of Goods and Supply of Services Act 1980, such as those in relation to contracts made away from business premises,[26] standard form contracts,[27] and the size of type in printed contracts,[28] were never brought into effect. Instead from the 1980s onwards, the development of consumer protection was dominated by a steady flow of EC/EU consumer protection measures in the form of directives, and the impetus for the further development of consumer law shifted from Ireland to Europe.

The Shift to Europe

The original founding treaty of the European Economic Community, the Treaty of Rome 1957, contained only five explicit references to consumers, all of which were essentially incidental in nature.[29] Nonetheless, as Weatherill shows, notwithstanding this 'barren Treaty background', European consumer policy began to develop in the years following the Treaty, through the application of core EC provisions on market integration and through the development

19. 1980 Act, s 10, which substitutes redrafted ss 10–15 into the 1893 Act.
20. 1980 Act, ss 12–13.
21. 1980 Act, ss 15–19.
22. 1980 Act, s 20, which substitutes redrafted ss 34–35 into the 1893 Act.
23. 1980 Act, s 21, which substitutes a redrafted s 53 into the 1893 Act.
24. 1980 Act, s 3 and s 22, which substituted a redrafted s 55 into the 1893 Act.
25. Indeed, various aspects of this legislation was recognised as progressive and innovative by the European Commission in its preparations for the consumer sales directive: see the Green Paper on Guarantees for Consumer Goods and After-Sales Services, COM(93)509, 6 and 96.
26. 1980 Act, s 50.
27. 1980 Act, s 52.
28. 1980 Act, s 53.
29. Stephen Weatherill, *EU Consumer Law and Policy* (Edward Elgar 2005) 3.

of 'soft' law initiatives and greater harmonisation of national laws.[30] It was, however, only in the mid-1970s that the European consumer protection agenda began to solidify with the introduction of a Council Resolution establishing a preliminary programme for a European consumer protection and information policy.[31] Progress on the European agenda was far from dramatic with only a small number of measures being introduced in the following 10 years, primarily relating to food labelling.[32] It was the mid-1980s before a more activist legislative agenda became evident, with the introduction of a number of consumer directives during this period.[33] These measures were introduced in the context of harmonisation and market integration. The measures were a reaction to the divergence in national legal systems, which were seen as barriers to trade and contrary to the perfection of the internal market.

It was not until the Maastricht Treaty in 1992 that specific legislative competence in respect of consumer protection was established. This competence derives from art 153(1) EC (now art 169 the Treaty on the Functioning of the European Union, hereinafter TFEU), which states that:

> In order to promote the interests of consumers and to ensure a high level of consumer protection, the Union shall contribute to protecting the health, safety and economic interests of consumers, as well as to promoting their right to information, education and to organise themselves in order to safeguard their interest.

The introduction of a specific consumer-protection competence was generally welcomed by consumer groups as providing 'a potential constitutional basis for the development of an EC strategy on consumer protection which is independent of harmonization policy in particular and the process of market integration in general'.[34] However, Weatherill argues that, in practice, the introduction of an explicit legislative competence did not impact to any significant extent on the nature of directives introduced. Instead, these continued to fit with a harmonisation/market integration agenda and a potentially more broad-based consumer agenda was not pursued.[35] The stream of directives continued post 1992,[36] leading

30. ibid 4.
31. Council Resolution [1975] C92/1. Chronologically, this mirrors the emerging Irish interest in this regard.
32. Weatherill, *EU Consumer Law*, 9.
33. See, eg, Council Directive 84/450/EEC on misleading advertising; Council Directive 85/374/EEC concerning liability for defective products; Council Directive 85/577/EEC to protect the consumer in respect of contracts negotiated away from business premises; Council Directives 87/102/EEC and 90/88/EEC concerning consumer credit; Council Directive 90/314/EEC on package travel, package holidays and package tours.
34. Weatherill, *EU Consumer Law*, 17.
35. ibid 18.
36. See, eg, Council Directive 93/13/EEC on unfair terms in consumer contracts; Council Directive 98/27/EC on injunctions for the protection of consumer interests; Council

to the establishment of a wide-ranging consumer *acquis*. Crucially, however, the European legislative agenda did not extend to the comprehensive regulation of consumer contracts.[37]

A number of features of early European consumer law, and of the Irish response to this, contributed to a stagnation in the development of the nascent Irish consumer law. First, inevitably, consumer protection directives constitute a compromise between the civil and common law.[38] This kind of cross-fertilisation results in the introduction of concepts into diverse legal systems in which there may be no conceptual grounding within existing frameworks. From a common law perspective, a classic example of this is the reliance in the unfair terms directive[39] on the civil law, and in particular, the German conception of 'good faith' (in German 'Treu und Glauben') which recognises an explicit requirement of fair and equitable dealing.[40] As has been pointed out by numerous commentators, this concept of 'good faith' does not sit comfortably within the common law tradition.[41] The difficulties with assimilating the concept into the common law tradition are evident in the decision of the House of Lords in *Director General of Fair Trading v First National Bank Plc*.[42] Here, Lord Bingham described the requirement of good faith as 'one of fair and open dealing'.[43] The House of Lords unanimously held that the applicable term met this standard notwithstanding that Lord Bingham had 'no hesitation' in accepting the submissions of the Director General of Fair Trading that the 'situation is unacceptable'[44] and that it was 'readily understandable that a borrower may be disagreeably surprised if he finds that his contractual interest obligation continues to mount despite his duly

---

Directive 97/7/EC on the protection of consumers in respect of distance contracts; Council Directive 99/44/EC on certain aspects of consumer sales and associated guarantees.

37. Hans Schulte-Nölke and Lubos Tichy (eds), *Perspectives for European Consumer Law: Towards a Directive on Consumer Rights and Beyond* (Sellier 2010) 1.
38. See Hans W Micklitz, Norbert Reich and Peter Rott, *Understanding European Consumer Law* (Intersentia 2008).
39. Directive 93/13/EEC on unfair terms in consumer contracts, [1993] OJ L 95/29.
40. art 3(1) of the Directive states that a term shall be regarded as unfair 'if, contrary to the requirement of good faith, it causes a significant imbalance in the parties' rights and obligations arising under the contract, to the detriment of the consumer' and the recitals to the Directive outline a set of factors to be taken into account in making an assessment of good faith.
41. See Roger Brownsword and Geraint Howells, 'The Implementation of the EC Directive on Unfair Terms in Consumer Contracts: Some Unresolved Questions' [1995] JBL 243; Roger Brownsword, 'Two Concepts of Good Faith' (1994) 7 JCL 197; Hugh Collins, 'Good Faith in European Contract Law' (1994) 14 OJLS 229.
42. [2001] UKHL 52.
43. [2001] UKHL 52 [17]. This description was also adopted by Lord Steyn at [36].
44. [2001] UKHL 52 [24].

paying the instalments ordered by the court'.[45] The decision has been criticised as failing 'to reassure consumers that the law really works for their protection or benefit'.[46] In Ireland, the European Communities (Unfair Terms in Consumer Contracts) Regulations 1995 (which transposes the unfair terms directive)[47] would appear to have had a very limited impact for consumers. There has been only one reported case involving the Regulations and the analysis in the case is limited.[48] The limited recourse to the Regulations in practice may derive from a similar difficulty with conceptual assimilation into Irish law.[49]

A second feature of early European consumer law, derived in part from the same foundation of necessary compromise, was the fragmented nature of the measures introduced. Consumer-protection directives generally applied only in specific areas, based around distribution methods[50] or particular contract types.[51] As described by Schulte-Nölke and Tichy, '[t]he individual directives are badly inter-coordinated. There are gaps and contradictions. The legislative quality of the directives is far below the usual quality of national legislation.'[52]

Many of these difficulties with European consumer law could have been addressed at a domestic level during the transposition process. The bulk of community directives in this early phase of development were minimum harmonising measures, harmonising consumer laws in Member States to a designated minimum level, leaving Member States the freedom to pursue a higher level of consumer protection in keeping with their particular

---

45. [2001] UKHL 52 [24]. The case concerned a term in a loan contact that allowed the lender to continue to charge the contractual rate of interest after judgment for default had been entered using language that was far from clear and accessible.
46. Meryll Dean, 'Defining Unfair Terms in Consumer Contracts – Crystal Ball Gazing *Director General of Fair Trading v First National Bank Plc*' (2002) 65 MLR 773, 780.
47. SI 27/1995 as amended by the European Communities (Unfair Terms in Consumer Contracts) (Amendment) Regulations 2000, SI 307/2000.
48. See *Marshall v Capitol Holdings Ltd* [2006] IEHC 271.
49. See Edoardo Ferrante, 'Contractual Disclosure and Remedies under the Unfair Contract Terms Directive' in Geraint Howells, André Janssen and Reiner Schulze (eds), *Information Rights and Obligations: A Challenge for Party Autonomy and Transactional Fairness* (Ashgate 2005) 115, who also suggests that the directive's 'easy reception into the German cultural environment' may be explained because it was so similar to German law.
50. See, eg, Council Directive 85/577 to protect the consumer in respect of contracts negotiated away from business premises; Council Directive 97/7 on the protection of consumers in respect of distance contracts (both now amended and consolidated in Directive 2011/83; Council Directive 2002/65 on the distance marketing of financial services.
51. See, eg, Council Directives 87/102/EC and 90/88/EC concerning consumer credit repealed and replaced by Council Directive 2008/48/EC; Council Directive 90/314/EC on package travel, package holidays and package tours.
52. Schulte-Nölke and Tichy, *Perspectives for European Consumer Law*, 1.

socio-economic circumstances and consumer needs and expectations. In general, however, the Irish approach was to harmonise to the minimum level only[53] and not to enhance consumer protection beyond that afforded at a European level.[54] This approach is in contrast with that taken by many other Member States that have been more prepared to expand, sometimes significantly, the protections afforded to consumers at transposition stage.[55] Thus, the compromises made at a European level, which were not intended to dictate the scope of domestic consumer protection measures, became reified in Irish law.

Other aspects of the Irish approach to transposition also contributed to the stagnation of Irish consumer protection law. Transposing measures tended, perhaps because of the introduction of unfamiliar concepts, to follow closely the original wording of the directive. As a result, any uncertainties about the meaning of terms or omissions in the directive are replicated in the Irish transposing measure and there is no attempt at clarification. This cautious approach may have meant that Ireland was not at any risk of being found to be in breach of its transposition obligations. However, it also meant that the necessary measures in order to integrate European legislation into domestic law were not taken. A further feature of the Irish approach to transposition was a preference for a standalone legal instrument, usually a statutory instrument, without any attempt to address or integrate into pre-existing legal rules. The result is a number of unconsolidated measures giving rise to inconsistencies and, at times, conflicts.[56]

Reactivating the Domestic Agenda

A number of domestic initiatives, which commenced midway through the last decade, led to a reactivation of the domestic consumer protection agenda. At around the same time, European institutions began to consolidate European consumer protection law.

The potential for conflict was inevitable and, as discussed below, this was played out in the protracted negotiations leading to the eventual adoption

53. One notable exception to this was the Consumer Credit Act 1995 which, in addition to transposing Directives 87/102 and 90/88, introduced detailed consumer-protection measures in respect of hire purchase, consumer hire and housing loans, and expanded considerably on the European legislation in many respects.
54. See Hans Schulte-Nölke et al (eds), *Consumer Law Compendium: The Consumer Acquis and its Transposition in the Member States* (Sellier 2008) 42.
55. For a state-by-state overview, see *Consumer Law Compendium* ibid.
56. See, eg, the Sale of Goods Act 1893, as amended by Part II of the Sale of Goods and Supply of Services Act 1980, and the European Community (Certain Aspects of the Sale of Consumer Goods and Associated Guarantees) Regulations 2003 (SI 11/2003). See further Fidelma White, 'The EC Directive on Certain Aspects of Consumer Sale and Associated Guarantees: One Step Forward, Two Steps Back?' (2000) 7 CLP 3.

of Directive 2011/83/EU on consumer rights.[57] First, however, the steps in the reactivation of the domestic agenda are reviewed.

Reinvigorating the Irish Agenda

The reinvigoration of the Irish consumer protection agenda came first in the context of financial services. The gaping lacunae in consumer protection in this context emerged in the wake of consumer-related scandals in the late 1990s.[58] The difficulties arose in part from the absence at this time of a clear consumer protection agenda in respect of financial services. Besides Directives 87/102/EC and 90/88/EC concerning consumer credit, there had been limited European initiatives in the broader financial services field. The European gap had not been filled at a domestic level. Instead, the task of consumer protection fell somewhere between the Central Bank (which was responsible for prudential regulation) and the Office of the Director of Consumer Affairs (which had limited expertise in the financial services sphere). Acknowledging the regulatory gap, the then Governor of the Central Bank noted that '[t]here is, somewhere, a cross-over point where prudential supervision ends and what I might describe as consumer protection begins. I have to admit this is a grey area.'[59]

The legislative response to the gap identified included the establishment of the Central Bank and Financial Services Regulatory Authority of Ireland,[60] which had a strong consumer protection agenda; the creation of the statutory position of Consumer Director;[61] the establishment of a Financial Services Consumer Consultative Panel;[62] and a statutory Financial Services Ombudsman (FSO) to provide consumer redress. One of the most significant innovations of the Consumer Director was the introduction of an enforceable Consumer Protection Code with a statutory basis.[63] Although a number of aspects of this

---

57. [2011] OJ L304/64.
58. The most prominent was the deliberate over-charging of customers at National Irish Bank (NIB). Following a journalistic investigation, inspectors were appointed (under s 8(1) of the Companies Act 1990) to investigate the way in which NIB had conducted its business. The investigation concluded that NIB had 'loaded' certain accounts of more troublesome customers in relation both to interest and bank charges: see *Report on the Investigations into the Affairs of National Irish Bank Ltd and National Irish Bank Financial Services Ltd by High Court Inspectors Mr Justice Blayney and Tom Grace FCA* (Office of Director of Corporate Enforcement 2004).
59. Speech by the Governor of the Central Bank, Mr Maurice O'Connell, to the *Joint Oireachtas Committee on Finance and the Public Service*.
60. Established by the Central Bank and Financial Services Authority of Ireland Act 2003.
61. Central Bank Act 1942, s 33S(1)(b), inserted by Central Bank and Financial Services Authority of Ireland Act 2003, s 26.
62. Central Bank Act 1942, s 57CW, inserted by CBFSAI Act 2004, s 17.
63. On the innovative nature of the Code, see Mary Donnelly, 'The Consumer Protection Code: A New Departure in the Regulation of Irish Financial Services Providers' (2006) 13 CLP 271; 'The Consumer Protection Code: Regulatory Innovation from the Irish

regime are now defunct,[64] both the Code and the FSO continue in operation,[65] with the Code having been substantially expanded in 2012.[66]

The establishment of a Consumer Strategy Group in 2004 to make proposals for the development of a national consumer strategy heralded a widening of the agenda beyond financial services. In its 2005 Report, *Make Consumers Count: A New Direction for Irish Consumers*, along with many sector specific recommendations (in relation to groceries, pharmaceuticals, and transport, for example) the Group recommended major structural change, which resulted in the establishment of an independent National Consumer Agency, on an interim basis,[67] to replace the Office of Director of Consumer Affairs, with direct responsibility for consumer research, advocacy, information, enforcement, and education and awareness.[68] Underlying many of the recommendations of the Group was a recognition that '[i]nformed and empowered consumers are a powerful social and economic force'.[69]

The momentum to review and reform continued with the establishment of an expert group, the Sales Law Review Group, in 2008. The Group's focus was on both commercial and consumer sales law and its remit included both domestic and European agendas. Thus, the Group was asked to review the general sales law provisions of the Sale of Goods Acts 1893 and 1980 and to make recommendations for an appropriate modern scheme and also to examine the provisions of the proposed consumer rights directive and to make recommendations as to 'how the Directive and Irish contract and sales law may best be integrated'.[70]

Financial Regulator' in Deborah Parry et al (eds), *Yearbook of Consumer Law 2009* (Ashgate 2008).

64. The office of Consumer Director (together with the Central Bank and Financial Services Authority of Ireland) and the Financial Services Consumer Consultative Panel were abolished by the Central Bank Reform Act 2010 and responsibility for aspects of consumer protection in financial services (proving information to consumers and promoting the development of financial education and capability) was transferred to the National Consumer Agency.
65. On the current operations of the FSO, see Mary Donnelly, 'The Financial Services Ombudsman: Asking the "Existential Question"' (2012) 35 DULJ 229.
66. See Mary Donnelly, 'Revisions to the Consumer Protection Code: Expanding the Scope of Financial Services Regulation' (2012) 19 CLP 3.
67. The Agency was put on a statutory basis in the Consumer Protection Act 2007, Part 2. The 2007 Act also transposed Directive 2005/29/EC on unfair business-to-consumer commercial practices into Irish law: see further Nathan Reilly, 'The Consumer Protection Act 2007: Rationalising the Regulation of Misleading Commercial Practices in Ireland' (2008) 6 CLP 127 and 157.
68. See further Consumer Protection Act 2007, s 8.
69. Consumer Strategy Group, *Make Consumers Count: A New Direction for Irish Consumers* (2005) viii.
70. Sales Law Review Group, *Report on the Legislation Governing the Sale of Goods and Supply of Services* (2011) Prn A11/1576, 7.

A Changing European Agenda: Moving towards Maximum Harmonisation

At around the same time as Irish consumer law was beginning to re-establish itself, the European institutions were seeking to bring a new level of coherence and direction to European consumer law as part of a 'more aggressive internal market strategy'.[71] This led to a shift in the European legislative agenda towards the introduction of 'full' or 'maximum' harmonising measures.[72] As described in the *Green Paper on the Review of the Consumer Acquis*, maximum harmonisation means that 'no Member State could apply stricter rules than the ones laid down at Community level'.[73] Thus, maximum harmonisation does not mean the introduction of a uniform law; rather, as Mak describes 'the degree of harmonisation can only be seen within the context, or indeed *within the scope* of regulation set down by the directive'.[74] This approach was favoured at a European institutional level because it was argued by the European Commission that it would lead to a more coherent legislative framework within the European Union, thereby encouraging cross-border shopping while at the same time ensuring a more competitive environment by reducing transaction costs and preventing consumer protection from being used as 'goldplating' in order to restrict new entrants in the market.[75] From 2005 on, a number of significant maximum harmonisation consumer protection measures were introduced. These included the Unfair Commercial Practices Directive[76]; the Consumer Credit Directive[77] and the Payment Services Directive.[78]

The move towards maximum harmonisation was inevitably controversial.[79] Generally, these kinds of measures aim to advance business interests by lowering transaction costs and increasing consumer confidence in cross-border shopping.[80] From a consumer perspective, there is considerably less enthusiasm. Critics argue

---

71. Norbert Reich, 'From Minimal to Full to "Half" Harmonisation' in James Devenney and Mel Kenny (eds), *European Consumer Protection: Theory and Practice* (Cambridge University Press 2012) 3.
72. See *Green Paper on the Review of the Consumer Acquis* COM (2006) 744 final (8 February 2007).
73. ibid 10.
74. Vanessa Mak, 'Review of the Consumer Acquis: Towards Maximum Harmonisation' (2009) 17 ERPL 55.
75. On the Commission's 'allocative efficiency' argument (and the underlying flaws with this argument), see Hans W Micklitz and Norbert Reich, 'Crónica de Una Muerta Anunciada: The Commission Proposal for a "Directive on Consumer Rights"' (2009) 46 CMLR 471, 474–76.
76. Directive 2005/29/EC [2005] OJ L 149/22.
77. Directive 2008/48/EC.
78. Directive 2007/64/EC.
79. Alexandre Duterque, 'Do We Really Want a *Ius Commune* for EU Consumer Protection?' (2012) 35 DULJ 72.
80. Iain Ramsay, 'Regulation and the Constitution of the Single Market: The Contribution of Consumer Law' (2010) 50 CBLJ 322.

that the maximum harmonisation project lacks a sufficiently strong empirical basis to support either the lower transactions costs or the increased cross-border consumer confidence arguments.[81] Even in a fully harmonised context, Member States have different interpretations of concepts (for example 'good faith') and different ways of giving effect to the law. Thus, from a trader's perspective, while the need to take legal advice on different jurisdictions before commencing to trade might be reduced, it would not be removed.[82] In respect of increased consumer confidence, it has been convincingly argued that the barriers to cross-border shopping derive primarily from psychological factors, based on language and culture, and that these are not addressed by formal legal harmonising measures.[83]

While the benefits for consumers from maximum harmonisation are questionable, the disadvantages from a consumer perspective are considerable. This is especially the case for consumers in more developed consumer societies, where the effect of maximum harmonisation may well be to lower consumer protection standards.[84] In an Irish context, the disapplication of much of the Consumer Protection Code in respect of consumers to whom the Consumer Credit Directive and the Payment Services Directive (both maximum harmonisation measures) apply shows the negative practical impact of maximum harmonisation from a consumer perspective.[85] Other difficulties derive from the complex apparatus of the European legislative framework, which means that law-making is unable to respond quickly to newly emerging situations. Additionally, because the measure is applicable across the EU, it is unable to take account of the specific contexts of consumer societies at different stages of development.[86]

---

81. See Geraint Howells and Thomas Wilhelmsson, 'EC Consumer Law: Has it Come of Age?' (2003) 28 ELR 370, 376.
82. See Marco Loos, 'Full Harmonisation as a Regulatory Concept and its Consequences for the National Legal Orders: The Example of the Consumer Rights Directive' (University of Amsterdam, Centre for the Study of European Contract Law, Working Papers Series 2010/03) 9.
83. See Gary Low, 'The (Ir)relevance of Harmonisation and Legal Diversity in European Contract Law: A Perspective from Psychology' (2010) 18 ERPL 288; see also Ramsay, 'Regulation', 335, who argues that the impact analysis for the proposed consumer rights directive had difficulty in linking low levels of cross-border shopping to legal regulation.
84. See Stephen Weatherill, 'Maximum versus Minimum Harmonisation: Choosing between Unity and Diversity in the Search for the Soul of the Internal Market' in Niamh Nic Shuibhne and Laurence Gormley (eds), *From Single Market to Economic Union: Essays in Memory of John Usher* (Oxford University Press 2012) 175.
85. See Consumer Protection Code 2012, 6. The disapplied measures in respect of consumer credit in CPC 2012 are more advantageous for consumers than those contained in Directive 2008/48/EC and transposed by the European Communities (Consumer Credit Agreements) Regulations 2010, SI 281/2010.
86. See Vanessa Mak, 'The Degree of Harmonisation in the Proposed Consumer Rights Directive: A Review in Light of Liability for Products' in Geraint Howells and Reiner Schulze (eds), *Modernising and Harmonising Consumer Contract Law* (Sellier 2009) 318.

Many of these concerns with the maximum harmonisation agenda came to the fore in the context of the proposals for a consumer rights directive.[87] These proposals emerged from the harmonisation agenda relating to European contract law that started in 2001, when the European Commission published a Communication on *European Contract Law*.[88] It is notable that 'European contract law', in so far as it existed at the time, did so largely in the form of consumer directives.[89] Subsequently, in 2003, the Commission issued an Action Plan proposing to improve the quality and coherence of European contract law by establishing a Common Frame of Reference (CFR) to act as a 'toolbox' or handbook containing common principles, terminology and model rules to be used by the European legislator when making or amending legislation.[90] It was also proposed to review the *acquis* in the area of consumer contract law, to remove inconsistencies and fill regulatory gaps.[91] As a result of this review, in October 2008, and before the CFR was finalised, the Commission submitted a proposal for a directive on consumer rights.[92] This proposal sought to amalgamate and rationalise four existing consumer directives (the door-step selling directive[93]; the distance selling directive[94]; the consumer sales directive[95]; and the unfair terms in consumer contracts directive[96]) into one new maximum harmonised consumer rights directive. Shortly thereafter,

87. Jan M Smits, 'Full Harmonisation of Consumer Law? A Critique of the Draft Directive on Consumer Rights' (2010) 1 ERPL 5 at 9.
88. COM(2001) 398 final. See further, eg, Robert Clark, 'Irish Contract Law Reform and the European Commission's Agenda' (2001) 7 BR 126; Walter Van Gerven, 'Codifying European Private Law? Yes, if ...!' (2002) 27 ELR 156. In 2010, the Commission published a new Green Paper on European Contract Law: COM(2010) 348 final. The policy options considered therein ranged from: non-binding model contract rules; to an optional (28th system) European contract law; to harmonisation of national contract law by means of a directive or regulation; to a fully fledged European Civil Code.
89. For example, between 1985 and 1999, seven consumer law directives dealing with contractual issues were adopted. Other directives addressing contractual issues but outside the consumer law remit include Directive 86/653/EEC on self-employed commercial agents; Directive 2000/31/EC on e-commerce and Directive 2000/35 on combating late payment in commercial transactions.
90. See, eg, Mel Kenny, 'The 2003 Action Plan on European Contract Law: Is the Commission Running Wild?' (2003) 28 ELR 538.
91. Commission Communication on European Contract Law and the Revision of the *Aquis*: The Way Forward, COM(2004) 651 final.
92. COM(2008) 614.
93. Directive 85/577 /EC [1985] OJ L 372/31.
94. Directive 97/7/EC [1997] OJ L 144/19.
95. Directive 1999/44/EC [1999] OJ L 171/12.
96. Directive 93/13/EC [1993] OJ L 95/29.

in 2009, following comparative research across the Member States of the European Community, the draft Common Frame of Reference was published.[97]

Maximum Harmonisation: A Step too Far?

Notwithstanding the re-emergence of a domestic consumer protection agenda at around the same time, there is little evidence that the encroachment on domestic competence brought about by maximum harmonisation was a source of initial Irish concern.[98] This changed, however, when the Sales Law Review Group (SLRG) examined the proposed consumer rights directive. In three of the four areas covered by the proposed directive – door-step selling; distance selling and unfair terms – there had been no prior Irish law when the three directives were originally transposed and so they were incorporated without any difficulty. Further, any revision to this legislation, in the form of the proposed consumer rights directive, would be equally easy to assimilate into Irish law.

However, the position in relation to consumer sales law was different. When Directive 1999/44 on consumer sales and associated guarantees was transposed into Irish law, this was done on the basis that the directive was a minimum harmonising measure and Member States were free to maintain higher levels of consumer protection. It was arguable that some aspects of domestic sales law, at that time, pursuant to the Sale of Goods Acts 1893 and 1980, provided a greater level of consumer protection, in particular as regards consumer remedies. Under the Sale of Goods Acts, the buyer's primary remedy when supplied with non-conforming or defective goods, is to reject the goods (and seek a refund of any price paid), thereby terminating the contract.[99] In contrast, the remedy regime found in Directive 1999/44 ranks the remedies of repair and replacement as primary remedies and leaves the right to repudiate or terminate the contract (and reject the goods) as a remedy of last resort.[100] When Directive 1999/44 was transposed into Irish law, consumers were offered the option to assert their rights and seek remedies under the tradition Sale of Goods Acts rules or

97. See Lucinda Miller, 'The Common Frame of Reference and the Feasibility of a Common Contract Law in Europe' [2007] JBL 378; Simon Whittaker, 'A Framework of Principle for European Contract Law?' (2009) 125 LQR 616; Reinhard Jansen and Nils Zimmermann, '"A European Civil Code in All but Name": Discussing the Nature and Purposes of the Draft Common Frame of Reference' (2010) 69 CLJ 98.
98. See, for example, the Irish response to the *Green Paper on the Consumer Acquis*, which was that it was too early to take a stance on the question of full harmonisation given the limited experience at that time: see Loos, 'Full Harmonisation', 6.
99. An additional action for damages for any loss suffered is also permissible: Sale of Goods Act 1893, s 53.
100. As per art 3(5) only where the rights of repair or replacement are impossible, disproportionate, or where the seller does not complete repair or replacement within a reasonable time, and without significant inconvenience to the consumer, can the consumer progress to the remaining remedies of price reduction or rescission.

the newer European rules.[101] The maintenance of the primary right to reject was permissible due to the minimum harmonising nature of Directive 1999/44. However, the consumer rights directive as proposed would require the Irish government to amend the law to remove the right to reject as a primary remedy for consumer buyers and instead to allow its use only as a last resort. On the advice of the Sales Law Review Group,[102] the Irish negotiators were not willing to agree such a change in the levels of consumer protection for Irish consumers.

Other governments were similarly minded, in particular the UK and French governments.[103] Others again were opposed to the maximum harmonising nature in relation to other aspects of the directive. Ultimately, in order to achieve agreement, large aspects of the proposal dealing with consumer sales and unfair terms were jettisoned and the final version of the directive adopted was a considerably more modest measure than that originally envisaged by the Commission.[104] Alongside this, the Commission proposed an optional Common European Sales Law in the form of a regulation. If adopted, this regulation will not replace national contract laws but will offer consumers and businesses an optional (28th system) of European sales law. The choice of a regulation reflects a growing recognition at a European level that directives (and in particular maximum harmonising measures) may not be the most effective way to achieve the economic goal of enhanced cross-border trade and that targeted regulations to deal with the particulars of this context may be preferable.[105] More generally, the Commission's experience in respect of the consumer rights directive means that it is unlikely to attempt a repeat on the scale in the original proposal. From an Irish perspective, too, the government's assertion of the specific concerns of the Irish consumer is to be welcomed.

Policy Convergence – Confident/Informed Consumer

Even if, at an operational level, the maximum harmonisation agenda has stalled, there is still a degree of policy convergence around the paradigm of 'consumer' at the heart of the European consumer agenda. This is the well-informed,

---

101. See the European Communities (Certain Aspects of the Sale of Consumer Goods and Associated Guarantees) Regulations 2003, SI 13/2003, regs 3(2)–3(4).
102. See Sales Law Review Group, *Position Paper on the Proposal for a Directive of the European Parliament and of the Council on Consumer Rights* (May 2009): see further <www.djei.ie/commerce/consumer/slrg.htm accessed 25 October 2013.
103. On the right to reject in French law see Lucinda Miller, 'The Common Frame of Reference and the Feasibility of a Common Contract Law in Europe' [2007] JBL 378, 391–96; Andrea Pinna, 'La Transposition en Droit Français' (2001) 9 ERPL 223.
104. Directive 2011/83 on consumer rights, [2011] OJ L304/64.
105. See Christian Twigg-Flesner, 'Goodbye Harmonisation by Directives, Hello Cross-Border Only Regulation? A Way Forward for EU Consumer Contract Law' (2011) 7 ERCL 235; Christoph Busch and Ronny Domröse, 'From a Horizontal Instrument to a Common European Sales' (2012) 1 JECML 48; Ewoud Hondius, 'Common European Sales Law: If It Does Not Help, It Won't Harm Either(?)' (2013) 21 ERPL 1.

confident, empowered consumer.[106] The creation of this kind of consumer through the provision of information is a cornerstone of European consumer protection law and policy.[107] In adopting this focus, European and Irish consumer law and policy are similar. The primary foundation for this model of consumer protection is economic growth rather than individual protection.[108] Thus, the Commission in its Consumer Policy Strategy 2007–2013 states: 'The Internal Market cannot function properly without consumer confidence. Adequate consumer protection is necessary for growth and competitiveness.'[109] The goal is to ensure that sufficient numbers of consumers have sufficient levels of confidence to engage in the market and achieve the economic goal of market growth.[110]

The choice of a policy focus on the confident consumer through information provision has been critiqued on a number of grounds.[111] At a very basic level, the information provided may never actually reach the consumer.[112] Secondly, drawing on insights derived from behavioural economics, critics challenge the presumption that consumers act rationally on the basis of information received.[113] Thirdly, behavioural economics also lends doubt to the view that more

---

106. Both case law and legislation subscribe to this stereotype. For instance, average consumers have been described as 'reasonably well informed and reasonably observant and circumspect': see Case 210/96 *Gut Springenheideb GmbH v Oberkreisdirektordes Kreises Steinfurt* [1998] ECR I–04657. See also Recital 18 of Directive 2005/29/EC, [2005] OJ L149/22 (the Unfair Commercial Practices Directive), which 'takes as a benchmark the average consumer, who is reasonably well-informed and reasonably observant and circumspect'.

107. See Michelle Everson, 'Legal Constructions of the Consumer' in Frank Trentmann (ed), *The Making of the Consumer: Knowledge, Power and Identity in the Modern World* (Berg 2006) 111.

108. Geraint Howells, 'The Potential and Limits of Consumer Empowerment by Information' (2005) 32 JLS 349, 350.

109. Commission Communication, 'Healthier, Safer, More Confident Citizens – A Health and Consumer Protection Strategy', COM (2005) 115 final.

110. See Wilhelmsson, 'Abuse'.

111. For a summary of the critiques, see Howells, 'Potential and Limits'; Iain Ramsay 'From Truth in Lending to Responsible Lending' in Howells et al (eds), *Information Rights*; Iain Ramsay, 'Consumer Protection in the Era of Informational Capitalism' in Thomas Wilhelmsson et al (eds), *Consumer Law in the Information Society* (Kluwer 2001); Mary Donnelly and Fidelma White, 'The Effect of Information Based Consumer Protection: Lessons from a Study of the Irish Online Market' in Christian Twigg-Flesner (ed), *Yearbook of Consumer Law 2007* (Ashgate 2008) 282–84.

112. Thomas Wilhelmsson, 'The Informed Consumer v the Vulnerable Consumer in European Unfair Commercial Practices Law – A Comment' in Geraint Howells (ed), *Yearbook of Consumer Law 2006* (Ashgate 2007) 211, 216.

113. See, in particular, Howells, 'Potential and Limits', 360, and Ramsay, 'From Truth in Lending', 52. For a general overview of this approach, see Cass Sunstein (ed), *Behavioural Law and Economics* (Cambridge University Press 2000).

information is better and suggest that too much information, or 'information overload', may decrease the individual's ability to make decisions.[114] Finally, and of particular relevance to the discussion in this article, the information provision model is critiqued because of its adoption of a 'one size fits all' approach that does not differentiate between types of consumer. Yet, studies have shown that information provision is most effective in the context of consumers from more 'privileged' socio-economic or education backgrounds and that consumers from 'less privileged' backgrounds stand to benefit less.[115] Underpinning all of these critiques is a recognition that consumer protection policy needs to respond to the needs of 'real world' consumers. A difficulty here is that, as Ramsay describes: 'There is unfortunately little empirical study of the effects, if any, of consumer law on consumer behaviour and the relationship of consumer law to other non-legal pressures on market behaviour.'[116]

The critiques of the paradigmatic informed, confident consumer have begun to impact on European consumer policy and there are signs of a policy move beyond a simple focus on informing consumers to take greater account of the broader requirements for consumer empowerment.[117] Underpinning this shift is a greater recognition of the need for an empirically based understanding of 'real world' consumers and the Eurobarometer study discussed in the next section represents a valuable first step in this direction.

Understanding the Irish Consumer

We contend that an Irish consumer protection agenda must recognise the nature and particular needs of the Irish consumer. Clearly, such an understanding can only be reached following detailed empirical investigation. This part of the article presents a range of available data that provides the beginnings of a picture of the Irish consumer, focusing on consumers' understanding of their legal rights. By way of background, a brief account of the nature and scope of the legal rights in respect of which consumers were tested is provided where relevant. The discussion draws in the first instance on the annual surveys published by the National Consumer Agency, which present a helpful longitudinal picture of consumers' self-perceptions. However, it is arguable that the contribution of

114. See Howells, 'Potential and Limits', 360; for an explanation of why difficulties with information overload apply, see Troy Parades, 'Blinded by the Light: Information Overload and Its Consequences for Securities Regulation' (2003) 81 Wash U L Quarterly 417.

115. See William Whitford, 'The Functions of Disclosure Regulation in Consumer Transactions' (1973) 2 Wisc L Rev 400; Iain Crow, Geraint Howells and Maureen Moroney, 'Credit and Debt: Choices for Poorer Consumers' in Crow, Howells and Moroney (eds), *Aspects of Credit and Debt: Choices for Poorer Consumers* (Sweet and Maxwell 1993).

116. Ramsay, 'Regulation', 335.

117. See European Commission Staff Working Paper *Consumer Empowerment in the EU* SEC (2011) 469 final.

these surveys is limited because they rely entirely on consumers' self-assessment and do not test the reality of consumers' understanding of the law. The 2010 Europe-wide Eurobarometer study on Consumer Empowerment addresses this limitation, providing information not just in respect of consumers' self-assessment but also testing consumers' actual knowledge. Inevitably, given its context, this study focuses entirely on evaluating consumers' knowledge of consumer rights arising under European law. Thus, it does not reflect the hybrid nature of Irish consumer law. The final study discussed here is the UCC study, which was conducted in November/December 2012 and which attempts to identify Irish consumers' knowledge of rights that derive from domestic rather than European law. Although the sample size is small relative to the Eurobarometer work, the study provides some interesting insights.

NCA Studies: How Irish Consumers Self-Identify

Beginning in 2007, the National Consumer Agency has commissioned a series of studies into Irish consumer empowerment and preparedness to complain.[118] Of particular relevance to the discussion in this article are the questions asked in respect of consumer rights awareness levels. These required consumers to self-identify in respect of their confidence as consumers; their knowledge as consumers and how protected they felt as consumers. The first survey was conducted in November/December 2007 (some six months after the statutory establishment of the NCA) and this provides the benchmark for the eight subsequent studies.[119] A consistent finding of the studies was that over three in four Irish consumers self-reported as being confident about their rights as a consumer, with only 10–11 per cent of consumers stating that they were not confident.[120] Slightly less than three in four consumers self-reported as being knowledgeable, with data indicating an increase of 10 per cent of consumers (from 62 per cent to 72 per cent) self-reporting as knowledgeable between the first study in November 2007 and the last study in the series, in March 2012.[121] Finally, approximately, three out of four consumers self-reported as feeling protected by the law.[122]

118. For details, see n 9. Studies were based on face-to-face interviews with 1,000 people aged between 15 and 74. In order to ensure that data was nationally representative, quotas were applied on the basis of age, gender, social class and region.
119. Subsequent studies were carried out in August 2008; November/December 2008; May/June 2009; November/December 2009; June 2010; November/December 2010; May/June 2011 and March 2012: for details, see NCA *Market Research Findings: Consumer Empowerment and Consumer Service* (March 2012) 4.
120. NCA *Market Research Findings 2012*, 6: the highest reported percentage of confident consumers occurred in March 2012 with 78 per cent self-reporting as confident, while the lowest reported percentage was in November 2007 with 70 per cent reporting as confident.
121. NCA *Market Research Findings 2012*, 7.
122. ibid.

Once again, this shows an ongoing and substantial improvement from the first study conducted, where 60 per cent of consumers reported feeling protected by the law, to the most recent study, where 76 per cent of consumers reported that they felt protected.

The consistent findings of these studies would seem to indicate that a substantial number of Irish consumers feel empowered[123] and that there has been a steady increase in consumers' feelings of empowerment over the period in which the studies were conducted. This longitudinal picture is very helpful and is certainly encouraging in terms of consumers' self-perceptions at any rate. The limit of these studies, however, is that consumers' self-assessment is not tested against objective fact. This is especially problematic in respect of self-reported levels of knowledge. In developing a domestic agenda for consumer law, reliance on self-assessment alone cannot be sufficient. The question that must be asked is whether Irish consumers are over- (or under-) estimating actual levels of knowledge. The two studies discussed below provide some objective data on this matter.

Eurobarometer: Testing Knowledge of Rights under European Law

Between February and April 2010, Eurobarometer, which undertakes surveys on behalf of the European Commission, undertook an extensive[124] EU-wide study, covering all Member States, of consumer empowerment, which sought to examine both consumers' self-perceptions in terms of empowerment and also their actual levels of knowledge and skills.

In terms of self-assessment, Irish consumers reported largely in accordance with the NCA studies discussed above. Thus, 83 per cent of Irish consumers self-reported as confident (compared with an EU27 average of 73 per cent, putting Irish consumers in the top tier of countries (alongside the Netherlands, Sweden, the United Kingdom, Demark, Slovenia, Belgium and Luxembourg).[125] Further, 77 per cent of Irish consumers self-reported as knowledgeable (compared with an EU27 average of 63 per cent), again placing Ireland in the top tier of countries in this regard (alongside the Netherlands, Sweden, the United Kingdom, Demark, Finland and Slovenia).[126] Finally, 70 per cent of Irish consumers reported feeling protected by the law (as compared to an EU27 average of 55 per cent), once again placing Ireland in the top tier of Member States (alongside Sweden, the Netherlands, Denmark, Finland and the United Kingdom). Thus, the encouraging

123. In the NCA studies, the measure of empowerment was calculated with reference to the three empowerment indicators of confidence, knowledge and protection: NCA *Market Research Findings 2012*, 8.

124. A total of 56,471 interviews were carried out as part of the survey, taking place in two waves. A total of 2,014 interviews were carried out in Ireland (by MRBI).

125. Eurobarometer, 12.

126. Eurobarometer, 14.

figures from the NCA commissioned studies are replicated (and indeed improved upon) across all measures.

However, when Irish consumers were actually tested, the findings evidenced significant deficiencies in knowledge (although as discussed below, some of the questions were ill-suited to Irish consumers). Of particular relevance to the discussion in this article are the seven questions that seek to identify consumers' awareness of EU consumer legislation.[127] The questions focused on four themes from European consumer law: unfair commercial practices; cooling-off periods; guarantee periods and cross-border transactions. To summarise the findings across the seven questions, in most respects, Irish interviewees were broadly in line, although slightly below, the EU27 average.[128] However, Ireland stood out as being one of the Member States with the highest number of respondents who could not answer even one question correctly. The fellow Member States in this category are rather different to the Member States that shared similar responses in respect of the self-assessed questions. Only Romania and Bulgaria have similar percentages of zero correct answers to Ireland.[129] When account was taken of respondents who could only answer one question correctly, Ireland is still in the bottom tier of Member States, this time sharing this category with Greece and Luxembourg (as well as Romania and Bulgaria).[130]

In terms of individual questions, three related to unfair commercial practices. These are regulated by Directive 2005/29/EC which, unusually for Ireland, is transposed by primary legislation, the Consumer Protection Act 2007. Directive 2005/29/EC deals with three kinds of commercial practices. These are first, 'unfair commercial practices' that are prohibited under art 5. A practice is 'unfair' if it is contrary to the requirements of due diligence and it 'materially distorts or is likely to materially distort the economic behaviour with regard to the product of the average consumer whom it reaches or to whom it is addressed'.[131] Secondly, the Directive prohibits misleading practices (both actions and omissions).

127. The study extends well beyond a focus on the law alone, including valuable data on all sorts of consumer empowerment matters, including arithmetic and financial skills; capacity to read labels and logos; levels of interest in consumer information; and preparedness to talk about purchasing experiences.
128. One per cent of Irish consumers (compared with 2 per cent of EU27) answered all seven questions correctly; 4 per cent (compared to EU27 average of 8 per cent) answered six questions correctly; 12 per cent (compared to an EU27 average of 15 per cent) answered five questions correctly; 21 per cent (compared to an EU27 average of 22 per cent) answered four questions correctly; 25 per cent (compared to an EU27 average of 23 per cent) answered three questions correctly; 20 per cent (compared to an EU27 average of 18 per cent) answered two questions correctly and 10 per cent (compared to an EU27 average of 9 per cent) answered one question correctly: see Eurobarometer, 101.
129. Eurobarometer, 103.
130. ibid.
131. Directive 2005/29/EC, art 5(2).

A commercial practice is defined as 'misleading' where it contains false information in respect of a designated list of factors and is as a result 'untruthful or in any way, including overall presentation, deceives or is likely to deceive the average consumer, even if the information is factually correct'.[132] In order to fall within the provision, the information in question must relate to the existence or nature of the product; the main characteristics of the product; the extent of the trader's commitments; the price or the manner in which the price is calculated; the need for a service, part, replacement or repair; the nature and attributes of the trader or his agent and, finally, the consumer's rights.[133] A practice may also be misleading if 'in its factual context, taking account of all its features and circumstances, it causes or is likely to cause the average consumer to take a transactional decision that he would not have taken otherwise' and it involves the marketing of the product or compliance with codes of conduct.[134] The third commercial practice targeted is 'aggressive' practice, which includes harassment, coercion and undue influence.[135]

The first question related to the legality of a newspaper offer of free sunglasses, which requires calling a very costly premium rate telephone number without mentioning the cost.[136] In response, 25 per cent of Irish consumers incorrectly identified this offer as legal and 18 per cent did not know whether or not this was legal. Thus, close to half (43 per cent) of Irish consumers would have difficulty asserting their legal rights in this regard. The equivalent EU27 average (comprising incorrect answers and consumers who did not know the answer) was 26 per cent. Interestingly, the only other common law jurisdiction, the United Kingdom, also had strikingly poor responses, with 33 per cent of United Kingdom consumers incorrectly identifying the practice as legal and 9 per cent not knowing.[137] This may reflect the conceptual unfamiliarity of aspects of Directive 2005/29/EC in common law jurisdictions.

The second unfair commercial practices question related to receipt of unsolicited DVDs together with a bill in the post.[138] In this case, 49 per cent of Irish consumers incorrectly responded that the recipient was not obliged to pay for the DVDs provided that they sent the DVDs back, with only 40 per cent giving the correct answer that there was no obligation to pay and

132. Directive 2005/29/EC, art 6(1).
133. Directive 2005/29/EC, art 6(1).
134. Directive 2005/29/EC, art 6(2).
135. Directive 2005/29/EC, art 9.
136. The question as asked was: 'An advertisement in your newspaper says: "Free sunglasses, just call this number to collect them". You call the number and later you discover that it is a very costly premium rate telephone number. Was the advertisement legal or illegal?': see Eurobarometer, 68.
137. Eurobarometer, 69.
138. The question as asked was: 'Imagine you receive by post two educational DVDs that you have not ordered, together with a 50 euro bill for the products. Are you obliged to pay the bill?': Eurobarometer, 72.

no obligation to return.[139] The responses were slightly better than the EU27 average (where 39 per cent gave a correct answer) but strikingly worse than the other Member States that had self-assessed as knowledgeable.[140] The final unfair practices question related to an airline pricing advertisement. Here, Irish consumers performed better than the EU27 average with 63 per cent (as compared to an EU27 average of 56 per cent) correctly stating that an advertisement must state the total amount to be paid, including taxes, fees and charges.[141] It is possible that, as an island nation, Irish consumers' particular dependence on the airline industry is a relevant factor in this stronger performance.

Two questions related to knowledge of cooling-off periods in distance selling, one of which related to Directive 97/7/EC on the protection of consumers in respect of distance contracts[142] and the other to Directive 2002/65/EC concerning the distance marketing of consumer financial services.[143] Article 6(1) of Directive 97/7/EC states that consumers who purchase goods at a distance, shall have a period of 'at least seven working dates in which to withdraw from the contract without penalty and without giving any reason'. In Directive 2002/65/EC, the right to withdraw is contained in art 6(1) and allows the consumer 14 calendar days to withdraw from the contract without penalty and without giving a reason. Under art 7(1), a consumer may be required to pay for any service actually performed by the supplier under the contract up until the time of withdrawal. However, art 7(2) states that Member States may provide that a consumer cannot be required to pay for services that have been provided under an insurance contract.

When questioned, 63 per cent of Irish consumers knew that there was a right to return goods bought at a distance (by post, phone or via the Internet) four days after delivery and to get money back without having to give a reason. This response was more or less in line with the EU27 response, although notably lower than other

139. Eurobarometer, 73.

140. In Denmark, 57 per cent of consumers gave correct answers, while in Finland, 55 per cent of answers were correct.

141. Eurobarometer, 79.

142. Directive 97/7/EC is repealed by Directive 2011/83/EU on consumer rights as of 13 July 2014. The current Irish transposing measure is the European Communities (Protection of Consumers in Respect of Contracts Made by Means of Distance Communication) Regulations 2001, SI 207/2001 as amended by the European Communities (Protection of Consumers in Respect of Contracts Made by Means of Distance Communication) (Amendment) Regulations 2010, SI 370/2010.

143. Transposed by the European Communities (Distance Marketing of Consumer Financial Services) Regulations 2004, SI 853/2004 as amended by the European Communities (Distance Marketing of Consumer Financial Services)(Amendment) Regulations 2005, SI 63/2005.

Member States where consumers self-assessed as knowledgeable.[144] In respect of the question on the cooling-off period in distance marketing of financial services, only 25 per cent of Irish consumers answered that a consumer could cancel a car insurance contract concluded at a distance (over the phone in the question asked) two days after the contract was concluded and get their money back. This maps fairly closely onto the EU27 data where 28 per cent gave this correct answer, as interpreted by Eurobarometer. Most Irish consumers (36 per cent) believed that they could cancel but that it was necessary to pay an administration fee, an answer which Eurobarometer categorised as incorrect. In fact, the position in Ireland is somewhat more complex than this suggests. As described earlier, although art 7(2) permitted Member States to provide that a consumer did not have to pay for an insurance service received prior to withdrawal, this option was not taken on transposition into Irish law[145] and therefore Irish consumers do have an obligation to repay the supplier for the service provided (in this case, the insurance cover). Thus, while the repayment cost cannot be accurately categorised as an administration fee, nor is it correct to state that the Irish consumer is entitled to cancel the contract and get all of their money back.

The final two questions related to 'doorstep' selling and to sales guarantees. 'Doorstep' selling is regulated by Directive 85/577 to protect the consumer in respect of contracts negotiated away from business premises.[146] Under art 5, a consumer has a right to cancel a contract concluded away from the trader's premises within seven days without giving a reason. In response to a question regarding whether or not a consumer has a right to return a vacuum cleaner bought at the door and get their money back without giving a reason, only 28 per cent of Irish consumers correctly answered yes, while 47 per cent answered no, and 18 per cent did not know.

Sales guarantees are covered by Directive 1999/44/EC on certain aspects of the sale of consumer goods and associated guarantees.[147] Under art 2, goods sold to consumers must be in conformity with the contract. Goods are presumed to conform with the contract if they meet a number of criteria, such as where they comply with the description provided by the seller and they are fit for their normal purpose. Article 3 states that the seller is liable to the consumer for any lack of conformity that exists at the time the goods were delivered and that, in that situation, the consumer is entitled to have the goods brought into

---

144. Eurobarometer, 83. The highest number of correct responses was from Germany, where 83 per cent answered correctly, with Finland and Denmark reporting 75 per cent and 74 per cent respectively.
145. See SI 853/2004, reg 15.
146. Directive 85/577 /EEC is repealed by Directive 2011/83/EU on consumer rights as of 13 July 2014. Transposed by the European Communities (Cancellation of Contracts Negotiated Away from the Business Premises) Regulations 1989, SI 224/1989.
147. Transposed by the European Communities (Certain Aspects of the Sale of Consumer Goods and Associated Guarantees) Regulations, 2003, SI 13/ 2003.

conformity by repair or replacement.[148] The Directive provides, in art 5, that the seller is liable for any non-conformity that arises within two years of delivery of the goods. The Eurobarometer question in respect of guarantees was, in the case of a fridge that broke down, and where an extended guarantee was not purchased, whether or not there was a right to repair or replacement 18 months after purchase. Only 30 per cent of Irish consumers correctly responded that they had such a right with 41 per cent stating that no such right existed. Again, as with question regarding the cooling-off period for online financial services, there may have been some confusion around this question in terms of its phraseology and its substance. The term 'guarantee' is actually not used in Directive 1999/44/EC (nor indeed the Irish sale of goods legislation) in relation to the *legal* quality standard with which goods must comply. Instead, the word 'guarantee' is more commonly used in relation to voluntary 'warranties' or 'guarantees' that may be offered by manufacturers and others, free or otherwise for variable periods. Moreover, when Ireland transposed Directive 1999/44/EC, the transposing measure did not implement the two-year time limit; rather it continued to apply the more generous six-year limitation period. In these circumstances, consumer confusion is understandable.

To summarise, Ireland receives specific mention as an outlier in the Eurobarometer study, at the top end in self-assessed levels of knowledge and at the lower end in objective assessment of knowledge, suggesting a dissonance between Irish consumers' self-perception and their actual knowledge. Of particular concern is the number of consumers who do not have any idea of their rights under European law and could not answer any questions correctly. The Eurobarometer study also reinforces the point, however, that legal rights operate differently across different Member States, with several of the questions asked not quite fitting the Irish context. Thus, some care needs to be taken with these findings (or indeed any European-wide findings) in the development of the Irish consumer agenda. A limitation of the Eurobarometer survey is that its focus is on European legislation. From an Irish perspective, consumer rights derived from the domestic foundation for Irish consumer law are not addressed. The study discussed in the next section attempts to integrate actual knowledge of this aspect of Irish consumer law into the analysis.

The UCC Study: Testing Knowledge of Rights under Domestic Law

The study discussed in this section was conducted in November–December 2012. The study builds on the Eurobarometer study in that it encompasses both consumer self-assessment and actual levels of consumer knowledge. However, the concern of this study is with rights that derive from domestic, rather than European, law and it investigates the hypothesis that Irish consumers are better informed in respect of

148. On the relationship between this right and the right to reject under the Sale of Goods Acts, see text to n 99.

these rights. This possibility arises because these rights are longer established and arguably, therefore, more ingrained in the Irish consumer psyche.

The sample size for this study is relatively small, comprising 262 face-to-face interviews with individuals at various locations throughout Cork City.[149] In evaluating the findings, account should be taken of the small sample size and the limited geographical coverage. For the purposes of this article, the relevant parts of the study are, first, consumers' self-assessment and, secondly, consumers' actual knowledge of their rights under domestic law.

In self-assessment, the findings in respect of confidence closely matched those of the NCA and Eurobarometer studies, with 83 per cent of respondents indicating that they felt very or quite confident. There was, however, a disparity between the NCA/Eurobarometer responses and those of this study in self-assessment regarding knowledge and feeling protected. Only 41 per cent of respondents self-assessed as feeling knowledgeable, while only 56 per cent described themselves as feeling protected by the law. These discrepancies may well be simply as a result of the small sample size. However, it is possible that the fact that the introduction to the survey expressly told consumers that they would be tested on their knowledge may have led to a somewhat more circumspect response.[150]

In evaluating actual levels of knowledge, the relevant parts of the study can be divided into knowledge about different aspects of consumer remedies in sale of goods transactions and knowledge about legal terms. All of the questions relate to rights arising under the Sale of Goods Acts 1893 and 1980. Under this legislation, various contractual terms (conditions) are implied into the contract of sale requiring that the goods supplied reach a certain minimum quality standard. For example, s 13 of the 1893 Act requires that where goods are sold by description, the goods supplied must comply with that description. Therefore, where goods are sold are described as '100 per cent beef burger' and they are found to contain horsemeat mixed with beef, there is a breach of s 13 and the legislation provides a series of remedies for the disappointed buyer. Another key implied term can be found in s 14(2) of the 1893 Act, which provides that where goods are sold in the course of a business, the goods supplied must be of

149. Locations were identified on the basis of socio-economic variation. All interviews took place in a public place: street or shopping centre. Demographic data was gathered in respect of gender, age and education. Breakdown was as follows: Gender: 54 per cent female and 46 per cent male; Age: 15–24 years: 22 per cent; 25–39 years: 35 per cent; 40–55 years: 24 per cent; 55 plus: 18 per cent; Education: up to 15 years: 2 per cent; 16–19 years: 37 per cent; 20 plus years: 47 per cent; Still studying: 14 per cent.

150. At the beginning of each interview, the interviewer read the following statement: 'This survey is being conducted on behalf the Law Faculty at UCC, and it asks questions about consumers' perceptions of themselves and their knowledge of the law. It takes between 5–10 minutes. Would you be willing to participate in this short survey? Please feel free to withdraw at any time.'

merchantable quality, defined as requiring reasonable fitness for purpose and durability, in light of any description applied to the goods, the price and any other relevant circumstances.[151]

Where any of the above implied terms are breached, the buyer is provided with a range of remedies. Because the statutory implied terms as to quality are classified as conditions, where any term or terms are breached, the buyer can terminate the contract, reject the goods (claiming a refund of any price paid) and claim damages for any loss. Alternatively, the buyer can opt to keep the goods, though not perfect, and sue for damages only. Importantly, the buyer can select whichever option suits his or her particular circumstances. Of these remedies, the right to reject (and seek a refund) is particularly powerful. It places the consumer buyer in a strong bargaining position (ie s/he can demand a refund on return of the goods) and its self-help nature makes it both easy and relatively cheap to operate. However, this right to reject does not continue indefinitely. Pursuant to the legislation the right to reject can be lost, in particular with the passing of time.[152] English case law suggests that the right to reject can be lost relatively quickly, as happened in *Bernstein v Pamsons Motors (Golders Green) Ltd*,[153] where a new car seized up after three weeks driving and 142 miles due to a blob of sealant in the lubrication system. While the court held that the car was unmerchantable, it also held that the buyer was too late to reject: he had lost his right to reject and was limited to a claim in damages only. In addition, since 1980, the consumer buyer may demand that the goods are repaired or replaced (known as a right of cure) under sale of goods legislation (and pursuant to Directive 1999/44/EC).[154] Importantly, though, it is the buyer's choice whether to seek to reject or cure the goods.

The results of the UCC study affirm the fundamental significance in Irish consumer law of the right to reject defective goods. When asked a question regarding the right to reject defective goods, 98 per cent of consumers gave a correct response, reflecting an almost perfect level of consumer knowledge about this aspect of the right to reject.[155] The study found that Irish consumers were less sure of their rights in respect of repair or replacement instead of rejection. When asked if a seller could insist on repair rather than return and refund,[156]

151. See 1893 Act, s 14(3): See Fidelma White, 'The Meaning of Merchantable Quality' (2012) 47 IJ 255. Other implied quality terms relate to fitness for particular purpose (s 14(4), 1893 Act); sales by sample (s 15, 1893 Act); and sales of motor vehicles (s 13, 1980 Act).
152. 1893 Act, ss 34–35.
153. [1987] 2 All ER 220.
154. 1893 Act, s 53(2).
155. The question asked was, 'Suppose you buy something in a shop (say a TV), and it turns out to be defective (ie it doesn't work), are you entitled in law to return it and get a refund?'
156. The question asked was, 'Suppose you buy a washing machine in a shop and within the first week, it stops working (because the heating element breaks). Can the seller

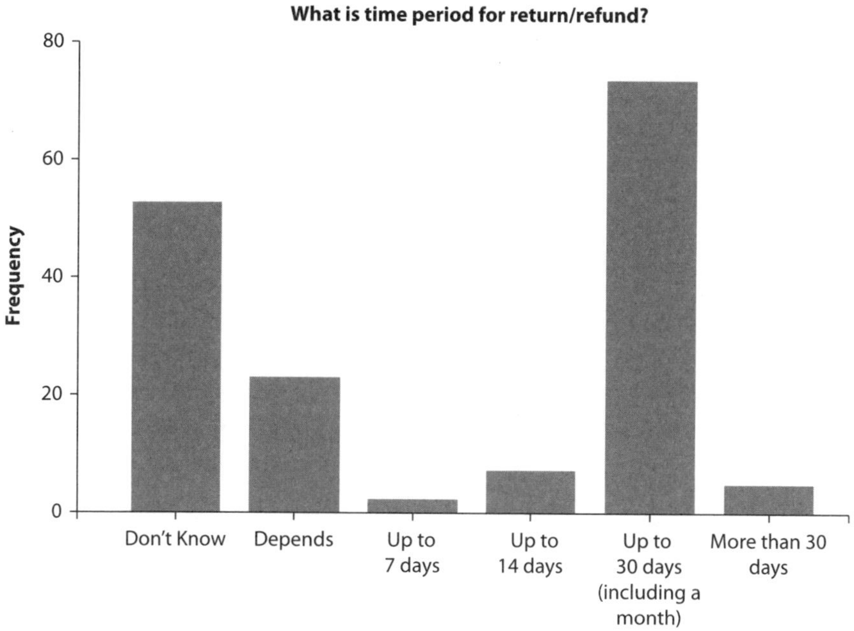

only 34 per cent of consumers gave the correct answer (which is that they could not), with 61 per cent saying that the seller could insist on repair and 5 per cent saying that they did not know. Thus, two-thirds of respondents do not know that the bargaining power rests with the consumer: it is the consumer who can select either rejection or cure.

Importantly, the right to reject under the Sale of Goods Acts 1893 and 1980 is typically only available where the goods are defective and hence are in breach of the statutory implied terms as to quality. A consumer does not have the right to reject/return goods merely because s/he changes his or her mind. The answers to a question about this showed clear evidence of consumer misunderstanding.[157] In response, 48 per cent of consumers correctly answered that there was not a right to refuse simply on the basis of a change of mind but a slightly greater percentage (49 per cent) incorrectly answered that there was. Only a very small number of respondents (3 per cent) stated that they did not know. The high number of incorrect responses here may reflect the business practice of many retailers who allow consumers to return goods without giving a reason. Further questions built on the exercise of the right to reject and, again, there was evidence of consumer confusion. Irish law does not specify a fixed time limit within which

insist on repairing or replacing of the washing machine instead of allowing you to return the washing machine and get a refund?'

157. The question asked was, 'Suppose you buy something in a shop (say a pair of shoes), and subsequently change your mind about them, does consumer law provide you with a right to return the shoes and get your money back?'

a consumer can reject/return defective goods. However, as described above, the right to reject is limited and a consumer can lose the right to reject with the passing of time. In response to the question of whether or not there was a time limit for the right to reject, 63 per cent of respondents correctly answered yes, with 6 per cent answering no and 31 per cent saying that they did not know. We then asked the respondents who knew that there was a time limit what this time limit was. Here, there was clear confusion with only 9 per cent giving the correct answer that it depended on the circumstances. As is clear from the graph below, there was a wide range of answers. Once again, it may well be that consumers' answers in this context are influenced by some retailers' business practices, which can leave consumers with a false sense of security.

We used two questions to assess consumers' recognition of legal terminology surrounding the sales of goods statutory framework. While recognition of terminology is clearly different to substantive understanding, it is nonetheless worthwhile to examine the extent to which terminology has entered the broader lexicon. There may also be practical benefits for a consumer who is able to articulate his or her rights against a supplier using the appropriate terminology. To this end, we asked respondents: 'Suppose you buy something in a shop, say a TV; there is a legal requirement that the TV must be of a certain quality: Do you know the legal term used to describe this quality?' A substantial majority (75 per cent) did not know the term. Of those who did know the term, 54 per cent identified the quality term correctly as merchantable quality; 35 per cent accurately described the quality terms in terms simply of 'fitness'; while 11 per cent used the more exact phrase 'fitness for purpose'. The second terminological question related to the commonly used term, especially in retail premises, 'does not affect your statutory rights'. When questioned, 77 per cent of respondents said that they had seen this term and, of these, 70 per cent could correctly explain what this term meant.[158] Thus, it would seem that this term has more effectively permeated consumer consciousness, probably because of its widespread usage in retail premises.

The final question asked was aimed at testing consumer awareness of the distinction between legal rights and business practices. All respondents were asked: are you legally entitled to a receipt when you purchase goods or services? The almost unanimous (99.6 per cent), and incorrect, response was yes. This finding accords with some of the earlier findings, which showed that consumers may be misled in respect of their legal rights by business practices which, in this context, almost inevitably involves the provision of receipts by retailers.

In summary, although the sample size is smaller, the UCC study reinforces the conclusion that emerged from the Eurobarometer study that a significant

158. All respondents who said that they had seen the term were asked by the interviewer to explain what the term meant and the responses were categorised by the interviewer as correct or incorrect.

proportion of Irish consumers lack of knowledge about their rights. It also suggests that, even though the sale of goods legislation is longer established, with the exception of the right to reject defective products, the protections afforded are not necessarily more embedded in the Irish consumer consciousness, thus disproving the hypothesis tested.

Conclusion

Under the TFEU, competence in the area of consumer protection is shared between the EU and the Member States, such as Ireland.[159] As well as this formal sharing of legal competences, it is clear that at a policy level the EU institutions and the relevant Irish institutions (government departments and the National Consumer Agency) also share a common strategy, which involves the creation of confident, well-informed consumers. Empirical data from the EU and Ireland, detailed above, shows that Irish consumers identify themselves as confident, knowledgeable about their rights and protected by the law, but significantly, objective testing of these self-perceptions displays a dissonance between consumers' perceived level of knowledge and their actual knowledge about their legal rights. As noted above, Ireland received specific mention in the Eurobarometer study, both in terms of self-reported levels of knowledge and in terms of actual lack of knowledge although, as also argued, the Eurobarometer study does not take account of differences between Member States in transposition and therefore some care should be taken with the findings. It is concerning, however, that Ireland stood out as being one of the Member States with the highest number of respondents who could not answer even one question correctly, suggesting that a significant number of Irish people may have little or no knowledge of their consumer rights. Perhaps these results in the Eurobarometer study could be explained by the fact that many of these EU rights are relatively new, and sometimes alien to our common law system, but the picture appears no better when we turn to consumer rights established under domestic sale of goods law, as illustrated by the UCC study. The detailed testing of the right to reject in Irish law illustrates poor penetration of the legal quality standard of 'merchantable quality' and confusion about the mechanics of the operation of the right.

The question is how to respond to the above findings and analysis. Clearly, law reform could help. The poor responses to questions about the Sales of Goods Acts 1893 and 1980 may derive in part at least from the continued use of archaic language, such as 'merchantable quality', and the lack of clarity in the law around the time-limit for rejection, as well as the complicated nature of the rights to reject and cure. And so, in this regard, the recommendation from the Sales Law Review Group to alter the quality standard from merchantable quality to 'satisfactory quality' is to be welcomed, along with their recommendation to introduce

159. TEFU, art 4.

a default 30-day rejection period and to better integrate consumer remedies.[160] These recommendations would modernise and simplify the law, and bring a greater level of clarity and certainty. In addition, more and better education of consumers about their rights is needed in Ireland and this is something the proposed Consumer and Competition body must address as a matter of urgency.

From a broader perspective, the analysis raises questions about the models of consumer protection adopted at European and Irish levels. It is arguable that we expect too much from consumers in terms of knowledge. Even if the recommendations to modernise and simplify the law, referred to above, are adopted, the reality is that consumer knowledge of the law is clearly affected by numerous factors.[161] One factor that emerges from the UCC study is that consumer knowledge is influenced by retail practices that may offer more favourable terms than the relevant legal regulation. Some degree of consumer confusion is therefore unavoidable and any policy that is based on a presumption of the achievement of 'perfect' consumer knowledge is inevitably flawed. Thus, consumer protection policies based primarily on the creation of the confident, informed consumer as an actor in promoting market growth are too limited. We would argue, therefore, that Irish law- and policy-makers need to develop an Irish consumer-protection policy that places the protection of consumers at its heart, with any resultant growth in the market to be seen as a welcome by-product. This approach to consumer policy is grounded in considerations of consumer welfare rather than solely fulfilling economic purposes. This is fundamentally different to the EU policy position, as discussed above, where internal market imperatives remain the key drivers and the consumer welfare agenda appears to be secondary.

Secondly, Irish law- and policy-makers must recognise the complex and distinct characteristics of Irish consumers: for example, they can be both confident and ill-informed, and their perceptions of the law derive as much from market practice as from legal regulation. Therefore, Irish legal regulation needs to be engaged, responsive, and flexible to address these complexities. For instance, greater use of codes of practice should be considered as an alternative way of delivering on consumer protection. The innovative Consumer Protection Code in relation to financial services, discussed above, presents a useful model. Thirdly, as was the case with the negotiations around the consumer rights directive, Irish negotiators must resist any attempts at maximum harmonisation that seek to stifle difference, innovation and experimentation. The input of the Sales Law Review Group provided Irish negotiators with expert opinion, thus enabling a more effective assertion of the domestic interest in the context of the proposed directive. Utilising these

160. Sales Law Review Group, *Report on the Legislation Governing the Sale of Goods and Supply of Services* (2011) Prn A11/1576, paras 4.43, 9.44, 9.53.
161. Relevant factors include amount of time spent shopping/comparing products/ reading terms and conditions: see Eurobarometer, 108 ff.

kinds of competencies and expertise must be key to the ongoing development of the Irish consumer-protection agenda within the European context.

Finally, in advancing the Irish consumer-protection agenda, it is necessary to revisit existing consumer-protection legislation and to engage critically with the choices made on transposition. One area that would clearly benefit from such an approach is the regulation of unfair contract terms. On transposition of the relevant directive, Ireland, unlike most other Member States, limited the scope of the regulations to standard form contracts only and utilised the core terms exemption to the full extent.[162] As a result, Irish consumers benefit from a lower level of protection in this respect than most other European citizens. This gap in regulation needs to be addressed in the context of a wide-ranging Consumer Contract Rights Act. A measure of this kind has been recommended by the Sales Law Review Group.[163] Such a measure would bring together the main provisions dealing with consumer contracts, supported by enforceable codes of practice, and must be a priority in asserting a distinct domestic agenda for Irish consumers.

162. See Mary Donnelly, 'Unfair Terms in Consumer Contracts: Time for Legislative Recalibration?' (2012) 19 CLP 115.

163. Sales Law Review Group, *Report on the Legislation Governing the Sale of Goods and Supply of Services* (2011) Prn A11/1576, para 14.14.

The Certificate of Registration and the Company Charge Register

Noel McGrath*

Abstract—This article considers the certificate issued by the Registrar of Companies on the registration of a company charge. It argues that the existing understanding of the effect of that certificate is flawed and suggests an alternative interpretation of the underlying provisions of the Companies Acts, which both respects the ordinary meaning of the words of the statute whilst at the same time better reflecting the purpose of the charge registration system.

Introduction

Part IV of the Companies Act 1963 establishes a system of registration for certain classes of charge created by companies over their property. The system has been in place since the passage of the Companies Act 1900 and requires that certain particulars of charges falling within a statutory list set out in s 99(2) be sent to the Registrar of Companies within 21 days of their creation. The courts have long recognised that the primary purpose of the registration system is to provide information to a company's creditors and prospective creditors about prior mortgages and charges granted by the company over its assets.[1]

The company charge register is one of several different systems of public registration for security interests in Irish law. Charges over registered[2] and unregistered[3] land, security bills of sale,[4] mortgages over agricultural chattels,[5] security interests over ships[6] and aircraft[7] as well as certain types of security

* Lecturer in Law, UCD Sutherland School of Law. The author would like to thank the anonymous reviewers for their helpful comments on earlier drafts of this article.

1. See *Re: Jackson and Bassford Ltd* [1906] 2 Ch 467, 476; *Re: Cardiff Workmen's Cottage Company Ltd* [1906] 2 Ch 627, 629; *Dublin City Distillery v Doherty* [1914] AC 823, 854.
2. See s 62 Registration of Title Act 1964 (as amended).
3. Part 3, Registration of Deeds and Title Act 2006, which re-enacts, with substantial amendments, the scheme of registration originally established by the Registration of Deeds Act 1707.
4. Bills of Sale (Ireland) Acts 1878–1883.
5. Part II, Agricultural Credit Act 1978.
6. ss 50–56 Mercantile Marine Act 1955.
7. See International Interests in Mobile Equipment Act 2005, which implements the provisions of the Cape Town Convention on International Interests in Mobile

interests over various classes of intellectual property[8] must all be disclosed to the public as a condition either of their validity or priority. When compared to these other systems of public registration, the company charge register has two unusual features. First, the formal obligation to register a charge falls on the company over whose property the charge is created, though registration can be, and in practice frequently is, carried out by the secured creditor. Second, when a charge is registered, the Registrar issues a certificate of registration of the charge. This certificate is deemed by s 104 of the Companies Act 1963 to be conclusive evidence that the requirements of the Act as to registration have been complied with.

This article will examine the judicial interpretation of the conclusive evidence rule. It will argue that the current interpretation of s 104 of the Companies Act 1963 is seriously flawed and is based on an incorrect reading of the statutory text. It will also contend that the current interpretation undermines the legislative policy behind the company register and that an alternative interpretation of the section would enhance the operation of registration system. The article is divided into three sections. The first section summarises the existing legislative provisions that established the system of company charge registration. The second section examines a number of reported Irish and English cases that have required the courts to consider the meaning of s 104 or its English equivalents in various different circumstances. The third section presents an alternative possibility for the interpretation of s 104 and argues that this alternative demonstrates greater fidelity to the statutory text as well as offering a more sensible policy outcome in the operation of the company charge register. A brief conclusion follows, which includes a discussion of the proposed changes to Irish company law in the Companies Consolidation and Reform Bill 2012.

The Company Charge Register

The company charge register was first established by the Companies Act 1900. When introducing the legislation at its second reading in the House of Commons, the then President of the Board of Trade, Charles Ritchie MP, stated that the purpose of the register was to provide the fullest possible publicity of any mortgages or charges over company property and thereby avoid the 'evil which at present exists… that when it comes to the winding up of some companies it is found that the whole of the available assets of the company are mortgaged, and there is nothing at all to divide among the unhappy creditors.'[9] The Companies Act 1900 provided for registration of four classes of charge: charges for the purposes of securing an issue of debentures; charges on the uncalled capital of

---

Equipment and its associated Protocol on Matters Specific to Aircraft Equipment into domestic law.

8. s 85 Patents Act 1992, s 29 Trade Marks Act 1996, and s 41 Industrial Designs Act 2001.
9. Hansard, HC Deb 26 June 1900, vol 84, col 1143.

the company; charges which, if registered by an individual, would require registration as a bill of sale and floating charges. The system was extended to charges over land wherever situate and charges over the company's book debts in 1907.[10] The Companies Act 1963 added charges over ships, charges over calls on share capital made but not paid and charges on intellectual property to the system in line with previous English legislation.[11] The Companies Act 1990 further extended the system to include charges over aircraft.[12]

At present, the principal legislative provisions for the registration of company charges in Ireland are to be found in ss 99–106 of the Companies Act 1963. The scheme can be briefly summarised as follows. Section 99(2) sets out a list of registrable charges. Section 99(1) states that a registrable charge is void against the liquidator and any creditor of the company unless certain information ('the particulars') about the charge is delivered to the CRO within 21 days of its creation. In effect, if the requirements of s 99 are not complied with, the secured creditor loses the benefit of the charge and becomes an unsecured creditor in the event of the company's default. In addition, non-compliance results in any monies secured by the charge becoming immediately repayable. With the exception of the sanction of invalidity, the provisions of Part IV do not affect the priority of registrable charges. For most types of charges, priority will be determined by the order in which the charge was created.[13]

Section 100 establishes that it is the duty of the company creating the charge to deliver the particulars in a timely manner and provides for a criminal sanction against the company and any officer in default in the event that the company's default results in a registrable charge going unregistered. Section 100 also permits any other person who has an interest in the charge to apply to have the charge registered and to recover the costs of doing so from the company.

The mechanics of the registration process are governed by ss 103–106. Section 103 requires the Registrar of Companies to maintain a register of charges in relation to each company, which must contain the following particulars: (a) the date of creation of the charge; (b) the amount secured by the charge; (c) short particulars of the property charged; and (d) the details of the person(s) entitled to the charge. Where a charge is to the benefit of the holders of a series of debentures the company must deliver a different set of

10. s 10 Companies Act 1907, re-enacted as s 93 Companies (Consolidation) Act 1908.
11. See s 43(1) Companies Act 1928, re-enacted by s 79 Companies Act 1929.
12. s 122 Companies Act 1990; the section also creates a power for the Minister for Enterprise, Jobs and Innovation to add, remove or vary the categories of registrable charge by statutory instrument. This power has never been used.
13. The priority rules vary depending on the nature of the competing charges and the order of creation rule does not apply to a conflict between a floating charge and later fixed charge see *Re: Russell Murphy* [1976] IR 15. For a summary of the present position see Mary Donnelly, *The Law of Credit and Security* (Round Hall 2011) [15–79]–[15–83].

particulars, including: (a) the total amount secured by the series of debenture; (b) the dates and resolutions that authorised the issue, together with the date of the covering deed by which the security is created or defined; (c) a general description of the property charged; and (d) the names of the trustees, if any, for the debenture holders. The Registrar is also required to enter a notice of satisfaction onto the register once supplied with evidence that the secured obligation has been discharged or that some or all of the charged property has been otherwise released from the charge.[14]

Unlike the equivalent provisions in force in England until 2013,[15] there is no requirement for a copy of the original charge documentation to be supplied to the Registrar. The English companies legislation is widely regarded as imposing an obligation on the Registrar of Companies to compare the particulars supplied against the original charge document before entering the correct particulars into the charge register.[16] This requirement has been frequently criticised in England as placing an unduly onerous burden on the Registrar and for potentially exposing the Registrar to liability in the event of an error made by the staff of the Registrar.[17] The absence of the requirement to supply the original charge document in all cases to the Registrar in Ireland is the result of an amendment to the Companies Bill 1962, taken at Committee Stage during the legislation's passage through Dáil Éireann. Introducing the amendment, the then Minister for Industry and Commerce, Jack Lynch, stated that the government intended it to implement the recommendations of the Jenkins Committee, which had criticised the checking function of the English Registrar of Companies.[18] It would seem, therefore, that in this jurisdiction the Registrar's role is purely mechanical and that there is no requirement for the Registrar to check the accuracy of the particulars prior to registering a charge.

In practice, the particulars of a charge are delivered using a statutory form, Form C1, which finds its legal basis in the Companies (Forms) Order 2001.[19] In contrast to the English position,[20] the text of s 99(1) of the Companies Act 1963

14. s 105 Companies Act 1963.
15. s 860 Companies Act 2006 as originally enacted; the system of company charge registration has been substantially altered by the introduction, in April 2013, of the Companies Act 2006 (Amendment of Part 25) Regulations 2013 (SI 600 of 2013). These Regulations establish a single system of company charge registration throughout the United Kingdom. The changes made to English charge registration by these regulations are extensive but, owing to considerations of space, they will not be considered in this article.
16. Hugh Beale et al, *The Law of Personal Property Securty* (OUP, 2007), 766–67. Gerard McCormack, *Registration of Company Charges* (3rd edn, Jordans 2009) 214.
17. Board of Trade, *Report of the Company Law Committee* (Cmnd 1749, HMSO 1962) [302]; Aubrey Diamond, *A Review of Security Interests in Property* (HMSO 1989) 98–101.
18. Dáil Deb, Special Committee on the Companies Bill 1962, 21 February 1962.
19. Companies (Forms) Order 2001, SI 466 of 2001.
20. See *R v Registrar of Companies, ex parte Central Bank of India* [1986] 1 QB 1114, 1171.

requires that the particulars of a charge be delivered in the prescribed manner and it would therefore appear that Form C1 must be used for this purpose. Form C1 requires the provision of the company's registered number and an indication of which of the registrable categories set out in s 99(2) the charge falls within. The form also requires the person delivering the particulars to sign the form in a section entitled 'Verification'. The guidance notes appended to the form indicate that where the form is signed on behalf of a company, the signature provided must be that of a director, secretary or solicitor acting for the company or of some other person duly authorised by the articles of association.

The legal consequences of the signature are not clear. Though the use of the term 'verification' might be taken to imply that the signature attests the accuracy of the particulars supplied, the form does not contain a statement to this effect. Instead it simply provides spaces for signatures, as well as a description of the signor's position and interest in the charge. Neither the Companies Acts, nor the Forms Order, specify any penalty for a person who, whether knowingly or otherwise, signs a Form C1 that contains false or inaccurate particulars. Either or both the chargor and chargee may sign the verification statement, but where only one signature is provided, the form states that a certified copy of the original charge document must be supplied along with the form.

Once the Form C1 has been delivered and the Registrar has registered the charge, a certificate of registration (which must include a statement of the amount secured thereby) is issued under s 104 of the 1963 Act. Section 104 provides that this certificate is conclusive evidence that the requirements of Part IV as to registration have been complied with. Finally, s 106 provides the High Court with a jurisdiction to order rectification of the register or to permit the registration of a charge outside the normal 21-day period for registration.

The Existing Interpretation of Section 104

The available parliamentary records do not definitively explain why the certificate of registration was included in the legislation providing for the establishment of the company charge register. Nonetheless it is fairly clear as a matter of logic that the purpose of the certificate is to give certainty to the parties to a charge that registration has been correctly carried out. Three reasons can be advanced in support of this proposition. First, though the Companies Acts formally place the duty to deliver the particulars on the company, the most serious sanction for failing to do so falls on the secured creditor, which loses the benefit of the charge against the liquidator and other creditors. Accordingly, it might be argued that the certificate of registration allows the company to furnish its creditor, or any other interested party, with proof that 'it has fulfilled its statutory duty'.[21] Secondly, under the initial text of the 1900 Act,[22] the company

21. William Gough, *Company Charges* (2nd edn, LexisNexis 1996) 716.

22. s 14(6) Companies Act 1900.

was required to include a copy of the certificate of registration on any debentures or certificates of debenture stock related to the charge.[23] Thirdly, and most importantly, the presence of the certificate reduces the risk to that the chargee will find itself unable to enforce its security because of an error in the registration process. The scope of this protection will be explored below.[24] It has also been suggested in the case law that the draftsperson may have included the certificate as a means of preventing the kind of challenges to security interests on technical grounds that had previously been encountered in the registration of bills of sale.[25] In addition, it should be noted that the certificates of registration have played a role in safeguarding the information contained on the register. In 1924, certificates of registration were used to reconstitute the company charge register after the destruction of the Public Record Office during the Irish Civil War.[26]

Section 104 states that the certificate of registration is 'conclusive evidence that the requirements of [Part IV of the Act] as to registration have been complied with'. As will be demonstrated below, the courts have interpreted the words 'conclusive evidence' in a literal manner. The meaning of this section has been explored by the courts in a number of cases, which broadly fall into two categories: cases where inaccurate particulars have been delivered to the Registrar, and cases where there has been an irregularity of one kind or another in the registration process.

Delivery of Inaccurate Particulars

Most of the case law on s 104 focuses on the delivery of inaccurate particulars to the Registrar. The leading English case in this area is *National Provincial and Union Bank of England v Charnley*,[27] in which the company had granted a charge over a leasehold interest in the land upon which one of its factories was built. The charge also covered the equipment used in or about the premises. The particulars delivered to the Registrar mentioned a charge on the land but made no reference to the equipment. The Registrar entered the particulars as delivered onto the register and issued a certificate of registration. The Registrar failed to notice that the particulars delivered incorrectly described the property that was the subject of the charge. In a subsequent dispute between the chargee and a judgment creditor of the company, the Court of Appeal held that:

> [O]nce the registrar has given his certificate that the registration was complete, and that the mortgage or charge was created by an instrument, identifying it, in my

---

23. This requirement has been retained in England under s 865 Companies Act 2006 but was repealed in Ireland in 1963.
24. See *Re: Yolland, Husson and Birkett Ltd* [1908] 1 Ch 152 at 158 per Cozens-Hardy MR, hereafter '*Yolland*'; *National Provincial and Union Bank of England v Charnley* [1924] 1 KB 431, 447–48 per Scrutton LJ, hereafter '*Charnley*'; and *Re: CL Nye Ltd* [1971] 1 Ch 442 at 470 per Harman LJ and 474 per Russell LJ, hereafter '*CL Nye*'.
25. See *Charnley*, 453, per Atkin LJ.
26. See ss 3–4 and Schedule 4 of the Companies (Re-Constitution of Records) Act 1924.
27. *Charnley*.

> opinion you have to go to the instrument to see what was actually charged, there being nothing in the statute which says that when once registration has taken place the register shall be the evidence of the extent of the charge.[28]

The effect of the judgment is that the certificate of registration 'must be understood as certifying the due registration of all the charges created by the instrument... the fact that the register was defective and misleading to a potential creditor of the company [will] not sway the court'.[29] A similar result was reached in Ireland in *Re: Valley Ice Cream (Ireland) Ltd*.[30] From a policy point of view, this outcome is entirely unsatisfactory as it results in a situation in which the information by the company charge register cannot be relied upon by interested parties who search the register.

The subsequent case law in England and in Ireland has applied the *Charnley* principle in several different contexts. In *Re: Mechanisations (Eaglescliff) Ltd*[31] and *Re: Shannonside Holdings Ltd*,[32] the courts considered a similar fact pattern in which the amount secured by the charge had been misstated in the particulars. In both cases it was held that the certificate of registration meant that the charges had been properly registered and were enforceable to the amount provided for in the charge documents rather than the amount mistakenly entered into the particulars. In *Re: Investment Options and Solutions Ltd*,[33] Laffoy J suggested *obiter* that the same reasoning would apply to a clerical error about the date of creation of the charge, a conclusion previously endorsed by the English courts in *Re: Eric Holmes (Property) Ltd*.[34]

Irregularities in the Registration Process

The second group of cases concerns a situation in which there has been an irregularity in the registration process. In contrast to the defective particulars cases where the error is made by the person filling out the particulars for delivery to the Registrar, the second category of cases will usually involve an allegation that the Registrar has acted improperly in registering the charge as he or she did. The leading case in this category is *Re: Yolland, Husson and Birkett Ltd*, in which the company had made two separate issues of a series of debentures supported by a single floating charge. The terms of series provided that the debentures numbered 1–84 were to have priority to later debentures in the series. Initially an attempt was made to register the two issues of the debenture series separately. It would appear that the Registrar objected to this course of action and that following discussions, the whole series was eventually

28. ibid 444–45.
29. McCormack, *Registration of Company Charges*, 215.
30. Unreported, High Court, McCracken J, 22 July 1998.
31. [1966] 1 Ch 20, hereafter '*Eric Holmes*'.
32. Unreported, High Court, Costello J, 20 May 1993.
33. [2010] IEHC 107.
34. [1965] 1 Ch 1052.

registered as a single charge.[35] The Registrar issued a certificate of registration that made no mention of the priority position of the different debentures in the series. In the Court of Appeal, counsel for the liquidator argued that a separate charge should be been registered for each separate debenture and that as a result the Registrar's certificate had been incorrectly issued.[36] The court rejected this argument, holding that the conclusive effect of the certificate prevented the court from looking behind it.

An important variation on the *Yolland* theme has been considered by the English courts in *CL Nye*[37] and in Ireland in *Lombard & Ulster Banking Ireland Ltd v Amurec Ltd*.[38] In *CL Nye* a charge was created over the company's property in February 1964. Owing to an oversight in the office of the solicitor for the chargee, the particulars of the charge were not delivered to the Registrar. The error was discovered on or about 18 June 1964, at which point the solicitor inserted that date into the charge document and then presented a set of particulars, also bearing that date to the Registrar. In *Amurec* the charge was created in November 1972. Delivery of the particulars was to be the responsibility of the company's solicitor, but this was not carried out immediately owing to a problem with the payment of stamp duty, which emerged after the completion of the transaction. In March 1974 the solicitor for the company decided to regularise the situation by dating the charge document 22 March 1974 and presenting the particulars for registration on 10 April 1974. In both cases the Registrar accepted the particulars and a certificate was duly issued. Both courts held that the wording of the legislation and the prior case law precluded the court from reaching any other conclusion than that the charges had been validly registered, though Hamilton J expressed 'considerable sympathy'[39] with the arguments of the liquidator that the particulars of the charge had not been delivered within the required time.

Applications for an Extension of Time or for Rectification of the Company Charge Register

Section 106 provides that the High Court may, on the application of the company or any person with an interest in the charge, make an order for the extension of time for registration or for rectification of the charge register on such terms as it considers just and expedient. Before making the order the court must be satisfied that that there has been an omission to register or that there has been an error or

35. See the detailed statement of facts in the headnote to the first instance decision at [1907] 2 Ch 471, 473.
36. *Charnley*, 155.
37. *CL Nye*.
38. [1976–1977] ILRM 222, hereafter '*Amurec*'.
39. ibid 224.

omission in one of the supplied particulars. The court must also be satisfied that one of the following conditions apply:

a. The error was accidental or due to inadvertence or some other sufficient cause; or,
b. The error is not of a nature to prejudice the position of the company's creditors or shareholders; or,
c. The making of an order is just and equitable on other grounds.

Relief under s 106 is discretionary and will not be ordered where it would be futile,[40] where the applicant has been guilty of some misconduct such as failing to disclose all relevant facts to the court,[41] or where the application has been brought after an undue delay.[42] The majority of reported applications under this section are for an extension of time for the delivery of particulars and such applications are usually granted unless a winding up has already commenced.[43] Where an extension of time is granted the order will usually be made subject to the so-called '*Joplin* provision' so that the order is without prejudice to the rights of the other secured parties who have acquired a competing charge before the actual delivery of the particulars to the Registrar.[44]

In view of the conclusive effect of the certificate, it is no surprise to find that applications for rectification of the register are uncommon. Previously the author of a leading Irish company law text book has suggested that an application for rectification should not be made where a certificate of registration has been issued, as doing so might expose the chargee to the imposition of conditions on the registration of the charge, which might adversely affect its position.[45] In *Re: Investments Options and Solutions Ltd*[46] the particulars of the charge that had been delivered to the Registrar misstated the date on which the charge had been created, though, in fact, the particulars had been delivered within time. A certificate of registration was issued. The successors in title to the chargee, who had appointed a receiver to the company, sought rectification of the error as they were concerned that the error might give rise to questions about the receiver's authority to sell the encumbered property. The High Court held that it was appropriate to order rectification since the particulars of the charge had in fact been registered within the relevant time period.

40. *Re: Farm Fresh Frozen Foods Ltd* [1980] ILRM 131, 136.
41. *Re: Telomatic Ltd* [1994] 1 BCLC 90, 94.
42. *Re: Ashputron Estates Ltd* [1983] Ch 110.
43. Beale and others (n 16), 350.
44. *Re: Joplin Brewery* [1902] 1 Ch 79.
45. Thomas Courtney, *Law of Private Companies* (2nd edn, LexisNexis 2002) [21.090]. Courtney's views have changed in light of *Re: Investment Options and Solutions Ltd*. See Thomas Courtney, *Law of Private Companies* (3rd edn, Bloomsbury Professional 2012) [19.092]. See also Lyndon McCann and Thomas Courtney (eds), *Companies Acts 1963–2006* (Bloomsbury Professional 2007) 225.
46. *Re: Investment Options and Solutions Ltd*.

Section 106 proceedings can cause other irregularities in the registration process, as was demonstrated in *Exeter Trust Ltd v Screenways Ltd*[47] and *Ali v Top Marques Car Rental Ltd.*[48] In *Exeter Trust* particulars of a registrable charge had not been delivered within the 21-day period. On 5 December 1988 the company issued a notice to its creditors of a creditors' meeting to take place on 21 December 1988 as part of the process of initiating a creditors' voluntary winding-up of the company. The chargee partnership received this notice and on 14 December 1988 it applied to the County Court, under the equivalent of s 106 of the Companies Act 1963 for an order to extend the time for delivery of the particulars. The application was grounded on the affidavit of one of the partners in the chargee, which explained the reasons for the failure to register on time but omitted to mention the impending creditors' meetings. An order extending the time was made on 19 December 1988, extending the deadline for delivery to 9 January 1989. The particulars were delivered on 21 December 1988 approximately 90 minutes before the commencement of the creditors' meeting and a certificate of registration was duly issued. In April 1989, the liquidator of the company successfully appealed the decision to extend the time for delivery and the court ordered that the register of charges be rectified by the deletion of the charge. In the Court of Appeal, the chargee argued that the certificate of registration precluded the court below from ordering rectification of the companies register. The Court of Appeal allowed the appeal. Delivering the unanimous judgment of the Court, Nourse LJ held that he was unable to distinguish this case from earlier decisions such as *Yolland* and *CL Nye*, in which the certificate had been held to be conclusive.[49]

In *Top Marques* the chargee had obtained an order extending time for delivery while the company was in administration. The order was made subject to the standard proviso in such cases ('a *Re: Charles* order'),[50] ie that the company's administrator or any creditor would be at liberty to apply to the court to discharge the order within 14 days. The secured creditor further gave an undertaking that it would submit to the jurisdiction of the court and would abide by any order made as a result of such an application to discharge the order. At a subsequent hearing, counsel for the administrator sought to have extension of time set aside on the basis that the company was insolvent at the date when the order was made and that it had no prospect of emerging from the administration restored to solvency.[51] Counsel for the chargee argued that there was no need for the court to consider this point, since the particulars had in fact been delivered and a certificate of registration had been issued before the expiry of the 14-day period. The Registrar

47. [1991] BCLC 888, hereafter '*Exeter Trust*'.
48. [2006] EWHC 109 (Ch), hereafter '*Top Marques*'.
49. *Exeter Trust*, 893.
50. See *Re: Charles (LH) & Co Ltd* [1935] WN 15.
51. On the significance of the company's solvency to the making of an order extending the time for registration, see *Re: Ashpurton Estates Ltd* and *Re: Resnoid & Mica Products Ltd* [1983] Ch 132 (decided in 1967). See also Beale, *Law of Personal Property Security*, 352; and McCormack, *Registration of Company Charges*, 224–25.

of Companies gave evidence that the certificate of registration had been issued in error and that the Registrar's normal practice in such cases was to delay issuing the certificate of registration until any time period specified in the extension order had expired.

The court held that in terms of the initial order, extending the time for delivery of the particulars amounted to an 'implied direction' to the Registrar not to issue a certificate while the order remained subject to review. However, having reviewed the earlier authorities the court held that it was 'constrained to the view' that once the certificate had been issued it was beyond the power of the court to order its recall and that the circumstances of the certificate's issue were not such as to undermine its conclusiveness.[52]

In Ireland, the courts appear to have reached a different conclusion on at least one occasion. In *Re: Telford Motors Ltd*,[53] an order extending the time for registration had likewise been made. At the time of the application, the commencement of a winding-up of the company was imminent and as such it was made a condition of the order that if the company was wound-up within 21 days of the date of the order, the company would be at liberty to apply to court to have the order discharged. The applicant committed to submit itself to the jurisdiction of the court and to abide by any order that might be made at that point for the removal of the late registration from the Registrar. The particulars were delivered to the Registrar and eight days later a liquidator was appointed to the company. The Registrar registered the charge two days after the appointment of the liquidator.

The court held that the charge had not been properly registered. Hamilton J stated that to regard the late registration as valid would be to disregard the terms of the court's original order and to treat the conditions of that order as an 'empty formula'.[54] It can be argued that *Re: Telford* represents a departure from the normal principle that a certificate of registration, once issued, is beyond recall. However, it must be noted that, unlike *Exeter Trust* and *Top Marques*, the court was dealing with a fresh application for directions from the liquidator and not a continuation of the proceedings surrounding the original s 106 application. Furthermore, from the judgment, it is not clear that the effect of the certificate of registration was canvassed in argument before the court.

Judicial Review Proceedings

The final aspect of the certificate of registration that needs to be considered is its impact in judicial review proceedings. In *R v Registrar of Companies, ex parte Central Bank of India*,[55] an attempt was made to utilise judicial review proceedings in order to evade the consequences of the certificate of registration. The judicial review

52. *Top Marques*, [29]–[30].
53. Unreported, High Court, 27 January 1978.
54. ibid, 10.
55. [1986] 1 QB 1114, hereafter '*Central Bank of India*'.

proceedings were taken by the company and a number of intervening creditors as an aspect of a broader set of plenary proceedings in which the applicants wished to dispute the validity of the registration of a charge.

The facts were as follows. The company had opened a series of documentary credits at Allied Arab Bank ('AAB'). The agreement required the company to provide security when called upon to do so by AAB. A call for security was made in February 1984 by the delivery of a draft debenture the company. The company refused to comply and AAB then obtained an order for specific performance requiring the company to provide the security required under the agreement. AAB took the view that the call for security, coupled with the order for specific performance, had the effect of creating a charge over the company's property, which required registration as of 4 February 1984. The bank delivered a copy of the charge document and the particulars on 29 February 1984. On 23 March 1984, one of the Registrar's officials contacted the bank's solicitors and stated that the particulars that had been submitted were unsatisfactory in a number of respects. It was agreed that the documents would be returned to the solicitors for amendment and resubmission. In line with the Registrar's practice at the time, it was further agreed that the resubmitted documents would be treated as a having been submitted on 29 February 1984. Revised particulars were resubmitted to the Registrar on 29 March 1984. A certificate of registration was duly issued, which recorded that the charge had been registered on 29 February 1984.

The company sought an order of *certiorari* to quash the registration of the charge together with the certificate of incorporation. At the hearing, three grounds were argued by the applicants:

(a) that the Registrar had exceeded his jurisdiction in considering the particulars delivered on 29 March because these particulars were delivered outside the 21-day time limit specified in the legislation;
(b) that there was an error on the face of the record in that the documents delivered on 29 February were in fact the prescribed particulars required by the Act;
(c) that there had been a breach of fair procedures in that in the peculiar circumstances of the case, the Registrar ought not to have taken a decision to register the charge without affording the company or other intervening creditors an opportunity to make representations as to the appropriate course of action;

At first instance the court held that in principle a decision of the Registrar of Companies to issue a certificate of registration is amenable to judicial review. Having considered *Yolland* and the other English cases that have examined the effect of the certificate in ordinary litigation, Mervyn-Davies J held that in judicial review proceedings, concerns about 'commercial uncertainty must give way to the policy that the decisions of public officials ought to be subject to… scrutiny'.[56] He went on to hold that in issuing the certificate based on the

56. ibid 1134.

amended particulars, the Registrar had assumed a jurisdiction that was not provided for by the statute and made an order quashing the Registrar's decision to register the charge and the certificate of registration issued pursuant to that decision.

The Registrar of Companies successfully appealed the decision of the High Court. In reversing the court below, the court accepted the submissions of counsel for the Registrar to the effect that conclusiveness of the certificate of registration is a rule of evidence and not a rule that exempts the Registrar from judicial review. On this view, if 'an unsecured creditor seeks judicial review solely on the ground that the chargee did not deliver the prescribed particulars he cannot put the necessary evidence before the court'.[57] Lawton LJ also recorded, without making a positive comment as to their validity, that counsel for the Registrar had suggested three limitations on this principle.

(a) Where an unsecured creditor seeks judicial review on other grounds, such as that the certificate was obtained by fraud, there might be a case for judicial review.
(b) Since the Companies Acts are not expressly binding on the Crown it might be open to the Attorney General to challenge the validity of a certificate of registration.
(c) A chargee who has failed to disclose information to the Registrar which might have affected his decision on whether to register the charge or not may find himself estopped from relying on the charge in proceedings with an unsecured creditor.

Central Bank of India suggests that there is little practical prospect of utilising public law remedies to alleviate the effect of the Registrar's certificate. Whether the Irish courts would take a similar view of the effect of the certificate in public law proceedings has never been judicially considered.

A Re-Interpretation of Section 104

The conclusive effect of the issue of a certificate of registration has obvious advantages when viewed from the perspective of a secured creditor. In light of the case law reviewed in the previous section it would appear that once a certificate is issued, there is virtually no risk whatsoever of the chargee being unable to enforce their security against the liquidator or a competing creditor as a result of a defect in the registration process. From the perspective of a person interested in promoting the broad policy objectives of the company charge register, however, the certificate of registration must be viewed very differently.

The purpose of the company charge register is to provide information to interested parties about the charges a company has granted over its property.

57. ibid 1169.

In *Yolland,* the 'mischief' that promoted the introduction of the system was described in the following terms:

> It was that companies were allowed to issue debentures, charging very frequently all their present and future assets, and there might be no means of ascertaining, at all events for a considerable time, whether any such debentures were issued; and therefore, for the protection of the general creditors of the company, or of persons desiring to trade with the company, it was thought fit to require that there should be a register of mortgages of that particular kind, not merely in the company's own books, but kept by the registrar.[58]

The certificate for registration actively undermines the ability of third parties to rely on the information obtained by a search of the register. Where erroneous information is given to the Registrar as in cases like *Charnley, Shannonside Holdings* and *Mechanisations*, there is a real and obvious risk that a person examining the register of company charges may be misled into believing that some or all of the company's assets are unencumbered when in fact this is not the case. In cases such *CL Nye* and *Amurec* the danger is even greater, in that interests that were not registered within the requisite time period may be validated as a result of a certificate of registration erroneously issued weeks or even months after the time for delivery of the particulars has passed. Since competing charges normally rank in order of their time of creation, this opens the possibility that a later creditor, who takes a subsequent charge before registration of the first charge actually occurs, may find himself losing priority to an earlier, undiscoverable, interest.

The courts have consistently answered arguments of this nature by stating that, as a matter of statutory interpretation, the wording of the statute requires the court to refrain from looking behind the certificate of registration. In some cases there is evidence of judicial discomfort with the consequences of the existing interpretation. For instance, Hamilton J in *Amurec* stated that he had considerable sympathy with the position of the liquidator who was seeking to set the certificate aside,[59] while Pennycuick J in *Eric Holmes* stated that he felt that there must be some 'lacuna' in the Acts that resulted in the Court having to uphold a certificate made on the basis of particulars which were incorrect and 'might even be fraudulent'.[60]

The purpose of this section is to challenge the view that there is no interpretation, other than the current one, open to a court when presented with a certificate of registration. Since this section of the article requires a close reading of the relevant provisions, it is necessary to reproduce some of the most significant sections of the Act here. Section 99(1) of the Companies

58. *Yolland*, 156.
59. *Amurec*, 227.
60. *Eric Holmes*, 1072.

Act 1963 establishes the requirement for charges to be registered and sets out two the consequences of a failure to register. It reads as follows:

> 99. —(1) Subject to the provisions of this Part, every charge created after the fixed date by a company, and being a charge to which this section applies, shall, so far as any security on the company's property or undertaking is conferred thereby, be void against the liquidator and any creditor of the company, unless the prescribed particulars of the charge, verified in the prescribed manner, are delivered to or received by the registrar of companies for registration in manner required by this Act within 21 days after the date of its creation, but without prejudice to any contract or obligation for repayment of the money thereby secured, and when a charge becomes void under this section, the money secured thereby shall immediately become payable.

Section 100 imposes a duty on the company to deliver the particulars of charges created over its property to the Registrar of Companies and provides for a criminal sanction where this step is not carried out. The relevant portions of the section read as follows:

> 100.—(1) It shall be the duty of a company to send to the registrar of companies for registration within the time required by section 99 the particulars of every charge created by the company, and of the issues of debentures of a series requiring registration under section 99, together with any documents required by that section, but registration of any such charge may be effected on the application of any person interested therein.

Section 103 requires the Registrar of Companies to maintain the company charge register and to enter onto the register the particulars of charges. The relevant subsection reads as follows:

> 103.—(1) The registrar of companies shall keep, in relation to each company, a register in the prescribed form of all the charges requiring registration under this Part, and shall, on payment of such fee as may be prescribed, enter in the register, in relation to such charges, the following particulars…

Section 104 provides for the issuing and effect of the certificate of registration and reads as follows:

> 104.—The registrar shall give a certificate under his hand of the registration of any charge registered in pursuance of this Part, stating the amount thereby secured, and the certificate shall be conclusive evidence that the requirements of this Part as to registration have been complied with.

A close reading of these sections suggests the following. A registrable charge is void under s 99(1) if, and only if, the prescribed particulars have not been 'delivered to or received by the registrar of companies' within the time limit provided. The purpose of making that delivery is to enable the Registrar of

Companies to register the charge. The statute does not, in fact, make the validity of the charge dependent on the particulars being registered.

Further support for this view can be found in s 100(1), which defines the duty of the company in terms of 'sending' the particulars to the Registrar and not in terms of carrying out registration. It is suggested that if a company or chargee could prove, for instance by *via voce* evidence, that the necessary particulars were in fact delivered to the Registrar, the charge would be valid even if the Registrar had taken no action whatsoever after the delivery had taken place. Authority for this point can be found in the decision of the High Court in *Re: Investment Options and Solutions Ltd* in which Laffoy J was satisfied, without need to refer to the certificate that a charge had been registered within time.[61] Additional support can be found in *Grove v Advantage Healthcare (T10)*.[62] There the particulars delivered to the Registrar were correct in all respects; however the form which was used misstated the company's registered number and instead bore the number of a related company, Advantage Healthcare (T9) Ltd. A certificate of registration was issued bearing T9's registered number. Lightman J held that the certificate was conclusive evidence that T9 had registered a charge but that with reference to T10 the certificate was a nullity. Nonetheless, the Court held that the company's number is not a prescribed particular, and since there was clear evidence that T10 had in fact delivered all of the particulars, the Court held that the charge was not invalidated by the equivalent of s 99(1). Finally it should be pointed out that the last clause in s 100(1) permits a third party with an interest in the charge to make an application to the Registrar to have the charge registered. It does not permit the third party to actually make the registration on its own behalf.

That the duty to attend to registration falls on the Registrar rather than the person who delivers the particulars seems to be beyond doubt in light of the wording of ss 99(2) and 100(1), both of which speak of delivering particulars to the Registrar 'for registration'. Further confirmation can be found in the wording of s 103, which imposes a dual duty on the Registrar: first to maintain a register of charges for each company and then to enter the particulars of each charge into that register on receiving payment of the required fee.

Once it is clearly understood that the Registrar is required to attend to registration of the charge and that the duty of the company is merely to deliver the particulars to the Registrar in order to facilitate the registration of the charge, s 104 can be read in a different light. Section 104 speaks of the certificate as being 'conclusive evidence that the requirements of this Part *as to registration* have been complied with' (emphasis added). If registration, as distinct from delivery of particulars, is the duty of the Registrar of Companies, then a literal reading of s 104 can only result in the conclusion that the certificate is evidence that the *Registrar* has complied with his duty under Part IV. On this view, the certificate of registration provides no evidence at all, much less evidence of a conclusive

61. [2010] IEHC 107, [9].
62. [2000] 1 BCLC 661.

nature, on the separate question of whether the company has complied with its duty to deliver the particulars to the Registrar.

Such an approach appears particularly apposite in the Irish context when it is borne in mind that in 1963 the Oireachtas removed the requirement that the Registrar be provided with the original charge document along with the prescribed particulars. The role of the Registrar in the Irish system is purely a mechanical one of receiving particulars and entering them on the register. In light of such a system, it is surely absurd to claim that the Oireachtas, having repealed the ability of the Registrar to verify the particulars, simultaneously intended that the Registrar would certify their veracity. Such a result, it is suggested, would require clear words to that effect to be located in the statute and no such words appear in s 104.

It can also be pointed out that there are at least are two cases in which the English courts seem to have ignored the conclusive effect of the certificate in a manner that would fit with proposed reinterpretation of s 104. In *Esberger & Son v Capital and Counties Bank*[63] a company deposited title deeds to its land together with a signed and sealed, though undated, memorandum of a charge, which was to secure certain future advances made by the bank. A series of advances were made by the bank under the arrangement. Some nine months after the deposit, a manager in the bank filled in that day's date into the memorandum and then proceeded to send details of the charge to the Registrar. In the High Court, Sargant J held that the charge had been created at the date on which the first advance had been made and that it was void for want of registration within 21 days of that date. The court did not offer any reason for ignoring the certificate of registration; indeed it would appear that the certificate point was not argued between the parties at the hearing and *Yolland* was not cited in argument. Similarly, in *Re: N Defries & Co*,[64] Buckley J examined considered whether or not, as a matter of fact, the charge in question had been registered within time despite the presence of a certificate of registration. *Defries* was not cited before the Court of Appeal in *Yolland.*

A reinterpretation of s 104 has the further advantage that it provides a more harmonious fit between ss 104 and 106. At present, the rectification mechanism provided for by s 106 is virtually redundant, since in all cases once a certificate of registration has been issued there can be no question but that the charge is valid no matter what errors may appear on the register. Under the reinterpretation contended for in this article, s 106 would have an important role to play in the registration of company charges. It would provide a mechanism for the correction of errors. At the same time it would allow for the protection of the reasonable expectations of those who rely in good faith on the accuracy of the register through the court's jurisdiction to impose conditions on an order for rectification.

63. [1913] 2 Ch 366.
64. [1904] 1 Ch 37.

While a fresh interpretation of s 104 would have several advantages, it is important to note there are limits to what a judicial rethink of the legislative framework can achieve. The certificate would continue to have conclusive effects as regards the actions of the registrar, with the result that in fact patterns such *Exeter Trust* and *Top Marques* it would probably continue to be beyond the reach of the courts to conclude that the charge had been properly registered. Similarly, it would appear that reinterpretation would not open the possibility of applications for a judicial review of the Registrar's decision-making since the certificate would continue to act as conclusive evidence that the Registrar had discharged his function correctly.

Two objections can be mounted to this interpretation of s 104. One is based on the decision in *Yolland* and the many cases that have followed it. The second is based on pragmatic considerations of policy.

In *Yolland* the Court of Appeal recognised that registration of a charge involves two steps, one of delivery and one of registration. It also recognised that the different parties to the process have different duties but said of the certificate:

> [It] means not merely that he has done his mechanical duties, but that that has been done which is required to be done by any person upon whom a duty is imposed by this Act in order to get the benefit of the security, including the company itself.[65]

The difficulty with this statement is twofold. First, Cozens-Hardy MR provides no textual basis in the statute itself for his assertion that the certificate is intended to provide evidence that persons other the Registrar have done their duty under the Act. Second, the statement must be regarded as an *obiter dictum*, because what was being decided in that case was whether the Registrar's decision to register a series of debentures under a single entry was correct or not. In other words the court was being asked to consider whether the Registrar had performed his duty or not. The question of whether the company had fulfilled its duty by sending (or 'filing' to use the language of s 14(6) of the Companies Act 1900 as it then stood) the prescribed particulars to the Registrar was not before the court.

The policy objection to the above is that if the certificate of registration is not conclusive evidence that a charge has been properly registered, then all company charges are at risk of being challenged by liquidators and creditors of companies. For chargees it might be claimed, this would be, as Cozens-Hardy MR put it in *Yolland*, 'an unendurable state of things'[66] and the spectre would be raised of the company charge register attracting the same sort of interminable litigation over the technical requirements of registration as has made the registration system for the bills of sale commercially unworkable.[67]

---

65. *Yolland*,159.
66. ibid 158.
67. For an overview of the experiences with the bills of sale register in Ireland, see Barbara Maguire, 'Bills of Sale: The Forgotten Relation?' (1997) 4 CLP 3. The

The extent to which it is appropriate to have regard to detailed arguments about the desirability of a particular policy outcome when engaged in statutory interpretation is of course open to question. Leaving that qualification to one side, however, several responses can be made to the policy argument. First, had the legislature wished to extend the protection of the certificate to the delivery of particulars it would have been easy do to so by inserting the words 'and delivery of particulars' after the word 'registration' in s 104.

Secondly, the requirements imposed on the company by ss 99 and 100 are nowhere near as complicated as those imposed on an individual seeking to register a security bill of sale under the Bills of Sale (Ireland) Acts 1879–1883. To take but one example, s 9 of Bills of Sale (Ireland) (1879) Amendment Act 1883 provides that every bill of sale must, as a condition of its validity' be drafted 'in accordance with' a sample bill set out in Schedule 1 to the Act. It is extremely difficult to define with a precision how far one can safely depart from the statutory form without infringing s 9.[68] There is no equivalent requirement for a company charge.

Thirdly, the loss of certainty that would be suffered by chargees under a revised interpretation of s 104 would be offset by the increased certainty produced for those who rely on the information provided by the register in their day-to-day dealings. It might also be said that the degree of uncertainty faced by chargees can be reduced by taking due care to ensure that particulars delivered to the Registrar are fully accurate. On this view, a chargee who loses their security as a result of an error in registration is the author of his own misfortune and has only himself (or his legal advisor) to blame. It is certainly easier for a chargee to ensure that the particulars are accurate when presented to the Registrar than it is for a member of the public to verify whether the information contained on the company charge register is correct. Since the avowed purpose of the company charge registration system is to provide information to the public, it is difficult to argue in favour of an interpretation of s 104 that undermines the accuracy of that information. Finally, as noted above, in the event that an error in the registered particulars is discovered, s 106 provides a mechanism whereby a chargee can seek to rectify the difficulty by application to court, a relief not afforded to the holder of an unregistered bill of sale.

The Companies Consolidation and Reform Bill 2012

The previous sections have argued for a judicial reconsideration of the interpretation of s 104 of the Companies Act 1963. The final section of this article will consider the impact of the proposed changes to the company charge registration system contained in the Companies Consolidation and Reform Bill 2012.

---

difficulties with the system are best summed up by Goode, who has claimed that 'it is easier for a camel to pass through the eye of a needle than for a bill of sale to be drafted which complies with all the technical requirements of the Acts', see Roy Goode, 'Removing the Obstacles to Commercial Law Reform' (2007) 123 LQR 602, 603.

68. See William Johnston, *Banking and Security Law in Ireland* (Butterworths 1996) 418–26.

In its Second Report on the reform of Irish company law, the Company Law Review Group ('CLRG') considered the impact of s 104 on the charge registration system. Focusing in particular on the existing requirement to describe the property subject to the charge, the CLRG acknowledged, under the present law, 'it is quite possible that… Certificates of Charge,… have been issued by the Registrar where the requirements [as to registration] have not in fact been complied with'.[69]

The CLRG made a number of recommendations for reform of the process for registering charges in Ireland. It argued for the abolition of the list of registrable charges currently provided in s 99 and its replacement with a general requirement that all charges be brought within the registration system.[70] The CLRG suggested extensive changes in the system of charge registration and argued for a transition to a wholly electronic system of registration in which the date of registration would be used in establishing priority between competing charges.[71] The CLRG also recommended substantial alterations to the particulars, which must be sent to the CRO in order to satisfy the registration requirement. The suggested particulars would omit the requirement to specify the category of the charge being registered and would omit the requirement to specify the amount secured by the charge. The requirement to supply a description of the property subject to the charge was retained; however the CLRG recommended that the law be changed so as to restrict to the conclusive effect to the certificate 'only as to the charges particulars of which have been filed'.

The changes recommended by the CLRG have found legislative expression in Part 7, Chapter 25 of the Companies Consolidation and Reform Bill 2012 ('the 2012 Bill').[72] While the 2012 Bill implements the reforms suggested by the CLRG, the drafting of the key provisions retains much of language and structure of the current legislation. In particular, much of the legislative language that has been analysed above in arguing that the present understanding of the effect of the certificate of registration is flawed is repeated in the new proposed legislation.

Clause 410 of the 2012 Bill establishes the principle that a charge is void against the liquidator and any creditor of the company unless one of two registration procedures has been followed. The two registration systems are designed to enable a charge to be registered either before or after a charge

69. Company Law Review Group, *Report on Second Work Programme of Company Law Review Group 2002–2003* (2004) [8.11.4].

70. ibid 8.2.5. The general principle of requiring registration is subject to an exception for financial collateral arrangements: see European Communities (Financial Collateral Arrangements) Regulations 2004 (SI 1/2004) and the European Communities (Financial Collateral Arrangements) (Amendment) (No 2) Regulations 2011 (SI 318/2011).

71. Company Law Review Group, *Second Work Programme* [8.3.11].

72. For a detailed consideration of the effect of the proposed legislation on the company charge register, see Noel McGrath, 'The Company Charge Register in Ireland: Some Reflections on the Reform Proposals in the Companies Consolidation and Reform Bill 2012' [2013] JBL 03.

has been created and both procedures involve a prescribed set of particulars in the prescribed form.[73] Under the first procedure ('the normal registration procedure') a charge is void unless the prescribed particulars are delivered within 21 days of the date of creation. Under the second procedure ('the early registration procedure'), a notice of an intention to create a charge may be delivered to the Registrar along with the prescribed particulars. Within 21 days of the delivery of notice, a second notice must be delivered to the Registrar confirming that the charge has been created. Where this is done, the charge is treated for priority purpsoes as having been registered at the date the initial notice was received. Where the second notice is not filed within a timely manner, the charge is declared void.

The prescribed particulars have not been specified in the primary legislation; however it would appear from the CLRG report and from Clause 415, which imposes a duty on the Registrar to maintain the charge register for each company, that the following particulars will be included:

a. The name and registered number of the company creating the charge;
b. The date of creation of the charge;
c. The name and contact details of the person presenting the particulars to the Registrar;
d. The name and contact details of the person entitled to the charge;
e. A description of the property subject to the charge.[74]

In setting out the procedures for carrying out registration, Clause 410(3) and 410(4) make it clear that the procedures for registration are completed when the Registrar of Companies has received the prescribed particulars. Thus, under the 2012 Bill, the actual registration of the charge itself remains the function of the Registrar.[75] Clause 416 provides for the issuing and effect of the certificate of registration and is worth setting out in full:

> 416.—(1) The Registrar shall give a certificate of the registration of any charge registered in pursuance of this Part.
>
> (2) Subject to subsection (3), such a certificate shall be conclusive evidence that the requirements of this Part as to the registration of the charge have been complied with.
>
> (3) To the extent that the particulars of a charge delivered to the Registrar in purported compliance with this Part omit the required 25 particulars in respect of one or more properties to which the charge relates, the evidential effect of the certificate provided under subsection (2) shall not extend to the particular property or properties in respect of which that omission occurs.
>
> (4) In subsection (3) 'property' includes an interest in, or right over, property.

73. See *cl* 410(3) and (4) Companies Consolidation and Reform Bill 2012.
74. See Company Law Review Group, *Second Work Programme*, [8.4.1]–[8.4.11].
75. See *cl* 415 Companies Consolidation and Reform Bill 2012, which is phrased in almost identical terms to s 100 Companies Act 1963.

The intended effect of this clause seems to be to disapply the (presumed) conclusive effect of the certificate of registration from descriptions of the property subject to the charge. Thus the outcomes of cases with fact patterns such as those in *Charnley*[76] and *Re: Valley Ice Cream*[77] will be reversed under the new legislation and such cases will be decided in accordance with the interpretation argued for in the previous sections. If passed, clause 416(3) will amount to a legislative rejection of the policy arguments presented by Cozens-Hardy MR in *Yolland* in that it will force those who send particulars to the Registrar to bear the consequences of errors in the documentation they supply – at least in so far as those errors relate to the description of the property that is subject to the charge.

While clause 416(3) clarifies the intention of the legislature in respect of errors relating to the description of the property subject to the charge, the courts will still have to determine the scope of protection afforded by the certificate of registration where other irregularities have occurred in the registration process. Errors relating to the date of creation of the charge provide an interesting example. Clause 410 retains the requirement that the particulars of a charge be presented within 21 days of the date of creation, or within 21 days of the filing of a notice of the intention to create a charge in the case of the early registration procedure. One effect of the inclusion of these 21-day time limits is that there remains a possibility of an *Amurec* type fact pattern emerging in which a certificate of registration is issued to a chargee who did not, as a matter of fact, deliver the particulars of the charge in time.

In such cases the courts will be faced with determining the meaning of clause 416(3) of the Bill, the language of which is drawn directly from the existing s 104 of the 1963 Act. Such a case will present the courts with an identical interpretive dilemma to that currently posed by the existing statutory text. Clause 410, the analogue of s 99 of the 1963 Act, states that a charge is void unless either the normal or early registration procedures have been carried out. These procedures are detailed in Clauses 410(3) and 410(4) respectively and involve the delivery of notices and particulars to the Registrar within defined time limits. Clause 415, the analogue of s 103 of the 1963 Act, imposes duties on the Registrar to companies to maintain registers and carry on registrations. Under the new legislation, therefore, the meaning of the phrase 'conclusive evidence that the requirements of this Part as to the registration of the charge have been complied with' will remain important in at least some cases.

Conclusion

This article has argued that the courts ought to reappraise the interpretation of s 104 of the Companies Act 1963. It has demonstrated that the existing authorities have accorded the certificate of registration a significance that is not envisaged

76. *Charnley.*
77. *Re: Valley Ice Cream Ltd.*

by a plain reading of the words of the statute and that is incompatible with the legislative policy underlying Part IV of the 1963 Act.

The interpretive dilemma addressed by this article has important consequences for the liquidation of Irish companies. Where a charge is void because of a failure to comply with the requirement to send particulars of registration to the Registrar, the assets that were the subject of that charge ought to be distributed to the company's general body of preferred and unsecured creditors rather than being delivered up to the charge holder.[78] It is suggested that the result of the present interpretation is unduly favourable to secured creditors whose charges have not been disclosed to the public in the manner intended by the Oireachtas. While it seems likely that the text of s 104 of the Companies Act 1963 will soon be consigned to history, it should be noted that clause 421 of the Companies Consolidation and Reform Bill 2012 provides that the terms of the 1963 Act will continue to apply to charges created prior to the repeal of the existing legislation. For this reason, the true meaning of s 104 will continue to be of concern to liquidators and creditors for some years to come.

This article has also argued that the changes to company charge registration proposed in the 2012 Bill, while clarifying the position in respect of the description of the property subject to the charge, will continue to present the courts the same problems of interpretation posed by previous versions of the Companies Acts. In interpreting statutes that seek to consolidate earlier enactments, the courts have long recognised that the state of the law before the new legislation was passed is a relevant factor in interpreting the meaning of the new section.[79] It is submitted, therefore, that the precise meaning and effect of s 104 will continue to be a matter of considerable practical importance after the passage of the 2012 Bill.

The meaning and effect of s 104 has been considered settled law for many years. Nonetheless, it is notable that neither the Supreme Court in this jurisdiction, nor the equivalent courts of final appeal in the United Kingdom have ever been presented with an opportunity to review the interpretations of s 104 propounded by High Court and Court of Appeal judges over the last century. The cases reviewed in this article have all taken as their starting point the statements of Cozens-Hardy MR in *Yolland* about the role of the certificate. This article has shown that those statements have been repeated in an uncritical manner by judges and commentators over the years and, perhaps by mere force of repetition, they have become to be regarded as definitive. Be that as it may, as Hardiman J has recently reminded the legal community, '[t]he judgment of a judge, however

78. See s 284(1) Companies Act 1963.

79. *Action Aid Ltd v Revenue Commissioners* Unreported, High Court, Costello J, 15 January 1997; *Attorney General (Fahy) v Bruen (No. 2)* [1937] IR 126; see also David Dodd, *Statutory Interpretation in Ireland* (Bloomsbury Professional, 2007), [8.42]–[8.65].

eminent, should not be construed as though it were a statute'.[80] It might be that a reinterpretation of s 104 would cause an unanticipated alteration of the law as it is presently understood to be but, it is respectfully submitted, that a careful, plain reading of the existing statute would require the judiciary to confine the decision in *Yolland* to its proper context and to reassess those cases that have broadened its impact. Such a reappraisal would, it is suggested, restore the Registrar's certificate to its proper function and would render the company charge register a more useful and reliable source of information about charges created by Irish companies.

80. *Re: Tralee Beef and Lamb Ltd* [2008] 3 IR 347, 358.

Financial Provision on Relationship Breakdown in Ireland: A Constitutional Lacuna?

Lucy-Ann Buckley*

Abstract—This article analyses the constitutional basis for financial provision orders on the breakdown of marriage, civil partnership and cohabitation in Ireland. Although a clear constitutional foundation exists for financial provision on divorce, this does not apply to judicial separation or non-marital relationships. Accordingly, the constitutionality of financial orders in these contexts is questionable. This article examines the constitutional provisions on the family, private property and equality as potential grounds for upholding redistributive mechanisms. It contends that appropriate provision for families in the relationship breakdown context is an important social policy objective which justifies the delimitation of constitutional proprietary interests, and that this is the only constitutional basis that offers equal potential for upholding financial provision measures in the marital, non-marital and same-sex contexts. Although recent case law has posited a new constitutional basis for financial orders on marital breakdown, the article contends that the reasoning adopted is both flawed and limited in application. Consequently, a significant lacuna remains in Irish constitutional law.

Introduction

In recent decades, legislation has had an extraordinary impact on personal property rights in the context of marital and relationship breakdown. Initially under the Judicial Separation and Family Law Reform Act 1989,[1] and subsequently under the Family Law Act 1995[2] and the Family Law (Divorce) Act 1996,[3] courts are empowered to make a wide range of ancillary property orders on judicial separation and divorce. These include orders for the sale or transfer of property, periodical payment orders, lump sum orders, pension adjustment orders and financial compensation orders. All of these orders are discretionary. Neither spouse has an entitlement to a particular share of the marital assets, and judges are required to consider particular criteria, largely based on resources,

* Lecturer in Law, National University of Ireland Galway. I am grateful to Dr Tom Hickey, Dublin City University, for his helpful comments on an earlier draft of this paper.

1. Hereafter 'the 1989 Act'.
2. Hereafter 'the 1995 Act'. Note that the 1995 Act largely repealed and replaced the 1989 Act.
3. Hereafter 'the 1996 Act'.

contributions and need, before making any order.[4] The overriding statutory requirement is that the court must be satisfied that 'proper' provision has been or will be made for both spouses and any dependent family member, but no order may be made unless it would be in the interests of justice.[5] Similar provisions have now been applied to the breakdown of civil partnerships, under the Civil Partnership and Certain Rights and Obligations of Cohabitants Act 2010.[6] The 2010 Act also provides for financial provision to be made for 'qualified' cohabitants (as defined)[7] on the termination of a cohabitational relationship, though the orders available are more limited than on the breakdown of formal legal relationships. Orders on the termination of cohabition are conditional on the existence of financial dependency arising from the relationship or its breakdown,[8] although the orders themselves are not explicitly limited to addressing financial need.[9] Furthermore, orders in the cohabitational context can only be made if the court is satisfied that it is 'just and equitable' to do so;[10] there is no requirement of 'proper' provision, as on the breakdown of a marriage or civil partnership.

There is no doubt that the changes brought about in respect of marital breakdown were greatly needed, and were essential measures both to combat post-separation poverty and to vindicate spousal marital contributions.[11]

---

4. s 20(2)(a)–(j) of the 1989 Act (now repealed) lists 10 such factors; s 16(2)(a)–(l) of the 1995 Act lists 12; and the 1996 Act lists 13 (s 20(2)(a)–(l), and s 20(3)). Criteria include the present or likely future 'income, earning capacity, property and other financial resources' and the 'financial needs' of each spouse.
5. s 20 of the 1996 Act and s 16 of the 1995 Act (as amended).
6. Hereafter 'the 2010 Act'. Section 129 again provides that provision must be 'proper', and lists the same factors for consideration as the 1996 Act.
7. s 172 of the 2010 Act.
8. s 173(2) of the 2010 Act. The orders available are orders for the transfer or settlement of property, orders for periodical or lump-sum payments, pension adjustment orders and orders for provision from a deceased cohabitant's estate.
9. Mee has argued that it is unclear whether the claimant cohabitant should be restored to 'bare financial independence' or whether the financial dependency criterion is merely the qualifying threshold for application. He considers the second alternative more plausible, though he highlights potential injustices that this interpretation entails. See John Mee, 'A Critique of the Cohabitation Provisions of the Civil Partnership Bill 2009' (2009) 4 IJFL 83, 88.
10. s 173(2) of the 2010 Act.
11. Prior to the current legislation, the principal protection for non-owning spouses was the right to a share of their deceased spouse's estate under the Succession Act 1965. Spouses received limited protection (though not ownership) under the Family Home Protection Act 1976. *Inter vivos*, spouses could only claim an interest in property owned by the other spouse under the resulting trusts doctrine. However, the scope of this doctrine was limited by judicial insistence that 'contributions' to the acquisition of property must be financial, combined with a refusal to attribute a financial value to domestic labour. See, eg, *RK v MK* (HC, 24 October 1978).

Marital breakdown is a significant social issue in Ireland: in 2011 alone, nearly 3,000 divorces were granted by the Circuit and High Courts, as well as over a thousand judicial separations.[12] The most recent census data, in 2011, found that nearly 88,000 people in Ireland were divorced, while a further 116,000 were separated.[13] Significantly more divorced and separated persons were women than men.[14] Both marital breakdown and the connected issue of lone parenthood are significant indicators of poverty.[15] Although a discussion of social gender roles is beyond the scope of this article, it should be noted that women, in particular, are financially vulnerable following divorce and separation, due to employment and childcare patterns.[16] Children also are at increased risk of poverty following divorce.[17] *Census 2011* found that there were over 215,000 lone-parent families in Ireland, and that 87 per cent of these families were headed by lone mothers. Although 40 per cent of lone parents were single, 31.8 per cent were separated or divorced.[18]

Civil partnership is a statutory registration scheme for same-sex couples. As civil partnership is a marriage-like relationship,[19] which may include children,

---

Even financial contributions might not be adequate, as the contribution had to be referable to the acquisition of the property; hence, contributions towards later improvements, or towards items such as furniture, were insufficient: see John Mee, 'Trusts of the Family Home: The Irish Experience' [1993] Conv (ns) 359, or Hilary Delany, *Equity and the Law of Trusts in Ireland* (5th edn, Round Hall 2011) 185–209, for an account of the law in this area.

12. In 2011, 3,330 applications for divorce were received by the Circuit Court in Ireland, and 2,777 divorces were granted. A further 28 divorce applications were received by the High Court in the same period, and 38 divorces were granted. The Circuit Court also received 1,352 applications for judicial separation in 2011, and granted orders in 1,006 cases, while the High Court received 27 applications for judicial separation and granted orders in 23 cases. See Courts Service, *Courts Service Annual Report 2011*, 57.
13. Central Statistics Office, *This is Ireland: Highlights from Census 2011, Part 1* (Stationery Office 2012) 23.
14. ibid.
15. See Dr Evelyn Mahon and Elena Moore, *Post-Separation Parenting: A Study of Separation and Divorce Agreements Made in the Family Law Circuit Courts of Ireland and their Implications for Parent-Child Contact and Family Lives* (Office of the Minister for Children and Youth Affairs 2011), 24–25.
16. ibid 24–25 and 53–54.
17. ibid 24–25.
18. *Census 2011*, fn 13, 27.
19. It is clear from s 5 of the 2010 Act that civil partnership, like marriage, is an exclusive and permanent relationship. For further analysis and contrasting views of the marriage-like status of committed same-sex relationships, see Lynn D Wardle, 'Form and Substance in Committed Relationships in American Law', and Robert Wintemute, 'Marriage or "Civil Partnership" for Same-Sex Couples: Will Ireland Lead or Follow the United Kingdom?', both in Oran Doyle and William Binchy, eds, *Committed Relationships and the Law* (Four Courts Press 2007).

it seems logical that similar measures are necessary and appropriate in that context also. As yet there are no data on the breakdown of civil partnerships in Ireland, but *Census 2011* found that there were over 4,000 same-sex couples living together in Ireland, of whom 166 indicated that they were married.[20] Two hundred thirty same-sex couples had children; the overwhelming majority of these couples were female.[21] Concerns regarding child and female poverty may therefore arise in this context also, quite apart from issues of fairness. However, it must be noted that the 2010 Act does not provide for orders in favour of children or other dependents of the civil partners (or indeed of cohabitants). The Act cannot therefore be justified in terms of addressing child poverty, except insofar as children may benefit incidentally from parental provision. Even so, the presence of children is still relevant insofar as children's needs greatly increase the economic burden on custodial parents, while simultaneously affecting their labour market participation.

The cohabitational measures of the 2010 Act are more controversial, as they may result in financial relief even though no formal legal or moral commitment was made by either party.[22] Assuming that a case can be made for legal intervention in this context,[23] it is worth noting that unmarried cohabitation is increasingly common in Ireland; *Census 2011* identified 143,600 cohabiting couples, an increase of 21,800 since 2006.[24] Although *Census 2011* noted that the majority (57.8 per cent) of cohabiting couples did not have children, the average number of children in cohabiting families was increasing.[25] It therefore seems reasonable to assume that many of the same financial concerns that arise on the breakdown of marital and civil relationships could arise in this context too, as the same issues regarding lone parenthood and employment and childcare patterns are also relevant here. However, it must be noted that cohabiting couples under the

20. The census notes that most of these couples may have married abroad, given that the 2010 Act had only recently been passed at the time the census data was compiled: *Census 2011*, fn 13, 27.
21. ibid.
22. Though in fact Mee argues that the cohabitation provisions in the 2010 Act are seriously flawed from a fairness perspective, and that many deserving claimants may be left without a remedy: Mee, 'Cohabitation Provisions', fn 9, 87–88.
23. The Law Reform Commission noted conflicting arguments on this point in its report on cohabitation: see Law Reform Commission, *Report on the Rights and Duties of Cohabitants* (LRC 82–2006) 15–16. However, a detailed discussion of why family commitments may justify legal financial obligations is beyond the scope of this paper, as is an analysis of the potential differences in this regard between marital and legal partnerships, and non-marital relationships.
24. *Census 2011*, fn 13, 27. It is not clear from the census data whether the total figure for cohabitants included same-sex couples; presumably it did, since the figures for same-sex couples includes both married and cohabiting couples.
25. There were 0.7 children per cohabiting couple in 2011, compared with 0.6 in 2006: *Census 2011*, fn 13, 27.

2010 Act may be of either the same or the opposite sex,[26] reducing the relevance of gender poverty concerns.

The very extensive powers granted to courts to make financial and property orders on relationship breakdown require a clear constitutional basis. Such a basis has been explicitly provided in relation to financial provision on divorce,[27] so that the only question there is whether the scheme of the 1996 Act accords with the constitutional mandate. However, the Constitution is silent on judicial separation, civil partnerships and cohabitation. How, then, can the current, radical power to make property and financial orders under the 1995 and 2010 Acts be justified? Is it, in fact, constitutional at all? Although recent case law has purported to answer these questions in the judicial separation context at least, this paper argues that there are significant flaws in the reasoning adopted, and that the constitutionality of the 1995 Act is not yet quite resolved. Furthermore, the principal justification advanced by the courts to justify provision in the judicial separation context does not apply to civil partnerships and cohabition, so that provision under the 2010 Act still lacks a constitutional foundation.

The first half of this article outlines the broad constitutional context, highlighting aspects of constitutional law of particular relevance to financial provision on relationship breakdown. The article begins by outlining the constitutional protection of the family in Ireland, and how this protection has been interpreted and applied in the context of family property issues. It then examines the significance of constitutional property rights in the context of financial provision on relationship breakdown. The article subsequently considers the potential utility of constitutional equality provisions and arguments for upholding financial redistribution mechanisms. It contends that, even without the special constitutional protection of the family, or the constitutional mandate for provision on divorce, appropriate provision for families in the relationship breakdown context is an important social policy objective that justifies the delimitation of proprietary interests, and as such is likely to be upheld on the basis of previous case law. The constitutional place of the family bolsters the importance of this objective, in the marital breakdown context at least, and this support should not necessarily be displaced by the constitutional significance attached to family autonomy. The article also contends that the family provision measures may also be supported by constitutional gender equality considerations, though this aspect must be of limited relevance in the civil partnership context.

The second half of the article examines the most recent litigation on the 'proper' provision issue, the *LB* cases.[28] The two High Court judgments in *LB* are significant as they confirm a new understanding of the basis for making

---

26. s 172(1) of the 2010 Act.
27. art 41.3.2° of the Constitution, discussed below.
28. *LB v Ireland* [2006] IEHC 275, [2008] 1 IR 134; and *LB v Ireland and the Attorney General and PB* [2012] IEHC 461.

financial orders in the marital breakdown context, drawing on conceptualisations of the constitutional family to give a clear justification for the encroachment on individual property rights. However, although the *LB* litigation purportedly confirmed the constitutionality of the judicial power to make 'proper' provision on both judicial separation and divorce, it is contended that the reasoning was flawed in both cases in respect of judicial separation. Furthermore, the reasoning cannot be used to justify upholding provision in the civil partnership and cohabitation contexts without significant constitutional change. Consequently, a considerable lacuna remains in Irish constitutional law. The article concludes by arguing that although the 1995 and 2010 Acts both should and probably would be considered constitutional, there is still some room for doubt.

Part A: The Constitutional Background to Financial Provision Measures in Ireland

Constitutional Protection of the Family and Its Implications for Property Rights

Article 41 of the Constitution 'recognises the Family as the natural primary and fundamental unit group of Society, and as a moral institution possessing inalienable and imprescriptible rights, antecedent and superior to all positive law'.[29] The State therefore guarantees to protect the family, and also the institution of marriage, 'on which the Family is founded'.[30] The State also 'recognises that by her life within the home, woman gives to the State a support without which the common good cannot be achieved'.[31] Consequently, the State must 'endeavour to ensure that mothers shall not be obliged by economic necessity to engage in labour to the neglect of their duties in the home'.[32]

The Constitution does not define the term 'family', but the Supreme Court has held that it means the marital family only.[33] The Constitution Review Group recommended that art 41 should be amended to include a specific permission for the Oireachtas to legislate in the interests of non-traditional relationships, arising out of social and demographic changes since the adoption of the Constitution.[34] To date, however, this has not happened, and the Oireachtas All Party Committee on the Constitution concluded that attempting to make such a change would be undesirably divisive.[35] The application of art 41 is therefore still restricted, and cannot, as it stands, apply to civil partnership or cohabitation, and cannot be used to support financial provision in those contexts. (Indeed, it is possible that

29. art 41.1.1°.
30. art 41.3.1°.
31. art 41.2.1°.
32. art 41.2.2°.
33. *State (Nicolaou) v An Bord Uchtála* [1966] IR 567 (SC); *McD v L* [2009] IESC 81; [2010] 2 IR 199.
34. *Report of the Constitution Review Group* (Government Publications 1996), 336.
35. All-Party Oireachtas Committee on the Constitution, *Tenth Progress Report: The Family* (Stationery Office 2006) 121–122.

art 41 might be used to impugn the constitutionality of the 2010 Act, if that Act were deemed to undermine the institution of marriage, though the Law Reform Commission considered this unlikely so long as non-marital relationships were not more favourably treated than marital ones.[36]) Furthermore, the recognition of work in the home is specifically based on what may be considered anachronistic gender roles. Accordingly, unless the Constitution were amended to recognise the value of all caring contributions (irrespective of the gender of the contributing partner), this aspect of art 41 must be irrelevant to male civil partnerships and cohabitational relationships at least.

Even if the constitutional interpretation of the family were to be broadened, judicially or otherwise, how much support might it offer to statutory financial provision measures? Taken at face value, art 41 appears to import a partnership ideology into Irish law in the marital context, which might be extended to civil partnership at least, if this were deemed equivalent to marriage. The family is clearly regarded as a unit and it is plainly envisaged that both spouses will make equally valuable marital contributions. Hogan and Whyte note that the Constitution, unlike common law, 'regards marriage as a union of equals'.[37] While the husband's role is implicit (as norms usually are), explicit recognition is given to the worth of homemaking and childcare, not only to the family but to society. This is consistent with the communitarian view that the marital partnership is akin to a joint enterprise.[38] For communitarians (advocating a marital community of property), each spouse has an equal stake in the marital partnership and each is equally entitled to share in the fruits of the marriage. Accordingly, one might well expect the Constitution to mandate at least a sharing approach to marital property, if not a community property regime as such.

However, the judicial interpretation given to art 41 has generally been quite restrictive, based on separationist rather than sharing principles and emphasising independence and free will.[39] It has therefore offered little substantive

36. Law Reform Commission, *Consultation Paper on the Rights and Duties of Cohabitees* (LRC CP 32–2004) 7–9. However, Mee has contended that the (albeit restricted) power to make orders affecting married cohabitants, under s 170(6) of the 2010 Act, casts some doubt on the reasoning of the Law Reform Commission: see Mee, 'Cohabitation Provisions', fn 9, 85.
37. Gerard Hogan and Gerry Whyte, *JM Kelly: The Irish Constitution* (4th edn, LexisNexis Butterworths 2003) para 7.6.36. This principle has been established in a series of cases where 'the doctrine of equality of spouses has resulted in the abolition or restriction of discriminatory rules or provisions' (ibid para 7.6.37), eg *Re Tilson, Infants* [1951] IR 1 (SC); *The State (DPP) v Walsh* [1981] IR 412 (SC); *W v W* [1993] 2 IR 476 (SC).
38. For a more detailed discussion of communitarian approaches, see Lucy-Ann Buckley, 'Matrimonial Property and Irish Law: A Case for Community?' (2002) 53 NILQ 39, 45.
39. Separationists consider that partnership principles have no role to play in the financial aspects of matrimony and the focus is individualistic rather than based on sharing.

benefit, even within the marital context. Article 41 is considered to protect the (marital) family against external forces; it does not create any internal rights, or confer individual family members with rights (such as property rights) against each other. Even the vaunted protection for wives and mothers has not conferred substantive rights in practice. In *L v L*,[40] the Supreme Court overturned a High Court ruling of Barr J that would have given a wife a constitutional right to a share in the family home; Barr J had held that this was necessary if the Constitution was to be given 'flesh and meaning'.[41] Holding that the philosophy of art 41 was that women should devote their time and attention to home duties, Barr J commented,

> It is… in harmony with that philosophy to regard marriage as an equal partnership in which a woman who elects to adopt the full-time role of wife and mother in the home may be obliged to make a sacrifice, both economic and emotional, in doing so. In return for that voluntary sacrifice… she should receive some reasonable economic security within the marriage…[A]s her role… precludes her from contributing, directly or indirectly, in money or money's worth from independent employment… towards the acquisition by the husband of the family home and contents, her work as home-maker and in caring for the family should be taken into account in calculating her contribution towards that acquisition – particularly as such work is of real monetary value.[42]

The Supreme Court, however, held that the redistribution of property rights within the marriage was not mandated by art 41, which merely entitled the State to make special provision for mothers. The Court sympathised with the plight of economically vulnerable homemakers, but held that it was not for the judiciary to provide a remedy. While an award of maintenance could be an appropriate means of ensuring that a mother was not obliged by economic necessity to work outside the home, the same could not be said of the award of a share in the home itself.

Following *L v L*, the Matrimonial Home Bill 1993 attempted to provide for the co-ownership of all family homes, but the Supreme Court held that this was also unconstitutional.[43] The Bill was not invalidated by its transference of property rights as such, but because imposing a regime of joint ownership breached the 'antecedent and superior' right of a married couple to determine who should own the family home. Imposing joint ownership on all matrimonial homes could interfere with positive decisions of the family. Although spouses could

---

Although husband and wife share emotions and experiences, they remain independent individuals in respect of their property entitlements and should not have their property rights adulterated without their express consent. See, eg, Buckley, 'Matrimonial Property', fn 38, 42.

40. *L v L* [1992] 2 IR 77 (SC).
41. ibid 98.
42. ibid 98–99.
43. *Re the Matrimonial Home Bill 1993* [1994] IESC 5; [1994] 1 IR 305.

contract out of the legislation, the need to readdress ownership issues could disturb the family's equilibrium and result in litigation. The Supreme Court therefore considered that the Bill did not constitute reasonably proportionate State intervention in the family's affairs, but instead amounted to a failure to protect the family's authority. Although the Supreme Court left open the possibility that provisions regarding the future acquisition of property by married couples would not be unconstitutional, particularly if contractual variation was permitted, this approach was not adopted by the legislature, perhaps because it would result in unequal protection for older spouses.[44]

It seems unlikely that the Supreme Court in *Re Matrimonial Home Bill 1993* intended to place family autonomy ahead of all social considerations and redistribution mechanisms. This would effectively prohibit all redistributive measures on marital breakdown, since it could always be argued that the ownership of particular property, including but not limited to the family home, had been agreed. No such argument was advanced in *TF v Ireland and the Attorney General and MF*,[45] one of the few constitutional cases in this area (discussed in detail below). The best interpretation of *Re Matrimonial Home Bill 1993* is probably that blanket measures, unjustified by reference to the particular facts of a given case, are constitutionally prohibited. However, proportionate intervention in family affairs, based on specific circumstances, may be upheld. It should also be noted that the 'family autonomy' argument would presumably be inapplicable in the civil partnership and cohabitation contexts, given that the constitutional family is marital only; to this extent, the 2010 Act is free from one doubt that might potentially affect the 1995 and 1996 Acts.

Article 41 might perhaps save other legislative measures that interfere with property rights. The Succession Act 1965 imposes a minimum level of provision for a surviving spouse and permits claims by a testator's children where they have not been properly provided for. These aspects of the 1965 Act have never been constitutionally challenged,[46] and Forde considers that any such attack 'most likely would founder on Article 41'[47] and 'most likely would be upheld as a measure that protects the family and... gives recognition to the contribution of married women as acknowledged in Article 41.2'.[48] The 1965 Act may be distinguished from the situation in *L v L* as it applies after death and does not affect the use or enjoyment of property by a living owner, though clearly curtailing the owner's testamentary powers. However, these distinguishing factors do not apply to orders made on marital breakdown or the termination of a civil partnership or cohabitating relationship.

44. Buckley, 'Matrimonial Property', fn 38, 71.
45. *TF v Ireland and the Attorney General and MF* [1995] 1 IR 321 (SC).
46. The sole challenge related to the rights of non-marital children: *O'B v S* [1984] IR 316 (SC).
47. Michael Forde, *Constitutional Law* (2nd edn, First Law 2004) 754.
48. ibid 684.

Could the 'family' and 'work in the home' aspects of art 41 also support the making of financial provision on marital breakdown? The constitutional recognition of work in the home was emphasised by the Supreme Court in *T v T*,[49] though that case concerned the correct approach to 'proper' provision on divorce rather than any constitutional issues as such. In *T v T*, Murray J considered that the constitutional guarantee 'recognises that work in the home is indispensable for the welfare of the family, husband, wife and children, where there are children', as well as to the welfare of the State.[50] This underscored the weight to be attached to work in the home in evaluating the appropriate level of financial provision, and reflects sharing and communitarian values. In this sense, Article 41 bolsters the extension of 'proper' provision to the recognition of domestic and caring contributions as well as need, albeit in the marital context only.

Of most relevance to the 1996 Act is the provision in art 41.3.2°[51] that divorce may only be granted where, *inter alia*, 'such provision as the Court considers proper having regard to the circumstances exists or will be made for the spouses, any children of either or both of them and any other person prescribed by law'. This clearly envisages financial provision of some kind, and in no way limits that provision to maintenance rather than capital redistribution. Indeed, capital redistribution may often be the only feasible means of providing for a family. Accordingly, while the Constitution does not, as interpreted, mandate asset redistribution during or because of marriage, or because of a person's status or contributions as a wife or mother, it permits provision on divorce, and does not delimit that provision other than providing that it must be 'proper'. However, it is clear that 'proper' provision is more than a mere standard for relief in Irish matrimonial law; it is a mandatory pre-condition for the granting of a divorce decree.[52] Indeed, it has been held that referring to 'ancillary relief' in the Irish context is 'somewhat of a misnomer', as provision here is the master of divorce, rather than the slave.[53] As noted previously, *Re Matrimonial Home Bill 1993* strongly suggests that that 'proper' provision is not something that can be dealt with in a generic or automatic manner, and must in some way be context-dependent. This actually fits well with the discretionary scheme adopted under the 1995, 1996 and 2010 Acts, and emphasised in the divorce context in *T v T*. It also accords with what Parkinson terms 'the principle of judicial restraint'[54] enshrined in all three Acts, since all specify that orders can only be made in the interests of justice.[55]

---

49. *T(D) v T(C)* [2002] IESC 68; [2002] 3 IR 334 (SC).
50. ibid 407.
51. Inserted in 1995 by the Fifteenth Amendment to the Constitution.
52. *JC v MC* (HC, 22 January 2007; *The Irish Times* (Dublin, 19 February 2007)).
53. ibid (Abbott J), discussed in Inge Clissman, 'Trends in Divorce: A Review of Recent Case Law', *Law Society of Ireland CPD Seminar: Divorce – Ten Years On* (February 2007), 64.
54. Patrick Parkinson, 'Quantifying the Homemaker Contribution in Family Property Law' (2003) 31 Fed L Rev 1, 23.
55. s 20 of the 1996 Act; s 16 of the 1995 Act (as amended); s 199(4) of the 2010 Act (civil partnership). Note that the cohabitation provisions are slightly different, as these

In summary, therefore, art 41 clearly not only permits proper provision on divorce, but informs the nature of that provision. It does not mandate proper provision on judicial separation or on the termination of a civil partnership or a cohabiting relationship. However, it may support provision in the judicial separation context insofar as domestic contributions are vindicated and family need is addressed. This is particularly the case since the spouses in a separated family are still married, and hence the family falls within the constitutional ambit. What is less clear is whether or not art 41 could, of itself, mandate a scheme for provision on judicial separation as extensive as that provided in the 1995 Act; without significant amendment, it clearly cannot justify provision under the 2010 Act at all.

The Constitutional Right to Private Property

L v L makes it clear that the right to private property may constitute a significant barrier to redistributive mechanisms.[56] This particularly applies in the context of judicial separation and the termination of civil partnerships and cohabiting relationships, given the lack of an explicit constitutional mandate for provision in this regard. 'Property' itself is not defined in the Constitution, but has been held to include tangible and at least some intangible assets.[57] The right to private property is enshrined in art 43 of the Constitution, which acknowledges private property as a 'natural right', 'antecedent to positive law'.[58] The State therefore guarantees not to infringe the right of private ownership or concomitant rights of transfer or inheritance. However, ownership rights may be regulated by 'principles of social justice',[59] and the State may 'delimit by law the exercise of the said rights with a view to reconciling their exercise with the exigencies of the common good'.[60] Article 43 is supplemented by a guarantee in art 40.3.2° that the State shall 'protect from unjust attack and, in the case of injustice done, vindicate the… property rights of every citizen'. The traditional view is that art 43 protects the institution of property from State interference, while breaches of individual citizens' particular property rights are dealt with under art 40.3.2°.[61] However, the Supreme Court has more recently held that both provisions may be relevant in considering whether a particular expropriation is valid.[62]

While art 43 permits the State to regulate and 'delimit' property rights, art 45.2.ii goes considerably further than this, requiring the State to 'direct its policy' towards

---

specify that orders for financial provision may not be made unless it would be 'just and equitable' to do so: s 173(2) of the 2010 Act.

56. *L v L* [1992] 2 IR 77 (SC).
57. See Forde, *Constitutional Law*, fn 47, 730.
58. art 43.1.1°.
59. art 43.2.1°.
60. art 43.2.2°.
61. *Blake v AG* [1982] IR 117 (SC).
62. *Re Part V of the Planning and Development Bill 1999* [2000] IESC 20; [2000] 2 IR 321.

the distribution of the 'ownership and control of the material resources of the community' among individuals and classes so 'as best to subserve the common good'. Article 45.4.1° also requires the State to 'safeguard with especial care the economic interests of the weaker sections of the community'. Although the social policy provisions of art 45 are stated not to be judicially cognisable, and to be simply for the guidance of the legislature, Walsh has demonstrated that the constitutional right to private property was originally intended to encompass broad principles of distributive justice.[63] However, fear of potential legal claims resulted in the separation of property rights and social policy concerns into different constitutional articles. Walsh contends that this 'de-coupling' inadvertently strengthened the individualistic appearance of art 43 and weakened the social principles intended to regulate that power.[64] She therefore contends that '[b]y removing the social context for the protection of private property that had been provided by the social principles, the drafters created a provision that appeared to favour the right to private ownership over the demands of the common good'.[65] She further suggests that this evidence of the framers' intentions could be 'constructively applied' to 'help to clarify the scope of the State's power to restrict property rights'.[66] She notes that art 45 has been successfully invoked to bolster the constitutionality of legislative social justice measures,[67] and argues that this is appropriate, given that the purpose of art 45 is to guide the legislature in its enactments.[68] Hence, she concludes that art 45 may be used to justify legislative restrictions on property rights under art 43, though not to impugn them.[69] If this is correct, art 45 might be used to uphold a financial provision scheme on relationship breakdown, even if such a scheme would otherwise constitute a breach of property rights.

With this in mind, what is the scope of the State's power to regulate or delimit property rights? Is it limited to State expropriations in the common interest, or can the State also redistribute property between individuals? In either case, does the validity of the infringement depend on compensation?

It is clear that limited State expropriations of property are permitted, if in accordance with law, though they are judicially reviewable.[70] Notably, and unlike

63. Rachael Walsh, 'Private Property Rights in the Drafting of the Irish Constitution: A Communitarian Compromise' (2011) 33 DULJ 86.
64. ibid 109.
65. ibid. Even so, as Walsh argues elsewhere, the courts have permitted great latitude to the legislature in the interpretation and implementation of social principles: Rachael Walsh, 'The Constitution, Property Rights and Proportionality: A Reappraisal' (2009) 31 DULJ 1.
66. Walsh, 'Communitarian Compromise', fn 63, 109; see further 113.
67. ibid 111. However, she also notes that no judicial decision has used art 45 in this way since 1984, and that the Supreme Court might decide against this approach in future (ibid 112).
68. ibid 111.
69. ibid.
70. *Buckley v AG* [1950] IR 67 (SC).

the 'Takings Clause' under the Fifth Amendment to the American Constitution, the Irish Constitution does not explicitly require that State (or other) expropriations of private property must be compensated, either wholly or in part. However, even without adequate compensation, it is rare for legislative measures to be struck down for breaching the private property guarantee.[71] The key issue is whether the expropriation is a proportionate means of achieving a legitimate and important social end (commonly referred to as the 'principle of proportionality'). Thus, in *Re Part V of the Planning and Development Bill 1999,*[72] the Supreme Court held that a scheme whereby up to 20 per cent of a developer's land could be expropriated for social housing, at less than the market rate in compensation, was not a disproportionate violation of property rights. Keane CJ considered that the statutory measure 'was rationally connected to an objective of sufficient importance to warrant interference with a constitutionally protected right and... undoubtedly relate[d] to concerns which, in a free and democratic society, should be regarded as pressing and substantial'.[73]

It also appears that property reallocations between individuals may be upheld, at least as part of a larger redistributive scheme. For instance, in *Shirley v A O'Gorman & Co Ltd,*[74] the claimant challenged legislative provisions that permitted qualified tenants to acquire their landlord's freehold interest in the property at a fraction of the market value.[75] The legislative policy was based on social justice for disadvantaged tenants, rather than superior use. Since the tenant in *Shirley* was a successful company, the landlord argued that the forced sale at an undervalue did not advance any social objectives but rather infringed the landlord's property rights. However, Peart J considered that it was sufficient that the scheme as a whole had a social justice objective, even if there were aberrant outcomes in particular cases.[76]

Notwithstanding the foregoing, Forde notes that '[i]t has not been resolved whether the State is permitted to take property merely in order to give it to some other individual..., who the State believes will make better use of the property and where that taking is not part of some general scheme for redistribution'.[77] The issue was partly addressed in the High Court decision of

71. Forde, *Constitutional Law*, fn 47, 734.
72. *Re Part V of the Planning and Development Bill 1999* [2000] IESC 20; [2000] 2 IR 321.
73. ibid 354.
74. *John E Shirley & Ors v A O'Gorman & Co Ltd* [2006] IEHC 27.
75. The provisions were s 8 Ground Rents (No 2) Act 1978 and s 7(4) of the Landlord and Tenant (Amendment) Act 1984.
76. On appeal, the Supreme Court held that the relevant statutory provisions could have been interpreted in such a way that the landlord was not obliged to sell the freehold interest at all. Hence, the landlord did not have *locus standi* to challenge the constitutionality of the provisions, and the Supreme Court did not deal with the constitutional issues raised. See *Shirley v A O'Gorman & Co Ltd* [2012] IESC 5.
77. Forde, *Constitutional Law*, fn 47, 736.

Clinton v An Bord Pleanála,[78] where Finnegan P accepted that 'compensation cannot validate an interference with property rights that is not justified by the exigencies of the common good'.[79] However, on the facts, he felt the common good was a matter to be determined by An Bord Pleanála, though it required some 'pressing social need'.[80] While stating that '[t]here must be a sufficient and proper public purpose for the acquisition… which purpose cannot be achieved by lesser means',[81] he upheld the compulsory purchase of the plaintiff's land on the grounds that fair procedures had been followed. Unfortunately, the Supreme Court did not ultimately address the constitutional point on appeal.[82]

Are financial orders on relationship breakdown State expropriations, and does it matter if they are? It might be contended that they are not, since the property at issue is not taken by the State for its own use, but rather transferred between private citizens for reasons of social justice. Nevertheless, the fact remains that the citizen is deprived of property at the behest of the State; the statutory financial provision schemes, by definition, do not operate on a voluntary basis. The judiciary is a branch of State power; it is applying measures enacted by the legislature (albeit in a discretionary manner); and there are State-enforced sanctions for failure to comply, in the form of criminal contempt proceedings. In this sense, therefore, all compulsory re-allocations of property between individuals are State expropriations. For instance, in *Re Part V of the Planning and Development Bill 1999*, one might argue that the social housing measures essentially entailed taking land from its owners and reallocating it to those deemed in greater need of it, albeit through a State intermediary. If the State intermediary were removed from the picture, and the re-allocation were made directly, would it still be a State expropriation? It is submitted that it would, and that the net effect is no different to financial provision on relationship breakdown, although the justification for the specific measures may differ (since financial provision on relationship breakdown may be compensatory as well as needs-based).[83]

In fact, however, and in line with the Constitution itself, most of the cases raising constitutional property issues do not use the language of State expropriation. For instance, in *BUPA Ireland Ltd & Anor v Health Insurance Authority & Ors*,[84] health

---

78. *Clinton v An Bord Pleanála & Ors* [2005] IEHC 84.
79. ibid citing Hogan and Whyte, *JM Kelly*, fn 37, para 7.7, 88.
80. *Clinton v An Bord Pleanála & Ors* [2005] IEHC 84, citing Budd J in *An Blascaod Mór v Commissioners of Public Works (No. 3)* [1999] IESC 4; [2000] 1 IR 6.
81. ibid.
82. *Clinton v An Bord Pleanála & Ors* [2007] IESC 19.
83. Although financial orders on the breakdown of a cohabiting relationship are conditional on financial dependency, the factors listed for judicial consideration with regard to whether an order is 'just and equitable' include compensatory factors, such as domestic contributions and contributions to the resources and earning power of the other cohabitant: s 173(3) of the 2010 Act.
84. *BUPA Ireland Ltd & Anor v Health Insurance Authority & Ors* [2006] IEHC 431.

insurance companies new to the Irish market were required to make payments to the VHI, a semi-state insurer with an older client base, under a risk equalisation scheme. McKechnie J's judgment does not discuss whether this was a State expropriation as such,[85] but rather addresses it as a restriction or 'infringement' of the plaintiff's property rights, which must be justified by reference to the common good.[86] Similarly, in *In Re Article 26 and the Employment Equality Bill 1996*, forcing employers to pay for accommodative measures for disabled workers was described as a 'delimitation' of their property rights, rather than a State expropriation.[87] Again, the State was required to justify this, which it failed to do, as the Bill essentially re-allocated social costs to a particular social group in an impermissible way. Accordingly, even if provision orders on relationship breakdown are not State expropriations but simply re-allocations of property between individuals, the key question appears to be whether the limitation or restriction of the transferor's property rights is justifiable as meeting a pressing social objective. This interpretation accords with the language of art 43 itself.

In determining whether delimitations of private property rights are justifiable, there is considerable deference for legislative views on social policy.[88] This is because, as Hanna J put it in *Pigs Marketing Board v Donnelly (Dublin) Ltd*,[89] what amounts to social justice involves 'questions of ethics, morals, economics and sociology' that are 'beyond the determination of a court of law', but may properly fall within the remit of the legislature.[90] Walsh contends, *contra* Hogan,[91] that the principle of proportionality has been applied in a way that 'privileges the public interest', and that the courts tend to give only cursory scrutiny to the impact of statutory measures on personal rights, once there appears to be any rational link with a legitimate social objective.[92]

If this is correct, it is highly likely that financial provision orders would be deemed justified by considerations of need and fairness, and as a reasonable

---

85. Arguably the semi-state nature of the transferee strengthens the case that it was a State expropriation, though McKechnie J's judgment does not address this point.
86. *BUPA Ireland Ltd & Anor v Health Insurance Authority & Ors* [2006] IEHC 431 [237–47] (McKechnie J).
87. *In Re Article 26 and the Employment Equality Bill 1996* [1997] IESC 118; [1997] 2 IR 321, 366.
88. Walsh, 'Proportionality', fn 65, 11.
89. *Pigs Marketing Board v Donnelly (Dublin) Ltd* [1939] IR 413 (HC).
90. ibid 418.
91. Gerard Hogan, 'The Constitution, Property Rights and Proportionality' (1997) 32 IJ (ns) 396.
92. Walsh, 'Proportionality', fn 65, 24. Indeed, Walsh goes so far as to argue that, under current law, the State may 'transfer property to another private individual or entity simply by invoking an ill-defined and indefinite public benefit such as "regeneration" or "development"': Rachael Walsh, '"The Principles of Social Justice": The Compulsory Acquisition of Private Property for Redevelopment in the United States and Ireland' (2010) 32 DULJ 1.

response to the pressing socio-economic concerns (outlined in the Introduction to this article) that arise on relationship breakdown.[93] This contention is supported by art 41 in the marital context, as discussed above, but in fact the same policy considerations would still apply under art 43, irrespective of art 41's provisions. In that sense, the explicit mandate for proper provision on divorce contained in art 41 is arguably unnecessary from the perspective of permitting a significant degree of financial redistribution in the marital breakdown context. The 'proper' provision requirement might therefore be better regarded as a precondition for divorce (as discussed above) rather than as a permission for financial reallocation, though it certainly supports this as well.

If art 43 is indeed sufficient in itself as a constitutional basis for financial provision measures, there is no reason to limit its application to marital breakdown only. Unlike art 41, it may still apply on the breakdown of non-marital relationships, providing that the problem addressed by the relevant statutory measures is sufficiently pressing. The strongest caveat that might arise here concerns cohabitation: unlike marriage or civil partnership, where the parties have made mutual commitments that might justify some level of mutual financial readjustment on the breakdown of the relationship, cohabiting couples have made no such formal commitment, and may indeed have consciously wished to avoid doing so. Hence, the basis for making the parties each other's insurers is questionable.[94] Surprisingly, the Law Reform Commission did not address the issue of constitutional property rights in its proposal for financial provision measures on the breakdown of either civil partnership or cohabitation. However, cases such as *Shirley* suggest that individuals may be required to transfer property interests to others for social justice reasons, even if there is no personal moral or legal commitment to justify such liability. In addition, it must be noted that there is no requirement to make financial provision orders on the breakdown of cohabitation (in contrast to the imperative of making

93. There are some caveats: for instance, it is clear that any expropriation provisions must be applied equally and cannot be directed against a particular class or group: *An Blascaod Mór Teo v Commissioners for Public Works (No 3)* [1999] IESC 4; [2000]1 IR 6. This suggests that any redistributive provisions must be gender neutral, as is also required by art 40.1. This aspect is discussed further in the section on constitutional equality. Expropriation might also be invalid if the same objective could easily be achieved by other means (Forde, *Constitutional Law*, fn 47, 737, considering the judgment of the European Court of Human Rights in *Sporrong v Lonröth* (1983) 5 EHRR 35). However, it is difficult to see how a family might otherwise be provided for other than by some form of redistributive mechanism, unless the entire burden is to be placed on the State. This would effectively require citizens to subsidise some families even where there was no lack of resources, which seems both unjust and impractical.

94. This concern was recognised by the Law Reform Commission itself: Law Reform Commission, *Consultation Paper on the Rights and Duties of Cohabitees* (LRC CP 32–2004) 20–24.

'proper' provision on the termination of marriage or civil partnership). On the contrary, the court is enjoined not to make any order unless justice requires it.[95] This suggests that the likelihood of financial provision orders must be significantly lower on cohabitation breakdown than on marital or civil partnership breakdown. As such, the financial provision measures for former cohabitants may be upheld as proportionate, even without the support of art 41 (in the marital context) or the legal and moral commitment made by the parties in either marriage or civil partnership.

Although there is as yet no case law on the breakdown of non-marital relationships in Ireland, decisions to date suggest that constitutional property rights would not bar redistributive mechanisms on marital breakdown, at least. In *TF v Ireland and the Attorney General and MF*,[96] the plaintiff alleged that the judicial power under the 1989 Act to confer sole occupation of the family home on one spouse breached the titleholder's constitutional property rights. Murphy J, in the High Court, held that the power to confer sole residence entitlements on one spouse could not be considered in isolation and must be viewed in the wider context of the Act. A right of residence conferred on one spouse might well be balanced by other orders, such as maintenance, in favour of the other spouse. He therefore concluded that the power to grant a sole right of residence 'is in no sense an unjust attack on the property rights of either party', but was

> merely one feature in the difficult and unhappy task of attempting to ensure that provision is made as far as practicable in the best interests of both spouses and their dependant children in the unhappy circumstances which have arisen and which will ordinarily create severe financial as well as emotional problems for them.[97]

This view was confirmed by the Supreme Court, although the Court's examination of the property issues in this case was disappointingly brief. Hamilton CJ emphasised that granting exclusive occupation to one spouse 'does not in any way purport to deprive the excluded spouse of such rights of ownership as he or she may enjoy in the family home'.[98] It also did not infringe a married couple's right jointly to determine the ownership of the matrimonial home, as stated in the Supreme Court's judgment in *Re the Matrimonial Home Bill 1993*.[99] Hamilton CJ also emphasised that the judicial powers 'are not arbitrary' but must be exercised in accordance with the legislative requirements. Furthermore, the order could be varied or discharged in appropriate circumstances. Hamilton CJ therefore concluded that the residence provision was not an unjust attack on

95. This caveat also applies to provision under the 1995 and 1996 Acts, and to the breakdown of civil partnerships under the 2010 Act, but only after a positive stipulation that 'proper' provision must be made.
96. *TF v Ireland and the Attorney General and MF* [1995] 1 IR 321 (SC).
97. ibid 345.
98. ibid 380.
99. *Re the Matrimonial Home Bill 1993* [1994] IESC 5; [1994] 1 IR 305.

the individual spouse's property rights, but rather 'an effort by the Oireachtas to protect so far as practicable the rights of the Family and members thereof'.[100]

The significance of the Supreme Court's decision in *TF* is limited, for a number of reasons. First, only two aspects of the 1989 Act's scheme for financial provision were at issue. These were ss 16(a) and 19 of the 1989 Act, both of which related to the court's power to confer on one spouse a sole right of residence in the family home. Although the Supreme Court held that these provisions must be considered in the context of the broader statutory scheme for financial provision, it is important to emphasise that the constitutionality of the broader scheme was not challenged, and the Supreme Court did not make any explicit pronouncements on this issue.

Second, *TF* related to the 1989 Act, which applies a different overall standard for provision to the 1995 and 1996 Acts, and for civil partnerships under the 2010 Act. Under the 1989 Act, provision must be 'adequate and reasonable' in the circumstances; under the 1995 and 1996 Acts, and for civil partnerships, it must be 'proper'.[101] It will be contended later in this article that these standards differ, and that the difference is significant. Therefore, even if the Supreme Court had held that the entirety of the 1989 scheme for financial provision was constitutional, the same would not automatically apply to the 1995 Act, or to civil partnerships under the 2010 Act.

Third, *TF* emphasised that granting a sole right of residence to the non-owning spouse did not actually deprive the home-owning spouse of ownership. This suggests that an actual deprivation of ownership (as commonly occurs under property adjustment orders, and not always on a reciprocal basis) might be viewed differently.

Fourth, the availability of blocking orders under the current legislation must also cast doubt on the weight attached by the court to the inconclusiveness of the orders. Blocking orders are a variety of provisions that can be utilised to prevent subsequent variation of particular ancillary property orders.[102] This suggests that the current judicial separation legislation is open to constitutional challenge. On the other hand, the Supreme Court also stressed in *TF* that the judicial powers under the statutory scheme were not arbitrary, and were for the benefit of the family as a whole. This might be sufficient to counteract the constitutional danger posed by the availability of blocking orders, at least in the context of divorce, given the explicit constitutional mandate for

---

100. *TF v Ireland and the Attorney General and MF* [1995] 1 IR 321 (SC), 381.

101. s 16(1) of the 1995 Act originally mandated the same standard as under the 1989 Act, ie provision was to be 'adequate and reasonable'. However, this was amended by s 52(h) of the 1996 Act.

102. Property adjustment orders, pension adjustment orders and applications for provision from the estate of a deceased spouse may all be barred from review: s 18(4) of the 1995 Act and s 22(4) of the 1996 Act. Similar orders are available on the breakdown of civil partnerships: s 131(5) of the 2010 Act.

provision in that event: the situation under the 1995 and 2010 Acts must be considered more tenuous.

The Constitution and Equality

Article 40.1 of the Constitution states that all citizens, 'as human persons', shall be equal before the law. However, the State may, in its enactments, 'have due regard to differences of capacity, physical and moral, and of social function'. Article 40.1 was initially restrictively interpreted to relate only to 'the essentials of human personality',[103] and did not relate to the treatment of persons other than in their human capacity. However, Forde notes that the reference to 'human persons' 'may be intended not as a restriction on the scope of the guaranteed equality but, instead, as a statement of the reason why the Constitution guarantees equality'.[104] Hence, all human individuals should be treated equally in equivalent circumstances. This would prohibit invidious discrimination on grounds of race, colour or social background, among other grounds.[105]

More problematic was the suggestion that the guarantee 'refers to human beings for what they are in themselves rather than to any lawful activities… which they may engage in….'[106] Hogan and Whyte comment that this 'virtually emasculated the guarantee of equality',[107] as it implied 'that the essential attributes of human personality operate to determine the *context* in which the principle of equality applies, as opposed to identifying the presumptively impermissible *bases* of discrimination'.[108] This could have excluded all commercial activities from the guarantee, and therefore 'seems to attribute to human personality an unrealistically small ambit'.[109] However, they suggest that this approach has now been 'implicitly abandoned'.[110]

The Constitution also provides that men and women have an equal right to an adequate means of livelihood,[111] but neither this nor a further stipulation that citizens should 'not be forced by economic necessity to enter avocations unsuited to their sex, age or strength'[112] is judicially cognisable.[113] There is no

103. *Murphy v Attorney General* [1982] IR 241 (SC), 283 (O'Higgins CJ).
104. Forde, *Constitutional Law*, fn 47, 371.
105. *Quinn's Supermarkets Ltd v Attorney General* [1972] IR 1 (SC), 14 (Walsh J).
106. ibid 13–14 (Walsh J).
107. Hogan and Whyte, *JM Kelly*, fn 37, para 7.2.40.
108. ibid para 7.2.42.
109. ibid para 7.2.43.
110. ibid para 7.2.48, discussing *Re Article 26 and the Employment Equality Bill 1996* [1997] IESC 6; [1997] 2 IR 321.
111. art 45.2.1°.
112. art 45.4.2°.
113. Even so, in *Murtagh Properties v Cleary* [1972] IR 330 (HC), Kenny J held that art 45.2 informed the meaning of art 40.3, so that attempts to prevent an employer from employing both men and women on the ground of sex only were unconstitutional.

blanket constitutional proscription on sex discrimination[114]; nevertheless, discriminatory common law rules for husbands and wives have been struck down on foot of the equality decree.[115] However, only once has a provision of an Act of the Oireachtas been struck down for unconstitutional sex discrimination.[116]

Differences in treatment may be upheld where they are based on real differences in situation: in *De Búrca v Attorney General*, Walsh J emphasised that the State may have regard to legitimate differences, but cannot assume that women as a group have a particular social function. He commented:

> ... it is not open to the State to discriminate in its enactments between the persons who are subject to its laws solely upon the ground of the sex of those persons. If a reference is to be made to the sex of a person, then the purpose of the law that makes such a discrimination should be to deal with some physical or moral capacity or social function that is related exclusively or very largely to that sex only.[117]

Do the constitutional equality provisions have any implications for the legislative mechanisms for financial provision on relationship breakdown? It might be argued that redistributive provisions of relationship breakdown legislation favour women, in practice if not in form. Men generally earn more than women and have a larger asset base,[118] making them more likely to give than to receive, even where legislation (like the 1995, 1996 and 2010 Acts) is apparently gender neutral. Hence, such legislation might indirectly discriminate against men, though if so, the discriminatory effect might be justified on social policy grounds, and by the 'special' role of the home-making wife and mother within the constitutional family (in the case of divorce or judicial separation).[119] In fact, even directly discriminatory measures have been upheld in Irish law.[120] In *Dennehy v Minister for Social Welfare*,[121] a provision that granted benefits for deserted wives but not for deserted husbands was upheld on the basis that it was not unjust, unreasonable or arbitrary to exclude men from the benefits.

---

114. Limited prohibitions are included, for instance, in relation to nationality and citizenship: art 9.1.3°.
115. For instance, the doctrine that a wife's domicile depended on that of her husband was rejected in *W v W* [1993] 2 IR 476 (SC).
116. Widowers wishing to adopt a child were less favourably treated than widows, on the basis of an 'idea of difference in capacity between men and women which has no foundation in fact', McMahon J, *O'G v Attorney General* [1985] ILRM 61, 65.
117. *De Búrca v Attorney General* [1976] IR 38 (SC), 71.
118. See, eg, Lucy-Ann Buckley, 'Irish Matrimonial Property Division in Practice: A Case Study' (2007) 21 Int'l JL Pol & Fam 48, 57–62.
119. The constitutional position regarding indirect discrimination, or disproportionate impact, is discussed below.
120. Direct and indirect discrimination theory, as understood in the labour law context, appears to differ from the approach in Irish constitutional law. For instance, direct discrimination seems to be justified by substantive equality considerations.
121. *Dennehy v Minister for Social Welfare* (HC, 26 July 1984).

This was because desertion by men was much more frequent than desertion by women, and homemaking mothers, who were engaged in childcare, were at a greater economic disadvantage in the labour market, and had greater financial needs, than their husbands. Similarly, in *Lowth v Minister for Social Welfare*,[122] it was held that there was ample justification for the Oireachtas to consider that deserted wives were generally in more need than deserted husbands. Whyte criticises this on the basis that the burden of proving gender discrimination by the State rests on the plaintiff in Ireland, while in the United States the onus lies on government to justify any gender-based classification. The standard of proof is also more onerous there, as 'instead of merely having to show the existence of facts which could reasonably justify the discrimination, the State has to prove the existence of a relationship between the classification and an important interest of government'.[123]

These cases related to the provision of State benefits, and the reallocation of private resources between spouses or former civil partners might be treated differently. In *Re Employment Equality Bill 1996*,[124] the Supreme Court held that the cost of meeting a particular social need (in that case, providing 'reasonable accommodation' for disabled workers) could not be imposed on a particular group (in that case, employers).[125] However, it is submitted that the relationship and mutual commitments of spouses and civil partners are very different to those of employers and employees, and it is therefore appropriate and reasonable to provide for inter-party financial provision on the breakdown of such relationships. As noted in the Introduction, the case for intervention in the cohabitational context is significantly weaker, so that an unequal gender impact might be harder to justify there. However, the 2010 Act's stipulation that the court must not make orders in favour of former cohabitants unless justice requires it, and the threshold requirement of financial dependency arising from the relationship or its breakdown, may overcome this difficulty.[126]

It is unclear in any event whether disproportionate impact, or indirect discrimination, is covered in the constitutional equality guarantee. Forde argues that the aggregation of married couples' incomes for tax purposes, which was struck down in *Murphy v Attorney General*,[127] could have been construed as having a disproportionate and discriminatory effect on married women by discour-

---

122. *Lowth v Minister for Social Welfare* [1998] IESC 1; [1998] 4 IR 321.
123. Gerry Whyte, 'Judicial Treatment of Social Welfare Issues', in Gerry Whyte, *Social Inclusion and the Legal System: Public Interest Law in Ireland* (Institute of Public Administration 2002) 160.
124. *Re Employment Equality Bill 1996* [1997] IESC 6; [1997] 2 IR 321.
125. This was so even though the relevant provision allowed for consideration of the financial circumstances of the employer.
126. However, the fact that financial dependency is apparently merely a threshold criterion, rather than informing the substantive content of orders, may undermine this view.
127. *Murphy v Attorney General* [1982] IR 241 (SC).

aging them from working outside the home.[128] However, this was not the basis of the decision, which was instead based on the provision's discouragement of marriage. A 'disproportionate impact' argument was rejected in *State (Nicolaou) v An Bord Uchtála,* where adoption provisions discriminating against unmarried fathers were upheld.[129] In *Draper v Attorney General*, electoral legislation with a disproportionate impact on a disabled woman, who was unable to vote in person and wished to vote by post, was upheld.[130] The Supreme Court considered that the State was merely obliged to act reasonably in the provision of voting entitlements and that prohibiting postal voting was not unreasonable, given the potential for abuse. This suggests that any disproportionate gender impact of redistributive provisions would probably be justified by overriding social needs, if indeed the concept of disproportionate impact were to be recognised at all.

However, an alternative view of equality might *require* redistribution, in the interests of distributive or substantive justice. Distributive justice stresses the just distribution of social goods. Substantive justice emphasises the unequal effect of apparently neutral measures; it then 'focuses on whether a group has been unjustly subordinated', and on 'group and societal responsibility for inequality'.[131] Doyle comments that this

> makes it possible to perceive the benefits which members of the dominant group collectively gain from the continuance of deep-seated patterns of social discrimination... [T]he substantive conception of equality sees itself as a response to forms of inequality and subordination that have historically been a problem in a particular society... [It] does not accept that the courts should be neutral as between competing groups in society.[132]

Women are a historically disadvantaged group within Irish society, and one might argue that it is a legitimate State aim to redress the effects of gender-based social and economic roles. However, as Doyle also states, 'Ireland is not renowned as an egalitarian society', and the courts have tended to take a narrow, process-oriented view of equality.[133] He notes that two arguments have been made in the case law against the judicial enforcement of socio-economic rights, which would require distributive justice. These are 'that judicial enforcement of distributive justice is undemocratic' (as judges are not elected and may be going against the wishes of the legislature) and that it is also 'pragmatically unwise' (as judges have no special expertise in social matters).[134]

---

128. Forde, *Constitutional Law*, fn 47, 379.
129. *State (Nicolaou) v An Bord Uchtála* [1966] IR 567 (SC).
130. *Draper v Attorney General* [1984] IR 277 (SC).
131. Doyle, *Constitutional Equality Law* (Thomson Round Hall 2004) 19.
132. ibid.
133. ibid 20.
134. ibid 42.

Both arguments were utilised in *O'Reilly v Limerick Corporation*,[135] where Costello J rejected the claim of members of the Traveller Community that the State was constitutionally obliged to provide them with a halting site. Costello J held that it was beyond the judicial function to evaluate and adjudicate between the many competing claims for public resources, both because judges were unqualified for this and because such an intervention breached the constitutional separation of powers.[136] Six years later, in *O'Brien v Wicklow UDC*,[137] Costello J found (on similar facts) for the plaintiffs. While his decision there was based on s 13 of the Housing Act 1988, Costello J also conceded that his views had changed in the interim.[138] However, his decision in *O'Reilly* was approved by the majority of the Supreme Court in *Sinnott v Minister for Education*,[139] where a young autistic man claimed that the State's failure to provide appropriately for his educational needs breached his educational rights under art 42 of the Constitution. Finding against the plaintiff, Hardiman J emphasised (*obiter*) the separate functions of the legislature and the judiciary, and that decisions on the allocation of public resources fell within the remit of the legislature and executive.[140] The separation of powers argument was again used in *TD v Minister for Education*,[141] where the Supreme Court rejected the claim of a minor with behavioural problems that the State had failed to provide him with the special care facilities he required, again on the basis of the separation of powers. Keane CJ expressed 'the gravest doubts' that the courts should recognise unenumerated socio-economic constitutional rights.[142] Even so, Doyle argues that the Constitution does not preclude the enforcement of socio-economic rights through judicial review – assuming, of course, that such rights are found to exist.[143] Similarly, Whyte contends that 'judicial intervention on behalf of marginalised groups whose pressing needs are studiously ignored by the political process can be defended as both constitutionally and politically legitimate'.[144] However, in the wake of the Supreme Court decisions in *Sinnott* and *TD*, Whyte concedes that 'the portents for public interest litigation targeting social exclusion in this jurisdiction are not good'.[145]

135. *O'Reilly v Limerick Corporation* [1989] ILRM 181 (HC).
136. *O'Reilly v Limerick Corporation* [1989] ILRM 181, 195 (HC).
137. *O'Brien v Wicklow UDC* (HC, 10 June 1994).
138. ibid 3–4.
139. *Sinnott v Minister for Education* [2001] IESC 63; [2001] 2 IR 505.
140. ibid 707–708.
141. *TD v Minister for Education* [2001] IESC 101; [2001] 4 IR 259.
142. ibid 282.
143. Doyle, *Constitutional Equality Law*, fn 131, 44. Doyle notes that the 'vast majority' of case law interpreting art 40.1 is 'wholly inconsistent with a substantive interpretation' of the Article, although the wording itself is not (at 230).
144. Whyte, *Social Inclusion*, fn 121, 57.
145. ibid 362.

The case law on this point all relates to claimants seeking to compel the State to benefit them, out of public resources. It is likely that similar reasoning would apply should an individual seek to compel the State to make provision out of private resources, even though this would not affect public revenue: in either case, the separation of powers would prevent judicial intervention. This, however, is not to say that the State could not itself determine to make such provision, and that such intervention could not be justified by the constitutional equality provisions. On the contrary, given the emphasis on the legislative prerogative in cases such as *Sinnott* and *TD*,[146] it seems highly probable that a positive exercise of legislative discretion might well be upheld provided that (unlike *Re Employment Equality Bill 1996*) there was sufficient justification for requiring provision to be made from private as opposed to public resources. Therefore, although it seems unlikely at present that constitutional equality arguments could be used to *compel* legislative measures for financial provision on relationship breakdown, they might well be used to *support* such measures. Gender equality theory might therefore supply at least a supplementary justification for provision on marital breakdown and the demise of heterosexual cohabiting relationships. However, gender equality theory could have no relevance to provision on the breakdown of civil partnerships or same-sex cohabitational relationships, since homemaking as such is not a recognised category of discrimination.

Part B: Recent Developments in the LB Litigation

The most recent insights into the constitutional aspects of 'proper' provision on marital breakdown derive from the *LB* litigation.[147] In a series of cases, the plaintiff initially challenged the constitutionality of various statutory provisions, including those permitting financial orders on divorce. Having failed there, the plaintiff subsequently sought various declarations and damages in respect of the alleged wrongful expropriation of his property by the State by means of the financial and property orders made on divorce. Both cases, featuring detailed High Court judgments by MacMenamin J and Hogan J respectively,[148] shed new light on the basis for upholding the legislative provisions on 'proper' provision on divorce. Although the decisions did not specifically apply to the making of 'proper' provision on judicial separation, it is

146. This emphasis on the legislative prerogative has continued post-*TD*; for instance, in *F v Minister for Education* [2007] IEHC 36, Smyth J stressed that, save as a 'last resort', courts 'should refrain from embarking' on 'questions related to distributive justice'.

147. *LB v Ireland* [2006] IEHC 275; [2008] 1 IR 134; and *LB v Ireland and the Attorney General and PB* [2012] IEHC 461; [2012] 11 JIC 0905.

148. Hogan J noted in *LB v Ireland and the Attorney General and PB* [2012] IEHC 461 that the earlier decision of MacMenamin J in *LB v Ireland* [2006] IEHC 275 was affirmed by the Supreme Court in July 2009. However, no written copy of the Supreme Court's judgment is available for analysis.

arguable that the same reasoning would apply in that context also, though not, for reasons that will be seen, to provision under the 2010 Act. However, even the application of the reasoning to the 1995 Act is not as straightforward as it might seem, since a number of additional factors might justify a different result in the separation context, and there are also considerations that partly undermine the authority of the *LB* decisions.

In the first case,[149] the plaintiff challenged (*inter alia*)[150] the constitutionality of the court's power to make ancillary financial orders on divorce under the 1996 Act, alleging that the orders made breached his constitutional property rights under art 43. Rejecting this contention, and in line with the arguments advanced in this article, MacMenamin J emphasised that rights could be regulated and limited for the common good, so long as such intervention was reasonable, proportionate and unoppressive.[151] MacMenamin J also considered that the Supreme Court had implicitly held in *TF* that 'any delimiting of personal rights as arose in the Act of 1989 were not oppressive and bore a reasonable and proportionate relationship between the benefit which the legislation would confer on family members on the one hand and the interference with the personal rights of the citizen on the other'.[152] This, however, may be more doubtful than MacMenamin J appeared to assume, since (as noted above) only two very limited and specific sections of the 1989 Act's financial provision scheme were at issue in *TF*.[153] Furthermore (again as noted above), although the Supreme Court in *TF* stressed that the challenged sections must be considered in light of the broader statutory scheme, it did so from the perspective that the orders made did not actually deprive the home owner of ownership.

Of most significance is MacMenamin J's emphasis on the nature of marriage as a civil contract that creates reciprocal obligations between the spouses.[154] In this regard, MacMenamin J's conceptualisation of the family built on that advanced in *T v T*.[155] In that case, Murray J emphasised that marriage automatically entails spousal obligations and liabilities, and that even on divorce, spouses might legally

149. Although this was the first case to raise a constitutional challenge, the claimant in *LB* had previously been involved in three cases: a judicial separation and a divorce in the Circuit Court, and a High Court appeal in respect of the orders made on divorce.

150. The Plaintiff also challenged the constitutionality of the court's power to grant a judicial separation under the 1989 Act and the court's power to order maintenance under the 1976 Act, but these aspects are not relevant for this article.

151. *LB v Ireland* [2006] IEHC 275 [43] (MacMenamin J); [2008] 1 IR 134, 147, citing the judgment of Kenny J in *Ryan v the Attorney General* [1965] IR 294 (SC) 312–313.

152. ibid.

153. ss 16(a) and 19 of the 1989 Act; see the discussion in *TF v Ireland* [1995] 1 IR 321 (SC) 380–381.

154. *LB v Ireland* [2006] IEHC 275 [42] (MacMenamin J); [2008] 1 IR 134, 147, citing MacCarthy J in *N (otherwise K) v K* [1985] IR 733 (SC), which was also cited by Hamilton CJ in *TF v Ireland* [1995] 1 IR 321 (SC) 373.

155. *T(D) v T(C)* [2002] IESC 68; [2002] 3 IR 334.

be required to continue to respect those marital obligations designed 'for their mutual protection and welfare'.[156] This was because marriage was, 'in principle, intended to be a lifetime commitment and… each spouse has fashioned his or her life on that premise'.[157] Essentially this was a reliance argument, based on legitimate expectations: if spouses could renege on their marital obligations when they divorced, this would undermine marriage itself. It would also show 'complete disregard' for the homemaker's role, since she would necessarily be the one to suffer most financially (a fairness and equality argument).[158] This was the reason for the constitutional requirement that 'proper' provision be made prior to divorce.

In terms of spousal obligations, MacMenamin J noted that there was a long-established right of spousal maintenance at common law and in the ecclesiastical courts. This was subsequently built on by legislation, including the 1989 Act, which granted more extensive powers of provision. Again placing particular reliance on *TF*, MacMenamin J concluded that 'such orders were appropriate, proportionate and in accord with the provisions of the Constitution of Ireland on the institution of marriage itself and the rights of each family member'.[159] In this way, MacMenamin J used art 41 to support proportionate delimitation of property rights.

In some respects MacMenamin J's reasoning is problematic. The common law right of support was extremely limited, effectively being restricted to the provision of necessities, for which an estranged wife could pledge her husband's credit.[160] It certainly did not include any power to transfer property between spouses. Any historical justification for the extensive powers of provision under the current legislation must therefore be doubtful. Furthermore, as has previously been noted, a strict perusal of *TF* does not provide a 'blanket' approval of the scheme of provision under the 1989 Act, though the general tone of the decision might be considered supportive.

MacMenamin J is of course on firmer ground when discussing the property aspects of divorce legislation, since the 1996 Act is supported by a constitutional imperative. It was therefore unsurprising that MacMenamin J concluded that the 1996 scheme was within the competence of the Oireachtas. MacMenamin J held that the 1996 provisions 'must be seen… as having been made to provide for and to balance the interests of the family as a whole and the members of that family unit'.[161] Relying on *T v T*, MacMenamin J noted that 'proper' provision must be based on a consideration of all the circumstances of

156. ibid 405.
157. ibid.
158. ibid.
159. *LB v Ireland* [2006] IEHC 275 [46] (MacMenamin J); [2008] 1 IR 134, 148.
160. See, eg, Nigel V Lowe and Gillian Douglas, *Bromley's Family Law* (10th edn, Butterworths 2006) 915–16 for an account of common law duties of financial support.
161. ibid [50] (MacMenamin J); [2008] 1 IR 134, 149.

the case, including those factors highlighted in the legislation.[162] Accordingly, he concluded that 'proper' provision under the 1996 Act was in fact 'a recognition of the constitutional obligation which the Act of 1996 was passed to serve', and was constitutionally mandated.[163]

While this reasoning is unexceptionable, MacMenamin J continued to stress the significance of *TF*, holding that:

> The provisions of the Act of 1996 with regard to financial relief are in harmony with the terms of the relief that may be granted by the court under the Act of 1989. Thus, insofar as the provisions of Act of 1989 are constitutional then, (unless some fundamental distinction in principle is shown) ipso facto, the Act of 1996 must also be constitutional in its provisions. No such distinction has been urged, identified or established herein.[164]

Again, however, this is questionable. Although the 1989 scheme is similar to that of the 1996 Act, the standard for provision differs (so are the two really 'in harmony'?).[165] Furthermore, as noted above, *TF* did not in fact hold that the entirety of the 1989 scheme was constitutional. Finally, it must be noted that MacMenamin J was not pronouncing on the significance of any possible distinction between the two Acts, since no such distinction was argued.

Although MacMenamin J's decision was apparently affirmed by the Supreme Court, no written Supreme Court judgment is available,[166] nor was the Supreme Court's reasoning explained in the subsequent decision of Hogan J (discussed below). Accordingly, the issues identified in this analysis lack definitive clarification.

In the most recent *LB* litigation, the plaintiff essentially contended that the various ancillary relief orders made on the parties' judicial separation and divorce constituted an unlawful expropriation of his assets by the State. As MacMenamin J had done before him, Hogan J emphasised the comments of Murray J in *T v T* regarding the nature and obligations of marriage, and the view that a failure to uphold these obligations between divorced persons would undermine the institution of marriage.[167]

Hogan J considered that the previous *LB* litigation had established that neither the 1989 nor the 1996 Act were unconstitutional insofar as they allowed courts to make proper provision on judicial separation or divorce;[168] such

162. ibid [52] (MacMenamin J); [2008] 1 IR 134, 150.
163. ibid [52] (MacMenamin J); [2008] 1 IR 134, 151.
164. ibid.
165. This issue is discussed further below.
166. In the second *LB* case, Hogan J states that the Supreme Court affirmed MacMenamin J's decision in July 2009, but does not provide further details of the Supreme Court's ruling. See *LB v Ireland and the Attorney General and PB* [2012] IEHC 461 [8] (Hogan J).
167. ibid [10] (Hogan J).
168. ibid [12] (Hogan J).

provision was not merely permitted but required, for the reasons identified by MacMenamin J. However, for reasons previously discussed, this is questionable to the extent that MacMenamin J relied on *TF* as authority for his views. Furthermore, even if MacMenamin J correctly held that financial provision under the 1989 Act was constitutional, due to *TF*, such an endorsement could not automatically be applied to the 1995 Act, given the change in the standard of provision in the that Act (as amended). For these reasons, it is worrying that Hogan J stated in passing that the previous litigation had entailed a challenge to ss 12–21 of the 1995 Act.[169] This was presumably an error, since the 1995 Act was not at issue in the previous litigation. Nor, indeed, had the claimant contested the constitutionality of the equivalent provisions of the 1989 Act, so in fact MacMenamin J's comments on the constitutionality of that Act were effectively *obiter*.

These caveats aside, it was noteworthy that Hogan J's decision, like that of MacMenamin J, was essentially based on the commitments undertaken by spouses in marriage, and on the need to uphold the family, which justified the limitation of personal property rights.[170] Indeed, Hogan J described the statutory provisions that permitted property to be transferred to P's wife as

> no more than giving effect to that which is inherent in the nature of marriage. Marriage, after all, involves mutual giving and sacrifice. In practical terms this means the sharing of outgoings, expenses and, in some respects, at least, the capital assets of the parties.[171]

Both judges therefore found that the justification for the delimitation of property rights in the marital breakdown context lay in the nature of the family itself rather than on the connected but distinct social policy objective of combating hardship and consequent social ills in the post-marital breakdown context. The basis for intervention therefore lay in art 41 rather than art 43, except insofar as upholding marital commitments can also be interpreted as an aspect of the common good and social justice under art 43. It is striking that neither judge referred to the broader social policy justifications that might also support or have influenced the financial provision measures on divorce or judicial separation,[172] though perhaps both felt that this was unnecessary since art 41 offered an appropriate basis for intervention in the particular case.

169. ibid [7] (Hogan J).
170. Neither judge adverted to gender equality concerns (other than a glancing and gender-neutral reference to the need to protect the homemaker).
171. *LB v Ireland and the Attorney General and PB* [2012] IEHC 461 [13] (Hogan J).
172. Dáil Debates reveal that the Matrimonial Home Bill 1993 was premised on concepts of marital partnership, but the policy behind the 1995 Act is less clear. No clear statement of purpose was made by the Minister for Equality and Law Reform, Mr Taylor, on introducing the Family Law Bill 1994 (later the 1995 Act) to the Dáil (Dáil Deb 23 February 1994, vol 439, cols 613–14). However, the 1989 Act, the

Hogan J distinguished between the automatic division of a couple's property in a particular way, and discretionary orders of the type permitted by the judicial separation and divorce legislation. The former was impermissible 'without compelling reasons'[173] (following the decision in *Re the Matrimonial Home Bill 1993*),[174] as it constituted an interference with the autonomous decision-making of the family without reference to any circumstances that might make such a decision injurious or unfair. However, Hogan J considered that 'different considerations would naturally obtain' where (as here) 'one spouse had potentially failed to discharge his or her duties to the other'.[175] This was no different to imposing maintenance obligations in respect of the other spouse or dependent children.[176] Of course, this depends on one's interpretation of spousal 'duties', since the payment of needs-based maintenance is arguably different in kind to the conferral of a proprietary interest in the property of another based on marital contributions and like considerations.[177]

Hogan J emphasised that support (and presumably, sharing) 'obligations stem from the very nature of marriage and parenthood itself and without them marriage and child-rearing would be all but impossible'.[178] Hence, the provisions permitting such provision actually upheld and safeguarded marriage, as constitutionally required by art 41.3.1. Seen in this light (and contrary to the view advanced earlier in this article), the legislation did not involve State expropriation of assets but rather 'the intra-spousal transfer of capital assets'.[179] In this respect, the State was 'doing no more than providing for an independent resolution mechanism (ie by means of the judicial system) of disputes between family members in respect of the extent of such proper financial provision'.[180]

Even if the making of 'proper' provision did involve such expropriation, or to the extent that it did so, Hogan J held that this was 'by definition not an

---

financial provisions of which were largely replicated by the 1995 Act, was clearly based on a desire to to ameliorate the invidious position of separated spouses, particularly wives. For instance, Senator Manning noted at the Second Stage that 'The basic purpose of this Bill is to minimise the hardship and distress that can occur when marriages break down… It confers new comprehensive powers on the courts to make financial lump sum and property transfer orders to provide additional protection, in particular for dependent wives and children, by enabling the court to give them a far greater degree of security than they can obtain at present' (Seanad Deb 1 March 1989, vol 122, col 326).

173. ibid [14] (Hogan J).
174. *Re the Matrimonial Home Bill 1993* [1994] IESC 5; [1994] 1 IR 305.
175. *LB v Ireland and the Attorney General and PB* [2012] IEHC 461 [16] (Hogan J).
176. ibid [17].
177. This issue is beyond the scope of this paper.
178. ibid [18] (Hogan J).
179. ibid [18] (Hogan J).
180. ibid [19] (Hogan J).

unjustified interference with the property rights of the affected spouse for the purposes of Article 40.3.2 since this legislation is designed to give effect to fundamental values cherished by Article 41 and is, in any event, sanctioned by Article 41.3.2'.[181] Again, this emphasises Hogan J's view that the basis for intervention lies in art 41 rather than art 43. Hogan J also held that there was no need for the State to compensate the transferring spouse, since this 'would mean that the State had assumed a responsibility in respect of the financial obligations which one spouse owes to the other'.[182] As well as noting that a compensatory obligation on the State would encourage spouses to default on their obligations towards other family members,[183] Hogan J also held that compensation by the State could not be payable since the State was not taking the plaintiff's assets, but simply providing a mechanism whereby inter-spousal financial relations were adjusted appropriately.[184]

In one respect, Hogan J's decision may have been *obiter*, since he acknowledged that the issues raised were largely *res judicata* insofar as similar issues had already been adjudicated in the plaintiff's previous High and Supreme Court proceedings.[185] Even so, his views are likely to be highly influential, particularly since both he and MacMenamin J have advanced a new constitutional justification for the reallocation of marital property in the marital breakdown context. It is therefore important to emphasise that the *LB* cases technically only address 'proper' provision in the divorce context, since (as explained above) neither the 1989 nor the 1995 Acts were actually at issue in either case. It is of course possible to make a strong argument that equivalent reasoning should apply in the judicial separation context: after all, the obligations of the marital contract and the need to protect the family are the same, whether a couple are divorcing or merely obtaining a separation order. The problem faced in both contexts is also essentially the same: the need to provide for what will henceforth be two households instead of one, from the same asset base. The provision schemes under the 1995 and 1996 Acts are almost identical, allowing 'proper' provision to be tailored to the relevant circumstances. Why then should the equal constitutionality of both Acts be in doubt?

The first important point is that, although (taken at face value) the *LB* judgments considered the 1989 provision scheme to be constitutional, they did not address the difference in the standards of provision between the 1989 and the 1995 Acts. As noted previously, the 1989 Act stipulates that financial provision on judicial separation must be 'adequate and reasonable', while the 1995 Act, as amended, requires that it must be 'proper' in the circumstances (the same

---

181. ibid [18] (Hogan J). Of course, art 41.3.2° applies to divorce only.
182. ibid [19] (Hogan J).
183. ibid [19] (Hogan J).
184. ibid [19] (Hogan J).
185. ibid [21] (Hogan J).

standard as for divorce). It must therefore be asked: do these standards differ, and if they do, does this matter?

The case law suggests that the term 'proper' provision entails a consideration of overall fairness as between the parties. In *T v T*, Murphy J considered that the term 'proper' provision and the statutory criteria adopted in the 1996 Act clearly meant that the provision to be made went 'far beyond mere "needs" and probably exceeds what is comprised in the alluring term of "reasonable requirements"'.[186] Similarly, Fennelly J considered that the term 'proper' was equivalent to 'appropriate', and that it was 'also synonymous with what is "fair" or "just"'.[187] The meaning of 'adequate and reasonable' provision has not been similarly expounded, but may be assumed to intimate a somewhat lower, perhaps more needs-based standard (though it should be noted that the factors for consideration by the court are largely the same under the 1989, 1995 and 1996 Acts). More recently, the Supreme Court has defined 'proper' provision as being 'reasonable in all the circumstances'.[188] This suggests a narrower approach than the previous emphasis on fairness and justice, though it should be noted that the Court did not advocate or refer to mere 'adequacy'. It is suggested here that 'adequate and reasonable' provision must necessarily differ from provision that is 'proper', if only because there would otherwise have been no reason to amend the 1995 Act.[189]

The distinction between 'proper' provision and that which is merely 'adequate and reasonable' may be meaningless in many cases, due to a lack of resources. Nevertheless, the distinction matters because a judicial separation is not in fact a divorce, and provision in this context is therefore not explicitly constitutionally mandated. Although the *LB* litigation confirms that 'proper' provision is constitutional under the 1996 Act, there is no clear authority that it is constitutional on judicial separation. While it might be contended that the lengthy waiting period for divorce makes it reasonable to apply the ultimate standard for provision at an earlier date,[190] it might equally well be argued that a lower standard of provision is appropriate where the marriage still technically subsists. After all, reconciliation may still be possible (if unlikely), and it may therefore be inappropriate to make 'final' orders at the separation stage. Furthermore, there is likely to be a lengthy period of adjustment, during which the parties' needs may remain fluid. In this sense, the lengthy waiting period for divorce may be both advantageous and disadvantageous – advantageous in permitting a realistic evaluation of the parties' future needs before making final

186. *T(D) v T(C)* [2002] IESC 68; [2002] 3 IR 334, 399.

187. ibid 413.

188. *G v G* [2011] IESC 40 [25] (Denham CJ).

189. There is no explanatory memorandum for the change, which was made in s 52(h) of the 1996 Act; nor was the change discussed in the Dáil prior to enactment.

190. Spouses must have lived apart for four of the five years preceding an application of divorce (s 5(1)(a) of the 1996 Act), but only for one year prior to a consensual judicial separation (s 2(1)(d) of the 1989 Act).

provision, but disadvantageous in making them wait so long for that provision. All of this weakens the degree of intervention that might be supported by art 41 on judicial separation.

It might be contended that the Constitution merely gives 'proper' provision as a necessary precondition for divorce, without however specifying how long previously that provision may be made. Article 41.3.2.iii states that the court must be satisfied that 'proper' provision 'exists or will be made'; why, then, should not that provision be made some years previously, on judicial separation? Viewed this way, 'proper' provision on judicial separation may be implicitly constitutionally sanctioned. This, however, seems unlikely. For instance, one can easily envisage a couple with religious scruples that prohibit divorce, who nevertheless wish to avail of judicial separation. Is 'proper' provision constitutional in this context? It is suggested that it must be questionable, at least, since the 'implied mandate' argument does not provide a stand-alone sanction for provision on judicial separation. The 'implied mandate' argument is further attenuated by the fact that the 1996 Act does not require the terms of a judicial separation order to be considered in making 'proper' provision on divorce, though it does specify that the terms of a valid and subsisting separation agreement must be considered.[191] While the courts in practice can and do take such prior orders into account,[192] the fact that there is no legislative requirement to do so undermines any implicit extension of the ambit of art 41.3.2.iii to the judicial separation stage.[193]

Overall, therefore, the potential distinctions between the divorce and judicial separation contexts weaken the utility of art 41 as the sole or primary constitutional basis for financial orders under the 1995 Act. It is submitted that the strongest argument in favour of proper provision on judicial separation is that it is a proportionate intervention in an important and pressing issue of social concern. Marital breakdown is both common and linked to issues of poverty and social justice. Consequently, legislative intervention is both appropriate and necessary, irrespective of whether the marriage is finally being dissolved. Although this article has emphasised how art 41 may support the necessary redistributive measures, both in terms of policy and as a mandate for distribution on divorce, it has also argued that art 41 is not in fact essential to permit such measures since art 43 already permits such intervention. Further constitutional support for the financial provision measures of both the 1995 and 1996 Acts may derive from the equality provisions, though again these aspects are best regarded as supplementary only, since they have only limited application to financial provision under the 2010 Act.

---

191. s 20(3) of the 1996 Act.
192. See, eg, *RG v CG* [2005] IEHC 202. In the Supreme Court decision of *SN v PO'D* [2009] IESC 61, Fennelly J seemed to treat a consent judicial separation as if it were a separation agreement, in terms of the statutory obligation to 'have regard' to the terms of the settlement.
193. Naturally, an 'implicit extension' justification for 'proper' provision could not apply in relation to the breakdown of a civil partnership; still less could it justify provision on the breakdown of a cohabitational relationship.

Financial Provision under the 2010 Act in the Wake of the *LB* Litigation

If there is doubt as to whether the *LB* reasoning would apply to judicial separation, what of civil partnerships and cohabitational relationships? A discretionary system of provision applies also on the breakdown of these relationships; indeed, the legislative provisions for financial orders on the termination of civil partnership are virtually identical to the provisions of the 1995 and 1996 Acts. The 'proper' provision standard applies also on the breakdown of civil partnerships, though not to the end of cohabitation; this distinction is presumably based on the 'marriage-like' status of civil partnerships, as compared with the lack of legal commitment of cohabitants. As noted in the Introduction to this article, many of the same problems may arise on the breakdown of both non-marital and marital relationships. Civil partnership (if not cohabitation) may be just as premised on expectations of mutual support as marriage itself; both civil partnership and cohabitation, like marriage, may entail personal and financial self-sacrifice by either partner.

Notwithstanding the close similarities, it seems clear that, to the extent that the *LB* decisions relied on art 41 and the need to support the institution of marriage, the reasoning could not apply to non-marital relationships. Therefore, assuming that the constitutional interpretation of the 'family' remains unchanged, art 41 cannot support redistributive measures under the 2010 Act, and the constitutional basis of that Act, if it exists, must lie elsewhere. This, of course, is entirely possible, though it would seem logical that the very similar measures in each Act should have similar justifications. Since art 41 cannot apply to non-marital relationships, and gender equality arguments cannot apply to same-sex relationships, it is contended that the only constitutional basis that offers equal potential for upholding financial provision measures under the 1995, 1996 and 2010 Acts is the delimitation of property rights to meet a pressing social concern, under art 43. It is therefore a matter of concern that this aspect was not addressed in the *LB* judgments.

Conclusion

The *LB* decisions provide a clear constitutional rationale for upholding very necessary provisions, at least in the marital breakdown context. Although the reasoning in both cases is flawed in some respects, the two High Court decisions confirm a new basis for upholding financial provision on marital breakdown, previously hinted at in *TF* and *T v T*. The judgments confirm that constitutional property rights are qualified in the interests of the family and society, albeit due to art 41 rather than art 43. This is certainly a viable basis for grounding the 1996 Act, and it may also be upheld in relation to the 1995 Act. However, due to the distinctions that may be drawn between judicial separation and divorce, it would have been useful if the judgments had placed a greater emphasis on social policy justifications for delimiting property rights under art 43, as well as using art 41 to support the redistributive mechanisms. This would also have permitted the reasoning to be extended to financial provision on the breakdown of civil partnership and cohabitation. As it stands, however, financial provision under the 2010 Act still lacks a clear constitutional basis.

There are good grounds of both policy and logic for extending the core reasoning in the *LB* cases to financial provision under the 1995 Act. However, since the judgments do not deal explicitly with that Act, a further constitutional lacuna remains. The gap cannot be filled simply by extending the deemed constitutionality of the 1989 Act to the 1995 Act, since (even if MacMenamin J's interpretation of *TF* is correct) the standard applied in both Acts is not the same. The constitutional void is a cause for concern because there are are significant differences between judicial separation and divorce, which might be held to justify the application of a different standard in each context. Overall, while the extension of the reasoning in the *LB* decisions to encompass the 1995 Act seems probable as well as desirable, the matter remains as yet unresolved.

Implementing Disability Rights in Education in Ireland: An Impossible Task?

Sarah Arduin*

Abstract—Over the past two decades, Ireland has seen an increased public interest in thinking about disability rights in education and in determining how Irish schools could deliver, in an inclusive environment, a quality education appropriate to the needs of every child, including children with learning difficulties and disabilities. Nonetheless, despite the evidence of a shift in its policy and the signature of the UN Convention on the Rights of Persons with Disabilities, the Irish approach to disability rights in education remains far from satisfactory.

This article intends to understand the inappropriateness and inadequacy of the Irish approach to disability rights in education. It intends to provide a comprehensive insight into the debate and into the challenges that remain to be overcome in order to transform the Irish approach, in line with international human rights law, into a human rights-based approach to disability rights in education; guaranteeing inclusive, equitable and quality education for all in a respectful learning environment.

Introduction

Over the past two decades, Ireland has seen an increased public interest in thinking about disability rights in education and determining how its schools could deliver, in an inclusive environment, a quality education appropriate to the needs of every child, including children with learning difficulties and disabilities. The approach of the Irish government to disability rights in education has significantly changed not only in its attitude in recognising persons with learning difficulties and disabilities as valuable citizens of the Irish State,[1] but also in establishing a legislative framework that encapsulates the ethos of an inclusive philosophy[2] and paves the way towards vindicating a right to quality education for all in the best-suited learning environment.[3] Now more than ever, educational

---

* PhD candidate, Trinity College Dublin. The author would like to thank Professor William Binchy, Professor Oran Doyle and David Quinn BL for their comments on earlier drafts. Any errors and omissions are the author's.

1. See *O'Donoghue v Minister for Health* (1996) 2 IR 20 at 59.
2. See, in particular, s 2 of the Education for Persons with Special Educational Needs Act (2004) No 30, which sets out the principle of inclusive education in Ireland. Further discussion on this section is provided below.
3. See below.

provisions for children with learning difficulties and disabilities are identified as being part of the wider education community. Their right to education is well established under the Irish Constitution[4] and has received official recognition through the enactment of a detailed legislative framework, culminating with the Education for Persons with Special Educational Needs Act (EPSEN Act).[5]

Nonetheless, despite the evidence of a shift in its policy and the signature of the UN Convention on the Rights of Persons with Disabilities (CRPD),[6] the Irish approach to disability rights in education remains far from satisfactory, particularly in the light of international developments.[7] As will be discussed in this article, the general trend in international human rights law is to advocate a human rights-based approach to disability rights in education, as exemplified by art 24 of the CRPD.[8] This approach centres the debate not so much on the type of

4. See art 42.4 of the Irish Constitution and its interpretation provided by the Judiciary in *Crowley v Ireland* [1980] IR 102 (SC); *O'Donoghue v Minister for Health* [1996] 2 IR 20 (HC); *O'Shiel v Minister for Education* [1999] 2 ILRM 241 (HC); and *Sinnott v Minister for Education* [2001] 2 IR 545 (SC).
5. (2004) No 30.
6. General Assembly resolution 61/106 (2007). Ireland signed the Convention on 30 March 2007, which entered into force on 3 May 2008. For further discussion on the Convention and its human rights-based approach, see Gerard Quinn and Theresia Degener, *Human Rights and Disability: The Current Use and Future Potential of United Nations Human Rights Instruments in the Context of Disability* (United Nations 2002); Michael Stein, 'Disability Human Rights' (2007) 95 Cal L Rev 75; and Michael Stein, 'Beyond Disability Civil Rights' (2006–07) 58 Hasting LJ 1203; Gerard Quinn and Oddny Mjoll Arnardóttir, *The UN Convention on the Rights of Persons with Disabilities: European and Scandinavian Perspectives* (vol 10, International Studies in Human Rights 2009); Marcia Rioux and Anne Carbert, 'Human Rights and Disability: The International Context' (2003) 10(2) J on Developmental Disabilities 1; Jenny Morris, 'Impairment and Disability: Constructing an Ethics of Care that Promotes Human Rights' (2001) 16(4) Hypatia 1.
7. See, for instance, the UN Declaration of Human Rights 1948; the UN International Covenant on Economic, Social and Cultural Rights, GA Res 2200 A (XXI), UN GAOR (1966); the Convention on the Rights of the Child, GA Res 44/25, UN GAOR, 44th Session (1989); and the UN Standard Rules on the Equalization of Opportunities for People with Disabilities, GA Res 48/96, UN GAOR, 48th Session (1993); and art 24 CRPD, which recognises the right of persons with disabilities to quality education in an inclusive environment.
8. art 24(1) CRPD reads as follows: 'States Parties recognize the right of persons with disabilities to education. With a view to realizing this right without discrimination and on the basis of equal opportunity, States Parties shall ensure an inclusive education system at all levels and life long learning directed to (a) the full development of human potential and sense of dignity and self-worth, and the strengthening of respect for human rights, fundamental freedoms and human diversity; (b) the development by persons with disabilities of their personality, talents and creativity, as well as their mental and physical abilities, to their fullest potential; (c) enabling persons with disabilities to participate effectively in a free society.'

rights to which persons with disabilities should be entitled, but rather on how society and, *a fortiori*, the law should accommodate human difference, diversity and plurality within its institutions.[9] Advocating disability rights in education is precisely about ensuring an effective and equal enjoyment of educational rights for every child in the best-suited learning environment, regardless of ability or disability, talent or difficulty, physical or intellectual capacity.

This article intends to understand the inappropriateness and inadequacy of the Irish 'special'[10] education law, policy and practice in light of international developments. It intends to provide a comprehensive insight into the debate and the challenges that remain to be overcome in order to transform the Irish approach, in line with international human rights law, into a human rights-based approach to disability rights in education, guaranteeing inclusive, equitable and quality education for all in a respectful learning environment.

This article is composed of four parts. The first part establishes the theoretical roots of the debate by analysing the content and purpose of a human rights-based approach to disability rights in education. The second part reviews the current Irish legislative framework, paying particular attention to the principles set down in the Education for Persons with Special Educational Needs Act. The third part outlines the theoretical inadequacies that directly stem from the legislative framework and the implications that these inadequacies have in practice for the education of children with learning difficulties and disabilities. The final part draws conclusions and suggests how the Irish legal framework could be improved in order to effectively guarantee the rights of children with learning difficulties and disabilities *within* education, and more precisely their right to quality education in an inclusive learning environment.

The Human Rights-Based Approach to Disability Rights in Education

The human rights-based approach to disability rights in education is a model that encompasses two progressive philosophies. First, it advocates a human rights-based approach to disability that emphasises the equal human dignity and equal human worth of persons with disabilities.[11] Secondly, it incorporates an ethical and inclusive approach to education that emphasises the humanistic and idiosyncratic nature of learning.[12] It suggests that education is about

9. For further details, see Quinn and Degener, *Human Rights and Disability*, 1.
10. The expression 'special education' and its inappropriate use will be further discussed below.
11. Quinn and Degener, *Human Rights and Disability*, 1.
12. For further discussion on the ethical approach to education, see Hans Skjervheim, *The Science of Man and the Philosophical Reflection* (Tanum 1964); Stephen Von Tetzchner and Karen Jensen, 'Interacting with People Who Have Severe Communication Problems: Ethical Considerations' (1999) 46(4) Int'l J of Disability, Development and Edu 453; John Vorhaus, 'Respecting Profoundly Disabled Learners' (2006) 40(3) J of Phil of Edu 313.

humanising difference and human diversity.[13] It is about valuing learners' background, knowledge, abilities, interests and life experience. In essence, the human rights-based approach to disability rights in education highlights the fact that children with disabilities are first and foremost children, and thereafter children with disabilities.[14] Respecting them as such and acknowledging their capacities to learn constitute the *sine qua non* condition for moving forward and implementing effectively this humanistic and inclusive ethos.

The Human Rights-Based Approach to Disability

Emerging alongside the civil rights movement,[15] the disability rights movement[16] has hastened the debate about disability, raised awareness about human diversity,[17] and emphasised the importance and benefits of a human rights-based approach to disability. In essence, this new perspective urges societies to move away from previous ontological assumptions and beliefs about disability, normality and difference towards adopting a more holistic understanding of disability as a sign of human diversity and as a human right.[18] Emphasising the complexity of disability and its multidimensional nature,[19] the

13. Lilia Bartolome, 'Beyond the Methods Fetish: Toward a Humanizing Pedagogy' (1994) 64(2) Harv Edu Rev 173.
14. Vorhaus, 'Respecting Profoundly Disabled Learners', 315.
15. See, for instance, Stein, who provides a comprehensive analysis of the emergence of the disability rights movement in the United States.
16. The slogan, to which it is often referred in order to characterise the disability rights movement, is borrowed from the title of a book from James Charlton, *Nothing About Us Without Us* (Charlton 1998). This slogan reflects the growing demand of persons with disabilities to be included in policy-making and disability research and become visible citizens with a voice that matters. For further details on the movement, see D Wasserman, LJ Davis, A Asch and RA Putnam, 'Disability: Definitions, Models, Experience', *The Stanford Encyclopedia of Philosophy* (Summer 2013 edn).
17. See art 8 CRPD, which provides a list of measures aimed at raising awareness, such as (a) initiating and maintaining effective public awareness campaigns designed to (i) nurture receptiveness to the rights of persons with disabilities; (ii) promote positive perceptions and greater social awareness towards persons with disabilities; and (iii) promote recognition of the skills, merits and abilities of persons with disabilities, and of their contributions to the workplace and the labour market; (b) fostering at all levels of the education system, including in all children from an early age, an attitude of respect for the rights of persons with disabilities; (c) encouraging all organs of the media to portray persons with disabilities in a manner consistent with the purpose of the present Convention; and (d) promoting awareness-training programmes regarding persons with disabilities and the rights of persons with disabilities.
18. See n 6.
19. Pointing out the interactionist nature of disability, the International Classification of Functioning, Disability and Health suggests a biopsychosocial model, according to

human rights model solicits governments to recognise persons with disabilities as subjects of rights, as opposed to charity objects.[20]

This model came about in reaction to the individualist and medical approach to disability (a) and the limits of its poststructuralist social version (b).

The Medical Model of Disability

The medical model of disability relies on ontological principles that distinguish the normal from the pathological.[21] It suggests that there exists a hierarchical ontological dichotomy in which impairment – as equalised to disability – is associated with 'deficit' or a flawed existence.[22] It posits that the essence of disability lies in the biomedical reality, which is determined by rational reflections and scientific methods used by physicians.[23] Only one real explanation of this phenomenon is provided: it is a biophysical deficit or impairment that is an inherent disorder, deficiency, dysfunction or abnormality located exclusively and inevitably within the individual's biological characteristics.[24] Disablement becomes a characteristic of a defective person – that is, someone who is 'functionally limited or anatomically abnormal, diseased, or pathoanatomical; someone who is neither whole nor healthy, fit nor flourishing, someone who is biologically inferior or subnormal'.[25]

As the medical model solely emphasises the medical nature of disability, it belittles people with disabilities and focuses on their rehabilitation, medication and cure with the hope to restore their body to the average standard from which it had deviated. Put another way, the medical model completely overlooks the social and environmental features of disablement.

---

which disability is the outcome of interactions between health conditions and contextual factors (see, ICF, *Towards a Common Language for Functioning, Disability and Health*, WHO, 2002, Geneva, WHO/EIP/GPE/CAS/01.3, 10).

20. Rannveig Traustadóttir, 'Disability Studies, the Social Model and Legal Developments' in Quinn and Arnardóttir, *UN Convention*, 3; and Quinn and Degener, *Human Rights and Disability*, 1.
21. See Jerome Bickenbach, 'The Biomedical Model of Disablement', in *Physical Disability and Social Policy* (University of Toronto Press Inc 1993), 65.
22. Bill Hughes, 'The Constitution of Impairment: Modernity and the Aesthetic of Oppression' (1999) 14(2) Dis & Soc, 155; Bill Hughes, 'Medicine and the Aesthetic Invalidation of Disabled People' (2000) 15(3) Dis & Soc, 555.
23. For further discussion, see Steve Smith, 'Equality, Identity and the Disability Rights Movement: From Policy to Practice and from Kant to Nietzsche in More than One Uneasy Move' (2005) 25 Crit Soc Pol 554.
24. It is important to note that the medical model of disability relies on the Kantian essentialist assumption, according to which there is an existential reality fixed across time and societies. This reality is constituted of delimited biophysical features that are present within the human body and that are therefore essential and not incidental to its existence (see ibid 560).
25. ibid.

The problem with this model is twofold. First, it sustains and further accentuates the myth according to which people with disabilities are sick and dependant individuals.[26] Secondly, the solutions advocated by the model diminish persons with disabilities to objects of charity, which at best may be rehabilitated or at worst excluded. Interestingly, talking about rehabilitation necessarily raises the question of what it is to be human and how the human body should look.[27] Rehabilitation conveys a sense of returning, bringing back or re-establishing a former situation or former state of being to the normal life by training or therapy.[28] As the medical model suggests that persons with disabilities have lost a function or an organ or have an abnormal biological characteristic, it believes that these individuals have also lost their place in society. The only way for them to regain their place within society is to endure some form of reconstruction of their disabled body or rehabilitation. To this end, an array of corrective devices are often provided, with the ultimate hope that these devices will eventually transform disabled people – as the medical model names them – into normal individuals, worthy of being integrated within society.[29] In essence, the medical solution of rehabilitation becomes the symbol of a culture that attempts to make identical individuals through the process of medicalisation and/or institutionalisation. It aims at eradicating the disabled body and, *a fortiori*, any human difference so that every member of a society is assimilated with the 'greater and single social whole'.[30]

In reaction to the limits of this model, a more social constructionist approach to disability is often advocated,[31] emphasising the sociological nature of

26. As suggested by Bickenbach, disablement becomes a characteristic of a defective person – that is, someone who is 'functionally limited or anatomically abnormal, diseased, or pathoanatomical; someone who is neither whole nor healthy, fit nor flourishing, someone who is biologically inferior or subnormal' ('Biomedical Model of Disablement' 61).
27. Ingunn Moser, 'Against Normalisation: Subverting Norms of Ability and Disability' (2000) 9(2) Science as Culture 201, 206.
28. ibid.
29. ibid 228.
30. ibid.
31. For a literature of the social model, see Gary Albrecht, Katherine Seelman and Michael Bury, *Handbook of Disability Study* (Sage Publications 2000); Colin Barnes, *Disabled People in Britain and Discrimination* (Hurst and Calgary 1991) 2; and Len Barton, *Disability and Society* (Longman 1996); Sara Goering, 'Beyond the Medical Model? Disability, Formal Justice, and the Exception for the "Profoundly Impaired"' (2002) 12(4) Kennedy Inst of Ethics J 373; Michael Oliver, 'If I Had a Hammer: The Social Model in Action' in John Swain, Sally French, Colin Barnes and Carol Thomas, *Disabling Barriers – Enabling Environments* (Sage Publications 2007); Tom Shakespeare, *Disability Rights and Wrongs* (Routledge 2006); and Carol Thomas, 'Disability Theory: Key Ideas, Issues and Thinkers' in Colin Barnes, Michael Oliver and Len Barton, *Disability Studies Today* (Polity Press 2002) 38.

impairment *and* disability.[32] This version adopts an anti-Cartesian perspective[33] and posits that impairment, like disability, is more a sociological and societal problem than a biomedical problem.[34] It suggests that disability, like impairment, is the idealist product of a society based on aesthetic and somatic values.[35]

The Social Constructionist Approach to Disability

Otherwise known as the poststructuralist model of disability, this approach posits that both concepts of disability and impairment are the product of cultural relativism – that is, of specific cultural conditions.[36] It argues that, although impairment may be constituted of biophysical characteristics, this phenomenon may be also constructed by social, cultural and political discourses.[37] In essence, the poststructuralist version argues that, whilst persons with disabilities have always been present in society, the degree to which they are included or excluded from mainstream activities varies depending on the predominant cultural interpretation of the concept of humane difference and therefore disability.[38]

Two important cultural phenomena have been identified as participating in this social and cultural construction.[39] They are the institutionalisation of linguistic and discursive practices on the one hand, and the aesthetic oppression of the non-disabled gaze in a somatic society based on 'the myth of bodily perfection'[40] – also called the 'tyranny of perfection'[41] – on the other hand. Both phenomena demonstrate that disability is experienced in, on and through the

32. It is important to note that the social model of disability is not a monolithic entity, but rather a plural entity that embodies a myriad of social-contextual approaches to disability. For the purpose of this article, only one type of social model of disability is analysed, namely the social constructionist approach.
33. An anti-Cartesian approach suggests that disability and impairment are not two separate entities. They both participate in a complex interpenetration of oppression and affliction. For further discussion on this topic, see Bill Hughes and Kevin Paterson, 'The Social Model of Disability and the Disappearing Body: Towards a Sociology of Impairment' (1997) 12(3) Disability and Soc 325, 330.
34. Tom Shakespeare and Miriam Corker, 'Mapping the Terrain' in *Disability/Postmodernity: Embodying Disability Theory* (Continuum 2002) 3.
35. Michael Priestley, 'Construction and Creations: Idealism, Materialism and Disability Theory' (1998) 13(1) Dis & Soc 75, 81.
36. ibid.
37. Hughes and Paterson, 'Social Model of Disability'.
38. Hughes, 'Constitution of Impairment'.
39. For the purpose of this article, these cultural phenomena are only mentioned, as a study of their content and implications would be outside the scope of this paper.
40. For further details, see Hughes, 'Medicine and the Aesthetic Invalidation of Disabled People', 560.
41. Barry Glassner, *Bodies: The Tyranny of Perfection* (Lowell House 1992).

body and the gaze of people without disabilities.[42] It is experienced from the perspective of impairment and from the social and aesthetic characteristics of a somatic society.

Under this version, the social environment of our society becomes the primary cause of disadvantage and discrimination against persons with disabilities. In response to these forms of exclusion, the social ontology favours the enactment of non-discriminatory measures that would remove social and environmental barriers and ultimately integrate persons with disabilities within society.[43] In this context, equality of treatment becomes the ethos upon which the social constructionist model of disability relies.[44] It posits that, by removing the environmental and structural barriers, people with disabilities can have access to the same societal services than people without disabilities and therefore participate within the mainstream society on an equal basis with others.

The problem with this formal conception of equality is that it does not challenge the traditional approach, according to which equality is assimilated to sameness and difference to otherness.[45] It protects equally all human beings from direct discrimination, but does not protect them from indirect discrimination, therefore avoiding real differences.[46] It fails to move beyond the 'equality as neutrality philosophy'[47] and to take the additional step of providing equality of opportunity.

This additional step is precisely provided by the human rights-based approach to disability.

---

42. Hughes and Paterson, 'Social Model of Disability', 335.
43. See, for example, Barnes, *Disabled People in Britain*; Stein, 'Beyond Disability Civil Rights', 1209; Stein, 'Disability Human Rights', 91.
44. This model is built upon the Aristotelian maxim, according to which like cases are treated alike and unlike cases unalike. In this context, equality becomes synonymous of sameness. When individuals are seen to be the same, but are not treated the same, their treatment is considered unreasonable and arbitrary and is prohibited by law as unequal under the 'likes alike' principle. However, if people are initially seen to be different, they can be treated differently without their treatment being considered as unequal – because they are unlike, they can be treated unalike. See, Aristotle, JL Ackrill and JO Urmson (eds), David Ross (trans), *Ethica Nicomachea* (vol. 3 Oxford University Press 1980) 112–17, 1131a–b; and Aristotle, Benjamin Jowett (trans), *The Politics* (The Modem Library 1943) 307 ('equality consists in the same treatment of similar persons'); Arnardóttir, 'A Future of Multidimensional Disadvantage Equality?' in Quinn and Amardottir (eds), *The UN Convention on the Rights of Persons with Disabilities: European and Scandinavian Perspectives* (International Studies in Human Rights 2009) 41; and Catherine A MacKinnon, *Sex Equality* (West 2001).
45. Arnardóttir, 'A Future of Multidimensional Disadvantage Equality?', 48.
46. ibid.
47. Quinn and Degener, 'The Moral Authority for Change: Human Rights Values and the Worldwide Process of Disability Reform' in *Human Rights and Disability* 16.

The Human Rights-Based Approach to Disability

Like the social constructionist model of disability, the human rights-based approach to disability highlights society's role in constructing the concept of disability through cultural and political discourses, on the one hand, and social and institutional environmental barriers on the other. Unlike the social version, the human rights perspective does not solely associate the concept of disability with a formal approach to equality.[48] It also recognises differences as an aspect of human diversity and argues for a substantive approach to equality that guarantees equality of opportunity, equity, social justice and respect for individual human rights.

The UN Convention on the Rights of Persons with Disabilities is the most prominent treaty embodying this humanistic philosophy. First, the Convention is an astounding example showing how to transcribe a positive and humanistic definition of disability. Although not defined expressly,[49] it is now well accepted that disability arises from the 'interaction with various barriers [that] may hinder [the] full and effective participation [of persons with disabilities] in society on an equal basis with others'.[50] This definition is the first at the international level to expressly reject ontological arguments on the essence and existence of disability. Moving away from the classification provided by the International Classification on Functionings, Health and Disability,[51] it transforms disability as a sign of 'human diversity and humanity'[52] and recognises persons with disabilities as human beings, with equal dignity, equal human worth and equal rights.[53]

Secondly, the Convention is particularly noteworthy for adopting the double approach to equality in its provisions. Not only does the Convention guarantee non-discriminatory measures by reaffirming that all persons are equal before and under the law and are entitled without discrimination to the equal protection

48. See Stein, 'Beyond Disability Civil Rights', 1209; Stein, 'Disability Human Rights', 91.
49. art 2 of the Convention does not provide any explicit reference to the term disability. For further details on this deliberate omission, see Gráinne de Búrca, 'The European Union in the Negotiation of the United Nations Disability Convention' (2010) 35(2) Euro L Rev 1.
50. art 1 CRPD.
51. The International Classification on Functioning adopts a 'biopsychosocial' model of disability by integrating both the medical and social models of disability. The problem with this approach is that it still operates a clear distinction between impairment, disability and handicap, whereby impairment refers to disease, disorders and disability to discrimination that persons with impairments face, and handicap to the inadequacy of the environmental structure. See, for further details, ICF, *Towards a Common Language for Functioning, Disability and Health* (World Health Organisation 2002, WHO/EIP/GPE/CAS/01.3).
52. art 3(d) CRPD.
53. arts 3, 5(1) and 12(1) CRPD.

and equal benefit of the law.[54] The Convention also recognises the right of persons with disabilities to benefit from equality of opportunity, acknowledging a more substantial approach to equality.[55] Article 24 of the CRPD is particularly patent for embodying these two approaches to equality. In guaranteeing the realisation of the right to education of persons with disabilities, s 1 of the Article specifies that this right must be implemented without discrimination and on the basis of equal opportunity.[56] This double guarantee, combined with the inclusive educational ethos of the Convention, constitutes the *sine qua non* condition for vindicating effectively and successfully disability rights in education.

The Inclusive Educational Ethos of the Human Rights-Based Approach to Disability Rights in Education

The inclusive approach to education underlines the need to respect and recognise all individuals as persons and subjects of rights. It acknowledges the individuality of every child as a unique learner with unique characteristics, interests, abilities and learning capacity.[57] In practice, this approach implies that schools, and in particular teachers, are required to go beyond the legal rule and act in accordance with their human duty.[58] This human duty refers to the duty of respecting every individual as a human being and, *a fortiori*, as a person, subject of rights.[59] A teacher who follows his or her human duty necessarily sees every child as a potential citizen and recognises children with learning difficulties and disabilities primarily as persons and subjects of rights, instead of expressions of human frailty or impairment.[60]

Under this inclusive approach to education, the goals of education are understood in a more progressive and pragmatic way. They are directed at the development of the child's talents, personality and creativity,[61] together with the 'respect for human rights, fundamental freedom and diversity'.[62] In essence, inclusive education fosters a child-centred and learner-friendly educational policy that understands learning as idiosyncratic.[63] It posits that every child, regardless of learning capacity, difficulty and/or disability, can learn meaningfully

54. art 5(1); see also arts 3(b), 4(1)(b) and (e) CRPD in relation to the right to equal treatment under the law.
55. arts 3(e) and 24(1).
56. art 24(1) CRPD.
57. See *Report of the Special Rapporteur on the Right to Education of Persons with Disabilities*, A/HRC/4/29 (10 February 2007) para 9.
58. Tetzchner and Jensen, 'Interacting with People Who Have Severe Communication Problems', 453.
59. ibid.
60. ibid.
61. art 24(1)(b) CRPD.
62. art 24(1)(a) CRPD.
63. *Report of the Special Rapporteur on the Right to Education of Persons with Disabilities*, para 9.

and successfully provided that this child benefits from equal educational opportunities to learn meaningfully and successfully and receives additional educational services appropriate to his or her individual educational needs in the best-suited learning environment.

The Convention on the Rights of Persons with Disabilities expressly embodies this humanistic and inclusive approach to education. As set down in art 24(1), with a view of being inclusive, education should aim *inter alia* at 'the full development of human potential and sense of dignity and self-worth, and the strengthening of respect for human rights, fundamental freedoms and human diversity'.[64] Article 24 further refers to the idiosyncratic nature of learning by ensuring that 'effective individualised' educational measures be provided for children with disabilities in 'environments which maximize academic and social development'.[65] It is noteworthy that, whilst the Convention refers to educational 'environments which maximize academic and social development',[66] it does not give any preference to the type of environment that would be better suited for educating children with disabilities. This omission is enlightening and unravels the ambiguity that is often brought on by the debate on inclusive education. The Salamanca principles affirm the right of every child to learn together, 'wherever possible, regardless of any difficulties or differences they may have'.[67] Some countries have interpreted this principle of inclusive education as referring to the place where the child should be taught,[68] whilst others have interpreted this principle of inclusion as referring to the right of the child to learn meaningfully and successfully in a best-suited, respectful learning environment.[69] The philosophy of the Convention leans towards the latter

64. art 24(1)(a) CRPD.
65. art 24(2)(e) CRPD.
66. ibid.
67. UNESCO, The Salamanca Statement and Framework for Action on Special Needs Education adopted by the World Conference on Special Needs Education: Access and Quality (7–10 June 1994) para 7.
68. As will be discussed in Part 3 of this article, Ireland is one of those countries, following the approach adopted in England. For further details on the English approach to inclusion, see M Ainscow, T Booth and J Dyson, 'Inclusion and the Standards Agenda: Negotiating Policy Pressures in England' (2006) 10(4–5) Int'l J of Inclusive Edu 295; J Baker, 'The British Government's Strategy for Special Educational Needs: Implications for the Role and Future Development of Special Schools' (2007) 22(2) Support for Learning 72; Ofsted, *Special Educational Needs and Disability: Towards Inclusive Schools* (Ofsted 2002); Thomas, 'A Review of Thinking and Research about Inclusive Education Policy with Suggestions for a New Kind of Inclusive Thinking' (2012) Brit Edu Research J 1.
69. Finland represents a manifest example in that regard. What matters in Finland is not where the child is being educated; rather what is at stake is how the child is being educated and therefore how a quality education may be provided for him or her. For further details on the Finnish approach to inclusive education, see Joel Kivirauma and Kari Ruoho, 'Excellence through Special Education? Lessons from

interpretation. Article 24(2)(d) and (e) focuses more on the support required for delivering a quality education than on the institutions that deliver it.[70] This is particularly patent when one reviews the vocabulary used in this Article. Instead of referring to 'mainstream education' and 'special education', art 24 refers to one type of education: general education.[71]

Very often, the place and the process of learning meaningfully coincide. Very often, a child will learn meaningfully and successfully alongside his or her peers. Nonetheless, in some cases, a child will learn more meaningfully and successfully in a separate setting, being a separate class or a separate school.[72] Article 24(3)(c) leaves the door open to this possibility.[73]

In essence, the Article conveys the idea that disability, inclusive education, difference and plurality all become synonymous with equity, social justice and respect for human rights. Inclusion becomes an outcome of a progressive, humanistic and ethical approach to disability rights in education. It suggests that establishing an inclusive educational policy requires more than just establishing non-discriminatory measures and ensuring equal participation in the learning environment . It requires a structure that ensures equality in learning.

As mentioned in the introduction of this paper, Ireland has signed the Convention on the Rights of Persons with Disabilities in 2007. Whilst it moves towards its ratification, one may query whether or not its legislative framework on disability rights in education is in compliance with the humanistic philosophy of the Convention and more precisely with the principles set down in art 24 of the CRPD.

The Irish Legislative Framework on Disability Rights in Education

The Irish legislative framework on disability rights in education is relatively recent. Its establishment is directly the product of two phenomena that became particularly patent in the 1990s: the surge of parental litigation against the State in relation to educational provisions for children with learning difficulties

---

the Finnish School Reform' (2007) 53 Rev of Edu 283; Charles Sabel, Anna Saxenian, Reijo Miettinen, Peer Hull Kristensen and Jarkko Hautamäki, *Individualised Service Provision in the New Welfare State: Lessons from Special Education in Finland* (Report prepared by SITRA, October 2010); Pasi Sahlberg, *Finnish Lessons: What Can the World Learn from Educational Change in Finland?* (Teachers College, Columbia University 2011).

70. art 24(2) reads as follows: '(d) Persons with disabilities receive the support required, within the general education system, to facilitate their effective education; (e) Effective individualized support measures are provided in environments that maximize academic and social development, consistent with the goal of full inclusion.'
71. See art 24(2)(d).
72. This observation is further suggested by the redaction of art 24(3)(c) CRPD, which refers to 'environments which maximise academic and social development'.
73. ibid.

and disabilities,[74] and the growing demand of the international community to establish equitable educational systems that would guarantee quality education for all and provide educational services appropriate to every child's individual educational needs in the best-suited learning environment.[75]

The first legislation that provides some statutory guarantees for children with learning difficulties and disabilities is the Education Act 1998.[76] The Act requires the Minister for Education to ensure that a level of quality education appropriate to meet the needs and abilities of each person residing in the State be available.[77] Endorsing the position of the Judiciary with regard to the right to education of children with learning difficulties and disabilities,[78] the Act reaffirms the State's duty to provide for[79] educational services to every child, regardless of disability, difficulty and/or learning capacity.[80]

---

74. See, for instance, *O'Donoghue v Minister for Health* [1996] 2 IR 20 (HC); *Comerford v Minister for Education* [1997] 2 ILRM 134 in which McGuinness J expressly acknowledged the principles set down by O'Hanlon J in the *O'Donoghue* case (see n 89) and went on to state that 'the right to free primary education extends to every child, although the education provided must vary in accordance with the child's abilities and needs' [1997] 2 ILRM 134 (HC) 143; *Sinnott v Minister for Education* [2001] 2 IR 545 (SC); *O'Carolan v Minister for Education* [2005] IEHC 296; *O'C v Minister for Education* [2007] IEHC 170; *McD v Minister for Education* [2008] IEHC 265; *McD v Minister for Education* [2013] IEHC 175.
75. See, *inter alia*, UNICEF, *A Human Rights-Based Approach to Education for All* (2007); UNESCO, *The Dakar Framework for Action – Education for All: Meeting our Collective Commitments*, adopted by the World Education Forum, Dakar, Senegal, 26–28 April 2000.
76. (1998) No 51.
77. s 7(1)(a).
78. In *O'Donoghue v Minister for Health* [1996] 2 IR 20 (HC), O'Hanlon J affirmed, for the first time, the existence of a constitutional right to free primary education for every child, including children with the most severe and profound learning difficulties. For a history on the education of children with learning difficulties prior to this decision, see Dympna Glendenning, 'Educational Provision for Children with Disability' in *Education and the Law* (Butterworths 1999) 142; Conor O'Mahony, *Educational Rights in Irish Law* (Thomson Round Hall 2006) 146; Gerard Whyte, *Social Inclusion and the Legal System: Public Interest Law in Ireland* (Institute of Public Administration 2002).
79. In *Crowley v Ireland* [1980] IR 102 (SC), the Supreme Court held that the first clause of art 42.4 of the Constitution, according to which the 'State shall provide for free primary education', imposes a duty on the State to provide for free primary education, and that this duty shall be normally interpreted as an indirect duty.
80. See, *inter alia*, s 6 of the Act, which states that 'Every person concerned in the implementation of this Act shall have regard to the following objects in pursuance of which the Oireachtas has enacted this Act: (a) to give practical effect to the constitutional rights of children, including children who have a disability or who have other special educational needs, as they relate to education; (b) to provide that, as far as is practicable and having regard to the resources available, there is made available to people resident in the State a level and quality of education appropriate to meeting the needs and abilities of those people.'

Although the Education Act 1998 provides the genesis of a structure that could guarantee quality education for all, the most prominent legislation with regard to the education of children[81] with learning difficulties and disabilities is the Education for Persons with Special Educational Needs Act 2004.[82] This Act represents an important step in establishing a legislative framework that could guarantee an effective and inclusive education accessible, available and adaptable to every child residing in Ireland.

Amongst its most important provisions, the Act sets out the principle according to which education of children with 'special educational needs'[83] shall take place, as far as possible, in an inclusive environment.[84] Whilst Ireland has been relatively slow, compared to other European countries,[85] in moving from an integrative approach[86] to an inclusive approach to education,[87] s 2 of the EPSEN Act manifests this philosophical shift in the nature of the debate.

81. This article is mostly concerned with the education of children with learning difficulties and disabilities, as opposed to the education of adults with disabilities. For this reason, the article does not provide an in-depth analysis of the Disability Act 2005, which deals with the education of persons with disabilities over the age of 18.
82. (2004) No 30.
83. Whilst the author of the article is reluctant to use this expression as will be further discussed below, this expression will be referred to when quoting the EPSEN Act.
84. s 2 of the 2004 Act.
85. For instance, England and Finland adopted the inclusive agenda in the 1990s. For England, see The Education Act 1996 and the Special Educational Needs Code of Practice 2001; for Finland, see The Basic Education Act 1998, which represents the unique legal authority in the Finnish education system.
86. According to the Special Education Review Committee Report, integration implies 'the participation of pupils with disabilities in school activities with other pupils, to the maximum extent which is consistent with the broader overall interests of both the pupils with disabilities and the other pupils in the class/group' (Government of Ireland 1993) 18. Put another way, integration refers to an educational system whereby individual additional supports to children with learning difficulties and disabilities are provided in order to enable these children to 'fit in' to mainstream society. In this sense, integration may be best understood as an assimilating model. It requires students to adapt or to assimilate to the existing educational structures. For further discussion, see Peter Farrell and Michael Ainscow, *Making Special Education Inclusive: From Research to Practice* (David Fulton Publishers 2002); Phádraig MacGiolla, 'Towards Inclusion: The Development of Provision for Children with Special Educational Needs in Ireland from 1991 to 2004' (2007) 26(3) Ir Edu Stud 289.
87. According to UNESCO, 'inclusion is seen as a process of addressing and responding to the diversity of needs of all learners through increasing participation in learning, cultures and communities, and reducing exclusion within and from education'. It is often referred to as embodying the four following features: 'Inclusion is a process: it has to be seen as a never-ending search to find better ways of responding to diversity. It is about learning how to live with difference and learning how to learn from difference. In this way differences come to be seen more positively as a stimulus for fostering learning, amongst children and adults; Inclusion is concerned with

The Act further lays down a certain number of key provisions that ensure that children with learning difficulties have the same educational rights as their peers.[88] For instance, s 10 of the Act provides that the National Council for Special Education (NCSE)[89] shall designate a particular school to which a child should be admitted, taking into account the needs of the child, the wishes of the parents and the capacity of the school to accommodate the child's needs.[90] Interestingly, this collaboration between school, parents and children constitutes a crucial aspect of an inclusive culture.

Perhaps the most prominent provision of the Act is the establishment of a detailed framework necessary for the development and implementation of an Individual Education Plan (IEP).[91] The Individual Education Plan is commonly understood as a tool that guarantees quality education appropriate to the individual needs of the child in an inclusive environment.[92] As described by the National Council for Special Education, it aims at 'identifying where the student is, where he/she is going, how he/she will get there, and how to tell if the journey

---

the identification and removal of barriers. Consequently, it involves collecting, collating and evaluating information from a wide variety of sources in order to plan for improvements in policy and practice. It is about using evidence of various kinds to stimulate creativity and problem solving; Inclusion is about the presence, participation and achievement of all students. Here "presence" is concerned with where children are educated, and how reliably and punctually they attend; "participation" relates to the quality of their experiences whilst they are there and, therefore, must incorporate the views of the learners themselves; and "achievement" is about the outcomes of learning across the curriculum, not merely test or examination results; and Inclusion involves a particular emphasis on those groups of learners who may be at risk of marginalization, exclusion or underachievement. This indicates the moral responsibility to ensure that those groups that are statistically most "at risk" are carefully monitored, and that, where necessary, steps are taken to ensure their presence, participation and achievement in the education system.' UNESCO, *Policy Guidelines on Inclusion in Education* (2009) 13, 15–16.

88. It is noteworthy that the Act is solely concerned with the issue relating to quality education in an inclusive environment. The Act does not cover the obligation of the State to provide reasonable accommodation, this obligation being considered in the Equal Status Act 2000 No 8. As the present paper focuses on educational rights of children with disabilities within education, and more precisely their right to quality education in an inclusive environment, issues relating to reasonable accommodation are not considered in full length. For further discussion on these issues, see *Cahill v Minister for Education and Science* [2010] IEHC 227 (HC).
89. New body established under the EPSEN Act and regulated under s 19.
90. Roisin Webb, *Country Report on the Equality of Educational and Training Opportunities for Young Disabled People* (2010) ANED, VT/2007/005, 4.
91. See section 9 onwards.
92. Sean Griffin and Michael Shevlin, *Responding to Special Educational Needs: An Irish Perspective* (Macmillan 2007).

is successful'.[93] It is child-centred, inclusive, holistic, collaborative and accessible to everyone who works directly with the individual child.[94] In essence, this individual programme helps children to realise their educational rights.[95] It helps them to realise their right to learn effectively and successfully in the best-suited learning environment, on an equal basis with others. In this sense, one has to bear in mind that IEPs, inclusion and quality education embody the same philosophy, that of equity in education, equality of opportunity and respect for individual human rights.

It is undeniable that all of these provisions represent a positive and significant change towards the implementation of a more progressive and inclusive approach to disability rights in education in Ireland. In the past, the common belief was that children with learning difficulties and disabilities could not cope with the learning tasks involved in the traditional curriculum and hence had to be provided with special restricted curriculum in secluded institutions.[96] The principles set down by the Education for Persons with Special Educational Needs Act expressly discredits this belief. The onus is now on national schools to revise their practice and structure in order to facilitate the delivery of quality education for every child, including children with learning difficulties and disabilities.

Nevertheless, beside these positive elements, the legislative framework remains insufficient in many respects. As pointed out by the Committee on the Rights of the Child, the Irish legal framework inadequately addresses the specific needs of children with disabilities and their access to educational facilities.[97] It is to the current inadequacies of the Irish legal framework that this article turns now its attention.

The Inappropriateness of the Irish Legislative Framework

This paper identifies two main inadequacies that significantly hamper the development of a human rights-based approach to disability rights in education in Ireland. First, it argues that the current legislation relies on inadequate definitions, which convey inappropriate beliefs and assumptions about disability and education. Secondly, it posits that the legislation misunderstands the concept of inclusion and seems to assimilate it with the concept of integration. The combinations of these two inadequacies contributes to the development of segregative practices observed at the local level and certainly justifies the persistence of negative attitudes and beliefs about disability, difference and inclusion.

93. NCSE, *Guidelines on the Individual Education Plan Process* (2006) 1.
94. ibid 5; see also Griffin and Shevlin, *Responding to Special Educational Needs*, 133.
95. UNESCO, *Policy Guidelines on Inclusion in Education*, 16.
96. See, for instance, the State's arguments in the *O'Donoghue* case, (1996) 2 IR 20 (HC) 25.
97. Committee on the Rights of the Child, 43rd Session, Consideration of Reports Submitted by States Parties under Article 44 of the Convention, Concluding Observations: Ireland (UN, CRC/C/IRL/CO/2, 29 September 2006) para 41.

A Legislative Framework Based on Inappropriate Definitions

As it stands, the Irish legislative framework relies on inadequate definitions. It fails to define the concept of education and its aims (a) and provides a very narrow approach to disability (b). Consequently, it creates an unequal system, under which disability becomes the prerequisite determinant for the allocation of additional resources for children with certain types of learning difficulties and disabilities (c).

The Failure to Define Education

The current legislative framework fails to provide any definition of what education is, what its aims are and, *a fortiori*, what special education is. The Education Act 1998 and the EPSEN Act 2004, which together regulate the entire Irish education system, both fail to explain what they mean by education. Both acts define in ss 2 and 1 respectively terms such as 'schools', 'student', 'child', 'principle', 'parents', but fail to consider 'education' or 'the aims of education'.[98]

This legislative lacuna has proved to be quite 'disabling' for the judiciary, which is left with the laborious duty of providing some elements of interpretation in relation to the aims of education and its content. A first interpretation was provided in *Ryan v Attorney General*, in which O'Dálaigh J referred to education as 'essentially the teaching and training of a child to make the best possible use of his inherent and potential capacities, physical, mental and moral'.[99]

Although this definition remained incomplete in light of international law, one could nevertheless applaud the attempt to provide some poststructuralist insights into the objectives of education. This interpretation would suggest that, by and large, education would have a double objective – an instructional objective, characterised by the 'teaching' or transfer of skills and knowledge; and a more humanistic objective, which would refer to the maximisation of the present and future learning capacity of the child through the 'training' of this child.

Interestingly, O'Hanlon J reiterated this poststructuralist definition in *O'Donoghue v Minister for Education*, although with a slight alteration.[100] Nonetheless, despite these two positive interpretations of the concept of education and its aims,[101] this issue did not reach a unanimous consensus in the Supreme Court in *Sinnott v Minister for Education*.[102] Instead of clarifying this question of definition, the divergent views held by the Supreme Court brought more confusion and ambiguity into the debate relating to the meaning of education. Murphy J and Hardiman J firmly believed that education, and more

98. See s 2 Education Act 1998 and s 1 EPSEN Act.
99. [1965] IR 294, 300.
100. [1996] 2 IR 20, 59.
101. Barr J adopted the same definition of education as O'Hanlon [2001] 2 IR 540, 571.
102. [2001] 2 IR 540.

precisely primary education, should be confined to its traditional and therefore scholastic nature.[103] To quote Murphy J,

> primary education is provided by teachers in classrooms. It was and is a basic scholastic education in the sense that it is a first stepping stone on a career which may lead to secondary level and ideally graduate to the third level.[104]

Disagreeing with this classical view, Murray J and Geoghegan J shared the view that, although the term education traditionally and historically referred to the classical education of scholastic nature provided in schools, this term should not be limited to this interpretation and should rather reflect the contemporary development, especially in relation to children with learning difficulties and disabilities.[105] Rejecting both views, Keane CJ was the only Judge adopting the definition provided by O'Hanlon J and reiterated by Barr J in the High Court,[106] Denham J and Fennelly J omitting to pronounce on the matter.

Accordingly, as it stands, the matter relating to the definition of education and its aims remains solely unclear. Some have argued that the approach taken by O'Hanlon J in *O'Donoghue* and subsequently reiterated by Barr J and Keane CJ in *Sinnott* should constitute the law on the issue.[107] Even though this view was correct, the definition of education provided would still remain wholly unsatisfactory because it is incomplete in the light of recent international developments.[108] One has to bear in mind that the concept of education is a multifaceted concept that has received many different types of interpretation. From the narrow-minded classical approach that emphasises scholastic matters[109] to the more utilitarian approach, which relies on the concept of efficiency and posits that education should be provided to individuals who will benefit the most from it and produce optimal average benefits to society,[110] the concept of education is not a unitary concept and, depending on the approach

103. ibid 670 for Murphy J and 693 for Hardiman J.
104. ibid 675.
105. ibid 682, 724.
106. ibid 628.
107. See Conor O'Mahony, 'The Right to Education and "Constitutionally Appropriate Provision"' (2006) 13(1) DULJ 422.
108. See, for instance, the General Comment issued by the UN Committee on the Rights of the Child on *Article 29(1): The Aims of Education, which Provides the Most Progressive Understanding of Education and its Aims* (CRC General Comment 1, 08/02/2001).
109. See John Locke, *Some Thoughts Concerning Education* (1693); Immanuel Kant, *Education* (University of Michigan Press 1960); and, more generally, Amy M Schmitter, Nathan Tarcov and Wendy Donner, 'Enlightenment Liberalism' in *A Companion to the Philosophy of Education* (Blackwell 2003) 73.
110. Benjamin Bentham, *Chrestomathia* (Clarendon Press 1983); Elissa S Itzkin, 'Bentham's Chrestomathia: Utilitarian Legacy to English Education' (1978) 39(2) J of the History of Ideas 303; FA Cavanagh, 'Jeremy Bentham on Education' (1933) 1 Int'l

adopted, its objectives and the attitude that it fosters towards children with learning difficulties and disabilities will differ significantly.

It is therefore disappointing that the Irish legislation does not provide any guideline in that regard, even more so considering that Ireland is a signatory of the UN Declaration of Human Rights[111] and the UN Convention on the Rights of Persons with Disabilities,[112] has ratified the International Covenant on Economic, Social and Cultural Rights[113] and, more importantly, the Convention on the Rights of the Child.[114] All these international documents provide a clear definition of education and its aims in a progressive and humanistic way.[115]

Interestingly, the Irish *Green Paper on Education* reaffirmed this human rights ethos and identified ten educational aims that should guide the Irish framework.[116] It suggested that education should aim *inter alia* at

> (i) fostering an understanding and critical appreciation of the values of the home and society generally; (ii) promoting self-esteem and self-worth, combined with a respect for the rights and beliefs of others; (iii) fostering intellectual development and the attainment of one's full educational potential; (iv) developing a spirit of inquiry; (v) developing expressive and creative abilities to the individual child's full capacity; (vi) providing students with the necessary skills to equip them for work and to unable them to function effectively in society; and (vii) creating tolerant, caring and politically aware members of society.[117]
>
> … an underlying educational aim is to assist or enable each individual to promote his or her development and personality and to achieve a sense of self-worth.[118]

This concluding statement could not be more progressive and humanistic in nature. Not only does it highlight the constructive dimension of education as a means to foster individual growth, but it also emphasises the humanistic

Edu Rev 412; and Patrick Bradley, 'Victorian Lessons: Education and Utilitarianism in Bentham, Mill and Dickens' (1999) The Concord Review 69.

111. Ireland signed the Declaration in 1948.
112. Ireland signed the Convention in 2007, but has not yet ratified it.
113. Ireland ratified the Covenant in December 1989.
114. Ireland ratified the Convention in September 1992.
115. For instance, art 29 of the Convention on the Rights of the Child (General Assembly resolution 44/25 of 20 November 1989) states that education should aim, *inter alia*, at: '(a) The development of the child's personality, talents and mental and physical abilities to their fullest potential; (b) The development of respect for human rights and fundamental freedoms, and for the principles enshrined in the Charter of the United Nations'.
116. Department of Education, Green Paper on Education: Education for a Changing World (1992).
117. Education should also aim at '(viii) fostering a spirit of self-reliance, of innovation and of enterprise; (ix) achieving standards of educational performance comparable to the highest internationally; and (x) ensuring that people are appropriately educated and trained to support the country's economic development' (33).
118. ibid 35.

dimension of education as an end in itself. One may wonder why the subsequent legislation has not reaffirmed this definition of education, considering that a clear and unambiguous approach was already provided and complied with international standard.

The result of not providing any definition of education is that the Irish government has a constitutional duty to provide for educational services for children with learning difficulties and disabilities without clear guidance on what education is, what its goals are and therefore what special education is. In this context, it is fair to query how a government can provide quality education, especially for children with learning difficulties and disabilities, without knowing the true meaning of education and its objectives and without understanding why special education is identified as being special.

The second concept that raises concern relates to the definition and interpretation of the concept of disability.

The Narrow Approach to Disability

As discussed in the first part of this paper, the language someone uses to name a phenomenon reflects his or her understanding of, and attitude toward, this phenomenon. It is commonly accepted that the process of defining disability is a difficult task. This is mainly so because of the complex and multifaceted nature of this concept.

This article advocates a human rights-based approach to disability. It suggests that disability should be recognised as an aspect of human diversity rather than an individual problem, located exclusively within the individual *per se*. Unfortunately, this approach is not the one that has been retained by the Irish legislation. The predominant imagery of disability as perceived in Ireland is the negative and stereotyped one of disability as a problem, a disease and a tragedy.

The Irish legislative framework embodies the medical model of disability, focusing solely upon the medical conditions and inabilities of the individual. It underlines the biomedical aspect of disability, which is often associated with impairment. For instance, the Education Act 1998 defines disability as follows:

> (a) The total or partial loss of a person's bodily or mental functions, including the loss of a part of the person's body, or
> (b) The presence in the body of organisms causing, or likely to cause, chronic disease or illness, or
> (c) The malfunction, malformation or disfigurement of a part of a person's body, or
> (d) A condition or malfunction which results in a person learning differently from a person without the condition or malfunction, or
> (e) A condition, illness or disease which affects a person's thought processes, perception of reality, emotions or judgement or which results in disturbed behaviour.[119]

119. s 2 Education Act 1998.

Interestingly, this definition is very similar, not to say identical, to the one provided in the Employment Equality Act 1998 and in the Equal Status Act 2000, which regulate the non-discriminatory framework in Ireland.[120] All three acts enumerate a list of potential medical factors or incapacities that may constitute impairment and, *a fortiori*, disability. Applied within the educational framework, learning difficulties become solely seen as the manifestation of the child's disability or impairment. Special educational needs are disability-related and do not relate to external factors, such as the environmental structure, the inadequacy of the teaching staff or the lack of adequate additional educational supports.[121]

The definition of disability adopted in the Disability Act 2005 differs slightly from the one provided in the three previous Acts. Instead of establishing a list of medical factors, s 2(1) of the Act 2005 defines disability as:

> a substantial restriction in the capacity of the person to carry on a profession, business or occupation in the State or to participate in social or cultural life in the State by reason of an enduring physical, sensory, mental health or intellectual impairment.[122]

If one may welcome the absence of any list of potential medical factors, one may still identify the presence of the medical philosophy in this definition. Section 2(1) of the Disability Act still highlights the personal condition or impairment of the individual as being the unique factor in the process of disablement. Like the previous definitions, it completely fails to recognise the predominant role society plays in further constructing the concept of disability and in further disabling this category of persons through social and environmental barriers and political and cultural discourses.

Interestingly, the Education for Persons with Special Educational Needs Act 2004 does not provide a definition of the concept of disability. Instead, the Act provides a definition of the expression 'special educational needs'. This definition is surprisingly similar to the definition of disability, as discussed above. Section 1 of the Act reads as follows:

> Special educational needs means, in relation to a person, a restriction in the capacity of the person to participate in and benefit from education on account of an enduring physical, sensory, mental health or learning disability, or any other condition which results in a person learning differently from a person without that condition and cognate words shall be construed accordingly.[123]

By reading this definition, one may be struck by the same references to 'restriction in the capacity of the person' or by reasons 'enduring physical, sensory, mental health or learning disability (or intellectual impairment)'. These

---

120. See respectively s 2 Employment Equality Act 1998 and s 2(1) Equal Status Act 2000.
121. s 1, EPSEN Act.
122. Disability Act 2005, s 2(1).
123. EPSEN Act 2004, s 1.

references are undeniably references to the individual medical conditions that restrict the child from learning effectively and 'normally' in a mainstream environment. They ignore the environmental influences on learning and overlook the complexity of 'special educational needs'.

The problem with using the expression 'special education' is twofold. First, the expression itself embodies the seeds of the medical model of disability. The adjective 'special' implies that those identified with special needs are different from those who do not have any and therefore should be separated from them. Put another way, this adjective is a clear and direct reference to the hierarchical ontological dichotomy of the medical model between what is normal and what is pathological – that is, special. It embodies a within-child model and conveys the idea that there exists a hierarchy between children's capacities to learn – those having special educational needs being necessarily at the bottom of such hierarchy. In this context, it introduces a new overarching, vague and impractical category, that of special needs.

The second problem that emerges from this expression is its definition itself. The Irish legislative framework confuses the three concepts of special educational needs, disability and impairment. This similitude between special educational needs and disability suggests that a child's special educational need is determined by his or her disability. It suggests that it is because he or she has a disability that he or she has special educational needs. Unfortunately, this correlation at best oversimplifies the complexity of the problem, at worst denies it. It omits the fact that some children may have some learning difficulties without having disabilities[124] and vice versa.[125]

As it stands, these definitions of disability and special educational needs under the Irish legislative framework are untenable. They are incongruous, slippery and should be replaced. They support the pessimistic view according to which having a disability is an inevitable and inherent characteristic of impairment possession and does not relate to any cultural or social phenomena, which are variable and contingent characteristics of this process of disablement. They associate disability with fixed essential characteristics, seen via the perspective of persons without disabilities, who generally interpret disability as being the exclusive cause of a life of personal loss or tragedy. In this context, they convey the message that persons with learning difficulties and disabilities have to adapt to society and its existing structures. The net effect is to segregate these persons more than include them within the community.[126]

124. For instance, dyslexia and dyscalculia are learning difficulties that do not result from an initial disability.

125. A physical disability, such as chronic fatigue syndrome, does not alter the learning capacity of the person, for instance.

126. Quinn and Degener, *Human Rights and Disability*, 1.

This legislative structure represents a clear step back from the more holistic view on disability as advocated in international human rights law.[127] Interestingly, the *Report of the Special Education Review Committee* provided a more comprehensive definition of the expression special educational needs.[128] Like the EPSEN Act, the report did not refer to the concept of disability. Unlike the EPSEN Act, the report did acknowledge the difficulty of defining the expression 'special educational needs', namely because of the wide scope this expression embodies.[129] Accordingly, the report opted for a broader approach to special educational needs, defining it as:

> disabilities *and/or circumstances* [that] prevent or hinder [children] from benefiting adequately from the education which is normally provided for pupils of the same age, or for whom the education which can generally be provided in the ordinary classroom is not sufficiently challenging.[130]

One will note that, by referring to the expression 'and/or circumstances', the report acknowledged the important role external factors, such as environmental, social, cultural and societal barriers, further play in disabling persons with learning difficulties and disabilities. It did identify special educational needs as being the result of the interaction between medical inabilities and inadequate educational structures. It is therefore regrettable that this definition has not been reaffirmed in the recent legislation as it would have clearly constituted a significant step in establishing a more progressive and humanistic approach to the issue.

Besides these definitional inadequacies stands another theoretical inappropriateness that is merely the direct consequence of adopting a medical approach to disability: the creation of a categorical system of assessment.

The Inadequacy of the Categorical System of Assessment

The practical consequence of adopting the medical model within the Irish legislation is twofold. First, it triggers the establishment of a system of assessment of special educational needs that is solely based on a categorical medical approach.[131] Special educational needs are currently categorised according to

127. Namely in the light of the CRPD.
128. Government of Ireland (1993).
129. As pointed out by Griffin and Shevlin, this concept covers a broad range of educational difficulties, ranging from those children who have mild and moderate learning difficulties and who require limited educational intervention, to those children, who, because of their severe or profound learning difficulties, require multi-disciplinary approaches (*Responding to Special Educational Needs*, 51).
130. Government of Ireland (1993) 18.
131. See s 4 of the EPSEN Act, which defines an assessment and establishes its proceedings.

the severity of their nature[132] and their identification is most of the time conducted by professionals belonging to the medical sector.[133] Despite the fact that the EPSEN Act mentions the participation of other professionals in assessing the special needs of a child,[134] in reality psychologists are the most frequently mentioned professionals when assessing the special needs of certain children with intellectual disabilities.[135]

The second problem with the Irish medical model of disability is that it has somehow established a link between the diagnosis of a disability and the allocation of additional resources.[136] In two circulars, the Department of Education and Science has established a categorical system, whereby children with special educational needs are divided into two groups, those with high-incidence special educational needs and those with low-incidence special educational needs.[137] On the one hand, children with high-incidence special educational needs are supported through a general allocation model (GAM)[138] – which provides schools with additional teaching resources on the basis of several factors.[139] Under this model, children do not need to apply individually. On the other hand, children with low-incidence special educational needs have to apply individually and be diagnosed with a certain type of disability in order to qualify for additional educational resources.[140]

The net effect of this categorical weighted system is that children with low-incidence special educational needs have to earn their right to receive an education by demonstrating that they belong to a certain category of special educational needs.[141] Special educational supports become a service that

---

132. See circulars 09/04 (2004) and 02/05 (2005) of the Department for Education, which have established two categories of special educational needs depending on the level of their incidence on school's activities.
133. According to s 5 of the EPSEN Act, persons involved in the assessment of a child's special educational needs belong essentially to the medical sector. There are psychologists, medical practitioners and/or therapists who are suitably qualified to provide support services in respect of the special educational needs of the child. Parents may also participate, but only if appropriate.
134. Mainly, the principal of the school concerned and an appropriate qualified social worker (see s 5(1)(c) and (d) EPSEN Act).
135. Martin Desforges and Geoff Lindsay, *Procedures Used to Diagnose a Disability and to Assess Special Educational Needs: An International Review* (NCSE Report 2010) 127.
136. See Paul Cooper and Barbara Jacobs, *Evidence of Best Practice Models and Outcomes in the Education of Children with Emotional Disturbance: An International Review* (NCSE report 2011) 11.
137. Department for Education and Science, circulars 09/04 (2004) and 02/05 (2005).
138. ibid; see also Desforges and Lindsay, *Procedures Used to Diagnose a Disability*, 120.
139. Those factors refer to school enrolment numbers, gender breakdown and disadvantaged status (circulars 09/04 (2004) and 02/05 (2005).
140. See Desforges and Lindsay, *Procedures Used to Diagnose a Disability*, 120.
141. Circulars 09/04 (2004) and 02/05 (2005).

needs to be earned by those who fit under the correct category more than a tool to guarantee quality education for all.

It is patent that this causal relationship is inappropriate, wrong and certainly at odds with the principles set down in art 24 of the CRPD. It identifies assessment as an end in itself, rather than a tool to an end – that of an inclusive and equitable education.[142] It reduces special education to an exceptional service that may be awarded in a special setting because of exceptional circumstances. As recently pointed out in the new report of the National Council for Special Education, the current allocation model does not provide all children with equitable access to educational supports.[143] It has become a high-stakes test to obtain additional resources for schools rather than to inform teaching and learning.[144]

In essence, the Irish approach reveals two things. First, it reveals its adoption of a 'special education paradigm' rather than an 'inclusive education paradigm'.[145] Instead of establishing a unitary legal and educational framework, the Irish system relies on two separate educational frameworks: one special for children with disabilities and one mainstream for children without disabilities. The most patent example illustrating this dichotomy resides in the legislation itself. Two acts govern the education system: the Education Act 1998 for mainstream education, and the EPSEN Act 2004 for the education of children with 'special' needs. By relying on a separate and distinctive Act that deals exclusively with the education of children with learning difficulties and disabilities, the government fosters the idea that general education and special education are still two different types of education, each one of them requiring a different legal structure with different principles and different educational settings.

Secondly, the Irish approach reveals that providing educational services for children with learning difficulties and disabilities is more a societal issue than a legal issue. Through the definition of legal concepts, the law embodies the values and beliefs upon which a society relies. As discussed in the first part, disability and education are two human rights. They are interconnected and complement each other. Accordingly, when a government adopts a medical approach to disability, it is necessarily bound to adopt the traditional, scholastic and segregational approach to education.

Within that framework, the Education for Persons with Special Educational Needs Act has introduced a new concept, that of inclusive education. Due to the previous inadequacies, it seems nevertheless that the concept of inclusion is being currently misinterpreted as the right to a mainstream placement rather than as the right to learn effectively and successfully in a respectful environment.

142. Desforges and Lindsay, *Procedures Used to Diagnose a Disability*, 120.
143. NCSE, *Supporting Students with Special Educational Needs in Schools* (Paper No 4, May 2013) 5.
144. ibid 50.
145. See *Report of the Special Rapporteur on the Right to Education of Persons with Disabilities*, para 11.

An Attempt to Move Towards an Inclusive Approach to Education?

Over a relatively short period of time, inclusive education has become the priority policy objective of liberal democracies.[146] Several international documents[147] and reports[148] manifest this strong ethos towards guaranteeing quality education for all[149] in an inclusive environment, regardless of difficulties, disabilities and learning capacities.[150]

This international trend has not been ignored by the Irish government. From the 1980s onwards, government-initiative reports introduced the concept of integration and discussed its merits. For instance, the *Special Education Review Committee Report* called for 'as much integration as is appropriate and feasible, and as little segregation as necessary',[151] whilst the *Green Paper on Education* advocated the 'valuable role of special schools' and advocated the development of an integrative system.[152] The novelty of the Education for Persons with Special Educational Needs Act is that it moves away from the integrative system

---

146. Eileen Winter and Paul O'Raw, *Literature Review of the Principles and Practices Relating to Inclusive Education for Children with Special Educational Needs* (NCSE report, ICEP Europe 2010) 3.
147. See art 23 of the Convention on the Rights of the Child (1989), which called for the child to be receive an education that would achieve the 'fullest possible social integration and individual development'; and art 24 of the Convention on the Rights of Persons with Disabilities (2006), which states that 'States Parties recognize the right of persons with disabilities to education. With a view to realizing this right without discrimination and on the basis of equal opportunity, States Parties shall ensure an inclusive education system at all levels and life long learning directed to: (a) the full development of human potential and sense of dignity and self-worth, and the strengthening of respect for human rights, fundamental freedoms and human diversity; (b) the development by persons with disabilities of their personality, talents and creativity, as well as their mental and physical abilities, to their fullest potential; (c) enabling persons with disabilities to participate effectively in a free society.'
148. See, namely, UNESCO, *Guidelines for Inclusion* (2005); *Policy Guidelines on Inclusion in Education* (2009); and UNESCO, *The Salamanca World Conference on Special Needs Education: Access and Quality* (1994), which is the most significant international document in special education, arguing that schools with an inclusive orientation are 'the most effective means of combating discriminatory attitudes building an inclusive society and achieving education for all'.
149. See UNESCO, *The World Declaration on Education for All and Framework for Action to Meet Basic Learning Needs: International Consultative Forum on Education for All* (1990) and UNESCO, *The Education for All Global Monitoring: The Quality Imperative* (2005).
150. Winter and O'Raw, *Literature Review*, 6.
151. Government of Ireland (1993) 22.
152. See Irish National Teachers' Organisation, *Green Paper on Education 1992* (Forum 1992) 40.

of the 1980s and suggests a more inclusive education system, as discussed in the second part of this paper.[153]

The problem that emerges from the EPSEN Act framework is that it is contradictory at its core. On the one hand, the Act emphasises the humanistic and inclusive nature of education through its reference to the individual educational plan.[154] On the other hand, the Act seems to confuse the philosophy of inclusion with that of integration. When one reviews s 2 of the EPSEN Act, one may be surprised by the sole emphasis on the place or 'environment'[155] where the child shall receive his or her education. The Section does not refer to the quality of education the child is entitled to receive in a respectful environment. Put another way, s 2 frames the question of inclusion in the following terms: Should a child be educated in a mainstream school or should he or she receive education in a special class or special school? This question summarises perfectly how inclusion is understood in Ireland. It is understood as the right to a placement in a mainstream school, unless this placement is inconsistent with (a) the best interests of the child, or (b) the effective provision of education for children with whom the child is to be educated.[156]

The right to be placed in a mainstream school is the aim of an integrative system. Integration aims at fitting children with learning difficulties and disabilities within mainstream activities.[157] It does not aim at guaranteeing the same educational opportunities on the same basis as to others. It embodies a formal approach to equality, but ignores its substantive component. It ignores the substantive right to learn effectively and successfully in the best-suited learning environment and the right to have one's dignity respected in a humanistic way.[158]

As it stands, inclusion in Ireland constitutes a major concern for parents, teachers and academics.[159] It is misunderstood as referring to the place where the child is being educated. It is identified as a placement issue, rather than an equitable issue. This misinterpretation is unsatisfactory and creates significant practical difficulties at the local level. In a study of 578 primary schools in

153. According to the first part of s 2 of the EPSEN Act, 'a child with special educational needs shall be educated in an inclusive environment with children who do not have such needs'.
154. ss 8 onwards EPSEN Act.
155. s 2 EPSEN Act.
156. s 2(a) and (b) EPSEN Act.
157. See n 86.
158. See *Report of the Special Rapporteur on the Right to Education of Persons with Disabilities*, para 41.
159. See, for instance, A Redahan, 'Implementing Inclusive Education in Mainstream Primary Schools: An Exploration of Parental Perspectives' (2006) 28 Learn 36; Sheelah Flatman-Watson, 'Barriers to Inclusive Education in Ireland: The Case for Pupils with a Diagnosis of Intellectual and/or Pervasive Developmental Disabilities' (2007) 37(4) Brit J of Learning Disabilities 277.

Dublin and Kildare conducted by Shevlin, Kenny and Loxley,[160] it was found that 34 per cent of primary schools had actually denied or deferred placements for children with learning difficulties.[161] They observed that these schools believed they could not cater for the needs of this category of children, because they did not have sufficient additional resources and appropriate qualified personnel, who would take 'care' of the needs these children may require and/or behaviour difficulties.[162] The authors concluded that, whilst schools seem to support the philosophy of developing an inclusive environment, the reality for parents of children with learning difficulties is that access to mainstream schooling is still fraught with many structural and attitudinal barriers – the ultimate decision relating to the admission of their child is exclusively conditional and dependent on the attitudes and beliefs of schools' principals, for instance.[163] As pointed out by one parent: 'You were always cap-in-hand, as in "I'm not entitled" or she wasn't entitled to the same treatment and it's the same thing about approaching schools. We did it but for a lot of parents it's a very difficult thing [...] and you're very vulnerable, if anyone says a wrong word you bring it to the grave with you'.[164]

This last comment highlights another practical difficulty, which arises once the first initial access issue to a mainstream placement has been overcome. Once a child with learning difficulties has been admitted to a mainstream school, it is not guaranteed that this child will actually receive a quality and effective education appropriate to his or her individual educational needs. In a study examining the inclusion of a child with a general learning difficulty in a multi-grade class of 30 pupils in a four-teacher mainstream primary school, located in rural Ireland, Ring and Travers observed that substantial challenges remained to the achievement of successful inclusion.[165] They observed in particular that the school lacked the necessary knowledge, skills and competence about the child's learning difficulties and had limited supports to accommodate the diverse individual educational needs of its students.[166] They concluded

160. Michael Shevlin, Mairin Kenny and Andrew Loxley, 'A Time of Transition: Exploring Special Educational Provision in the Republic of Ireland' (2008) 8(3) J of Res in Sp Edu Needs 141.
161. ibid 142.
162. ibid.
163. Richard Rose, Michael Shevlin, Eileen Winter and Paul O'Raw, 'Special and Inclusive Education in Ireland: Reviewing the Literature from 2000 to 2009' (2010) 25(4) Euro J of Sp Edu Needs 359.
164. Michael Shevlin, Patricia Noonan Walsh, Mairin Kenny, E McNeela and R Molloy, 'Experiencing Mainstream Education: Exploring the Perspectives of Parents of Young People who Have Down Syndrome' (2003) 17(1) REACH: J of Sp Needs Edu in Ir 3, 7; see also Griffin and Shevlin, *Responding to Special Educational Needs*, 85.
165. Emer Ring and Joseph Travers, 'Barriers to Inclusion: A Case Study of a Pupil with Severe Learning Difficulties in Ireland' (2005) 20(1) Euro J of Sp Needs Edu 41.
166. ibid.

that, whilst the child with severe learning difficulties seemed reasonably happy in the mainstream school, it was manifest that this child was not fully included socially and that several barriers prevented him from benefiting effectively from a quality education appropriate to his individual educational needs.[167]

These concerns have been recently expressed in the last report of the National Council for Special Education.[168] Parents and advocacy groups manifest their unease regarding current school enrolment policies and practices that are manifestly less than fully inclusive.[169] Some policies were reported as containing caveats suggesting that students with special educational needs will be enrolled only if resources are in place or if their behaviour does not adversely affect other students.[170] Others were reported as placing 'soft' barriers to enrolment by advising parents that a different school may be more suitable for their child or would have more resources for supporting him or her.[171] This is so despite the fact that all schools are resourced in the same manner.[172]

Interestingly, this reference to the availability of resources as an excuse for a school to reject the application of a child with learning difficulty and/or disability stems directly from the EPSEN Act. In s 13, the Act sets down the availability of resources principle.[173] This Section requires the Minister for Education to provide the necessary resources to implement special educational services 'with the consent of the Minister for Finance' and 'out of moneys provided by the Oireachtas'.[174] This suggests that, in the event of insufficient funds being voted through by the Oireachtas to meet the needs of children with learning difficulties or the Minister for Finance refusing to give his approval to a particular allocation of resources, the Minister of Education is unable to provide for the implementation of additional educational supports, at the disadvantage of children with learning difficulties and disabilities.[175] One may query the

167. For instance, there was unanimous agreement among the teachers that common curricular goals presented serious difficulty for the child concerned, especially in the context of large pupil-teacher ratios and multi-grade classes. Similarly, they observed that the teachers were concerned about the lack of specialist teaching materials available to them (ibid).
168. NCSE, *Supporting Students with Special Educational Needs*, 90.
169. ibid.
170. ibid.
171. ibid.
172. ibid; see also circulars 09/04 (2004) and 02/05 (2005) of the Department for Education.
173. s 13(1) reads as follows: 'The Minister and the Minister for Health and Children shall each, with the consent of the Minister for Finance, out of moneys provided by the Oireachtas, provide such moneys and other resources as are determined by him or her for the purposes of the preparation and implementation of education plans prepared in respect of children with special educational needs.'
174. O'Mahony, 'Right to Education', 108.
175. ibid.

compatibility of this principle with the international obligation of Ireland to ensure that adequate resources be available for the full realisation of educational rights.[176] As it stands, many families and associations believe that additional educational services are allocated on the basis of the structural state of the Irish economy rather than on the individual educational needs of the children concerned.[177]

Accordingly, it is manifest that the Irish approach to inclusion is significantly at odds with the human rights-based approach to disability rights in education and more precisely with art 24 of the CRPD. Too many schools, teachers, and other educational staffs still ignore the meaning of disability and inclusion.[178] As a result, teachers have low expectations for these children and feel powerless when it comes to their education in an inclusive environment.[179] They hold pessimistic beliefs and assumptions about disability, learning capacity and difference and therefore experience significant anxiety and stress when faced with the prospect of including children with learning difficulties and disabilities in their classroom.[180]

Although the EPSEN Act provides some provisions that may be in line with a progressive, inclusive and humanistic approach to disability rights in education, its key provisions are yet to be commenced and implemented. The Irish government had initially committed to a five-year implementation phase of the provisions of the Act to be completed by 1 October 2010.[181] In November 2008, the government announced an indefinite deferral of this implementation.[182] Given the current economic situation in Ireland, it is very likely that the provisions of the Act will be delayed for a number of additional years,[183] this deferral being at odds with the obligation of the State to progressively implement the educational rights of children with disabilities.[184]

---

176. See, for instance, art 4(2) CRPD, which reads as follows: 'With regard to economic, social and cultural rights, each State Party undertakes to take measures to the maximum of its available resources and, where needed, within the framework of international cooperation, with a view to achieving progressively the full realization of these rights, without prejudice to those obligations contained in the present Convention that are immediately applicable according to international law.'
177. For further details, see NCSE, *Supporting Students with Special Educational Needs*, 87–88.
178. See *Report of the Special Rapporteur on the Right to Education of Persons with Disabilities*, para 25.
179. ibid.
180. Winter and O'Raw, *Literature Review*, 28.
181. Department of Education, Circular 00/51 (2007).
182. Webb, *Country Report*, 5.
183. ibid.
184. This obligation is expressly set down in art 4(2) CRPD.

How Can Ireland Implement a Human Rights-Based Approach to Disability Rights in Education?

This article has sought to demonstrate that, in spite of the good intentions of the Irish government to develop the infrastructures necessary for establishing an inclusive learning environment accessible, available and adaptable to everyone, this remains insufficient. Too many barriers remain at the national level and consequently at the local level.

Two changes may be considered in order to overcome these inadequacies and establish, in compliance with human rights law, an inclusive legal framework guaranteeing quality education for every child in the best-suited learning environment. The first change is concerned with the definitions provided in the legislation. One has to bear in mind that definitions embody epistemological beliefs about disability, normality and education, which subsequently shape the values of one's society and influence the structure of its education system, its legal framework and the attitude of its teaching workforce. Refining these assumptions through new definitions is a *sine qua non* condition for transforming attitudes and beliefs about disability and education.[185] Accordingly, it is desirable that a definition of education and its aims be provided in the legislation. It is further suggested that this definition be in compliance with the human rights-based philosophy and more precisely with art 24(1) of the CRPD.

The second concept that would require some clarification in the legislation is the concept of inclusion. It should be clarified that an inclusive education does not refer to the place where the child receives his or her education. Nor should an inclusive education be understood as jeopardising the existence and role of special schools. Instead, inclusion should be interpreted as referring to the quality of education that a child receives in the best-suited learning environment, be it in a mainstream school, a special class or a special school. In this sense, the legislation should specify that inclusion and special schools are not at opposite poles, but rather converge toward the same goal – that of a quality education for all. Both concepts should be identified as tools for guaranteeing and implementing equity in education, as suggested by art 24(3)(c) of the CRPD.[186]

The last concept that would need to be refined in the current Irish legislation is the concept of disability. The medical definition provided in the Irish

---

185. It is noteworthy that the State is under an international obligation to raise awareness and 'to combat stereotypes, prejudices and harmful practices relating to persons with disabilities, including those based on sex and age, in all areas of life' (art 8(1)(b) CRPD).

186. In relation to children with hearing and sight difficulties, the Convention requires the State to deliver educational services in the 'most appropriate languages and modes and means of communication for the individual, and in environments which maximize academic and social development' (art 24(3)(c) CRPD).

legislation is wholly inadequate and significantly at odds with the CRPD[187] and the current European trend initiated by the European Court of Justice. In the recent case of *Ring and Skouboe Werge*,[188] the second Chamber of the European Court of Justice was asked to provide a preliminary ruling regarding the correct interpretation of the concept of disability in the context of the Council Directive 2000/78/EC establishing a general framework for equal treatment in employment and occupation.[189] Referring to the definition provided in the UN Convention, which was approved on behalf of the European Council in 2010,[190] the Court held that

> the concept of disability must be understood as referring to a limitation which results in particular from physical, mental or psychological impairments which, in interaction with various barriers, may hinder the full and effective participation of the person concerned in professional life on an equal basis with other workers.[191]

This ruling, which departs from the previous definition provided in *Chacón Navas*,[192] constitutes a landmark decision in the area of disability rights. Adopting the humanistic approach to disability embodied in the UN Convention, the Court manifests its clear attention to participate in and materialise the current attitudinal shift that is taking place at the international level. In this context, it is desirable that the Irish legislation align its policy, politics and practice with the current international trend and change its current definition so as to be in compliance with the UN Convention and with the recent decision of the European Court of Justice. In particular, it is recommended that a clear distinction be made between having an impairment and being disabled. Whilst the former refers to biophysical factors that modify the physical structure of one's body and its organic function, the latter is the result of the interaction between these biophysical characteristics and the presence of external societal, environmental and social barriers that further disable the individual concerned. Legislating for this distinction would be a first significant step towards adopting a more human rights-based approach to disability in Ireland.

---

187. See preamble, paragraph (e) of the Convention, which recognises disability as being the interaction between having an impairment and attitudinal and environmental barriers that hinder the full and effective participation of persons with disabilities in society on an equal basis with others.
188. Joined cases against DAB, in which two women were dismissed from employment when they returned to work following a period of sick leave (2nd Chamber, 11/04/2013).
189. OJ L303, 02/12/2000 P 0016–0022.
190. See Council Decision 2010/48/EC of 26/11/09 (OJ 2010 L 23) 35.
191. para 38.
192. European Court of Justice, Grand Chamber, 11/07/2006, in which the court held that 'the concept of disability must be understood as referring to a limitation which results in particular from physical, mental or psychological impairments and which hinders the participation of the person concerned in professional life' para 43.

In line with the latter point, it is further recommended that a distinction be established between disability and special educational needs. As demonstrated in this paper, the assimilation of the two concepts in the legislation is incongruous. It underestimates the complexity of most learning difficulties and does not reflect the reality that children with individual educational needs experience on a daily basis. In this context, it is advised that the expression 'special educational needs' be replaced by a more pedagogical expression such as 'individual educational needs'.[193] As mentioned in this paper, the reference to the term 'special' implies that there still exists a hierarchy between those who are special and those who are normal. This expression is stigmatising, demeaning and at odds with the philosophy of a human rights-based approach. Changing expressions would have significant positive impacts on the way society understands diversity, plurality and differentiation. Special education would become a tool, rather than a service, aimed at enhancing early, rightly timed and planned proactive support for the learning and growth of every child. It would highlight the idiosyncratic nature of learning and the pedagogical nature of additional supports. It is believed that this change would eventually contribute to the eradication of medical terms such as 'normal' and 'special' education and lead to the unification of the education system.

The second change is solely directed at the teaching workforce. The UN Special Rapporteur on the Right to Education[194] and art 24(4) of the CRPD[195] emphasise the importance of developing programmes that would inform and challenge misconceptions about disability amongst the teaching workforce. It is suggested that teaching students with learning difficulties does not require additional knowledge or skills, nor does it require a special education system on the margin of the general education system. It only requires a shift in attitude about human difference, a shift in belief about learning capacity and a shift in teaching methods.

Conclusion

Reforms of the Irish educational system have hitherto proved insufficient for the purpose of guaranteeing a quality education for all, including children with learning difficulties and disabilities. A commitment to education for all matters, as does the belief that every student can improve his or her learning capacity, regardless of his or her socio-economic background, disability or learning difficulty. The legal framework has to reflect and enact this belief if it wants to

---

193. This expression is used in international reports, such as the *Report of the Special Rapporteur on the Right to Education of Persons with Disabilities*, para 41.
194. ibid para 25.
195. The second provision requires States Parties to incorporate within the training of teachers 'disability awareness and the use of appropriate augmentative and alternative modes, means and formats of communication, educational techniques and materials to support persons with disabilities'.

ensure that every student benefits from equal opportunities to learn meaningfully and successfully. As correctly pointed out by the OECD, placing a high value on education can only get a country so far if teachers, parents and the government of that country believe that only a minority of students can reach a high educational standard.[196]

With the current economic and financial crisis, the Irish government is at a crossroads. Either it continues to foster its traditional approach to education with the risk of undermining the educational rights of children with learning difficulties and disabilities; or it uses this crisis as an opportunity to radically change everything and create a sustainable legal structure that would promote disability rights in education, equity, inclusion and social justice.[197] This article advocates the second option and believes that the time has now come to change attitudes, recognise and accept differences and make available to everyone what is accessible for some, at the exclusion of the others. Irish law should be an instrument to reach this ideal and effectively vindicate disability rights in education.

---

196. OECD, *PISA 2009 Results: What Makes a School Successful? Resources, Policies and Practices* (vol IV, OECD 2010) 104.
197. See the comments of Irina Bokova in *Education for All Global Monitoring Report 2010 – Reaching the Marginalised* (UNESCO, Oxford University Press 2010) i.

Why It's Better to be Sorry than Safe: The Case for Apology Protection Legislation

Val Corbett*

Abstract—Societal norms dictate that where one has wronged another, a genuine apology should be made by the wrongdoer to the victim. In such circumstances, wrongdoers are encouraged to acknowledge their wrongdoing, express remorse for its occurrence and promise such behaviour will not reoccur. In so doing, it is hoped that the relationship between the parties can be restored. The power of a genuine apology to repair relationships harmed by wrongdoing has long been recognised by sociologists and psychologists alike. Yet when such disputes enter the legal arena, the wrongdoer is positively discouraged from acknowledging any wrongdoing or apologising for his or her role in the commission of the wrong. While the adversarial system may promote the search for truth in litigation, it also has the effect of chilling expressions of apology. In a system where no quarter is asked or given, the opportunity to resolve some disputes earlier and less expensively is lost.

This article evaluates the role of apology as a method of facilitating the resolution of civil disputes. It examines the importance of apology to society and the positive impact the communication of a genuine apology can have on the concerns and interests of individual litigants. Despite these advantages, apologies are chronically under-used as a means of resolving disputes, partly because of the fear that an apology might be construed as an admission of guilt on the part of wrongdoer, thereby exposing him or her to liability. This article identifies and examines the underlying reasons for the under-use of apology in these cases and analyses whether these concerns are real or exaggerated. To promote the greater use of apology, other common law jurisdictions have introduced 'apology protection' legislation, which provides the giver of an apology with immunity relating to potential liability that might arise from it. This article examines such legislation and poses the question whether or not such an approach should be adopted in the Irish jurisdiction as the most appropriate method of encouraging the greater use of apology to resolve such disputes.

* Head of School, Independent College Dublin. The author would like to thank the editors and reviewers for their helpful comments on an earlier draft of this work.

'Never apologize, mister, it's a sign of weakness.'[1]

Introduction

As children we are taught that when we injure another through our inappropriate behaviour we should apologise to that person. We learn that apologising when we have done wrong is one of the most appropriate and effective ways of repairing a relationship damaged by our actions. Yet, as adults when our bad behaviour injures another, we are advised – usually by insurance companies and lawyers alike – that saying 'I'm sorry' is the last thing we should do. It would seem that these contradictory messages are justified simply on the basis that once we leave the playground and the wrongs become more serious, the stakes become much higher. The reality is that in such circumstances where our conduct causes injury, questions of legal liability (and the financial consequences arising therefrom) come to the fore.

The current state of the Irish legal system and its tort law positively discourages the use of apology as a possible remedy to a legal claim or its use as a means of efficiently facilitating the resolution of certain disputes between litigants. Aside from the cultural barriers, where apologising is perceived as a sign of weakness, there are very real legal hurdles that deter defendants from openly and honestly acknowledging their wrongful behaviour and apologising to the plaintiff for it. In particular, there is a fear from defendants that by apologising they will incur legal responsibility for the plaintiff's injuries. As a consequence, the Irish system is one whereby all parties are advised to keep their own counsel until a settlement is made or the court makes a determination as to the matter. This 'wall of silence'[2] can prove incredibly frustrating for both parties to the dispute. The defendant may feel that he has a moral responsibility to apologise and may feel guilt and shame not only for his role in causing the injury but also for his failure to admit that to the plaintiff. The plaintiff, on the other hand, may find that his negative feelings towards the defendant for causing the injury are exacerbated because the defendant refuses to communicate with him. In these circumstances, it is unlikely that the parties are of a mindset to explore alternative avenues by which the dispute between them can be resolved amicably and in the best interests of all.

The response from other jurisdictions to this conundrum has been to introduce what has become known as apology protection legislation. Such legislation essentially provides that where a defendant apologises for his wrongdoing after the event, his admission cannot be used as evidence against him in any subsequent civil proceedings relating to that event. The purpose of such legislation is to promote the greater use of apology not only as a remedy but also as a means of reducing the instances of litigation and the costs associated

1. Frank S Nugent (1908–1965), US screenwriter, Laurence Stallings, and John Ford, Capt Nathan Brittles (John Wayne), *She Wore a Yellow Ribbon* (1949).
2. Willie Dunne, 'Seeking a Clear Focus on Openness' *The Irish Times* (Dublin, 17 November 2009).

therewith. In its recent report on *Alternative Dispute Resolution: Mediation and Conciliation*, the Law Reform Commission recommended the limited introduction of apology protection legislation in Ireland to instances involving medical professionals and their patients. In its recommendation the Commission proposed that an apology delivered by or on behalf of a person in the medical context should not constitute an express or implied admission of civil liability by that party and should not be relevant to the determination of liability in an action.[3] It is noteworthy, however, that this recommendation was not adopted by the government in its subsequent publication of the draft Mediation Bill 2012, where all references to apology protection were omitted.

This article argues that the Law Reform Commission did not go far enough in its recommendation regarding the introduction of statutory protection for apologies. Certainly, the benefits of apology legislation are most evident in the medical context where trust between the medical professional and patient is essential and where the disclosure of mistakes can be crucial to the patient's ongoing treatment. However, it is submitted in this article that the benefits of apology are not limited to such relationships and that such protection should extend to all wrongdoers and their victims even if it can be argued that the need for such statutory protection is possibly greatest in the case of medical professionals and their patients. By removing all reference to apology protection in the draft Mediation Bill 2012, an opportunity to begin a process of reform has been lost.

This article proceeds in four parts. Part I presents an analysis of the benefits associated with an apology when made by a defendant to a plaintiff, including the potential for such an apology to facilitate the early (and less costly) resolution of disputes between parties. Part II examines the nature of an apology and what is required in terms of its content, timing and delivery if it is to be effective and deemed to be sincere. Part III explores the reasons why, notwithstanding its benefits, apologies voluntarily given are so rare in Irish law, and in particular it identifies the legal and cultural impediments to the greater use of apology in this regard. Finally, Part IV provides a critique of apology protection legislation before ultimately proposing that similar legislation should be adopted in the Irish jurisdiction.

1. The Benefits of Apology

A meaningful apology involves an acknowledgment by the wrongdoer that he has violated a social norm of behaviour shared by the parties who are members of a community.[4] The violation by the wrongdoer of that community norm creates an imbalance in the relationship between the parties

---

3. Law Reform Commission, *Report on Alternative Dispute Resolution: Mediation and Conciliation* (LRC–2010), para 7.47.
4. Prue Vines, 'The Power of Apology: Mercy, Forgiveness or Corrective Justice in the Civil Liability Arena?' (2007) 1 Pub Space, J L and Soc Just 1, 9; Erin A O'Hara and Douglas Yarn, 'On Apology and Consilience' (2002) 77 Wash L Rev 1121, 1136.

because the victim has suffered an uncorrected indignity at the hands of the wrongdoer. In some of these cases, an apology may be the most effective way of restoring the victim's status, as it can result in the realignment of the relationship between the wrongdoer and the victim.[5] By offering an authentic apology the wrongdoer explicitly recognises, through a 'ritual of humiliation',[6] his behaviour as wrongful and in doing so reasserts the dignity of the victim.[7] The equilibrium in the relationship that existed prior to the violation of the norm is restored as the wrongdoer, by making the apology, relinquishes power to the victim, who can decide whether to accept the apology or not. In this way, apologies act as 'an exchange of shame and power between the offender and the offended'.[8]

While an apology is essentially a moral act, it also has a number of other positive benefits. A sincere and genuine apology can commence a process of healing for both parties.[9] From the victim's point of view the apology is a sign of respect from the wrongdoer, who acknowledges – through the apology – the pain he has caused while also signalling that, despite his wrongdoing, he does value his relationship with the victim.[10] This process in turn promotes the emotional well-being of the victim as not only does it include an acceptance that a wrong was committed, it also makes it known that the victim was not responsible for its occurrence.[11] The apology act is also significant for the victim as it involves the wrongdoer seeking forgiveness from the victim and in so doing it restores power to the victim and leaves the wrongdoer vulnerable to the victim's rejection. White has observed that this process will assist the emotional recovery of the victim as he will understand the suffering the wrongdoer has undergone by making the apology.[12]

Where accepted, the apology acts to dissipate feelings of anger and resentment that the victim may have developed towards the wrongdoer as a result of his offensive actions. The delivery of a meaningful apology by the wrongdoer may commence a process of forgiveness that can lead to

---

5. Lee Taft, 'Apology Subverted: The Commodification of Apology' (2000) 109 Yale LJ 1135.
6. William Ian Miller, *Faking It* (Cambridge University Press 2003) 92.
7. Brent T White, 'Say You're Sorry: Court-Ordered Apologies as a Civil Rights Remedy' (2005–2006) 91 Cornell L Rev 1261.
8. Aviva Orenstein, 'Apology Excepted: Incorporating a Feminist Analysis into Evidence Policy Where You Would Least Expect It' (1998–1999) 28 Sw U L Rev 221. However, as Latif has noted, this shaming exercise will depend on whether the wrongdoer places a value on his place in society or whether he cares what other members of that society think of him. See: Elizabeth Latif, 'Apologetic Justice: Evaluating Apologies Tailored Toward Legal Solutions' (2001) 81 BU L Rev 289, 314.
9. Aaron Lazare, *On Apology* (Oxford University Press 2004).
10. O'Hara and Yarn, 'On Apology', 1137.
11. White, 'Say You're Sorry'.
12. ibid 1278.

reconciliation and a restoration of the relationship with the victim.[13] Taft has pinpointed the granting of forgiveness as being the determining feature of a successful apology.[14] He opines that feelings of resentment that the victim might feel towards the wrongdoer following the commission of a wrong are natural and serve to protect the 'critical value of self-respect'[15] of the victim. Consequently, in his view, 'one who does not resent moral injuries is lacking in self-respect'.[16] An apology for those injuries made to the victim provides that party with a 'legitimate moral reason' to forgive the wrongdoer.[17]

The apology act is also of emotional/psychological benefit to the wrongdoer. First, by voluntarily making a meaningful apology the wrongdoer restores his integrity following the commission of the wrong by accepting the consequences of his own wrongdoing.[18] Secondly, the apology can assuage the wrongdoer's feelings of guilt by shifting 'the moral burden from transgressors to victim to either forgive or justify a refusal to do so'.[19] The wrongdoer, in taking the first step at reconciliation by apologising, will be 'at peace' when the victim forgives him and no longer resents him. However, even if the victim chooses not to forgive, the wrongdoer will at least have the consolation of knowing that he tried. Thirdly, the apology allows 'the wrongdoer to rehabilitate his reputation, reinstate his self-worth, and assert that the improper behaviour was not intentional'.[20]

The apology act not only benefits the parties to the dispute by assisting in reconciliation, it can also benefit society, particularly in legal systems that encourage its use. By apologising, the wrongdoer not only seeks the forgiveness of the victim, he is also seeking re-admittance into the moral community. Through the act of apology the wrongdoer not only restores dignity and self-respect to the victim, he is also acknowledging membership of that moral community and respect for its norms are important to him.[21] In this way, the apology serves to communicate 'more broadly to society what constitutes moral or immoral behaviour'.[22] Thus, an apology educates as to norms of civil behaviour expected in a moral community.[23] As a meaningful

13. O'Hara and Yarn, 'On Apology', 1137.
14. Taft, 'Apology Subverted', 1143–46.
15. ibid 1144.
16. ibid.
17. ibid.
18. Lee Taft, 'Apology and Medical Mistake: Opportunity or Foil?' (2005) 14 Annals Health L 55, 83.
19. O'Hara and Yarn, 'On Apology'.
20. Aviva Orenstein, 'Apology Excepted', 244.
21. Latif, 'Apologetic Justice'.
22. Claire Truesdale, 'Apology Accepted: How the *Apology Act* Reveals the Law's Deference to the Power of Apologetic Discourse' (2012) 17 Appeal Rev Current L and L Reform 83, 87.
23. Orenstein, 'Apology Excepted'.

apology will involve an admission that mistakes were made,[24] the community can learn from those mistakes and make sure they are never repeated, or at the very least that their occurrence is minimised.[25] Consequently, a legal system that 'chills' the use of apology can be detrimental to societal interests. Take the medical profession as one specific example. In that field, medical professionals are placed in an almost impossible situation 'where the physician was completely aware of the error and its effects, yet shackled and silenced by a system and its advisors'.[26] A failure to offer apology protection places the medical community in an unenviable position, '… [c]onceal a mistake, and you violate your professional ethics. Admit a mistake, and you may give a patient ammo for a malpractice suit'.[27] A system that encourages openness and transparency surrounding medical mistakes will benefit the community as a whole. It is only when mistakes are admitted that we can begin to learn from them. Admitting mistakes builds trust between the patient and doctor, which in turn should improve patient care and consequently benefit society as a whole.

Aside from that specific example, society benefits when the use of apology is promoted by discouraging the wronged party from seeking violent revenge as a remedial response to the injury he has suffered.[28] Whilst the institution of tort law provides the victim with an avenue of civil recourse as a replacement for revenge, in appropriate cases an apology is a much simpler and inexpensive method of ameliorating the victim's violent thoughts of retribution.[29]

Apologies can also facilitate the swift and efficient resolution of disputes. Empirical studies have proven that a properly delivered, authentic and timely apology can lead to the earlier (and less costly) resolution of disputes as an alternative to pursuing expensive and time-consuming litigation.[30] Jennifer Robbennolt in particular has carried out a number of studies examining the impact that authentic

24. ibid 254.
25. Orenstein, 'Apology Excepted'; Taft, 'Apology and Medical Mistake'.
26. Taft, 'Apology and Medical Mistake', 58–59.
27. Orenstein, 'Apology Excepted', 265.
28. ibid.
29. Benjamin C Zipursky, 'Rights, Wrongs, and Recourse in the Law of Torts' (1998) 51 V and L Rev 1.
30. Jennifer K Robbennolt, 'Apologies and Legal Settlement: An Empirical Examination' (2003–2004) 102 Mich L Rev 460, 485–486 (where full apology was offered 73 per cent of respondents were inclined to accept the offer of settlement compared to 52 per cent where no apology was offered); Charles Vincent et al, 'Why Do People Sue Doctors? A Study of Patients and Relatives Taking Legal Action' (1994) 343 Lancet 1609, 1612 (where 37 per cent of respondents stated that they would not have instigated a claim in negligence had there been an apology and admission of wrongdoing); Margareth Etienne and Jennifer K Robbennolt, 'Apologies and Plea Bargaining' (2007–2008) 91 Marq L Rev 295; Brian H Bornstein et al, 'The Effects of Defendant Remorse on Mock Juror Decisions in a Malpractice Case' (2002) 20 Behav Sci and L 393; Amy B Whitman et al, 'How Do Patients Want Physicians to Handle Mistakes?' (1996) 156 Archives of Internal Medicine 2565, 2566 (where 98 per cent

apologies can have on influencing early settlement of disputes.[31] In the course of her research, Robbennolt randomly selected 556 staff members from a university to participate in an experiment. The participants were asked to read a scenario involving a pedestrian who was injured when struck by a cyclist. The participants were asked to negotiate a legal settlement on behalf of the injured pedestrian. As part of this process they were asked *inter alia* to assess the sufficiency of the apology provided by the cyclist. Contextual variables were changed, ie in some cases a full responsibility-accepting apology was given and in others a partial apology involving an expression of sympathy and no more was offered. In some cases the apology was granted legal protection so that it could not be used as an admission of liability in subsequent litigation and in others it was not.[32] From the results of her study, Robbennolt concluded that, '... apologies can alter perceptions, attributions, and judgments in ways that increase the likelihood of settlement – specifically that apologies result in more positive perceptions and attributions and influence settlement levers in ways that make settlement more likely'.[33]

The study also indicated that those apologies that involved the wrongdoer accepting responsibility for his wrongdoing had the strongest positive effect on the injured party.[34] Moreover, the study indicated that an apology could offset the costs of settlement by reducing the financial compensation that might otherwise be payable.[35] In other words, the apology was seen as lowering the cost of the financial settlement as it was deemed – particularly in relation to the emotional/psychological impact of the accident on the plaintiff – to be a more appropriate remedy that satisfied the victim's needs. Robbennolt also found that apologies, where positively received, can 'lower claimants' aspirations... [who] may feel bound by norms of reciprocity to respond favorably to an apology'.[36] Notwithstanding the fact that the 'results are open to criticism in that mere participants reading a scenario on a computer screen will react differently than someone with an actual injury',[37] the research conducted by Robbennolt has at the very least conclusively established a correlation between apologies and the early settlement of disputes.

A concrete – and oft-quoted – example of the positive influence that a policy of full disclosure accompanied by an expression of remorse in the form

---

of respondents expected or wished for some acknowledgment of the error by the medical practitioner).

31. Jennifer K Robbennolt, 'Apologies and Settlement Levers' (2006) 3 J Empirical Legal Stud 333; Jennifer K Robbennolt, 'Apologies and Legal Settlement: An Empirical Examination' (2003–2004) 102 Mich L Rev 460.
32. Robbennolt, 'Apologies and Settlement Levers', 356.
33. ibid 335.
34. ibid.
35. ibid 369.
36. ibid 355.
37. Matthew Pillsbury, 'Say Sorry and Save: A Practical Argument for a Greater Role for Apologies in Medical Malpractice Law' (2006) 1 S New Eng Roundtable Symp LJ 171, 182.

of an apology can have on the settlement of claims is that which occurred with the Veterans' Administration hospital (VA) in Lexington, Kentucky, in the United States.[38] In response to a number of costly medical negligence claims against it, the hospital implemented a new policy of voluntarily disclosing medical errors to patients. Such disclosures would be made at a meeting with the patient by the hospital's chief of staff who would express regret for what had occurred, outline the steps that would be undertaken by the hospital to correct or ameliorate the error (including compensation) and explain the procedures that would be adopted to ensure similar errors were not repeated. This change in policy towards medical errors adopted by the hospital coincided with significant improvements in the costs of malpractice awards.[39]

Notwithstanding the apparent success of the open disclosure policy adopted by the VA in Lexington, Taft has sounded a note of caution regarding these (financially) positive results. In particular, he observed that the patients of the VA were for the most part older men who generally might not be as litigious as other members of society and who might have lower expectations than patients in a private hospital.[40] Wu has also noted that this example must be viewed through a critical filter, particularly as VA doctors are legally protected from personal liability in such cases.[41] Nonetheless, and despite these caveats, the Lexington VA hospital experience provides compelling evidence in favour of the power of apology.

2. The Nature of Apology

Not all apologies result in the beneficial outcomes highlighted above. Sometimes, the injuries suffered by the plaintiff are too great to be resolved by apology alone regardless of how heartfelt it is. Sometimes, however, the apology is simply not accepted by the plaintiff because the defendant is just not believed or is interpreted as being insincere. The value of insincere apologies is a matter of some debate. We all can recall incidents from childhood where a teacher forces two squabbling children to apologise to one another in front of the entire class or face the consequences. Sulking, the children would invariably, albeit grudgingly, mutter

---

38. Steven S Kraman and Ginny Hamm, 'Risk Management: Extreme Honesty May Be the Best Policy' (1999) 131 Annals of Internal Med 963; Taft, 'Apology and Medical Mistake', 83.
39. Taft, 'Apology and Medical Mistake', 84, where the author noted that: 'In 1999, the median malpractice settlement in the private sector was $497,412 while Lexington's was only $98,150. In a concentrated study that focused only on the years 1990–1996, "the Lexington facility had 88 malpractice claims" and paid an average of $15,622 per claim. Additionally, only eight claims were filed in court, seven of which were dismissed before trial, and the VA won the only case that proceeded to trial.'
40. ibid 85.
41. Albert W Wu, 'Handling Hospital Errors: Is Disclosure the Best Defense?' (1999) 131 Annals of Internal Med 970, 971.

an apology to one another. Is such an apology effective? Does it satisfy the needs of the warring children? Does the apology made in front of the class – grudging or otherwise – serve as a 'teachable' moment for the entire class?

Sociologists would argue that the success of an apology is dependent on whether it is sincere, or at least appears to be sincere to the victim.[42] If the apology is perceived as anything other than genuine by the victim it is likely to exacerbate an already fraught situation. If the victim interprets the apology as lacking in sincerity or is somehow incomplete, it is likely to add insult to the injury already suffered by the victim. This, in turn, will only serve to further antagonise the victim, thereby decreasing the chances of an amicable settlement between the parties.

Research would indicate that the defining features of a valid apology can be identified as including the expression of regret and the acceptance of responsibility by the wrongdoer.[43] Sociologists such as Lazare have identified the key elements to an effective apology as involving the acknowledgement by the wrongdoer of the offence, communicating remorse for that offence, providing an explanation for what occurred and a commitment to making reparation.[44] Tavuchis has identified that an authentic apology consists of two elements. First, the wrongdoer must be sorry for the wrong done and second, she must say so.[45] While O'Hara and Yarn have noted that 'a consistent strand running through… [an effective apology]… is that the offender accepts blame for the wrongful act and thus bears responsibility for future forbearance and reparations'.[46]

Therefore, an attempt at apology that does not explicitly recognise the wrong and the wrongdoer's responsibility for the commission of the wrong, while also assuring the victim that it will not be repeated, is more likely to fail as a means of reconciliation. By explicitly acknowledging the wrong and his fault in it, the wrongdoer is making it clear that the victim is not to blame. Moreover, it communicates to the victim that the wrongdoer has respect for him and their relationship, thereby restoring dignity to the victim.[47]

By contrast, an incomplete or partial apology is one that deflects responsibility and merely expresses sympathy. Such apologies might convey that the wrongdoer is sorry for what has happened to the victim without acknowledging his own role in the wrongdoing and are unlikely to satisfy the needs of the

42. Taft, 'Apology Subverted', 1144.
43. ibid 1140; Daniel W Shuman, 'The Role of Apology in Tort Law'(1999–2000) 83 Judicature 180, 185.
44. Aaron Lazare, 'The Healing Forces of Apology in Medical Practice and Beyond' (2007–2008) 57 DePaul L Rev 251.
45. Nicholas Tavuchis, *Mea Culpa: A Sociology of Apology and Reconciliation* (Stanford University Press 1991) 17.
46. O'Hara and Yarn, 'On Apology and Consilience', 1137.
47. Latif, 'Apologetic Justice', 306.

victim.[48] In a similar manner, 'argumentative apologies'[49] are also unlikely to prove successful in the resolution of the dispute between the parties. Such apologies are of the qualified variety where the apology 'is intended to convey reasonableness and to usurp the moral high ground rather than to express remorse'.[50] The difficulty with such statements is that the healing qualities associated with an apology, it is argued, will only materialise where the apology is complete and sincere. The 'expression of fault is needed in an apology as it opens up the door to healing'.[51] Anything less, such as a 'non-apology, apology' is unlikely to promote healing between the parties and is likely to worsen an already fractured relationship.

While the content of the apology is essential in determining its authenticity, the timing of the delivery of the apology can also be critical to the chances of its success. It would seem that the apology should only be delivered after a period of thoughtful consideration but not so late that the victim's grievance is allowed to fester and develop into resentment.[52]

Thus, if an apology is delivered too quickly after the wrong has been committed, it may be devalued as it might be interpreted as given without adequate thought or consideration. On the other hand, wait too long after the event – and after a denial of responsibility for it – and the apology might be interpreted as grudgingly given.[53] Therefore, an apology should be delivered in a period of time after the event has occurred where the wrongdoer has had the opportunity to consider the import of his wrongdoing and its impact on the victim. During this period of soul-searching the wrongdoer should question himself as to his behaviour and how such behaviour has negatively affected the victim.[54] Moreover, during that period the victim will be afforded the opportunity of

48. O'Hara and Yarn, 'On Apology and Consilience', 1138; Jonathan R Cohen, 'Legislating Apology: The Pros and Cons' (2001–2002) 70 U Cin L Rev 819, 838.
49. O'Hara and Yarn, 'On Apology and Consilience', 1138.
50. ibid.
51. Lazare, *On Apology*.
52. Jennifer G Brown, 'The Role of Apology in Negotiation' (2003–2004) 87 Marq L Rev 665, 669–670; where the author commented that: 'Almost everyone seems to agree that an apology should be the result of some analysis and introspection on the part of the offender – if it comes too spontaneously or off-the-cuff it loses power and legitimacy. This can create a tension. The offender may need time in order to reflect upon the harm done, form true remorse for the offense, and prepare a heartfelt apology, but the more an apology is delayed the more profound the offense may seem in the eyes of the victim.'
53. Max Bolstad, 'Learning from Japan: The Case for Increased Use of Apology in Mediation' (2000) 48 Clev St L Rev 545; Stephen B Goldberg, 'Saying You're Sorry' (1987) 3 Negotiation J 221, 223.
54. Brown, 'Apology in Negotiation', 670 (citing Blanchard and McBride).

'telling his story' so that any apology delivered after that period will also take into consideration the full impact it had on the victim.[55]

How the apology is delivered – in what form and by whom – is also a key factor in determining the likelihood of its acceptance and, therefore, its success. An apology is an emotional act. When making an apology, the wrongdoer is expressing regret and seeking forgiveness. From the victim's point of view, the victim is forced to decide whether to let go of his resentment and forgive the wrongdoer. Given the emotions involved it is not surprising that some view that the most appropriate method by which to deliver an apology is orally and in person. What better way of judging the sincerity of an expression of contrition than by looking the wrongdoer in the eye when he is doing so?[56] By delivering the apology orally and in person, the victim is in a better position to observe 'the demeanour and facial expressions of the apologizer' and 'can better gauge whether or not the offender truly regrets his act'.[57] Hence, Tavuchis has described the apology as a 'speech act'.[58] While in many cases the delivery of an apology in this way may be the most effective way of communicating, it is not necessarily the only way by which an apology should be delivered. In certain cases, the injured party may wish for something more formal and permanent, ie a written letter or a public statement.[59] Thus, the method of communication can be key as 'meaning is found not only in context, but in shared beliefs, behaviors, values, customs and experience'.[60]

The identity of the person delivering the apology can also be a relevant factor in determining whether it will be deemed acceptable to the victim. The apology should 'be made by the person with the moral authority to make it'.[61] An apology directly given by the wrongdoer and not through an intermediary is more likely to be accepted by the victim because '[t]he apologizee is in a better position to judge the underlying emotions of the apologizer'.[62]

55. Deborah L Levi, 'The Role of Apology in Mediation' (1997) 72 NYU L Rev 1165, 1191.
56. ibid 23.
57. Bolstad, 'Learning from Japan', 549.
58. Nicholas Tavuchis, *Mea Culpa: A Sociology of Apology and Reconciliation* (Stanford University Press 1991) 21.
59. For example, some 50 years after one of the biggest medical disasters in the world, hundreds of survivors of the thalidomide scandal received a public apology from Britain's Minister of Health, Mike O'Brien, and a new £20 million compensation package. 'The apology is just as important as the financial settlement,' said Guy Tweedy, one of the thalidomiders leading the campaign for a better deal: Sarah Boseley, '50 Years On an Apology to Thalidomide Scandal Survivors' *The Guardian* (London 14 January 2010).
60. Peter H Rehm and Denise R Beatty, 'Legal Consequences of Apologizing' (1996) J Disp Resol 115, 117.
61. Catherine Regis and Jean Poitras, 'Healthcare Mediation and the Need for Apologies' (2010) 18 Health LJ 31.
62. Bolstad, 'Learning from Japan', 577.

Moreover, if the wrongdoer personally delivers the apology it is more likely that the victim will accept it as the wrongdoer has shown integrity by subjecting himself to the 'ritual of humiliation' of asking the victim for forgiveness.[63]

3. The Reluctance to Apologise

If an apology is capable of producing benefits such as bringing healing to the victim and encouraging the earlier resolution of disputes, why then is there an apparent reluctance to make apologies when one has wronged another? The root cause of such reticence appears to be both legal and cultural. First, there is a fear that by apologising, one is admitting liability for the wrong that has occurred and that the statement of apology can be admitted as evidence against a defendant as proof of his guilt. Second, there are cultural barriers in most Western societies that make apologies less likely. In such societies, making an apology is interpreted as an exercise in humiliation and consequently there is a great reluctance in admitting when one has done wrong.

Perhaps the biggest obstacle to the greater use of apology in disputes between litigants is a legal one grounded in the rules of evidence. In accordance with the hearsay rule of evidence, 'an assertion other than one made by a person while giving oral evidence in the proceedings is inadmissible as evidence of any fact asserted'.[64] Thus, as a general rule, a statement made by a party outside of the courtroom is inadmissible, other than by that party's own direct testimony, as evidence of the truth of the facts asserted in that statement. However, there are a number of exceptions to the principle and evidence of a non-testimonial statement (such as an apology) made by the defendant will be admitted as evidence in certain circumstances. For example, such evidence will be admissible where one party is testifying regarding statements made by the defendant outside of the courtroom that are adverse to the defendant's case, ie admissions of liability made by the defendant.[65] Orenstein has described the rationale behind this exception as one which 'emanates as much from the law of the sandbox, as from the law of rationality. Its premise is: "Ha, ha, you said it, now you're stuck with your own admission."'[66] In the context of apologies, therefore, a defendant might be fearful that should he apologise or make any other statement expressly or implicitly assuming responsibility for the incident that that statement could be rendered admissible as evidence of his liability in any subsequent litigation. Not surprisingly, apologies or expressions of contrition

---

63. William Ian Miller, *Faking It* (Cambridge University Press 2003) 92; Jennifer K. Robbennolt, 'Apologies and Settlement Levers'.
64. Colin Tapper, *Cross and Tapper on Evidence* (8th edn, Butterworths 1995) 564; Declan McGrath, *Evidence* (Thomson Round Hall 2005) 213.
65. ibid 642.
66. Orenstein, 'Apology Excepted', 249.

are in short supply in these circumstances even where the defendant might feel that it was the appropriate thing to do.[67]

While it may be the case that evidence of statements made by the defendant against his own self-interest, such as the defendant apologising for his role in causing the plaintiff's injury, are admissible, it does not necessarily automatically follow that such evidence without more is conclusive evidence of the defendant's liability. Whether an apology amounts to conclusive evidence of guilt is a nuanced one. However, at the outset it can be said that issues of liability are for the courts and not the parties to the dispute to determine.[68] As Vines has observed, 'a statement as to a legal conclusion by a party cannot be relied on to establish that conclusion, because that is the role of the court'.[69] An early example of this point arose in *Muir v Glasgow Corporation*.[70] In that case, a number of children were burned in a tea room when a tea urn carried by an employee of the appellant fell and its contents scalded them. Mrs Alexander, the manageress of the tea room, had authorised the transportation of the urn. In determining whether Mrs Alexander had acted negligently, Lord Thankerton emphasised that the determination of whether Mrs Alexander had failed to take reasonable care was an objective test of a legal standard and one for the court to make:

> The court must be careful to place itself in the position of the person charged with the duty, and to consider what he or she should have reasonably anticipated as a natural and probable consequence of neglect, and not to give undue weight to the fact that a distressing accident has happened or that witnesses in the witness box are prone to express regret, *ex post facto*, that they did not take some step, which it is now realized would definitely have prevented the accident. In my opinion, the learned judges of the majority have made far too much of that which Lord Moncrieff... regarded as an admission by Mrs Alexander. It is not an admission in the sense that it can bind the appellants, though it may be of some evidential value as to what the ordinary person would regard as a reasonable standard of care...[71]

Thus, Lord Thankerton recognised that, while in certain circumstances an admission might be of probative value in determining liability, he was slow to conclude from Mrs Alexander's expression of regret anything more than that it was an indication of her feelings of sorrow for what had occurred. That was quite different from arguing that in using those words she was admitting legal

67. Thomas H Gallagher et al, 'Patients' and Physicians' Attitudes Regarding the Disclosure of Medical Errors' (2003) 289 JAMA 1001, 1005.
68. *Muir v Glasgow Corporation* [1943] AC 448 (HL). See Jeffrey S Helmreich, 'Does "Sorry" Incriminate? Evidence, Harm and the Protection of Apology' (2012) 21 Cornell JL and Public Policy 567.
69. Prue Vines, 'Apologies and Civil Liability in the UK: A View from Elsewhere' (2008) 12 Edinburgh L Rev 200.
70. [1943] AC 448 (HL).
71. ibid 455.

liability for the accident. While she might subjectively have been of the opinion that she was to blame, the test for liability in negligence was an objective one to be determined by the court.

In a similar manner, the Supreme Court of Vermont in the US case of *Senesac v Associates in Obstetrics and Gynecology*[72] held that evidence that the defendant had expressed remorse and regret for causing injury was not necessarily conclusive evidence that she was guilty of negligence. In that case, the plaintiff underwent a therapeutic abortion performed by the defendant's physician. During the procedure the plaintiff's uterus was perforated, which required her to undergo an emergency hysterectomy. The central issue in the subsequent action in negligence was an admission by the defendant's physician who stated in cross-examination that she was sorry for what had happened and that such a mistake had not ever happened to her before. One of the questions before the court was whether the doctor's admission was sufficient evidence to establish that she had acted in a manner not in accordance with general approved practice at that time. The court concluded that the doctor's admission:

> Does not establish a departure from the standard of care ordinarily exercised by a reasonably skilful gynaecologist. The fact the physician may have believed, and, if so, verbalized the belief that her performance was not in accordance with her own personal standards of care and skill, is not sufficient in the absence of expert medical evidence showing a departure from the standards of care and skill ordinarily exercised by physicians in similar cases.[73]

The doctor's statement that she was sorry for what had happened and her explanation that it had not happened to her before was interpreted by the court as a simple expression of remorse and an admission that she had made a mistake. That was not the same thing as proving that her mistake was, in law, a negligent one. As Helmreich has explained, the defendant may simply be expressing a 'self-critical view of the harm done',[74] which does not necessarily equate with an acceptance of moral or legal responsibility for that harm. He concludes that wrongdoers feel compelled to make such statements:

> ... because harming others, even blamelessly, constitutes a misuse or misfire of one's considerable efforts to avoid doing so, efforts in whose success moral agents are deeply invested. When they harm someone, then, they appropriately regard their injurious conduct with criticism, if not guilt or blame.[75]

The court will place great significance on the context and the meaning of the apology when determining whether it is an admission of liability. Certainly, admissions

---

72. 449 a2d 900 (Vt 1982).
73. ibid 903.
74. Helmreich, 'Does "Sorry" Incriminate?', 579.
75. ibid 581.

regarding particular facts may go towards proving liability, but admissions or expressions of regret of themselves do not automatically lead to the conclusion that the defendant is liable. Take, for example, a negligence claim that emanates from the defendant's actions in driving his car. If the defendant were to admit to the plaintiff, 'I'm sorry, I knew what the speed limit was and yet I drove above that speed and could not brake in time,' such a statement might be evidence going towards the defendant's liability. It goes further than the negligent driver simply expressing remorse by saying, 'I'm sorry, it was my fault,' which may be a personal (and not objective) view of his liability. However, the negligent driver's actual statement admits facts that go towards establishing objective fault – *I knew what the speed limit was and I knowingly broke that speed limit.*

The question of how apparent admissions of liability by the defendant should be treated in evidentiary terms arose in the Australian case of *Dovuro Pty Ltd v Wilkins.*[76] In that case, the appellants had sold canola seeds described as containing certain weeds and as being of 'minimum 99% purity'. At the time the appellants had imported and distributed these seeds, they had fully complied with the governmental regulatory schemes that were in place at that time. After these seeds had been purchased and planted by growers, the Western Australian agricultural authorities became concerned about the potential harm that could be caused by the weeds and prohibited their use. The crops were not damaged, but the growers brought an action in negligence against the appellants in order to recover the financial losses and expense that they [the growers] had incurred as they were required to take certain precautionary measures because of the presence of the weeds in the seed.

In their defence, the appellants argued that they had acted reasonably at all times when importing and distributing the seeds. At the time of importation, there was nothing to suggest that the canola seeds were defective and at that time they were not under an obligation to inform the growers that the seeds contained the weeds in question. Following the event, the appellants issued a media release apologising to the growers. In the media statement, the appellants stated that the situation should not have occurred but that given demand for the seeds the appellants had been forced to contract seed production outside of the country. A second apology was made in the form of a letter stating that their decision to import the seeds did 'not excuse Dovuro in failing in its duty of care to inform growers as to the presence of these weed seeds. We got it wrong in this case...'. It was claimed that both the media release and letter were evidence (by admission) that the appellants should have informed the growers of the presence of the weed seeds and were consequently liable. As to the probative value of the appellants' admissions, Gleeson CJ considered:

> [T]he care that needs to be taken in identifying the precise significance of admissions, especially when made by someone who has a private or commercial

76. (2003) 201 ALR 139.

> reason to seek to retain the goodwill of the person or persons to whom the admissions are made. Common sense may dictate that they be used with caution by a fact-finder. And it is always necessary for the fact-finder to consider precisely what it is that is being admitted... The statement that the appellant '[failed] in its duty of care to inform growers as to the presence of these weed seeds' cannot be an admission of law, and it is not useful as an admission of failure to comply with a legal standard of conduct. There is no evidence that the author of the statement knew the legal standard.[77]

In other words, the so-called admission by the appellants could not automatically be taken as conclusive evidence that they had breached the legal standard of care. In particular, the issuing of a media release containing the admission was most likely motivated by the appellants' need to maintain customer loyalty. The admissions were considered to be an exercise in public relations designed to protect the appellants' future business rather than any admission of legal wrongdoing on their part.[78]

There is no doubt that under the current state of evidence law, making an apology following involvement in an accident is fraught with legal peril for the offender. While the dangers associated with apologies are exaggerated, there is greater comfort for defendants in adopting the approach 'it's better to be safe, than to *say* you're sorry'. Context, meaning and the form of words used are all crucial. Certainly, mere expressions of sympathy or remorse will not normally give rise to liability. Even if such statements go so far as the defendant subjectively accepting blame for the accident, they are unlikely to be sufficient evidence by themselves of the defendant's objective liability. However, matters may be complicated in circumstances where, in making an apology, the defendant admits objective facts that might go towards establishing his liability. Given the level of uncertainty that exists in this regard, it is little wonder that the legal advice offered to the defendant in such circumstances is to say nothing at all. To resolve such uncertainty – and thereby increase the use of apologies – the introduction of statutory protection of such admissions is necessary. Only with such certainty can real change be effected.

The legal impediments surrounding apology are not only evidentiary. Concerns also arise in circumstances where the incident that caused the harm falls within the terms of a contract of insurance. Many insurance policies will contain a term that prohibits the policyholder from assuming any responsibility for the incident. It is conceivable that an admission by way of apology by the injured wrongdoer may be deemed to be a breach of the contract of insurance, thereby rendering

---

77. ibid para 25.
78. See also the decision in *Rhone-Poulenc Agrochimie SA v UIM Chemical Services P L* (1986) 12 FLR 477; where the court also refused to accept that the admissions made by a Mr Waugh (an employee of the defendant) during cross-examination that the defendant had engaged in 'misleading' and 'deceptive' conduct in selling products was conclusive evidence of the defendant's liability. Such legal conclusions were for the court to make and not for witnesses.

it void.[79] In such circumstances the insured wrongdoer could be exposed to the full legal and financial repercussions of his admission. While this might be an unlikely outcome, it is nevertheless a theoretical factor that will only further chill the use of apology as a response to such events.

Another great barrier to the more frequent use of apology in most common law jurisdictions would appear to be a cultural one.[80] The act of apology can be potentially humiliating for the offender and may be viewed by certain members of society as a sign of weakness on their part. By apologising and seeking forgiveness from another, one is placing one's self at the mercy of that other.[81] In a sense, one is dependent on them accepting the apology and granting forgiveness.[82] People do not naturally admit when they are wrong as, in the words of Lazare, 'it is antithetical to the ever-pervasive values of winning, success, and perfection'.[83] In the case of a professional who has wrongfully injured another in the course of providing a professional service, the incentives not to apologise are even greater. By apologising, the professional runs the risk of ruining his reputation, thereby suffering professional humiliation piled upon personal shame.

Feminist theorists of apology have argued that the gender of the offender can also be determinative as to whether an apology is likely to be forthcoming or not.[84] Orenstein, for example, has argued that 'there is much anecdotal evidence and some empirical data that the apologizers of this world – those who are empathetic, quick to accept blame, and concerned with harmony – are more likely to be women'.[85] Thus, because women are more likely to apologise, they are more likely to fall foul of the rules of evidence in jurisdictions where the consequences of such apologies are not legislatively protected. In this way, it could be argued that the failure to provide apology protection legislation disproportionately impacts on female wrongdoers in a negative manner.

Not all societies view apology in this way. In a fascinating study, Wagatsuma and Rosett examined the differing approaches and cultural attitudes towards the issue of apology in both the United States and Japan.[86] The authors found that in cases where one party was injured, Japanese people were much more likely to formally apologise than their American counterparts.[87] In such circumstances,

---

79. Jonathan R Cohen, 'Advising Clients to Apologize' (1999) 72 S Cal L Rev 1027, 1025–1026.
80. Taft, 'Apology Subverted', 1142.
81. Orenstein, 'Apology Excepted', 245–46.
82. Hiroshi Wagatsuma and Arthur Rosett, 'The Implications of Apology: Law and Culture in Japan and the United States' (1986) 20 L and Soc Rev 461, 468.
83. Aaron Lazare, 'Go Ahead Say You're Sorry' (January–February 1995) Psych Today 78.
84. Deborah Tannen, *You Just Don't Understand: Women and Men in Conversation* (Harper Collins 2001) 231–33.
85. Orenstein, 'Apology Excepted', 221, 250.
86. Wagatsuma and Rosett, 'The Implications of Apology'.
87. ibid 462.

the authors observed that, 'Americans typically will deny or challenge the claim or may try to explain and justify their actions.'[88] These differences, according to Wagatsuma and Rosett, are rooted in Japanese culture, where there is much greater interdependence among people within society. This phenomenon can be contrasted with that which arises in American culture where the independence of the individual is paramount:

> Apology may be given a lower legal priority in the United States because American society does not place as high a value on group membership, conformity, and harmonious relationships among people as Japanese society does. In a social context that highly values group hierarchy and harmony, the appearance of conflict is likely to trigger a search for accommodation and compromise that will restore the sense of group coherence. An emphasis on individual autonomy, in contrast, is likely to lead to the vigorous assertion of narrowly defined personal interests that will appear in polar conflict with the rights of others. Compensation for the economic damage done may thus become more important to the hurt party than the restoration of the relationship that has been threatened.[89]

To compound matters, the adversarial nature of the common law legal system does not lend itself well to encouraging acts of apology. In this system, the litigants are locked in something akin to a gladiatorial contest where there will only be one winner and one loser. The law, in this regard, as Truesdale has observed, 'does not seek to reconcile the relationship, only to reward the successful individual litigant. Rather than bringing people together, it forces them apart'.[90] In this arena, apologies are actively discouraged as they are viewed as being tantamount to conceding defeat. Wagatsuma and Rosett have noted that such legal systems are evidence of 'the degree to which other, individualistic values – most notably compensation, declaration of right, punishment, professional self-interest, and administrative convenience – have been elevated at the expense of the restorative capacity of law and social ceremony'.[91] Hence, in such a system, apologies tend not to be used very often as a method of resolving such matters.

The emphasis on compensation as the primary remedy for civil wrongs in common law legal systems may also be a factor explaining the limited use of the apology as a means of resolving such disputes.[92] Traditionally, the courts in this jurisdiction, like similar common law systems, have had little difficulty awarding financial compensation in cases where the loss was tangible and easily quantifiable in monetary terms. However, when presented with cases where the loss was not so easily calculated, ie cases of pure economic loss or

88. ibid.
89. ibid 493.
90. Truesdale, 'Apology Accepted', 94.
91. Wagatsuma and Rosett, 'The Implications of Apology', 494.
92. ibid 464.

psychiatric damage/emotional distress, the courts have struggled to respond. The inability of the courts to adequately remedy claims that were not easily reducible to a monetary figure coincides with the infrequent use of the apology as an alternative remedy.[93]

4. Apology Legislation

Evidence would suggest that the promotion of apology as a dispute-resolution mechanism is a good thing and should be encouraged rather than discouraged. The potential benefits from apology accrue not only to the victim but can also encompass the wrongdoer and society generally. That is not to say that the apology is a panacea. There are certain wrongs that can never be righted through words and acts of contrition alone. However, even in such cases, an apology can have a powerful effect in healing hurt feelings and changing victims' attitudes towards the wrongdoer. Together with the award of compensation an apology can be much more satisfying to the victim rather than compensation alone. Moreover, an apology may lead to lower awards of compensation as the plaintiff's resentment towards the defendant may be neutralised somewhat by the defendant's acknowledgement of his wrongdoing. This is particularly so, Vines has observed, where 'the non-economic parts of the award, such as that for pain and suffering, might be better repaired by an apology than an award of money'.[94]

It is equally clear that given the apparent legal and cultural impediments, the use of apology in facilitating the resolution of disputes will not become the norm unless some external intervention or encouragement occurs. Aside from cultural concerns, individuals fear the apology from a legal point of view. While it is by no means certain that a simple apology following an involvement in an accident that has caused injury to another will result in liability being fixed on the apologiser, sufficient uncertainty exists under the current state of the law that can inhibit an individual's natural inclination to express remorse for having wronged the victim. Until that uncertainty is removed, defendants and lawyers alike are unlikely to apologise or encourage apology in such circumstances.

---

93. For example, the Law Reform Commission in its *Report on Alternative Dispute Resolution: Mediation and Conciliation* (LRC–2010) cited the decision of the Irish Supreme Court in *Devlin v National Maternity Hospital* [2007] IESC 50 as an example of the inadequacy of the law in this regard. In that case, the plaintiffs were parents of a deceased child who were later informed that the hospital had retained the organs of the child without their knowledge. Upon receipt of this news the mother of the child suffered a psychiatric illness. The Supreme Court, in a strict interpretation of the law on this issue, held that as the mother had not 'perceived the injury' to her child, damages for her injury were not recoverable. As noted at para 7.45 of the Law Reform Commission in its *Report on Alternative Dispute Resolution: Mediation and Conciliation* (LRC–2010), had an apology and explanation been given to the plaintiffs prior to the proceedings, the litigation might have been avoided.
94. Vines, 'Power of Apology', 22.

Other jurisdictions have sought to remedy this situation by introducing apology protection legislation. The aim of such legislation is to encourage the use of apology as a dispute resolution mechanism. Such legislation would prohibit the plaintiff in any action for personal injury caused by the defendant from using the fact that the defendant apologised for his role in causing that injury. Thus, under such legislation, the defendant would be free to apologise for the accident, safe in the knowledge that any such apology would not be admissible as evidence of his liability in any subsequent legal action. Similar legislation has been introduced in various guises in Massachusetts,[95] British Columbia,[96] England and Wales,[97] while other jurisdictions such as Scotland[98] and Ireland[99] have sought to reform the law in a similar manner.

If such legislation is to be introduced it must provide full protection for apologies. It cannot be a 'halfway house' approach such as that adopted in Massachusetts, which only renders inadmissible expressions of sympathy by the defendant as evidence of an admission.[100] Such partial apology protection will not achieve the goal of encouraging the greater use of apologies. Instead, there is a danger that legislation merely protecting expressions of sympathy will be viewed with suspicion by litigants and may only add fuel to the plaintiff's anger where such apology does not include an admission of wrongdoing. Moreover, it may not always be clear where the line between expressing concern or sympathy ends and where an admission of liability begins. This uncertainty

95. Massachusetts General Laws Title II Chapter 233, s 23D provides that: 'Statements, writings or benevolent gestures expressing sympathy or a general sense of benevolence relating to the pain, suffering or death of a person involved in an accident and made to such person or to the family of such person shall be inadmissible as evidence of an admission of liability in a civil action.'
96. s 2(1) of the Apology Act 2006 provides that an apology: '(a) does not constitute an express or implied admission of fault or liability by the person in connection with that matter, (b) does not constitute a confirmation of a cause of action in relation to that matter for the purposes of section 5 of the *Limitation Act*, (c) does not, despite any wording to the contrary in any contract of insurance and despite any other enactment, void, impair or otherwise affect any insurance coverage that is available, or that would, but for the apology, be available, to the person in connection with that matter, and (d) must not be taken into account in any determination of fault or liability in connection with that matter'. Section 2(2) further provides that, '[d]espite any other enactment, evidence of an apology made by or on behalf of a person in connection with any matter is not admissible in any court as evidence of the fault or liability of the person in connection with that matter'.
97. s 2 of the Compensation Act 2006 provides 'An apology, an offer of treatment or other redress, shall not of itself amount to an admission of negligence or breach of statutory duty.'
98. Apologies (Scotland) Bill 2012.
99. Law Reform Commission, *Report on Alternative Dispute Resolution: Mediation and Conciliation* (LRC–2010).
100. Massachusetts General Laws Title II Chapter 233, s 23D.

will only 'chill' the use of apology rather than encourage it. It is submitted that legislation similar to that adopted in British Columbia in the form of the Apology Act 2006, providing comprehensive protection to apology, should be introduced. Such a development would remove all legal ambiguity surrounding the apology process and thereby remove a major obstacle to the delivery of apologies. The legislation should provide broad protection of apologies and should provide for a statutory definition of apology that includes an expression of remorse and an acknowledgement of fault; a clear statement that an apology does not constitute an express or implied admission of fault or liability, nor is it evidence by itself of negligence; that an apology does not constitute confirmation of a cause of action for the purposes of the Statute of Limitations; and that an apology does not void any applicable contract of insurance. Finally, such legislation should only apply to civil actions involving personal injury.

Critics of 'safe harbour' legislation for apologies have argued that it destroys the essence of an apology. Such critics would contend that the provision of a 'safety net' for those who apologise by protecting them from the legal consequences of such an act, strips apology of its integrity and will result in an increase in strategic – and not genuine – apologies. If the victim interprets the apology as insincere, there is a real danger that the wrongdoer's actions will 'rub salt in the wounds' of the victim and as a consequence make resolution of the dispute even more difficult.

Taft is a proponent of the view that once an apology enters the legal arena it becomes corrupted.[101] In his view, apology is a moral act and once it forms part of the negotiation between the parties who are attempting to settle a dispute, it becomes a bargaining chip or an 'object of exchange'.[102] In other words, apology stripped of its moral meaning loses its healing force and becomes subverted. Thus, when apology is viewed in 'utilitarian terms',[103] its moral force and ability to heal is greatly diminished:

> In this exchange scenario, apology becomes part of a bargain that requires two independent parties. In this transaction, '[t]he injured party depends on the offender's taking responsibility for the offensive act, and the offender depends on the injured party for absolution' for the mediation to succeed. Success here is measured by settlement rather than by moral restoration. Cast in this way, the apology itself becomes an 'exchangeable good.' The apology is seen to produce a 'happy ending' because each party saves time and fees... Missing from the exchange model is 'the moral climate or sensibility required for authentic and effective apologetic discourse.' From a moral perspective, the bargained-for apology... is not an authentic apology. This is because authentic 'apology cannot come about and do its work under conditions where the primary function of speech is defensive or purely instrumental and where legalities take precedence over moral imperatives.'[104]

101. Taft, 'Apology Subverted', 1157.
102. ibid 1149.
103. Taft, 'Apology Subverted'.
104. ibid 1149.

In Taft's view, the morality of apology lies in the fact that not only does the offender acknowledge that he has committed a wrong but also in the fact that he accepts responsibility for the harm he has caused.[105] Legislation that protects the offender from the consequences of his wrongdoing undermines the power and morality of apology. Taft laments the fact that – as he sees it – those jurisdictions that protect apologies 'place more value on the settlement of lawsuits than on accepting responsibility for the harms we have caused'.[106] However, Taft's view fails to take into consideration the fact that the wrongdoer may have good reasons to apologise without wishing to accept the legal consequences that may attach to such an apology. In this regard, Helmreich has noted that:

> Many apologizers may be in no position to compensate their victim and, in any event, they may legitimately expect that the liability likely to be imposed on them following litigation would be excessive. They may, in other words, admit and be willing to take moral responsibility but not necessarily the extent of legal responsibility they expect to be assigned. Thus they may seek to fulfil their moral duty to apologize but have good reasons to resist legal liability.[107]

Thus, while the defendant may have been an agent in causing the plaintiff's injuries, he may not have been legally to blame. Nevertheless, the defendant may feel that he is responsible for the damage and may wish to apologise for his role in bringing the damage about. In such circumstances, why should he expose himself to the risk of a damages award simply where his moral code dictates that he should apologise?

In addition to questions of morality, legislation that attempts to protect apology may cause greater harm than good in terms of bringing about reconciliation. Indeed, Latif has observed that a legally protected apology may be 'inimical'[108] to resolving such disputes. She notes that where an apology has been made by one of the parties, which is not admitted as evidence on the basis that it is legally protected, the court may, nevertheless, learn of the existence of the apology and consequently 'may lower damage awards under the idea that the apology was a partial remedy for the dispute'.[109] This may be so, even where the victim may not have wanted the apology in the first place and had rejected it.

It may be the case that the introduction of legislation that protects apologies may encourage the use of strategic and less-than-genuine admissions. However, there is no evidence that the use of strategic apologies will increase. Moreover, this threat alone is not a sufficient justification to ignore the benefits that will accrue with

105. Lee Taft, 'Apology Within a Moral Dialectic: A Reply to Professor Robbennolt' (2004–2005) 103 Mich L Rev 1010.
106. ibid 1017.
107. Helmreich, 'Does "Sorry" Incriminate?', 580.
108. Latif, 'Apologetic Justice', 310.
109. ibid.

the passing of such legislation. While for many people the healing force of apology lies in the fact that 'the law attaches consequences to apologizing',[110] apologies can also have a positive impact in resolving disputes even in circumstances where the apology is not risk-laden for the offender. Apology legislation may lead to an increase in strategic apologies, some of which may be unlikely to affect reconciliation between the litigants; however, it will also encourage the 'stampede'[111] of genuine and heartfelt apologies that will promote resolution of disputes. An apology will also lead to the reduction of awards where the apology assists in the victim's psychological healing.[112] Apologies open the door to reconciliation between the parties. By apologising, the offender can commence a dialogue with the victim that may ultimately lead to a resolution of the dispute between the parties. However, without apology legislation the offender is unwilling to take that first step:

> There is a natural, human way of dealing with injuries: talking directly with the other person about what has happened. Apologies are a key part of those conversations. By allowing apologies to be admitted in court, our laws inhibit the natural dialogue. Instead of people talking with one another directly after injuries, in our culture all too often they *begin by or soon start* talking through lawyers. The fact that apologies can be used as proof in court inhibits people from entering that human dialogue, that human encounter. And that's precisely when disputes escalate. *The issue is not the sincerity or insincerity of the apology, as you call it, but whether that dialogue takes place.*[113]

Taft is correct when he states that an apology is an essentially moral act and that its moral basis may be undermined where the offender is protected from the legal consequences of his apology. However, the value of apology does not solely lie in the fact that its maker is not shielded from the legal consequences of his apology. As Helmreich has pointed out, apology protection legislation will not necessarily destroy apology's moral value. Instead, it will facilitate and encourage those who genuinely wish to acknowledge their mistake and accept responsibility for it.

The Irish legislature has already recognised the merits of statutory intervention in this area. Section 24(1) of the Defamation Act 2009 provides that an apology made by a defendant in the context of a defamation action may be used as evidence in mitigation of damage. Crucially, however, s 24(3) provides that where such an apology is made it cannot constitute an express or implied admission of liability by the defendant and would not be deemed relevant to the question of liability in the case. In such circumstances, it is difficult to justify

110. Cohen, 'Legislating Apology', 847–48.
111. Truesdale, 'Apology Accepted', 90.
112. ibid.
113. Cohen, 'Legislating Apology', 848.

the refusal to extend such protection to other areas of tort law, such as those involving personal injury.

The introduction of such legislation will encourage the making of more apologies, not just strategic ones. In this way dialogue is encouraged at an early stage of the dispute and should facilitate a resolution of the dispute without resorting to litigation. The fact that in some limited cases the wrongdoer might deliver a transparently insincere apology that could inflame tensions and escalate the conflict between the parties is an unjustifiable reason not to protect those who genuinely wish to express their remorse and acknowledge their wrongdoing. As Cohen commented, 'the law should not punish people from taking a moral step'.[114] Moreover, in a society where apologies are encouraged, it is more likely that mistakes will be corrected and less likely that those mistakes will be repeated than in a society where secrecy prevails because admissions may be punishable by the law. Furthermore, much can also be learned from strategically delivered apologies – even where insincerely delivered – as they can act as 'teachable moments' for the rest of society. By apologising when he does not want to, the defendant sends a signal to the rest of society that he realises that his behaviour was not acceptable.

While apology protection legislation may encourage strategic apologies, there is no evidence that such apologies will succeed.[115] Nor would evidence suggest that an apology protected by legislation would be perceived any differently by the victim.[116] This is because the power still remains with the victim as he is the only party who can decide whether or not to grant the wrongdoer forgiveness. This remains the case regardless of whether the apology is protected by legislation or not. Apology protection legislation will not force an offender to make an apology – the decision to apologise will still be his to make. Delivering an apology – genuinely or otherwise – still involves a shaming ritual where the offender is placing himself at the mercy of the victim in seeking the victim's forgiveness. In this way, the offender acknowledges his wrongdoing and the victim's status in the community is restored. Thus, on certain occasions, a victim will 'feel satisfaction in seeing a defendant make an apology that she did not want to make'.[117] In this way, the making of the apology regardless of the motives behind it can act as a catalyst for the victim's healing.

Notwithstanding the existence of legislation, lawyers will have a critical role to play in settlement negotiations that include an apology.[118] Studies have

---

114. Cohen, 'Legislating Apology'.
115. Prue Vines, 'Apologising to Avoid Liability: Cynical Civility or Practical Morality?' (2005) 21 Sydney L Rev 483.
116. Robbennolt, 'Apologies and Legal Settlement'.
117. White, 'Say You're Sorry'.
118. Russell Korobkin and Chris Guthrie, 'Psychology, Economics, and Settlement: A New Look at the Role of the Lawyer' (1997) 76 Tex L Rev 77, 81.

shown that lawyers are likely to have a major influence on settlement decisions made by clients.[119] Because the lawyers representing the parties are not invested personally in the dispute they have a certain emotional detachment that might facilitate the resolution of the dispute and they will be more likely to identify the sincerity or otherwise of the apology on offer.[120] This emotional detachment also means that the lawyer will be less likely to feel obliged to accept an apology made by the other side and will protect his vulnerable client from accepting a strategic apology designed to avoid paying the victim appropriate compensation. However, when acting for clients in settlement negotiations, lawyers must be conscious of the fact that their training can inhibit rather than facilitate settlements involving apologies. The typical lawyer's negotiation style is adversarial, where one is trained to reveal or concede little. Moreover, lawyers typically put a different outcome value on negotiations than a layperson tends to. Whereas a lawyer might be focused on protecting his client's legal rights and entitlements, the client might be more concerned with vindication.[121] As Riskin observed:

> Lawyers are trained to put people and events into categories that are legally meaningful, to think in terms of rights and duties established by rules, to focus on acts more than persons. This view requires a strong development of cognitive capabilities, which is often attended by the under-cultivation of emotional faculties.[122]

Thus, it is critical that lawyers maintain a broader view of the dispute involving their client in order that they may protect his psychological/emotional interests as well as his legal ones. As part of this process it is essential that the lawyer identifies what it is that the client hopes to achieve from the negotiation.[123] Only then can he craft a solution likely to meet those needs.[124] Finally, where an apology is sought from his client, the lawyer must be mindful of the fact that it is much more likely to be accepted if delivered by the client rather than through his lawyer.[125]

---

119. Jennifer K Robbennolt, 'Attorneys, Apologies, and Settlement Negotiation' (2008) 13 Harv Negot L Rev 349.
120. ibid.
121. Craig A McEwen et al, 'Lawyers, Mediation, and the Management of Divorce Practice' (1994) 28 Law and Soc Rev 149; Korobkin and Guthrie, 'Psychology, Economics, and Settlement', 82.
122. Chris Guthrie, 'The Lawyers' Philosophical Map and the Disputant's Perceptual Map: Impediments to Facilitative Mediation and Lawyering' (2001) 6 Harv Negot L Rev 145.
123. Russell B Korobkin, 'Aspirations and Settlement' (2002) 88 Cornell L Rev 1.
124. See generally, William L Ury, Jeanne M Brett and Stephen B Goldberg, *Getting Disputes Resolved: Designing Systems to Cut the Costs of Conflict* (Jolley–Bass 1988).
125. Jennifer K Robbennolt, 'The Effects of Negotiated and Delegated Apologies in Settlement Negotiation' (2013) 37 Law and Human Behavior 28.

Conclusion

Too often after suffering an injury at the hands of a wrongdoer, the victim is left to deal with the consequences on his own. Whether he wishes to apologise or not, the wrongdoer is taught that apologising is a sign of weakness. The law as it currently stands discourages wrongdoers from taking a positive step such as accepting responsibility and expressing contrition for injuries caused. In particular, there is a fear among defendants that any admission of responsibility will attract civil liability for their role in the events in question. As we have seen, such fears are exaggerated but nevertheless uncertainty does exist that has the effect of chilling the greater use of apology in such circumstances.

The power of apology to mend relationships, heal psychological scars and facilitate the resolution of disputes before they escalate into a costly legal battle has been recognised by lawyers and sociologists alike. An apology can restore dignity to the victim, integrity to the wrongdoer and educate society generally on acceptable and unacceptable behaviour. As a society, we should actively promote the use of apology to assist in the resolution of disputes between parties. It will not resolve all such disputes, particularly where the injuries are catastrophic. However, even in such circumstances it will go some way towards repairing the relationship between the parties; it may possibly restore the status of the wrongdoer within the community and may heal some of the psychological pain suffered by the plaintiff. In cases where the physical injuries are not as severe, but the emotional trauma real, an apology might be the most appropriate remedy.

The promotion of apologies in the legal setting can most effectively be done by the introduction of apology protection legislation similar to that recommended in the LRC report on *Alternative Dispute Resolution: Mediation and Conciliation*. However, unlike that report, such legislation should not be limited to medical professionals and should be open to all. It is only through the implementation of a clear legislative framework that the cultural and legal barriers that currently prevent the use of apology will be overcome.

Critics of legislative intervention argue that offering such protection to an apology destroys its very essence and will only encourage cynical and strategic apologies. However, an argument that such legislation should not be introduced simply on the basis that there exists the possibility that some defendants will abuse its protection and attempt to manipulate the plaintiff by cynically apologising is not a justifiable excuse for failing to act in this area. While such legislation might encourage the greater use of strategic apology, it will also free those who genuinely wish to apologise from the shackles in which they currently find themselves. Even with the protection of such legislation, offering a cynical apology is a high-risk strategy for the defendant. First, there is no evidence that such apologies will work. There is a real danger that if the plaintiff considers the apology to be insincere, it will only worsen the situation for the defendant as it may serve to further anger the plaintiff, strengthen his resolve to follow through with his action and consequently might lead to an increase in the quantum of damages that the defendant must pay. Second, the simple fact that the defendant has apologised – especially if publicly – will sometimes be sufficient for the plaintiff even where he knows it is insincere. For the plaintiff, there may be some satisfaction in knowing that he has regained some power over the defendant by forcing him into an apology he otherwise may not have been inclined to make. Sometimes healing comes from the act itself. In fact, as Orenstein has commented, '… the better question is not why some people issue insincere apologies, but rather why, given the benefits of apologies, do so many people fail to issue them at all'.[126]

Apologies are not appropriate for everyone and cannot erase all wrongs. On the other hand, '[t]he practice of never apologizing is not in the public interest because it leads to litigation rather than reconciliation'.[127] The introduction of apology protection legislation will do no more than encourage those of us who wish to listen to the better angels of our nature and act accordingly. Apology protection legislation will not force any individual into doing something that they do not wish to do. Ultimately, the power to forgive rests with the victim and it is for them to decide whether the wrongdoer's apology is acceptable or not. However, by providing litigants with the space to open dialogue without fear of legal sanction, we create an environment where disputes can be better resolved to the satisfaction of all concerned. Apology can be the vital first step in that healing process and we must do more to promote its use in such circumstances. Only statutory intervention can provide the certainty that is required.

---

126. Orenstein, 'Apology Excepted', 245.
127. Rehm and Beatty, 'Legal Consequences' (1996) J Disp Resol 115, 119.

Reappraising the Constitutional Justification for Intentionalism and Literalism in Statutory Interpretation

Cathal Curran* and Eoin Daly**

Abstract—It is widely assumed that a constitutional principle of legislative supremacy confines judges, in interpreting statutes, to the modest role of effectuating legislative intention. In this article, however, we argue that statutory meaning is inevitably determined by constitutional and normative desiderata which are irreducible to legislative intention. Moreover, the prevailing account of statutory interpretation masks this by positing literal meaning as the default expression of legislative intent. The public values which inevitably inform statutory interpretation cannot be imputed to legislative intent. Constitutional principles cannot be conceived of solely as a 'trump' on legislative intent in 'frontier' cases where legislation is invalidated; they are also constitutive of statutory meaning across a much wider range of cases, independently of legislative intent. We argue that since the principle of legislative supremacy is so strongly qualified in the Irish context, it cannot support a theory of intentionalism in statutory interpretation.

Introduction

It is a truism that principles of statutory interpretation are derivative of constitutional theory. In the common law world, the conventional theories are based on legislative supremacy as a constitutional principle. Thus, in interpreting statutes, courts are to assume a mechanical and uncreative role in ascertaining parliamentary intent, thereby respecting the constitutional pre-eminence of the legislature as a deliberative, accountable lawmaking authority. Therefore, while intentionalism suggests that statutory meaning is determined by the legislature's intent, this is grounded in normative as well as interpretive theory: for courts to supplant legislative intent is seen as fundamentally undemocratic. It is commonly held that the default method of discovering parliamentary intent is a literalist approach to interpreting statutes, whereby the 'plain meaning' of statutory words is to be privileged subject to certain exceptions. However, even where literal meaning is departed from or qualified, alternative sources of statutory meaning are still routinely attributed to legislative intent. Thus, while

* PhD candidate, Trinity College Dublin.

** Lecturer, University College Dublin.

the Irish courts do not purport to apply a strictly literalist approach in statutory interpretation, their commitment to intentionalism is quite unyielding. Indeed, the prevailing account presupposes an inherent link between literalism and the effectuation of legislative intent.[1] Literalism in statutory interpretation – while not itself absolutist – is merely derivative of intentionalism and in turn, intentionalism is rooted in the legislative supremacy of parliament as a central constitutional principle. In contrast, constitutional interpretation is thought to be necessarily 'broader', given the wider scope of constitutional provisions as the political–moral framework for a state.[2]

There are numerous objections, rooted in hermeneutic and semantic theory, to literalism and intentionalism as theories of statutory interpretation.[3] In this article, however, we question their constitutional justification specifically. On the one hand, we argue that the location of these doctrines in the constitutional separation of powers is incoherent at least in the context of a codified constitution where the doctrine of legislative supremacy exists only in a very qualified and diluted form: hemmed in, most notably, by the principle of constitutional supremacy itself. Whereas standard accounts seek to justify intentionalism and literalism based on a constitutional theory of institutional competence, the broader principle of constitutional supremacy means that various constitutional principles will be used in ascertaining statutory meaning. Specifically, we argue that constitutional supremacy is given expression not only through the invalidation of unconstitutional statutes: it also requires statutes to be read through the lens of constitutional principle. Moreover, contrary to the prevailing doctrines, the constitutional principles that inform statutory meaning are irreducible to legislative intent. In turn, this undermines intentionalism as an overarching theory of statutory interpretation.

We aim to illustrate how, in Ireland, judicial interpretations of constitutional right – and other normative standards external to legislative intent – already play a strong (albeit unacknowledged) role in statutory interpretation in a manner that undermines the prevailing intentionalist theory. In particular, the 'presumption of constitutionality' – the requirement to give constitutionally contestable statutes a narrower, constitutional reading – means that judicial interpretations of constitutional principle already represent an important source of statutory meaning. Despite protestations of formalistic restraint, this grants judges more autonomy and latitude than the prevailing intentionalism can accommodate – because the constitutional dimensions of statutory meaning simply cannot be subsumed within legislative intent as an overarching default source. In this light, intentionalism may serve simply to obscure the role of normative desiderata in statutory interpretation.

1. See David Dodd, *Statutory Interpretation in Ireland* (Tottel Publishing 2008) ch 5.
2. See, eg, *Sullivan v Robinson* [1954] IR 161.
3. See generally Andre Marmor, *Interpretation and Legal Theory* (Clarendon Press 1994), and particularly Ian MacLean, 'Responsibility and the Act of Interpretation' in Ian MacLean, Alan Montefiore and Peter Winch (eds), *The Political Responsibility of Intellectuals* (Cambridge University Press 1992).

In turn, we also challenge the prevailing view that constitutional and statutory interpretation operate in distinctive spheres. Constitutional principle should not be viewed solely as a 'trump' on statutory validity in the context of judicial review of legislation: rather it should also be conceived of as partly constitutive of statutory meaning, at least in a broad range of cases.

Part 1 describes how literalist approaches to statutory interpretation have been grounded in a broader theory of intentionalism, which portrays statutory interpretation as a process of recovering legislative intent. Part 2 considers the origins of intentionalism in constitutional principles of parliamentary sovereignty (in Britain) and correspondingly legislative supremacy (in Ireland). However, Part 3 argues that principles of statutory interpretation cannot be grounded in a constitutional principle of legislative supremacy. It illustrates various ways in which, despite the prevailing intentionalist doctrine, existing methods of statutory interpretation rely on normative sources that are irreducible to legislative intent. The theoretical implications of this argument are then considered.

1. Intentionalism and Literalism in the Orthodox Approach to Statutory Interpretation

Under the prevailing doctrine, as a general rule the point of departure for courts in interpreting statutes is to effectuate legislative intention by articulating the literal meaning of the statutory text.[4] The standard account of statutory interpretation holds that where a literal or plain meaning is forthcoming the interpreter gives effect to that meaning, and by extension the intent of the legislature, and does not engage in any further interpretation. Per *Driedger on the Construction of Statutes*:

> 1. Courts are obliged to give effect to the intention of the legislature as revealed by the literal meaning of the legislative text.
> 2. Where the literal meaning of the text is clear or 'plain', the task of interpretation is done and the court should not worry about legislative purpose or look to other aids to interpretation…
> 3. Where the literal meaning of the text is clear or plain, this meaning governs regardless of consequences…[5]

---

4. This foundational presupposition is not a specifically Irish phenomenon; it can also be found in discussion of the British and Canadian approaches to statutory interpretation. While the arguments considered here point to problems in the default preference for literalism in the Irish context; at a conceptual level in the UK and Canada, literalism also acts as an operative presupposition from which statutory interpretations begin, despite the obvious constitutional differences across these legal systems. Thus, while we discuss the default position of the literal approach in Ireland, and the considerable authority for such a presupposition, it is beyond the scope of this paper to delve into the distinct constitutional features that necessarily affect this starting point – for example, the difference between legislative supremacy denoted by the separation of powers in Ireland, and the principle of parliamentary sovereignty in the UK, and how these affect the interpretative approaches of respective courts.
5. Ruth Sullivan, *Dreidger on the Construction of Statutes* (3rd edn, Butterworths 1994) 1.

It is said that as a default if not absolutist position, the Irish courts endorse the objective intention of the legislature through a strictly literal interpretation of the statutory text.[6] In *Crilly v T & J Farrington Ltd*,[7] a seminal Irish case in the context of statutory interpretation, the court had to consider whether parliamentary debates and other extrinsic materials could be taken into account in articulating the intention of the legislature. In that case textual ambiguity as to the calculation of a charge under s 2 of the Health (Amendment) Act 1986 required the court to consider the doctrinal approach to statutory interpretation in Ireland, and whether the courts should countenance altering the default position of the literal rule in that regard. In considering the question of legislative intent, the court underlined the importance of looking to the objective intention of parliament in the context of the plain meaning rule, affirming a consistent link between the two concepts:

> ... what the courts in this country have always sought to ascertain is the objective intent or will of the legislature. This is evident for example from the rule of construction according to which when the meaning of the statute is clear and definite and open to one interpretation only in the context of the statute as a whole, that is the meaning to be attributed to it.

The orthodox view thus implies a necessary connection between literal meaning and legislative intention, despite the clear tension between what we might term the 'formal realisation of determinate language' under the literal rule as denoted by the second point from Dreidger above, and the wholly different goal of effectuating the aims encapsulated or 'intended' in legislation.[8] Accordingly, no conceptual distinction seems to be made between legislative intention on the one hand, and the *meaning* effectuated by the statutory language on the other, these being presumed – somewhat peculiarly – to be mutually inclusive. Proponents of conventional theory such as FAR Bennion[9] and David Dodd,[10]

---

6. As was held in *People (Attorney General) v Dwyer* [1972] IR 416: Dodd, *Statutory Interpretation*, 22. For a discussion of the literal rule in Ireland see also Raymond Byrne and Paul McCutcheon, *Byrne and McCutcheon on the Irish Legal System* (5th edn, Bloomsbury Professional 2009) paras 14.20–14.23, 562–63. See also the judgment of Blayney J in *Howard v Commissioner of Public Works in Ireland* [1994] IR 101, 151, a case regarded by Justice Hugh Geoghegan as one of the most significant in the Irish context of statutory interpretation, in *Statutory Interpretation in the Context of the Irish Constitution* <http://www.statutelawsociety.org/data/assets/pdf_file/0003/84702/Statutory_Interpretation_in_the_context of_the_Irish_Constitution._Mr_Justice_Hugh_Geoghegan.pdf> 5, accessed 29 April 2013.
7. [2001] 3 IR 251.
8. This points to a considerable debate between textualists and intentionalists who differ in their conceptualisation of statutory interpretation. We argue that an interpretation cannot simultaneously speak to literal meaning and intention, as these concern divergent outcomes.
9. Francis Bennion, *Bennion on Statutory Interpretation* (5th edn, Butterworths 2008) 469.
10. Dodd, *Statutory Interpretation*, 25.

outlining the UK and Irish positions respectively, assume this position, stating that effectuating the literal meaning of the statute and the legislative intention are both the starting point and the end towards which statutory interpretation is aimed, one facilitating the other (notwithstanding well-known exceptions to the literal rule). However, this disregards the creative nature of judicial interpretation and presents a deductive process comparable to rule formalism. This idea implies that the meaning of the law is 'immanently intelligible',[11] intimating that statutes do not require judicial interpretation for legislative meaning or intent to be discerned.[12] Therefore, it seems that the conventional theory of statutory interpretation as outlined – with its default (if not automatic) recourse to literal meaning as expressive of legislative intent – ignores the inevitable creative aspects of adjudication which, in reality, underlie an inevitable decoupling of statutory meaning and legislative intent.

By this argument 'plain' meaning might be imagined to exist independently of the selection of any interpretative criteria. This, however, implies that the literal approach exists separately from other interpretative methods, as if literal meaning somehow precedes interpretation itself.[13] Indeed, the foundational rationale behind the literal rule as a means of ascertaining legislative intention suggests that literalism is inherently un-interpretative. The standard approach, then, is undermined by the fact that courts retain quite a degree of discretion in applying interpretative criteria on their own merits in particular cases, a fact acknowledged by Dodd in the Irish context.[14] This discretionary application, described by Bell and Engle in *Cross* as a 'statement of attitude or approach'[15] by the courts, undermines the sense that the rules of statutory interpretation, such as the literal rule, manifest themselves as actual 'rules' *per se*.[16]

---

11. Dennis Patterson, *Law & Truth* (Oxford University Press 1996) 25.
12. For a thorough analysis of formalist and realist perspectives on adjudication in the context of the interpretation of statutes see Richard Posner, 'Legal Formalism, Legal Realism, and the Interpretation of Statutes and the Constitution' (1986–87) 37 Case W Res L Rev 179.
13. Neil McCormick et al, *Interpreting Statutes* (Aldershot 1991) 466.
14. Dodd, *Statutory Interpretation*, 36, in relation to the judgment of the court in *Gooden v St Otteran's Hospital* [2005] 3 IR 617, 639. See Antonin Scalia, *A Matter of Interpretation, Federal Courts and the Law* (Princeton University Press 1998), rejecting the discretionary picture that realists such as Karl Llewellyn paint of the application of the canons of construction, see Karl Llewellyn, 'Remarks on the Theory of Appellate Decisions and the Rules or Canons about how Statutes Are to Be Construed' (1950) 3 Vanderbilt L Rev 395. Scalia has observed that arguments such as Llewellyn's do not unhinge the relevance or importance of the interpretative criteria; rather, Llewellyn succeeds merely in showing that no one canon of construction is absolute, see Scalia, A *Matter of Interpretation*, 27.
15. John Bell and George Engle, *Cross on Statutory Interpretation* (3rd edn, Butterworths 1995) 42.
16. This issue was explicitly adverted to by Murray J in *Crilly v T & J Farrington Ltd*, where it was stated: '...the use of any rule of construction as evidenced in judgments of the

Thus, there is a divergence in accounts of the operation of the literal rule – as between a rule denoting the formal application of rules of language, and an attitudinal or contextual approach to statutory terms, which has at its end point the articulation of the legislative intention. However, in the Irish context, the court in *McGrath v McDermott* stressed the necessity of limiting judicial deviation from the statutory text, implying that while the 'literal rule' does not necessarily require the formal realisation of language, the courts will follow the words of the text as far as possible, taking contextual issues into account:

> The function of the Courts in interpreting a statute of the Oireachtas [parliament] is... strictly confined to ascertaining the true meaning of each statutory provision, resorting in cases of doubt or ambiguity to a consideration of the purpose and intention of the legislature to be inferred from other provisions of the statute involved, or even other statutes expressed to be construed with it. The Courts have not got a function to add to or leave from express statutory provisions so as to achieve the objectives which to the court seem desirable. In rare or limited circumstances words or phrases may be implied into statutory provisions solely for the purpose of making them effective to achieve their expressly avowed objective.[17]

While this might assert a common-sense approach to the plain meaning rule, it is nonetheless problematic in necessitating a departure from the mechanical conception of the literal rule in the resort to context. That is, on using the literal or plain meaning rule, the question arises whether we are speaking to the purposes of the statute generally in articulating the legislative intention, or whether intention in this context refers to intended meaning. Given that the literal rule is said to concern the language of the statute and not the statutory aims, it seems appropriate that judges consider the intended meaning of the language of the statutory text.[18] However, the courts do not take an absolute position on this, insisting that discerning intention is the ultimate end of statutory interpretation.[19]

This quandary is highlighted in *Rahill v Brady*,[20] in which the court considered whether a cattle mart held twice a week over a year qualified for a 'special event' licence under the Intoxicating Liquor Act 1962. This is regarded as a 'classic statement of the literal rule'[21] in Irish jurisprudence, although it has been

---

courts is rarely other than an ad hoc illustration of its use rather than a decision in principle'. [2001] 3 IR 251.

17. [1998] 1 IR 258, 276.
18. Dodd, however, has suggested that intention in this context refers to the intended *application* of the statute. This seems incorrect, as speaking to intended application then blurs the distinction between legislative intent and the *purpose* of legislation, a separate interpretative device. Dodd, *Statutory Interpretation*, 115.
19. See, for example, the judgment of Denham J in *Lawlor v Flood* [1999] 3 IR 107, 136–37.
20. [1971] IR 69 (SC).
21. Law Reform Commission, 'Report on Statutory Drafting and Interpretation: Plain Language and the Law' [61–2000] 11.

described as a conservative articulation of it.[22] The Supreme Court found that the case hinged primarily on a contextual reading of the section, given that there was no statutory definition for the phrase 'special event' in s 11(1). The court applied the ordinary meaning of the word 'special' in the sense of something that was not commonplace, or out of the ordinary. Per Budd J:

> In the absence of some special technical or acquired meaning, the language of a statute should be construed according to its ordinary meaning and in accordance with the rules of grammar. While the literal construction generally has *prima facie* preference, there is also the further rule that in seeking the true construction of a section of an Act the whole Act must be looked at in order to see what the objects and intention of the legislature were; but the ordinary meaning of words should not be departed from unless adequate grounds can be found in the context in which the words are used to indicate that a literal interpretation would not give the real intention of the legislature.

Considering the literal rule as articulated under the prevailing theory, this conception proves awkward in that it lays down a *condition precedent* concerning the application of literal meaning – requiring that the court first take contextual issues into account, apart from the mere language of the text, in construing the Act as a whole. This involves the interplay of literal interpretation and what could very loosely be described as a form of purposive interpretation, as a means of arriving at the 'ordinary' or plain meaning. How the literal approach retains a default interpretative status or a *prima facie* preference in light of this interplay is open to question, given that the additional criteria or contextual matters that must be taken into account seem contingent on the use of the literal approach, and vice versa. There is ample evidence in academic commentary[23] as well as case law like *Rahill* to suggest that the terms 'literal meaning' and 'plain meaning' have, consistently and misleadingly, been conflated, although it is far from clear that those labels speak to the same kinds of meaning.[24] Thus, literalism is to prevail up until an indeterminate point where context is needed, but this means, in turn, that some purposive, contextual or non-literalist appraisal precedes and circumscribes the actual remit of the default literalism. The extent of

---

22. Sean Patrick Donlan and Ronán Kennedy, 'A Flood of Light?: Comments on the Interpretation Act 2005' (2006) 6 Judicial Studies Institute Journal 1, 114.
23. [1971] IR 69, 86.
24. ibid. Ruth Sullivan has argued that the labels 'literal', 'plain' and 'ordinary' meaning are often used to denote the same types of meaning, but are not necessarily inclusive: see Ruth Sullivan, 'Statutory Interpretation in the Supreme Court of Canada' (1998–99) 30 *Ottawa L Rev* 1–45. Indeed, Summers and Marshall propose quite a discrete interpretative argument from the platform of 'ordinary meaning', highlighting the minute differences between ordinary and plain meaning in Robert S. Summers and Geoffrey Marshall, 'The Argument from Ordinary Meaning in Statutory Interpretation' (1992) 43 NI Legal Quarterly 213.

the pre-eminence of the literal meaning must, in fact, spring from an eminently purposive or contextual assessment.

In light of these inconsistencies, then, the point at which literalism can be said to no longer apply tells us much about the operation of the literal rule; whether or not it can legitimately be said to occupy the default interpretative position as provided for under the principle of legislative supremacy, and in turn whether the purported differences between statutory and constitutional interpretation are in fact plausible. Where the court cannot arrive at a plain or literal meaning of the statutory text – that is, where a literal interpretation would give rise to ambiguity or absurdity – it must engage in a purposive reading of the statute to ascertain the legislative intent. Thus, Dodd argues: 'if a provision is found to be entirely plain and incapable of bearing more than one meaning, effect must normally be given to that plain meaning, and purpose will play little or no role'.[25] However, this seems incorrect because it assumes that the method by which we ascertain a provision's plain meaning is superseded by the fact that a meaning is arrived at; that is, the result proves more important than the procedure. This presupposes the idea of plain meaning as a given; thus, the hypothesis becomes the premise. If the courts are to effectuate plain meaning, the question must first be asked: 'Is this statutory provision absurd, or does the language of the section include any absurdity?' This is inversely purposive: it is, in effect, a purposive question – essentially we are asking 'Does the language of this section permit straightforward application?' or 'Will it be formally realised?', but in order to do so, we must first conceive of the intended contextual application of the provision.[26] A contextual appraisal of intention *precedes* any ascertainment of 'plain' meaning; thus, literalism can no longer be viewed as a default expression of intention.

The paradox can thus be expressed as follows: literal meaning is supposed to convey legislative intent unless, in context, it appears contrary to the legislature's aims – yet this requires an appraisal of legislative aims *antecedent* to the statute's literal meaning. This assumes that there is always a need to inquire as to potential absurdities and accordingly undermines the notion that there is in most instances an institutionally validated, legitimate plain meaning that precedes independent appraisal by the courts. If it is not possible to observe absurdity without resort to purpose, and if our default interpretative position is the literal approach, purpose must then be ascertained in all cases.[27] Thus, literal interpretations rely on a purposive methodology. On this understanding we cannot interpret literally at all, and the conception of statutory interpretation as necessarily uncreative collapses.

---

25. Dodd, *Statutory Interpretation*, 168.
26. However, Dodd notes this incongruity in another section of his book: ibid 190, 195.
27. For a detailed analysis of the foundational role played by the resort to absurdity and purpose in the interpretation of statutes, see John Manning, 'The Absurdity Doctrine' (2002–03) 116 Harv L Rev 2387.

The Irish courts have attempted to circumvent this predicament by suggesting there is a need to respect a balance between the competing alternatives of literal meaning and purpose – as suggested in the judgment of Denham J in the case of *DPP (Ivers) v Murphy*.[28] In that case Denham J found that while it was essential for the courts to identify and engage a clear statutory purpose when encountering absurdity, she nevertheless adverted that the courts in interpreting legislation had to respect constitutionally protected institutional competences:

> While no method of statutory interpretation could be adopted which would impinge upon the constitutional role of the Oireachtas as the legislative organ of the State, if the court adopted a literal approach to the interpretation of s.6 of the 1997 Act it would produce the absurd result of requiring the presence of a Garda in court to prove that his presence was not required. Therefore, the court was entitled to look at the purpose for which the provision was enacted...

While Denham J's rationale here points to the obvious need to balance the dangers of injustices produced by unyielding literalism against the spectre of judicial legislation,[29] this seems to undermine the default position of literalism under the prevailing theory, as the courts themselves implicitly recognise the limitations of the literal rule, and the correlative requirement, in certain circumstances, to engage in corrective forms of adjudication in order to effectuate the intentions of the legislature. Indeed, Brady's claim that the attempt to 'regulate' departures from the literal rule under s 5 of the Interpretation Act 2005 has failed to alter the courts' interpretative procedures[30] should further entrench an intuitive distrust of the primacy afforded to literalism, as it is incongruent with actual practice in any event.

2. Legislative Supremacy as the Constitutional Basis for Intentionalism in Statutory Interpretation

Whereas the literal approach stems from an intentionalist understanding of statutory interpretation, intentionalism in turn is conventionally understood as being grounded in a constitutional principle of legislative supremacy. In the British constitutional tradition, this is historically understood in terms of parliamentary sovereignty. Historical English decisions point to a dissonance between interpretations running along restrictive lines, in cases such as

---

28. *DPP (Ivers) v Murphy* [1999] ILRM 46, concerning a textual absurdity in the context of s 6(1) Criminal Justice (Miscellaneous Provisions) Act 1997.
29. This danger was adverted to by Murray J in *Crilly v Farrington* [2002] 3 ILRM 161, 18.
30. See Paul Brady, 'Constitutional Interpretation and the Irish Supreme Court: Some Reflections on a Neighbouring Common Law Court's Approaches to Interpretation', conference paper, Statute Law Society Conference 2010: 'Legislation and the Supreme Court' (Supreme Court, London, 9 October 2010) <http://www.statutelawsociety.org/__data/assets/pdf_file/0004/93586/Paul_Brady.pdf> 2, accessed 14 August 2013.

Stradling v Morgan (1570), and extensive or purposive interpretation such as in *Heydon's Case* (1584).[31] It is noted in *Cross* that such judicial divergence predated the emergence of a strict understanding of parliamentary sovereignty in Britain. Thereafter, until the seminal decision in *Pepper v Hart*,[32] the primary object of statutory interpretation was understood as the technical meaning of English language or, in short, a narrow version of the plain meaning rule.[33]

This is significant in the Irish context because the principle of legislative supremacy is still, similarly, understood as a constitutional justification for intentionalist and literalist approaches to statutory interpretation. It is sometimes asserted that the preference for a default literalist approach in Ireland stems from the exclusive legislative power of the Oireachtas under art 15.2.1° of the Constitution.[34] Thus, the courts are called upon to articulate literal meaning as the presumed expression of legislative intent, and not speculate as to alternative legislative intent, or deliver value judgments as to what the meaning of a particular legislative enactment should be. In *Lawlor v Flood*[35] Denham J highlighted the significance of constitutional restraints for courts articulating statutory meaning:

> In applying the ordinary meaning of the words the Court is enforcing the clear intention of the legislature. This aspect of statutory construction is an essential part of the separation of powers… an illustration of the appropriate respect by one organ of government to another.[36]

Therefore, intentionalism is thought to be constitutionally grounded. In turn, the literal rule – which is justified in intentionalist terms – is understood as a controlling mechanism on judicial power as well as a bulwark for the representative democracy envisaged by the Constitution. Thus, whereas statutory meaning is thought to stem from parliamentary intent, whose default expression, in turn, is said to be literal meaning, this is a normative as well as descriptive claim – it is based on the parliament's legislative supremacy both in constitutional law as well as on grounds of democratic legitimacy.[37] It is assumed that since the

31. Bell and Engle, *Cross*, 11.
32. [1992] UKHL 3.
33. ibid 11–12, 18.
34. Dodd, *Statutory Interpretation*, 117.
35. [1999] 3 IR 107.
36. ibid 117.
37. On the principle against judicial legislation, see *Norris v Attorney General* [1984] IR 36 and the judgment of the Supreme Court *O'Reilly v Limerick Corporation* [1989] ILRM 181, where the Court gave a detailed account of why the courts should not engage in strained interpretations to the point that the courts enter the legislative sphere. See also Michael Freeman, 'Positivism and Statutory Construction: An Essay in the Retrieval of Democracy' in Stephen Guest (ed), *Positivism Today* (Darthmouth Publishing Company 1997).

legislature is familiar with the courts' interpretative criteria, the default resort to literalism facilitates it in effectuating its will (a somewhat circular logic).[38]

Despite the undoubted significance of these democratic ideas that link representative democracy to legislative intent, it is by no means self-evident that they ought to support a theory of intentionalism in the context of statutory interpretation. On the one hand, it might be queried why, as a general proposition, legislative supremacy ought to translate specifically to a doctrine of intentionalism, given the various theoretical problems associated with the idea of group or collective intentions. Yet more narrowly, legislative supremacy has a highly qualified status in the Irish constitutional order – particularly by virtue of what might be termed the principle of constitutional supremacy.[39] Therefore, a doctrine of intentionalism which developed under a strong principle of legislative supremacy (linked to parliamentary sovereignty) may be more difficult to justify within the weaker understanding of legislative supremacy that prevails in Irish constitutional law. Legislative supremacy enjoys a more prominent role in British constitutional theory,[40] and might therefore offer a plausible constitutional justification for an unbridled intentionalism in that system (notwithstanding its potential weaknesses on other grounds). However, the intentionalist orthodoxy sits uneasily with Ireland's different constitutional framework.

Indeed, the constitutional trajectory of post-independence Ireland discarded many of the positivist, Diceyan inheritances of the British constitutional tradition. This was evident, for example, in the endorsement of natural law theory, but most notably, perhaps, in the early introduction of strong-form judicial review – in the guise of an explicit jurisdiction to invalidate unconstitutional statutes (partly reflecting the influence of American constitutional thought). Yet in fact, this was just one expression of a broader attempt to fashion a distinctive constitutional theory – or, perhaps, a mythology – based on popular constituent power. In turn this was informed by a theory of popular sovereignty which necessarily negated or at least qualified the doctrine of parliamentary supremacy as it existed in the

38. Freeman, *Positivism and Statutory Construction*, at 31, See also Manning, 'Absurdity Doctrine', fn 285.
39. It was stated in *State (Walshe) v Murphy* [1981] IR 275, 310 by the High Court that 'the power of legislation is absolute and all-embracing, *subject to the qualifications imposed on it by the Constitution*' (emphasis added). This offers a narrow definition of the principle of constitutional supremacy, although appropriate for current purposes.
40. See, eg, Trevor Allan, *Law, Liberty and Justice: the Foundations of British Constitutionalism* (Clarendon 1994); 'Parliamentary Sovereignty: Law, Politics and Revolution' (1997) 113 LQR 443; 'Parliament's Will and the Justice of the Common Law: The Human Rights Act in Constitutional Perspective' (2006) 59 CLP 27; Vernon Bogdanor, 'Imprisoned by a Doctrine: The Modern Defence of Parliamentary Sovereignty' (2012) 32 OJLS 179; Jeffrey Goldsworthy, *Parliamentary Sovereignty: Contemporary Debates* (Cambridge University Press 2010).

United Kingdom.[41] This appeal to popular sovereignty was partly a nationalist imperative in the context of de Valera's campaign against the post-independence political settlement. Nonetheless, the principle of popular sovereignty – and indeed, the appeal to a mythologised, unitary 'people' unknown to British constitutional theory – also had concrete implications in the form and conception of Irish constitutionalism. This attempt to forge an alternative constitutional theory of popular sovereignty – or at least a conception that was distinct from parliamentary sovereignty – was evident in the Irish Free State Constitution, for example, in the provisions envisaging the creation of vocational councils and referendums by popular initiative[42] as well as the provision for judicial review of legislation (despite these provisions having all eventually been subverted or removed).[43]

Thus O'Cinnéide notes an early 'desire to give substantive effect to the idea of popular sovereignty [which] led the drafters of both constitutions to experiment with different methods of ensuring greater popular participation'.[44] Popular sovereignty provided a source of moral legitimacy in a context where considerable doubt existed concerning the legality of the enactment process of the 1937 Constitution. The authority of the 1937 Constitution was consciously predicated on a direct appeal to popular constituent power, but correspondingly the legislative authority of the Oireachtas was more firmly bounded, in both rhetorical and practical terms, within the Constitution's substantive rights provisions. In contrast to the United Kingdom, the people's democratic power was thought to be captured in the provisions of the codified Constitution itself, not in the unbridled sovereignty of the legislature. The Constitution itself, then, is conceived of as a foundational legislative charter – described by de Valera as 'the foundation law of the sovereign people'.[45] In the *Abortion Information* case, the Supreme Court posited the 'sovereignty of the people' as an overarching constitutional principle.[46] Indeed, popular sovereignty is almost mythologised in judicial and political discourse – for example, in de Valera's description of

41. David Gwynn Morgan, *Constitutional Law of Ireland* (Gill and Macmillan 1990) 22.
42. arts 45, 48.
43. The 1922 Constitution initially specified that the Constitution could be amended for a transitory eight-year period using ordinary parliamentary legislation, and thereafter could only be amended by referendum. However, the Oireachtas used this provision to extend the transitory period itself, and so the Constitution could be amended by ordinary legislation for the entirety of its lifespan. The transitory amendment procedure was used to remove the direct democracy provisions through Amendment 10 (1928). The extension of the transitory amendment procedure itself was upheld in *State (Ryan) v Lennon* [1935] IR 170.
44. Colm O'Cinnéide, 'The People Are the Masters: The Paradox of Constitutionalism and the Uncertain Status of Popular Sovereignty within the Irish Constitutional Order' (2012) Irish Jurist 249, 273.
45. Dáil Éireann debates 11 May 1937, vol 67, cols 74–76.
46. *Re Article 26 and the Regulation of Information (Services Outside the State for Termination of Pregnancies) Bill 1995* [1995] 1 IR 1.

the 'people' as 'masters' in the Oireachtas debates on the draft Constitution. Therefore, with art 6 affirming all powers of government are derived – albeit 'under God' – from the 'people', the theory of parliamentary sovereignty is unambiguously rejected (indeed O'Flaherty J described the Constitution as embodying elements of 'plebiscitary' as well as representative democracy).[47]

Any residual concept of parliamentary supremacy is extensively qualified in comparison to the British constitutional doctrine. Whereas art 15 describes the Oireachtas as the 'sole and exclusive' legislative body, this legislative power is, obviously, subject to the provisions of the Constitution itself.[48] Legislative authority is depicted as a power held on trust from the people and subject to their overriding jurisdiction as constitutional legislators, enforced by judicial review. In *Abbeylara*,[49] the Supreme Court affirmed that the separation of powers effected by the 1922 and 1937 Constitutions in no way stemmed from the preceding, conventional British framework. This, in turn, has implications for the scope and extent of legislative supremacy that the Constitution implies.

How, specifically, should this different understanding of the constitutional framework inform statutory interpretation? Most obviously, the principle of legislative supremacy necessarily has a different scope in light of the principle of constitutional supremacy itself. In Ireland it is conventionally assumed that the main relevance of constitutional supremacy for statutory law pertains to statutory validity – that is, that the principle is given effect primarily through the jurisdiction of the courts to invalidate unconstitutional statutes.[50] However, constitutional supremacy can be understood as equally requiring that statutory meaning should be informed by constitutional principles across a broader range of cases, not merely where the constitutionality of statutes is directly in question. Thus, an implication of constitutional supremacy is that constitutional principles may partly determine statutory *meaning* as well as statutory validity and methods of statutory interpretation. While this might ostensibly seem an uncontroversial proposition, it is impossible to reconcile with the prevailing idea that statutory meaning derives exclusively from legislative intent. The principle of constitutional supremacy cannot accommodate intentionalism as an overarching doctrine of statutory interpretation – simply because the constitutional principles that are to inform statutory meaning are irreducible to legislative intention. In turn, it seems obvious that literal or plain meaning cannot capture the extraneous public values that will be partly constitute of statutory meaning. In fact constitutional supremacy precludes that statutory meaning could be considered entirely a function of legislative intent. Therefore, rather than the Constitution requiring deference to legislative intent – as

47. *McKenna v An Taoiseach (no 2)* [1995] 2 IR 10, 43.
48. See arts 26, 34, Constitution of Ireland.
49. *Maguire v Ardagh* [2002] 1 IR 385.
50. See art 34.3.2°, Constitution of Ireland. See generally Oran Doyle, 'Legal validity: Reflections on the Irish Constitution' (2003) 26 DULJ 56.

the traditional British-influenced theory suggests – in fact it demands that legislative intent be read against, and hedged by, substantive constitutional principles. In this alternative understanding, statutory ambiguities are read against the background of constitutional principle, at least in certain cases as will be detailed in Part 3.

In this understanding, statutory meaning as well as statutory validity will hinge partly on judicial interpretations of constitutional principle that are irreducible to legislative intention. In fact this is already a feature of statutory interpretation in existing practice, although it is unacknowledged and glossed over. This undermines the orthodox account of statutory interpretation as a strictly formalist, mechanical and non-creative exercise understood as the retrieval of legislative intent.[51] Statutory interpretation continues to be portrayed as an exercise in uncovering parliamentary intent, in the vein of the British constitutional tradition – and if constitutional desiderata are used in interpreting statutes, these are routinely attributed, as detailed in Part 3, to legislative intent. The prevailing account seems to suggest that constitutional principles represent a 'trump' on legislative intentions in outlier cases where statutes are invalidated, but that legislative intent remains undisturbed in all other cases. Constitutional supremacy, then, is somehow thought compatible with an unyielding account of intentionalism in statutory interpretation. Yet intentionalism is harder to justify, constitutionally, within the weaker principle of legislative supremacy that applies in Ireland, and its uncompromising formulation in case law may be understood partly as an incongruous residue of the British constitutional principle of parliamentary sovereignty.

3. The Role of Constitutional Norms in Statutory Interpretation

Our claim is partly that constitutional norms have a bearing on the meaning as well as the validity of statutes in ways that are not fully articulated or acknowledged in existing doctrine. The aim of this section is both to describe more fully how this occurs within existing practice and to offer some suggestions as to how it might be theoretically understood or justified. It considers the role of intentionalism in the prevailing understanding of the presumption of constitutionality doctrine, the normative basis for the presumption of constitutionality, and the theoretical issues raised by the idea of a judicial responsibility to read statutes in light of constitutional norms.

51. By formalism in this sense, we mean the theory that legal reasoning can and/or should operate independently of normative considerations external to the law. Thus Unger describes formalism as 'a belief in the possibility of, a method of legal justification that can be clearly contrasted to open-ended disputes about the basic terms of social life, disputes that people call ideological, philosophical, or visionary'. See Roberto Unger, 'The Critical Legal Studies Movement' (1983) 96 Harv L Rev 561, 563. For a broader discussion on the meaning of formalism see Brian Leiter, 'Positivism, Formalism, Realism' (1999) 99 Columbia L Rev 1138.

Intentionalism and the Presumption of Constitutionality

In one sense, the salience of constitutional norms in statutory interpretation stems from the background possibility of the provisions in question being declared unconstitutional. Invalidation is effectively considered a last resort: statutes are to be struck down only where no plausible constitutional interpretation is available.[52] Consequently, the literalist doctrine has been significantly qualified by the 'presumption of constitutionality' doctrine, as courts may depart from an apparently plain meaning in order to uphold an impugned provision.[53] In fact this presumption of constitutionality principle embraces two distinct components. First, it is assumed, in the case of post-1937 legislation at least, that the Oireachtas intended to respect constitutional requirements; therefore, the burden of proof falls on plaintiffs challenging the constitutionality of legislation. Effectively, this is a doctrine of deference. Secondly, and more importantly for current purposes, the 'double construction' rule means that where alternative constructions of a statute are available, the court must select that which is compatible with the Constitution, thereby upholding the constitutionality of the statute by attributing it this (usually narrower) meaning. In Hogan and Whyte's terms, 'only if the words of the statute admit no course of events other than a constitutionally objectionable one… is the presumption in favour of the Act… disappointed'.[54]

It follows from the 'double construction' rule, specifically, that constitutional norms are used not only to invalidate statutes, but also to *vary* their meaning, in a manner that is inconsistent with intentionalist doctrine. Constitutional supremacy is observed through the use of constitutional principle in statutory interpretation – not only as a guide to methods of statutory interpretation, but also as a source of statutory meaning. In turn, insofar as such constitutional principle is *judicially* derived, this will involve statutory meaning departing significantly from legislative intent, and intentionalism, as an overarching interpretive theory, then seems unsustainable. Effectively this means that judicially derived constitutional principles counteract and potentially compete with legislative intent, notwithstanding judicial protestations of neutrality and restraint. Therefore, the Constitution does not simply prescribe statutory-interpretive-methodology, it also offers a (partial) source of statutory meaning. Whereas the prevailing account portrays statutory interpretation as the retrieval of legislative intent, it would be more coherent, in this lens, to view parliament and the courts as co-agents in the construction of statutory meaning.[55]

---

52. See, eg, *Cooke v Walshe* [1984] IR 710.
53. Brian Foley, 'Presuming the Legislature Acts Constitutionally: Legislative Process and Constitutional Decision-Making' (2007) 29 DULJ 141.
54. Gerard Hogan and Gerry Whyte, *JM Kelly: The Irish Constitution* (4th edn, Butterworths 2001) 6.2.217.
55. As Allan argues, 'Co-operation with the statutory purpose therefore engages the moral judgment appropriate to furtherance of the common good.' Trevor Allan,

Yet the prevailing account presents the relationship between statutory meaning, legislative intent and constitutional principle as something along the following lines. First, where statutes are struck down, it is accepted that parliamentary intent is effectively trumped by constitutional principle, as constitutional supremacy requires. Second, where statutes are not invalidated, legislative intent is fully preserved – even where their meaning or *vires* are based partly on judicial interpretations of constitutional principle. Legislative intent is presented as being fully determinative of statutory meaning in all instances other than the (comparatively rare) invalidation remedy: in a somewhat simplistic binary conception, legislative intent is either trumped completely though constitutional invalidation, or held up as the exclusive determinant of statutory meaning. This obscures an important third category, where statutes are upheld but their meaning is determined partly by judicial interpretations of constitutional principle (or other background public norms). Under this category the courts respect the primacy of the Constitution without resorting to invalidation. Legislative 'intent' is then effectively overridden, altered or supplemented by the courts, yet in current doctrine, this corrective to legislative intent is presented as somehow an expression of it.[56]

Thus the presumption of constitutionality is presented and understood in the terms of the prevailing intentionalism: where statutory meaning is grafted to constitutional requirements, this is attributed to the legislature's presumed *intention* that the Constitution should be respected. However, these constitutional determinants of statutory meaning cannot plausibly be attributed to the legislature's intentions, because these are interpreted and derived independently by judges and cannot plausibly be imputed to legislative intent (a claim elaborated on below). At first glance, the presumption of constitutionality is simply a variant of the wider idea that parliament's intent, and thus statutory meaning, must be understood as encompassing widely accepted background public values.[57] Parliament, it can be assumed, intended such values to prevail. Constitutional principles might simply represent a particular species of the broader set of values that inform statutory meaning. Yet as explored below, judicial interpretations of constitutional principle are not only portrayed and understood as the product of an expert knowledge; they are often controversial, unexpected, and unforeseeable by the legislature. Therefore, the role of constitutional principles cannot be accounted for within an intentionalist theory as neatly as consensual 'public values'.

'Legislative Supremacy and Legislative Intention: Interpretation, Meaning and Authority' (2004) 63 CLJ 685, 687.

56. This suggests that legislative intent, assumed under the prevailing theory as the point at which interpretation begins, by which it is guided, and the end which interpretations ultimately reflect, might well be a judicial artefact and not the foundation from which statutory interpretation proceeds. This seems to confirm our contention that the literalist paradigm is inherently flawed, and that consequently, statutory interpretations are essentially creative.

57. Allan, 'Legislative Supremacy'.

Why does this seeming anomaly undermine intentionalism as a theory of statutory interpretation? It is hardly novel to contend that constitutional considerations influence statutory interpretation in cases where the constitutionality of statutes may be in question. It might then be argued that the attribution of these constitutional influences to legislative intent is a mere rhetorical flourish with no real importance. However, where statutory meaning is determined partly on the basis of interpretations of constitutional principle – and assuming these are judicially derived independently of legislative intent – their attribution to legislative intent serves to obscure, and evade public justification of this important exercise of judicial power. An *explicit* justification of these latent normative desiderata is needed. Additionally, constitutional principles might guide statutory interpretation across a broader range of situations where the validity of the relevant provisions is not in question, and the 'double construction' rule as such does not apply.

Of course, a clear legislative intent will often exist in routine cases of statutory interpretation – particularly in statutes of a technical nature – making it unnecessary for judges to resort of constitutional or other public norms. However, this type of interpretation may be necessitated where statutes are framed by open-textured normative standards. For example, ambiguities in equality legislation are typically read against a legislative balancing of conflicting public values – in particular, freedom of association and equality – values which, in turn, are constitutionally defined and protected. The courts will normally defer to the balancing solution the Oireachtas has effectuated (within the boundaries of proportionality). Yet the application of ambiguous equality-law provisions in specific 'hard cases' inevitably invites fresh appraisals of this normative 'balancing': the legislature's appraisal cannot carry through in a fully determinative way to the adjudicative stage. Referring to legislative intent to resolve such ambiguities – as occurred, for example, in *Portmarnock*[58] – is deeply unsatisfactory. It is too indeterminate to be conclusive, particularly since legislators will naturally have attached different weight and priority to the competing norms balanced by the legislation. *Portmarnock* turned primarily on the meaning of 'discriminating club' under ss 8–9 of the Equal Status Act 2000, and correspondingly, on the interpretation of the terms 'needs' – of the male-only members of the golf club – and the 'principal purpose' of the club, in so catering for their needs. Intentionalism suggests that these ambiguities can be resolved with reference to the legislature's intent as to how the competing public values at stake are to be balanced. Yet this problematically assumes both that

58. *Equality Authority v Portmarnock Golf Club* [2010] IR 671. The Equality Authority had instigated proceedings against the defendant as a 'discriminating club' for the purposes of ss 8 and 9 of the Equal Status Act 2000, given that membership of the golf course was confined to men (women were allowed access to club facilities as non-members). The case turned on the interpretation of the word 'needs', and the phrase 'principal purpose' under s 9 of the 2000 Act. Under s 9, a club is not defined as a 'discriminating club' if 'its principal purpose is to cater only for the needs of… persons of a particular gender…'.

the legislation reflects a conclusive and determinate intention as to how these values are balanced, and that this determinate intention can yield determinate constructions of the legislation in particular 'hard cases' without judges engaging in any independent normative appraisal.

Indeed it is clear from Hardiman J's piquant *obiter* remarks on equality in the *Portmarnock* judgment that such normative appraisals played a role in the construction of the relevant section. In turn, the attribution of these desiderata to a legislative intent presumed to be embodied in 'plain meaning' ignores that these political–moral considerations are irreducible to any singular, corporate legislative intent. The reference to legislative purpose to support the claimed 'plain meaning' serves to lend a façade of normative neutrality. That is, the consideration as to when it is necessary to consult purpose or context to clarify 'literal' meaning seems undergirded by an implicit normative baseline as to what is reasonable or just. 'Literal meaning' and 'purpose' cannot be ordered so as to yield statutory constructions for particular fact scenarios without the use of some normative appraisal that is independent of legislative intent. Thus, intentionalist terminology obscures these latent normative desiderata informing statutory interpretation. However, if, semantically, the relevant section can support different constructions, we suggest that the explicit use of constitutional principle to justify a determinate conclusion at least ensures that such moral desiderata – ordinarily latent, at best, in statutory interpretation – are at least brought to the surface and more rigorously justified.

It is true that absent a written Constitution, English courts, for example, may often depart from literal meaning or read statutes in accordance with international treaties or common law principles.[59] For example, they will assume parliament intended that statutory powers are to be exercised in accordance with natural justice.[60] However, while these interpretations do explicitly depart from literal meaning, they may nonetheless be attributed (however implausibly) to parliamentary intention. Thus departures from literalism are perfectly consistent with an uncompromising intentionalism. Yet in Ireland the written Constitution offers courts a much wider range of normative principles for imputing fictional intentions to parliament,[61] and this strains the intentionalist

59. Allan outlines how in one understanding 'an Act of Parliament is a contribution to an existing order of (common law) justice, which it supplements and modifies but never wholly supplants. It takes its true meaning from an understanding of the law as a whole'. Allan, 'Legislative Supremacy', 686.
60. See generally Trevor Allan, 'Parliament's Will and the Justice of the Common Law: The Human Rights Act in Constitutional Perspective' (2006) 59 CLP 27.
61. It should be noted that despite the doctrine of parliamentary sovereignty, Allan has argued that legislative supremacy concedes a degree of judicial autonomy in weighing the competing values and principles informing statutory enactments. Thus 'legislative supremacy is confined by judicial appraisal of the reasons that inform and explain the Act, or properly qualify its meaning and application'. Allan, 'Legislative Supremacy', 689.

doctrine to a much greater extent. Restrictions on statutory meaning deriving from substantive constitutional principle cannot plausibly be attributed to parliamentary *intention*, given the autonomous role of the judiciary in their exposition. Where a statutory provision is upheld by being given a constitutionally valid (narrower) reading, the narrowed meaning cannot then be attributed to legislative intent except through a rather outlandish fiction – that the legislature envisaged and intended the constitutional restriction the court will have imposed on the statute. Given the well-established and relatively uncontroversial content of natural justice, there is probably a reasonable basis for presuming that the British legislature does not in fact intend to legislate against these rights, or at least it is aware it must explicitly provide for this if such is intended. But the intention of constitutional compliance that Irish courts impute to statutes covers a much broader range of constitutional norms whose interpretation by courts the legislature could not have anticipated, never mind willingly respected. Of course in reality, constitutional restrictions on statutory vires are judicially derived, and may not even be foreseen, never mind intended, by parliament. Presenting such restrictions as a function of legislative 'intent' simply serves to obscure the independent normative appraisal judges will conduct in constructing many statutes.

Why Is Legislation Presumed Constitutional?

Foley notes that the presumption of constitutionality sometimes amounts to the 'relatively simple presumption that the legislature does, in fact, consider constitutional questions when legislating'.[62] The courts then owe respect to what is presumed to have been a good-faith attempt by the legislature to regulate the area in question while observing its understanding of constitutional requirements. An alternative understanding is that legislation deserves a degree of deference or circumspection from judges based on democratic legitimacy, irrespective of whether the parliament has actually considered constitutional requirements. Foley has speculated: 'this deference may be justified on the basis that the democratic organs of state should be entitled to pride of place in deciding important constitutional questions because their decisions are democratically infused in a way in which judicial decisions are not'.[63] But there is no necessary connection between the democratic or deliberative nature of legislative enactments and the likelihood of their constitutionality (in the sense of their compatibility with constitutional restrictions that courts derive).[64] It seems unlikely that the doctrine is understood as stemming from a conception of the Oireachtas as a subsidiary agent of constitutional interpretation that conducts

62. Foley, 'Presuming the Legislature', 142.
63. ibid 149.
64. Perhaps its main underlying motivation is not respect for democratic legitimacy or institutional comity, but rather the value of *stability*, as it enhances predictability and certainty.

independent constitutional appraisals. Thus, given the reality of executive dominance, the Oireachtas will perform little independent constitutional analysis, with deputies typically accepting the advice conveyed by the relevant minister.[65] Effectively, the doctrine then extends deference (or respect) not to parliament, but the government.

More pertinently, while parliamentarians (as well as legislative drafters) might anticipate constitutional difficulties in bills, they cannot necessarily foresee specific judicial interpretations of constitutional principle,[66] and so the eventual constitutional restrictions imposed on the statute, by courts, can hardly be attributed to legislative intent; in fact they may well contradict it. Hogan and Whyte argue that 'the basis for the presumption [of constitutionality] is that the legislator must be presumed to have been aware of the limits imposed by the Constitution',[67] but amongst other problems, this assumes that constitutional restrictions are determinate and foreseeable in advance of constitutional litigation.

This fiction was evident in *Doherty v Government of Ireland*,[68] where the High Court held that the government's delay in allowing a by-election to be held was unconstitutional.[69] Although neither the Constitution nor the relevant statute mentioned any time requirement for the holding of by-elections, the Court cited background constitutional precepts, including the '"constitutional contract" between the citizen and the State'.[70] Yet despite the wholly novel and essentially judge-made nature of this constitutional proposition, the Court invoked the presumption of constitutionality to impute the requirement to the relevant statute.[71] Never mind intending this restriction, the parliament could barely have anticipated it had it consulted constitutional lawyers; in fact, it would seem more obvious to infer from the absence of this explicit statutory time limitation that precisely the opposite was intended by the legislature.

Therefore, the attribution of constitutional restrictions on *vires* to parliamentary foresight relies not only on an unrealistic conception of parliamentary practice, but also on a fiction of constitutional determinacy: essentially, judicial interpretations of constitutional right are fictionally presented as actual parliamentary intent.

---

65. Foley, 'Presuming the Legislature'.
66. It is implied in orthodox theory, however, that the legislature is 'fully aware' as to the manner in which the court applies its interpretative methodologies – as a means of ensuring that judicial departures from texts are legitimate and can be pre-determined. It seems an implicit, but untenable assumption. Dodd, *Statutory Interpretation*, 31.
67. Hogan and Whyte, *JM Kelly*, 6.2.
68. [2010] IEHC 369.
69. For analysis of this judgment see David Prendergast, 'By-elections and the Filling of Dáil Vacancies within a Reasonable Time: A Note on *Doherty v Ireland*' (2011) 34 DULJ 242. Prendergast notes 'an alternative determination of the Doherty case would have been to simply strike down section 39(2) of the 1992 Act as unconstitutional' (249).
70. [2010] IEHC 369.
71. Electoral Act 1992, s 39(2).

It is sometimes unclear whether the presumption of constitutionality is based on an assumption that the Oireachtas has conducted an independent exercise in constitutional interpretation, which deserves a certain degree of deference in its own right, or simply stems from deference to its central democratic status under the constitutional framework. In *Buckley v Attorney General* it was said the doctrine stems from 'that respect which one great organ of the State owes to another'[72] – and not, then, implicitly, from any conception of parliament as enjoying a subsidiary competence of constitutional interpretation. However, it appears the doctrine is sometimes based not on a policy of deference towards parliament at all – whether as an agent of constitutional interpretation or as a democratic institution – but rather on a crude fiction that constitutional propositions formulated by courts are logically determinate, non-controversial, antecedently *true* – and therefore foreseeable by the legislature and capable of being intended by it.

It is difficult to resist Foley's assertion that the presumption of constitutionality doctrine stems from a 'largely hypothetical and unrealistic conception of legislative decision-making'.[73] However it also serves to illustrate the incoherence of intentionalism within the framework of Irish constitutionalism. The doctrine qualifies the literal approach, yet without bringing into question the status of legislative intention as the end-point of statutory interpretation. It is portrayed as simply another exception to the rule whereby literal meaning is to be taken as the default expression of legislative intent. Yet the doctrine obscures the true degree of judicial autonomy, discretion and activism that inhere in statutory interpretation. The qualification, correction and development of parliamentary intent is misleadingly presented as its mere discovery. Thus constitutional supremacy and intentionalism in statutory interpretation equally receive lip-service, but with no acknowledgment of their inherent tension.[74] While the constitutional restrictions judges impose on statutory meaning are portrayed as an expression of parliamentary intent itself – restrictions parliament is imagined to have intended – this sidesteps the question of how potentially controversial interpretations of constitutional right, misleadingly imputed to parliamentary intent, can be justified as *independent* sources of statutory meaning.

In effect, then, the 'double construction' doctrine obscures how courts effectively introduce constitutional correctives to statutes quite independently of legislative intent. In *McDonald v Bord na gCon (no 2)*,[75] the Supreme Court held that the statute allowing the defendant body to issue a range of exclusion orders within the greyhound industry included implicit restrictions based on principles of constitutional justice. This restriction is *rhetorically* attributed to the intention of the Oireachtas, but in reality, is independently formulated

72. [1950] IR 67, 80.
73. Foley, 'Presuming the Legislature', 147.
74. On the relationship between constitutional supremacy and legislative intent see Allan, 'Legislative Supremacy'.
75. [1965] IR 217.

by judges. Again, its attribution to legislative intent depends on a rather simplistic formalist fiction – that the constitutional restriction is somehow antecedent to or independent of its formulation by the Court.[76] Similarly, in *East Donegal Co-operative v Att Gen*,[77] the Supreme Court affirmed: '*the Oireachtas intended* that proceedings, procedures, discretions and adjudications which are permitted, provided for prescribed by an Act... are to be conducted in accordance with the principles of constitutional justice [departures from which] would be... corrected by the courts'.[78] Again, the legislature is imagined to have prospectively intended to restrict statutory vires on the basis of future judicial interpretations of constitutional principle – and so intentionalism is awkwardly squared with constitutional supremacy.

Interpreting Statutes in Light of Constitutional Principle: Methodological and Normative Challenges

While constitutional principle has in a minimal sense been acknowledged as a source of statutory meaning, this has been attributed to legislative intent in a reflexive genuflection to the orthodoxies of common-law intentionalism. In turn, there is a marked reluctance to recognise and defend the role of judicially derived constitutional propositions as freestanding, independent sources of statutory meaning that are irreducible to legislative intent. This analysis raises the question of how, in practice, ambiguous statutory provisions might be interpreted in light of constitutional principles. Clearly, a narrower constitutional reading can be used to avoid the spectre of invalidation, although we have argued this narrowed meaning cannot be attributed to legislative intent. However, we have also argued that constitutional principles may inform statutory meaning beyond the relatively narrow range of cases in which doubts around constitutional validity require the double construction rule to be applied. Various statutes can be understood as implementing and balancing foundational public values. We have already used the example of equality legislation. Courts following the approach we advocate would abandon any claim to discern a determinate legislative intent based on literal or plain meaning (even allowing for oblique references to context) – and instead explicitly recognise and expound the specific constitutional ethos and traditions from which anti-discrimination legislation might emerge (and perhaps the historical experience of discrimination underlying it), as well as the values and principles it aims to reconcile.[79] In short, this approach would reject any idea that a determinate legislative intent as to how competing public values are balanced can prove dispositive in 'hard cases', and correspondingly,

76. See *State (Quinn) v Ryan* [1965] IR 70.
77. [1970] IR 317, 368.
78. ibid, emphasis added.
79. A somewhat converse approach was taken to the interpretation of equality law in *Equality Authority v Portmarnock Golf Club* [2010] IR 671.

it would require courts to acknowledge the inevitability of these public values being independently (and transparently) appraised at the adjudicative stage.

This analysis has clear echoes of Ronald Dworkin's constructivist theory of adjudication – his claim that interpretation is never simply a retrieval of intent, but an effort to make the law the 'best it can be' in light of a community's institutional values and history. Indeed, in *Justice for Hedgehogs*, he argues that statutory interpretation, specifically, 'aims to make the governance of the pertinent community fairer, wiser, and more just' – judges must decide 'which of the semantically available interpretations of a controversial statute would produce the best law'.[80] More specifically, he argues that judges must consider which interpretation of statutes 'ties the language the legislature used to its constitutional responsibilities'.[81] Our argument is not solely that the use of normative desiderata in statutory interpretation is normatively and constitutionally defensible – it is also that this already occurs, by virtue of the double construction rule in particular, but without being properly articulated or justified. The remainder of the article aims to consider how this might be justified.

In contrast to statutory interpretation, it is widely accepted that constitutional interpretation requires a 'broad' approach that recognises the role of the Constitution as a foundational political charter.[82] Constitutional provisions are not to be read solely on the basis of their literal meaning or their presumed intent, but also (partly) with reference to the background political–moral values understood as underlying and informing the Constitution. Similarly, William Eskridge notes that in the US context, there has been a remarkable disparity between the acceptance that constitutional interpretation relies partly on the 'fundamental underlying precepts for our polity' and a reluctance to read statutes in a similar light.[83] Similarly, while in Ireland there has been a certain willingness to read constitutional provisions in light of a background public philosophy,[84] statutes are viewed as embodying more discrete, mundane policy purposes or intentions.

Thus it is assumed that whereas the Constitution captures public philosophy, legislation embodies policy, whose content is reducible to parliamentary intent. Implicitly, then, statutes are thought unsuitable for 'principled' or constructivist interpretation because of their different role, in the institutional framework, compared to constitutional provisions. Eskridge argues that although less 'dramatic', statutes can, like constitutional provisions, sometimes be read as

80. Ronald Dworkin, *Justice for Hedgehogs* (Harvard University Press 2010) 85.
81. Ronald Dworkin, *Taking Rights Seriously* (Harvard University Press 1977) 108.
82. See *Attorney General v Paperlink Ltd* [1984] ILRM 37.
83. William Eskridge, 'Public Values in Statutory Interpretation' (1989) 137 U of Penn L Rev 1007.
84. See, for example, *McKenna v An Taoiseach (no 2)* [1995] 2 IR 10. Hamilton J, at 42, invoked 'the democratic nature of the state' and the status of the people as the 'guardians of the Constitution'. Similarly, the Supreme Court, in *Webb v Ireland* [1988] IR 353 invoked a political theory of sovereignty, beyond the narrow provisions of the constitutional text, to ground the State's legal claim to ownership of historical artefacts.

expressing public values, and not solely as 'ad hoc' policy responses.[85] In Ireland, there has been frequent departure from the literal meaning of the Constitution – with reference to its underlying philosophy or even 'spirit'[86] – but never any acknowledgment that statutes might sometimes be read in a similar way. Yet there seems to be little justification for this rigid dichotomy between statutory and constitutional interpretation. Statutes, too, might be read as expressions of public philosophy; they will contain 'open-textured' norms and aspirations as well as 'rules' – standards that invite appraisals of a political–moral nature.[87] This might arise both where statutes openly invite adjudicators to make open-ended normative appraisals – for example, where statutes use terms such 'reasonable' – but more pertinently, perhaps, where a statute is addressed to an area of regulation (such as equality) in which competing constitutional norms are being balanced or reconciled.

Intentionalism might seem to constrain judicial power with reference to a democratically legitimate source – the collective intentions of an elected assembly as effectuated in legislation. However, since legislative intention is inconclusive and malleable, its invocation obscures an underlying judicial discretion. Indeed, whereas statutes read semantically afford judges a good deal of discretion or latitude, the responsibility to interpret in light of background constitutional norms may in fact represent a constraint on judicial power, insofar as it forces judges to justify the exercise of this discretion with reference to a publicly available set of norms. In political-theory terms, it better satisfies the criterion of publicity compared with the prevailing intentionalism. By obscuring the normative standards used, intentionalism leads to a weaker process of public justification in this important area of judicial power. The invocation of legislative intent lends statutory interpretation an allure of unconstestability, whereas an approach framed with reference to constitutional justifications would arguably help bring to the surface the latent policies, norms, aims and presuppositions informing statutory interpretation, rendering these contestable, and judicial power, more accountable. Therefore, a conclusion that legislative intent does not meaningfully exist (or alternatively, that it cannot be determinative of statutory meaning) does not necessarily imply a corresponding concession to unaccountable judicial power.

While irreducible to legislative intent, the public values used in statutory interpretation are located in the background public philosophy of which the Constitution is partly an expression, and within which legislative process and history are set.[88] These principles may not prove determinative in routine cases

85. Eskridge, 'Public Values', 1036.

86. *Doherty v Government of Ireland* [2010] IEHC 369.

87. Eskridge argues: 'in many instances Congress' enactment of an open-textured statute may constitute an implicit legislative delegation of lawmaking authority to the Court'. Eskridge, 'Public Values', 1063.

88. It is important to clarify that 'public values' might be used as a guide to statutory interpretation merely to inform and better illuminate the discovery of legislative *intention*. Thus, Allan argues: 'it is a requirement of the rule of law… that a statute

of statutory interpretation, but might play an important role at appellate level in the exposition of open-textured statutory provisions, for which intentionalist theories seem particularly unsatisfactory. It is in this limited sense that judges do not simply retrieve statutory meaning, but rather participate in its construction with reference to the background public culture; once more, this rejects the notion of legislative intent as the (exclusive) underlying object of statutory interpretation. Eskridge argues 'the interpreter should explicitly consider not just the text and legislative history of a statute, but also its entire public law context and current concepts of reasonableness and justice... These values may have their source in the Constitution, in other statutes, or in the common law.'[89]

It might well be argued that parliaments, not courts, should be the institutional custodians and articulators of 'public values'. Yet this ignores the point that parliaments' expression and choice of such values (through legislation) are insufficiently determinate and conclusive to prove dispositive at the adjudicative level. Intentionalism ignores this. Courts are needed to ensure coherence at the adjudicative level: parliaments simply cannot project exclusive conceptions of 'public values' upon the hypothetical future fact scenarios to which generally applicable statutory provisions will be applied. Whatever doctrine of adjudication is adopted or endorsed, judges will inevitably enjoy some degree of latitude, and accordingly, a responsibility to justify at least a certain range of statutory interpretations in constitutional terms best serves the political values of contestation, publicity and accountability. Background constitutional principles or public values may well be equally as diverse, contradictory and inconclusive as legislative intentions. But the normative virtue of this approach is not necessarily that (as per Dworkin) 'principle' yields determinacy or exclusive 'rights answers'. In fact it may well be no more constraining than intentionalism; however it eschews intentionalism's portrayal of statutory interpretation as an almost mechanical, formalist process. Unlike intentionalism, it is normatively transparent.

---

should be interpreted so far as possible consistently with the general body of rules and principles with which it belongs, understood as a reasonably coherent whole'. Thus, he argues 'we best conform to legislative intention when we acknowledge the context in which the text was approved'. In this understanding, public values simply illuminate legislative intention; however we argue that, in the Irish context at least, statutory interpretation will depend partly on interpretations of constitutional principle that are quite independent of legislative intention. See Allan, 'Legislative Supremacy', 687. Additionally, constitutional principles are simply a sub-set of the broader set of public values that inform legislative intent; thus Allan notes, 'the legislative endeavour will be itself interpreted, most plausibly, in the light of *those fundamental values or commitments that the constitution is normally understood to protect*', 688, emphasis added. However, in the Irish context (and other comparable constitutional contexts), constitutional principles acquire a special significance in this respect; additionally their role cannot be understood solely in terms of the illumination of legislative intention.

89. ibid 1017. Thus, while more familiar in constitutional interpretation, 'public values' are 'often equally important as background context for statutory interpretation'.

Dworkin extends his conception of 'integrity' in legal interpretation to statutory interpretation.[90] He argues that judges' role is not to mechanically retrieve legislative intention, pristine and intact; rather, they constructively contribute to statutory meaning using the background political–moral philosophy. The retrieval of a pristine legislative intention is a fiction: judges are more like 'authors in a chain novel', thus, 'the intentions of the legislature are relevant, but not necessarily dispositive'.[91] Moreover, where statutory meaning appears vague or incomplete, judges do not 'fill gaps' simply by exercising discretion as 'deputy' legislators, but rather appeal to a deeper level of public 'principle' transcending discrete policy questions. The 'public values' approach to statutory interpretation assumes the existence of a 'community of principle', such that 'legal values arise from the public values of the body politic'.[92] Again, it might be argued that this problematically identifies courts as arbiters of politically controversial values that are not amenable to resolution by any judicial standard. In particular, a salient risk is that when competing visions of public values are weighted and prioritised, this will insidiously clothe the political biases of judges – with ordinary politicking given a mystifying juristic gloss. As many critical legal scholars have argued, 'the spectrum of ideological controversy in politics is reproduced in the law'.[93] Indeed, critical scholars attack the liberal idea of law as 'integrity' – a coherent moral vision that judges can discern – as a naïve misrecognition of the baser matrix of ideologies and power relations that law encapsulates.[94] Yet as argued, where statutory interpretation is framed with reference to constitutional principle, these normative debates are at least brought to the surface and rendered contestable – whereas intentionalism portrays interpretation as a mechanical process of retrieval – a narrow expertist, technical process giving the illusion of normative neutrality.

On the other hand, the use of constitutional or public values in statutory interpretation need not necessarily be viewed as subversive of legislative intent, with all the normative dilemmas this raises. Sometimes, for example, disparate and conflicting legislative intentions or purposes may 'push the Court in different directions',[95] and a background scale of public values might be used to resolve this. Thus, 'statutory interpretation, in a community of integrity, ought

90. Dworkin, , *Justice for Hedgehogs*. Indeed, Dworkin could be criticised for intimating that under this moral vision, judges enjoy a monopoly on the articulation and formulation of background 'principle'.
91. Earl M Maltz, 'Statutory Interpretation and Legislative Power: The Case for a Modified Intentionalist Approach' (1988) Tulane L Rev 1, 10.
92. Eskridge, 'Public Values', 1016.
93. Andrew Altman, 'Legal Realism, Critical Legal Studies and Dworkin' (1986) 15 Philosophy and Public Affairs 205, 229.
94. See, eg, ibid; Jack *Balkin*, '*Taking Ideology Seriously*: Ronald Dworkin and the CLS Critique' (1987) 55 UMKC L Rev 392; Mark Tushnet, 'Following the Rules Laid Down: A Critique of Intepretivism and Neutral Principles' (1983) 96 Harv L Rev 781.
95. Eskridge, 'Public Values', 1064. Thus, Eskridge argues that in certain cases public values beyond the statutory text might operate as 'tiebreakers'.

not needlessly flaunt the deliberative decisions made by the legislature... but it does have the capacity for harmonizing statutes with changing values and policies over time'.[96] This might answer one possible objection to the use of 'public values' in statutory interpretation – that by injecting uncertainty in the form of normative 'wild cards', it undermines the rule of law. Background values might provide some degree of continuity and stability within the otherwise erratic interplay of 'plain' meaning and context.

Conclusion

The argument we have outlined suggests a remarkable disparity between courts' description of statutory interpretation as a mechanical, uncreative process centred around the retrieval of legislative intent, and the far-reaching judicial power inherent in the use of constitutional principles (as well as other public values) as supplementary sources of statutory meaning. The prevailing doctrines understate judges' independent role in shaping statutory meaning, while unrealistically attributing the constitutional sources of statutory meaning to legislative intent. This tendency to understate the role of normative appraisal in adjudication is present in other areas of jurisprudence. Yet arguably it is peculiarly acute in the context of statutory interpretation. There is a need for a more rigorous theoretical justification of judges' use of constitutional principle as an external source of statutory meaning that is irreducible to parliamentary intent.

A good deal has been written about the dilemmas of judicial review in relation to judicial review of legislation, but much less about what role constitutional norms should play in statutory interpretation – even though this raises similar normative questions. The tendency to attribute constitutional sources of statutory meaning to legislative intentions is borne primarily of a concern for democratic legitimacy. However, it is questionable to what extent this value is well served by a doctrinal approach whose effect is to divest judges of the responsibility to rigorously justify, on constitutional grounds, the political–moral appraisals underlying statutory interpretation. Legislative intent is too elusive to serve as an appropriate standard of justification for judicial power. Therefore, we have argued it would be more coherent to understand courts as interpreting statutes through a lens of constitutional principle derived independently of legislative intention. A potential problem in this argument is its implications for legislative centrality in the constitutional separation of powers, with the questions of democratic legitimacy this raises. However we have highlighted how, in the Irish context, the qualified status of legislative supremacy leans against the orthodox intentionalism.[97] Additionally, the narrower sources of statutory meaning favoured by formalist, traditional methods – primarily, text

96. ibid 1073.
97. Additionally, Eskridge points out, in the US context, 'the use of public values to interpret, rather than invalidate, statutes seems more acceptable politically', entailing 'less friction' between judiciary and legislature. Eskridge, 'Public Values', 1017.

and intent – are in any case already sufficiently indeterminate to afford a great deal of latitude to judges – such that in effect, they operate as something of a 'post-hoc rationalisation' for decisions that are in reality, largely intuitive or discretionary.[98] Thus, the democratic credentials of the prevailing intentionalism are largely illusory, and insofar as it is accepted that factors beyond parliamentary intent already determine statutory-interpretive processes, it is better these should be brought to the surface and properly explicated.

98. See generally Mark Tushnet, 'Critical Legal Studies: A Political History' (1991) 100 Yale LJ 1515.

The Proposed Common European Sales Law: A New Direction for European Contract Law?

Caterina Gardiner*

Abstract—The European Commission's proposal for a Regulation on a Common European Sales Law (CESL) envisages the establishment of a uniform sales law across Member States, not by requiring amendments to the pre-existing national contract law, but by creating within each Member State's national law a second optional contract law regime for contracts covered by its scope. The European Commission's use of an optional instrument appears to signal a move away from the difficult path of full harmonisation as a means of avoiding problems of fragmentation of national consumer contract laws. This article examines the provisions of the proposed optional instrument, assesses its prospects for success, and considers its potential impact on Irish businesses and consumers.

Introduction

On 11 October 2011, the European Commission published its proposal for a regulation on a Common European Sales Law (CESL).[1] This proposal envisages a 'second regime' of contract law introducing a set of rules for cross-border sales transactions, which would be common to all Member States and where choice of this second regime would be voluntary. Under the proposal, a trader would be free to choose to offer a contract under the regime or to remain with existing national contract law. In other words, the proposal introduces an 'opt-in' system of sales law, which would exist alongside Member States' domestic sales law.

In setting out the context of its proposal, the EU Commission refers to the difficulties for traders caused by differences between contract laws of the different

---

* Lecturer, School of Law, National University of Ireland, Galway.

1. *Proposal for a Regulation of the European Parliament and of the Council on a Common European Sales Law* (Brussels 11 October 2011) COM [2011] 636 final. The Proposal consists of three main parts: a Regulation; Annex I to the Regulation, containing the contract law rules (the Common European Sales Law); and Annex II, containing a Standard Information Notice. The Commission has based its proposal on art 114 TFEU, which constitutes the main Treaty Article used to enact harmonisation measures. According to art 114(1) TFEU, the Union may adopt 'measures for the approximation of the provisions laid down by law, regulation or administrative action in Member States which have as their object the establishment and functioning of the internal market'.

Member States.[2] Traders entering cross-border transactions are exposed to the different contract law requirements of foreign laws and are potentially faced with significant transaction costs associated with obtaining legal advice as to the different mandatory requirements. The Commission also cites difficulties for consumers who are hesitant and uncertain of their legal rights and remedies should the transaction go wrong, and the significant deterrent effect that this has in relation to their decision whether or not to enter cross-border transactions.[3] In cross-border transactions, traders must also deal with the added complication of art 6(2) of the Rome I Regulation, which provides protection to consumers in relation to choice of law. In a consumer contract, the trader may choose the law that applies to the contract, however, where a trader directs its activities to the consumer's country of residence, the choice of law cannot deprive the consumer of the protection of the mandatory laws of his home country. The effect of this provision is that the trader may have to amend its standard terms and conditions to comply with the requirements of several different countries and could involve a complex hybrid application of the applicable law of the contract and the mandatory rules of the consumer's residence. The Regulation has a particularly strong impact on internet traders who could fall within art 6(2) by offering goods for sale through a website in different languages or currencies. The choice of CESL as the law governing the contract would by-pass art 6 of the Rome Regulation as it would effectively be a choice of the law of the consumer's habitual residence.

The proposal undoubtedly also has its origins in the failure of the Consumer Rights Directive[4] to achieve full harmonisation in relation to all areas that were part of the original proposal. In the Commission's first proposal, the Consumer Rights Directive envisaged the consolidation of four directives: The Doorstep Selling Directive,[5] the Unfair Terms Directive,[6] the Distance Selling Directive[7]

2. *Communication from the Commission to the European Parliament, the Council, the European Economic and Social Committee and the Committee of the Regions. A Common European Sales Law to Facilitate Cross-Border Transactions in the Single Market* (Brussels 11 October 2011) COM [2011] 636 final.
3. ibid 3.
4. Directive 2011/83/EU of the European Parliament and of the Council of 25 October 2011 on consumer rights, amending Council Directive 93/13/EEC and Directive 1999/44/EC of the European Parliament and of the Council and repealing Council Directive 85/577/EEC and Directive 97/7/EC of the European Parliament and of the Council Directive 2011/83/EU of 22.11.2011, [2011] OJ L 304/64.
5. Council Directive 85/577/EEC of 20 December 1985 to protect the consumer in respect of contracts negotiated away from business premises [1985] OJ L 372.
6. Council Directive 93/13/EEC of 5 April 1993 on unfair terms in consumer contracts [1993] OJ L 95.
7. Directive 97/7/EC of the European Parliament and of the Council of 20 May 1997 on the protection of consumers in respect of distance contracts [1997] OJ L 144.

and the Consumer Sales Directive.[8] There was also to be a shift from minimum to full harmonisation, the aim being to 'merge these four Directives into a single horizontal instrument regulating the common aspects in a systematic fashion, simplifying and updating the existing rules, removing inconsistencies and closing gaps'.[9] The negotiation of this Directive was lengthy and difficult, many Member States fearing that the full harmonisation approach interfered too much with national laws. The final Directive is now a pared-down version applying to distance and off-premises contracts only. The fate of the Consumer Rights Directive appears to have heralded a change in direction for European consumer contract law. The Commission has moved away from the difficult path of full harmonisation as a way of avoiding the difficulties posed by differences in laws between Member States. The approach now favoured seems to be to complement rather than harmonise national laws.[10]

The proposed CESL is the product of this new directional change. It provides for the establishment of a uniform sales law across Member States not by requiring amendments to the pre-existing national contract law, but by creating within each Member State's national law a second optional contract law regime for contracts covered by its scope. This article will examine the scope and content of the proposed CESL, its potential impact in the context of business to consumer (B2C) contracts and also the impact of the decision to extend its scope to business to business (B2B) contracts where one of the parties is a small or medium-sized enterprise (SME). Extending the scope of the CESL to B2B contracts means that the CESL will compete with the Vienna Convention on the International Sale of Goods (CISG), which also contains a set of uniform rules for the regulation of international B2B sales contracts. The article compares the two instruments and analyses the likelihood of businesses choosing the CESL to apply to their commercial sales transactions. Finally, the article considers the impact of the proposed optional instrument in Ireland where the existing landscape of commercial and consumer sales law is complex and assesses the potential problems of providing a further choice of law in the form of the CESL.

Scope of the CESL

The CESL focuses on cross-border sales transactions, as this is where the Commission sees the problems of transaction costs and legal complexity arising.[11]

8. Directive 1999/44/EC of the European Parliament and of the Council of 25 May 1999 on certain aspects of the sale of consumer goods and associated guarantees [1999] OJ L 12.
9. *Proposal for a Directive of the European Parliament and of the Council on Consumer Rights* COM [2008] 614 final.
10. See further Christoph Busch and Ronny Domrose, 'From a Horizontal Instrument to a Common European Sales Law: The Development of European Consumer and Market Law in 2011' (2012) 1 Journal of European Consumer and Market Law 48–53.
11. *Communication from the Commission* COM [2011] 636 final.

However, discretion is given to Member States to extend the regime to domestic contracts. For the purposes of the Regulation, a contract between traders is a cross-border contract if the parties have their habitual residence in different countries of which at least one is a Member State. A contract between a trader and a consumer is a cross-border contract if either the address indicated by the consumer, the delivery address for goods or the billing address are located in a country other than the country of the trader's habitual residence; and at least one of those countries is a Member State.[12] The rules will obviously be particularly relevant to internet sales of goods contracts.

The regime will apply to B2C contracts and also to B2B contracts where at least one party is an SME. Contracts between private individuals and contracts between traders where neither of the parties is an SME are not included. Member States have the option, however, to make the CESL available for all B2B contracts.

The proposed CESL will apply to sale of goods contracts and contracts for related services (such as repair and installation of goods). It does not apply to 'mixed-purpose' contracts, ie contracts containing any element other than a sale of goods or related services. It also excludes contracts linked to consumer credit.[13]

Importantly, digital content contracts fall within the scope of the proposed new regime. Although 'goods' are defined as tangible movable items,[14] it was decided to include contracts for digital content as a separate type of transaction that will fall within the scope of the CESL. This means that, where the CESL is chosen, it will apply to sales of downloaded music, films, software and other applications. The inclusion of digital content contracts is very significant. The need for regulation of digital content contracts has been repeatedly highlighted and the situation with regard to classification of such contracts as either goods or services or as generic contracts is uncertain in most Member States.[15] While there is no Irish authority on this point, in the UK, the case of *St Albans City and District Council v International Computers Ltd*[16] addressed the question of whether, in the absence of any express term, a contract for the supply of software was subject to any implied term as to quality or fitness for purpose. Sir Iain Glidewell expressed the view obiter that, where software was supplied on a computer disk, that physical medium was within the definition of goods for the purpose of the sale of goods legislation, while the computer program itself 'being instructions or commands telling the computer hardware what to do' was not.[17]

12. art 4.
13. art 5.
14. art 2(h).
15. See further Chantal Mak, 'The Regulation of Digital Content Contracts in the Optional Instrument of Contract Law' (2011) 6 European Rev of Private Law 729.
16. [1996] All ER 481.
17. In *London Borough of Southwark v IBM (UK) Ltd* [2011] EWHC 549 (TCC), Akenhead J stated *obiter* that, in principle, software could be goods. He based this view on the

Accordingly, when a defective program is encoded and sold or hired on a disk, the seller or hirer of the disk will be in breach of the implied terms as to quality and fitness in the Sale of Goods Act. In this case, an employee of the defendant went to the plaintiff's premises and installed the program directly into the plaintiff's computer system. In Sir Iain Glidewell's view, there was no transfer of goods and there could consequently be no statutory implication of terms as to quality or fitness for purpose. He was of the opinion, however, that, in the absence of an express term, such a contract would be subject to an implied term under general contract law that the program would be reasonably fit for purpose.

The unsatisfactory result of the *St Albans'* decision is that the buyer's rights differ depending on the method of delivery of the digital content. If software is to be treated as goods, it must be contained on a tangible medium. Software or other digital content that is downloaded from the internet or transferred to the end user by e-mail cannot be classified as goods. It seems that such contracts could be categorised as either supply of services, or as contracts sui generis to which statutory rules do not apply. The buyer of defective software delivered online is left uncertain as to his rights under the contract.

It has been generally been agreed that the lack of a legal framework for digital content contracts is detrimental to the consumer.[18] Whether or not the

---

fact that a CD is a physical object and is hence goods. The fact that a CD is impressed with electrons to add functions to it simply gives it a particular attribute and, just as a CD containing music is goods for the purpose of the Act and is required to be of satisfactory quality, a CD containing software is no different in this respect. Unlike the *St Albans'* judgment, which distinguished between the software program and the disc carrying the program, the judgment in this case appeared not to think it necessary to distinguish or separate the two. Akenhead J's statement appears to be limited, however, to cases where software is contained on a physical medium such as a CD and to have no application to cases where software is downloaded from the internet or supplied by e-mail or some other non-tangible medium.

18. The Irish Sales Law Review Group considered the question of the classification of software in its recent report. While highlighting the anomalous situation with regard to contracts for digital content, it did not recommend amending the definition of 'goods' in the Sale of Goods Act to include computer software. Rather the report recommends that a consultative process should be undertaken to address the issues involved with treating software as goods. It concluded that it would be inadvisable to propose far-reaching national reforms until the outcome of the EU Commission's work on producing a proposal for a legal framework in this area. See *Report on the Legislation Governing the Sale of Goods and Supply of Services* (Prn A11/1576, 2011) 60 <www.djei.ie/commerce/consumer/slrg.htm>, accessed 29 October 2013. The European Commission has commissioned two studies: University of Amsterdam, Study on the Legal Framework for Digital Content Services for Consumers (2011), and Europe Economics: Digital Content Services for Consumers: Assessment of Problems Experienced by Consumers (2011). These studies are intended to assist the Commission in its work to produce a legal framework for digital content contracts.

terms of the CESL, particularly with regard to remedies for non-conforming digital content, are appropriate may be debated.[19] Nevertheless, there is no doubt that the consumer will benefit from the inclusion of digital content contracts in the CESL.

The Content of the CESL

Annex I to the Regulation sets out the substantive rules of the CESL. The rules are comprehensive and include a wide range of contract law issues such as remedies for non-performance, pre-contractual information, conclusion of the contract, right to withdraw, unfair contract terms, delivery, conformity of the goods, mistake, termination, passing of risk, damages and interest, restitution and prescription. Certain issues are not included either because they are considered 'very important for national laws'[20] or because they are not relevant to cross-border contracts. So, for example, rules on legal capacity, transfer of ownership, illegality/immorality and public policy are not addressed; these issues will continue to be governed by the rules of the national law that applies to the contract.

Article 2 of the CESL – Good Faith

Of particular interest is the inclusion of a general requirement of 'good faith'. Article 2 of the CESL provides that each party has a duty to act in accordance with good faith and fair dealing. Parties in breach of this duty may be precluded from exercising or relying on a right, remedy or defence that they otherwise would have, or they may be held liable for any loss caused by the breach. The application of this duty of good faith cannot be excluded or varied by the parties. This notion of a good-faith duty is one that is likely to cause common lawyers in Ireland and the UK some difficulty. The English common law tradition does not recognise a generally applicable doctrine of good faith in contract law.[21] However, good faith is not a completely foreign concept

---

Both studies are available at: <http://ec.europa.eu/justice/newsroom/consumer-marketing/events/digital_conf_en.htm≥, accessed 29 October 2013.

19. See further Chantal Mak, 'Remedies for Buyers in Case of Contracts for the Supply of Digital Content', Briefing Paper for the European Parliament's Committee on Legal Affairs, May 2012, PE 462.459, 25 Amsterdam Law School Research Paper No. 2012–71 Centre for the Study of European Contract Law Working Paper Series No 2012–08 <http://papers.ssrn.com/sol3/papers.cfm?abstract_id=2087626##>, accessed 29 October 2013.
20. See *Communication from the Commission* COM [2011] 636 final, para 2.1.
21. *Walford v Miles* [1992] 2 AC 128 (HL) per Ackner LJ at 138: '[T]he concept of a duty to carry on negotiations in good faith is inherently repugnant to the adversarial position of the parties when involved in negotiations. Each party to the negotiations is entitled to pursue his (or her) own interest so long as he avoids making misrepresentations. A duty to negotiate in good faith is as unworkable in practice

and a duty of good faith has been recognised in specific contexts.[22] It is also the case that more recently, English courts have appeared to be more willing to imply good-faith duties into contracts, especially long-term commercial contracts.[23] Nevertheless, an overriding general duty of good faith such as that to be found in the CESL is not known at common law. Indeed, it is a well-known characteristic of common law that it favours concrete legal solutions to specific problems as opposed to general broad principles and so prefers concise technical language and drafting. There is a view that this use of indefinite legal concepts and abstract principles may lead to uncertainty in the law, something which is especially undesirable in the tradition of commercial law. Some of the responses to the proposed CESL have made reference to the open-textured nature of the good faith duty and express concerns that it may allow too much interference with the parties' freedom to contract.[24]

---

as it is inherently inconsistent with the position of a negotiating party.' For a more detailed analysis of the role of good faith in English contract law, see Richard Hooley, 'Controlling Contractual Discretion' (2013) 72 Cambridge LJ 65.

22. *Interfoto Picture Library Ltd v Stiletto Visual Programmes Ltd* [1989] 1 QB 433, per Bingham LJ at 439: 'In many civil law systems, and perhaps in most legal systems outside the common law world, the law of obligations recognises and enforces an overriding principle that in making and carrying out contracts parties should act in good faith. This does not simply mean that they should not deceive each other, a principle which any legal system must recognise; its effect is perhaps most aptly conveyed by such metaphorical colloquialisms as "playing fair", "coming clean", "putting one's cards face upwards on the table". It is in essence a principle of fair open dealing... English law has, characteristically, committed itself to no such overriding principle but has developed piecemeal solutions in response to demonstrated problems of unfairness.'
23. In the recent judgment of *Yam Seng Pte Ltd v International Trade Corporation Ltd* [2013] EWHC 111, for example, the judge found that a duty of good faith and fair dealing could be implied in a distributorship agreement.
24. For example, see comments of The Bar Council of England and Wales: '... some of the substantive provisions of the CESL (e.g. those concerned with good faith) are likely to impose even greater legal costs than those which the proposal seeks to avoid...': 'Proposed Common European Sales Law Preliminary Position Paper on Legal Basis' 6 <http://www.barcouncil.org.uk/media/112927/bar_council_of_e_w_preliminary_views_on_cesl_legal_basis_-_january_2012.pdf, accessed 29 October 2013. See also, Law Commission, *An Optional Common European Sales Law: Advantages and Problems, Advice to the UK Government* (2011) s 44, which states: 'All systems of commercial contract law must grapple with the tension between certainty and fairness. English and Scots law have a reputation for leaning towards the certainty end of the scale. By contrast, the CESL is firmly towards the fairness end. It sets high standards of good faith and fair dealing and provides many discretionary remedies to a party who has suffered from a lack of good faith. This may protect a weaker party in negotiations – though this is less helpful in an optional regime, where a weaker party may have a choice of law imposed on them. The open ended nature of the discretion may

Aside from the general duty of good faith in art 2, the concept of good faith appears in other provisions of the CESL. For example, art 23 provides that the seller has a duty to disclose information concerning the main characteristics of the goods or services which 'it would be contrary to good faith and fair dealing not to disclose'.[25] Under art 55 (when read along with art 48), a party who has made a mistake of fact or law can claim damages against another party who 'knew or could be expected to have known of the mistake' but who failed to point out the relevant information contrary to the requirement of good faith and fair dealing. Under art 86, a court may strike out a term in a set of standard terms if it 'grossly deviates from good commercial practice, contrary to good faith and fair dealing'. Under art 59, when a court interprets a contract, it can have regard to good faith, and under art 68, good faith can be taken into account in deciding whether or not a term can be implied into a contract.

Recital 31 of the CESL does give some guidance on interpretation of these good faith obligations. It provides that:

> The principle of good faith and fair dealing should provide guidance on the way parties have to cooperate. As some rules constitute specific manifestations of the general principle of good faith and fair dealing, they should take precedent over the general principle. The general principle should therefore not be used as a tool to amend the specific rights and obligations of parties as set out in the specific rules. The concrete requirements resulting from the principle of good faith and fair dealing should depend, amongst others, on the relative level of expertise of the parties and should therefore be different in business-to-consumer transactions and in business-to-business transactions. In transactions between traders, good commercial practice in the specific situation concerned should be a relevant factor in this context.

While Recital 31 may provide general guidance on the *use* of the principle of good faith and fair dealing, it does not clarify its *meaning*. UK and Irish courts are still likely to struggle to interpret the concept. UK courts have had some experience of interpreting the good faith provisions of the Unfair Contract Terms Directive.[26] One of the leading cases on the application of the good-faith criterion that is part of the fairness test under the Directive is *Director-General of Fair Trading v First National Bank*.[27] In this case, the House of Lords set out

---

also disadvantage the party least able to litigate.' <http://lawcommission.justice.gov.uk/docs/Common_European_Sales_Law_Advice.pdf, accessed 29 October 2013.

25. art 23(f).
26. Council Directive 93/13/EEC of 5 April 1993 on unfair terms in consumer contracts [1993] OJ L 95. Under art 3(2) of the Directive, a term is unfair 'if contrary to the requirement of good faith, it causes a significant imbalance in the parties' rights and obligations under the contract to the detriment of the consumer'.
27. [2001] UKHL 52. For analysis of UK case law on the Unfair Contract Terms Directive, see Christian Twigg-Flesner, 'The Implementation of the Unfair Contract Terms Directive in the United Kingdom' (2007) Contemporary Issues in Law SSRN: <http://ssrn.com/abstract=1399631> accessed 25 October 2013.

guidelines as to how the unfairness test in the Directive and implementing Regulations should be applied. Bingham LJ emphasised that the aim of the Directive was to harmonise the law among all Member States that have no common concept of fairness or good faith. Therefore the legislation should be interpreted according to the clear language of the text disregarding any pre-existing national laws on fairness. According to Bingham LJ good faith involves:

> ... fair and open dealing. Openness requires that terms should be expressed fully, clearly and legibly, containing no concealed pitfalls no traps... Good Faith in this context is not an artificial or technical concept... It looks to good standards of commercial morality and practice...[28]

Unfortunately, the House of Lords did not use the preliminary reference procedure in Article 234 EC to obtain a ruling from the European Court of Justice as to an appropriate interpretation of 'good faith' so it is not clear whether or not the decision of the UK court on the meaning of the term would accord with a European approach to the concept of good faith.[29]

This points up another difficulty with this and other kinds of open-ended provisions in the CESL. It seems inevitable that these provisions will be subject to variable interpretations in the different Member States. Differing social, legal and economic traditions among the various countries may impact on the interpretation of these concepts. It is more likely, for example, that an English or Irish judge interpreting the duty of good faith would take a more narrow approach to interpretation, whereas courts in in other countries, eg Germany, which have a tradition of good faith rules in their contract law codes, would have a natural tendency to interpret the CESL rules with reference to their pre-existing domestic laws.[30] Granted, courts do have the opportunity to seek a preliminary ruling from the European Court of Justice and get an authoritative interpretation of such concepts but the UK courts, in particular, have shown a reluctance to make such references. This is particularly apparent in the case

28. [2001] UKHL at [17].
29. See Twigg-Flesner, 'Implementation', 13: 'It is an extremely valuable decision in that it provides a relatively clear interpretation of the various components of the unfairness test, and yet one cannot help but wonder if the European Court of Justice would have shared this approach, had it been given an opportunity to express its views.'
30. For further discussion of this issue and the 'good faith' provisions of the CESL, see Stephan Balthaser, 'The Draft CESL – Overview and Analysis' (2013) 24 Int Company and Commercial L Rev 43. The problem of divergent interpretation of uniform law has also been highlighted with reference to the Vienna Convention on International Sale of Goods, see further: Lisa Ryan, 'The Convention on Contracts for the International Sale of Goods: Divergent Interpretations' (1996) 4 Tul J Int'l and Comp L 99; Monica Kilian, 'CISG and the Problem with Common Law Jurisdictions' (2001) 10 Journal of Transnational Law and Policy 217.

of the interpretation of the Unfair Terms Directive.[31] In addition, the reference procedure may result in considerable delay in dispute resolution.

These issues may give traders cause for concern about use of the CESL for their cross-border transactions. It is possible for parties to contract out of or vary the terms of these particular provisions at least in B2B contracts.[32] However, it must be noted that the general duty of good faith in art 2 cannot be contracted out of,[33] nor can the duty in relation to standard terms in art 86.

Conclusion of the Contract

The general principles of offer and acceptance are set out in art 30 and fit well with the same concepts under Irish law. Article 31 outlines the requirements for the conclusion of a contract. It provides that a contract is concluded if the parties reach an agreement that is intended to have legal effect and has sufficient content and certainty to be given legal effect. Article 31 clarifies the question of offer and acceptance in internet sales. This is an area that remains uncertain in Irish and UK law. The question is whether a website advertisement is an offer that is accepted when a customer places an order, or is merely an invitation to treat, in which case the customer makes the offer when placing the order and the trader accepts by acting on that order. Article 31(3) provides that: 'A proposal made to the public is not an offer, unless the circumstances indicate otherwise.' This essentially means that the website is an invitation to treat and the consumer makes the offer by making the order, which the trader can then accept or reject. In relation to acceptance, art 34(1) provides that: 'Any form of statement or conduct by the offeree is an acceptance if it indicates assent to the offer,' and art 34(2) states that: 'silence or inactivity does not in itself constitute acceptance'. This corresponds with current practice in internet trading. Traders are often concerned not to be seen to accept an offer until they are in a position to check stock and ensure that there has been no pricing error.[34] Most traders will provide in their terms and conditions that an automatic e-mail response to an order does not constitute acceptance and that acceptance does not occur until the goods are dispatched. Article 34 therefore corresponds with this practice and a contract will not be formed by statement unless it indicates that it is assent to the offer.

---

31. There was much academic criticism of the failure of the Supreme Court to refer a preliminary ruling to the ECJ in relation to the Abbey National case. See Law Commission *Issues Paper on Unfair Contract Terms* 2012, which summarises the academic commentary <http://lawcommission.justice.gov.uk/consultations/unfair_consumer_contracts.htm> accessed 29 October 2013.
32. Article 1 allows the exclusion or variation of the provisions of the CESL subject to any applicable mandatory rules.
33. art 2(3).
34. On pricing errors, generally, see Ter Kah Leng, 'Website Pricing Errors, Who Bears the Risk of Mistake?' (2004) 20 Computer Law and Security Report 4, commenting on *Chwee Kin Keong & Ors v Digilandmall.com Pte Ltd* [2004] SGHC 71.

A further issue is whether or not the taking of payment by the trader would amount to acceptance by conduct under art 34(1). For example, a situation may arise where a customer submits an order giving credit card details, the trader obtains payment from the credit card company but fails to dispatch the goods. The correct interpretation of art 34(1) may be that a contract has been formed by the trader's conduct in taking payment for the goods. This interpretation gives rise to the best protection for the consumer. In this situation, the customer has a clear remedy for non-performance in art 106(1)(c), which allows the consumer to terminate the contract and claim return of payment. If accepting payment is not considered to be 'acceptance by conduct' under art 34, then in the absence of a contract, the consumer does not have a right to return of payment under the CESL. There would be a right to restitution under Irish contract law the consumer could rely on in the absence of such rules under the CESL. The UK Law Commission, in its Advice to the UK Government, has welcomed these provisions on contract formation and has suggested that the wording of art 34 in relation to acceptance by conduct could be interpreted in this way, but has called for clarification of the issue.[35]

Choice of CESL Excludes National Consumer Law

Article 11 of the CESL Regulation provides that where the parties choose the CESL for a contract, the CESL is the only applicable law for the matters addressed in its rules. This means that a state's mandatory consumer contract protection laws would not apply. Instead, the CESL's mandatory consumer protection provisions would apply. For consumer advocates, this has given rise to some concern. If, for example, the mandatory rules of the consumer's home country offer better protection than the CESL, then the choice of the CESL deprives the consumer of the benefit of art 6 of the Rome 1 Regulation, which provides that although the parties are free to choose the law that would apply to their contract, that choice cannot deprive the consumer of the protection of the mandatory consumer protection laws of his habitual residence. Although the European Commission has stated that the 'overall' level of consumer protection in the CESL is very high,[36] consumer groups have argued that the CESL provides a variable level of protection and in some instances, national laws may provide a higher level of protection than the draft CESL.[37] In the Irish context, a number of

---

35. Law Commission, *An Optional Common European Sales Law: Advantages and Problems, Advice to the UK Government* (2011) 4.52–4.57 <http://lawcommission.justice.gov.uk/docs/Common_European_Sales_Law_Advice.pdf>.
36. See *Communication from the Commission* COM [2011] 636 final, 33.
37. BEUC, the European Consumer Organisation, has undertaken a comparative analysis of the proposed CESL with national laws showing that CESL provides a variable level of protection. BEUC, Common European Sales Law, Preliminary Position, Annex A <http://www.beuc.org/content/default.asp?Pagename=Index&incFile=Index_314_23996.htm>, accessed 29 October 2013.

areas can be highlighted where consumers might be at a disadvantage if CESL is chosen to apply to their transaction. Under art 114(2) of the draft CESL, the consumer's right to terminate is excluded if the non-conformity is 'insignificant'. Existing Irish law does not specifically provide for appearance and finish of goods as part of the quality standard expected of conforming goods, however, the recent report of the Irish Sales Law Review Group recommends allowing the right to reject for 'minor defects'.[38] In a further example, the draft CESL does not allow damages for distress or inconvenience. This is clear from the definition of 'loss' under art 2(c). 'Loss' means 'economic loss and non-economic loss in the form of pain and suffering, excluding other forms of non-economic loss such as impairment of the quality of life and loss of enjoyment'. This would also represent a reduction in consumer protection as compared with Irish law where an exception can be made to the rule of non-recovery for mental distress damages where the main purpose of the contract is to provide pleasure or avoid distress. The main instance where consumers have been allowed to recover damages in this context has been in relation entertainment and travel services, and in particular, spoilt holidays,[39] however one could envisage situations where this might apply to sales of goods, for example a shoddy wedding dress or substandard wedding bouquet. A further example occurs under art 174(c) of the draft CESL, which provides that the trader may make a 'deduction for use' when a consumer terminates the contract for non-conformity if they were 'aware of the ground for termination but delayed taking action', or if it would be 'inequitable to allow the recipient free use' of the goods. This provision could lead to uncertainty as to its scope and has the potential to disadvantage Irish consumers where there is no corresponding provision in relation to rejection of goods under current Irish law.[40]

Nevertheless, in some important areas, the CESL does provide the consumer with high levels of protection. For example, unlike the Consumer Sales Directive,[41] under the CESL, it is proposed that consumers will have a free choice of remedies in the case of non-conforming goods, providing the consumer with the right to terminate the contract without first seeking repair or replacement of the goods. This, according to the Commission, will give consumers the confidence and incentive to buy products in other EU countries.[42]

---

38. See Sales Law Review Group, *Report on the Legislation Governing the Sale of Goods and Supply of Services* (Prn A11/1576, 2011) 280 <http://www.djei.ie/commerce/consumer/slrg.htm> accessed 25 October 2013. See further para 3.6 below.
39. See *Jarvis v Swans Tours* [1973] 2 QB 233; *Hynes & Hynes v Happy Holidays Ltd*, Irish Independent, 28 March 1985 (Circuit Court). See further R Clark, *Contract Law in Ireland* (6th edn, Thomson Round Hall 2008) 480.
40. See further para 3.7 below.
41. Directive 99/44/EC on Certain Aspects of the Sale of Consumer Goods and Associated Guarantees.
42. *Communication from the Commission* COM [2011] 636 final.

In setting the level of consumer protection, it is obvious that the Commission has had to balance the interests of consumers and businesses. If the Commission had chosen the highest level of protection from each Member State for inclusion in the CESL, then it is unlikely that businesses would opt in. The compromise does set a relatively high overall level of consumer protection, although some commentators have referred to the possibility that this high level of protection may be eroded before the final CESL text emerges.[43]

The Agreement to Opt In

Another concern relates to the consumer's agreement to opt in to the CESL. The most likely scenario is that the consumer will be presented with a standard term contract, which includes the trader's choice of CESL without the option of negotiating that choice. The trader is unlikely to allow the consumer a choice of contracting under the CESL or their own national laws as this would increase cost and complexity for the trader. The problems of standard term contracts for consumers are well known and reported.[44] A number of regulatory strategies are typically employed to offset the problems of illusory consumer consent to standard terms and conditions. The most common strategy and the one that is employed by the CESL is to give the consumer the information necessary to make an informed decision and thereby restore or reinforce autonomy so that the consumer can make the best choice. Article 8(2) of the Regulation requires consumer consent by explicit statement separate from the statement indicating the agreement to conclude a contract. The then EU Justice Commissioner, Viviane Reding, in a speech to a conference in Leuven on 3 June 2011 referred to the need for the consumer to make their own informed choice. In this regard, she approved of the idea of a 'blue button' on the trader's website, which would make the choice very visible to the consumer. The button would state that '*if you click here, then you contract under European Contract Law, not your national law*'. While agreeing with this idea, she also stated that it needed to be complemented with a legal requirement to inform the consumer about the most important features of the CESL in laymen's terms.[45] This is provided for under art 9, under which the

---

43. Hector McQueen, Charles Garland, Afson Barekat and Emma Boffey, 'Legislative Comment, The Proposed Common European Sales Law' (2012) Scots Law Times 65.
44. Perhaps best summarised by Reid LJ in *Suisse Atlantique Societe d'Armement Maritime SA v Rotterdamsche Kolen Centrale* [1967] 1 AC 361 [406]: 'In the ordinary way the customer has no time to read them, and if he did read them he would probably not understand them. And if he did understand and object to any of them, he would generally be told he could take it or leave it. And if he then went to another supplier the result would be the same.'
45. Viviane Reding, 'The Next Steps to a European Contract Law for Businesses and Consumers', Keynote Speech at the Conference Towards a European Contract Law co-organised by the Study Centre for Consumer Law of the Catholic University of Leuven and the Centre for European Private Law of the University of Munster

trader is required to provide the consumer with the 'standard information notice' set out in Annex II. This information notice sets out the core rights provided for in the CESL. Article 9 also provides that where the agreement to use the CESL is concluded by telephone or by any other means that do not make it possible to provide the consumer with the information notice, or where the trader has failed to provide the information notice, the consumer shall not be bound by the agreement until the consumer has received the confirmation referred to in art 8(2) accompanied by the information notice and has expressly consented subsequently to the use of the CESL. If the information notice is given in electronic form, it must contain a hyperlink or include the indication of a website through which the text of the CESL can be obtained free of charge.[46]

These provisions are clearly designed to ensure that the consumer can make a fully informed decision to accept the application of the CESL to the contract. There has been much academic commentary and debate on the effectiveness of information and mandatory disclosure as a consumer-protection device.[47] Hillman outlines the potential benefits of disclosure as a strategy for dealing with the problem of electronic standard forms. It allows the consumer to educate himself by being able to peruse and compare terms in an unhurried fashion. Even if disclosure fails to increase reading, it has symbolic value by demonstrating that the law makes efforts to make business to consumer transactions fairer. According to Hillman,

> ... disclosure laws in the context of e-standard form contracts would mean that law makers were making an effort to turn into something more meaningful the 'apologetic' legal fiction that consumers understand and assent to the terms of their e-standard form contracts.[48]

Other commentators argue that disclosure of information does not provide any benefits to consumers and is costly and ineffective. Bar-Gill and Ben-Shahar, for example, commenting on the CESL disclosure requirements, state:

> CESL's contract disclosures are likely to fail because consumers will not pay attention to them. People do not pay attention to standard forms, neither long nor short, in

---

(Leuven 3 June 2011) <http://europa.eu/rapid/pressReleasesAction.do?reference-=SPEECH/11/411> accessed 29 October 2013.

46. art 9(2).
47. See, for example, Stephen Weatherill, 'The Role of the Informed Consumer in European Community Law' (1994) 2 Consumer LJ 49; Geraint Howells, 'The Potential and Limits of Consumer Empowerment by Information' (2005) 32 J of L and Soc 349; Robert Hillman, 'Online Boilerplate: Would Mandatory Website Disclosure of E-Standard Terms Backfire?' (2006) 104 Mich L Rev 837; Omri Ben-Shahar and Carl Schneider, 'The Failure of Mandated Disclosure' 159 U of Penn L Rev (2011); Oren Bar Gill and Omri Ben-Shahar, 'Regulatory Techniques in Consumer Protection: A Critique of the Common European Sales Law' (2013) 50 Common Market L Rev 109.
48. Hillman, 'Online Boilerplate', 845–47.

> plain language or in legalese, written or oral, separately signed or unified into one document, handed out in advance, or ex-post. The failure of consumers to attend to mandated disclosures packaged in pre-drafted language, like ones CESL utilizes, has been documented thoroughly, in area after area of consumer transactions, medical 'informed consent', privacy, financial literacy, and much more.[49]

Further, the authors suggest that the mandatory disclosure scheme provided by the CESL is not only futile but may be harmful and more costly. They argue that it would be more costly as it increases transaction costs forcing traders to provide extra forms, signatures, clicks and thereby extending the time involved in a standard form exchange. It is more harmful, they argue, because the presumption that the consumer has provided informed consent may prevent a court from striking down hidden terms if consumers are presumed to be aware of their content.[50]

Nevertheless, it is clear that the Commission in drafting arts 8 and 9 is concerned with the quality of consumers' consent to use of the CESL. It may be the case, as Ben-Shahar and Bar-Gill argue, that consumers may not pay attention to mandated disclosure in pre-drafted language. However, if careful consideration is given to the quality of the information and how the information is presented, it may have value. The main problem with the standard information notice required by art 8 is that the notice does not contain the information the consumer really needs in order to make an informed choice. The standard information notice contains information on the core terms of the CESL, but does not educate the consumer as to the difference between his rights under the CESL and his rights under the laws of his habitual residence. It may not be at all clear to the consumer reading the standard information notice that by choosing to be governed by the CESL, he may lose the protection of his own national laws. In addition, presenting the consumer with the text of the CESL by way of hyperlink is unlikely to aid the consumer in understanding the impact of a choice of CESL. The text of the CESL is dense and complex and difficult to navigate.

The procedure itself, as set out in arts 8 and 9 on the agreement to opt in, has been criticised as being 'rather heavy' and 'a complicated mechanism' involving several parts – ie prior qualified information by submitting the notice of Annex II, existence of an agreement, in case of impossibility of prior information, later confirmation accompanied by the information notice and express consent.[51] Further, the consequences of an ineffective agreement and the sanctions for failure to use the procedure in arts 8 and 9 are unclear and may result in legal uncertainty as to the validity of the contract.[52]

---

49. Bar Gill and Ben-Shahar, 'Regulatory Techniques' 117.
50. ibid 118.
51. Hans W Micklitz and Norbert Reich, 'The Commission Proposal for a "Regulation on a Common European Sales Law (CESL)" – Too Broad or Not Enough?' EU Working Paper Law 2012/04 Department of Law, European University Institute, Florence.
52. Caroline Harvey and Michael Schillig, 'Consequences of an Ineffective Agreement to Use the CESL', 25 August 2012, ssrn: <http://ssrn.com/abstract=2136086>

Unfortunately, it is also still apparent that even where good quality information is provided in a clear way so that a consumer can make an informed decision, a consumer may have little choice where alternative terms are not available. Consumers who want to contract with a particular trader in order to get particular goods at a particular price will effectively have to accept the trader's standard terms, including the application of CESL to the contract.

Pre-contract Information Duties

The trader's duty to inform the consumer as to the agreement to opt in is just one of the many information duties contained in the CESL. A further range of pre-contractual information duties are provided for in arts 13 to 19 of the draft CESL and in arts 24 and 25. These duties of the CESL are divided into those applying in B2C contracts and duties applying in B2B contracts. They are also classified according to whether the contract is a distance/off-premises contract or a general sales contract. Articles 13–19 contain requirements in relation to pre-contract information in distance and off-premises B2C sales. These follow closely the provisions of the Consumer Rights Directive, which are already fully harmonised and will apply as part of national laws from 2014.[53] So, the trader must provide information about the main characteristics of the goods, digital content or related services to be supplied (art 13), the total price and additional charges and costs (art 14), the identity and address of the trader (art 15), the contract terms (art 16), the rights of withdrawal (art 17), the existence and the conditions of the trader's after-sale customer assistance, after-sale services, commercial guarantees and complaints handling policy (art 13), the possibility of having recourse to an Alternative Dispute Resolution mechanism to which the trader is subject and the methods for having access to it (art 13), the functionality, including applicable technical protection measures, of digital content; and any relevant interoperability of digital content with hardware and software which the trader is aware of or can be expected to have been aware of (art 13). Article 19 provides for additional information and requirements in relation to telephone sales and distance sales where the medium allows limited space to display the required information.

---

accessed 29 October 2013. The authors point out the inconsistencies surrounding the validity of the contract where there the mechanism to opt in to the CESL has not been complied with; and see also Simon Whittaker, 'The Proposed "Common European Sales Law": Legal Framework and the Agreement of the Parties' (2012) 75 Modern L Rev 578. Whittaker criticises the mechanism for consumer consent to opt-in and in particular its relationship with private international law rules.

53. Directive 2011/83/EU of the European Parliament and of the Council of 25 October 2011 on consumer rights, amending Council Directive 93/13/EEC and Directive 1999/44/EC of the European Parliament and of the Council and repealing Council Directive 85/577/EEC and Directive 97/7/EC of the European Parliament and of the Council Directive 2011/83/EU of 22 November 2011 [2011] OJ L 304/64. The Directive will apply to contracts concluded after 13 June 2014.

There are also pre-contract information duties for other sales aside from distance and off-premises contracts. The trader has a duty to provide information as to the main characteristics of the goods, digital content or related services, the total price and additional charges and costs, the identity, geographical address and telephone number of trader, contract terms and conditions of any after-sale services, guarantees or complaints policy. In relation to digital content, the trader must provide information as to its functionality including any technical protection measures and interoperability issues the trader is aware of. These information duties are not applicable where the contract involves 'a day-to-day transaction and is performed immediately at the time of its conclusion'.[54] There are additional duties contained in arts 24 and 25 to provide information in relation to contracts concluded by electronic means. These pre-contract information requirements are mandatory and cannot be excluded or varied by the parties. The remedy for failure to comply with these provisions is liability for loss caused to the other party by failure to comply.[55]

Non-Conformity

Existing Irish law on conformity of the goods with the contract is governed by ss 13–15 of the Sale of Goods Acts 1893 and 1980, which contain implied undertakings as to description, quality and fitness for purpose of the goods and also by the EC (Certain Aspects of the Sale of Consumer Goods and Guarantees) Regulations 2003,[56] which give effect to the Consumer Sales Directive.[57] Like many of the other European consumer directives, the Consumer Sales Directive was transposed into Irish law as a stand-alone statutory instrument, with no attempt to integrate it into the existing statutory framework. The result is that for consumer sales, there is a dual regime in relation to conformity of the goods. As the Consumer Sales Directive is a minimum harmonisation measure, Irish consumers can choose to apply either the Regulations or the Act. The legislative landscape in Ireland is therefore complex and difficult for consumers to access. There are different rules on conformity and also different and complex remedial schemes.[58]

Section 13 of the 1893 Act provides that there is an implied condition that where goods are sold by description there is an implied condition that they will correspond with that description. Section 14(2) provides that there

54. arts 20–22.
55. art 29.
56. SI 2003/11.
57. Directive 1999/44/EC of the European Parliament and of the Council of 25 May 1999 on certain aspects of the sale of consumer goods and associated guarantees [1999] OJ L 12, art 2.
58. For a more detailed analysis of the interplay between Irish rules on conformity and the Consumer Sales Directive, see Fidelma White, 'The EC Directive on Certain Aspects of Consumer Sales and Associated Guarantees: One Step Forward, Two Steps Back?' (2000) 7(1) Commercial Law Practitioner 3.

is an implied condition that the goods supplied under the contract are of merchantable quality. Section 14(4) provides that there is an implied term that where a particular purpose has been made known by the buyer, that the goods will be fit for that purpose; and s 15 provides that where goods are sold by sample, the goods will correspond with the sample in quality and the buyer has reasonable opportunity to compare bulk with sample.

Under s 14(3), goods are of merchantable quality if they are as fit for the purpose or purposes for which goods of that kind are commonly bought and as durable as is reasonable to expect having regard to any description applied to them, the price, and all other relevant circumstances.[59]

The provisions on conformity in the Consumer Sales Directive (implemented in Ireland by the 2003 Regulations) are set out in art 2. In summary, goods are deemed to be in conformity with the contract if:

- they comply with the description given by the seller and possess the qualities of the product which the seller has held out to the consumer as a sample or model;
- they are fit for the purposes for which goods of the same type are normally used;
- they are fit for any particular purpose for which the consumer requires them and which was made known to the seller at the time of conclusion of the contract, and accepted by the seller;
- their quality and performance are satisfactory, given the nature of the goods and taking into account the public statements made about them by the seller, the producer or his representative.

The basic provisions on conformity in the draft CESL are set out in art 100. In order to conform with the contract, the goods or digital content must:

(a) be fit for any particular purpose made known to the seller at the time of the conclusion of the contract, except where the circumstances show

59. There has been very little Irish case law on the merchantable quality provision in s 14 of the Sale of Goods Act 1893. As a result, commentators and courts have tended to rely on UK case law for guidance. However, UK and Irish law on quality standards in sales contracts are no longer the same, the UK having changed its standard from 'merchantable quality' to 'satisfactory quality' and adopted a different definition in s 14 of the UK Sale of Goods Act 1979, as amended by s 7 of the Sale and Supply of Goods Act 1994. However, despite the differences in terminology, there may be little difference in the interpretation of the two standards. See Fidelma White, 'The Meaning of "Merchantable Quality": *James Elliot Construction Ltd v Irish Asphalt Ltd*' (2012) 47 Irish Jurist 225. See also, Cowan Ervine, 'Satisfactory Quality: What Does it Mean?' (2004) J of Bus L 684; and Michael Bridge, 'What Is to Be Done about Sale of Goods?' (2003) 119 L Quarterly Rev 173. For a detailed analysis of the development of the law on merchantable quality in Ireland and the UK, see *Sales Law Review Group Report on the Legislation Governing the Sale of Goods and Supply of Services* (Prn A11/1576, 2011) 148–62 <http://www.djei.ie/commerce/consumer/slrg.htm>.

that the buyer did not rely, or that it was unreasonable for the buyer to rely, on the seller's skill and judgment;

(b) be fit for the purposes for which goods or digital content of the same description would ordinarily be used;

(c) possess the qualities of goods or digital content which the seller held out to the buyer as a sample or model;

(d) be contained or packaged in the manner usual for such goods or, where there is no such manner, in a manner adequate to preserve and protect the goods;

(e) be supplied along with such accessories, installation instructions or other instructions as the buyer may expect to receive;

(f) possess the qualities and performance capabilities indicated in any pre-contractual statement which forms part of the contract terms by virtue of Article 69; and

(g) possess such qualities and performance capabilities as the buyer may expect. When determining what the consumer may expect of the digital content, regard is to be had to whether or not the digital content was supplied in exchange for the payment of a price.

It appears that art 100, containing familiar provisions on quality and fitness for purpose, is broadly similar to existing Irish law on conformity. Indeed, arguably it provides stronger provisions on conformity than existing law. For example, the reference to packaging in art 100(d) is a new provision.[60] Article 100(e), which deals with accessories, is also new. If the goods arrive without accessories and instructions that the buyer may reasonably expect, then the consumer has the full range of remedies under the CESL.

One potentially important difference is that art 100 does not contain any specific reference to appearance, finish or freedom from minor defects. This is something the Law Commission has raised concerns about in their advice to the UK government.[61] The UK Sale of Goods Act 1979 provides that aspects of quality may include 'fitness for all the purposes for which the goods are commonly supplied, appearance and finish, freedom from minor defects, safety and durability'.[62] No similar provision exists in the Irish sale of goods legislation, however, a recent report by the Sales Law Review Group,[63] which

60. Packaging is not specifically referenced in the existing statutory rules on conformity of the goods in Irish law, however case law suggests that s 14 covers not only the goods actually bought by the buyer but also packages and containers in which the goods are sold. See, for example, *Geddling v Marsh* [1920] 1 KB 668.

61. Law Commission, *An Optional Common European Sales Law: Advantages and Problems. Advice to the UK Government* (10 November 2011) 54 <http://www.justice.gov.uk/lawcommission/publications/1698.htm>.

62. s 14(2B) Sale of Goods Act 1979.

63. *Sales Law Review Group Report on the Legislation Governing the Sale of Goods and Supply of Services* (Prn. A11/1576, 2011) 280 <http://www.djei.ie/commerce/consumer/slrg.htm>.

was established to make recommendations for the reform and modernisation of Irish sales law, recommends that the quality provision in s 14 of the Act should be amended substituting a test of 'satisfactory quality' for the existing provision and including an indicative list of specific aspects of quality, which should apply alongside the general definition *viz* appearance and finish; freedom from minor defects; safety and durability.[64]

The absence of a provision on appearance and finish of the goods is likely to give rise to some concern that the CESL does not provide adequate levels of protection in relation to minor defects. It is possible, however, that if a consumer is unhappy with the appearance and finish of the goods, they could claim that the goods do not possess the qualities and performance capabilities they might reasonably expect under art 100(g). In effect, therefore, this concern may be overstated. More controversial is the provision in the CESL providing that the consumer's right to terminate is excluded if the non-conformity is 'insignificant'.[65] This is in line with the Consumer Sales Directive, which does not allow the consumer to rescind the contract where the lack of conformity is 'minor'. However, the recommendation of the Sales Law Review Group for future Irish consumer sales legislation is to allow the right to reject for so-called 'minor' defects.[66] It is also unclear what is meant in the CESL by the term 'insignificant' and arguably this provision could lead to uncertainty about what is insignificant in relation to the conformity of the goods.

Remedies

So how does the CESL compare with existing Irish law on remedies for non-conforming goods? Under existing Irish law, the consumer's remedies are set out in the EC (Certain Aspects of the Sale of Consumer Goods and Guarantees) Regulations 2003 and in the Sale of Goods Act 1893. Under the Regulations, at the outset, the consumer is only entitled to a repair or replacement of non-conforming goods, but may rescind the contract if a repair or replacement cannot be provided without unreasonable delay or significant inconvenience. Under the Sale of Goods Act, the consumer also has a right to reject the goods and receive a refund without first seeking repair or replacement from the seller. This right to reject is lost where the buyer is deemed to have accepted the goods under certain conditions, including where, without sufficient reason, he retains the goods without intimating to the seller that he has rejected them.[67]

---

64. ibid 126.
65. art 114(2).
66. According to the Report: 'the appearance and finish of consumer goods is often integral to their overall quality and a provision that limits the remedies available to consumers for defects of this nature would be unjustifiably detrimental to consumer interests', *Sales Law Review Group Report* 282.
67. ss 11, 34 and 35 Sale of Goods Act 1893.

The right to reject the goods as a first-tier remedy is considered to be extremely important in the consumer sales law provisions of Ireland and the UK. The Irish Sales Law Review Group Report recommends integrating the existing scheme of remedies for consumers under the Sale of Goods Acts and the Consumer Sales Regulations. It recommends that three remedies of first resort would be available to consumers for goods not in conformity with the contract. These remedies would consist of: termination of the contract and full refund of the price within a normal 30-day period; replacement of the goods or repair of the goods. Where the consumer opts for repair or replacement, he would be entitled to proceed to the remedy of rejection and refund where repair or replacement was not completed within a reasonable time or without significant inconvenience, or where the lack of conformity was not remedied by the first repair or replacement.[68]

A further recommendation of the Sales Law Review Group Report is to remove the uncertainty surrounding acceptance of the goods and the loss of the right to reject by stipulating that the time period for the exercise of the right to reject goods not in conformity with the contract should normally be 30 days in the case of consumer contracts.[69] A similar recommendation has been made by the Law Commission.[70]

The draft CESL also proposes to give the consumer a free choice of remedies. These remedies include the right:

a) to repair or replacement;
b) to a reduction of the price;
c) to terminate the contract and claim the return of any price paid; and
d) to claim damages.[71]

There has been a broad welcome from consumer groups and others in relation to this choice of remedies provided for in the CESL and the inclusion of the right to reject the goods as a first-tier remedy. However, surprisingly, the right to terminate the contract under the proposed CESL is open-ended in relation to consumer contracts. Article 119 states that in B2B contracts, notice of termination must be given within a 'reasonable' time but there is no such stipulation in B2C contracts. The only time limit appears to be the prescription period in arts 179 and 180, which provides that the consumer must act within two years of the time that they knew or ought to have known of the fault, or within 10 years of the sale if this is a shorter period. It is, however, possible that prolonged delay by the consumer in notifying the trader of a fault may constitute a lack of good

68. *Sales Law Review Group Report on the Legislation Governing the Sale of Goods and Supply of Services* (Prn A11/1576, 2011) 319.
69. ibid 274.
70. *Consumer Remedies for Faulty Goods* (2009) Law Com No 317 and Scot Law Com No 216.
71. art 106.

faith under art 2, thereby making the remedy unavailable. A trader may also make a deduction for use when refunding the consumer if the consumer was 'aware of the ground for avoidance or termination' but delayed taking action, or if 'it would be inequitable to allow the recipient the free use' of these goods.[72]

This extended right to terminate has attracted adverse comment. Although an extended termination period provides a high level of protection, it may place an undue burden on traders, who might be deterred as a result from using the CESL. The questions of whether or not the consumer has acted in good faith or should give allowance for use are criticised as being likely to lead to uncertainty and scope for dispute between the parties.[73] Given the extent of criticism in relation to this particular provision, it is seems likely to be re-negotiated before the final version of the CESL emerges.[74]

Unfair Terms

The provisions on unfair terms in consumer contracts are largely similar to those provided for in the Unfair Terms Directive[75] implemented in Ireland by the EC (Unfair Terms in Consumer Contract) Regulations.[76] It is clear that arts 82–85 are based on the Directive. A term is unfair if it 'causes a significant imbalance in the parties' rights and obligations arising under the contract to

72. art 174.
73. According to the Law Commission in its Advice to the UK Government: '... the right to reject is a powerful weapon which should be kept for faults that manifest themselves immediately or after a short period of use. After the product has been used for a while, the primary remedy should be a repair or replacement.' *Advice to the UK Government* (10 November 2011) 62 <http://www.justice.gov.uk/lawcommission/publications/1698.htm>. See also OFT response to the call for evidence on a Common European Sales Law for the European Union – *A Proposal for a Regulation from the European Commission* www.oft.gov.uk/shared_oft/reports/oft_response_to.../CESL1.pdf, accessed 29 October 2013 and Regine Feltkamp and Frederic Vanbosselle, 'The Optional Common European Sales Law: Better Buyer's Remedies for Seller's Non-Performance in Sales of Goods? (2011) 6 Euro Rev of Private Law 873.
74. The Legal Affairs Committee of the European Parliament has approved an amended version of the CESL based on its Rapporteurs' Report. In response to the criticisms in relation to the right to terminate, the amended version provides that the buyer loses the right to terminate if notice of termination is not given within two months from when the right arose or the buyer became aware of the non-performance, whichever is later. This would not apply where no performance at all has been rendered. See Final Report as voted on by the Legal Affairs Committee on 17 September 2013, available at: http://www.europarl.europa.eu/document/activities/cont/201309/20130925ATT71873/20130925ATT71873EN.pdf , accessed 29 October 2013.
75. Council Directive 93/13/EEC on unfair terms in consumer contracts [1993] OJ L 95.
76. SI 1995/27 European Communities (Unfair Terms in Consumer Contracts) Regulations 1995.

the detriment of the consumer contrary to good faith and fair dealing'.[77] There are also familiar black and grey lists of unfair terms.[78]

However, the Unfair Terms Directive only contains protection in relation to content of terms. The CESL, while providing similar controls in relation to the content of standard term contracts, also contains rules on the incorporation of non-negotiated terms into a contract. Article 70 is very significant and provides for a specific duty to raise awareness of non-individually negotiated contract terms. It provides that non-negotiated terms may not be invoked against a consumer unless the consumer was aware of them or if the trader took reasonable steps to draw the other party's attention to them before or at the time the contract was concluded.

Moreover, art 70(2) provides that in relations between a trader and a consumer, contract terms are not sufficiently brought to the consumer's attention by a mere reference to them in a contract document, even if the consumer signs the document. This provision will apply regardless of the substance of the term. The term does not have to be shown to be unfair. If the trader failed to take reasonable steps to draw the term to the consumer's attention, then it will not be binding on the consumer.

This provision goes further than the Unfair Contract Terms Directive to protect the consumer. Arguably, it also goes further than existing common law contract principles on incorporation of terms. At common law, standard terms can be enforced without the signature of either party if reasonable notice of the terms are given to the other party at the time the contract is made.[79] Whether reasonable notice has been given depends on the facts of the case. It is also settled that where a condition is particularly onerous or unusual, the party seeking to enforce it must show that the condition was fairly brought to the notice of the other party.[80] Article 70 applies to all terms regardless of whether they are particularly onerous or unusual. Article 70(2) provides that even where there is a signature, reasonable steps must be taken to draw the consumer's attention to the terms.

This provision in the CESL may have particular relevance in the context of website trading. The question of incorporation of terms in standard term 'click-wrap' and 'browse-wrap' was at issue in the Irish case of *Ryanair v Billigfleuge*.[81] In this case, Ryanair was seeking to enforce an exclusive jurisdiction clause in its standard contract terms. The clause was contained in its terms of use on its website, highlighted by a hyperlink. The court referred to the jurisprudence of US courts on the issue of incorporation of online terms and conditions.

77. art 83.
78. arts 84 and 85.
79. *Parker v South Eastern Railways Ltd* (1877) 2 CPD 416; *Carroll v An Post National Lottery* [1996] 1 IR 443.
80. *Interfoto Picture Library Ltd v Stiletto Visual Programmes Ltd* [1989] QB 433.
81. *Ryanair Ltd v Billigfluege.de GMBH* [2010] IEHC 47.

In particular, Hanna J cited *Specht v Netscape*, where it was held that reasonable notice of the licence terms for free software was not given as the terms were placed below the download button and users were not likely to scroll down the webpage sufficiently to read the terms before downloading the software. Hanna J also referred to traditional contract law cases such as *Thornton v Shoe Lane Parking Ltd*,[82] in which it was held that the defendant had not taken sufficient steps to ensure that the notice containing the exclusion clause was brought to the attention of customers of the car park before they bought their ticket. He also made reference to the *Interfoto*[83] case and found that if terms were unusual or onerous, the party seeking to enforce the terms must show that the condition was fairly brought to the attention of the other party. Applying these authorities to the facts of the case, Hanna J found that the terms of use on Ryanair's website were 'fairly brought to the attention of the other party'. The terms were accessible by way of a hyperlink, which was clearly visible to users of the site. The terms were not hidden in an awkward part of the screen or in any way concealed or difficult to find.

It is not clear how art 70 might apply in the context of website standard term contracting. The crucial question is what is meant by '*reasonable steps*' in that Article. It seems that it may not be enough to simply provide a hyperlink to the terms of use as was done in the *Ryanair* case and that a more prominent warning as to the existence of the standard terms would be necessary even where the consumer has signed or 'clicked' to accept the terms. It is important that this issue is clarified. The area of cross-border internet consumer sales is where the CESL is likely to have its greatest impact. If traders are uncertain as to whether their standard terms are incorporated through their website standard terms and conditions, they may be reluctant to use the optional instrument.

Use of CESL in B2B Contracts

The proposal for the optional instrument envisages that choice of the CESL is not limited to B2C contracts but also can be used in cross-border contracts between traders. However, art 7(1) provides that for B2B contracts, use of CESL is restricted to cases where one party is a small or medium-sized enterprise or 'SME'.[84] Notwithstanding this restriction, Member States are given the choice to make the CESL also available for B2B contracts where neither of the parties is an SME, where a Member State considers this to be appropriate.

The explanatory memorandum to the Proposal sets out the rationale for the extension of the CESL to contracts between traders where one of the parties is an SME. It refers to the significant impact of contract law related

82. [1971] 2 QB 163.
83. *Interfoto Picture Library Ltd v Stiletto Visual Programmes Ltd* [1989] QB 433.
84. Article 7(2) provides that an SME is a trader that employs fewer than 250 persons and has an annual turnover not exceeding Eur 50 million or an annual balance sheet total not exceeding Eur 43 million.

transaction costs and legal obstacles in cross-border transactions stemming from differences in national contract laws, these costs having the greatest impact on SMEs. In their relations with larger companies, SMEs generally have to agree to apply the law of their business partner and bear the costs of finding out about the content of the foreign law applicable to the contract and of complying with it. In contracts between SMEs, according to the Commission, the need to negotiate the applicable law is a significant obstacle to cross-border trade and these additional transaction costs may even be disproportionate to the value of the transaction. These barriers may dissuade businesses from entering new markets and trading across borders.[85]

In her speech at Leuven, Commissioner Reding also referred to the fact that SMEs make up 99 per cent of the businesses in the European Union and to the importance of making transactions in the single market easier and legally more certain for them. She also made reference to the fact that they can often be the weaker party in a business-to-business context and therefore need protection against use of unfair terms being imposed.[86]

Whether the choice of CESL should be restricted to SMEs must be questioned. It adds a layer of complexity to the application of the CESL that is unnecessary. Article 7 defines an SME as 'a trader which employs fewer than 250 persons and has an annual turnover not exceeding Eur 50 million or an annual balance sheet total not exceeding Eur 43 million'. Recital 21 of the Proposal states that the definition must be applied according with Recommendation 2003/361.[87] This Recommendation applies a complicated set of criteria to the assessment of SMEs, including provisions in relation to counting employees and calculating turnover. This could create an undesirable level of uncertainty in B2B transactions as to whether or not the choice of the CESL is open to a particular party. Moreover, there seem no obvious advantages to maintaining a restriction on the use of CESL in all B2B transactions. Why not simplify the rules and allow all businesses to make a free choice of law, which would include the CESL?

In practice, given the relative bargaining strengths in contracts between SMEs and large businesses, whether there would be a real choice for the smaller business is questionable. It is more likely that the stronger party would be able to insist on its choice of law, which may not be the CESL. In effect, the success of the CESL in B2B contracts would be very much dependent on whether or not the business sector embraces the CESL and is willing to use the CESL for their cross-border contracts in place of their current choice of law.

A business deciding whether or not to use the CESL for their B2B cross-border trading activities needs to consider to what extent it creates a cost saving or

---

85. *Proposal for a Regulation of the European Parliament* COM [2011] 636 final, Explanatory Memorandum, 3.
86. Speech to Conference 'Towards a European Contract Law' (Leuven 3 June 2011) 19.
87. Commission Recommendation of 6 May 2003 concerning the definition of micro, small and medium-sized enterprises (2003/361/EC).

brings legal certainty to the contractual arrangements between the parties. While the CESL does contain a comprehensive code for sales transactions, many of its provisions could be considered to be open-ended and perhaps could lead to dispute and litigation at the cost of legal certainty. Many of these provisions are unknown to Irish sales law and unfamiliar to traders and their legal advisers.

The prime example of an open-ended provision in the CESL is the duty of good faith and fair dealing in art 2.[88] This duty is mandatory wherever the CESL is chosen. Breach of the duty could give rise to the party who is in breach being prevented from exercising a legal right or remedy or a defence that they otherwise would have had, at the discretion of the court. The standard of good faith is assessed according to the relative expertise of the parties and differs in the commercial or consumer context. The duty of good faith also arises in the context of art 23. It imposes a duty of disclosure on traders in B2B contracts to disclose such characteristics of goods and services that it would be contrary to good faith not to disclose. Choice of CESL would also allow for rules on unfair terms in contracts between traders. Article 86 provides that a term is unfair if it is not individually negotiated and 'it is of such a nature that its use grossly deviates from good commercial practice, contrary to good faith and fair dealing'. Further reference to good faith principles appears in art 89, which contains rules on performance of the contract. Where 'performance becomes excessively onerous because of an exceptional change of circumstances', there is a duty to negotiate in good faith with a view to adapting or terminating the contract. If the parties fail to do so within a reasonable time, then at the request of either party, the court may effectively intervene and rewrite the contract.

It is seems likely that these open-ended norms in the CESL will be a deterrent to businesses considering switching to CESL as their choice of law for B2B contracts. Businesses may fear that these uncertain and open-ended provisions will result in prolonged litigation or will allow judges to intervene to rewrite their agreed terms. There is a degree of uncertainty as to how these provisions will be interpreted by the courts and this lack of predictability may impact the decision of a trader to opt in to the CESL. Businesses concerned about the application of the good-faith duties may choose to exclude some of these rules; however, this would require businesses to incur further legal costs in rewriting the provisions of the CESL. It seems unlikely that a business would choose to do this rather than choose its existing national law, which would have the advantage of being known and being predictable. In addition, some of these rules are stated to be mandatory and cannot be excluded. The duty of good faith in art 2, for example, is mandatory, as is art 86 on terms that are regarded as unfair.

Perhaps the greatest market for the CESL in the B2B context will be in contracts between SMEs. In these situations, the parties generally use standard forms and in many cases wish to avoid the legal costs associated with negotiating contracts. For SMEs, the use of CESL terms would allow them a neutral choice of law, involving a

88. See above para 3.1.

single contract law system and may allow them increased opportunities to trade and to expand into new markets.

The CISG and the CESL Compared

A further point must be made about the relationship between the CESL and the Vienna Convention on the International Sale of Goods (CISG). The CISG also contains a set of uniform substantive rules for the regulation of international sales contracts involving parties with a place of business in contracting states. The CISG is narrower in scope than the CESL as it only applies to B2B cross-border transactions and has no application in the consumer context. The CISG has been ratified by 76 states in total, including all of the world's main trading economies. All EU Member States have ratified the Convention except for Ireland, the UK, Portugal and Malta. Ireland has not yet acceded to the Convention despite a recommendation to that effect from the Law Reform Commission in 1992.[89] In 2011, the Sales Law Review Group also recommended that Ireland should ratify and it seems likely that the provisions necessary to accede to the CISG will be included in the amended legislation on sale of goods whenever that is introduced.[90]

The CISG applies to contracts of sale of goods between parties whose places of business are in different states where both parties are in contracting states, or the rules of private international law lead to the application of the law of a contracting state.[91] For Irish businesses, and for businesses from the other states who have not ratified the Convention, the parties may choose to use the CISG if the other party is from a contracting state. They may also use the CISG by choosing the law of a country that fully incorporates the CISG. So, for most EU states, the CISG is the default regime for B2B cross-border sales contracts. However, the principles of the Convention are based on party autonomy and therefore Art 6 provides that the parties may exclude the application of the Convention in whole or in part and choose another law. As such, therefore, the CISG, like the CESL is an optional instrument where the parties may agree to 'opt out' as opposed to 'opt in' in the case of the CESL. The Sales Law Review Group in its Report finds that opting out of the CISG is a fairly wide practice by the parties to international sales contracts and that 'the standard form contracts of many leading trade associations expressly exclude CISG as do those of the large oil companies'.[92] This raises the obvious question: If parties to the CISG are opting out of the CISG, are they any more likely to opt in to the CESL?

---

89. Law Reform Commission, *Report on United Nations (Vienna) Convention on Contracts for the International Sale of Goods* LRC 42–1992.
90. *Sales Law Review Group Report on the Legislation Governing the Sale of Goods and Supply of Services* (Prn A11/1576, 2011), ch 15, 449.
91. art 1(1).
92. *Sales Law Review Group Report* 280, ch 15, 449.

In its favour, in terms of content, the CESL contains a more comprehensive set of rules covering the whole lifecycle of a contract. For example, unlike the CESL, the CISG does not cover the validity of a contract, nor does it contain any provisions on unfair terms or information duties. The principle of good faith appears in the CISG in art 7(1), however, it is to be used as an interpretive principle and not a specific duty leading to specific consequences in the event of breach as it is in the CESL. The CISG has no detailed provisions on conflicting standard terms or 'the battle of the forms' as has art 39 of the CESL.

One of the main considerations for a business in choosing the law that will apply to its transactions is legal certainty and predictability of the law in the event of a dispute. Perhaps a drawback for the CISG is that it does not have its own court and is subject to rulings of national courts, which can lead to inconsistent interpretation of its rules. This could be a reason why so many parties opt out of the CISG. The CESL has an advantage in this regard in that disagreement about its interpretation can be resolved by the European Court of Justice. Recognising the importance of legal certainty as to the interpretation of its provisions, the Commission proposes that a publicly available database of European and national decisions will be set up. Member States are required to ensure that national judgments are communicated to the Commission for this purpose.[93] Nevertheless it remains the case that many of the provisions of the CESL are open-ended and many businesses may fear that the text leaves too much room for varying interpretations. In the first instance, it is still national courts that must make decisions and interpret the provisions of the CESL. There is likely to be a great deal of uncertainty in relation to the interpretation of its provisions, especially those that are unfamiliar in Ireland and the UK, such as the duty of good faith.[94] A large number of preliminary rulings may arise in the early years and it may take some years before a body of jurisprudence builds up to provide the certainty and continuity that the parties to such contracts require.[95]

So, it seems that the CISG and the CESL will co-exist. The CISG will remain the default regime for cross-border B2B transactions but the parties will be free to explicitly 'opt in' to the CESL. Article 25 of the Preamble provides that where the CISG would otherwise apply to the contract, the choice of CESL should imply an agreement of the parties to exclude the CISG. Rather than displacing the CISG, the CESL simply provides an additional choice for businesses. In the long term, the market will decide which regime it prefers. Whether businesses will

93. art 14 CESL.
94. See above para 3.1.
95. See further, Nicole Kornet, 'The Common European Sales Law and the CISG – Complicating or Simplifying the Legal Environment?', Maastricht European Private Law Institute Working Paper No 2012/4 <http://papers.ssrn.com/sol3/papers.cfm?abstract_id=2012310>, accessed 29 October 2013. See also Jan Smits, 'The Common European Sales Law Beyond Party Choice', Maastricht European Private Law Institute Working Paper No 2012/11 <http://papers.ssrn.com/sol3/papers.cfm?abstract_id=2039345>.

choose to use the CESL may depend on a number of factors. It may prove to be a practical and effective neutral choice for SMEs contracting on standard terms. Confidence in the effectiveness of its terms may be boosted by involvement of the European Court of Justice in interpreting its provisions. However, businesses may also be deterred by the lack of certainty in the initial years and concerned at some of the unfamiliar, open-ended rules. The extension of the optional instrument to B2B transactions has met with a mixed response. The Law Commission Advice to the UK Government is concerned that

> The CESL offers the parties a free choice – which we welcome. Even if we are right to be pessimistic, and the CESL is hardly ever used, no harm would be done. On the other hand, we are not convinced that developing a CESL for commercial parties should be seen as a priority for the European Commission's scarce resources...[96]

Impact in Ireland

The remaining question is how the CESL will fit in with Irish sales law. The existing landscape of commercial and consumer sales law is already complex. Commercial and consumer sales are both governed by the Sale of Goods Acts 1893 and 1980. However, a number of European consumer protection directives have also been implemented in Irish law by means of Statutory Instrument. In particular, the Consumer Sales and Related Guarantees Directive[97] was transposed as a standalone piece of legislation without integrating it into existing sales law in Ireland. The result is that the European Communities (Certain Aspects of the Sale of Consumer Goods and Associated Guarantees) Regulations 2003[98] provide for a separate regime of consumer sales law, which differs from the Sale of Goods Acts in relation to a number of important matters, such as quality standards for goods and buyers' remedies. Consumer buyers must choose to pursue their legal rights under the Regulations or under the Sale of Goods Act. This requires the consumer to be able to compare the rights and remedies under the two regimes and make a choice as to which is the best option, a task that would prove difficult even for even an experienced lawyer.

This unsatisfactory situation was referred to by the Sales Law Review Group in its recent Report. It recommended that a separate statute should be enacted to consolidate the law in relation to core provisions applicable to consumer contracts. This 'Consumer Rights Act' would incorporate the main statutory provisions applicable to consumer contracts, including the provisions of the

96. *An Optional Common European Sales Law: Advantages and Problems. Advice to the UK Government* (10 November 2011) 114 <http://www.justice.gov.uk/lawcommission/publications/1698.htm>, accessed 29 October 2013.
97. Directive 1999/44/EC of the European Parliament and of the Council of 25 May 1999 on certain aspects of the sale of consumer goods and associated guarantees [1999] OJ L 12.
98. SI 2003/11.

Consumer Rights Directive, the Directive on Consumer Sales and Associated Guarantees, the Directive on Unfair Contract Terms and relevant consumer provisions in the Sale of Goods Acts 1893 and 1980. Provisions relating to non-core aspects of consumer sales, such as transfer of property, transfer of title and rights of the unpaid seller against the goods, would continue to be dealt with together with all provisions relating to commercial contracts in a separate Sale and Supply of Goods and Supply of Services Act. According to the Report, '… there would be considerable benefit to both consumers and businesses in bringing together in an accessible way the main statutory provisions applicable to consumer contract rights'.[99]

There is no doubt that the proposal to consolidate consumer contract rights into one statute will serve greatly to enhance the transparency and accessibility of consumer sales law in Ireland. However, we must now consider the impact on the Irish legislative landscape of an additional optional instrument in the form of the CESL. The proposed CESL is presented in the form of a Regulation and will therefore be directly applicable in the Member States without the need for implementing measures. There will be no necessity or opportunity to integrate the CESL into the existing statutory regime. Consumers will again have a choice for cross-border contracts (and for domestic contracts should Ireland decide to exercise its discretion to extend choice of CESL to all contracts). For consumers, this potentially removes the advantage that a single consolidated consumer sales law would bring. Are we asking consumers to become comparative lawyers, able to make rational decisions about the most effective choice of law? To ensure that this does not become a burden for consumers and does not complicate the landscape of consumer rights, it is imperative that national legislatures ensure that appropriate comparative information is made available to consumers in a simple and accessible format.[100] Consumers need to be able to clearly distinguish between the legal regimes and understand the practical effect of their choice. In this regard, the National Consumer Agency will play a vital role in informing as to the benefits for the consumer of a choice of the CESL. The more information and endorsement as to the effectiveness of CESL as a choice, the more likely it is that the CESL will become trusted by

99. *Sales Law Review Group Report on the Legislation Governing the Sale of Goods and Supply of Services* (Prn A11/1576, 2011) summary para 63.

100. See further Jan Smits, 'The Common European Sales Law (CESL) Beyond Party Choice', Maastricht European Private Law Institute Working Paper No 2012/11 <http://papers.ssrn.com/sol3/papers.cfm?abstract_id=2039345>, accessed 29 October 2013. Smits proposes that new technologies could be used to provide alternative methods of informing consumers and businesses. People should be able to share experiences on the use of the CESL in comparison with other legal systems and for this purpose: he suggests an interactive website that would offer rankings of jurisdictions based on their attractiveness for parties where experiences could be shared in relation to the use of the various options.

consumers and businesses alike and will gain the necessary critical mass to become an effective regime for consumer cross-border sales.

Despite being presented in the form of a Regulation, Member States retain some discretion in relation to the scope of the CESL and so Ireland will need to make a number of choices. First, whether the CESL should be made available for domestic contracts as well as cross-border contracts; and second, whether it should be made available for all B2B contracts without a requirement that one of them be an SME.

From a business perspective, in order to enhance efficiency of transactions, Ireland should use the option of making the CESL available for domestic transactions as well as cross-border transactions. Part of the rationale behind the CESL is to reduce transaction costs by simplifying and providing a uniform set of contract law rules for contracts. If a business has to distinguish between domestic and cross-border transactions and apply different rules to each, then this would complicate its business structure. It would clearly be beneficial to traders, particularly internet traders, to use one system of law for all their sales.

Likewise, Ireland should also exercise its discretion to make the CESL available for contracts between traders where neither party is an SME. The requirement that in B2B contracts one of the traders must be an SME adds an unnecessary level of complexity to the choice of law. The definition of an SME is technical and may prove difficult to apply in practice. It isn't really clear why choice of CESL should be removed in large business transactions. Why not allow parties in B2B transactions a free choice of law, which would include the CESL? It may be difficult to see why a choice of CESL would be made in B2B transactions given the relatively uncertainty likely to exist in relation to the interpretation of its provisions. Nevertheless, there seems no reason to complicate the scope of the CESL in this way.

Conclusion

Undoubtedly, the case for the optional instrument is stronger in B2C than in B2B transactions. Attempts at maximum harmonisation of consumer sales law have not been successful. Businesses engaged in cross-border transactions with consumers are subject to the consumer-friendly provisions of art 6 of the Rome I Regulation and must therefore deal with different mandatory consumer protection rules of the consumer's habitual residence across the Member States regardless of the choice of law. The CESL attempts to solve this problem by providing a comprehensive uniform set of rules to apply in all consumer transactions. For the most part, the CESL as now drafted should provide the consumer with the advantage of a high level of protection in relation to cross-border transactions. With use, over time, consumers may associate it with a set of terms that can be trusted and it may therefore encourage confidence in cross-border transactions. While the CESL contains provisions to ensure that the consumer is informed, there remains a question mark over the extent to which the consumer has a real choice when presented with a trader's standard terms. Despite the existence of a 'blue button' and a standard information notice, the question of the consumer's real consent to the terms is a worrying issue. National consumer organisations will play an important role in ensuring that consumers are informed as to their core rights under the terms of the CESL.

Given the existence of the CISG, the case for another uniform set of laws for B2B contracts is not very compelling. It is difficult to envisage why parties to a B2B contract would make a choice of CESL. Its most likely sphere of application may be in the case of SMEs by making negotiations of the applicable law easier and reducing the costs associated with cross-border contracts. In that regard, the extension of the proposal to B2B contracts is useful and there seems to be little to be lost in offering it as another choice for businesses in relation to cross-border transactions. Ireland should exercise the option of extending to all B2B transactions regardless of whether one party is an SME.

So, what are the prospects for success for the CESL? Will the CESL be embraced by businesses and consumers for their cross-border contracts in sufficient numbers to give the optional instrument the momentum it needs to become established as the appropriate choice of law? From the point of view of the consumer, the CESL as drafted gives a high level of protection and so can be looked on positively. However, businesses may be concerned at this high level of protection and particularly provisions such as that allowing for an extended termination period in the case of non-conforming goods. Of course, businesses will also need to know that the CESL's provisions are predictable and certain. In this regard, many may have concerns as to some of the CESL's more open-ended provisions, including concepts such as good faith, previously unknown and untested in this country. In addition, for any business contemplating new terms, costs of start-up may be high and this would undoubtedly also be a factor in a decision to use the CESL.

To allay concerns as to the application and interpretation of the provisions of the CESL, the Commission has proposed enacting so-called 'flanking measures'.[101] So, it proposes developing 'European model contract terms' for specialist areas of trade or sectors of activity. This would be a model contract that has standard terms and conditions available in all official languages of the European Union. The Commission also envisages the setting up of a database of European and national decisions that have a bearing on the interpretation of the instrument. Finally, the Commission proposes to organise training sessions for legal practitioners who use the CESL.

The Commission views the CESL as 'a concrete solution for a tangible problem for businesses and consumers: costs and legal uncertainty when buying or selling cross-border in Europe's internal market'. It also hails the CESL as an innovative solution that gives businesses a uniform optional instrument whilst still preserving Member States' legal traditions and cultures.[102] Final agreement on the optional instrument is still some way off. The Legal Affairs Committee of the European

101. See *Communication from the Commission* COM [2011] 636 final, para 2.4.
102. ibid para 3.

Parliament has produced a draft report that proposes a number of amendments to the Commission's text and a majority of Committee members have voted in favour of this amended proposal.[103] The Committee negotiators have now received a mandate to start negotiations with the European Council where a final decision will be made. It seems likely, however, that the Commission's proposal for an optional instrument will be adopted largely in its present form, having been already endorsed in principle by a convincing majority in the European Parliament in 2011 and again by its Legal Affairs Committee in 2013.[104] Once adopted, the success of the CESL will depend on how the parties will react in practice to the existence of another choice of law as the basis for their contracts. In the end, the market will be the final arbiter of this new approach to European contract law.

103. Final Report as voted on by the Legal Affairs Committee on 17 September 2013, available at: http://www.europarl.europa.eu/document/activities/cont/201309/20130925ATT71873/20130925ATT71873EN.pdf , accessed 29 October 2013. The most significant of these proposed amendments is the proposal to limit the scope of the optional instrument to distance contracts. In effect, this limitation would not necessarily have a major impact on the material sphere of application of the optional instrument, as it is in the area of online sales that the Commission sees the main use for the CESL. However, at a public hearing on the draft report of the Legal Affairs Committee, opposition was expressed to this proposed limitation by a number of speakers. See, for example, comments of Ursula Pachl of BEUC who was concerned that the limitation in scope would lead to increased fragmentation; and Professor Hugh Beale who comments that the CESL should be aimed primarily at distance contracts, but not necessarily limited to them. (The Proposal for a Common European Sales Law, Work in Progress: Presentations to the Legal Affairs Committee of the European Parliament), 19 March 2013. Available at: http://www.europarl.europa.eu/committees/en/juri/events.html, accessed 29 October 2013.

104. See *European Commission Press Release* (8 June 2011) <http://europa.eu/rapid/press-release_IP-11-683_en.htm?locale=en> accessed 29 October 2013,

Sanctions and Financial Regulation: A Meditation upon 'Natural Necessity'

Shaun Elder*

Abstract—The relationship between law and regulation and the markets where crises are endemic is complex. Market society is inherently criminogenic, necessitating deterrent sanction. Punishment is fundamental to criminal law and practice and is impacted by social, political and cultural trends. From historical origin both market and criminal law theory are underpinned by the conflict between individual self-interest and community interest as reflected in the social and political public interest. Issues in criminal practice and the markets assisted the rise of the 'regulatory state'. Criminal law and regulation are a binary that police the financial market regulatory control domain. The interplay between criminal and administrative sanction is a crucial element in repression of illegal, and regulation of legal, markets. New transformational interplay approaches are called for.

> Lagarde[1]: '...we need a stronger and safer financial sector that puts societal interest ahead of its own financial gain. This means better, and more coordinated, regulation... We simply cannot carry on with the financial sector that gave us the global financial crisis.'

Introduction

The genesis of this article is the global financial crisis (GFC) and its ongoing aftermath effects, where in its initial phase at least, an unruly market domain exceeded the regulatory control domain. Hard lessons learned have included that the global economy is incredibly complicated and interconnected, and that it is riven by financial fault lines capable of transmitting economic tremors at both lightning speed and in all directions.[2]

One of the key challenges to emerge concerns the relevance or efficacy of criminal law enforcement in controlling corporate and individual financial market behaviour around supply side financial innovation, such as product innovation (especially derivatives), business plans, and the use of superfast technology.

---

* PhD Candidate, University of Limerick.

1. The author acknowledges the kind assistance of the two peer reviewers and is grateful for their helpful comments.
Christine Lagarde, *Opening Remarks* (address to the IMF/CFP Policy Roundtable on the Future of Financial Regulation, Washington DC, 17 April 2012).

2. Nemat Shafik, *Global Economic Challenges and Fostering Future Prosperity* (address at the University of Iceland, Reykjavik, 28 October 2011).

However, the relationship between law and regulation and the markets, where crises are endemic, is complex and contingent with dynamic tensions and interconnections paradoxically commingling.[3] Market failure is a primary rationale for government regulatory intervention and the origin of the post-crisis regulatory response.[4] The broad thrust of the impact of such regulation, and especially regulatory reform where sanctions are a vital foundation, has been described by Macrory:

> Regulation almost by definition is introduced where the unconstrained market cannot by itself guarantee goals that society wishes. An effective system of sanctions underpins any regulatory structure...[5]

Financial regulation is tasked to fulfil many interlocking roles, including societal and economic protection and prevention, ensuring market efficiency and correction, and punishing market wrongdoers. The Irish Central Bank as financial regulator oversees 14 separate categories of financial service provider, which require licence authorisation or approval, including professional bodies, retail intermediaries, credit institutions (including banks), insurance undertakings, investment firms and those operating in regulated markets.

Market society is inherently criminogenic necessitating deterrent sanction.[6] Punishment is fundamental to criminal law and practise and is impacted by social, political and cultural trends. From historical origin both market and criminal law theory are underpinned by the conflict between individual self-interest and community interest as reflected in the social and political public interest. Issues in criminal practice and the markets have assisted the rise of what some describe as the 'regulatory state'.

Criminal law and regulation are a binary that police the financial market control domain.[7] Thus, the interplay between criminal and administrative sanction within this binary is a crucial element in repression of illegal, and regulation of legal, markets. Responsive Regulation techniques dominate explicitly or implicitly, with criminal sanction, however, sometimes sandwiched between administrative penalties and with criminal prosecutions rare. Modern regulatory strategies, it has been claimed, have resulted in the acceptance of the normality

---

3. Carmen M Reinhart and Kenneth S Rogoff, *This Time Is Different: Eight Centuries of Financial Folly* (Princeton University Press 2009); Julia Black, 'Empirical Legal Studies in Financial Markets: What Have We Learned' (2010) LSE Law, Society and Economy Working Papers 4/2010.
4. Arie Freiberg, *The Tools of Regulation* (The Federation Press 2010).
5. Richard Macrory, 'Reforming Regulatory Sanctions – Designing a Systematic Approach' in Dawn Oliver, Tony Prosser and Richard Rawlings (eds), *The Regulatory State* (Oxford University Press 2010) 229.
6. Ian Taylor, *Crime in Context: A Critical Criminology of Market Societies* (Polity Press 1999).
7. Celia Wells, 'Corporate Crime: Opening the Eyes of the Sentry' (2010) 30(3) Legal Studies 370.

of crime. Negotiated settlements for corporate offenders have become the norm. The prison messaging icon has been marginalised by double jeopardy and other considerations. Such a milieu begs the question: Are criminal law and regulation really incompatible 'black boxes' requiring a concerted connective tissue?[8]

The identification and growth of a 'risk society' has led to the responsive deployment of public resources to the control, deterrence or the minimisation of hazard in a way known as the 'new penology' based around economic or 'actuarial' considerations,[9] a remove from the traditional social or community underpinning of the criminal dimension. One of these 'economic risks' that arose pre-crisis was a compounding regulatory failure with disastrous results globally. Post GFC, reforms, therefore, have brought increased institutionalisation and new control mechanisms, regulatory reform weighed down by systemic risk, where targeting – a counterpart of actuarial justice – is a hallmark response, amid demands for increased criminal law deterrence messaging. Financial regulation as social control in such an environment, while crucially important to both national and global economies, and societies, nonetheless is problematic.

Husak's somewhat obvious statement that: 'In deciding what behaviours are deserving of penal sanctions we decide what conduct we want to deter,'[10] begs the issue: What economic self-interest does society really wish to deter and by what means?

This article draws from cross-disciplinary sources to examine these issues mainly from the criminal law vantage of the binary. A wobbling paradigm is revealed awaiting equilibrium. Set against an often unruly market background, I argue a case for transformational change in the use of the criminal law within the sanction binary, and as a beneficial improvement of financial regulation generally. The criminal law paradigm is discussed and found to be in flux, and this restlessness provides an ideal opportunity to consider and implement transformative regulatory reform, beyond procedural tampering, into more substantive areas.

I commence with an examination of criminogenic financial markets as a discussional back-drop. It must be acknowledged that the rational actor is a long-standing trope in both criminology and economics, although in my view market actors pre-crisis acted rationally but were negligent/mistaken, reckless and in that perhaps irrational, or downright criminal. Seeking to establish the argument for transformational change we move to a consideration of deterrent sanctioning, its rationale and underpinning values and beliefs within such markets, and which ground the sanction paradigm itself. I review the concept of 'managing

8. Gunther Teubner, 'After Legal Instrumentalism? Strategic Models of Post-Regulatory Law' (1984) 12 Int'l J of the Sociology of L 375.
9. Malcolm M Feeley and Jonathan Simon, 'The New Penology: Notes on the Emerging Strategy of Corrections and its Implications' (1992) 30 Criminology 449; Malcolm M Feeley and Jonathan Simon, 'Actuarial Justice: The Emerging New Criminal Law' in David Nelken (ed), *The Futures of Criminology* (Sage Publications 1994).
10. Douglas Husak, *The Philosophy of Criminal Law: Selected Essays* (Oxford University Press 2010) 3.

crime' within the regulatory state, and examine the relationship between conduct and punishment, identifying a need for an integrated binary sanctioning approach. Moving to sanction operationalisation, I contemplate Responsive Regulation and its in-built strategies as a valid sanctioning medium, and finally, seek to locate the continuing role of the criminal law within the binary.

The Backdrop: Criminogenic Financial Markets

A little over a decade ago, and pre-GFC, Taylor highlighted the 'specific relationship between the explosive development of market society and the problem of social order itself'.[11] For him a fundamental transformation in the organisation of economic life in most Western societies had occurred in the previous quarter century, a movement from economies organised around production to economies organised around consumption, and where involvement with financial markets moved from an elite to a mainstream activity. He sought to examine the ways that the 'postmodern' cultural market place, articulated around the sovereignty of the dynamic, innovative and constant-change-accepting individual as a consumer of private goods, play into what he described as, 'the spiralling sense of anxiety and danger' as a feature of such market society.[12] Presciently, he speculated about some forms of contemporary crime being 'market phenomena' complicit with unregulated marketing of particular products – and I speculate perhaps including 'debt as a consumer product' as suggested by Kaletsky[13] – and where competitive individualism is actively encouraged by such markets. For Taylor, this market society culture included an accelerating inequality of economic prospects, which was expressed in increased property crime, and in a burgeoning transnational hidden economy of capital accumulation.

Schanze has argued that due regard must be had to the dynamism of counter-reaction to market regulation.[14] He asserted that at the borders of legitimate markets new innovative markets spring up and escape regulation. These lie beyond the recognised regulatory structure and the governing legislation. This diligent evasion is tolerated by the courts, in Schanze's view, as a regulatory bifurcation – a clear departure from universal application of criminal law theories – since regulation tends to be partial in any case. He opined that, '... courts, wise legislators, and administrative agencies display sympathy with those who smartly escape the regulatory regime'.[15]

Thus there is a perennial tension between financial market risk-taking and innovation, the reflexive relationship of law and market innovation, the highly

11. Taylor, *Crime in Context*, 7.
12. ibid 6, 61.
13. Anatole Kaletsky, *Capitalism 4.0: The Birth of a New Economy* (Bloomsbury 2010).
14. Erich Schanze, 'Hare and Hedgehog Revisited: The Regulation of Markets that Have Escaped Regulated Markets' (1995) 151 J of Institutional and Theoretical Economics 162.
15. ibid 165.

competitive and powerful corporate sector, the combined commercial and political pressures regulators find difficult to fend off, regulatory power itself, and the ever-present and recurring financial crises.[16] Nelken has explained the origins and manifestations of criminal activity as follows:

> ... much white-collar and financial crime grows out of the opportunities to exploit objective changes in organizational forms of business trading (particularly marked in a period of increasing global competition) in ways which the law, especially national laws, are slow to deal with or incapable of catching in time. Other crimes are connected to the cycles of boom and bust which seem inherent in global capitalist expansion.[17]

Such concerns and observations concerning the criminogenic nature of market capitalism are central to the consideration, not only of the causes of the GFC itself, but also the ongoing control by the use of sanctions of such a highly charged, competitive, and individualised market society post-crisis. Norrie has observed of the orthodox theory of law: 'The logic of law is a logic of individual right and self-interest, in a social world presented as resting upon a consensus of individuals.'[18] Indeed, making a market connection, Adam Smith declared over 230 years ago that the classical market system is grounded in such individual self-interest, which by an unseen hand directs personal wealth into the wealth of nations.[19] The relationship between law and regulation and the markets is thus grounded in contingency, complexity, dynamic adaptability, and unpredictability.[20] To this may be added reflexivity and recursivity.

For Ireland particularly, the financial crisis and its dramatic transformation of huge banking debt into sovereign debt has become a social crisis, and one where commentators and its citizenry are very much concerned with the blaming and shaming of individuals exhibiting the values of absolute asocial individualism. What role then can legal sanctions play in reining in asocial behaviour in the financial regulatory sector? Providing a general answer, Gill[21] has argued that state intervention regarding crime is aimed formally at the *repression* of illegal markets and *regulating* legal ones. Norrie recognised criminal law protection of particular social interests through a language that is universal and

---

16. William S Laufer, 'Secrecy, Silence, and Corporate Crime Reforms' (2010) 9(3) Crim & Pub Pol 455; Reinhart and Rogoff, *This Time is Different*.
17. David Nelken, 'White-Collar Crime' in Maguire *et al* (eds), *Oxford Handbook of Criminology* (Oxford University Press 2002) 871.
18. Alan Norrie, *Crime, Reason and History* (Butterworths 2001) 23, 222.
19. Adam Smith, *An Inquiry into the Nature and Causes of the Wealth of Nations* (1776; Kathryn Sutherland ed, Oxford University Press 1993).
20. Black, 'Empirical Legal Studies'.
21. Peter Gill, 'Policing and Regulation: What Is the Difference?' (2002) 11(4) Soc and L Stud 523.

general, and cast in terms of respect for individuals.[22] As of yet, no Irish banker has been successfully prosecuted.

Three years before the crisis unfolded, Baldwin critically identified a 'new punitive regulation',[23] where greater emphasis was placed upon criminal sanctions, and he argued that one alternative approach, which today post-crisis would likely be derided, was to move towards more corporate self-regulation. Nonetheless he did warn that such control may lack legitimacy, prove unfair, and be exclusive and inefficient. Norrie has asserted the legitimacy of deterrent penal policy formed and implemented to deal with particular offenders, in peculiar time-relevant circumstances, where a display of firmness and vigour is necessary.[24] I argue that dealing with white-collar criminals in the financial sector – and particularly bankers – where systemic risk is the peculiarity sits squarely within such rubric.

In summary, market capitalism is both crisis- and crime-ridden, is dynamically innovative and difficult to police save in arrears, and yet it requires regulation of both legal and illegal strands. Penal policy must be tailored to current demands, and even particular offenders, where firm and effective sanctions are mandatory. Criminal law in theory protects social interests having a community rationale, yet prosecutes individuals subject to fair procedure. Coercive enforcement is the paramount control technique, a step beyond the civil law's declaratory style, as evidenced, for instance, in the distinction between company law past conduct offence enforcement, and the future protectionist role of disqualification of directors. While as shown, the potential offender pool includes both corporate entities and individuals, it must be acknowledged that the motivations, decision-making processes and reactions to sanction of each are significantly different. Although culture, lure, inadequate oversight and opportunity are conducive to crime causation in financial markets, counter-intuitively, however, criminal sanctioning has been peripheralised in Ireland. The Irish financial regulator's administrative sanction regime is virtually the sole enforcement medium. Although it may perhaps be inferred that regulatory crime is a clearly understood concept, this is not the case. Thus, from a transformative reform scenario this article examines what role, if any, may be expected for criminal enforcement. In the next section I commence with exploration of the rationale for the confrontational deterrence sanction strategy the criminal law legitimately exercises.

Criminal Deterrent Sanction: The Rationale

For Hart, who regarded sanctions as a 'natural necessity',[25] characteristic criminal law technique designates guiding behavioural standards by rule for members of society generally, or for special classes within it. This includes those

22. Norrie, *Crime, Reason and History*, 23.
23. Robert Baldwin, 'The New Punitive Regulation' (2004) 67(3) Mod L Rev 351.
24. Norrie, *Crime, Reason and History*.
25. HLA Hart, *The Concept of Law* (Clarendon Press 1961).

regulated within the financial sector purposed to the protection of those with whom they deal. Without the aid or intervention of officials, the expectation is that those affected will understand the rule, determine whether or not it applies to them and conform. Only when the rule of law is broken does officialdom identify the fact of breach, and impose the threatened sanction. Thus, the sanctioning process is borne of failure, a failure to understand the law or its application, or a failure to conform. Life out of court because of failure very much becomes life in court upon the charge-prosecution-conviction-sentence merry-go-round. As Hart argued, citizens voluntarily cooperate in a coercive system based upon the existence of sanctions that function as a *guarantee* that the compliant shall not be sacrificed to the disobedient.[26]

Hart's liberal view that the criminal law coexists with a consensual world according to Norrie, however, can only operate if the deep social and political conflicts in society are kept out of judicial rulings and sentencing. Norrie argued that responsibility and punishment relative thereto cannot be judged as an apolitical, asocial, and amoral abstraction. In his view crime control is primarily about the social and political elite controlling the lowest social classes, who are not free and equal subjects, a classical 'them and us' divide. If this is so, can the principles accumulated over the centuries validly inform a criminal/regulatory binary, concerned with business or white-collar infringers or criminals, apparently drawn from the ranks of that same elite? Here may lie the diversity in approach to criminality and sanctioning of blue- and white-collar offending: 'them' theories cannot be applied to 'us'.

A person of high status who commits a criminal act is usually less likely to be labelled and eventually attributed a deviant character than is a low-status person, while most people – upper, middle, and lower statuses – have trouble thinking of high-status individuals as deviant or criminal, no matter what they do.[27] Wells[28] has argued that the crimes of the powerful are differentially enforced within a rhetoric of clampdown and control. The Irish compliance-oriented approach has created a two-tier legal system privileging corporate elites in the financial sector.[29] All of this is amply expressed post-GFC within the recognition among governance scholars that elite cultures are as crucial to financial regulatory reform as the economics of the markets.[30] Pragmatically this may be so, but whether or not they deserve such a role and whether or not their involvement may stymie such reform are matters for considerable thought.

26. ibid; see also David Garland, *The Culture of Control: Crime and Social Order in Contemporary Society* (Oxford University Press 2001).
27. Charles R Tittle and Raymond Paternoster, *Social Deviance and Crime: An Organizational and Theoretical Approach* (Roxbury 2000).
28. Wells, 'Corporate Crime'.
29. Joe McGrath, 'Two-Tier System Puts Corporate Criminals above Law' *The Irish Times* (Dublin, 21 December 2010).
30. Christopher Arup,'The Global Financial Crisis: Learning from Regulatory and Governance Studies' (2010) 32(3) L & Pol 363.

However, in any event, as Norrie explained, since 'street crime' committed by actual individuals dominates the harm focus, corporate harm finds itself doubly removed in that corporations are hard to perceive as criminals, and further, hard to capture within the law's individual forms.

In Norrie's argument, the state through its courts applies the logic of subjective individual right as a principle, while at the same time perceived community or socio-political imperatives are systemically reflected in political policy, whereupon policy prevails within a rhetoric of abstract individualism. Reflecting yields acceptance of this argument, but with little effective choice for society and its authorities, legitimately seeking societal protection. Nonetheless, in my view a greater transparency about policy, the factors that inform it, and the allowance of defence lawyers to test its probative usefulness and value within the context of the criminal trial process, as well as sentencing, may afford some measure of redress to the accused 'individual' within the community setting where his/her offending occurred. Collaterally it may perhaps extend protection and consideration to the 'victim' also. Concerning corporates the institution of a new and transparent policy – both rhetoric and implementation – one that is not subject to change resistance by either political forces (especially lobbying) or judicial authority (as Schanze suggested), would be a clear step to establishing new sanctioning norms.

Recognising the criminal law – despite its flaws – as crucial and powerful, Norrie argued: 'Criminal law is an expression of a social and political practice, and it bears the marks of the conflicts within that practice.'[31] He went on to accuse the 'liberal legal project' of being 'unachievable' and 'inherently flawed'. He argued that the liberal approach has merely tinkered around the edges. In terms of sentencing replete with wide discretion, Norrie[32] concluded that it is the culmination of a particular historical form of social control that confirmed his central thesis that, 'the criminal law is founded on ideological principles that are in their essence contradictory, so that rationalistic readings of the law are bound to fail'.

So what is Norrie's solution? He openly acknowledged that he could not indicate how the problems would ultimately be resolved, but rightly suggested that pointing up the issues would nonetheless assist. This is a course this article also follows regarding the future location of criminal law within the binary. Responsibility for Norrie is much more complex than legal individualism can allow, and the deduction of legal rules and application thereof, once deducted, must be much less rational than orthodox legal theory is prepared to recognise. There is every incentive, he argued, to seek a deeper critique that can understand the underlying contradictions that operate. I similarly argue that a transformative approach to the operation of the criminal law for business crime as a targeted, discrete group is required post crisis, to re-embed the societal guarantee, albeit with a legitimacy that a sufficient mass of the elite will accept.

31. Norrie, *Crime, Reason and History*, 225, 231.
32. ibid 231.

Describing criminal law theory as a form of knowledge, a 'praxiology', grounded in social and historical practice, and inherently bound by its concepts, practices and outcomes means that the broader picture is blurred, asserted Norrie. I may add, in the language of Paul the Apostle to the Corinthians[33]: it is observation 'through a glass, darkly'. Norrie further asserted that those concepts cannot be transcended, and the underlying conundrums resolved. He thus called for a transformational move away from legal knowledge tied to punishing the 'individual' towards recognition of the social dimension of individual agency, and additionally, for recognition of the role of political judgment within the legitimating rational legal process. This would appear to reflect Madame Lagarde's viewpoint concerning the future of financial regulation, where self-interest financial gain is superceded by societal interest. And also the massively accentuated post-crisis intervention of government to secure economic stability and regulatory reform.

Back-tracking somewhat, on the criminal law side the cornerstone of the modern costs and benefits concept of 'deterrence', which itself occupies a central place in the criminal law structure, lies in the mid-19th-century expression of the British Law Commissioners when they stated: 'The great object of the penal law is to deter men… by holding out privation and suffering as the consequences of transgression.'[34] To this day this notion grounded in Benthamite utilitarianism underpins the common law penal tradition and practice. The original sanction objective was graded punishment according to the crime, while the overall goal was envisioned to establish different degrees of aggravation of offences, executing appropriate punishment after allowing the sentencing court a limited discretion.[35] In practice, in Ireland 'just deserts' (retributivism) is the key concept in sanction practice (sentencing) tinged by elements of rehabilitation, whereas elsewhere, especially the US and UK 'just desserts' rules.[36]

Sanctions in the regulatory sphere are a fundamental legally grounded state control mechanism, or enforcement tool, normally specifically and legislatively provided for, and imposed as a result of a breach of rule, either by a lawfully appointed judge or administrative authority exercising lawful discretion, directed to infringers motivated to apply rules to themselves, by dint of those sanctions attaching to such rules. They are secondary rules that provide the centralised official 'sanctions' of the legal system. Coercive in nature, they take many forms, whether punitive, privatory or preventive, including criminal sanctions such as imprisonment, fines and obligatory criminal registration, as well as separately applied administrative/civil sanctions, including monetary penalties,

---

33. 1 Corinthians 13:12.
34. Criminal Law Commissioners, *Seventh Report* (Parliamentary Papers XIX – 1843) 92.
35. Criminal Law Commissioners, *First Report* (Parliamentary Papers XXVI – 1834); Norrie, *Crime Reason and History*.
36. Thomas O'Malley, *Sentencing Law and Practice* (2nd edn, Thompson Round Hall 2006).

levies, cautions/reprimands and disqualifications.[37] While the sanction suites differ at the apex, incapacitation is the aim whether imprisonment on the criminal law side or disqualification and it's similar on the administrative side. In the administrative regime, corporate entities and individuals are treated differently as far as the maxima for monetary penalty is concerned. The need for new and specific civil sanction tools to add to the mix was highlighted as essential even for pre-crisis Irish financial regulatory control and this has continued post crisis.[38] The sanction paradigm mimics the criminal justice/regulation paradigm, but does not, however, provide a single transversal sanction suite. Sanctions are of the very essence of a criminal justice/regulatory system, and bear a relationship to offences or prescribed contraventions themselves, the breach of which provokes the sanction. They are distinguished on the 'real' crime side as inherently wrong or *mala in se,* and on the regulatory side as *mala prohibita* or, as some observers put it, 'technically' illegal, a difference that emerged from industrialisation in the 19th and 20th centuries.

At adjudication level, sentencing or sanction guidelines are utilised in some jurisdictions to set out relevant principles or stipulations for the sentencing authority to use when imposing sanction, including incentives to plead guilty. However, they are not utilised in Ireland on the criminal side where judicially set-out principles are the norm.[39] Interestingly, post-crisis the Irish Court of Criminal Appeal in Murray has established social solidarity, within the context of the crisis and its social effects implicitly within Durkheim's logic, as a new deterrent

37. The Irish financial regulator acts upon complaints or upon its own initiative, acts through authorised officers, may apply to the courts to appoint examiners, may appoint inspectors, and may impose administrative civil sanctions – the administrative sanction suite – including: caution or reprimand, issue directions to refund/withhold payment, monetary penalty, disqualify from management, direct contravention seizure, impose costs, may publish sanction guidelines, establish an enquiry, may issue a supervisory warning, may issue an evidentiary notice; may issue a suspension and/or prohibition notice, may enter into a settlement agreement, may publish adverse decisions; and on the criminal side may prosecute minor or summary offences, and may refer serious offences to the Garda Síochána/DPP. See Niamh Connery and David Hodnett, *Regulatory Law in Ireland* (Tottel 2009) ch 4; Central Bank Reform Act 2010, Part 3.
38. Report of the Advisory Group on the Establishment of a Single Regulatory Authority for the Financial Services Sector (McDowell Report 1999); see also M Butler *et al* (eds), *Criminal Litigation* (Cambridge University Press 2011); James Hamilton, 'Do We Need a System of Administrative Sanctions in Ireland?' (Two-Tier Criminal Law System Conference Common Law and Regulatory Enforcement: Is the Traditional Role of the DPP Diminishing? Law Society Dublin, 25 April 2009); Shelly Horan, *Corporate Crime* (Bloomsbury 2011); Michael McDowell, 'Non-Criminal Penalties and Criminal Sanctions in Irish Regulatory Law' (Two-Tier Criminal Law System Conference Common Law and Regulatory Enforcement: Is the Traditional Role of the DPP Diminishing? Law Society Dublin, 25 April 2009).
39. Thomas O'Malley, *The Criminal Processes* (Round Hall 2009).

sentencing principle in frauds against the public purse.[40] Paradoxically, non-statutory sentence guidelines are operated on the financial regulatory side as devised by the financial regulator.

Insofar as Taylor recognised that the liberalising, and in his view divisive, consequences of marketisation, all perhaps amply demonstrated by pre-crisis excesses, such as uncontrollable global capital movements, outlandish bankers' bonuses and unsustainable business models, disorientated the value-commitments of social commentators, and may I add market 'players', the opposite is also true. Thus, the occurrence of a financial crisis, which struck the very core of the capitalist financial system, has rapidly focused those same commentators, players and their regulators upon the need for beefed-up regulatory intervention, including sanctioning powers and their implementation. Re-resourcing and re-packing the tool-kit, floodlighting the sometime heretofore hidden playing paddock, and examining the dynamics of infringement and sanction – the gamesmanship – are all highly relevant objectives at this identifiable swing-point of new departure. Thus, a thorough discussion and evaluation of both historical practice and Norrie's acute critique both assists and informs ultimate conclusions.

In considering what sovereign states do in the face of activities perceived as damaging to dominant economic, political and social interests, Gill identified three broad actions: (1) criminal law protection against harms affecting property and personal rights; (2) economic regulation governing the terms of entry and competition in particular markets tasked at ensuring honesty and efficiency or securing the possibilities of accumulation; (3) social regulation to protect workers and the community in relation to both food consumption and the environment.[41] Financial regulation is mainly concerned with the first two, but may also impact the latter, while the main focus of this article lies in the role, if any, of the criminal law, which includes its interplay with civil/administrative sanctioning, particularly in relation to category two.

In carrying out a recent survey concerning the availability, procedural modes and enforcement of sanctions (administrative, civil or criminal), Faure *et al* identified five different national models of enforcement policy.[42] They found the key characteristics determining such models include proactive monitoring by regulatory agencies, and whether financial penalty imposition originates from an administrative, civil or criminal source. The national choice was impacted by national culture and legal tradition. Common law jurisdictions favoured significant monitoring, and criminal law involvement, although there was a perceived inadequate deterrence for serious cases.

40. *DPP v Paul Murray* [2012] IECCA 60, Finnegan J.
41. Gill, 'Policing and Regulation'.
42. Michael Faure, Anthony Ogus, and Niels Philipsen, 'Curbing Consumer Financial Losses: The Economics of Regulatory Enforcement' (2009) 31(2) L & Pol 161.

In summary, targeted sanctioning is legitimate, and the economic elite whose culture is crucial to reform are not alone not exempt but must be involved. New sanctioning approaches are demanded (and tentatively emerging) as necessary to enable success within a difficult political and social environment. Community policy attitudes to 'real' crime encompass dangers for future corporate and individual white-collar criminal infringement, and require reassessment. Transparency protections may assuage elite fears. Gradated sanctioning responses have been operated for almost two centuries: they come in many forms across both criminal and administrative territory, and plea incentives are an in-built mechanism. But there is a lack of commonality across the binary. Deeper critique of present modes is called for. Common law jurisdictions in general favour criminal law involvement, but with limitations, while in Ireland the administrative regime is almost exclusively used for financial contravention. Taking these findings around foundational sanctions values and beliefs forward, I now examine the sit-atop sanction paradigm itself.

The Sanction Paradigm

The sanction paradigm has recently been forensically examined from a UK perspective by Ashworth and Zedner,[43] who argued that change has occurred in the relationship between the citizen and the state, and indeed in the state itself, which they attribute to jostling between the authoritarian state, the preventive state and the regulatory state. Garland[44] framed one of these changes as the delegation of social tasks in punishment to specialised agencies on the margins of social life, resulting in them becoming hidden. This is an apt reference to forms of sanctioning in the financial regulatory sector, where much is conducted in private, with non-universal publication of outcomes, and where publication, if effected, is generally by electronic means, requiring those interested in actively seeking out the information. In Garland's view, the 'open, ritualised dialogue'[45] between community and offender has become a much more oblique communication.

Bearing up the liberal tradition, Ashworth and Zedner started their review from the proposition that the purpose of criminal law is the censure and sentencing of those who commit wrongs, which have been justifiably criminalised, under circumstances where the wrongdoers' individual autonomy and dignity are respected. However, they argued that of more recent vintage, the need to comply with human rights provisions has led to the state skirting the more onerous procedural requirements applicable to the criminal process, by

43. Andrew Ashworth and Lucia Zedner, 'Defending the Criminal Law: Reflections on the Changing Character of Crime, Procedure and Sanctions' (2008) 2 Crim L & Phil 21.
44. David Garland, *Punishment and Modern Society* (Oxford University Press 1990).
45. ibid 186–87.

stimulating the development of alternative channels of control. They identified the greater use of seven major trends as exemplars:

(1) Diversion (mainly by police caution)
(2) Fixed penalties
(3) Summary trials
(4) Hybrid civil–criminal processes (civil orders where breach is enforced by criminal penalty)
(5) Strict criminal liability
(6) Incentives to plead guilty (reinforced in sentencing guidelines)
(7) Preventive orders (eg disqualifications or restrictions)

For Ashworth and Zedner:

> Conviction of an individual for an offence is the strongest form of condemnation of conduct that the state can muster. Conviction for an offence also opens the possibility of a coercive sentence, ordered by a court within the limits of what legislation permits. To justify the creation of a certain crime is therefore to justify the imposition of the censure of conviction and the imposition of a punishment.[46]

They argued that five negative challenges surrounding the criminal-trial process have emerged to what they called 'the paradigmatic sequence of prosecution-trial-conviction-sentence'. These are: not cost-effective; not preventive; not necessary; not appropriate; not effective.

Clearly these issues, the jostling between citizen and state, the oblique communication of punishment, the development of alternative channels of control, and negative challenges affecting the traditional trial process, not alone affect the movement towards greater administrative sanctioning, but also impact the way in which prosecutors approach the handling of difficult financial crime.

As far as Ireland is concerned, the complex nature of criminal fraud trials was examined by Murphy.[47] Clearly exhibiting lacunae in legal practice, when compared with jurisdictions such as the US, he concluded that a number of areas of Irish prosecutorial practice in the area of white-collar crime required urgent review. He outlined seven specific target areas for reform, including the increased use of technology; the implementation of 10-year-old already statutorily existent legislation allowing judges to order the provision of documentary evidence to juries; the adoption of a protocol, including immunity, based around encouraging informants including whistleblowers to give evidence against fellow conspirators; the earlier engagement of legal counsel in the investigative process; the greater use of agreed pre-trial admissions; the development of court rules to enhance pre-trial case management; and, from a sanctions viewpoint, the wider invocation of the confiscation powers jurisdiction

46. Ashworth and Zedner, 'Defending the Criminal Law', 48.
47. Shane Murphy, 'The Trial of Complex Fraud Cases' (12th Annual National Prosecutors' Conference, Dublin Castle Conference Centre, 28 May 2011).

held by the Irish DPP, especially for cases involving fraud or dishonesty. Murphy did not, however, advocate a transparent published policy or strategy governing the use of criminal law as opposed to the administrative stream, nor the expansion of the criminal sanction suite to include enforceable undertakings, for instance, where a form of co-regulation between state and the newly convicted would benefit non-custodial sanction policy and potentially past and potential future victims.

In summary, the sanction paradigm has increasingly seen sanctioning, where criminal procedure is under pressure to deliver, delegated to agencies within a burgeoning regulatory state, including within the financial services sector. How these new authorities determine the respective roles of criminal and administrative sanctioning, to date a neglected enterprise, impacts both deterrence and compliance, signalling where publicity is paramount. The preferred adjudication process and sanction suite must not alone be effective but clearly must also uphold fair procedure norms. The cost calculus has increasingly been applied to examine regulatory efficiency and has adversely impacted the use of criminal deterrence. So then, what role does this truncated paradigm play within the modern regulatory state?

The Sanction Paradigm and the Regulatory State

Ashworth and Zedner[48] drew upon noted authorities in considering the 'regulatory state', where the rationale is that the state governs more effectively at a distance, withdrawing from the active delivery of services ('rowing') to their direction ('steering'). They argued that a prominent feature of regulatory strategies is the acceptance of the normality of crime. This policy viewpoint results in a larger culture of 'managing crime', rather than responding to it as aberrant or to be suppressed. Ashworth and Zedner cited the significant influence of neo-liberal economics, which characterised wrongdoers as rational actors motivated by the desire to maximise their own self-interest. Braithwaite described a neo-regulatory state, in a shift from a welfare focus, and premised upon a combination of market competition, privatised institutions and decentred forms of regulation.[49] Crime within such is not regarded as a moral wrong, but instead as a cost to be calculated in, and thus efforts aimed at reducing such cost, including the payment of restitution, are deemed worthy of all acceptation.

Ashworth and Zedner described this as a 'managerialist tendency', most prevalent at the lower end of the sanction tariff, where the cost argument is deemed more appropriate, and which results in the lower forms of infraction being hived off to administrative channels, resulting in administrative sanctions.

48. Ashworth and Zedner, 'Defending the Criminal Law'.

49. John Braithwaite, 'The New Regulatory State and the Transformation of Criminology' (2000) 40 Brit J of Crim 222.

Pat O'Malley[50] has recently described a 'hard zone' of simulated justice, a world of offender profiles on which risk-based policing is founded, of actuarial justice where lengthy prison sentences are matched to risk predictors, an area characterised by 'risk targeting', a prominent feature of new forms of financial regulatory practice. In Ireland, all financial regulatory contraventions, upper and lower end, since the introduction of sanctioning in autumn 2004, have been the subject of settlement agreements, although on a number of occasions monetary penalties in excess of €2 million have been imposed.

For McGrath Irish jurisprudence has failed to fully recognise that there are two interwoven strands to the criminal law: the first, which is recognised by Irish courts, is the 'expressive, symbolic, moral judgement that reflects community values and which inflicts punishment and just deserts on offenders'; the second, and the one neglected, is 'regulatory, instrumental and utilitarian'.[51] He argued that this second strand is often compliance-oriented, aimed at deterring offenders regarding their future behaviour, and places reliance on fines as a compensator for wrongdoing, both generally regarded as features of the civil law. He stated: 'regulatory crime as a concept has no fixed meaning in Irish law, nor is there a rich common law history in the area'.[52] In McGrath's view, the Irish courts in defining crime have only juxtaposed conventional criminal law and civil law, whereas he argued there is a need to contrast regulatory crime with conventional crime, and also regulatory crime with civil sanctions. He reflected that unless a proper distinction is recognised, and drawn, that misbehaviour may not receive its proper status, and thus appropriate punishment. More needs to be done to understand the nature and characteristics of regulatory criminal law, and to study why it is becoming an increasingly prominent tool of law enforcement, he advocated, before concluding by way of warning – and in direct contrast to the Ashworth and Zedner view – 'Not all regulatory offences address minor matters or punish with small penalties'.[53]

Examples from the financial regulatory sector spring readily to mind in that Irish corporates may be administratively fined up to a maximum of €5 million at present[54]; and offences may involve multiple acts with multiple 'victims'. For instance, Allied Irish Banks Plc – a bank nationalised during the financial crisis – in December 2010, was fined €2 million by the Irish Financial Regulator for breaches of the Consumer Protection Code, and the European Communities

50. Pat O'Malley, 'Simulated Justice: Risk, Money and Telemetric Policing' (2010) 50 Brit J of Crim 795.
51. Joe McGrath, 'The Colonisation of Real Crime in the Name of All Crime: The Traditional Court Approach to the Definition of Crime' in Shane Kilcommins and Ursula Kilkelly (eds), *Regulatory Crime in Ireland* (First Law 2010) 48.
52. ibid 49.
53. ibid 51.
54. Part IIIC Central Bank Act 1942 as amended.

(Licensing and Supervision of Credit Institutions) Regulations 1992.[55] The bank failed for a number of years to have robust governance arrangements in place, specifically failing to have adequate internal control mechanisms to prevent and rectify frequent and many instances of overcharging.

In summary, pre-GFC a new criminal normality emerged, and even some forms of 'real' crime became a societal or business 'cost'. Regulatory crime that increased in occurence grew to encompass 'targeting' and 'cost' features, but is not a recognised discrete crime category in common law jurisdictions. There is a need to develop strategy around the contrast, or even a new comparison between regulatory crime with conventional crime, and also regulatory crime with civil sanctions. This is the heart of the criminal/administrative enforcement and sanctioning interplay issue. Recognition that regulatory offences may have major impact, and both involve multiple acts, and affect multiple victims, is essential. In addition to this spatial awareness, the temporality of such offending, whether short or long-term, must be factored in. Criminal behaviour must receive its proper status and appropriate punishment. To achieve this status, a move towards greater regulatory 'steering' on the part of the state, and its agencies, is required. So then, what is the proper origin and status of criminal punishment?

Conduct and Punishment: Tension and Leakage

There is a refreshingly true simplicity then to Husak's earlier quoted statement that: 'In deciding what behaviours are deserving of penal sanctions we decide what conduct we want to deter.'[56] Fifty years ago Hart had explained: 'In the case of a rule of criminal law we can identify and distinguish two things: a certain type of conduct which the rule prohibits, and a sanction intended to discourage it.'[57] For Kelsen, 'Law is the primary norm which stipulates the sanction.'[58] Norrie, however, concluded that while the law protects and defends the individual and his rights in principle, it also oppresses, being a means of social control over conflicts grounded in social inequities.

I may add, because individual wealth creation, and especially its success, which is often termed 'greed', is a notable cause of social distemper, this tension that Norrie identified may well manifest itself in the framing of offences, enforcement implementation or lack of it, sanctions applied, and the interpretations rendered, and discretions exercised, by the prevailing authority. Norrie argued that general criminal law principles have, from historical roots, crucially

55. Publicity Notice of Settlement Agreement between Central Bank of Ireland and Allied Irish Banks Plc effective 17 December 2010 <https://www.centralbank.ie/publications/Documents/101217%20-%20Publicity%20Statement%20-%20AIB%20plc.pdf> accessed 6 June 2013.
56. Husak, *Philosophy of Criminal Law*, 3.
57. Hart, *Concept of Law*, 34.
58. Hans Kelsen, *General Theory of Law and State* (1949) 63.

been shaped by the tension between individual responsibility and a world where actions are socially structured and conditioned, effectively where self-interest meets public interest head-on, and where, he asserted, there lies the 'persistent threat of social and political leakage into the process of state judgement and punishment'.[59] This latter point sings loudly throughout the theoretical formulation, enactment, implementation and reform of financial regulation post GFC both in Ireland and elsewhere.

Ashworth and Zedner have argued that punishment is both the consequence and the *raison d'être* of the criminal law, and that it has operated as a carefully calibrated and time-limited curtailment of the rights of the individual. However, Williams, although acknowledging that if a single test of crime was applied, 'punishment' was undoubtedly the best, reflected that in UK law at any rate there was no way to distinguish between the punitive fine and the civil penalty, or between punitive imprisonment and civil coercive imprisonment, except in terms of procedure.[60] This is an important observation in that monetary penalties are the most common administrative remedy for businesses.[61] The notion of the distinction between criminal and civil sanctions that so exercised the UK Macrory Review,[62] the relevant consequences, and the stigma attaching to either or both, go to the root of the interplay between criminal and administrative sanctioning for financial regulatory infringement. They are regarded as distinct systems on procedural grounds.

Forty-five years ago, in the first of his nine essays, the classic *Prolegomenon to the Principles of Punishment,* Hart, when confronting the definition of punishment, identified five essential elements: (1) pain or unpleasant consequence – the British Law Commissioners (1843) 'privation and suffering' conceptualisation; (2) an offence against legal rule; (3) punishment applied to an actual or supposed offender; (4) intentional administration by other humans; and (5) imposition by legal authority against which the offending behaviour was directed (note not the individual 'victim').[63]

Such punishment, for Hart, was justified where there was breach of legal standards of behaviour (whether or not moral standards) established by criminal legislation and not merely purposed to extract a penalty. John Gardner, in the introduction to the second edition of Hart's work in 2008, synopsised Hart's view as: 'Any action or practice that has costs – and what does not? – needs to pay its way in countervailing benefits.'[64] Gardner went on to pose the tricky question – so then what constitutes a 'countervailing benefit'? For Hart, according to Gardner, the thwarted future wrongs never committed constituted such

59. Norrie, *Crime, Reason and History*, 24.
60. Glanville Williams, 'The Definition of Crime' (1955) 8 Current L Prob 107.
61. Macrory, 'Reforming Regulatory Sanctions'.
62. Macrory Review, *Final Report on Regulatory Justice: Making Sanctions Effective* (November 2006).
63. HLA Hart, *Punishment and Responsibility* (2nd edn, Oxford University Press 2008).
64. ibid xii.

benefit. Perhaps it may then be asked: for financial regulation, how can a legally grounded criminal sanction suite attain such a result, other than by a strict deterrence/compliance strategy (replete with flexible sanctions), whether or not socially inequitable? And further, if solely future oriented (including rehabilitation) is the retributive aim redundant or, if not redundant, merely a messaging system for future consumption?

For Zedner, the form and functions of punishment vary over time and reflect changes in society,[65] and thus, explanations for it are an exercise in social theory as Taylor argued in relation to the market society, and as Norrie reflected upon concerning both social and political 'leakage'. This surely entails the amendment of not alone societal attitudes towards sanctioning and punishment, as has been noticed post GFC, but also the forms it uses to express its social and political theory, whether in changes to legislation or practises. Punishment is mainly a mechanism for maintaining social order, a legal and administrative disciplinary device – formal bureaucratic governance with formal code, rules of procedure and adjudication, functionaries and institutions – a means of expressing outrage, and thus, is most concerned with society, not individual offenders or victims, and more recently has been recognised as part of culture.[66]

Why, then, is it necessary that conduct necessitating punishment be classified as criminal or civil, other than by reference to its procedural pageantry and outflows? Is it not possible to conceive of penalties as 'sanctions' *per se* and to ditch the criminal/civil divide? It is not impossible for one single standard of proof, that of proof beyond reasonable doubt as Macrory recommended,[67] to apply to all sanctioning events, although of course well-resourced corporates may gain an increased protection? Indeed, nor is it impossible for all sanction results or orders, whether criminal or administrative, to be reposited in a single sanction/punishment register. It is all punishment after all! And a fine is increasingly the most oft-used weapon, the sanction for those 'in and of' the market.[68]

As an illumination to the ongoing discourse, Macrory stated of his UK Review:

> Where the Review and… the Government broke new ground was to set [statutory reforms[69]] within a clear set of principles concerning the rationale for sanctions that combined and integrated both criminal and civil approaches.[70]

In respect of such a combination and integration, if the question 'what' concerning the criminal law in relation to financial regulation, and also its answer *inform*, then the 'why' question, why involve the criminal law, has *transformational power* when such criminal law is applied. In such application, financial

65. Lucia Zedner, *Criminal Justice* (Oxford University Press 2004).
66. ibid.
67. Macrory Review, *Financial Report*.
68. Pat O'Malley, 'Theorizing Fines' (2009) 11 Punishment & Soc 67.
69. The Regulatory Enforcement and Sanctions Act 2008.
70. Macrory, 'Reforming Regulatory Sanctions', 241.

regulation is transformed into something more. It is effective and strong, sending a clear signal as to standards that must be met at peril of sanction.

For Simester and von Hirsch,[71] between the two poles of criminal law being that involves fines and imprisonment, rather than injunctions and damages, punishment is imposed with censure as an integral aspect, responding to the fact that its subject has done something wrong, with the level of sentence one measure of opprobrium. They concluded that the crime-preventive aspect of the criminal law, and of its sanctions, is significant evidence of deterrent effect. Relating to a central theme of this article, the interplay of administrative and criminal sanctions, they argued that criminal law is a special regulatory tool for influencing behaviour, having a social significance beyond civil law. Here conviction and sanction send clearly understood messages with the criminal law embodying a qualitatively unique and more significant moral communicative voice lacking in the civil arena.

Criminal law incorporates a moral imperative transcending man-made rule. There is a finding of guilt. It is proven beyond a reasonable doubt. It is deeply personal, a matter of central concern to the business elite. Legally grounded, independent, and yet interlinked institutions, exercise arrest and charge, and a real jail-time potential both pre-trial and post-conviction. A public shaming is pronounced by a consensually acknowledged legitimate authority, and a record is kept for all to see and publicise.

In summary, infringing conduct and sanction go hand in hand. Thus, stipulating the conduct and proving it lead on to both future sanction messaging, and past conduct punishment. Wealth accumulation practices should not override regulation in sanction suite choice or discretionary implementation. Public interest must outweigh self-interest and future conduct control is a legitimate aim. Criminal sanction influences future behaviour and sends a qualitatively unique and strong moral message. A newer punishment 'culture' may validly reflect a combination and integration of criminal and civil/administrative approaches, where nonetheless, the strength of traditional criminal law messaging persists. For such a transformational move to ensue, however, how will sanctioning be operationalised?

Sanction Operationalisation: Responsive Regulation and the Pyramid Strategy

A quarter of a century ago, Gunningham[72] categorised two main enforcement strategies along a single continuum: confrontational deterrence and cooperative compliance. These were amalgamated from the Australian experience,

---

71. AP Simester and Andreas von Hirsch, *Crimes, Harms, and Wrongs on the Principles of Criminalisation* (Hart Publishing 2011).
72. Neil Gunningham, 'Negotiated Non-Compliance: A Case Study of Regulatory Failure' (1987) 9 L & Pol 69.

principally by Ayres and Braithwaite,[73] for business regulatory purposes and became known as the hybrid 'Responsive Regulation'. This conceptualisation, which mixes punishment and persuasion, and more recently restorative justice in a business-friendly manner, over the last two decades has globally been adopted by regulators.[74]

Deterrence is confrontational, sanctions rule-breaking behaviour, is adversarial and accusatory, and focuses upon detection, guilt establishment, and penalising prior offending, and where sanctioning all breaches is espoused.[75]

Contrastingly, compliance favours prevention, repair and results, focuses upon attaining broad legislative aims, rarely seeks legal recourse, and is characterised by bargaining and negotiation.[76] A compliance enforcement strategy occurs, where regulators inform the regulatee how to comply in the future, instead of imposing sanctions for past indiscretions, and allows for discretionary waivers and exemptions.[77]

For those truly committed to responsive compliance, all deterrence is geared towards gaining compliance, a changing of behaviour for future benefit, a concept in harmony with Hart's 'countervailing benefits', but not with retributive aims. Compliance theory, a significant remove from Bentham's deterrence-based compliance, is a relative newcomer, finding its feet in the separate work of Reiss,[78] springing into regulation from a criminal law source and from environmental protection concerns.[79] Compliance clearly sits at the regulatory or 'softer' end of binary enforcement and, as predicted by Reiss,[80] more and more systems of social control are based around it.

The principal framework advocated by 'responsive regulation' from a sanctioning viewpoint is the Enforcement Pyramid. Enforcement strategies within such practise were originally arrayed in a five-level ascending and descending

73. Ian Ayres and John Braithwaite, *Responsive Regulation: Transcending the Deregulation Debate* (Oxford University Press 1992).
74. John Braithwaite, *Restorative Justice and Responsive Regulation* (Oxford University Press 2002); Charlotte Wood, Mary Ivec, Jenny Job, and Valerie Braithwaite, 'Applications of Responsive Regulatory Theory in Australia and Overseas' (2010) Occasional Paper RegNet ANU Canberra, 15 June 2010.
75. Gunningham , 'Negotiated Non-Compliance '; Julia Black, *Rules and Regulators* (Clarendon Press 1997).
76. Gunningham, 'Negotiated Non-Compliance'; Keith Hawkins, *Environment and Enforcement: Regulation and the Social Definition of Pollution* (Clarendon Press 1984).
77. Black, *Rules and Regulators*.
78. Albert J Reiss jr, 'Selecting Strategies of Social Control over Organisational Life' in Keith Hawkins and John M Thomas (eds), *Enforcing Regulation* (Kluwer–Nijhoff 1984); see also Albert J Reiss jr and David J Bordua, 'Environment and Organisation: A Perspective on the Police' in David Bordua (ed), *The Police: Six Sociological Essays* (John Wiley 1967).
79. Hawkins, *Environment and Enforcement*; see also Keith Hawkins, *Environmant and Enforcement* (Oxford University Press 1987).
80. Reiss, 'Selecting Strategies'.

dynamic pyramidal approach, with criminal penalty two rungs below apex where the removal/restriction of authorisation or licence lurks, and where the objective – the presumptive preference – is to maintain as much enforcement activity as possible at the educational base. More recently, Braithwaite[81] has explained that 'the ideas of pyramids of supports and of sanctions' lie at the heart of the responsive 'project'.

One critique has centred upon licence revocation as a misfiring 'big gun', since the larger financial institutions are too big or important to fail. Later manifestations of the pyramid, including in the financial regulatory sector, have seen criminal prosecution gain the apex.[82] In such instances, the issue of the policy balance in the pyramid between a tough top – criminal deterrence – and an educational bottom – responsive compliance – requires redress. For Kingsford Smith the responsive approach has not yet flourished in the financial services sector, inhabited by securities and investment firms, where traditional criminal law adversarial and legalistic rights-based postures are defensively adopted by those regulated. She argues that more resources, more appropriate powers and a change in regulatory culture are all required.[83] This correction accords with Braithwaite's view that responsive regulation is 'a natural social process',[84] and reaffirms the need to re-engineer the interplay space, and to clearly define the pyramidal balance.

Scott has critiqued the responsive approach generally as selective, responsive, oriented towards the regulator's instrumental objectives and in conflict with 'real' crime universal application principles.[85] With the 'real' crime rationale being the public interest or common good based in a community or social contract, as opposed to financial regulation's economic rationale and disputed regulatory contract underpinning, there is some merit in Scott's argument. Braithwaite himself post crisis has highlighted that white-collar crime is more under-deterred than other forms of crime, and suffers more under-investment in prevention and preventive policing.[86] Indeed, for Yeung, the 'real' crime responsibility paradigm punishes intended individual wrongdoing, whereas regulation aims at collective welfare deterrence with

81. John Braithwaite, 'The Essence of Responsive Regulation' (2011) 44 U of Brit Columbia L Rev 475, 475.
82. Wood *et al*, 'Applications of Responsive Regulatory Theory'.
83. Dimity Kingsford Smith, 'A Harder Nut to Crack? Responsive Regulation in the Financial Services Sector' (2011) 44 U of Brit Columbia L Rev 695.
84. Braithwaite, 'Essence of Responsive Regulation' 519.
85. Colin Scott, 'Regulatory Crime: History, Functions, Problems, Solutions' (July 2009) UCD Working Papers in Law, Criminology & Socio-Legal Studies Research Paper No 13.
86. John Braithwaite, 'Diagnostics of White-Collar Crime Prevention' (2010) 9(3) Crim & Pub Pol 621.

a lesser punishment.[87] In practice, as far as monetary penalties are concerned, this lesser penalty approach is no longer the case for financial regulation but of course is definitely still the case insofar as administrative regimes are denied access to imprisonment/incarceration as significant sanction signalling.

In the UK, the Macrory Review looked at some of these issues. Writing four years later Macrory suggested he took a more flexible approach,[88] like a number of other commentators have done.[89] Macrory said, apparently advocating a model focusing upon individual circumstances, rather than collective sectoral responsibility:

> The Macrory Review built upon [the Braithwaite enforcement pyramid approach] but moved away from the type of graduated response inherent in the pyramid structure to one that allowed for different responses to different types of businesses and the different circumstances of the breach [and] grounded within a set of more coherent principles of regulatory governance emphasising transparency and accountability.[90]

Braithwaite, who from the outset had advocated flexibility, when writing after Macrory's contribution, characterised responsive theory as a principles-based, dynamic and 'cumulative creation'.[91] He emphasised that in designing the regulatory pyramid that a partnership approach between regulator and regulated is possible, and concluded:

> The paradox of responsive regulation is that by having a capability to escalate to tough enforcement, most regulation can be about collaborative capacity building. Most of the action can fall within a strengths-based pyramid, a pyramid of supports for business compliance and continuous improvement.[92]

Within the original responsive enforcement pyramid criminal law sanction was sandwiched between administrative options, with incapacitation in the form of disqualification or licence removal at apex, and monetary penalty on rung

87. Karen Yeung, 'Quantifying Regulatory Penalties: Australian Competition Law Penalties in Perspective' (1999) 23 Melbourne L Rev 440.
88. Macrory, 'Reforming Regulatory Sanctions'.
89. See Neil Gunningham and Peter Grabosky, *Smart Regulation: Designing Environmental Policy* (Oxford University Press 1998); Robert Baldwin and Julia Black, 'Really Responsive Regulation' (2008) 71(1) Mod L Rev 59; Gary Lynch-Wood and David Williamson, 'Regulatory Compliance: Organizational Capacities and Regulatory Strategies for Environmental Protection' in Hannah Quirk, Toby Seddon and Graham Smith (eds), *Regulation and Criminal Justice: Innovations in Policy and Research* (Cambridge University Press 2010).
90. Macrory, 'Reforming Regulatory Sanctions', 241.
91. Braithwaite, 'The Essence of Responsive Regulation'.
92. ibid 475.

three. Even in later versions the role of criminal law is viewed by some regulatory experts as peripheral and effectively non-apex in effectiveness.[93] Nonetheless, Braithwaite, right from his pre-responsive paradigm days, in considering coal-mine legislation made it clear that there must be a role for both civil penalty and criminal sanction.[94] The key issue is the interplay between both, in a collaborative, dynamic design that will garner legitimacy and industry buy-in, change with circumstances, and involve both a tough top where criminal law lurks and a balanced middle.

The objective of this paper, therefore, is to develop a framework around Responsive Regulatory Theory, and more particularly the Enforcement Pyramid, enabling the criminal law to become a transformation agent in relation to the reform of financial regulation as a potential universal model. Within such objective regulatory approaches exhibit a swing towards individualised sanctioning response within a societal welfare culture, the requirement for a tough top and balanced middle criminal law presence, where a supportive pyramidal approach incorporating greater investment and resources in prevention and preventive policing provides optimum benefit. Thus, I now move to consideration of sanction interplay issues.

Criminal and Administrative Sanctioning Interplay

The validity of positioning criminal penalties below apex, or regarding them as below apex effective, however, raises reasonable query. Extrapolated from the criminal law sphere, and emphasised to the carceral form of punishment, Ashworth, in discussing a penal 'ladder' concept of hierarchy of sentencing options, argued:

> ... custody should not simply be seen as the top rung of a ladder which starts with discharges and runs upwards through fines and community penalties. The imposition of a custodial sentence restricts liberty to a far greater degree than any other sentence, and for that reason should require special justification.[95]

A number of points arise. First, Ashworth's enunciation clearly shows the criminal sentencer's mindset is to move in an upwards direction as regards penalty choices, whereas Responsive Regulation admits commencement anywhere

93. See Peter Grabosky, 'On the Interface of Criminal Justice and Regulation', Anthony Ogus, 'Regulation and its Relationship with the Criminal Justice Process', and Graham Smith, Toby Seddon and Hannah Quirk, 'Regulation and Criminal Justice: Exploring the Connections and Disconnections' in Smith, Seddon and Quirk (eds), *Regulation and Criminal Justice: Innovations in Policy and Research* (Cambridge University Press 2010).
94. John Braithwaite, *Punish or Persuade: Enforcement of Coal Mine Safety* (State University of New York Press 1985).
95. Andrew Ashworth, *Sentencing and Criminal Justice* (4th edn, Cambridge University Press 2005) 269.

on the ladder, and permits both upward and downward movement. Secondly, for traditional criminal policy-makers jail is the ultimate sentence, whereas for businessmen the loss of livelihood entailed in disqualification or restriction – their capital punishment – may prove such. Thirdly, there are gradations of punishment, and the criminal and the regulatory spheres have different views as to the composition and ordering of components. Fourthly, the conceptualisation of a penalty framework by way of shape or simulation assists in indicating the primary focus for sanctioners. For instance, the more educational and compliance-oriented wider, lower tier of the pyramid is where most activity is encouraged by Responsive Regulation. Fifthly, Ashworth views custody as the top-rung sentence, a sanction absent from most administrative sanction suites. And, finally, the imposition of severe penalties requires particular evidence-based consideration.

Ireland, like the EU where it has competence, has favoured an administrative approach to sanctioning in the financial regulatory sector. My survey of the 59 settlement agreements[96] entered into between the Irish financial regulator and those regulated between the commencement of sanctioning in 2004 and December 2012 revealed an implicit empirical enforcement pyramid broadly in line with the 'responsive regulation' model. Criminal penalties are absent, however, since, like the UK, there is a double-jeopardy administrative and criminal-procedure prohibition,[97] a far cry from the US parallel-proceedings approach.[98] In Ireland revocation, disqualification, fine and reprimand are the downward pyramid flow while the reprimand at the base of the pyramid is the most frequent accompaniment to a monetary penalty.

In the EU context, where punitive sanction involves exclusion from future benefits or pecuniary penalty, both the EU Commission, and the ECJ on review, have not shirked imposition at a higher than base level for an observable Treaty-specified pyramid, even for inadvertence, where potential serious consequences are concerned.[99] Financial regulatory enforcement, based on *effective, proportionate and dissuasive* sanctions,[100] is regarded by the EU Commission as one of four intrinsically linked priority principles grounding post-GFC reforms.[101] The EU Commission have opined that criminal sanctions, when appropriately applied, in particular imprisonment, send a strong message of disapproval

96. See <www.centralbank.ie>.
97. For Ireland see s 33 AT 1942 Central Bank Act 1942 as inserted by Central Bank and Financial Services Authority of Ireland Act 2004.
98. Hank J Brightman, *Today's White-Collar Crime: Legal, Investigative, and Theoretical Perspectives* (Routledge 2009).
99. Takis Tridimas, *The General Principles of EU Law* (2nd edn, Oxford University Press 2006); and see Case C–308/90 *Advanced Nuclear Fuels v Commission* [1993] ECR 1–309.
100. Case C–68/88 *Commission v Greece* [1989] ECR 2965 (*Greek maize case*).
101. EU Commission, 'Regulating Financial Services for Sustainable Growth' (Communication) COM June 2010/301, 4.

that could increase the dissuasiveness of sanctions, and further recommended introducing criminal sanctions for the most serious violations.[102] The EU has been the primary source for Irish financial regulatory legislation since the introduction of the international treaty known as the Single European Act in 1986.

From an Australian context, Freiberg[103] has argued that the responsive regulation model is a replacement for a rule-enforcement and deterrence-based compliance approach. In his view, the approach is premised on an ongoing dyadic relationship between regulator and regulated, and requires – in line with Macrory – the regulator to be aware of the different motivations, backgrounds and objectives of such regulatees, as well as the broader regulatory environment. The Australian Law Reform Commission[104] has described enforcement methods arrayed across a continuum of coerciveness, an explicit enforcement pyramid, where tougher measures are only used when lesser measures have failed in a tit-for-tat escalating response.

Freiberg has also argued, in contrast to generally accepted criminal law sentence practice, but also in line with the Macrory approach, that in the use of sanctions the regulator:

> ... should consider the effects on the regulatee in terms of markets and... the administrative burdens imposed, as well as the resources required to employ the option and the consequences if no action is taken.[105]

Baldwin and Black have critiqued responsive regulation, within the context of advocating their own 'really responsive' approach, under three headings: 1) the policy or conceptual: including arguing that step-by-step escalation up the pyramid may not be appropriate for catastrophic risk; 2) the practical: including the lack of repeat interactions in some dyadic relationships or within the relevant industry sector; and 3) the principled: including that 'responsive' strategies lack formalism, and undermine the rule of law and broader constitutional values.[106]

The tension dilemma, that prosecution is public whereas administrative penalties are confidential, thus encouraging the payment of heavy penalties to avoid publicity, a criminal record and imprisonment, has been highlighted by Levi.[107] Civil sanction may be cheaper, quicker and more predictable, but it creates a sense of unfairness and social privilege – a dangerous downside affecting

---

102. EU Commission, 'Reinforcing Sanction Regimes in the Financial Services Sector' (Communication) COM 2010/716, 14; and EU Commission (Impact Assessment) SEC (2010) 1497, 7 final.
103. Freiberg, *Tools of Regulation*.
104. Australian Law Reform Commission, *Report on Principled Regulation: Federal Civil and Administrative Penalties in Australia* (ALRC 95 – 2003).
105. Freiberg, *Tools of Regulation*, 98.
106. Baldwin and Black, 'Really Responsive Regulation'.
107. Michael Levi, 'Serious Tax Fraud and Noncompliance' (2010) 9(3) Crim & Pub Pol 493.

sanction efficacy – while stigma and criminal process are a big deterrent to 'the respectable'.[108] Lacey emphasised, on the other hand, imprisonment's 'uniquely intrusive, stigmatizing, psychologically painful, and expensive nature',[109] while Braithwaite, even post-crisis, perhaps unsurprisingly, argued that the public is overly pre-occupied with the imprisonment of the guilty as a crime remedy despite prison not being the most cost-effective way to reduce crime.[110]

And yet beyond the unarguable financial prison–cost analysis, Luban has forcefully argued the real power of the criminal law:

> ... criminal penalties aid in regulatory enforcement. Would-be corporate offenders know that they might be facing not only an over-burdened regulatory agency, but also tough and capable professional prosecutors – prosecutors who have a powerful investigative tool in their hands, namely the threat of jail time...[111]

In summary, the presence and positioning of the criminal law 'jail-time' big gun is crucial to enforcement in any pyramid or other preferred structure; a pyramid better reflects the operability of sanction options; incarceration may not be the 'ultimate' penalty in all cases; interplay policy formulation must reflect both the presence and absence of an ongoing dyadic exchange and catastrophic risk; and, cost-effective sanctions including publicity, equity and stigmatisation are mandatory inclusions.

Workable Interplay Policy Options

Seventy years ago Pound, in a US yet common law context, argued that law is the paramount agency of social control, which itself is primarily the function of the state, and that the ultimate effectiveness of law depended upon the application of force (punishment) exercised by bodies, agencies and officials established or chosen for that purpose.[112] For Findlay and Henham, law's moral power in sentencing is achieved through its capacity to shape social reality through the recursively organised practices of the criminal process.[113] This includes discretionary judicial sentencing based in technique and analysis, reflects legal concepts (eg culpability) in sanction choice, is grounded in sentence guidelines, and normatively operationalises policy-justified principles of punishment. At judicial level, albeit within the criminal law frame, Morris and Tonry

108. Hart, *Concept of Law*; ibid.
109. Nicola Lacey, 'Principles, Politics, and Criminal Justice' in Andrew Ashworth and Lucia Zedner (eds), *The Criminological Foundations of Penal Policy: Essays in Honour of Roger Hood* (Oxford University Press 2003) 97.
110. Braithwaite, 'Diagnostics of White-Collar Crime Prevention'.
111. David Luban, 'The Publicity of Law and the Regulatory State' (2002) 10(3) J of Pol Phil 296, 312.
112. Roscoe Pound, *Social Control through Law* (Yale University Press 1942).
113. Mark Findlay and Ralph Henham, *Transforming International Criminal Justice* (Willan 2005).

highlighted the need for 'interchangeability of punishments' two decades ago, advocating that a just and efficient sentencing system should include a range of punishments, and not merely a choice between imprisonment at the top and probation at the base, where a variety of intermediate punishments, along with appropriate treatment conditions, are part of a comprehensive, integrated system of sentencing and punishment.[114]

Almost 40 years ago and writing his seminal work, also from a US and common law context, Donald Black argued that within the context of legal control, legal mobilisation mediated both between legal prescriptions and case disposition, and between rules and their application.[115] Within the linkage between the law and the people served or controlled by it, he identified two distinct sequences of mobilisation first, that commenced by the citizenry, which was *reactive*, and second, that commenced by the state, which was *proactive,* and where the major examples are regulatory and criminal law. While clearly both sequences engage state apparatus, they reinforce a *civil v criminal* divide where there is no inter-mixture. For Reiss the logical shift for deterrent law enforcement is to escalate proactive mobilisation and especially where instrumental to compliance strategies.[116] More recently Pat O'Malley, within the wider common law criminal law 'proactive' context, has argued that two zones of simulated justice, one 'soft' and one 'hard', where monetised justice based around risk-based technologies, a particular feature of more modern financial regulatory practice, have bifurcated from the judicial apparatus.[117]

Within the EU single integrated financial market context, where political and economic rationales are pre-eminent, and where 'serious' crime is the main focus, a central theme emerging from financial regulatory reform deliberations is the issue of the interplay between civil and criminal penalties.[118] The development of a workable policy or strategy dealing with interplay issues – policy-justified principles of punishment – is thus a matter of some importance. In Ireland and the UK (and Australia), for instance, there are double-jeopardy provisions, preventing both administrative and criminal penalty upon the same facts, while in the US parallel proceedings in the form of both federal and state simultaneous administrative/criminal/and private suit are regularly commenced. Although the global regulatory space thus seems destined to non-convergence, a newer approach at a national level is not precluded.

Taking the Australian regulatory context, for instance, and readily identifiable elsewhere, Freiberg highlighted that under some legislation enforcement agencies are empowered to take simultaneous or sequential, administrative,

114. Norval Morris and Michael Tonry, *Between Prison and Probation* (Oxford University Press 1990).
115. Donald J Black, 'The Mobilization of Law' (1973) 2 J L Stud 125.
116. Reiss, 'Selecting Strategies'.
117. Pat O'Malley, 'Simulated Justice'.
118. COM 2010/716; Brightman, *Today's White-Collar Crime.*

civil or criminal action in respect of the same conduct.[119] Four models or pathways of penalty enforcement have been identified[120]:

- Parallel criminal liability and civil penalties for the same conduct, the US approach;
- Separate schemes of civil and criminal penalties, a throwback to Donald Black's empirical observations;
- Administrative penalties that arise automatically by operation of legislation, a feature of Pat O'Malley's simulated justice concept; and
- Parallel criminal liability and quasi-penalties (eg licence suspension or removal), which resonates with aspects of Braithwaite's responsive pyramid.

Irrespective of legal jurisdiction, generally the grounding legislation will set out the relevant and statute-specific pathway, stipulate the priority of sanction models, provide for any stay on proceedings where an alternative procedure has become operative, or direct that one procedure cannot be maintained if another has been completed.[121] The format often adopted is that a civil pecuniary/monetary penalty cannot be imposed if a criminal conviction or acquittal upon substantially the same facts has occurred, that civil proceedings are stayed where contemporaneous criminal proceedings are instituted, and sometimes that if a civil monetary/pecuniary penalty is imposed that no criminal proceedings may lie. The relevant issues, therefore, arise in the context of the administrative/civil/criminal sanction interplay and concern joint proceedings, double jeopardy, and, elections and bars to proceedings.

The reasoning in favour of the availability of multiple penalties is the flexibility it provides both to the regulator and the regulated.[122] Downside risks include multiple punishment as triply being potentially oppressive and unfair, cost injurious to the regulated, and time-delaying 'finality'; the use of evidence gathered in one proceeding entailing discrete safe-guards and procedures before being used in another if at all; and penalty or sanction across the binary differing in speed of application, process, severity and purpose.

In addition, enforcement distinction may be drawn, for instance, when considering 'hard-core collusive behaviour', the size or scale of a business organisation, and the geographical impact or operability of such business, matters falling within the Macrory flexibility. The catastrophic and recidivist infringement cases equally impact interplay policy. Issues also potentially exist around the subjective nature of some criminal proofs, the imposition of strict liability offences where 'moral culpability' is absent, the use of reverse burdens of proof, and the admixture of 'bi-polar' civil and criminal approaches (one paradigm

119. Freiberg, *The Tools of Regulation.*

120. Australian Law Reform Commission, *Report on Principled Regulation.*

121. Freiberg, *The Tools of Regulation.*

122. Australian Law Reform Commission, *Report on Principled Regulation*

based in compensation and the other in punishment) resulting, some claim, in no regulation of the middle-ground.[123]

Equally reflective of the position of 'victims' in the financial regulatory space, Findlay and Henham, who from an international context criticised 'symbolic and rhetorical' repositioning of penality as insufficient, have called for an ideological realignment, synthesised from an engagement between the morality informing the ideology of justice, and the morally legitimate expectations of such crime victims and the crime context.[124]

In summary, an ideological realignment or transformational change is advocated. Identified binary 'opposites' must be accommodated or circumvented; a choice between four pathways must be made or a pathway synthesis developed; such strategy development – a combined and integrated approach – must establish policy-justified principles of punishment; a clear implementation route must be signalled; the 'inter-changeability of punishments' or sanction suite must be in-built; proactive mobilisation must escalate towards compliance strategies. The law, a principled and legally grounded regulatory system, has the capacity to shape social reality through the recursively organised practices of the criminal process, and especially the moral power of punishment.

Final Thoughts

Within the traditional criminal law paradigm, it is clear that significant transformational change has occurred over the last three decades. Such change has impacted sanction suite capability and operationalisation. However, it remains the case that there is still a significant role for the criminal law. I argue that further transformational change must be applied to the interplay between administrative and criminal law sanctioning in relation to financial regulation, and that the financial crisis and its aftermath present an ideal opportunity and motivation to do so.

As at the present, however, a lesser route has been advocated or adopted but with hope for the future. In the UK, both the Hampton Report[125] and the subsequent Macrory Review,[126] echoing the Responsive Regulation philosophy, accepted that the most effective approach to preventing regulatory breach will in many cases be advice on how best to ensure compliance.[127] Macrory, however, warned:

> But without the power to sanction, even a regulator's advisory functions are likely to have little effect… sanctions are an important tool for ensuring compliance but… it does not necessarily follow that risks are automatically decreased.[128]

123. ibid.
124. Findlay and Henham, *Transforming International Criminal Justice.*
125. Hampton Report, *Reducing Administrative Burdens: Effective Inspection and Enforcement* (HM Treasury/HMSO – 2005).
126. Macrory Review.
127. Macrory, 'Reforming Regulatory Sanctions'.
128. Macrory, 'Reforming Regulatory Sanctions', 230–31.

The Macrory review found that civil penalties are common to the financial regulation and competition areas in the UK, US, Australia and many continental European jurisdictions, and clearly from my research the same applies to Ireland. Nonetheless, Macrory advocated broader monetary penalty categories to round out the regulatory sanctions arsenal.

Within the criminal law regulatory sector, where, in Macrory's view,[129] traditional UK approaches left the criminal law with a great deal of work, he found that in nearly every regulatory field the core sanction was a criminal offence, and usually one expressed in strict liability terms. Thus, the Macrory cReview made recommendations for change/ improvement of the criminal system including [130]: improved training for court officials in regulatory offences, specialising criminal courts to specific areas, the provision of a richer range of sentencing options, including publicity orders, corporate rehabilitation orders, enforcement undertakings that allow the offender to propose their own sanction, eg staff retraining or compensation for victims, the application of proof beyond reasonable doubt in all regulatory enforcement, and the introduction of forms of restorative justice (victim involvement). But beyond this prescription, no meaningful interplay combination and integration enforcement policy or strategy was suggested.

A wobbling paradigm was characterised awaiting equilibrium. Yet, the reform actions proposed suggest a possible generalised but limited stabilisation. Whether it may validly extend to encompass the financial sector remains to be seen, since, for the most part, there is already so little criminal law involvement, and what is more very little industry-led appetite for it. Will it be confined to the most egregious breaches or the most serious offences? Will it include recidivists? Will market innovators be exempt? Can a discernible line be drawn between reckless culpability and lesser negligence? Will a separate regulatory offence category emerge? Will prescribed contraventions and offences be mirrored? Will a realistic interplay policy or strategy emerge at all? If so, will a conjunction (one sanction suite) or even transversality of administrative and criminal sanctions be utilised?

Braithwaite has advocated that the key to progress is to constantly construct new paradigms that sweep across disciplines, new paradigms responsive to new world realities, which themselves dynamically shift when even newer realities emerge.[131] The dynamically complex intersecting world of finance and law, where politics and history enmesh, is, however, a tough nut to crack.

In perhaps a suitable place to end what for me is an ongoing enquiry into the interplay between the administrative and the criminal dimensions, Macrory, espousing a traditional administrative and criminal divide, expressed the hope that:

---

129. ibid.

130. Macrory Review.

131. Braithwaite, 'New Regulatory State'.

> … the changes taking place should lead to a system where the criminal law is more focused on the truly criminal, where sanctions better reflect the range of circumstances involved in regulatory breaches, and where they encourage restoration and improved compliance in a more sophisticated way.[132]

Of course, irrespective of the optimal interplay policy, what the 'truly criminal' consists of, who determines its parameters, and what 'sophistication' entails, are all individually and collectively completely another matter! Let the debate begin.

132. Macrory, 'Reforming Regulatory Sanctions', 242.

Polygamous Marriages and Potentially Polygamous Marriages in Irish Law: A Critical Reappraisal

Kieran Walsh*

Abstract—The Irish courts have recently begun to engage with the challenges posed by polygamous and potentially polygamous marriages validly entered into abroad. Claims relating to the recognisability and validity of these marriages have arisen in contexts ranging from refugee law to family law, via the problematic doctrine of common law marriage. Essentially, the problem is reducible to two questions: What are the appropriate rules of private international law to be applied, and what is the interaction between private international law, public policy and the Constitution? This article critically analyses these decisions in an attempt to disentangle the relevant legal principles, and to highlight the differences between actually and potentially polygamous marriages. It concludes that this latter category of marriages ought to be treated as significantly different from actually polygamous relationships, largely due to the harm often associated with actually polygamous marriages, harm that is recognised within international human rights law.

Introduction

The Irish courts have recently begun to engage with the challenges posed to traditional understandings of family life by the development of a more culturally diverse society. As this article will outline, the recognition of foreign marriages by the Irish courts has had a chequered history – not only have the courts sometimes asked the wrong questions, they have also relied on a traditionalist approach to marriage. This has caused problems when the marriage under consideration has deviated from the forms and practices that are familiar in Ireland, such as marriages that take place by proxy, marriages that are potentially polygamous and marriages that are actually polygamous. It is important to distinguish these two forms of 'polygamous' marriages. Marriages that are actually polygamous are those involving more than two spouses, for instance where a man has two wives. Potentially polygamous marriages differ in that the legal system under which the marriage was contracted permits the formation

---

* Senior Lecturer, Griffith College Cork. I would like to thank Sarah Atkins, Nicholas McMurray, Robert O'Brien and Dr Fergus Ryan for their comments on earlier drafts of this article. Any errors remain my own.

of actually polygamous marriages, but at the time when a legal controversy arises over the status of the marriages, there are only two spouses involved. Indeed, the couples concerned may have no intention of ever transforming their factually monogamous relationship into a polygamous one, despite the legal ability to do so. This latter type of marriage will play a significant role in the case law discussed below, as marriages contracted under in legal systems permitting polygamy have been considered in Irish law at the point at which there is a single husband and wife.

The majority of claims for recognition of foreign marriages that have come before the courts in recent years originated as immigration claims, adding a further layer of legal complexity to proceedings. However, the issues in these cases can be reduced to two relatively straightforward questions – What are the rules of private international law to be applied and are there any public policy considerations that should be brought to bear on the consideration of those rules? In answering these questions, this article will critically examine the decisions to date. It will then interrogate the manner in which public policy considerations have been used and it will be demonstrated that the way in which this issue has been used in Ireland is not only legally questionable but culturally problematic. While a full discussion of how Irish law should treat forms of marriage that are different from traditionalist understandings will not be entered into, the discussion will be more narrowly focussed on the role culture, and assumptions about culture, played in one judgment in this area, while suggesting that the addition of what amounts of a 'cultural gloss' to the private international law questions relating to unfamiliar marriage forms may be more problematic than beneficial. The discussion of this issue points out more tentatively some ideas that should be borne in mind should recourse to cultural discourse be relevant.

The final matter to be considered is the role of international human rights law when considering private international law problems. It will be argued that, at least in the context of actually polygamous marriages, it is acceptable to refuse to recognise many of these marriages due to the demonstrable harms associated with them. Potentially polygamous marriages, on the other hand, ought not to be treated the same way. In arguing for a differentiation between actually and potentially polygamous marriages, the article will critique the approach traditionally taken by the courts to potentially polygamous marriages, which has emphasised the form of the marriage rather than the relationship between the parties.

The Recognition of Foreign Marriages in Ireland

Irish law only permits monogamous marriage as, generally speaking, Ireland adopts a traditional understanding of marriage. As outlined in *Hyde v Hyde*,[1]

1. (1866) LR 1 P & D 130. On the rules relating to foreign marriages and private international law in Ireland generally, see Law Reform Commission, *Report of the Law Reform Commission on Private International Law Aspects of Capacity to Marry and Choice of*

and *B v R*,[2] marriage, in the Irish context, is deemed to be monogamous, in line with the traditional Christian understanding of marriage. This was reinforced by s 2(2)(b) of the Civil Registration Act 2004, which states that it shall be an impediment to marriage if one of the parties is already married. In addition, both *Murray v Ireland*,[3] and *TF v Ireland*,[4] described marriage in Irish law as having been based on the 'Christian notion of partnership'. Such explicitly religious language has not been adopted in recent cases,[5] although in the most recent review of the issue in *Zappone v Revenue Commissioners*, the High Court adopted a deferential approach whereby Dunne J relied on the 2004 Act to highlight the continued importance of the traditional understanding of marriage.[6]

While polygamous marriages are clearly prohibited by a traditional understanding of marriage based on Christian principles, potentially polygamous marriages exist in the space between these two marital forms, as the relationship is in fact monogamous. The difficulty for a state like Ireland, which professes equality of the sexes as a basic norm of public policy, is how to classify and accommodate non-traditional marital relationships. As will be discussed below, polygamy can cause severe harm to those involved, based in part on the power imbalances between spouses. Yet there is a clear necessity for the law to assess how it deals with these marriages – while polygamous marriages may not occur within Ireland, they do occur in other jurisdictions and the parties to these marriages may seek to migrate here.[7] Given the standing of women within the

---

Law in Proceedings for Nullity of Marriage (LRC 19–1985). This Report, however, does not deal with polygamous marriages.

2. [1995] 1 ILRM 491 (HC).
3. [1985] IR 532 (HC).
4. [1995] 1 IR 321 (SC).
5. See, for example, the decisions in *DT v CT* [2002] 3 IR 334 (SC) and *Foy v An tÁrd Chláiraitheoir (No 1)* [2002] IEHC 116.
6. *Zappone v Revenue Commissioners* [2008] 2 IR 417 (HC) 504–07. For criticism of this approach, see in particular Conor O'Mahony, 'Societal Change and Constitutional Interpretation' (2010) 1(2) Ir J of L Stud 71.
7. Amy Kaufman, 'Polygamous Marriages in Canada' (2005) 21 Can J of Fam L 315. Islam is among the religions that permit polygamous marriage, and many of the cases that have come before the Irish courts originate in marriages conducted according to Islamic rites. The Islamic approach to polygamy is seen in The Koran, IV:3, which reads, 'If you fear that you shall not be able to deal justly with orphans [left without parents after the battle of Uhud in 625 CE] marry women of your choice, two, three or four. But if ye fear that ye shall not be able to deal justly [with them] then only one.' Traditionally, this has been seen as sanctioning marriage of up to four wives, but the caveat is that a man must be able to treat all equally. Venketraman argues that the Koranic stance on polygamy is not purely permissive. It should be read as seeking to limit a man to four wives and to curtail the pre-Islamic Arabian customary practice of taking many wives and treating them unequally – this is supported by quoting IV:129 – 'Ye are never able to be fair and just as between women, even if that were your ardent desire.' See Bharathi Anandhi Venketraman, 'Islamic States and the

societies where polygamy is practiced, refusal to countenance the existence of these relationships and the dynamics that underpin them is a course of action that risks doubly endangering the second, third and fourth spouses by denying them certain legal protections afforded exclusively to spouses.[8]

Under private international law rules, the recognition of marriages is dependent on two factors – the domicile of the persons entering the marriage and the rules relating to marriage in the jurisdiction where the marriage is contracted. Traditionally, the formalities of marriage and the capacity to marry were governed by the law of the country in which the marriage is celebrated.[9] However, according to the rule set down in *Brook v Brook*, private international law regards a person's capacity to marry as being regulated by the law of their domicile (*lex domicilii*), while the formalities prescribed for the ceremony are regulated by the law of the jurisdiction where the marriage takes place (*lex loci celebrationis*).[10] In *Sottomayor v De Barros (No 1)*, it was held that '[t]he law of a country where a marriage is solemnised must alone decide all questions relating to the validity of the ceremony by which the marriage is alleged to have been constituted'.[11] Similarly, in *Berthiaune v Dastous* the Privy Council held that

> [i]f a marriage is good by the laws of the country where it is effected, it is good all the world over, no matter where the proceedings or ceremony which constituted marriage according to the law of the place would not constitute marriage in the country of the domicile of one or other of the spouses. If the so called marriage is no marriage in the place where it is celebrated, there is no marriage anywhere, although the ceremony or proceedings is conducted in the place of the parties domicile would be considered a good marriage.[12]

There are several exceptions to this general rule. The most important when considering polygamy is the public policy exception. This provides that, even though a marriage may be regarded as recognisable under conflicts rules, the court from which recognition is sought retains a residual jurisdiction to decline to recognise it. This jurisdiction is, however, to be exercised sparingly.[13]

United Nations Convention on the Elimination of All Forms of Discrimination Against Women: Are the Shari'a and the Convention Compatible?' (1995) 44 Am UL Rev 1949.

8. As the term 'potentially polygamous' is the one used most often by the courts, it will be adopted in this article. However, it can be justifiably argued that the decision to adopt either this phrase or to describe them as polygamous marriages belies a normative view as to the acceptability of such marriages within the legal system; therefore the search should continue for more neutral descriptors.
9. This concept appeared, *obiter*, in *Omychund v Barker* (1744) 1 Atk 22, 26 ER 15 and was fully recognised in *Scrimshire v Scrimshire* (1752) 2 Hag Con 395, 161 ER 782.
10. (1861) 9 HL Cas 193.
11. (1877) 3 PD 1, 5.
12. [1930] AC 79 (PC) 83.
13. *Vervaeke v Smith* [1983] 1 AC (HL) 145.

In *Cheni v Cheni*,[14] a marriage between a Jewish uncle and niece, both domiciled in Egypt at the time of the marriage, was recognised by the English courts. This marriage would usually be within the prohibited degrees of relationship, and it was argued that recognition ought to be denied because incestuous marriages were regarded as invalid 'by the common consent of all Christendom or of civilised nations'. However, it was valid under the religious law of the parties and the law of their domicile. The English court recognised the marriage, and outlined the following test: 'the courts… will exceptionally refuse to recognise and give effect to a capacity or incapacity to marry by the law of the domicile on the ground that to give it recognition and effect would be unconscionable in the circumstances in question'.[15] Similarly, in *Mohamed v Knott*, which dealt with a potentially polygamous marriage, it was stated that 'a polygamous marriage will be recognised in England as a valid marriage unless there is some strong reason to the contrary'.[16] In addition to this, the English decision of *Apt v Apt* clarified the position with respect to proxy marriages – if a proxy marriage occurs in a foreign jurisdiction, which complies with the formalities imposed by local law, and will not be regarded as contrary to public policy given the method of giving consent, as opposed to the fact of consent, is essentially a matter for local law.[17] Therefore, the public policy exception appears to only be justifiable as a defence of last resort.

Prior to 2010, actually polygamous marriages had not been considered by the Irish courts, but potentially polygamous marriages had received some limited attention. With respect to actually polygamous marriages, Binchy has argued that if we accept that our *ordre public* does not prevent us from affording recognition to them under the *lex domicilii*, it is then necessary to decide how the legal entitlements that usually arise for spouses on entry to a monogamous marriage may be applied. It would, he contends, be inappropriate to treat the word 'spouse' as if it had a single meaning in the conflicts of laws, indicating that a person may not be regarded as a 'spouse' for all legal purposes.[18] This does two important things. First, it recognises that it is not necessarily the case that a polygamous marriage being considered by an Irish court will come within the public policy exception to *Brook*. It secondly implies that recognition of a marriage for one purpose does not mean that it will be recognised for all

14. [1965] P 85 (PDA).
15. ibid 98.
16. [1969] 1 QB 1 (DC) 13–14. The judgment approves the statement made in Dicey that a marriage would usually be considered polygamous, and which is not rendered invalid due to it being celebrated in England without any attending civil ceremony or because either of the parties is domiciled in England at the time of the marriage will be recognised as valid in English law. See now AV Dicey, JHC Morris and Lawrence Collins, *The Conflict of Laws* (14th edn, Thomson Sweet and Maxwell 2006) Rules 69–73.
17. [1948] P 83 (PDA).
18. William Binchy, *Irish Conflicts of Laws* (Butterworths 1988) 215. This reflects the discussion in Dicey et al, *Conflict of Laws*, Rule 73 about the effects of recognition of a marriage.

purposes. Therefore, it may be possible to recognise a polygamous marriage in order to regularise a person's immigration status, while at the same time denying them the full range of reliefs available to married couples.

The issue of common law marriage has also arisen in several of the recent decisions in this area. It is sometimes thought that marriage could take place by the simple exchange of words of consent in the present tense, otherwise known as a marriage *per verba de praesenti*.[19] Several late nineteenth- and early twentieth-century cases considered whether or not, in light of the provisions of the Clandestine Marriages Act 1753, it was necessary for an episcopally ordained priest in holy orders to be present at the ceremony,[20] and whether or not a marriage could be valid despite not being properly witnessed.[21] The best evidence indicates that the idea that marriages could ever have been entered into by a simple exchange of vows is a misconception,[22] and the later decisions dealing with so-called common law marriages have been heavily criticised.[23] As will be seen, however, this abstruse area of legal history has enjoyed a revival in the Irish case law on foreign marriages.

The term 'common law marriage' is also used in private international law, but it carries a different meaning. In this context, it indicates a marriage that will be recognised by the courts in circumstances where the formalities of marriage required by local law have not been complied with by the couple. Several such exceptions exist: they may arise where the common law is in force in the country in which the marriage took place,[24] where there is an insuperable difficulty in complying with the formalities,[25] where the marriage takes place in a jurisdiction under belligerent occupation,[26] or where it takes place at sea.[27] Often the courts will, for policy reasons, recognise marriages where local laws impose what are regarded as unjustifiable restrictions on the right to marry: preventing a person from marrying at all due to a link between state and religious law,[28]

19. Alan Shatter, *Family Law in the Republic of Ireland* (3rd edn, Butterworths 1986) 82–83.
20. *R v Millis* (1844) 10 Cl & Fin 534 (HL).
21. *Ussher v Ussher* [1912] 2 IR 445 (HC).
22. Rebecca Probert, *Marriage Law and Practice in the Long Eighteenth Century: A Reassessment* (Cambridge University Press 2009).
23. Rebecca Probert, 'Common-Law Marriage: Myths and Misunderstandings' (2008) 20 Child & Fam L Quarterly 1; Rebecca Probert, '*R v Millis* Reconsidered: Binding Contracts and Bigamous Marriages' (2008) Leg Stud 337.
24. There was a general rule stemming from the early days of British colonialism that British settlers took the common law with them, but only so much of it as was applicable to their specific situation. See *Wolfenden v Wolfenden* [1946] P 61 (PDA) and *Penhas v Tan Soo Eng* [1953] AC 304 (PC).
25. *Kent v Burgess* (1840) 11 Sim 361, 59 ER 913.
26. *Taczanowska v Taczanowski* [1957] P 301 (PDA), *Kochanski v Kochanska* [1958] P 147 (PDA) and *Merker v Merker* [1963] P 283 (DC).
27. *Du Moulin v Druitt* (1860) 13 ICLR 212.
28. *Sottomayor v De Barros (No 2)* (1879) 5 PD 94.

restrictions based on religious rules,[29] caste,[30] or race.[31] It is important that when discussing 'common law marriage' in the context of foreign marriages, the term should be properly understood as implying that one or more of the exceptions to the rule in *Brook v Brook* apply to the marriage, thereby enabling its recognition.

The interaction between polygamous marriages and immigration law is highlighted by the EU's Family Reunification Directive.[32] This permits states to adopt 'restrictive measures' when assessing family reunification claims by persons who have entered polygamous relationships.[33] In particular, art 4(4) states that '[i]n the event of a polygamous marriage, where the sponsor already has a spouse living with him in the territory of a Member State, the Member State concerned shall not authorise the family reunification of a further spouse'. It further stipulates that Member States 'may limit the family reunification of minor children of a further spouse of the sponsor'. This makes clear that the EU's policy is that, while Member States may recognise polygamous marriages if they wish, family reunification may not be afforded to more than one spouse. It does so out of concern and respect for the rights of women and children. However, a problem may arise if the children of a second wife are granted permission to enter and reside in the EU, but their mother cannot be granted such permission, thereby preventing the children from being cared for by their own mother. It should be noted that the Directive is not applicable in Ireland, the United Kingdom or Denmark, but it has been cited by the Irish courts in recent decisions as indicative of contemporary approaches to polygamous marriage.[34]

The Decision in *Conlon v Mohamed*

Conlon v Mohamed was the first occasion on which Irish courts had considered the validity of a potentially polygamous marriage conducted under Islamic rites.[35] The plaintiff was domiciled in Ireland, while the defendant was domiciled in South Africa. The couple married in South Africa in an Islamic ritual. According to the dictates of this ritual, no women were present at the religious ceremony and so the plaintiff was represented by a male friend of the family. The couple later celebrated at the home of the defendant's mother and at this celebration, the couple exchanged marriage vows and wedding rings. It was agreed that, on returning to their home in Ireland, they would have a civil marriage ceremony,

29. *Gray (otherwise Formosa) v Formosa* [1963] P 259 (CA); *Lepre v Lepre* [1965] P 52 (PDA).
30. *Chetti v Chetti* [1909] P 67 (PDA).
31. *Sottomayor v De Barros*.
32. Council Directive 2003/86/EC of 22 September 2003 on the right to family reunification [2003] OJL 251/12.
33. ibid [11].
34. See *HAH v SAA* [2010] IEHC 497.
35. [1987] ILRM 172 (HC); [1989] ILRM 523 (SC). As the High Court judgment is more extensive, this judgment will form the basis of discussion unless otherwise indicated.

but this never occurred. In addition, they were not validly married under South African law as mixed-race marriages, as this was considered to have been, were prohibited.[36] The couple knew this but they did, however, appear to regard themselves as married. A dispute later arose in relation to the property in which the couple lived, the solution to which turned on the question of whether or not their marriage could be recognised as valid under Irish law.

The High Court did not regard the exchange of rings and vows as a separate ceremony and so the question became, in the Court's eyes, whether the marriage in the mosque could be regarded as a valid common law marriage or not. Significant attention was focused on the issue of whether or not an episcopally ordained priest was a necessary requirement for a common law marriage and whether the validity of the marriage was affected by their belief that it was not valid in South Africa.[37] Having established that the presence of a priest was not necessary and that the intention of the couple to be bound by the ceremony was more important than their belief as to its validity, the Court dealt with the issue of potential polygamy in Islamic marriages in a rather brusque manner, with Barron J stating, 'Since it is accepted that such a marriage is potentially polygamous, it follows that the essential ingredients of a common law marriage were not present.'[38] This implicitly refers to the requirement in *Hyde v Hyde* that marriage be monogamous. It is implicit from Barron J's statement that a marriage under Islamic rites that is potentially polygamous cannot be recognised as a common law marriage under Irish law.

The matter was appealed to the Supreme Court where, in a rather brief decision, it was held that the High Court had correctly found that the mosque marriage was potentially polygamous, therefore precluding any further inquiry. The Supreme Court acknowledged that a number of ancillary matters, such as the precise standing of a common law marriage and the problems caused by the interaction of the *lex domicilii* and the *lex loci celebrationis*, had arisen but believed that it was not necessary to address them. In fact, these questions are essential to a proper understanding of the case.

The courts in *Conlon* made a number of problematic assumptions. First, it was accepted that each spouse had the capacity to marry. While the plaintiff possessed capacity to marry generally, it is not necessarily the case that she had the capacity to enter this particular marriage. As her capacity to marry is determined by the law prevailing in her antenuptial domicile, her capacity to marry should have been based on Irish laws on marital capacity. It appears from *Hyde* that an Irish domiciled person cannot enter a marriage that is not monogamous, yet this can be taken two ways. First, it can be said that person does not have the capacity to marry when they are a party to an already subsisting valid marriage. This much seems uncontroversial. Secondly, it could be taken to mean

---

36. See the Prohibition of Mixed Marriages Act 1949.
37. *R v Millis*.
38. *Conlon v Mohamed* 180.

that an Irish domiciled person cannot enter a marriage that is polygamous, a logical extension of the rule of private international law whereby questions relating to a person's status are being determined by their law of the country of domicile, and a view supported by Binchy.[39] Where it becomes controversial is whether or not an Irish domiciled person is capable of entering a marriage that was potentially polygamous, even though it was in fact monogamous. Older cases seemed to believe that once a marriage was potentially polygamous, it was to be treated by the law as polygamous for all purposes,[40] but this view no longer has significant support.[41]

Binchy states that the approach of the Irish court is unclear, and that the issue did not arise in *Conlon* because the plaintiff was at all times domiciled in Ireland.[42] But it is precisely because the plaintiff was domiciled in Ireland that the question should have been considered. If a factually monogamous, but potentially polygamous, marriage was forever regarded as polygamous, an Irish domiciled person would never possess capacity to marry in an Islamic marriage abroad. Therefore, the *Conlon* judgment should have focussed on the question of capacity rather than on the requirement for an episcopally ordained priest and the relevance of the parties' intention. On the other hand, if the marriage could somehow be converted into a monogamous marriage at law, matching its factual status, the court should have asked how this could be done. Either way, the court asked the wrong questions.

Another problem with the judgment is that it discussed the concept of common law marriage in a confusing way. The decisions in *Wolfenden*[43] and *Penhas*,[44] which deal with the common law exceptions to the rule in *Brook*, were relied upon heavily by Barron J. However, the decisions in *R v Millis*[45] and *Ussher v Ussher*[46] were also relied upon. These decisions do not deal with the rule in *Brook* but with the now discredited concept of marriage *per verba de praesenti* and the related problems of the requirement for witnesses and the presence of an episcopally ordained priest in holy orders. As such, these two sets of judgments deal with the two different meanings of the term 'common law marriage' and it was a mistake to conflate them. By collapsing the distinction between the two meanings of the term common law marriage, the High Court in *Conlon* added significantly to the confusion in this area. It should have focused on whether or not the marriage fell within one of the public policy exceptions to *Brook*, and in particular on whether or not the South African legislation prevent-

39. Binchy, *Irish Conflicts of Laws*, 213.
40. *Hyde v Hyde; Mehta v Mehta* [1945] 2 All ER 690 (PDA).
41. *The Sinha Peerage Claim* (1939) 171 Lords' J 350; *Ali v Ali* [1968] P 564 (PDA); *R v Sagoo* [1975] QB 885 (CA).
42. Binchy, *Irish Conflicts of Laws*, 214.
43. *Wolfenden v Wolfenden.*
44. *Penhas v Tan Soo Eng.*
45. *R v Millis.*
46. *Ussher v Ussher.*

ing inter-racial marriage presented an insuperable obstacle to marriage that would otherwise be recognisable at common law. This approach would also have forced the court to consider the question of Ms Conlon's domicile, given that the marriage could only be recognisable as an exception to *Brook* if she possessed the requisite capacity. The judgments in *Millis* and *Ussher* were simply not relevant to the factual scenario presented in *Conlon* and, indeed, their relevance to any marriage contracted abroad is limited.[47]

The Legislative Framework Relating to Family Reunification and Declarations as to Marital Status

Four recent decisions point to the development of a more sophisticated approach to the issue of polygamous marriages than was evident in *Conlon*. The marriages in these cases were contracted abroad and mostly arose in the context of family reunification following the grant of refugee status. In three of the four cases, *HAH v SAA* being the only exception,[48] the marriages were potentially polygamous but actually monogamous. Before describing the reasoning in the cases, it would be helpful to set out the legislative framework involved. Two statutory regimes have to be considered – the regime applying to family reunification within refugee law, and the determination of marital status under the Family Law Act 1995.

Family reunification is governed by the Refugee Act 1996.[49] According to s 18(1), a refugee may be granted permission to have a member of their family enter and reside in the State.[50] Subsection 3 establishes the scope of the reunification scheme, indicating that it applies to the spouse of the refugee if the marriage is subsisting at the date of the application, the child of the refugee if that child is under 18 and not married, or, if the refugee is a child, they may be joined by their parents. Where this subsection applies, permission 'shall'

---

47. James Fawcett, Janeen Carruthers (Peter North, consultant ed), *Cheshire, North & Fawcett: Private International Law* (14th edn, Oxford University Press 2008) 887–95.
48. *HAH v SAA*.
49. It should also be noted that although there is an EU directive governing family reunification, Ireland has not opted into this. See Council Directive 2003/86/EC of 22 September 2003 on the right to family reunification (OJL 251/12 of 3 October 2003). The UN High Commission on Refugees also regards family reunification as an essential right of refugees – see 'UNHCR Resettlement Handbook (Geneva, November 2004)'; the 'UNHCR Guidelines on Reunification of Refugee Families 1983' and the 'Conclusions of the UNHCR Executive Committee on Family Reunification of 21 October 1981.
50. When an application is made, it is referred to the Refugee Applications Commissioner (s 18(1)), who will then, according to s 18(2), 'investigate the application and… submit a report in writing to the Minister and such report shall set out the relationship between the refugee concerned and the person the subject of the application and the domestic circumstances of the person'.

be granted, unless the exception created by sub-s 5 is relevant, due to a the presence of a national security or public policy reason for refusing permission, or if the Refugee Appeals Commissioner indicates that it is a false claim. Subsection 4 also permits entry and residence rights to be granted to another dependent member of the refugee's family at the discretion of the Minister for Justice. This broader category applies to 'any grandparent, parent, brother, sister, child, grandchild, ward or guardian of the refugee who is dependent on the refugee or is suffering from a mental or physical disability to such extent that it is not reasonable for him or her to maintain himself or herself fully'. Clearly then, sub-s 3 is drafted in mandatory language, as the Minister has no discretion to refuse the application unless one of the two narrow exemptions apply, whereas sub-s 4, however, is drafted so as to grant much greater discretion to the Minister. Therefore, the likelihood of success of a claim for family reunification depends largely on whether sub-s 3 or sub-s 4 applies to the claim.

The difficulty for the applicants in all four of the recent decisions is that, because of the decision in *Conlon*, it was uncertain whether or not the circumstances under which the applicants had married could create marriages that could be regarded as valid under Irish law, and so they did not necessarily qualify as spouses for the purposes of sub-s 3. Instead, the applicants were urged to seek a declaration that their marriages were valid under s 29 of the Family Law Act 1995. This provision is used to determine a person's marital status under Irish law, and is typically the basis on which nullity claims are initiated. If the marriages were deemed valid in Irish law, then sub-s 3 of the 1996 Act could then be applied. However, given the exclusive nature of the list provided in sub-s 4, if the marriages were not recognised as valid, there would be no statutory basis on which family reunification could be granted under the 1996 Act, given that the person being sponsored was neither a spouse nor a person to whom sub-s 4 applied. This problem can be easily circumvented by realising that a marriage can be valid for one purpose but not for another, and so s 29 appears to be rather blunt instrument for the purpose at hand. As person's capacity to marry is determined according to their antenuptial domicile, the Irish courts are capable of deciding that a marriage contracted abroad, which complied with both the *lex loci celebrationis* and the *lex domicilii*, is recognisable by the Irish courts even though it would not have been a valid marriage if it had occurred in Ireland.

The Case Law Relating to Family Reunification

The first case that needs to be considered is *Hamza v Minister for Justice*.[51] The applicant had married in Sudan, where he was originally domiciled, and was later granted refugee status in Ireland. He sought permission for his wife and children to join him under the family reunification scheme. His application was rejected

51. [2010] IEHC 427.

partly on the basis that his marriage was a proxy marriage, which was viewed as invalid under Irish law. The applicant contended that this was not a proxy marriage in the true sense, as his wife, although not present in the mosque when the ceremony took place, was represented by a male relative who indicated her consent to the marriage.[52] Cooke J reasoned that the ceremony need not be categorised as a proxy marriage in the strict sense, and that proxy marriages need not be necessarily excluded from recognition as valid in Irish law.

He also held, critically for this case, that recognition of the marriage as having validity under Irish law is not the exclusive test for recognition of the marriage for family reunification purposes. Relying on *Sottomayor* and *Apt*, he held that a marriage, celebrated in accordance with local law, will be recognised in Ireland assuming that each party had capacity to enter into it and there is no public policy rationale to prevent recognition. This is further strengthened by the fact that both parties were domiciled in Sudan at the time of the marriage, meaning that both certainly had capacity to enter a proxy marriage, as well as proxy marriage being in compliance with the *lex loci*.[53]

With respect to the question of whether or not a marriage must be recognisable as fully valid under Irish law in order to be recognisable for family reunification purposes, Cooke J reasoned that a purposive approach should be taken to the interpretation of the 1996 Act. He cited the purposive approach to reunification seen in the Council Directive on Family Reunification and the UNHCR Guidelines on Reunification of Refugee Families, and reasoned that in the absence of any express indication to the contrary in the 1996 Act, it ought to be interpreted in accordance with the principles established in the Directive and the Guidelines.[54] This has significant impact on the question of polygamous marriages as *Conlon* was the only previous occasion on which consideration was given to the issue. Seeing as *Conlon* did not deal with the manner in a satisfactory way, Cooke J relied on these more specialised sources of guidance. As stated above, art 4(4) of the Directive states: 'In the event of a polygamous marriage, where the sponsor already has a spouse living with him in the territory of a Member State, the Member State concerned shall not authorise the family reunification of a further spouse.'[55] This implies that potentially polygamous marriages can qualify for family reunification purposes. States are prevented from according reunification where the marriage is actually polygamous, yet that does not prevent actually monogamous but potentially polygamous marriages from being recognised for family reunification purposes.

52. Marriages contracted under Islamic law in Sudan required as a formality that the woman did not enter the mosque. However, Cooke J did not view this a 'proxy' marriage in the strict sense. See *Hamza*, ibid [17–23].
53. Indeed, *Apt* provides some authority for the proposition that a person domiciled in one country can validly enter a proxy marriage in another under certain circumstances.
54. Such an approach should even hold where there are deficiencies in the formal proof of marriage, given the conditions pertaining in the state from which a person has fled.
55. Council Directive 2003/86/EC art 4(4).

Indeed Cooke J expressly attacked the decision in *Conlon* on this basis, stating that its assertion that a polygamous marriage could never be recognised also means that a potentially polygamous marriage is similarly not recognisable should not be taken to be a general proposition. Instead, he argued that 'the better view of the general conflict of laws issue is that a foreign marriage validly solemnised in accordance with the *lex loci* may be recognisable as valid in Irish law, even if it was potentially polygamous according to that law, provided neither party was domiciled in Ireland at the time and neither has also been married to a second spouse, either then or since'.[56]

This attacks *Conlon* in two ways. First, and most obviously, it recognises that the Irish courts can treat potentially polygamous but actually monogamous marriages as valid for certain purposes. Secondly, Irish domiciled persons are incapable of having such a marriage recognised, thereby highlighting that although the right decision was reached in *Conlon*, it was decided on the wrong basis. Instead of engaging in the mired question of whether or not the presence of an episcopally ordained priest is an essential ingredient in a common law marriage, it could have been disposed of much more simply by pointing out that the wife lacked the capacity to enter a potentially polygamous marriage.

In the Supreme Court, Fennelly J upheld the High Court decision. While not expressing any clear opinion on the questions raised by Cooke J over the *Conlon* decision, he did clarify the role of the Minister in s 18 applications. In particular, he clarified that a declaration of marital status under s 29 of the Family Law Act is not an alternative means of satisfying the requirements of the Refugee Act.[57] This implicitly recognises that idea that the sections provide for mutually exclusive aims, with one determining a person's marital status in Irish law, while the other determines the existence of a familial relationship for a limited and specific purpose. Fennelly J also expressly upheld Cooke J's decision that a marriage conducted by proxy, which complies with the *lex loci celebrationis*, is capable of being recognised in Irish law, at least for family reunification purposes.[58] This at the very least clarifies the position of foreign proxy marriages in Irish law.

Further clarity in the law was afforded by the decision in *Hassan v Minister for Justice*,[59] delivered on the same day as *Hamza*. The applicant married in Somalia according to Islamic rites.[60] As in *Hamza*, his application to be reunited with his wife was rejected. What is interesting in *Hassan* is the way in which

56. *Hamza v Minister for Justice* [42].
57. [2013] IESC 9 [44].
58. ibid [53]–[54].
59. [2010] IEHC 426.
60. Due to the fact that Somalia had not had an effective government and bureaucracy for over a decade, the applicant was unable to present documentary evidence of the marriage. This is a matter of public knowledge, and so should not prevent the marriage being recognised. To demand such documentation would place an unreasonable burden on an applicant by expecting them to produce documentation that is essentially unobtainable. See Hassan ibid [15].

the Court dealt with the vexed question of common law marriage, which had occupied such a central role in the *Conlon* case. As a preliminary to this question, Cooke J stated firmly that the wife in *Conlon* did not have the capacity to enter a potentially polygamous marriage as she was domiciled in Ireland.[61] This clarifies the capacity question in *Conlon*, as it appears that the original decision was based on the belief that common law marriage demanded a monogamous relationship, thereby preventing a potentially polygamous relationship from coming within its ambit. By focusing on the question of the wife's antenuptial domicile, the uncertainty over the capacity of Irish domiciled persons to enter potentially polygamous marriages abroad has been removed.

Hassan enters more difficult terrain when it revives the idea of common law marriage. Referring to the *Conlon* decision, Cooke J stated that

> [i]t would seem that, had it not been for the potentially polygamous nature of the Islamic marriage, a monogamous religious marriage would be recognised as valid in Irish law as a common law marriage, notwithstanding non-compliance with formal requirements of the civil law in the *lex loci*. It appears clear to the Court that had the marriage in question taken the form of a non-Islamic religious service according to a rite requiring monogamy, it would have been valid as a common law marriage in Ireland although prohibited as an inter-race union in South Africa at that time.[62]

Building on this, he states that the view that religious marriage contracted abroad can be recognised as valid in Ireland. This is because a common law marriage may exist even where formal requirements imposed by the *lex loci* were not complied with or are now impossible to determine.[63] It would appear that Cooke J, despite using the term 'common law marriage', was in fact attempting to clarify the law relating to the common law exemptions from having to comply with the formal rules required by the *lex loci celebrationis*. Therefore, Cooke J's analysis of the legal rules is correct, even though the terminology he adopted was somewhat misleading.

The confusion was compounded however, by the Supreme Court decision. Fennelly J expressly stated that while any remarks in the judgments should be regarded as *obiter*, it was nonetheless important to discuss them given the representative nature of the decision.[64] He outlined the history of common law marriage in Ireland, arguing that such marriages were possible due to the fact that the Clandestine Marriages Act 1753 was not applicable in Ireland.[65] More problematically, however, he proceeded to adopt an approach similar to that of Barron J in *Conlon* whereby the different meanings of common law marriage were conflated. In particular, he discussed the issue of 'common law marriages

61. *Hassan* ibid [17].
62. ibid.
63. ibid [18].
64. *Hassan* [2013] IESC 8 [37].
65. ibid [39]–[40].

contracted abroad', rather than the circumstances in which the common law recognises an exception to the general rules governing the form of a foreign marriage.[66] The concurring comments by Murray J were also concerning. He cast doubt of the ability of persons resident in Somalia, which had never been subject to the common law, to enter a common law marriage. However, the correct question is not whether or not this couple entered a common law marriage, but whether or not their marriage complied with the local rules relating to the form of a marriage, and, if they did not, whether this marriage can be recognised under the exceptions provided for in private international law or not.

The Case Law on Determination of Marital Status under the Family Law Act

The cases outlined above do not attempt to determine the civil status of the marriages in question under Irish law. In fact, *Hamza* and *Hassan* were predicated on the basis that the Minister for Justice had acted *ultra vires* in attempting to have the parties seek such a determination before proceeding with their family reunification applications. However, the question of civil status did arise in two subsequent decisions, one of which dealt with an actually polygamous marriage, while the other considered a potentially polygamous marriage.

In *HAH v SAA*,[67] the Irish courts dealt for the first time with an actually polygamous marriage. The applicant had married twice in Lebanon, where all parties were domiciled, and both marriages were valid according to Lebanese law. He was granted refugee status in Ireland. The husband and both wives argued that, given their compliance with both the *lex domicilii* and the *lex loci celebrationis* and, more importantly, the lack of any public policy rationale preventing the recognition of the marriages, they should be regarded as valid in Irish law. Dunne J accepted that both marriages were valid under Lebanese law. She categorised the first marriage as having been potentially polygamous at its inception, which is critical to a proper understanding of the s 29 declaration as s 29 asks whether or not the marriage was valid at its inception. Therefore, the question arises as to whether a marriage that is valid at its inception is rendered invalid by the second marriage or whether it is unaffected. Unfortunately, Dunne J did not consider this. Additionally, there is a problem with using s 29 for cases such as this, quite apart from the issue of the Minister's *vires* as addressed in *Hamza* and *Hassan*. In order to properly interpret this section, it may be necessary to have recourse to Irish constitutional principles in proceedings that are really about a conflict of laws issue. As already indicated, s 29 seeks to determine the validity of a marriage under Irish law rather than under foreign law. The more logical approach may have been to determine the matter under conflicts rules and by

66. ibid [47]–[48].
67. *HAH v SAA*.

asking whether or not a once-valid marriage can be subsequently invalidated, rather than resorting to s 29 and, as a consequence, constitutional principles.

As a result of the introduction of constitutional questions, the main issue addressed in the judgment is the role of public policy. The applicant and both wives argued that public policy ought to be considered only as a measure of last resort. In particular, they noted the gradual relaxation of the rule, first established in *Hyde*,[68] that no polygamous or potentially polygamous marriage could be recognised by English law. The *Hyde* decision is a striking example of Victorian Christian ideals, and the idea that such marriages were against Christian principles heavily influenced not only the outcome, but the reasoning in that case. Gradually, the rule was relaxed, and so polygamous marriages were increasingly recognised, whereas public policy exceptions became increasingly rare. Many of the cases relied on by the applicant originated in British colonies. However, Dunne J sought to characterise the relaxation of the rule against polygamous marriages as being a necessary part of the administration of a multi-ethnic Empire, rather than the gradual development of a legal principle, and so saw this attitudinal change towards polygamous marriages as irrelevant in an Irish context.[69]

The construction of art 41 of the Irish Constitution played a central role in the *HAH* decision, as it was argued that the marriage ought to be recognised unless it was contrary to public policy or it was incompatible with the Constitution. This raises the thorny questions of the extent to which a constitution can be said to adequately represent public policy and the interrelationship between private international law and the Constitution. While there is limited case law on this issue, perhaps the most important decision for present purposes is *Nottinghamshire County Council v B*.[70] This decision concerned the abduction of children from the United Kingdom into Ireland and the application of the Hague Convention on International Child Abduction. It was alleged by the children's parents that the Irish courts could not order the return of the children to the UK as to do so would result in the adoption of the children in breach of the rights conferred by art 41 of the Constitution.

O'Donnell J asked in 'what circumstances does the Constitution have regard to and/or attribute legal significance, to events occurring abroad? In particular, when can acts occurring abroad be said to be in breach of the Irish Constitution?'[71] While much of the discussion may be restricted to the interaction between art 20 of Hague Convention and the Irish Constitution, some limited guidance may be drawn from the decision as to the general principles governing the relationship between the Constitution and private international law. When considering the interaction between foreign actions and Irish con-

---

68. *Hyde v Hyde*.
69. ibid 64.
70. [2011] IESC 48.
71. ibid [13].

stitutional law, the question to be asked is whether or not what is done in this jurisdiction is contrary to the Constitution. This focuses attention on the question of whether or not the Irish Constitution distinguishes between events occurring abroad and events occurring within this jurisdiction, but there is no clear answer to this question.[72] With respect to the determination of a person's status, O'Donnell J posits that if an act, such as an adoption, is properly carried out in the UK and a question later arose in the Irish courts as to the status of that act, the courts would likely recognise the act as validly done. Where the Irish courts are part of a process, the end point of which could be the making of an order by a foreign court that would breach the Constitution if the order were made in Ireland, the Irish courts have to consider whether their own actions could lead to a later breach of constitutional rights. However, this point is of no relevance to the recognition of an existing relationship. It is only when subjecting a person to a foreign court or administrative procedure that is contrary to the scheme of rights envisaged by the Constitution that the Irish courts should invoke Irish constitutional principles. To this end, the courts should only in exceptional cases seek to inhibit the application of, for example, 'French law to French citizens'.[73] In particular, the statement in *Nottinghamshire* that 'the Irish Constitution does not demand the imposition of Irish constitutional standards upon other countries or require that those countries adopt our standards as a price for interaction with us' was explicitly endorsed in the context of foreign marriage in *Aslam v Minister for Justice*.[74]

Although this judgment was delivered after the decision in *HAH*, it casts significant doubt on the approach adopted by Dunne J. The *Nottinghamshire* decision outlines the general principle that people ought to be subject to the law of their own domicile, and that this would fulfil the aims of art 29 of the Constitution.[75] It is only where there is a risk of exposing a person to a breach of their rights that the Irish courts should intervene, and even then only where there is a close causal connection between a decision of the Irish courts and that breach of rights. Therefore, in matters pertaining to the determination of personal status acquired aboard and with no earlier involvement by the Irish courts, the Irish Constitution should not be invoked, and the law of a person's domicile should be regarded as of fundamental importance. More general public policy concerns should play a minimal role.

This raises the question of whether it is legitimate to invoke the Constitution in order to refuse recognition to a polygamous marriage. Dunne J proceeded to assess whether the Lebanese marriage was compatible with the Irish

72. ibid [61].
73. ibid [66].
74. [2011] IEHC 512.
75. This Article deals with the interaction between international law and the Irish legal system, and establishes Ireland as a dualist state.

Constitution's understanding of marriage.[76] The idea that the Irish Constitution relies on a Christian understanding of marriage, derived from *Murray v Ireland*,[77] was held to be important for a proper understanding of a marriage under s 29 of the 1995 Act, as a reading of that statute that was not in line with constitutional principles would be impossible. Indeed 'to interpret the word "marriage" in section 29(1)(a) as including polygamous marriage would be to give it an interpretation which is simply not compatible with the constitutional understanding of marriage'.[78] Therefore, it was 'impossible to equate polygamous marriage with marriage as understood in the Constitution'.[79] It appears that instead of public policy being regarded as a matter of last resort, where local law should only be set aside if the rule under consideration is unconscionable, the court treated the Constitution as a trump card whereby a particular understanding of a constitutional provision automatically prevented the recognition of the marriage. Dunne J therefore assumed that to recognise any relationship form that was not compatible with ideology of this article would be unconscionable in Irish law.

The belief that an argument based on incompatibility with a traditionalist understanding of the constitutional meaning of marriage could be used to refuse recognition of that marriage is not without its difficulties, as it effectively adds a cultural gloss to proceedings that may succeed in establishing a rather rigid and binary way of categorising marriages as culturally acceptable or not, rather than facilitating a more nuanced discussion of relationship forms that are unfamiliar to traditional approaches. There is a danger in courts invoking public policy as if it were a clear, universally knowable and universally acknowledged concept, especially where the policy in question cleaves to an ideologically traditional understanding. This is particularly problematic when applied to problems of family life, where the very meanings of terms is so culturally constructed that understanding their meaning requires a deep level of cultural inquiry into how those meanings came to be.

The imposition of Irish constitutional standards on foreign institutions or individuals, especially in an area so culturally constructed as marriage, would effectively amount to a form of judicial cultural imperialism.[80] As Freeman has observed in a different context, 'the so-called dominant understanding is in reality the understanding of the dominant'.[81] To claim that a particular definition of marriage is evident within public policy when the only evidence advanced to support this proposition comes from other court judgments is to

76. *HAH v SAA* [65].
77. *Murray v Ireland.*
78. *HAH v SAA* [70].
79. ibid.
80. John Murphy, 'Rationality and Cultural Pluralism in the Non-Recognition of Foreign Marriages' (2000) 49 Int and Comparative L Quarterly 643.
81. Michael Freeman, 'Images of Child Welfare in Abduction Appeals', in John Murphy (ed), *Ethnic Minorities, their Families and the Law* (Hart Publishing 2000).

give a peculiarly narrow meaning to the term 'public policy'.[82] Indeed, it would seem to indicate an approach that aggrandises the role of courts in determining policy. Given the level of disagreement that exists in wider policy discourse over the question of what defines marriage, courts ought to tread carefully if invoking the nebulous public policy ground when considering marriage so as not to appear culturally imperialist; as Murphy argues 'as a minimum, explicit acknowledgement of (minority) cultural value[s]... ought to be provided if the decision is to appear both rational and non-ethnocentric'.[83] This is not to argue that all cultural values must necessarily be treated as incommensurable and that cultural relativism must prevail; merely that the failure to acknowledge competing values in any meaningful sense can, especially when dealing with the values of immigrants, appear ethno-centric and imperialist.[84]

Several difficulties of this nature are made evident by the last two paragraphs of the *HAH* judgment. First, Dunne J explicitly acknowledges the changes that have occurred in Irish society since the Constitution came into force, especially with respect to family life, yet asserts that the basic understanding of and concept of marriage has remained unchanged.[85] This is not necessarily the case. More problematic is her belief that increased immigration and the development of 'a multi-cultural and pluralist society' will inevitably lead to 'a clash of cultures'.[86] This rhetoric is deeply troubling. First, it presupposes that certain views or approaches to family life are essential elements of a particular culture. This has the effect of reducing disparate and diffuse cultures to a homogenised essence, an idea that is particularly problematic given that this case concerned the highly diverse state

82. This is particularly troubling in the present context, as Dunne J in *HAH* relied heavily on the decision in *Zappone v Revenue Commissioners* (n 6), a judgment that she herself delivered.
83. Murphy, 'Rationality', 649.
84. Indeed, Murphy argues that judgments can be based on a pre-commitment to a particular domestic value that is not commensurable with a foreign value, and that these can even be necessitated. However, it is arguable that the context in which this argument is made, that of the recognition of child marriage, undermines his more general point as even within domestic legal systems, value A (the protection of children) can be regarded as more important than value B (the promotion of autonomy interests). He attempts to circumvent this by locating both values under the general umbrella of children's interests, but this does not assist in determining questions involving other kinds of interests, such as the recognition of adult relationships. Fundamentally, there is no way to determine the priority courts should give to competing domestic values that involve only adults, and so, as will be argued below, one must instead attempt to create space within which a variety of different intimacies can be regonised once it is clear that no harm has occurred. Even this proposition relies on the *a priori* assumption that the prevention of harm is a good for which legal systems ought to strive, an assumption that, despite its clear appeal, suffers from the same metaphysical defect found in all arguments based on *a priori* assumptions.
85. *HAH v SAA* [72].
86. ibid [73].

and multi-confessional state of Lebanon.[87] Such approaches are best regarded as reductive.[88] Secondly, it assumes mutual incompatibility between these assumed cultures. Making such an assumption is unsound, relying as it does on the supposition of cultural essentialism. Thirdly, it is premised on a misunderstanding of both multiculturalism and pluralism. These are not just simple descriptive labels indicating the multiplicity of cultures within a jurisdiction but a commitment to developing cross-cultural dialogue, participation in political life by all communities, a positive endorsement of diversity and the realisation that no one 'culture' can dominate others. Therefore, cultural clash is absent from a multicultural and pluralist society properly understood. While is uncertain that a discussion of culture was necessary to resolve the case, it is unfortunate that such errors provided the foundation for the single reference to cultural politics within the judgment. Not only that, but the concept of cultural clash is predicated on the construction of a rather rigid binary division that may inhibit rather than facilitate the development of a nuanced discourse surrounding relationships and culture in situations where that discourse is necessary. Consequentially, the judgment can, perhaps, be regarded as something of a problematic precedent not only in terms of the applicable legal principles but also in terms of whether or not and how the idea culture should be deployed by the courts.

The decision in *HAH* is further undermined by the later decision in *DM v CF*.[89] A Zimbabwean couple had married according to customary law, which permitted polygamy. The relationship was factually monogamous. The husband was granted refugee status in Ireland and was eventually joined here by his two children. However, his wife was denied the right to enter and reside here under the family reunification scheme and so he sought a s 29 declaration. The declaration was granted at first instance as both parties had the capacity to marry and the formalities established by the *lex loci* had been fulfilled. However, the Attorney General appealed on the basis that a potentially polygamous marriage could not be regarded as a valid marriage, even at its inception, under Irish law.

The judgment of Clark J is notable in that it seeks to expressly decouple the question of recognition of polygamous or potentially polygamous marriages from the issue of family reunification. As a result, the State's argument that the *Conlon* decision prevented the recognition of potentially polygamous marriages was rejected, as Clark J did not regard it as relevant to family reunification cases or to s 29 cases. As *Conlon* centred on the question of whether or not matrimonial relief could be sought by the parties, and given that no such relief was at stake in the present case, all that was required was an assessment of whether or not the couple had the requisite capacity and complied with the

87. There are at least 17 different religious communities recognised by the Lebanese state – see Rania Maktabi, 'The Lebanese Census of 1932 Revisited: Who are the Lebanese?' (1999) 26 Brit J of Mid East Stud 219.
88. Edward Said, 'The Clash of Ignorance' (October 2001) The Nation.
89. [2011] IEHC 415.

formalities established under local law. This is because 'the applicable principles for the recognition of a refugee's marriage for family reunification purposes are found in private international law and not in s 29 of the Family Law Act 1995 or other Irish legislation or the Constitution'.[90] Interestingly, *HAH* was dealt with in a rather cursory fashion. Citing *Hamza* and *Hassan*, Clark J reiterated that a foreign marriage between two foreign domiciliaries would be regarded as valid unless public policy holds against recognition. She argued that *HAH* reached exactly the same conclusion, which, as the earlier analysis highlighted, is only superficially true given the significance of the public policy issue within *HAH*. Clearly, Clark J believed that cases such as this should only be dealt with as family reunification matters, with recourse to s 29 regarded as 'inappropriate'.[91] She also distinguished *HAH* on the basis that it concerned an actually polygamous marriage, and so public policy concerns automatically prevented its recognition. However, no discussion was entered into about the appropriateness of the public policy analysis undertaken by Dunne J, meaning that the questions of culture raised in the earlier judgment could be sidestepped.

While the finding of the European Commission on Human Rights in *RB v United Kingdom* was cited to demonstrate that the non-recognition of actually polygamous marriages does not infringe art 8 ECHR,[92] Clark J upheld the earlier order that this potentially polygamous marriage was a valid marriage at its inception and so upheld the s 29 order. This seems to indicate that while a potentially polygamous marriage will be valid under s 29, an actually polygamous marriage will not. This further weakens the *HAH* decision due to the fact that no distinction was made in that case between potentially and actually polygamous marriages with respect to the public policy concerns supposedly raised by art 41 of the Constitution. Dunne J failed to question whether a potentially polygamous, but factually monogamous, marriage could be recognised as valid under the constitutional definition or not. The more recent decision of *Aslam* provides further guidance on this, however, stating that 'our conflict of law rules should be open-minded, tolerant, flexible and accommodating of different legal cultures and traditions'.[93]

Is the Distinction between Polygamous and Potentially Polygamous Justifiable?

Given the importance of the distinction between actually and potentially polygamous marriages, it must be asked whether or not the distinction is justifiable. In doing so it is necessary to assess whether polygamy itself causes or significantly contributes to significant harm, thereby justifying its separate consideration from merely potentially polygamous marriages. It is strongly arguable

90. ibid [27].
91. See, in particular, the comments at [39].
92. *RB v United Kingdom*, application no 19628/92, 29/06/1992.
93. *Aslam v Minister for Justice* [22].

that polygamy, and polygyny (the practice of taking multiple wives) in particular, is a form of discrimination that international human rights law requires states to eliminate, based on evidence that indicates that it is a harmful practice.[94] Given that the majority of polygamous marriages are in fact polygynous marriages, this section will concentrate on polygyny.

The principle of gender equality, both before the law and within marriage, has been central to international human rights law since its formalisation in the mid-twentieth century.[95] The Convention on the Elimination of All Forms of Discrimination against Women (CEDAW) is specifically designed to combat gender inequality. Article 5 is central to CEDAW's attempts to encourage genuine equality of power relations between men and women rather than being satisfied with mere formal equality. It requires states to 'modify the social and cultural patterns of conduct of men and women, with a view to achieving the elimination of prejudices and customary and all other practices which are based on the idea of the inferiority or the superiority of either of the sexes or on stereotyped roles for men and women'. Therefore, any attempt to portray a violation of women's rights as part of cultural tradition will result in the breach of one of core obligations imposed on States parties by CEDAW. The question then remains – is the cultural tradition and contemporary practice of polygyny a violation of women's rights?

Article 16 of CEDAW envisages a version of marriage based on the equality of spouses. Deller Ross makes the argument that in polygynous marriages, a husband has multiple wives, but each wife essentially has only a fraction of a husband, leading to the unequal division of resources between husbands and wives during marriage and at its dissolution.[96] In particular, General Recommendation 21 on Equality in Marriage and Family Relations makes clear that

> Polygamous marriage contravenes a woman's right to equality with men, and can have such serious emotional and financial consequences for her and her dependents that such marriages ought to be discouraged and prohibited. The Committee notes with concern that some States parties, whose constitutions guarantee equal rights, permit polygamous marriage in accordance with personal or customary law. This violates the constitutional rights of women, and breaches the provisions of article 5(a) of the Convention.[97]

94. Rebecca Cook and Liz Kelly, *Polygyny and Canada's Obligations under International Human Rights Law* (Department of Justice 2006) 22–23.
95. See, for example, art 55 of the Charter of the United Nations; art 16 of the Universal Declaration of Human Rights; arts 2(1), 3, and 23(4) of the International Covenant on Civil and Political Rights; and arts 2 and 3 of the International Covenant on Economic, Social and Cultural Rights.
96. Susan Deller Ross, 'Polygyny as a Violation of Women's Right to Equality in Marriage: An Historical, Comparative, and International Human Rights Overview' (2002) 24 Delhi L Rev 22, 34.
97. United Nations Committee on the Elimination of All Forms of Discrimination Against Women, 'General Recommendation 21: Equality in Marriage and Family Relations' (1994) UN Doc A/49/38 [14].

The aim of these instruments is to prevent the asymmetry of power relations between men and women. Yet in polygynous relationships, women are often reduced to a solely reproductive stereotype, with Weinbrod making the argument that polygynous practices often resemble slavery.[98] One woman who had left a polygamous relationship spoke about how religious doctrine maintained that she, like all girls and women, had the duty to contribute to the 'production' of an abundance of children through polygynous marriage in order for the community in which she lived to survive.[99] Such stereotyping is clearly in breach of both art 16 and General Recommendation 21. The principle that marriages must be freely consented to is also violated in polygynous marriages, as women and young girls can be 'assigned' to husbands by community leaders.[100]

Polygyny can also be regarded as a violation of women's security and the right to be free from gender-based violence. General Recommendation 19 on violence against women defines gender-based violence as 'violence that is directed against a woman because she is a woman or that affects women disproportionately'.[101] In addition to the gendered violence often associated with polygyny, polygyny itself can be a form of gender-based violence. The UN Special Rapporteur on Violence against Women has noted that 'several... forms of threat or violence are used to ensure that women stay obedient within a marriage, for example the threat of the husband taking another wife'.[102] Given the detrimental effect of gender violence on women's health, permitting polygyny can also be regarded as a violation of women's rights to the highest available standard of health as provided for in art 12 of the International Covenant on Economic, Social and Cultural Rights. General Recommendation 24 of CEDAW on Women and Health places an obligation on states to 'prevent and impose sanctions for violations of rights by private persons and organizations'.[103] This is

98. Carol Weisbrod, 'Universals and Particulars: A Comment on Women's Human Rights and Religious Marriage Contracts' (1999) 9 S Cal Rev of L and Women's Stud 77.
99. Cook and Kelly, *Polygyny*.
100. Daphne Bramham, 'Religious Tyrants Twist Tolerance for their Own Ends' *The Vancouver Sun* (Vancouver, 17 July 2004) C7.
101. United Nations Committee on the Elimination of All Forms of Discrimination Against Women, 'General Recommendation 19: Violence against Women' (1992) UN Doc A/47/38 [6]. This can also be linked to violations of women's right to be free from cruel, inhuman or degrading treatment under art 7 of the ICCPR.
102. UN Special Rapporteur on Violence Against Women, *Cultural Practices in the Family that are Violent towards Women* (2002) UN ESCOR, 48th sess, UN Doc E/CN4/2002/83 [63]. See also the findings of Law and Advocacy for Women in Uganda, 'Project Report on the Domestic Violence Study', as cited in Human Rights Watch, *Just Die Quietly: Domestic Violence and Women's Vulnerability to HIV in Uganda* (Human Rights Watch 2003) 51, which found that in two focus groups of Ugandan women, 80 per cent and 86.7 per cent reported that polygyny was a cause of domestic abuse.
103. United Nations Committee on the Elimination of All Forms of Discrimination Against Women, 'General Recommendation 24: Women and Health' (1999) UN Doc A/54/38/Rev 1, ch I [15].

especially important in the context of polygyny. Clearly, polygyny is practiced by non-state actors, but this does not remove the obligation on the state to take positive steps to outlaw the practice, given its clear deleterious effects.

The Empirical Evidence on the Harms Caused by Polygamy

As discussed above, one of the most common harms associated with polygamy, and polygyny in particular, is the link between the practice of multiple marriage and gender inequality. Polygyny is often found within patriarchal social structures, and it is therefore apparent that states that permit the practice effectively endorse power imbalances between the sexes.[104] A useful definition of patriarchy is provided by Rifkin, who describes it as 'any kind of group organization in which males hold dominant power and determine what part females shall and shall not play, and in which capabilities assigned to women are relegated generally to the mystical and aesthetic and excluded from the practical and political realms, these realms being regarded as separate and mutually exclusive'.[105]

The charge that polygyny is patriarchal has been met in two ways: first, that polygyny actually serves a protective function, and secondly, that power imbalances are also found in societies that only permit monogamous marriage. Advocates of the belief that polygamy has a protective function point to both its historic roots and its contemporary practice. The Islamic roots of polygyny are often linked to the Battle of Uhud in 625, in which approximately 10 per cent of the male Muslim population was killed. Therefore, a man was permitted to marry up to four wives, thereby ensuring that care could be provided for vulnerable women and orphans.[106] A similar practice was also permitted by some European Protestant churches at the end of the Thirty Years' War in 1648.[107] With respect to its current protective purpose, Rehman argues that until such time as constitutional and state laws close the socio-economic gap that exists between men and women in contemporary Islamic society, polygyny could 'serve to protect those women who would otherwise be condemned, discarded or abandoned in that society through the operation of divorce or nullity laws'.[108] With respect to the possibility that monogamous marriages can also reinforce

104. Cook and Kelly, *Polygyny*, 7–10; Mark Shurtleff and Terry Goddard, *The Primer: Helping Victims of Domestic Violence and Child Abuse in Polygamous Communities* (Utah Attorney General's Office and Arizona Attorney General's Office 2006) 31.
105. Janet Rifkin, 'Toward a Theory of Law and Patriarchy' (1980) 3 Harv Women's LJ 83.
106. Javid Rehman, 'The Sharia, Islamic Family Law and International Human Rights Law: Examining the Theory and Practice of Polygamy and Talaq' (2007) 21 Int J of L, Policy and the Family 108; and Urfan Khaliq, 'Beyond the Veil? An Analysis of the Provisions of the Women's Convention in the Law as Stipulated in Shari'ah' (1995) Buffalo J of Int L 1.
107. Irwin Altman and Joseph Ginat, *Polygamous Families in Contemporary Society* (Cambridge University Press 1996) 42.
108. Rehman, 'The Sharia', 115.

patriarchal norms and gender imbalances, Kaganas and Murray argue that it is not self-evident that monogamous relationships can bring about spousal equality. They point out that it is the relative lack of capacity and agency enjoyed by women that is problematic, rather than the practice of multiple marriage itself.[109]

While it may be conceded that it is theoretically possible to have a form of multiple marriage that embraces an equality of power between all parties, it appears to be more mythical than practical when the experience of women in polygyny is taken into account. It should be noted that, given the patriarchal and isolated conditions in which many women who experience polygyny live, the harms they face cannot be explained by their experience of polygyny alone. However, the prevalence of polygynous relationships is one of the most important ecological factors that contribute to these harms.

It is frequently argued that polygynous marriages are demeaning of women and that they most often occur in patriarchal societies where women have lower societal standing. Bennion argues that 'in these patriarchal religious polygamous groups is a dominant male structure that inhibits the full expression of female power, and women are forced to structure their understanding of the world through the model of the dominant group'.[110] Okin highlights evidence that demonstrates that polygyny tends to occur when it serves men's self-interest, while at the same time providing a mechanism whereby women can be controlled.[111] Women are reduced to reproductive stereotypes, thereby ensuring that their life chances are restricted to a particular role that has been deemed fit for them by men. While this may also occur within monogamous relationships, the experience of women in monogamous and polygynous relationships indicates that there is a higher chance of women being able to assert their agency in monogamous relationships. This is most apparent within the context of religiously and culturally informed rules whereby women are obliged to obey their husbands. In such situations, women are often unable to express their own autonomous social and political interests.[112] This is also evident in

---

109. Felicity Kaganas and Christina Murray, 'Law, Women and the Family: The Question of Polygyny in a New South Africa' (1991) 1 Acta Juridica 116.
110. Janet Bennion, *Women of Principle: Female Networking in Contemporary Mormon Polygyny* (Oxford University Press 1998) 7.
111. Susan Moller Okin, *Is Multiculturalism Bad for Women?* (Princeton University Press 1999); Suleman Dangor, 'Historical Perspective, Current Literature and an Opinion Survey among Muslim Women in Contemporary South Africa: A Case Study' (2001) 21 J of Muslim Minority Affairs 109; and Sangeetha Madhavan, 'Best of Friends and Worst of Enemies: Competition and Collaboration in Polygyny' (2002) 41 Ethnology 69.
112. Courtney Howland, 'Safeguarding Women's Political Freedoms under the International Covenant on Civil and Political Rights in the Face of Religious Fundamentalism' in Courtney Howland (ed), *Religious Fundamentalism and the Human Rights of Women* (St Martin's Press 1999).

the prevalence of domestic abuse within polygamous relationships.[113] While domestic abuse and other forms of gender-based violence are prevalent within non-polygamous relationships, the traits characteristic of abusive relationships – such as the use of power, control, domination and fear to control partners – are not only common in polygamous relationships but are exacerbated by the isolated conditions in which many polygamous families live.[114]

Polygyny can have serious, harmful effects on women. Anthropological evidence indicates that polygyny often results in problematic relationships between co-wives. While it has been suggested that such relationships can be cooperative,[115] most of the literature indicates that the polygyny fosters stressful relationships. Often, this manifests itself in higher rates of low self-esteem, depression and anxiety.[116] Concerns have also been raised about the role of polygamy in the spread of sexually transmitted diseases.[117] Many polygamous families cannot afford multiple residences, and so the tensions that may already exist between sub-groups within families are exacerbated.[118]

Children born into polygamous families also tend to experience negative consequences, such as lower levels of socio-economic status, academic achievement, and self-esteem, as well as higher levels of reported family dysfunction.[119] Children also face significant problems caused by the lack of parental bonding and assistance, which impact negatively on the child's development.[120] These developmental problems usually result in educational disadvantage.[121] Children born into polygamous communities may also be married at an early age, sometimes as young as 14, to older men selected by community

113. Shurtleff and Goddard, *The Primer*, 32–38; and Cassiah M Ward, 'I Now Pronounce You Husband and Wives: *Lawrence v. Texas* and the Practice of Polygamy in Modern America' (2004) 11 William and Mary Journal of Women and the Law 131.
114. Shurtleff and Goddard, *The Primer*; and Committee on Polygamous Issues, *Life in Bountiful: A Report on the Lifestyle of a Polygamous Community* (British Columbia Ministry of Women's Equality 1993).
115. Altman and Ginat, *Polygamous Families*, 341; and Madhavan, 'Best of Friends'.
116. Alean Al-Krenawi, 'Women from Polygamous and Monogamous Marriages in an Out-Patient Psychiatric Clinic' (2001) 38 Transcultural Psych 187.
117. Esther Mayambala, 'Changing the Terms of the Debate: Polygamy and the Rights of Women in Kenya and Uganda' (1998) 3 East African J of Peace & Human Rights 200.
118. Sonja Starr and Lea Brilmayer, 'Family Separation as a Violation of International Law' (2003) 21 Berkeley J of Int L 213; and Adrien Katherine Wing, 'Polygamy from Southern Africa to Black Britannia to Black America: Global Critical Race Feminism as Legal Reform for the Twenty-First Century' (2001) 11 J of Cont L Issues 811.
119. Alean Al-Krenawi et al, 'Mental Health Aspects of Arab-Israeli Adolescents from Polygamous versus Monogamous Families' (2002) 142 J of Soc Psych 446.
120. Committee on Polygamous Issues, *Life is Bountiful*.
121. VI Cherian, 'Academic Achievement of Children from Monogamous and Polygynous Families' (1989) 130 J of Soc Psych 117; and VI Cherian, 'Corporal Punishment and Academic Achievement of Xhosa Children form Polygynous and Monogamous Families' (1994) 134 J of Soc Psych 387.

leaders.[122] The negative effects of child abuse, when it occurs within polygamous groups, can also be exacerbated by the fact that many children in such families are brought up to fear government intervention of any kind.[123] Rigid barriers are drawn by polygamous community leaders between 'insiders' and 'outsiders', with children taught not to trust outsiders and to lie to them in order to protect their families.[124] Given that many of these families, at least in Western states, exist in isolation from the rest of society, intervention is more difficult due to a lack of information about the conditions in which children live.

Given this data, it is evident that courts are right to treat polygamous relationships as a class apart from potentially polygamous ones. It may be countered that a legal system that allows polygamy creates conditions of possibility in which this more problematic relationship may be formed, and that the permissibility of such a relationship indicates that patriarchy is deeply engrained within that culture. However, this charge can be met in the following ways. First, it lapses back on the culturally essentialist arguments used to criticise the decision in *HAH*. Secondly, it ignores the particularity of individual relationships, preferring to consider form over substance. Just because a particular legal system permits polygamous marriage does not necessarily mean that any potentially polygamous marriage may become actually polygamous. The nature of that individual relationship must be assessed, rather than its potential for change under the law of the state in which it was contracted.

This leaves one further question. Having argued that actually polygamous relationships ought to be considered differently from merely potentially polygamous ones, is it ever permissible to invoke a public policy exception when considering a polygamous marriage's recognition under private international law? Leaving aside the manner in which the exception was invoked in *HAH*, could it be argued that, in light of the empirical evidence just outlined, courts should refuse recognition based on the public policy ground of not wishing to implicitly condone practices that may be considered to be in breach of international human rights law? As a general proposition, it can be legitimately argued that actually polygamous marriages ought to be treated with a greater amount of circumspection but without relying on the cultural gloss introduced in *HAH*. Given the clear evidence that the suffering of women and children is compounded within such relationships, there is perhaps good reason to invoke the public policy exception to recognition, whereas to invoke it on cultural grounds is both circular and ethnocentric. Yet there remains the possibility that an individual polygamous relationship may seek recognition in circumstances where none of these harms are evident. It may be that several people have chosen,

---

122. Alean Al-Krenawi and John Graham, 'The Story of Bedouin-Arab Women in a Polygamous Marriage' (1999) 22 Women's Stud Int Forum 497; and Debbie Palmer and Dave Perrin, *Keep Sweet: Children of Polygamy* (Dave's Press 1994).
123. Shurtleff and Goddard, *The Primer*, 42.
124. ibid 43–44, 47–48.

in accordance with the law of their domicile, to regulate their intimacy through multiple marriage.[125] Recalling the view expressed in *Aslam* that conflicts of rules ought to be interpreted in an open-minded and tolerant way, it may be possible for such a relationship to be recognised and accommodated within the legal space. Before that is done, however, greater clarity is needed on the role of public-policy exemptions in private international law, but also on the ways in which the rights and interests of the parties involved may be met.

Conclusion

This article has sought to critique the approach taken by the Irish courts to polygamous and potentially polygamous marriages. While polygamy, and polygyny in particular, is a practice that brings with it serious levels of physical, economic, and psychological harm for spouses and children, potentially polygamous marriages do not necessarily carry these same consequences. While withholding recognition from actually polygamous marriages on public policy grounds due to the human rights concerns that they raise may be justifiable, potentially polygamous marriages should be treated differently. The private international law rules are designed to mediate between legal systems, and so a potentially polygamous but factually monogamous marriage should be capable of transitioning reasonably seamlessly from one legal system to another. Yet the Irish courts have struggled at times to grasp the nature of the private international law rules, while at the same time signalling the potential development of a rigid, binary approach to cultural questions surrounding marriage practices. While early decisions found themselves distracted by the red herring of common law marriage, the *HAH* decision extends the problematic consequences for a traditional understanding of marriage to inter-cultural dialogue. Not only is greater clarity on the operation of these complex legal rules needed, but the courts also need to realise that if a cultural gloss is to be added to the discussion in the name of determining public policy, adopting a traditionalist and binary approach to unfamiliar forms of marriage may be damaging in itself.

125. On intimacy generally, see Antony Giddens, *The Transformation of Intimacy: Sexuality, Love and Eroticism in Modern Societies* (Stanford University Press 1993).

The EU Charter of Fundamental Rights and the Member States: An Originalist Analysis

Stephen Brittain*

Abstract—This article advocates the adoption of an originalist approach in the interpretation of Article 51 of the Charter of Fundamental Rights (CFR). The latter provides that the CFR shall apply to Member States 'only when they are implementing Union law'. The first part of the article describes and critiques the teleological approach to interpretation of the European Court of Justice (ECJ). The second part considers the arguments in favour of and against the adoption of an originalist approach to interpretation, concluding that an originalist approach ought to be adopted in the interpretation of the CFR. Parts 3 to 5 of the article carry out an originalist analysis of Article 51 CFR, concluding that that article requires Member States to abide by the provisions of the CFR only when they are acting as agents of the EU. Part 6 considers how Article 51 CFR has been interpreted since its adoption, and concludes that the ECJ's reading has been considerably broader than its wording allows. Part 7 accordingly argues that the Court's interpretation of Article 51 CFR undermines certain crucial values, including the rule of law and democracy.

Introduction

The EU Charter of Fundamental Rights (CFR) entered into force on 1 December 2009. It is equal in status to the Treaty on European Union and the Treaty on the Functioning of the European Union and, thus, forms part of the fundamental law of the EU.[1] The CFR protects many different rights, which are divided into seven chapters, including rights as diverse as the right to dignity (art 1), the right to freedom of expression (art 11), and the right to collective bargaining (art 28).

In this article, I shall confine my attention to art 51, ch VII, thereof, which sets out its 'field of application'. Article 51 of the CFR states that '[t]he provisions of this Charter are addressed to… the Member States only when they are implementing Union law'. There is a fundamental difference of opinion as to the meaning of the phrase 'implementing Union law'. One side in the debate suggests that 'implementing Union law' has a narrow meaning and only covers situations where the Member States are acting as agents of the EU, eg when

---

* Stephen Brittain, PhD Candidate, Trinity College Dublin. This article is based on doctoral research, the funding for which was provided by the Irish Research Council. I would like to thank Kate de Contreras, Professor Catherine Donnelly, Professor David Prendergast, and the anonymous DULJ reviewers for helpful comments on earlier drafts of this article. Responsibility for any errors or omissions lies with the author.

1. art 6.1, Treaty on European Union [2010] OJ C83/13 (TEU).

applying provisions of EU secondary legislation. The other side in the debate suggests that 'implementing Union law' is synonymous with the phrase 'within the scope of Union law'. Situations that have been adjudged to fall within the scope of the EU extend far beyond agency cases and include, in addition, cases in which the Member States derogate from EU law, ie cases in which they seek to justify restrictions they have imposed on rights deriving from the EU Treaties.[2]

The debate over whether or not Member State derogations from EU law are covered by art 51 of the CFR is a matter of great significance. It is possible to argue that any divergence between national regulations has an impact on the conditions under which citizens exercise their free movement rights under the Treaties. Thus, if derogations from EU law are held to be included under the 'implementing Union law' formula used in art 51 CFR, it may mean that Member States will have to comply with EU fundamental rights in every sphere of their activities. Peter Huber has observed that, if art 51 is held to include derogations, it will mean that there will be 'virtually no area of life left' that does not come within the scope of the CFR.[3] For instance, in the *Zambrano*[4] and *Dereci*[5] cases, discussed in detail below, Member States were prevented from applying the provisions of domestic immigration law to a significant number of third-country nationals. These decisions emasculated the autonomy traditionally enjoyed by Member States in the field of immigration law.[6] By contrast, if it is held that only agency-type situations are covered by art 51, it will be necessary to show that the Member State measure sought to be reviewed under the CFR was specifically aimed at giving effect to a provision of EU law or was necessary to give effect thereto, a much narrower field of application. The stakes in the debate over the meaning of art 51, therefore, are exceedingly high.

In Part 1 of this article, I shall briefly describe the ECJ's teleological approach to interpretation. I shall show that the Court frequently goes beyond or even contradicts the text of the law being interpreted. I shall also attempt to demonstrate that the arguments that have frequently been put forward to justify the Court's approach do not stand up to scrutiny. I argue that the teleological approach of the Court violates a number of fundamental values to which the EU legal order is committed, most notably democracy and the rule of law.

In Part 2 I shall argue that an originalist approach to interpretation would be a preferable alternative to the ECJ's teleological method in the interpretation

2. These are the Treaty on the Functioning of the European Union [2010] OJ C83/47 (TFEU) and TEU.
3. Peter M Huber, 'The Unitary Effect of the Community's Fundamental Rights: The ERT–Doctrine Needs to be Reviewed' (2008) 14 Eur Pub L 323, 327.
4. C-34/09 *Gerardo Ruiz Zambrano v Office national de l'emploi* (*ONEM*) (ECJ, 8 March 2011).
5. C-256/11 *Murat Dereci, Vishaka Heiml, Alban Kokollari, Izunna Emmanuel Maduike, Dragica Stevic v Bundesministerium für Inneres* (ECJ, 15 November 2011).
6. For discussion see Anja Lasbergen and Nina Miller, 'European citizenship rights in internal situations: an ambiguous revolution? Decision of 8 March 2011, Case C-34/09 Gerardo Ruiz Zambrano v Office national de l'emploi (ONEM)' (2011) 7 ECL Rev 287, 301.

of the CFR. I shall begin by describing the nature of the originalist enterprise as I understand it. I shall then briefly sketch some normative arguments in favour of originalism. I shall argue that originalism safeguards a number of essential interpretative values, such as predictability and democratic legitimacy. In this part I shall also seek to respond to some of the criticisms that have been advanced against originalist interpretation.

Having established that an originalist approach ought to be adopted in the interpretation of the CFR, I shall proceed to carry out an originalist analysis of art 51 CFR. In parts 3 to 5 of this article I shall carry out an originalist analysis of art 51 CFR. Originalists seek to discern the meaning of legal texts by reference to four principal *indicia*: text, pre-drafting law and usage, drafting and ratification history, and post-ratification interpretations of the text. Part 3 of this article shall be devoted to a consideration of the text of the CFR; Part 4 shall examine the law in effect prior to its adoption and pre-ratification usages of the phrase 'implementing Union law'; Part 5 shall examine the drafting and ratification history of the CFR; and Part 6 shall examine post-ratification interpretations of art 51. In this section I shall discuss how the ECJ has interpreted art 51 CFR and I will show how their interpretation has veered far from its original meaning. In Part 7 I shall show that the Court has thereby undermined several crucial interpretative values, which originalism seeks to safeguard.

1. The Teleological Approach of the ECJ: A Critique

1.1. The Nature of the Court's Approach

Trevor Hartley divides decisions of the ECJ into three categories: decisions that are within the text of the law, decisions that are beyond the text of the law, and decisions that are against the text of the law.[7] The debate on the ECJ's methods of interpretation largely concerns the legitimacy of decisions that fall within the second and third of Hartley's categories; decisions within the first category are generally considered unexceptionable. In Part 1.1.1 of this article I shall provide examples of decisions that go beyond the text of the law. In Part 1.1.2 I shall provide examples of decisions that contradict the text. Due to constraints of space, I shall discuss a single example of each type of case. In Part 1.2 I shall seek to demonstrate that none of the arguments that have been put forward in defence of the Court's approach to interpretation stand up to close scrutiny, and in Part 1.3 I shall show that teleological interpretation undermines certain values that all legal systems should seek to safeguard.

1.1.1. Decisions Beyond the Text

As is well-known, prior to the ratification of the Lisbon Treaty, the ECJ developed a body of case law on human rights, without there being any EU bill of rights to

7. Trevor Hartley, 'The European Court, Judicial Objectivity and the Constitution of the European Union' (1996) 112 LQR 95, 96.

base it on. In the case of *Costa v ENEL*[8] the Court held that EU law had supremacy over national law in the event of a conflict between the two. The ECJ's postulation of EU law supremacy over national law caused certain national constitutional courts to express concern at the absence of human rights protection under EU law.[9] These courts suggested that provisions of EU law would be held invalid if they were found to infringe rights guaranteed by national constitutions.[10]

In *Internationale Handelsgesellschaft mbH v Einfuhr- und Vorratsstelle für Getreide und Futtermittel*,[11] the Court reiterated its position that the validity of EU law could not assessed in light of any species of national law, including national constitutions. The Court reasoned that this would have 'an adverse effect on the uniformity and efficacy of Community law'.[12] However, in a concession to national constitutional courts, the ECJ stated that human rights formed part of the general principles of law, the observance of which the Court ensured.[13] The decision of the ECJ lacked any firm textual basis because the Treaty of Rome did not expressly empower the Court to protect human rights.

1.1.2. Decisions Against the Text

Article 173 of the Treaty of Rome originally provided that actions for annulment could be brought by 'a Member State, the Council or the Commission' and by '[a]ny natural or legal person against a decision addressed to that person or... against a decision which... is of direct and individual concern to the former'. The coverage in art 173, judging by its extensive listing of those entitled to take actions for annulment, was plainly intended to be exhaustive. Thus, in the *Comitology* case,[14] the ECJ held that the European Parliament (EP) did not have the capacity to bring an action for annulment. However, in the *Chernobyl* case[15] the Court reversed *Comitology* and held that the EP was entitled to bring an action for annulment.[16] The Court reasoned that if the EP were not permitted to take such an action a 'procedural gap' would exist, which would upset the 'institutional balance laid down by the Treaties'.[17] It is plain that, in *Chernobyl*, the broad objective of 'institutional balance' was invoked in order to arrive at a result that was contrary to the text of art 173.[18]

8. Case 6/64; [1964] ECR 585.
9. See, Case 1/58 *Stork v High Authority* [1959] ECR 17.
10. See, *Solange I*, BVerfGE 37, 271 2 BvL 52/71(German Constitutional Court); *Spa Fragd v Amministrazione delle Finanze*, Dec 232 of 21 April 1989 (1989) 72 RDI (Italian Constitutional Court).
11. Case 11/70; [1970] ECR 1125.
12. ibid para 3.
13. ibid para 4.
14. Case 302/87; [1988] ECR 5615.
15. Case 70/88; [1991] ECR I–4529.
16. ibid para 27. See Mitchel De S-O-l'E Lasser, *Judicial Deliberations: A Comparative Analysis of Judicial Transparency and Legitimacy* (Oxford University Press 2004) 225–27.
17. ibid para 26.
18. See Lasser, *Judicial Deliberations*, 225–27. For further examples of decisions against the text, see Case 149/79 *Commission v Belgium* [1980] ECR 3881; C–176/03 *Commis-*

1.2. Justifications for the Court's Approach: An Evaluation

Numerous arguments have been put forward to justify the teleological approach of the ECJ. Due to constraints of space, it will only be possible to discuss the most important of these.

1.2.1. European Integration

It has been argued that the framers of the Treaties were committed to European integration and that their vision in this regard should inform the interpretative approach of the Court. The preamble of the TEU, which proclaims that the Member States of the EU are 'RESOLVED to continue the process of creating an ever closer union among the peoples of Europe' is frequently cited in this regard.[19]

Use of the preamble to the TEU in the service of integrationist interpretations of EU law has been criticised on a number of grounds. First, it has been said that the language of the preamble is too vague to serve as a guide to judicial decision-making.[20] It is not clear that the phrase 'ever closer union' necessarily refers to the political integration of the Member States. Near-identical language has been used to describe traditional diplomatic cooperation between states. For example, when a proposal for an Anglo-German alliance was mooted in 1898, Arthur Balfour, a member of the British Cabinet, described the German Foreign Secretary, Prince Bernhard von Bülow, as 'being in favour of a closer union between the countries'.[21] This use of the phrase plainly did not carry any integrationist signification.

Secondly, Stuart Scheingold notes that the fundamental principles of the Treaty 'provide something for everyone', which reflects the deep divisions among the founding fathers on the nature of the project they were setting in motion.[22] The EEC Treaty was considerably less integrationist than the previously proposed EPC Treaty, which failed after Member State objections to its federalising tendencies.[23] When this fact is considered, it becomes impossible to attribute to the framers of the Treaties an unqualified commitment to European integration.

---

sion v Parliament and Council [2005] ECR I–7879.

19. See, for example, Henry G Schermers and Denis F Waelbroeck, *Judicial Protection in the European Union* (6th edn, Kluwer Law International 2001) 21; Oreste Pollicino, 'Legal Reasoning of the Court of Justice in the Context of Principle of Equality between Judicial Activism and Self-Restraint' (2004) 5 German LJ 283, 289.
20. Stuart A Scheingold, *The Rule of Law in European Integration: The Path of the Schuman Plan* (Yale University Press 1965) 17.
21. See Niall Ferguson, *The House of Rothschild* (vol 2, Penguin Books 2000) 389.
22. Roger-Michel Chevallier, 'Methods and Reasoning of the European Court in its Interpretation of Community Law' (1964) 2 Common Market L Rev 21, 30.
23. Gráinne de Búrca, 'The Evolution of EU Human Rights Law', ch 16 in Paul Craig and Gráinne de Búrca (eds), *The Evolution of EU Law* (Oxford University Press 2011).

1.2.2. Vagueness

Renaud Dehousse has stated that 'the open-textured character of many provisions, together with the purpose-oriented nature of the Treaty, lent itself quite well to the kind of teleological interpretation proposed by the ECJ'.[24]

However, the argument that the Treaties' vagueness justifies the teleological approach of the ECJ cannot be sustained. For example, the decision of the Court in *Internationale Handelsgesellschaft* finds no support in the text of the Treaties. The Treaty did not mention fundamental rights at all. Moreover, it is plain from the historical background to the Treaty of Rome that this was an intentional omission.[25] Thus, it is impossible to justify *Internationale Handelsgesellschaft* on the basis of the vagueness of the Treaty. Similarly, in *Chernobyl*, the provisions of the Treaty implied with unmistakeable clarity that the Parliament did not have standing to bring an action for annulment in respect of decisions of the Council.

1.2.3. Effectiveness

It is often argued that the effectiveness of EU law would be compromised if any other method were to be adopted.[26] Anna Bredimas has noted that, when the ECJ seeks to justify a particular decision by reference to the need to ensure the effectiveness of EU law, 'it puts together certain Treaty provisions and combines them in order to deduce a result that cannot be imputed with precision to either of these'.[27] For example, in *Amministrazione delle finanze dello Stato v Simmenthal*,[28] the Court re- reiterated the view it had expressed in *Costa v ENEL*[29] that EU law had primacy over any contrary provisions of national law.[30] The Court emphasised that the effectiveness of EU law would be undermined otherwise.[31] No provision of the EEC Treaty expressly provided that EEC law was to prevail over contradictory national law. The Court also ignored the applicable principles of international law, under which it was left to national law to determine the extent to which international legal norms would apply directly in the national legal order.[32]

Thus, it is clear that any argument that enhances the power of EU institutions, amplifies the obligations imposed by EU law, or widens the scope of the

---

24. Renaud Dehousse, *The European Court of Justice* (Macmillan Press 1998) 76.
25. de Búrca, 'Evolution of EU Human Rights Law'.
26. See, for example, Gordon Slynn, 'The Court of Justice of the European Communities' (1984) 33 Int'l & Comp L Q 409, 416–18.
27. Anna Bredimas, *Methods of Interpretation and Community Law* (North Holland Publishing Co 1978) 78.
28. Case 106/77; [1978] ECR 629.
29. Case 6/64; [1964] ECR 585.
30. ibid para 21.
31. ibid para 20.
32. See, for example, Juha Raitio, 'The Interpretation of Community Law' (1996) 7 Finnish YB Int'l L 369, 376.

remedies available for its breach, is capable of being justified on effectiveness grounds. To accede to the effectiveness argument in favour of teleological interpretation is to accept unlimited judicial law-making power.[33] Thus, the argument that the teleological approach of the ECJ may be justified by the need to ensure the effectiveness of EU law must be rejected.

1.2.4. The Multilingual Nature of EU Law

The EU Treaties are authentic in 23 different languages, with each language version carrying equal weight.[34] Timothy Millett has stated that 'the multilingual nature of Community legislation necessarily reduces the importance of the literal method of interpretation'.[35] It is certainly true that divergences among the different language versions are commonplace.[36] However, the claim that the multilingual nature of EU law necessitates the adoption of a teleological method of interpretation cannot be sustained.

First, as Nial Fennelly has observed, '[l]inguistic conflict or ambiguity is not, in any sense, a pre-condition for the application of the teleological or schematic approach'.[37] Thus, many of the decisions of the ECJ that exemplify its teleological approach cannot be justified on the basis of a divergence between the different language versions of the Treaty.[38] For example, as I shall discuss below, the conclusion of the ECJ in *Åkerberg Fransson*[39] that the phrase 'implementing Union law' can encompass derogations from EU law cannot be justified by reference to any of the authentic language versions of the CFR.

Secondly, even in cases that do involve a genuine divergence among the different language versions of the Treaty, it is not clear that teleological interpretation is necessary to bridge such divergences. Mattias Derlén identifies three approaches to resolving divergences between the different language versions of a text: classical reconciliation, reconciliation and examination of purpose, and a teleological approach.[40] Thus, the conclusion that a teleological method of interpretation must be adopted due to the multilingual character of the law being interpreted is not axiomatic.

33. Trevor Hartley, *Constitutional Problems of the European Union* (Hart Publishing 1999) 60.
34. See art 55 TEU.
35. Timothy Millett, 'Rules of Interpretation of EEC Legislation' (1989) 10 Statute L Rev 163, 164–65.
36. For an example, see Hartley, *Constitutional Problems*, 72.
37. Nial Fennelly, 'Legal Interpretation at the European Court of Justice' (1996–97) 20 Fordham Int'l LJ 656, 665.
38. For the view that the Court exceeds the meaning of the text in all language versions on occasion, see Jens Rinze, 'Methods of Interpretation in EC Law' (1994) 26 BLJ 57, 60.
39. C–617/10 *Åklagaren v Hans Åkerberg Fransson* (ECJ, 26 February 2013).
40. Mattias Derlén, *Multilingual Interpretation of European Union Law* (Walters Kluwer 2009) 43–45.

1.3. Criticisms of the Court's Approach

1.3.1. Teleological Interpretation and Multiple Purposes

Laws generally reflect a compromise among competing purposes, which means that an exclusive focus on one of these is inappropriate.[41] For example, in the case of *Statens Kontrol Med Aedle Metaller v Larsen*[42] the ECJ held that a ban on import taxes contained in the Treaty suggested that the latter sought 'to guarantee generally the neutrality of systems of internal taxation with regard to intra-Community trade' and, therefore, that discriminatory taxes on exports were also prohibited.[43] There may have been a variety of reasons why the framers of the Treaty of Rome prohibited taxes on imports but not on exports. Perhaps they wished to reduce the volume of exports of goods that were 'particularly valuable or especially sought after'.[44] Either way, it cannot be concluded that, because a single legal provision pursues a particular objective up to a certain point, it is solely concerned with that objective.

1.3.2. Teleological Interpretation and the Level of Generality Problem

The ECJ frequently states the purpose of the law at an extremely high level of generality.[45] This widens the range of the Court's interpretative options, and enables it to arrive at the conclusion it deems to be most desirable on policy grounds.[46] In *Commission v Council* (*'ERTA'*),[47] the Court held that the Member States, by conferring on the EU authority to create common rules in the field of transport, had alienated their right to enter into agreements with third parties in the same field. The Court held that the retention by Member States of a power to enter into such agreements would compromise 'the unity of the Common Market and uniform application of Community law'.[48] No provision of the Treaty conferred a competence on the EU to enter into international agreements in the field of transportation.[49] In spite of this fact, the Court held that the Member States could no longer unilaterally enter into international agreements in the field of transportation,[50] and that the EU had exclusive competence in the

41. Trevor Hartley, *The Foundations of EC Law* (6th edn, Oxford University Press 2007) 74.
42. Case 142/77; [1978] ECR 1543.
43. ibid para 23.
44. ibid para 26.
45. Lasser, *Judicial Deliberations*, 207–36.
46. For a thorough description of the highly general nature of the Court's teleological approach, see ibid.
47. Case 22/70; [1971] ECR 263.
48. ibid para 30.
49. ibid para 48. However, the Court noted that art 3 of Regulation No 543/69 on the harmonisation of certain social legislation relating to road transport [1969] OJ L 77 had conferred a limited competence to enter into international agreements necessary to give effect to that regulation.
50. ibid para 30.

field. Thus, in *ERTA* the Court relied on the 'meta-purpose' of uniformity in order to claim a competence the Treaties did not confer on the EU.

1.3.3. Teleological Interpretation and the Rule of Law

To permit unambiguous text to be overridden by reference to purpose is contrary to the rule of law because it upsets the expectations of citizens.[51] For example, the case of *Defrenne v SABENA*[52] concerned the interpretation of art 119 of the Treaty of Rome, which guaranteed equal pay for equal work between men and women. The text of the provision was addressed exclusively to Member States. However, the Court stated that the effectiveness of art 119 would be compromised if it were not also applicable to private parties.[53] This outcome was excluded by necessary implication by the text of art 119. Thus, the *Defrenne* decision is an example of a case in which the Court's teleological approach to interpretation disrupted private arrangements by ascribing a meaning to the text of art 119 that could not reasonably have been predicted beforehand.

1.3.4. Teleological Interpretation and Democratic Self-Government

Article 10.1 TEU provides that '[t]he functioning of the Union shall be founded on representative democracy'. Thus, it is plain that the EU conceives of itself as a democracy.[54] However, the nature of democracy in the EU is heavily contested.[55] Any attempt to contribute to this debate would be beyond the scope of this article. Whatever conception of democracy one adopts, however, 'democracy seems to require that the interpretative perspective of the judiciary and that of the legislative… authority must converge substantially'.[56] Due to the indeterminacy of the Court's teleological approach, it is impossible for the EU legislature to predict how its enactments will be interpreted by the Court.

For example, in *Internationale Handelsgesellschaft mbH v Einfuhr- und Vorratsstelle für Getreide und Futtermittel*,[57] discussed above, the ECJ stated that human rights, though not explicitly mentioned in the Treaty, formed part of the general principles of law, the observance of which the Court ensured. The interpretation of the Court contradicted the intentions of the Member States at the time the Treaty of Rome was adopted.

---

51. Frederick Schauer, 'Formalism' (1988) 97 Yale LJ 509, 534.
52. Case 43/75 *Defrenne v SABENA* [1978] ECR 1365.
53. ibid paras 30–40.
54. See also references to democracy in the Preamble and arts 2, 10.2, 10.3, 10.4, 21.1, 21.2 TEU, and arts 165.2 and 222.1, TFEU.
55. See, for example, Martin Nettesheim, 'Developing a Theory of Democracy for the European Union' (2005) 23 Berkeley J Int'l L 358.
56. Gerard Conway, *The Limits of Legal Reasoning and the European Court of Justice* (Cambridge University Press 2012) 94.
57. *Internationale Handelsgesellschaft* (n 11).

That Treaty was drafted and ratified in the aftermath of the failure of the European Political Community (EPC) and European Defence Community (EDC). The former had included provisions to empower the Supreme Court of the EPC to review the activities of the EPC institutions for compliance with human rights standards.[58] These twin projects failed after objections were made by certain Member States, most prominently the French, that the arrangements contained therein were too supranational. No provisions relating to human rights were included in the Treaty of Rome. For this reason, we may conclude without any doubt that, in the movement from the EPC to the EEC Treaty, there was a clear intention to exclude human rights protection under the latter.[59] *Internationale Handelsgesellschaft* shows that the teleological approach of the Court can lead to results that find support in neither the text of the law nor the intention of its makers. In this respect, the approach of the Court is undemocratic.

2. The Case for an Originalist Approach

2.1. The Nature of Originalism

David Langwaller identifies several distinct varieties of originalism. First, he defines 'old originalism' as a 'search for the intention of the founding fathers'.[60] Secondly, he notes that 'new originalism' 'has as its central idea that the meaning of the constitution is the original public meaning of the document. . .'.[61] Thirdly, he distinguishes between 'original meaning' and 'original expected application'. He says:

> *Original Expected Application* binds us to the intention of our forefathers (assuming we can assess same). *Original Meaning* gives us a text which we show attention and fidelity to and which provides a blueprint for future generations.[62]

In this article I shall adopt a 'new originalist' approach to the interpretation of art 51 CFR. 'Old originalism' seeks to identify the intentions of the law's drafters. Since it was not the drafters of the CFR that had the authority to ratify it, an old originalist approach should not be adopted in the interpretation of the CFR. That authority belonged to the ratifiers of the CFR, ie the parliaments of the various EU Member States and the Irish electorate. Thus, 'new originalism', which accords priority to the words of the document rather than the intention of its framers, ought to be adopted in the interpretation of the CFR. An original public meaning approach is also to be preferred to one based on original expected application. This is because legal texts inevitably say both more and less than

58. art 45, Draft Treaty on European Political Community.
59. de Búrca, 'Evolution of EU Human Rights Law'.
60. David Langwaller, 'The Incoherence of Historicism and Originalism in Irish Constitutional Interpretation' (2008) 4 Ind L Rev 17, 20.
61. ibid 20.
62. ibid 21.

their drafters intended.[63] Because the text ultimately adopted is law, and the intention of the law-maker is not, the former ought to be followed in the event of divergence.

Thus, in what remains of this article, I shall adopt a 'new originalist' approach to interpretation. Such an approach is exemplified in the jurisprudence of Justice Scalia and Justice Thomas of the US Supreme Court. In *District of Columbia v Heller*,[64] Justice Scalia stated his understanding of the originalist enterprise:

> In interpreting this text, we are guided by the principle that the Constitution was written to be understood by the voters; its words and phrases were used in their normal and ordinary… meaning.[65]

This focus on the conventional meaning of the text means that originalist interpreters are not confined to the period during which the Constitution was framed and adopted in their selection of interpretative materials. In fact, new originalists refer to four different kinds of material in attempting to discern the original meaning of the Constitution: text, pre-ratification law and usage, drafting and ratification history, and post-ratification interpretations. I shall discuss each of these indicia of meaning in my analysis of art 51 CFR below. First, however, it must be determined whether or not originalism is a desirable method of interpretation.

2.2. Arguments in Favour of Originalism

The first and most important argument in favour of originalism is that it gives effect to the expectations citizens had when they ratified the text being interpreted, which ensures that interpretation of the fundamental law will be democratically legitimate.[66] This is important because the CFR was itself approved by a democratic process, ie by the unanimous approval of the Member States of the EU.[67] It would be extraordinary, given that such a cumbersome procedure was adopted in the ratification of the CFR, if its meaning could be changed by the ECJ by means of expansive interpretation.[68] In the remainder of this article I shall seek to demonstrate that the Court's interpretation of its jurisdiction under art 51 CFR has been broader than its wording allows and also broader than the people of Europe sought to confer. For this reason, the Court's interpretation of art 51 CFR is deeply undemocratic.

---

63. Joseph Raz, *Between Authority and Interpretation* (Oxford University Press 2009) 230.
64. 554 US 570 (2008). See also Justice Thomas *McDonald v Chicago* 561 US 3025 (2010).
65. ibid (internal quotation marks omitted).
66. ibid 403–10. Frank H Easterbrook, 'Alternatives to Originalism?' (1996) 19 Harv J L Pub Pol'y 479, 479.
67. TEU, art 48.4.
68. For a similar argument see Steven G Calabresi and Livia Fine, 'Two Cheers for Professor Balkin's Originalism' (2009) 103 Nw U L Rev 663, 683.

Secondly, by according supremacy to the text of the law being interpreted, originalism helps to attain legal certainty.[69] Citizens should be able to find out easily what their rights are and governments should know the extent of their powers. As I shall demonstrate below, by adopting a purposive approach to the interpretation of art 51 CFR, the ECJ has created uncertainty as to the scope of EU citizens' rights. Such uncertainty spawns litigation and undermines the principle of legality itself.

Thirdly, by insisting upon a strict adherence to text, originalism recognises that the drafters of the text chose the words they used advisedly.[70] The Convention at which the CFR was drafted deliberated at great length over its wording. The discussion in Part 5 of the drafting of art 51 should demonstrate this clearly. For this reason an interpreter should not lightly assume that they did not intend what they said. This is precisely the error the ECJ has thus far made in its interpretation of art 51 of the CFR.

Fourthly, by according priority to text, originalism causes the meaning of the Constitution to be clarified.[71] Randy Barnett has explained that: 'When a writing can be contradicted by testimony of a differing understanding, the purposes for which the agreement was put in writing in the first place is undercut.'[72] Below, I shall discuss the Explanations of the CFR, which are in tension with the text of art 51 thereof. I shall argue that clear text must prevail over all such extrinsic indications of meaning.

Fifthly, because most texts have a core of meaning about which there can be no disagreement,[73] adherence to the text constrains judicial discretion.[74] Although there is certainly some room for disagreement as to the meaning of particular words or phrases, there are certain meanings that a text simply cannot bear. My discussion below of the linguistic meaning of art 51, and the determination of purposivist judges and commentators to ignore it, should underline this point.

2.3. Arguments Against Originalism

2.3.1. Textual Ambiguity

Originalism has been criticised on four main grounds. First, Samantha Miller has stated that textualism requires appraisals every bit as subjective as

---

69. Randy E Barnett, *Restoring the Lost Constitution* (Princeton University Press 2004) 101–2.
70. Barnett, *Restoring the Lost Constitution*, 101–2.
71. Calabresi and Fine, 'Two Cheers', 671.
72. Barnett, *Restoring the Lost Constitution*, 101–2.
73. ibid.
74. Antonin Scalia and Bryan A Garner, *Reading Law: The Interpretation of Legal Texts* (Thomson/West 2012) 69–77.

non-textualism.[75] It is surely an overstatement, however, to suggest that all textual readings are contestable and problematic; words do 'have a limited range of meaning, and no interpretation that goes beyond that range is permissible'.[76]

For instance, Bryan Wildenthal has argued that Scalia's dissenting opinion in *Maryland v Craig*[77] demonstrates the capacity of textualism to constrain judges.[78] The case concerned the meaning of the Confrontation Clause of the Sixth Amendment to the United States Constitution. The latter states, 'In all criminal prosecutions, the accused shall enjoy the right... to be confronted with the witnesses against him.' In a five-to-four majority decision the Court construed the clause to guarantee merely 'the reliability of the testimony' presented at trial. In the view of the majority it did not necessarily extend a right to confront witnesses face-to-face. Justice Scalia wrote a dissent in which three of his colleagues joined, upholding a right to face-to-face confrontation. Thus, in *Maryland v Craig*, Justice Scalia's preference for close adherence to the text of the Constitution led him to a more robust defence of the right to confrontation than some of his colleagues, who thought the spectacle of a child victim of sexual abuse being confronted by her abuser distasteful.

2.3.2. Historical Ambiguity

Michael Perry has argued that '[t]he originalist approach does not entail a minimalist judicial role because... there is often more than one plausible conclusion to the inquiry into the original meaning of a constitutional provision'.[79] This argument suggests that, because of the indeterminacy of historical investigation, those who purport to adhere to the original meaning are covertly giving effect to their own political preferences.

However, it is worth observing that many of the scholars who have criticised the originalist justices for particular decisions they have made have suggested that the historical materials supported a different outcome,[80] thus proving that if Justice Scalia and Justice Thomas are imperfect practitioners of originalism, correct answers are possible under an originalist approach. Moreover, other scholars have endorsed historical analyses undertaken by Justice Thomas and

75. Samantha Miller, 'Interpreting Intent: An Analysis of the Doctrine of Originalism' (2007) 5 Dartmouth LJ 226, 234–35.
76. Antonin Scalia, *A Matter of Interpretation: Federal Courts and the Law* (Princeton University Press 1997) 24.
77. 497 US 836 (1990).
78. Bryan A Wildenthal, 'The Right of Confrontation, Justice Scalia, and the Power and Limits of Textualism' (1991) 48 Wash & Lee L Rev 1323, 1390.
79. Michael J Perry, *The Constitution in the Courts: Law or Politics?* (Oxford University Press 1994) 56–59.
80. William G Merkel, '*District of Columbia v Heller* and Antonin Scalia's Perverse Sense of Originalism' (2009) 13 Lewis & Clark L Rev 349.

Justice Scalia.[81] The appropriate response to flawed historical analyses by originalists is to try to learn from their errors and to improve standards of historical analysis, not to abandon historical analysis.[82]

Historical obscurity, therefore, is no embarrassment to originalism. The originalist justices acknowledge the occasional existence of historical obscurity and have developed methods of dealing with it. In *McIntyre v Ohio Elections Comm'n*,[83] Justice Scalia stated that, because the original meaning of the First Amendment was hopelessly obscure on the question as to whether anonymous political speech was protected, the Court should defer to the longstanding tradition under which such speech had been proscribed. Thus, Justice Scalia's judgment in *McIntyre* suggests that the Court should defer to the political branches where the original meaning of the Constitution is unclear.[84] Justice Thomas expressed a similar view in *Deck v Missouri*.[85]

2.3.3. The 'Dead Hand' of the Past

Secondly, Joseph Raz suggests that the democratic argument in favour of recognising the authority of lawmakers is of little force in the case of old laws, the original makers of which are long dead.[86] Thus, it must be shown why judicial adherence to laws enacted by dead generations is a democratic necessity. Michael McConnell attempts to do so by rejecting the notion of self-government in the present in favour of 'self-government over time'.[87] On this conception of self-government the laws in force do not derive their authority from the existing society in which they currently operate but, rather, from the authority of the generation that enacted them.[88] Self-government over time recognises that each generation can add to, and alter, the laws enacted its predecessors. The innovations of each generation, however, owe their continuing legal validity, even after the passing of the generation that brought them about, to the authority of that generation to amend the law.[89] The current generation's agreement to be bound

81. Price Marshall, 'No Political Truth: *The Federalist* and Justice Scalia on the Separation of Powers' (1989–90) 12 U Ark Little Rock LJ 245, 262–64.
82. Calabresi and Fine, 'Two Cheers', 335.
83. 514 US 334 (1995). See also *Michael H v Gerald D* 491 US 110 (1989).
84. Ralph A Rossum, *Antonin Scalia's Jurisprudence: Text and Tradition* (Kansas University Press 2006) 46–47.
85. Justice Thomas, *Deck v Missouri* 544 US 622 (2005). However, it is important to note that he disagreed Justice Scalia in *McIntyre* and has generally been less deferential to democratic institutions.
86. Raz, *Between Authority and Interpretation*, 295–97.
87. Michael W McConnell, 'Textualism and the Dead Hand of the Past' (1997) 66 George Wash L Rev 1127.
88. For the view that Justice Scalia's opinions indicate an adherence to the theory of 'self-government over time', see Tony Cole, 'Scalia and the Institutional Approach to Law' (2003) 34 U Tol L Rev 559, 569.
89. McConnell, 'Dead Hand of the Past', 1135–36.

by the enactments of past generations carries the corollary that it enjoys a right to bind future generations.

The principal benefit of self-government over time is that it enables citizens to plan their affairs more effectively, secure in the knowledge that the rights they enjoy today will also be secured to them tomorrow.[90] Moreover, it is to be observed that those who object to the rule of dead generations are not typically arguing that current legislative majorities should be at large concerning what policies to adopt. Rather, they are arguing that judges should be permitted to impose limits on current majorities on a basis other than the authority of the people, dead or alive.[91]

3. Text

3.1. Text in Originalist Exegesis

In seeking to discern the meaning of a law, new originalists accord priority to its text. If the text on its most linguistically reasonable interpretation compels a particular result, an originalist interpreter is bound by that interpretation regardless of the consequences.[92]

Dictionaries seek to reflect the conventional understanding of words and phrases by particular linguistic communities. Therefore, the starting point in seeking to discern the linguistic meaning of a text is with an examination of the dictionary meaning of the disputed terms.[93]

I shall examine the dictionary definitions of the various parts of art 51 in reverse order. The meaning of the word 'law' in this context is uncontroversial: it refers to 'the enforceable body of rules that govern any society'.[94] The European Union consists of: '[t]he 27 nations… that have joined together to form an economic community with common monetary, political, and social aspirations'.[95]

Thus, the meaning of 'Union law' is uncontroversial. The only point of controversy therefore, centres upon the meaning of the verb 'to implement'.

---

90. Steven G Calabresi, 'Introduction' in Steven G Calabresi (ed), *Originalism: A Quarter-Century of Debate* (Regnery Publishing Inc 2007) 8.
91. Robert H Bork, speech at the University of San Diego Law School, 18 November 1985: ibid 88.
92. Justice Scalia, *Maryland v Craig* 497 US 836, 870 (1990); Justice Thomas, *United States v International Business Machines Corp* 517 US 843, 861 (1996).
93. Scalia and Garner, *Reading Law*, 72. For guidance on the use of dictionaries, see pp 418–19.
94. *Oxford Dictionary of Law* (Oxford University Press 2012) <http://www.oxfordreference.com.elib.tcd.ie/view/10.1093/acref/9780199551248.001.0001/acref-9780199551248-e-2186?rskey=WaR7Zx&result=1&q=law> accessed 25 October 2012.
95. ibid.

3.2. 'To implement': A Semantic Analysis

3.2.1. Etymology

HW Fowler in his celebrated *Modern English Usage* noted that the verb 'to implement' is 'derived from the barbarous jargon of the Scotish [*sic*] bar'.[96] He also notes that the word is synonymous with the phrase 'to carry out'.[97]

3.2.2. General Dictionaries

The *Oxford English Dictionary* defines the verb 'to implement' in the following terms: '1.a. *trans.* To complete, perform, carry into effect (a contract, agreement, etc.); to fulfil (an engagement or promise)'. The *American Heritage Dictionary of the English Language* contains the following entry: '1. To put into practical effect; carry out: implement the new procedures'. The *Merriam-Webster Collegiate Dictionary* uses similar terms: '1: carry out, accomplish; *especially*: to give practical effect to and ensure of actual fulfilment by concrete measures'.

All of these dictionaries indicate that the verb 'to implement' refers to an affirmative action, as opposed to an omission. It is doubtful, therefore, whether the wording of art 51 of the CFR could refer to a Member State that had not taken some positive action designed to give effect to a provision of EU law.

3.2.3. Legal Dictionaries

The *Oxford Dictionary of Law* contains the following entry for the noun 'implementation': '[t]he process of bringing any piece of legislation into force....'[98]

This entry seems to suggest that the phrase 'implementing Union law' should be understood to mean the transposition and application of EU legislation. The formulation '*any* piece of legislation' encompasses all EU secondary legislation and, possibly, directly effective Treaty provisions. *Garner's Dictionary of Legal Usage* states disparagingly that 'implement' is: 'a vogue word beloved by jargon-mongers, in whose language *policies are implemented*. The phrase *carry out* is usually better, and certainly less vague.'[99] Although Garner condemns its vagueness, his equation of the verb 'to implement' with the phrase 'carry out' confirms that it refers to an affirmative action rather than to a situation in whichMember States have been entirely passive.

---

96. HW Fowler, *Modern English Usage* (1st edn, Oxford University Press 1926) 260; quoting David Irving's *Elements of English Composition* (11th edn, 1841).
97. ibid 259.
98. *Oxford Dictionary of Law*.
99. Bryan A Garner, *Garner's Dictionary of Legal Usage* (3rd edn, Oxford University Press 2011) 429.

3.2.4. Other Language Versions

Because the 'text' of art 51 consists of all 23 language versions of the CFR,[100] it is important to ensure that the other language versions support, or at least do not contradict, the reading of art 51.1 laid out above.

Multiple languages were used in the drafting of the CFR. For reasons of space, I shall discuss only a small selection of the authentic language versions in the main body of the text and shall confine the remainder to footnotes. No lawyer is fluent in all 23 of the official languages of the EU; therefore, reliance must be placed on multilingual dictionaries. Though these are useful aids, they are a poor substitute for fluency in a language. Nonetheless, the only alternative option to using them is to ignore the fact that the EU Treaties are authentic in 23 different languages, an approach that would violate art 55 TEU.

All of the language versions, however, appear to confirm that an affirmative action by the Member States, designed to give effect to a provision of EU law, is required in order for Member State activity to be reviewable under the CFR. The French version of art 51 uses the phrase '*mettre en oeuvre*', which has been recognised as a synonym for the verb 'to implement'.[101] The German version uses the phrase '*Durchführung*', which has been translated as 'carrying out... performing'.[102] Similarly, the Italian version of the CFR uses the word '*attuazione*' to describe the circumstances in which Member States are bound by the CFR. This word translates as 'implementation... carrying out'.[103] The Spanish version is expressed in similar terms. It uses the verb '*aplicar*', which translates as 'to put into practice, apply'.[104] The other language versions strongly support the view that, in order to be bound by the CFR, the Member States must be engaged in some positive activity designed to give effect to a provision of EU law.[105]

---

100. art 55 TEU provides as follows: '1. This Treaty, drawn up in a single original in the Bulgarian, Czech, Danish, Dutch, English, Estonian, Finnish, French, German, Greek, Hungarian, Irish, Italian, Latvian, Lithuanian, Maltese, Polish, Portuguese, Romanian, Slovak, Slovenian, Spanish and Swedish languages, the texts in each of these languages being equally authentic, shall be deposited in the archives of the Government of the Italian Republic, which will transmit a certified copy to each of the governments of the other signatory States.'
101. *Oxford Hachette French Dictionary* (Oxford University Press 1997) 556.
102. *Concise Oxford German Dictionary* (Oxford University Press 2005) 139.
103. *Oxford Italian Dictionary* (Oxford University Press 1997).
104. *Oxford Spanish Dictionary* (Oxford University Press 2008) 57.
105. The Portuguese version of art 51 uses the verb '*aplicar*', which has been translated as meaning 'to apply': *Oxford Essential Portuguese Dictionary* (Oxford University Press 2009) 195. The Dutch version of the CFR uses the phrase '*ten uitvoer brengen*', which has been translated as meaning 'to implement': *The New Routledge Dutch Dictionary* (Routledge 2003) 643. The Danish version of art 51 uses the verb '*gennemforer*', which has been translated variously as 'to implement', 'to carry through', and 'carry through;... carry out; implement... effect... go through with... finish': Jens Axelsen, *The Standard Danish–English/English–Danish Dictionary*

Derogating from EU law involves a limited negation of some EU law principle or other, usually with the objective of securing a policy objective deemed important by national authorities. For this reason it would be linguistically curious to describe a Member State derogating from EU law as being involved in the implementation of EU law.

(Cassell 1994) 174. The Swedish version uses the verb '*tillampa*', which means 'to apply': *Swedish Dictionary* (Routledge 1995) 32; Ole Roger Reuter *Swedish–English Dictionary* (George Allen & Unwin Ltd 1964) 10. The Finnish version uses the verb '*soveltao*', which has been translated as 'to apply': Raija Hurme, Maritta Pesonen, Olli Syvaoja (eds), *English–Finnish General Dictionary* (3rd edn, Werner Sodestrom Osakeyhtio) 46. The Estonian version uses the verb 'kohaldama', which means 'to apply'. See, Paul F Saagpakk, *Estonian–English Dictionary* (Koolibri 1992) 303. The Lithuanian version uses the verb '*igyvendinti*', which has been translated to mean 'to implement': Bronius Piesarkas and Bronius Svecevicius (eds), *Lithuanian Dictionary: English–Lithuanian / Lithuanian–English* (Routledge 1995). The Latvian version uses the verb '*istenat*', which has been translated as meaning 'to realize, to carry out, to put into practice': E Turnika, *Latviesu – Anglen Vordnica* (Avats 1982) 179. The Irish version uses the phrase '*cur chun feidhme*'. This phrase is a variant of the more typically used phrase '*cur i bhfeidhm*', which means 'put sth into operation': Tomás de Bhaldraithe, *Niall Ó Dónaill: Foclóir Gaeilge–Béarla* (Government of Ireland 1977) 530. The Hungarian version uses the verb '*végrehajt*', which has been translated to mean 'execute, effect, fulfil… carry/follow out… enforce' and 'to enforce;… to fulfil… to implement': *Magyar–Angal Keziszotar* (7th edn, Akademioi Kiado 1976) 103. The Romanian version uses the verb '*aplica*', which has been translated to mean 'to apply; to implement; to put into practice' and 'to bring/put the law into operation': Mihai Miroiu, *Romanian–English/English–Romanian Dictionary* (Hippocrene Books 1996) 26. The Maltese version uses the verb '*implement*', which translates as 'implementation… To implement; to fulfil… to put into effect': *Maltese–English Dictionary* (vol 1, Midsea Books Ltd 1987). The Polish version uses the verb '*stosowac*', which translates as 'to apply;… to administer'. See also Iwo Cyprian Pogonowsk, *Unabridged Polish–English Dictionary* (Hippocrene Books 1997) 2391, which translates '*stosowac*' in the following terms: 'use; employ; resort to (force, etc); observe; to put into practice; put into operation; adopt; suit; apply…' The Slovene version uses the word '*izvajanje*', which translates as 'execution, executing, performing… carrying out, implementation, deduction; derivation;… implementation of policy': Anton Grad and Henry Leeming, *Slovene–English Dictionary* (DZS 1993). The Czech version uses the verb '*uplatnit*', which translates as 'apply, put across,… enforce': *Anglicko–Cesky/Cesko–Anglicky Velky Slovnik* (Lingea 2010) 1446. The Slovenian version uses the verb '*vykonot*', which translates as 'to execute… to perform,… to achieve… to do… to carry out': Dr J Vilikovska and P Vilkovsky, *Slovenso–Angliky Slovnik* (Slovenski Pedagogicko Nokladatelstvo 1971) 456. The Greek version uses the word 'εφαρ-μόζουν', which means 'to apply, put into practice': George A Magosis, *Standard Greek Dictionary* (Langenscheidt 1990) 592. In the Bulgarian version, the word 'прилагат' is translated as '1. Apply, execute, exercise; enforce a law/ a decree;… application, execution': *Bulgarian–English Dictionary* (vol II, 3rd edn, Nauka I Izkoustvo,1990).

3.3. 'To Implement': A Contextual Analysis

3.3.1. Usage in the CFR, TFEU, and TEU

In seeking to discern the meaning of the phrase 'implementing Union law' it is useful to examine other usages of the phrase in the three texts that together constitute the EU Treaty system, the CFR as well as the Treaty on the Functioning of the European Union (TFEU) and the Treaty on European Union (TEU).[106] The same word should be presumed to bear the same meaning throughout a text unless the context indicates otherwise.[107]

I shall begin by attempting to discern what light, if any, the text of the CFR and the TFEU can shed on the meaning of the verb 'to implement'. Aside from art 51, the verb 'to implement' is used once more in the CFR and repeatedly in the TFEU. Beginning with the CFR, art 35 thereof states in relevant part as follows:

> A high level of human health protection shall be ensured in the definition and implementation of all Union policies and activities.

In this provision, the verb 'to implement' seems to refer principally to EU secondary legislation, since EU policies are generally given effect by means of such legislation. However, it probably also embraces the application of directly effective Treaty provisions, since these are sometimes applied without the need for intervening secondary legislation.

The usages of the verb 'to implement' in the TFEU also confirm that it must be understood to embrace the application of EU secondary legislation[108] and directly effective Treaty provisions.[109] The verb 'to implement' has also been

---

106. Scalia and Garner, *Reading Law*, 252.
107. Henry Campbell Black, *Handbook on the Construction and Interpretation of the Laws* (2nd edn, West Publishing 1911) 42.
108. See, Title I, arts 26.2, 28.1, 31, 32, 36, 42.5, 45.1 of the TFEU speaks of the implementation of decisions of the Council in relation to the Common Foreign and Security Policy; Title II, arts 164 and 178 empower the European Parliament and Council to adopt 'implementing regulations'; Title II, art 207.2 refers to the implementation of regulations; Title II, art 311 speaks of the Council adopting 'implementing measures… by means of regulations'; Title II, art 322 speaks of 'implementing the budget… by means of regulations'. Article 51.9 of Protocol No 3 of the Treaties on the Statute of the Court of Justice of the European Union speaks of the implementation of a Council decision.
109. Title I, art 11 of the TFEU, which creates for a right of petition for EU citizens, speaks of 'implementing the Treaties'; Title II, art 91, TFEU speaks of the implementation of 'Article 90' of the TFEU; Title II, art 95.3 TFEU speaks of the implementation of the rule contained in art 95.1 thereof; Title II, art 225, speaks of 'implementing the Treaties'.

used to refer to measures adopted by the Commission[110] and those adopted under national law designed to give effect to EU law.[111]

Some provisions of the TFEU in which the verb is used do not specify the particular form of law to which they relate: for instance arts 9, 10, and 12, Title II, TFEU speak of the implementation of the Union's 'policies and activities'; Title II, arts 13, 43 TFEU thereof speak of the implementation of the Union's 'policies'; Title II, arts 182.3, 185, 186 to the implementation of a framework programme, to be devised by the European Parliament and Council, and to include all of the activities of the Union; and Title II, art 263 speaks somewhat opaquely of 'implementing measures'.

Usages of the phrase in the TEU also confirm the inference that the verb 'to implement' applies to application of secondary legislation[112] and directly effective Treaty provisions.[113] In addition, art 8.2 of the TEU speaks of implementing agreements with neighbouring countries. Many articles of the TEU speak of implementing the common foreign and security policy.[114] Certain usages of the word 'to implement' in the TEU, like the TFEU, are ambiguous, though none of these can be taken to refer to Member State derogations.[115]

3.3.2. Declarations

The Declaration by the Czech Republic on the Charter of Fundamental Rights states that 'its provisions are addressed to the Member States only when they are implementing Union law, and not when they are adopting and implementing national law independently from Union law'. It is arguable that this formulation supports the view that the provisions of the CFR do not apply to Member States when derogating from EU law since, as noted above, in cases of derogation, Member States are engaged in a discrete negation of some EU law principle or other.

3.3.3. Explanations Relating to the CFR

One major item of evidence as to the meaning of 'implementing', which has been said to contradict the lexicographical and contextual evidence adduced above, is contained in the Explanations Relating to the CFR prepared by the

---

110. Title II, art 291.2 states that '[w]here uniform conditions for implementing legally binding Union acts are needed, those acts shall confer implementing powers on the Commission'.
111. Title II, art 291.1 speaks of 'measures of national law necessary to implement legally binding Union acts.
112. art 22.1 TEU speaks of the implementation of Council decisions.
113. art 11.4 TEU speaks of 'implementing the Treaties'.
114. arts 24, 25, 26, 27, 28, 31, 35, 36, 38, 40, 41, 42, 43, 44, 45 TEU.
115. The preamble of the TEU speaks twice of implementing policies; art 12(c) TEU deals with the role of national parliaments in monitoring the implementation of Union policies; art 12.3 TEU speaks of the implementation of Union external policy.

Convention that drafted the CFR. The status of these Explanations is somewhat anomalous. Article 6(1) TEU provides as follows:

> The rights, freedoms and principles in the Charter shall be interpreted in accordance with the general provisions in Title VII of the Charter governing its interpretation and application and with due regard to the explanations referred to in the Charter, that set out the sources of those provisions.[116]

Thus, although there is no strict requirement that the CFR be interpreted in accordance with the Explanations, the ECJ must have 'due regard' to the Explanations in its interpretation of the CFR.

Let us, therefore, consider what light the Explanations may throw on the meaning of the phrase 'implementing Union law'. They provide in relevant part as follows:

> As regards the Member States, it follows unambiguously from the case-law of the Court of Justice that the requirement to respect fundamental rights defined in the context of the Union is only binding on the Member States when they act in the scope of Union law...[117]

By equating the phrase 'implementing Union law', contained in art 51 CFR, with 'acting within the scope of Union law', used in the jurisprudence of the ECJ, and by specifically invoking the *ERT* case, which involved a derogation from EU law, the Explanations could be taken to suggest that Member State derogations from EU law should be held to fall within the scope of the CFR.

We have already seen that the semantic meaning of the phrase 'Member States only when they are implementing Union law' indicates that an affirmative action by a Member State, designed to give effect to an EU law principle, is required to subject Member State activity to review under the CFR.

Therefore, there certainly appears to be a divergence between the text of art 51 and the Explanations. This justifies recourse to the other indicia of original meaning discussed above.

4. Pre-Ratification Law and Usage

4.1. Pre-Ratification Law and Usage in Originalist Exegesis

Referring to the background law against which a provision was adopted can indicate both the origins of the provision under construction and the mischief with which it was intended to deal.[118] It is important to note, however,

116. See also art 52.7 CFR.
117. Explanations Relating to the Charter of Fundamental Rights [2007] OJ C303/02.
118. *Heydon's Case* (1584) 3 Rep 7a. For an example of background law being cited in originalist exegesis, see Justice Scalia in *Summers v Earth Island Institute* 129 S Ct 1142 (2009).

that pre-ratification law cannot trump text as evidence of original meaning, as this would undermine the purpose of putting the law into writing, which is to inform citizens of their rights and obligations. Pre-ratification usage refers to the manner in which the disputed words or phrases in the law being interpreted were used prior to its ratification.

4.2. The Law Prior to the Ratification of art 51 CFR

I shall begin my discussion of the meaning of art 51 CFR with a description of the state of the law prior to the ratification of the Lisbon Treaty.

As discussed above, between 1957 and 2009 the EU did not have a legally enforceable bill of rights.[119] Nonetheless, after a period of some uncertainty, it was held by the ECJ that it was a condition of the legality of Union action that it respected such rights. In this section I intend to focus exclusively on the scope of the obligations that jurisprudence imposed on Member States.

Once the Court had recognised human rights as general principles of EU law, which it was the duty of the Court to protect, it was rapidly accepted that the Court would review Member States' implementation of EU law for compliance with human rights.[120] In the *ERT* case[121] it was held that derogations were also subject to human rights review by the ECJ.[122] Thus, the text of art 51 of the CFR is considerably narrower, in terms of the scope of its application to Member States, than the pre-Lisbon case law of the ECJ.

4.3. Pre-Ratification Usage in Originalist Exegesis

Pre-ratification usage denotes the manner in which the word or phrase, the meaning of which is in dispute, was used prior to its inclusion in the text. From an originalist perspective, the justification for examining such prior usage is that, if a particular word or phrase bore a clear legal meaning before the adoption of the text under construction, it is reasonable to presume that the usage of the word in the text corresponds to that pre-existing legal meaning.[123]

4.4. 'Implementing Union Law': Pre-CFR Usage

4.4.1. ECJ Cases

Due to constraints of space, it is not possible to include all pre-ratification usages of the phrase 'implementing Union law' in this article. Instead, I will give examples to illustrate the meaning of the phrase. In many cases decided

119. For discussion see de Búrca, 'Evolution of EU Human Rights Law'.
120. See, for example, Case 222/84 *Marguerite Johnston v Chief Constable of the Royal Ulster Constabulary* [1986] ECR 1651.
121. C–260/89 *ERT* [1991] ECR I–2925, para 43.
122. ibid.
123. Scalia and Garner, *Reading Law*, 320–21.

prior to the drafting of the CFR, the phrase 'implementing Union law' or close variants thereof were used by members of the Court to describe Member State activities. In none of these cases was it used to describe a situation in which a Member State was derogating from EU law.

The phrase 'implementing Union law' and its variants did not apply to derogations from EU law. The phrase and its variants seem to have been used to describe measures giving effect to all species of secondary EU legislation, including regulations[124] and directives.[125] They were also used to describe actions taken by Member States designed to give effect to directly effective Treaty provisions.[126]

4.4.2. Secondary Legislation

An examination of secondary legislation prior to the drafting of the CFR tends to confirm the view that the phrase applied to Member State efforts to give effect to such legislation.[127]

4.4.3. Other Official Documents

An analysis of usages of the phrase and its variants in other official documents confirms what I have said above: the provisions of the CFR apply to Member States where they give effect to EU secondary legislation – directives,[128] regulations,[129] decisions,[130] and directly effective Treaty provisions.[131] It is also

---

124. C–213/99, *José Teodoro de Andrade v Director da Alfandega de Lexoes* [2000] ECR I–11083, Opinion of Advocate General Fennelly, para 43.
125. C–300/95 *Commission of the European Communities v United Kingdom of Great Britain and Northern Ireland* [1997] ECR I–2649.
126. Case 51/71 *International Fruit Company* [1971] ECR 1107, Opinion of Advocate General Roemer at 1121.
127. See, for example, Directive 89/665 of 21 December 1989 on the coordination of the laws, regulations and administrative provisions relating to the application of review procedures to the award of public supply and public works contracts [1989] OJ L 395, art 1.
128. There are numerous usages of the verb 'to implement' to describe the Member States giving effect to directives in official documents. See, for example, the sixteenth annual report on monitoring the application of Community law of 07/12/1999, COM/99/0301.
129. See, for example, Report from the Commission for the Biarritz European Council on the Community's strategy for safety at sea, COM/2000/0603 final, 4.
130. European Union Preparatory Report from the Commission to the Council, the European Parliament and the Economic and Social Committee on the implementation of Decision 3052/95/CE 1997 and 1998.
131. See, for example, European Union Preparatory Acts Opinion of the Economic and Social Committee on the 'White Paper on Modernisation of the Rules Implementing Articles 81 and 82 of the EC Treaty – Commission Programme No 99/027' [2000] OJ C51/55, 2–7.

plain that Member State regulatory measures designed to supplement a legal regime established by EU law may also be understood as 'implementing Union law'.[132]

4.4.4. Scholarly Commentary

Pre-CFR scholarly commentary also uniformly employed the phrase 'implementing Union law' and analogous phrases to mean the implementation of directives,[133] regulations,[134] decisions,[135] and directly effective Treaty provisions.[136] I have uncovered no instance in which a Member State derogating from EU law was described as implementing that law.

4.4.5. Conclusion

My research has uncovered no instance in which the phrase 'implementing Union law,' or any variant thereof, was used prior to the drafting of the CFR to describe a Member State derogating from EU law. This constitutes strong evidence that the phrase was not understood to encompass such derogations at the time of the drafting of the CFR.

5. Drafting and Ratification History

5.1. Drafting and Ratification History in Originalist Exegesis

Below, I shall consider only the drafting history of the CFR. A full treatment of the ratification history of the CFR, incorporating all public discussion surrounding its adoption in every Member State, would be, for linguistic reasons, beyond the capacity of any single scholar. Each Member States was, however, represented in the Convention at which the CFR was drafted.[137] Thus, by confining my analysis to the drafting history of the CFR, the views of the Member States are, in fact, taken into account.

---

132. See, for example, European Union Information and Notices Council Resolution on 20 June 1994 on the electronic dissemination of Community law and national implementing laws and on improved access conditions [1994] OJ C179, 1.
133. See, for example, Edward T Swaine, 'Subsidiarity and Self-Interest: Federalism at the European Court of Justice' (2000) 41 Harv Int'l LJ 1, 23.
134. See, for example, John P Flaherty and Maureen E Lally-Green, 'Fundamental Rights in the European Union' (1997–98) 36 Duq L Rev 249, 265, 318–19.
135. See, for example, Jules Lonbay, 'The Single European Act' (1988) 11 BC Int'l & Comp L Rev 31, 61.
136. See, for example, Patrick Tangney, 'The New Internationalism: The Cession of Sovereign Competences to Supranational Organizations and Constitutional Change in the United States and Germany' (1996) 21 Yale J Int'l L 395, 419–21.
137. The countries which had yet to accede to the EU were granted the right to make observations in the Convention and, thus, were able to make known their views as to the meaning of the CFR.

The drafting history of a provision provides especially significant evidence of its original meaning. This is because it gives an interpreter an insight into the way in which the disputed words in the text were understood in the specific context in which they were used.[138] It is important, however, to note that the search is not for the intention of a single flesh and blood author; most legal texts, including the CFR, are the work of collective bodies. Therefore, it is necessary to treat the legislature *as if* it were a single author, by examining all data related to the enactment process, with a view to determining what a reasonable author would have had in mind when using the words that were ultimately included in the text.[139] However, it is important to be clear that the beliefs and ideals of its drafters have authority only to the extent that they received concrete expression in the CFR itself.[140]

5.2. The Drafting History of art 51 CFR

The CFR was drafted at a Convention consisting of representatives of the European Parliament, of national parliaments, of Member State governments, and of the European Commission. The Convention also included observers from the European Court of Justice, the Committee of the Regions, the Economic and Social Committee, the Ombudsman, and the Council of Europe. The records of the proceedings of the Convention strongly support the view that the drafters' use of the phrase 'implementing Union law' represented an attempt to narrow the scope of application of the ECJ's human rights jurisdiction.

It was at the Cologne European Council of 3–4 June 1999 that the decision was made to establish a body to draft a human rights charter for the EU.[141] Annex IV of the Cologne European Council Presidency Conclusions states that the Council 'recognises that fundamental rights are indivisible by making the charter... (g) binding upon the Member States when applying or transposing provisions of Community law'.[142] Thus, the Council's mandate empowering the body to draft a charter of fundamental rights required that the latter be confined, in its application to Member States, to circumstances in which they were implementing EU law.

At the First Meeting of the Body Responsible for Preparing a Draft Charter of Fundamental Rights of the EU, on 17 December 1999,[143] later renamed 'the

138. For a case in which the originalist justices examined the Constitution's drafting history, see Justice Scalia in *Morrisson v Olson* 487 US 654 (1988).
139. Vasan Kesavan and Michael Stokes Paulsen, 'The Interpretive Force of the Constitution's Secret Drafting History' (2003) 91 Geo LJ 1113, 1118.
140. *District of Columbia v Heller* 554 US 570 (2008).
141. Cologne European Council Presidency Conclusions, Annex IV.
142. ibid Part F; First Meeting of the Body Responsible for Preparing a Draft Charter of Fundamental Rights of the EU (17 December 1999) 12–21.
143. 14073/99 (Presse 418).

Convention', Roman Herzog, chairman of the newly created body, stated that the CFR would be principally addressed to the institutions of the EU.[144]

Other members of the Convention had more expansive ambitions. For instance, Mr Mendez de Vigo, the EP's representative, suggested that the CFR should be applicable to Member State governments without restriction.[145] Thus, the battle lines were drawn early between those in the Convention who wished to see the proposed charter apply to all Member States activities and those who envisaged its having a narrower scope of application. The rest of the CFR's drafting history makes it clear that the latter faction prevailed.

Early drafts of art 51 used a broader formulation than 'implementing Union law'. The Secretariat Paper on Horizontal Questions of 20 January 2000 adopted the wording used in the jurisprudence of the ECJ and proposed that the CFR should apply to Member States when they act 'within the scope of EU law'.[146]

Draft Charter Articles presented to the Convention by the Praesidium on 15 February 2000 adopted a narrower formulation, stating that the provisions of the proposed charter 'are binding on the Member States only where the latter transpose or apply the law of the Union....'[147]

The representatives of several Member State governments made proposals in response to this initial Praesidium draft, in which they expressed concerns over the potential of the charter project to interfere with the autonomy of Member States. Lord Goldsmith QC, the representative of the United Kingdom government, proposed a much narrower formulation under which the provisions of the CFR would be 'addressed to the bodies and institutions of the European Union in the exercise of the responsibilities and tasks assigned to them by the Treaties'.[148]

While Member States representatives worried about the CFR's potential to reduce their autonomy, the EP was keen to ensure that Member States not be given an entirely free hand either. The EP passed a resolution, which stated that it would lend its support to the CFR on condition *inter alia* that it be made: 'binding upon the Member States when applying or transposing provisions of Community law....'[149]

---

144. ibid 9.
145. ibid 12. See also, Letter from Mr Buttiglione to Mr Mendez de Vigo, 21 February 2000, CHARTE 4118/1/00 Rev. 1, Contrib 14, 2.
146. Secretariat Paper on Horizontal Questions, 20 January 2000, CHARTE 4111/00 Body 3, 2, para 4.
147. Draft Charter Articles from the Praesidium, 15 February 2000, CHARTE 4123/1/00 Rev 1, Convent 5, 9.
148. Lord Goldsmith, 6 March 2000, CHARTE 4146/00, Contrib 36. See also, Contribution from Mr Erling Olsen, Personal Representative of the Government of Denmark, 20 March, 2000, CHARTE 4181/00, Convent 64, 2–3.
149. European Parliament Resolution (Report by Mr Duff and Mr Voggenhuber), 5 March 2000, CHARTE 4199/00, Contrib 80, 2.

Perhaps in response to such submissions, on 15 February 2000, the Praesidium submitted an amended draft to the Convention for its consideration, which provided that '[t]he provisions of this Charter shall be applicable... to the Member States when implementing Community law'.[150] In a draft submitted to the Convention on 18 April 2000, the Praesidium changed this wording slightly to 'within the framework of implementing Community law'.[151]

Several other drafts defining the scope of application of the CFR were submitted to the Convention, which would have made it applicable to all Member State activities.[152]

Although such radical proposals were not accepted, the Praesidium vacillated somewhat between broad and narrow formulations. On 16 May 2000, the 'implementing Community law' formulation of 15 February and 18 April drafts was replaced. The working draft now read as follows: 'The provisions of the Charter are addressed... to the Member States exclusively within the scope of Union law.'

This restored the formulation contained in the draft of 20 January and again employed the language the ECJ had used up to that point in its case law, under which both Member State implementation and Member State derogation from EU were deemed to fall within the scope of EU law. Accordingly, had this version of art 51 been adopted it would have been impossible to deny that the CFR's scope of application was co-extensive with the scope of application of the Court's pre-Lisbon human rights jurisprudence.

In a later draft the Praesidium, submitted on 23 June and described as a 'Compromise proposal', altered this wording, reverting to the original formulation used in the 15 February and 18 April drafts. This new version provided in relevant part as follows:

> 1. The provisions of this Charter are addressed, with due regard for the principle of subsidiarity, to the institutions and bodies of the Union and to the Member States exclusively when they implement Union law.[153]

This was the wording, with one slight and inconsequential change,[154] which found its way into the final draft of the CFR.

---

150. Praesidium Draft Charter of Fundamental Rights of the European Union – New Proposal for Articles 1 to 12 (now 1 to 16), 8 March 2000, CHARTE 4123/1/00 Rev 1, Convent 5, and CHARTE 4137/00, Convent 8, 2.
151. Draft Horizontal Articles Praesidium, 18 April 2000, CHARTE 4235/00, Convent 27.
152. See Motion Tabled by PDS in German Bundestag, 24 March 2000, CHARTE 4189/00, Contrib 72, 9; Submission by Amnesty International, on the 10 of May 2000, CHARTE 4290/00, Contrib 162, 6; Platform of European Social NGOs on the 12 May 2000, CHARTE 4286/00, Contrib 158.
153. Compromise proposal submitted by the Praesidium for arts 31 to 40 (social rights and horizontal clauses), 23 June 2000, CHARTE 4316/00, Convent 34, 5.
154. A later draft, submitted on 28 July 2000, substituted the words 'only when they are implementing Union law' for 'exclusively when they implement Union law', which

It is reasonable to suppose that the Convention was familiar with the semantic meaning, and the pattern of usage, of the phrase 'implementing Union law', which does not include Member State derogations from EU law. Thus, in its conscious decision to opt for the phrase 'implementing Union law' in preference to 'within the scope of Union law', the latter of which certainly includes derogations, it is very likely that the Convention intended Member State derogations to be excluded from the scope of the CFR. Thus, the drafting history of the CFR clearly demonstrates that the members of the Convention understood the difference between acting 'within the scope of Union law' and 'implementing Union law'. In choosing the latter formulation the Convention chose to give the CFR a narrower scope than the pre-existing human rights jurisprudence of the ECJ.

6. Post-Ratification Interpretations

6.1. Post-Ratification Interpretations in Originalist Exegesis

By post-ratification interpretations I mean the manner in which the disputed words in the text have been interpreted since their ratification by courts and others. Post-ratification interpretations ought to be considered in originalist exegesis, as they alert the interpreter to how other reasonable interpreters have understood the text. However, the views of such interpreters cannot override the plain meaning of the text.[155]

6.2. 'Implementing Union Law': Post-Ratification Interpretations

6.2.1. Case Law

Article 51 of the CFR has been cited in numerous cases since the Lisbon Treaty. The ECJ has confirmed that the CFR applies to Member States in the implementation of decisions,[156] regulations,[157] directives,[158] directly effective Treaty provisions,[159] and to national law measures designed to give effect to EU law.[160]

Several judgments of the Court and opinions of Advocates General suggest that art 51 should be given a broad interpretation and should be held to apply,

---

are linguistically synonymous. See also the Praesidium draft of 14 September 2000, CHARTE 4470/00, Convent 47, 17.

155. Justice Scalia *United States v Gaudin* 515 US 506, 519 (1995).

156. C–483/09 and C–1/10 *Magatte Gueye and Valentín Salmerón Sánchez* [2011] ECR I–8263, Opinion of Advocate General Kokott paras 75–79.

157. See, for example, C–571/10 *Kamberaj v Instituto per L'Edilizia Sociale della Provincia Autonoma di Balzano (IPES)* (ECJ, 24 April 2012) para 80.

158. See, for example, ibid para 85.

159. See, for example, C–372/09 and C–373/09 *Josep Peñarroja Fa*, [2011] ECR I–1785, paras 48–65.

160. C–489/10 *Prokurator Generalny v Łukasz Marcin Bonda* (ECJ, 15 December 2011) Opinion of Advocate General Kokott paras 17–20.

not only to the implementation of secondary EU legislation and directly effective Treaty provisions, but also to Member State derogations from EU law. In addition, several Court decisions have expanded the CFR's scope even beyond the bounds established by the Court's pre-Lisbon human rights jurisprudence. In this respect the decisions of the ECJ have followed the prior pattern of interpretation, described above, under which text of the law was contradicted in the service of objectives the Court deemed important.

In the case of *Åklagaren v Hans Åkerberg Fransson*,[161] the ECJ interpreted art 51 CFR as a codification of the position prior to the Lisbon Treaty. The Court stated that Member States were bound by the CFR when they acted 'within the scope of European Union law'.[162] The Court cited the Explanations to the CFR in support of this conclusion. However, as noted above, the Explanations are not law and, thus, cannot have the effect of overriding the plain text of the CFR.

Åkerberg Fransson did not involve a Member State derogation from EU law. The issue in the case was whether the Sweden authorities were 'implementing Union law' or not when they prosecuted the plaintiff for evasion of VAT. The Court noted that the Member States were obliged, under the TEU, the TFEU, and secondary legislation to prevent evasion of VAT, which was also the objective of the national legislation in issue. For these reasons, the Court held that the case involved the implementation of EU law.[163] As mentioned above, Title II, art 291.1 TFEU mentions 'measures of national law necessary to implement legally binding Union acts'. This wording implies that it is possible for national legislation to be considered an EU law implementing measure, even where that legislation is not specifically described as such, provided such legislation is 'necessary' to the Member States' implementation of EU law. In *Åkerberg Fransson* the national legislation in issue aimed to ensure *inter alia* the effectiveness of VAT collection, and thus was partially aimed at fulfilling Sweden's obligations under the Treaties. Thus, the conclusion in *Åkerberg Fransson* is justified on an originalist interpretation of art 51 CFR. The reasoning of the Court is defective, however, in suggesting that the phrase 'implementing Union law' is synonymous with the significantly broader formula 'within the scope of Union law'.

Advocate General Cruz Villalón expressed a view similar to that of the Court as to the meaning of art 51 CFR. He said that the Explanations to the CFR 'point to continuity rather than conflict' and that the ECJ's pre-Lisbon jurisprudence received 'concrete expression in the Charter'.[164] In AG Cruz Villalón's view, art 51 permitted the CFR to be applied to the activities of Member States in circumstances 'where it is legitimate that the Union's interest in leaving its mark – its

---

161. *Åkerberg Fransson*.
162. ibid paras 16–23.
163. *Åkerberg Fransson* paras 24–28. For an endorsement of the view that the situation in *Åkerberg Fransson* does come within the traditional concept of implementation, see Filippo Fontanelli, '*Hic sunt nationes*: The Elusive Limits of the EU Charter and the German Constitutional Watchdog' (2013) 9 ECL Rev 315, 326.
164. ibid para 25.

conception of the fundamental right – should take priority over that of each of the Member States. . ..'[165] On the specific facts of the case, and in contrast to the ECJ, AG Cruz Villalón held that Sweden was not bound by the CFR in its collection of VAT. This was because VAT was merely one among many different kinds of tax collected by the Swedish authorities. In the view of the Advocate General it would be disproportionate for the Court to review the entire Swedish taxation system for compliance with the CFR.[166] However, this is a false dichotomy. It would have been perfectly legitimate for the ECJ to have held that the tax collection law in issue in *Åkerberg Fransson* constituted a measure implementing Union law to the extent that it applied to VAT collection, which is required by EU law to be effective, but not to the extent that it applied to the collection of purely domestic taxes.

The tendency to expansively interpret art 51 CFR is also evident in other cases. The most significant in this regard are *Gerardo Ruiz Zambrano v Office national de l'emploi (ONEM)*[167] and *Murat Dereci, Vishaka Heiml, Alban Kokollari, Izunna Emmanuel Maduike, Dragica Stevic v Bundesministerium für Inneres.*[168] In the *Zambrano* and *Dereci* cases the ECJ held that the CFR applied to all situations that were 'covered by EU law'.[169] According to the pre-Lisbon jurisprudence of the Court a citizen who had exercised their free movement rights automatically came within the scope of EU law.[170] However, in the *Zambrano* and *Dereci* cases the Court held that the CFR could be relied upon by an EU citizen who had not exercised their right to free movement. *Zambrano* and *Dereci* thus represent an expansion of the Court's human rights jurisdiction, in spite of the fact that art 51 of the CFR plainly envisaged retrenchment.

As discussed above, this interpretation of art 51 CFR contradicts the original meaning of the phrase 'implementing Union law'. Moreover, insofar as *Åkerberg Fransson*, *Zambrano*, and *Dereci* cumulatively suggest that there is no area of Member State activity that can be identified *a priori* as falling outside the scope of the CFR, it contradicts the word 'only' used in art 51 thereof. Use of this word in the phrase 'only when they are implementing Union law' suggests that some Member State activities are *not* embraced by the term 'implementing Union law'. To the extent *Åkerberg Fransson*, *Zambrano*, and *Dereci* contradict this logic, they are contrary to the original meaning of art 51 CFR.

In *Yoshikazu Iida v Stadt Ulm*,[171] Advocate General Trstenjak echoed the sentiments expressed by the Court in *Åkerberg Fransson*, once more citing the Explanations as supporting a broad reading of art 51 CFR.[172] In *Ivana Scattolon*

165. ibid para 41.
166. ibid paras 62–63.
167. C–34/09; [2011] ECR I–1177.
168. C–256/11 (ECJ, 15 November 2011).
169. ibid para 72.
170. C–60/00 *Carpenter* [2002] ECR I–6279 paras 14, 17, and 39.
171. C–40/11 (ECJ, 8 November 2012).
172. ibid para 74. Advocate General.

v Ministero dell'Istruzione, dell'Università e della Ricerca,[173] Advocate General Bot argued, on the basis of the Explanations, that art 51 should be interpreted broadly.[174] He also argued that a restrictive reading of art 51 CFR:

> could be regarded as being contrary to the wording of Article 53 of the Charter, which provides... that '[n]othing in [the] Charter shall be interpreted as restricting or adversely affecting human rights and fundamental freedoms as recognised, in their respective fields of application, by Union law...'[175]

This latter argument is fundamentally unsound and, indeed, linguistically indefensible. Article 53 proscribes any interpretation of the CFR that would weaken the level of human rights protection under international law, Union law, the ECHR, and national constitutional law, but this injunction only applies 'in their respective fields of application'. Article 51 of the CFR purports to set out its 'field of application'.[176] Thus, to invoke art 53 in order to justify a broad interpretation of art 51 of the CFR is to beg the question.

The decisions made by the ECJ, and the opinions issued by its Advocates General, since the ratification of the Lisbon Treaty have uniformly rejected the original meaning of art 51 of the CFR. That Article required retrenchment in the Court's jurisprudence. However, rather than follow the original meaning of that provision, the ECJ has in fact expanded the scope of its human rights jurisdiction. This disregard of the plain meaning of the CFR's text constitutes an illegitimate arrogation of power by the Court.

6.2.2. Scholarly Commentary

It is generally accepted among scholars that the phrase 'implementing Union law', on a purely linguistic reading, excludes derogations from EU law from its scope.[177]

However, certain scholars have advanced textual arguments in support of the opposite position, none of which is convincing. Nick Grief argues that art 6(1) TEU, which provides that the CFR has 'the same legal value of the Treaties', means that the CFR must have 'the same domestic reach as the principles

173. C–108/10; [2011] ECR I–7491.
174. ibid para 118.
175. ibid.
176. *Oxford English Dictionary* <http://www.oed.com.elibin .tcd.ie/view/Entry/69922?rskey=RFm6QR&result=1&isAdvanced=false#eid> accessed 22 October 2012.
177. See, for example, Sionaidh Douglas-Scott, 'The Charter of Fundamental Rights as a Constitutional Document' (2004) EHRLR 37, 50; Gráinne de Búrca, 'The Drafting of the European Union Charter of Fundamental Rights' (2001) EL Rev 126, 138; Francis G Jacobs, 'Human Rights in the European Union: The Role of the Court of Justice' (2001) EL Rev 331, 338.

enshrined in the Treaties'.[178] However, the fact that the CFR has the same legal value as the Treaties, ie that it is equal to the Treaties in the hierarchy of legal norms, cannot have any bearing on the meaning of its provisions.

Paul Craig argues that when Member States derogate from EU law they rely on a defence provided by that law and should therefore be bound by the CFR.[179] However, relying on defences provided by EU law has always been described as 'derogating' from EU law. By contrast, the term 'implementing' has always been understood as referring exclusively to situations in which the Member States acted as agents of EU law. When the phrase 'within the scope of EU law' was used, it was understood to include both derogations and implementing measures. Had the drafters of the CFR employed the phrase 'within the scope of EU law' there could have been no doubt but that derogations were included. However, by instead employing the phrase 'implementing Union law', they indicated a desire to limit the scope of application of EU fundamental rights to agency-type situations. Craig's suggestion that 'implementing Union law' includes derogations is, therefore, unsound. Indeed, Craig recognised this fact in his earlier writings, in which he described Member State derogations as 'far from implementing Community law'.[180] Thus, prior to the distinction between implementation and derogation having any practical significance, Craig recognised and employed it himself. However, when it became desirable 'in normative terms'[181] to conflate the two, so as to ascribe to the CFR a broader scope of application than its wording fairly allows, he did so. Thus, Craig's reading of art 51 CFR is results-driven and unconvincing.

7. An Originalist Critique

The meaning ascribed to art 51 CFR by the ECJ is much broader than its plain language allows. In this subsection I shall summarise my criticisms of this reading and shall seek to demonstrate that it undermines each of the objectives originalism seeks to attain, as set out in Part 2.

First, by ascribing to the verb 'to implement' a meaning it never had before, the Court has upset the expectations of those who ratified the CFR, and has thereby behaved undemocratically.

Secondly, after cases such as *Åkerberg Fransson, Dereci,* and *Zambrano* it is unclear in what circumstances Member States will be bound by the CFR. Such uncertainty undermines the clarity of the law and positively encourages litigation.

---

178. Nick Grief, 'The Domestic Reach of General Principles of Law: First City Trading Revisited' (2007–08) 10 Cambridge YB Eur Legal Stud 199, 208–9.

179. Paul Craig, *The Lisbon Treaty: Law, Politics, and Treaty Reform* (Oxford University Press 2010) 211.

180. Paul Craig and Gráinne de Búrca, *EU Law: Text, Cases and Materials* (Oxford University Press 1998) 323.

181. Craig, *Lisbon Treaty*, 211.

Thirdly, the ECJ's insistence that 'implementing Union law' means exactly the same as acting 'within the scope of EU law' ignores the fact that this latter formulation was rejected in the Convention at which the CFR was drafted. Thus, it renders pointless the careful labour of the CFR's drafters.

Fourthly, the willingness of the ECJ to prioritise indications of meaning derived from extrinsic sources, over the plain text of art 51 CFR, undermines the purpose of having attempted to encapsulate the limits of the Court's human rights jurisdiction in writing.

Fifthly, because it is now difficult to identify any area of Member State activity that can be identified *a priori* as falling outside the scope of the CFR, the Court will enjoy excessive discretionary power in deciding which Member State acts are reviewable under the CFR, a discretion that would have been curbed by adhering to the plain text of art 51 CFR.

Conclusion

My objective in this article has been to demonstrate that the phrase 'implementing Union law' used in art 51 of the CFR, in its original meaning, refers to situations in which the Member States are acting as agents of the EU, by giving effect to directives, regulations, decisions, and directly effective Treaty provisions, but that the CFR does not apply to derogations from EU law.

In Part 1 I discussed the teleological method of interpretation of the ECJ. I showed that the Court goes beyond the text of the law, and even contradicts it, when this is deemed necessary to achieve objectives the Court considers important. I showed that the arguments that have been put forward in favour of the Court's approach are unconvincing and that the Court's approach is fundamentally flawed.

In Part 2 I discussed originalism as a possible alternative to the Court's teleological approach. I first defined what I meant by originalism and then put forward some normative arguments in favour of originalism, as well as responding to some criticisms that have been levelled against the originalist approach.

In Part 3 I carried out a linguistic analysis of art 51 of the CFR and concluded that the phrase 'implementing Union law' does not embrace Member State derogations from EU law but, rather, applies exclusively where Member States are acting as agents of the EU.

In Part 4 I gave the legal background against which the CFR was adopted and showed that the pre-Lisbon fundamental rights jurisprudence of the ECJ applied to Member States both when they were implementing Union law and when they were derogating therefrom.

In Part 5 I analysed the CFR's drafting history. I concluded that the phrase 'implementing Union law' was deliberately adopted, in direct preference to 'within the scope of EU law', to describe the field of the CFR's application. Thus, given that the latter formula was used in the Court's pre-CFR jurisprudence, I concluded that the drafters of the CFR intended to narrow the scope of EU law fundamental rights.

In Part 6 I examined the manner in which the CFR has been interpreted since it entered into force in 2009. It was only after the drafting of the CFR, I noted, that any suggestion was ever made that the phrase 'implementing Union law' applied to derogations. Nonetheless, the ECJ has accepted this reading of art 51.

In Part 7 I showed that this conclusion rests on a perversion of the CFR's clear language and, therefore, undermines democracy, legal certainty and the care and attention shown by the CFR's draftsmen in choosing how to express themselves. Moreover, the expansive interpretation of art 51 CFR by the ECJ may ultimately vest the Court with the truly awesome power of deciding whether *all* Member State laws respect fundamental rights.

Case Notes and Recent Developments

Originalism Enabled? The Role of Historical Records in Constitutional Adjudication

---

Of all of the reasons why the doctrine of originalism has never commanded consistent or authoritative support in Ireland, it is perhaps instructive that the first of those identified by the authors of *JM Kelly: The Irish Constitution* was one based on pragmatism rather than principle – namely, the unavailability of relevant recordings of the drafters' original intent. This paucity of primary evidence contrasted with the position in the United States where, of course, originalism has had a substantial impact on both academic and judicial discourse.

> [D]ocumentary material which might assist with an objective assessment of the framers' intentions has hitherto not generally been available. Unlike the United States – where the courts have available to them the detailed workings of the Constitutional Convention of 1787 – the drafting of the 1937 Constitution took place in secret and the subsequent Dáil debates, frequently marred by partisan squabbling, often do not reveal the thinking of the drafters.[1]

This practical constraint on originalist analysis in Ireland meant, however, that the question of its normative or constitutional appropriateness was left domestically unaddressed. Aside from the occasional academic discussion of the doctrine,[2] judicial interest in the esoteric question of how the courts might deal with such material was limited by the issue's practical irrelevance.

The publication last year by the Royal Irish Academy of the superb *The Origins of the Irish Constitution 1928–1941*[3] has, however, made the irrelevant relevant. The book provides a comprehensive and scholarly account of the genesis of the 1937 text, which includes much fresh and fascinating information about the external influences and internal deliberations that shaped the drafting process. The archival research behind the publication has brought a range of documents to public attention for the first time, in a manner that will undoubtedly facilitate further academic exploration of many previously unappreciated features of Ireland's constitutional history.

---

1. Gerard Hogan and Gerry Whyte, *JM Kelly: The Irish Constitution* (4th edn, LexisNexis Butterworths 2003) 29.
2. Adrian Twomey, 'Bork's Originalism: Reconciling Judicial Constitutional Interpretation with the Rule of Law' (1996) 14 ILT 278.
3. Gerard Hogan, *The Origins of the Irish Constitution 1928–1941* (Royal Irish Academy 2012). This is referred to as '*Origins*' in the remainder of the piece.

All of this is unquestionably of substantial academic and public value. A distinct question arises, however, as to whether this scholarship should also be of interest for our courts. In the short time since its publication, the book has already been cited on two occasions in the Supreme Court.[4] Yet, there has been little, if any, discussion thus far of whether this type of documentation is or should be relevant to contemporary constitutional adjudication.

Given the extensive scholarship on originalism that exists in the US, it is beyond a comment piece such as this to provide a definitive analysis of whether originalism – in any or all of its myriad guises – can or should ever be relevant to Irish constitutional law. What this short piece seeks to suggest, however, is that the use of contemporary historical records as an interpretive aid in constitutional litigation raises specific issues from both a practical and conceptual point of view. This type of documentation is of a different character to that to which the Irish courts have previously had regard, with the consequence that its use could have implications for the conduct and content of future constitutional litigation. The purpose of this piece, therefore, is to identify the issues the courts should take into account before endorsing the use of this sort of historical documentation as an appropriate source of constitutional meaning.

Why Originalism?

The first and perhaps most fundamental issue to consider is how access to documentation relevant to the drafting of the Constitution might assist the courts in their interpretation of the Constitution. The basic aim of interpretation is to ascertain or extract meaning from the words that appear in the text itself. It is a truism of legal commentary that the search for meaning is an imprecise and potentially unreliable process that is made more difficult in the constitutional context by the open-textured character of the Constitution's provisions. 'The meaning of many of the provisions of the Constitution are indeterminate and the task of the interpreter is to elicit more precise criteria by which these principles can be understood.'[5]

The development of such uniform criteria or methodologies is intended to reduce the scope for inconsistency or unpredictability by ensuring that the interpretive task is approached in the same way and on the basis of the same principles. Originalism ostensibly assists in that process by identifying the intentions of the framers in crafting the constitutional text. 'When the originalist encounters an ambiguity in the text he turns to an external source for guidance. That source, obviously enough, is the original intention of the framers.'[6] Originalism – to the extent that it represents a single school of thought – tends to trust in the accessibility and interpretive legitimacy of this 'original intention'. 'Although the originalist position itself covers a variety of views, the core tenet of originalism... holds that the principal task of judges called upon to interpret

4. *Pringle v Ireland* [2012] IESC 47; *McGowan v Labour Court* [2013] IESC 21.
5. Aileen Kavanagh, 'The Quest for Legitimacy in Constitutional Interpretation' (1997) Ir Jur 195–216.
6. Twomey, 'Bork's Originalism', 281.

the Constitution is to ascertain and give effect to the original intentions of the framers and ratifiers of the Constitution.[7] The presumed coherence of these individuals' original intentions means that they should, in theory, provide a stable and consistent source of determinate guidance. This imparts a technical or instrumental value to originalism.

In addition, the assumed consistency of this guidance, when combined with the inherent authorial legitimacy of the framers, has led advocates of originalism to claim a normative or democratic value for the theory. This is based on the assertion that it reduces or avoids the scope for judges to exploit the ambiguity of the text in order to give effect to their own subjective or otherwise illegitimate views. As Bork summarised it, 'only the approach of original understanding meets the criteria that any theory of constitutional adjudication must meet in order to possess democratic legitimacy'.[8]

This account of originalism as a reliable and legitimate source of guidance is deceptively simple. Gardner's core tenet of originalism – that judges should ascertain and give effect to the original intentions of the framers and ratifiers of the Constitution – belies the complex and multi-stage nature of that exercise. Even leaving aside the broader question of why the courts should take account of such views, Gardner's determinedly neutral summary of the originalist process implicitly identifies areas of ambiguity and doubt.

Is there a difference, for example, between framers and ratifiers? Should the courts look to one or both as a legitimate source of guidance? If so, which of their views should carry more weight in cases of conflict or inconsistency?

The definition also draws attention to the fact that constitutional litigation involves both the identification of meaning and the application of that meaning to a specific set of circumstances. Is the originalist enquiry a search for their understanding of the word in question? Or of how it would have applied at the time of enactment? Is it a matter of identifying meaning? Or identifying intent? Or even identifying how the framers (or ratifiers) would have decided the case at hand?

And what of the formulation's pregnant claim that judges 'should' give effect to the framers views? Does that apply only in cases of ambiguity or does it involve a more wide-ranging assertion of normative might? Is original intention one[9] of many permissible methodologies, first above all others or, as some have suggested, the only[10] legitimate means of identifying constitutional meaning?

---

7. James A Gardner, 'The Positivist Foundations of Originalism: An Account and Critique' (1991) 71 BU L Rev 1, 3.
8. Robert H Bork, *The Tempting of America: The Political Seduction of the Law* (Free Press 1997) 143.
9. For example, see David A Strauss, 'Common Law Constitutional Interpretation' (1996) 63 U Chi L Rev 877, where he opined at 881 that 'virtually everyone agrees that the specific intentions of the Framers count for something'.
10. Or, as some would have it, 'not simply one method of interpretation among many – it is the only method that is suited to discovering the actual meaning of the relevant text'. Gary Lawson, 'The Rise and Rise of the Administrative State' (1994) 107 Harv L Rev 1231, 1250.

What Originalism?

The practical complexity of actually applying originalism is well illustrated by the fractured state of the American scholarship. Berman, in an admittedly sceptical summary of the state of the field, suggested that there are now at least 72 flavours of originalist thought.[11] Many of the more recent models of originalism – so-called 'new new originalism' – scarcely seem like originalism at all.[12] Much of the current focus of this US scholarship is on a distinction drawn by Balkin,[13] amongst others, between interpretation-as-ascertainment and interpretation-as-construction.

> Balkin, Barnett, Lawrence Solum, and Whittington have all noted that because the objective meaning of the constitutional text often is vague or 'underdetermined', originalism, which is a theory only of interpretation, simply cannot produce answers to many questions of constitutional law. In such cases, these theorists have argued, the questions can be resolved only by construction, which is 'outside the domain of originalism' and necessarily requires an act of creativity beyond interpretation.[14]

Save to the extent that this development suggests an implicit rejection[15] of the traditional notion of originalism as a search for semantic meaning, this distinction is peripheral to the question here of whether the Irish courts ought to have regard to *Origins*' new research. This reflects the fact that the material in *Origins* seems more relevant to 'interpretation-as-ascertainment' than 'interpretation-as-construction'. Their value is precisely that they shed light on the discussions that occurred within the government during the years leading up to the enactment of the Constitution.

The documentation contained within the book includes various drafts of the text, some with handwritten annotations, departmental memoranda, submissions from non-governmental bodies such as religious organisations, and minutes of relevant meetings. These documents are mainly, if not wholly, concerned with meaning – with the text of certain provisions or articles, with

---

11. Mitchell N Berman, 'Originalism is Bunk' (2009) 84 NYU L Rev 1, 14–15.
12. Peter Smith has argued that 'new new originalism is, at least in practice, not meaningfully different from non-originalism'. Peter J Smith, 'How Different Are Originalism and Non-Originalism?' (2011) 62 Hastings LJ 707, 721.
13. Jack M Balkin, *Living Originalism* (Harvard University Press 2011).
14. Smith, 'How Different?', 716–17, citing Keith E Whittington, 'Constitutional Interpretation: Textual Meaning, Original Intent, and Judicial Review' (1999) 7, 5–14; Jack M Balkin, 'Framework Originalism and the Living Constitution' (2009) 103 Nw U L Rev 549, 553; Randy E Barnett, 'Trumping Precedent with Original Meaning: Not as Radical as It Sounds' (2005) 22 Const Comment 257, 264–65; Lawrence B Solum, '*District of Columbia v Heller* and Originalism' (2009) 103 Nw U L Rev 923, 974.
15. Which explains in part why there is a controversy about whether this is originalism at all. More traditional originalists would not necessarily accept this distinction or the implication identified here.

how they might be interpreted by the courts, and with what that would mean in practice for the future operation of government. This type of material seems most pertinent to more traditional conceptions of originalism as an enquiry into what the drafters were actually thinking when undertaking their work. It is these with which the remainder of this piece is concerned.

Origins and Originalism

From this perspective, the material published in *Origins* might be thought to assist the courts in identifying how the constitutional text was intended to be interpreted, thereby avoiding the unreliability or subjectivity that might otherwise be involved in construing its ambiguous terms. Even a short examination of *Origins* indicates, however, that it does not – and does not purport to – provide an objective record of the drafters' intent.

First of all, the book is the product of an editorial process that inescapably involves subjective decisions about structure, content, analysis, inclusion or exclusion. Any such process cannot but be influenced by the perceptions or preoccupations of contemporary minds. Material or comments that may have seemed unimportant to the framers can seem misleadingly portentous with the hindsight of several decades of jurisprudential developments. The very act of including, excluding or arranging material will always involve the potential juxtaposition of records with other documents or editorial comments in a way that may not have been originally intended. That these editorial decisions are likely to appear reasonable to modern readers carries with it the additional danger that today's determination of original meaning may reflect not the primary material but this secondary assessment and presentation of it.

Secondly, the process is inevitably incomplete. The work's preface records that '[t]he original version of this work… was deemed to be simply too large for publication', with the result that it was 'adapt[ed]' and 'judicious[ly] edit[ed]' by Professor Ronan Fanning.[16] That the final version excludes material that was, at one point, thought to be relevant confirms that the work provides only select guidance to parts of the historical record. Furthermore, that historical record may itself be incomplete. It is notable, for example, that the archives provide little concrete evidence about the intended scope of art 40.3.1. The eventual provisions of the Article appear to have originated in a handwritten amendment by John Hearne, which seems to have been unaccompanied by any further comment or explanation. As Hogan observes:

> This re-casting of the language was of some importance and perhaps even Hearne probably did not then appreciate its potential significance. It is particularly

16. Thereby introducing another set of personal and disciplinary values into the editorial process.

> unfortunate that there appears to have been no memorandum prepared by him which sought to explain the objectives of this provision.[17]

That this section goes on to draw partial conclusions – about what, it will be recalled, remains one of the most central and contentious questions in Irish constitutional law – from the fact that a version provided to de Valera included an extended dictionary definition of the term 'vindicate' underscores both the points being made here.

It is a tribute to the disciplinary rigour of the author that the analysis contained in *Origins* is frequently accompanied by a specific caveat about the incomplete or indeterminate character of the archival records. Indeed, the commentary itself often sounds a cautiously self-critical note, specifically drawing the reader's attention to situations where the author feels a conclusion may risk over-emphasising the significance of a particular phrase or document. The point being made, however, is not that there are difficulties with *Origins* itself – on the contrary, it is one of those rare and impressive works of scholarship that is likely to have a genuinely transformational impact on its academic field. The point is that it is in the nature of archival research, no matter how carefully undertaken, that it cannot plausibly provide the complete or objective guidance a strict belief in originalism would demand. Where the documentary record is ambiguous or incomplete, the conclusions drawn from it must inevitably be contingent, contentious or susceptible to analytical over-reach.

The Role of Historical Research in Constitutional Adjudication

The main issue raised by these considerations concerns the role and status of historical research and of legal-historical analysis in constitutional adjudication. The identification, collation and interpretation of documentary records in order to better comprehend the views and attitudes of individuals is, as Justice Scalia conceded, 'a task sometimes better suited to the historian than the lawyer'.[18] Yet as Tushnet comments, '[w]here the originalist seeks certainty and clarity, the historian finds ambiguity'.[19] As is the cases with most academic disciplines, historians may disagree about the methodologies used, the factors taken or not taken into account, the frame of reference applied, and the conclusions drawn.

This raises obvious concerns, however, about the capacity or willingness of the courts to engage with and adjudicate upon what are essentially debates about historical methodologies. If the material contained in *Origins* is considered to be relevant to the court's interpretive task, so logically must be any other archival material from the period that might explain, to some degree, the sentiments of the various participants in the drafting process. Yet, this would

17. *Origins*, 354.
18. Antonin Scalia, 'Originalism: The Lesser Evil' (1989) 57 U Cin L Rev 849, 857.
19. Mark Tushnet, *Red, White and Blue: A Critical Analysis of Constitutional Law* (Harvard University Press 1988) 36.

seem to raise the prospect of historians fulfilling a role similar to that formerly performed by religious theorists in cases involving the potential interpretation or application of natural law.[20] It would also seem to suggest that archival research and historical analysis should form part of a lawyer's preparation for a constitutional case. Just as the courts ultimately deprecated the relevance (and presumably also the cost) of allowing religious theorists give evidence about the correct meaning of the Constitution, similar concerns might be expressed about any analogous efforts to subordinate the courts' interpretive task to the views or disciplinary vagaries of historians. It is doubtful whether courtroom arguments about the indeterminacy of the constitutional text should be replaced by arguments about the indeterminacy of historical methodologies or analyses.[21]

Disputes could also arise regarding the type and category of material to which the courts might legitimately have regard. The documents contained in *Origins* are, by and large, connected with the official drafting process. As material that was and remained unpublished for several decades, it seems clear that it was not created in the contemplation that it would ultimately be used by the courts as an interpretive aid. This is evidenced by its incomplete and sometimes ambiguous character. Its value, accordingly, seems to derive not from its content *per se* but from the insights it provides into the mindset, attitudes and opinions of those involved in the drafting. Yet, if that is the case, there does not appear to be any particular reason to deny interpretive value to other, less-official documentation. The private papers or correspondence of any of the individuals might also contain information about their personal motivations or beliefs during the relevant period. Is there any reason to assume that this would be any less illustrative than, for example, the ambiguous inscription by de Valera of 'United States, Czechoslovakia, Portugal' on the cover of a draft brought with him to Zurich?[22]

This not only underlines again concerns about the potential cost of normalising wide-ranging archival research but also draws attention to the problem

20. *McGee v AG* [1974] IR 284, and see especially the critical comments of Walsh J, 318.
21. That does not deny that there may be situations where historical records may be determinate. However, it should be borne in mind that this piece is primarily concerned with the type of records contained in *Origins*, and with the potential use of such material as evidence of what may have been the intention or understanding of those individuals. Such material is always likely to leave some scope for contestation. This is because the records were not designed to provide such evidence and, as such, could not be said to put the matter beyond doubt. More fundamentally, the intention or understanding of individuals is essentially unknowable, given the possibility that even a clear statement of intention may reflect political calculation rather than personal conviction. This may leave open scope for historians to disagree about how reliable any one document or set of documents might be as evidence of a subjectively held belief.
22. *Origins*, 279, fn 38.

of post-originalist research. This occurs where new documents or analysis undermine the basis upon which a previous court adopted an interpretation of the Constitution by applying originalist techniques. As Emil Kleinhaus has pointed out, this has arisen on several occasions in the US, not least because the initial judicial determination thereby incentivises those interested in or opposed to the outcome to seek out contradictory historical data.

> Despite the best efforts of historians to reach decisive historical conclusions, the most plausible interpretation of a historical text changes over time. Historians' understanding of the Constitution and its amendments develops as they interpret and synthesize documentary evidence. Further, since research about particular historical questions intensifies after Justices 'declare' history, historical conclusions that are incorporated into the law can be particularly vulnerable. To the extent that Justices rely on historians when they declare history, Justices' conception of the document's original meaning must change along with historians'. Moreover, to the extent that Justices engage in independent historical inquiries, their conception of the document's original meaning can change even more dramatically as they encounter previously overlooked documents or compelling secondary interpretations of those documents... Ultimately, the more Justices use historical research as a decisive interpretative tool, the more substantial the body of law that one scholar has called the 'common law of history' becomes, and the more vulnerable the Court itself becomes to extralegal historical criticism.[23]

Once again, the claimed consistency of originalist analysis seems, on closer scrutiny, exaggerated, if not wholly misconceived.

The Case for Originalism?

If the content and analysis of historical records cannot supply the consistency or neutrality that is sometimes claimed, what remains of the case for originalism? The technical or instrumental case for an originalism based on contemporary documents contended, it will be recalled, that it could assist the courts by reducing ambiguity or indeterminacy. For all of the reasons outlined above – the hermeneutic bias of modern analysis, the inevitably incomplete nature of the documentary record, the editorial and analytical subjectivity of any attempt to make sense of such an array of material – caution would seem to be required in employing any such material as an interpretive guide to the meaning of the constitutional text.

Yet the normative or democratic claims for originalism also seem questionable in the Irish context. It seems reasonable to suggest that one of the reasons why this material provides such uncertain interpretive guidance is because it was never intended to be used in this way. The aim of the drafting process is to reduce the intentions of the rule-creators to concrete terms so that the law, and those subject

23. Emil A Kleinhaus, 'History as Precedent: The Post-Originalist Problem in Constitutional Law' (2000) 110 Yale LJ 121, 123–124.

to it, are governed by concrete terms rather than undeveloped thoughts. The process of identifying and articulating agreed legal terms secures the publicity and generality that are important components of the rule of law. The point of drafting is to reduce the potential influence of the sort of unannounced subjectivity that the material in *Origins* arguably reveals.

This is particularly true with a constitution that was ratified by the public. Jefferson's well-known objection to the intergenerational application of constitutional provisions was that 'the earth belongs... to the living'.[24] Yet, to look for the meaning of a publicly endorsed provision in the confidential discussions of the drafters goes further in conferring interpretative status, from the public's point of view, on neither the living nor the dead. Instead, the public's constitution remains, in part, the property of the dead drafter. This would be inconsistent with at least one account of originalism as consent-based positivism:

> For the originalist, ultimate authority in our society is lodged in the people. The Constitution is the vehicle by which the people consent to the creation of a government and spell out its various powers and the limitations on those powers. The Constitution thus creates a government whose officials are 'the servants of the people.' Precisely because they are servants whose power to bind the people is confined to 'laws which are made pursuant to and in accord with the Constitution's command,' government officials such as judges are powerless to deviate from the terms of 'popular consent' expressed in the Constitution. Any such deviations, even if benignly motivated, are 'usurpations' by the agents of the sovereign people.[25]

Furthermore, it would also presumably be inconsistent with the intentions of the drafters themselves. There is an evident peculiarity in adopting an approach that treats the drafters' original intentions as having at least persuasive interpretive value but simultaneously does so by reference to documents that they themselves kept confidential.

For these reasons, originalists in America have tended in recent decades to downplay the status or influence of the framers' views in preference to the opinions or attitudes of the public at the time. '[M]any self-described originalists have shifted their allegiance from original intent to original public meaning',[26] leading them to 'distinguish between three types of originalism: framers' intent originalism, ratifiers' understanding originalism, and original public meaning originalism'.[27] It is this latter form that has become most influential, reflecting perhaps the difficulty

24. Letter by Thomas Jefferson to James Madison, 6 September 1789.
25. Gardner, 'Positivist Foundations', 7–8, citing Rehnquist, 'The Notion of a Living Constitution' (1976) 54 Tex L Rev 693, 695–96; R Berger, 'Neutral Principles and Some First Amendment Problems' (1971) 47 Indiana LJ 1, 4; Meese, 'Toward a Jurisprudence of Original Intent' (1988) 11 Harv J L and Public Policy 5.
26. Berman, 'Originalism is Bunk', 4.
27. ibid 9.

for originalists in asserting its superior democratic credentials while deriving content from the presumptive positions of an historical elite.

This also means, however, that this approach encourages reliance on a wider range of historical materials. If the attitudes of the many are the criteria of interpretive relevance, there is no reason to confining the courts' examination to documents associated with the few. This, unsurprisingly, exacerbates the problems of indeterminacy and unreliability identified above.

> 'Original public meaning' can become a kind of black hole… [W]hat can happen is that the proponent of 'original public meaning' disappears into the archives, assembles some evidence from the founding period, and announces that he has discovered the 'original public meaning' without ever explaining how, exactly, one figures out what that is.[28]

In the context of the discussion here, it seems questionable whether *Origins* could plausibly be used as evidence of the original public meaning of the 1937 text. The Irish courts have previously had regard to certain historical factors when interpreting certain provisions of the Constitution. These have tended to be certain legal or institutional procedures with which it might be assumed people were familiar.[29] That is not the case with much of the material or deliberations contained in *Origins*. That work suggests, for example, that the drafters were substantially influenced by other European constitutions of the era, especially that of Weimar Germany. It seems unrealistic, however, to infer from that a wider comparative sophistication on the part of the public as a whole.

More generally, to rely on individual documents produced by a select number of individuals as part of an ongoing and evolving process of drafting as evidence of collective intention would risk engaging in the sort of errors identified by McGuinness J in *Crilly v Farrington*:

> The process of legislation by the Oireachtas is essentially collective. It is the Oireachtas *as a whole* which legislates. It would in my view be a misleading oversimplification of this process to rely, in interpreting a statute, on ministerial statements alone. Particularly in the case of more complex statutes, which pass through a lengthy committee stage, contributions come from all sides of both Houses of the Oireachtas. The statute as finally enacted may well have been extensively amended and may differ crucially from the bill as introduced by the Minister's initial introductory statement at the second stage. For the courts to rely on ministerial statements in interpreting statutes would not, therefore, reflect the will of the Oireachtas as a whole.[30]

---

28. David Strauss, 'Can Originalism Be Saved?' (2012) 92 BU L Rev 1161, 1166.
29. See, for example, the use of historical circumstances in *Sinnott v Minister for Education* [2001] 2 IR 545 or *Maguire v Ardagh* [2002] IR 385. The key point of distinction here is that these authorities relied on historical material as evidence of institutional fact. This then provided a background.
30. [2001] 3 IR 251, 302. Original emphasis.

The concern over the reliability of inferring collective intention from individual comments obviously applies with even greater force when dealing with the larger and more diverse concept of 'public' meaning.

Broadly speaking, the analogy with the treatment of parliamentary debates is instructive. The Supreme Court held in *Crilly* that ministerial statements would rarely be admitted as evidence of legislative intent. To do so would, in the Court's view, be costly, potentially misleading and contrary to the core 'principle of objective intent [that is] at the root of the role of the courts in interpreting statutes'.[31] To these concerns might be added, in the constitutional context, the democratic dubiousness of construing the popular will as expressed in documents of which the public were generally unaware. If it is impermissible to use parliamentary debates that take place in public as evidence of objective intent, it would seem highly illogical to treat confidential documents as indicative of the public's original meaning.

Conclusion

The consequence of this, however, is that it is unclear what, if any, guidance secret historical records can or should provide to the courts' interpretation of the 1937 Constitution. *Origins*, like the future scholarship it seems likely to encourage, provides an academically valuable insight into an important episode of Ireland's legal history. That does not mean, however, that archival research should now become a feature of the quite different exercise of constitutional adjudication. It seems unreliable for confidential documents to be used as evidence of the public's original intent. Yet, the obvious alternative use of it as evidence of the drafter's internal deliberations is open to objection on both technical and normative grounds. From a technical perspective, it is interesting but incomplete and potentially unreliable. From a normative perspective, it is democratically suspect and internally incoherent.

Furthermore, even if it could be taken as a consistent and objective record of the drafters' original intent, this would still leave unresolved various issues concerning the precise status of intent as a source of constitutional meaning. Would it be relevant, for example, to the meaning of the term at issue or to its application to the case at hand? Should the courts look to it at the first stage of interpreting meaning or at the second stage of applying that meaning to the facts? And what if the implications of an originalist analysis differ to those produced by an alternative interpretive approach? These are the kinds of issues the courts would have to address as part of any acceptance of archival records as an interpretive guide.

What this shows is that evidence about what the drafters may have intended is not simply an alternative or value-neutral source of information. Its use involves particular choices about the basic character of the Constitution, the

31. [2001] 3 IR 251, 296 per Murray J.

respective status of the drafters and ratifiers of the text, and the relevance of public knowledge or deliberation in constitutional interpretation. These choices are not only contentious but may also have an effect on the direction and outcome of constitutional litigation. It is important, therefore, that they are – at the very least – taken with full consideration of these issues. The risk is that the availability and erudition of the research in *Origins* may lead the courts to repeatedly invoke it without any detailed examination of the potential long-term implications of that practice, particularly in terms of encouraging alternative archival research, analysis or argumentation on original intention as an aspect of constitutional litigation. The complex and controversial nature of the US debates should, by themselves, serve as a warning against any unconscious incorporation of original intention by the back door.

EOIN CAROLAN*

Recent Developments in the Right of the Person in Article 40.3: *Fleming v Ireland* and the Spectre of Unenumerated Rights

---

An interesting recent development in constitutional rights jurisprudence has been the resurrection of a constitutional provision that has rarely been invoked by the courts. The right of the person[1] is protected in art 40.3.2°. The Article reads:

> The State shall, in particular, by its laws protect as best it may from unjust attack and, in the case of injustice done, vindicate the life, person, good name, and property rights of every citizen.

Hogan J has rescued the right of the person from obscurity, and given it a broad meaning, raising the possibility that the provision could lead to a significant and novel development in the protection of personal rights under the Constitution. I wish to examine this in Part 1 of this note.

---

* Lecturer, University College Dublin.

1. It is difficult to title this right succinctly. The 'right to the protection of the person' is used by Hogan and Whyte. Gerard Hogan and Gerry Whyte, *JM Kelly: The Irish Constitution* (4th edn, Butterworths 2004) 1403. I will use 'the right of the person', although this is still cumbersome.

However, this new development raises a fundamental question for the Irish constitutional order: What is the scope for, and the legitimacy of, judicial innovation and creativity in interpreting constitutional rights after the demise of the unenumerated rights doctrine? At its broadest, in the High Court judgment in *Fleming v Ireland*,[2] the right of the person seemed closely to resemble aspects of that doctrine. However, after the Supreme Court appeal in that case,[3] this broadest reading seems to have been circumscribed. This will be discussed in Part 2.

The question then becomes: What of the rest of the jurisprudence on the right of the person, which is not as expansive? Can some novel readings of constitutional rights avoid the allegations of illegitimacy that doomed unenumerated rights? In Part 3, I tentatively suggest that the right of the person may be a legitimate and interesting development in the enforcement of constitutional rights, which has the potential to expand the reach of the Constitution into areas where it has had less influence than it should have, while distinguishing itself from unenumerated rights, and avoiding the problems suffered by that doctrine.

The Meaning of the Right of the Person

Unclear Origins and Limited Judicial Invocation

The right of the person appeared, as if from nowhere, in the February 1937 draft of the Constitution.[4] It is not immediately clear what meaning the right was intended to have by those who drafted the Constitution. Hogan reproduces, in his recent work on the origins of the document, a version of the February 1937 draft with handwritten notations by de Valera.[5] The right of the person is underlined; there is a small question mark drawn beside it.

Unlike many of the rights provisions of arts 40–44, this right does not seem to have any direct inspiration from a papal encyclical.[6] Nor do we know the

---

2. [2013] IEHC 2.
3. [2013] IESC 19.
4. Gerard Hogan, *Origins of the Irish Constitution 1928–41* (RIA 2012) 310, 276–78. Numbered art 38.2.2°, it read: 'The State shall, in particular, protect, as best it may, from unjust attack, and, in the case of injustice done, vindicate the person, life, good, name and property rights of every citizen.'
5. Hogan, *Origins*, 318; UCDA, P 150/2387. Hogan at 277 identifies this as the earliest known version of what would become art 40.3.2°.
6. ibid 278–9. Recent scholarship suggests that the inclusion of human dignity in the Preamble of the Constitution may be attributable to *Divini Redemptoris*, an encyclical of Pope Pius XI, which also stressed importance of human personality rights as a response to the threat of communism. Samuel Moyn, 'The Secret History of Constitutional Dignity', 18–19 <http://ssrn.com/abstract=2159248> accessed 10 April 2013. However, it is not clear that the right of person was inspired by this sudden (and, according to Moyn, largely unforeseen) shift in Catholic thought, as

history of its drafting; recent research on the drafting of the Constitution has uncovered no memorandum or other correspondence to shed light on the inspiration behind art 40.3.2.[7] Further historical research, or analysis of the meaning of personhood in an international human rights context, might shed some light on possible meanings of the right. For the moment, however, we are in the dark.

Perhaps because of this ambiguity, the right of the person in art 40.3.2° has had little impact on the jurisprudence of the Irish courts. The clause could have been an alternative source of some of the unenumerated rights recognised under art 40.3, such as the right of bodily integrity[8] and the right against torture.[9] Instead, there have been few cases where the right has been invoked. Gavan Duffy J cited it in *State (Burke) v Lennon*,[10] striking down the internment provisions of the Offences Against the State Act. It was relied on to bolster a decision on the scope of the High Court's wardship jurisdiction in lunacy cases.[11] Denham J in dissent in *DG v Eastern Health Board*[12] argued that detention in a penal institution of someone not convicted or charged with a crime was a violation of, *inter alia*, the right of the person. None of these cases considered the meaning of the provision in any significant way.

The underdevelopment of this textual right left it open for judicial interpretation and reinvigoration. Hogan J has taken this opportunity in a series of recent cases.

The Physical Person

The right of the person has been held to protect the physical person – one's body. In *A v Refugee Appeals Tribunal*,[13] Hogan J relied on the right of the person to quash a decision of the Refugee Appeals Tribunal, which had not sufficiently regarded the risk that *A*, a minor, would be subject to female genital mutilation if she were deported to Nigeria.

---

the inclusion of this right seems to predate by a short period the publication of the encyclical on 19 March 1937. The lack of documentation on the drafting of art 40.3 renders it impossible to know whether or not this played a role.

7. Hogan, *Origins*, 354.
8. *Ryan v Attorney General* [1965] IR 294. This is suggested by Aileen Kavanagh, 'Natural Law, Christian Values, and the Ideal of Justice' (2012) 48 Irish Jurist 71,74.
9. *State (C) v Frawley* [1976] IR 365. Hogan and Whyte, *JM Kelly*, 1403, go further, suggesting it could have substituted for many rights that protect those 'normal dimensions which human existence in society entails'.
10. [1940] IR 136.
11. *Re D and the Midland Health Board* [1987] IR 499. See Hogan and Whyte, *JM Kelly*, 1403–4.
12. [1997] 3 IR 511, 533–35.
13. [2011] IEHC 373.

> The subjection of any female to FGM is an open assault on her person, the very right which by Article 40.3.2 of the Constitution the State expressly undertakes to defend and vindicate in so far as it is practicable to do so.[14]

The Tribunal had not had sufficient regard to this right, and its decision was quashed.[15]

The right was similarly invoked to protect physical wellbeing in *H v HSE*, where Hogan J ordered the detention of a disturbed young man in St Patrick's Institution not for any punitive reason, but for his own safety and welfare.[16] In another instance, it was used to justify the inherent power of the High Court to make an order for a blood transfusion to save the life of a child whose Jehovah's Witness parents objected to the transfusion on religious grounds.[17] Hogan J also cited the right in denying immediate release to an art 40.4 applicant whose detention in the Central Mental Hospital had been found to be unlawful, but whose severe paranoid schizophrenia would have presented 'a very serious threat to himself, identifiable individuals and to the general public were he to be released from custody'.[18]

The protection of physical integrity is surely the very least that this right could mean, though its application to particular cases could be a matter of dispute, and it is surely subject to limitation. It is significant that Hogan J chose to rely on the right of the person in these cases, as opposed to bodily integrity. Despite its lack of textual basis, the right to bodily integrity has a better pedigree in Irish constitutional law, having been recognised 50 years ago in one of the most famous Irish constitutional cases.[19] Hogan J seemingly wished to ground these rights claims in the text of art 40.3 rather than on an unenumerated right. It is unclear from these cases whether the right of the person protects the physical person more extensively than bodily integrity does.

Mental Integrity and Human Personality

The protection of the person, in Hogan J's view, goes well beyond the body or physical person; it includes mental and psychological integrity as well. In *Kinsella v Governor of Mountjoy Prison*,[20] Wayne Kinsella challenged, under art 40.4, the legality of his detention in Mountjoy Prison, where he was awaiting trail for murder. Mr Kinsella's life was in danger amongst the general prison

---

14. ibid [15].
15. ibid [20].
16. [2011] IEHC 297.
17. *Temple St v D* [2011] IEHC 1 [38].
18. *FX v Clinical Director of the Central Mental Hospital* [2012] IEHC 272 [2]. Hogan J previously found his detention unlawful; [2012] IEHC 271.
19. *Ryan v Attorney General* [1965] IR 294.
20. [2011] IEHC 235.

population. To protect him, the prison authorities kept him for 11 days in solitary confinement in an unfurnished padded cell that was used to observe those at risk of self-harm. He had no reading material, no radio or television, and no toilet facilities beyond a cardboard box. His only contact with the outside world was one six-minute phone call per day.

Even though this detention was necessary for Mr Kinsella's welfare, Hogan J said that these conditions violated his constitutional rights.

> [I]t is the State's duty to protect and vindicate the person of Mr. Kinsella which is principally engaged here… [I]t is undeniable that detention in a padded cell of this kind involves a form of sensory deprivation in that the prisoner is denied the opportunity of any meaningful interaction with his human faculties of sight, sound and speech – an interaction that is vital if the integrity of the human personality is to be maintained…
>
> By solemnly committing the State to protecting the person, Article 40.3.2 protects not simply the integrity of the human body, but also the integrity of the human mind and personality… [O]ne does not need to be a psychologist to envisage the mental anguish which would be entailed by a more or less permanent lock-up under such conditions for an eleven day period. Nor, for that matter, does one need to be a psychiatrist to recognise that extended detention over weeks under such conditions could expose the prisoner to the risk of psychiatric disturbance.[21]

Mr Kinsella's detention violated the basic minimum standards needed for the protection of his person, which included his mental fortitude.[22]

In *Sullivan v Boylan (No 1)*,[23] Ms Sullivan had been subject to threats and intimidation by a debt collector, Mr McCartan, which included repeated phone calls, emails, and text messages, and the besetting of her home. Hogan J ordered an injunction restraining him from this conduct, as it violated two constitutional rights – art 40.5's inviolability of the dwelling, and art 40.3.2°'s protection of the person:

> [I]t requires little imagination to visualise the acute mental distress which Ms. Sullivan suffered as a result of this this [sic] outrageous conduct. The citizen's right to the security of his or her person necessarily implies that the subjection by unlawful means of any person to what would objectively be regarded as acute mental distress must be regarded as amounting in itself to a breach of Article 40.3.2.[24]

---

21. ibid [8]–[9].
22. As in *FX v Clinical Director*, Hogan J decided to wait to see if the prison could improve conditions rather than insisting on immediate release. They found him a place in Cloverhill the next day.
23. [2012] IEHC 389.
24. ibid [23].

In a later judgment, he awarded damages against Mr McCartan for breach of these constitutional rights.[25]

There have been other instances where mental integrity was highlighted as an aspect of the right.[26] In *DF v Garda Commissioner*,[27] Hogan J suggested it would be unnecessary to seek an ECHR Act remedy for inhuman and degrading treatment, which includes protection for both mind and body, 'since the express constitutional protection of the person necessarily precludes treatment of this sort'.[28]

Mental integrity could be interpreted in a fairly narrow way: as a negative entitlement, preventing treatment that would jeopardise the psychological well-being of individuals, as in *Kinsella* and *Sullivan*. But it is apparent that this could be a broad protection: once meaningful interaction with human faculties is mentioned, as it was in *Kinsella*, one can conceive of this right as an entitlement to act in any way that is, in the view of a judge, essential for self-actualisation or human flourishing. One judgment in particular took this broad view of the right.

Fleming v Ireland

The broadest invocation of the right of the person was by the High Court in *Fleming v Ireland*.[29] This judgment went far beyond *Kinsella*, suggesting a sweeping constitutional protection of personal autonomy in decision-making. Marie Fleming claimed that a statute preventing assisted suicide was an unconstitutional violation of her rights as a terminally ill individual whose condition made her unable to take her own life without the assistance of another party. Hogan J was a member of the three-judge Divisional High Court; Kearns P gave the judgment of the Court.

> At the heart of the plaintiff's case is her contention that inasmuch as Article 40.3.2 of the Constitution protects her 'person', this also necessarily embraces decisions concerning her personal welfare, including medical treatment. It is, of course, perfectly clear that the protection of personal autonomy in matters of this kind is a core constitutional value.[30]

The Court found that the decision that Ms Fleming wished to take, being central to her personal welfare, was '*in principle* engaged by the right to personal autonomy which lies at the core of the protection of the person by Article 40.3.2'.[31] The Court held that this claim was 'not really properly to be regarded as either an implied constitutional right' but 'rather a facet of that personal

---

25. *Sullivan v Boylan (No 2)* [2013] IEHC 104 [24].
26. It was suggested in *H v HSE*.
27. [2013] IEHC 5.
28. ibid [12].
29. [2013] IEHC 2.
30. ibid [49].
31. ibid [52].

autonomy which is necessarily protected by the express words of Article 40.3.2 with regard to the protection of the person'.[32] However, the Court ultimately held that the restriction on the right was proportionate, as public policy considerations and the State's duty to safeguard life justified the legislative prohibition.[33]

The right of the person was interpreted as in principle guaranteeing autonomy in decision-making related to personal welfare. This is, in theory, an astonishingly wide protection. Though ultimately the right was balanced against countervailing interests, the Court said that justifying a restriction of the right in this context 'requires compelling justification', suggesting it would not be easy to limit the right.[34]

As I will argue later, this invocation of the right is qualitatively different to that in *Kinsella*. The High Court went out of its way to disclaim that this was an implied right – it was rather a facet of the express right of the person. But whatever one calls it, the right of the person as interpreted in *Fleming* resembled the unenumerated rights jurisprudence of the past. A general constitutional entitlement to freedom of action in decisions relating to personal welfare would render any law interfering with such decisions *prima facie* unconstitutional,[35] greatly expanding the scope of constitutional review, and essentially embracing new unenumerated rights by way of an exceedingly broad interpretation of an express right.

The Right of the Person and Unenumerated Rights

In this section, I will recount briefly the rise and fall of unenumerated rights in Ireland; ask if the right of the person as interpreted by the High Court in *Fleming* suffers from the same problems as this doctrine; and look at how the Supreme Court judgment in that case seems to preclude this developing further.

Unenumerated Rights

The unenumerated rights doctrine was espoused in the landmark case of *Ryan v Attorney General*,[36] when Kenny J famously read the words 'in particular' in art 40.3 as guaranteeing rights beyond those expressly listed in the Constitution. Kelly described this piece of reasoning as 'logically faultless',[37] and Hogan and

32. ibid.
33. ibid [72]. *Cf* [74].
34. ibid.
35. That the law in *Fleming* was *prima facie* unconstitutional hinged on an unorthodox application of the burden of proof in proportionality analysis, the correctness of which the Supreme expressly reserved for another case; *Fleming v Ireland* [2013] IESC 19 [140]. This aside, it would render any such law at least constitutionally suspect.
36. *Ryan v Attorney General*.
37. JM Kelly, *Fundamental Rights in the Irish Law and Constitution* (Alan Figgis 1967) 42.

Whyte said it 'can hardly be questioned',[38] though it has been questioned and logically faulted.[39] It led to dozens of rights being recognised as springing from these two words, including the right to earn a livelihood,[40] the right to marital privacy,[41] and the right of access to the courts.[42] Various methods were used to identify these unenumerated rights. In *Ryan*, Kenny J used the Christian and Democratic Nature of the State to derive the right to bodily integrity, quoting from a papal encyclical.[43] Later, the rights were chiefly derived from the natural law,[44] or the human personality of the citizen.[45]

The doctrine of unenumerated rights ultimately came to be treated with suspicion for three related reasons.[46] First, the particular rights recognised often lacked textual grounding.[47] The text might suggest that other rights existed, but it did not suggest what they might be.[48] Secondly, none of the techniques used to identify these implied constitutional rights seemed to give any objective guide to what rights were contained within the Constitution. Rather, these techniques may have allowed judges to recognise rights in accordance with their own preferences. Walsh J explicitly stated that judges had to rely on their own view of prudence, justice, and charity to establish what rights the natural law protected.[49] Hogan, writing as an academic, was a critic of the doctrine on this ground, saying the doctrine 'seriously undermine[d] the important legal values of objectivity and certainty' and 'resulted in a vast – and, it must be said, unprincipled – expansion of the power of judicial review'.[50] Of course, constitutional interpretation is rarely entirely free from value judgments,[51] but

---

38. Hogan and Whyte, *JM Kelly*, 1418–19.
39. Desmond Clarke, 'Unenumerated Rights in Constitutional Law' (2011) 34 DULJ 101; Gerard Casey, 'The "Faultless" Argument for Unenumerated Rights in the Constitution' (2004) 22 ILT 246.
40. *Murphy v Stewart* [1973] IR 97.
41. *McGee v Attorney General* [1974] IR 284.
42. *Macauley v Minister for Posts and Telegraphs* [1966] IR 345.
43. He quoted *Pacem in Terris*, encyclical of Pope John XXIII; *Ryan v Attorney General*, 313–14.
44. See *State (Nicolau) v An Bord Uchtála* [1966] IR 567, 642; *McGee v Attorney General*, 289, 317; *G v An Bord Uchtála* [1980] IR 32.
45. *Norris v Attorney General* [1984] IR 36.
46. Most of these concerns were adumbrated by Kelly, *Fundamental Rights*, 41–48 shortly after *Ryan*.
47. Gerard Hogan, 'Unenumerated Personal Rights: Ryan's Case Re-Evaluated' (1990–92) 25–27 Irish Jurist 95, 114.
48. Gerard Hogan, 'Constitutional Interpretation' in Frank Litton (ed), *The Constitution of Ireland 1937–1987* (IPA 1988).
49. *McGee v Attorney General* 318–19.
50. Hogan, 'Constitutional Interpretation', 114.
51. See Aileen Kavanagh, 'The Quest for Legitimacy in Constitutional Interpretation' (1998) 32 Irish Jurist 195.

the breadth of this discretion eclipsed the discretion ordinarily afforded in interpreting ambiguous text.

Finally, the lack of objectivity in recognition of rights raised concerns of democratic legitimacy. All judicial review of legislation is anti-democratic to some degree,[52] but democratic concerns are more pronounced due to the lack of textual link or objective method of ascertaining the rights. The Constitutional Review Group raised concerns about the separation of powers: when unelected judges recognised new rights and used them to invalidate laws, the courts often set social policy, and seemed to make law, a power exclusively reserved for the Oireachtas.[53]

Due to these concerns, Hogan suggested that the courts should be slow to recongnise new rights 'unless they can point to *other* constitutional provisions (ie, quite independent of Article 40.3) to support this conclusion'.[54] Though some defended the doctrine, and the use of the natural law,[55] ultimately the Irish courts came to agree with Hogan's view.

The doctrine was never formally rejected, instead gradually falling into disuse after the Supreme Court held that the natural law, though acknowledged as superior to positive law by the Constitution, could not be interpreted and applied by judges.[56] As Kavanagh puts it, 'it seemed that the influence of the natural law on constitutional jurisprudence had been stopped in its tracks'.[57] With this 'death of the natural law'[58] came doubts that judges could recognise and enforce unenumerated rights. This scepticism was first expressed by Keane J in *O'T v B*.[59] He said that courts had not been able to establish a coherent and principled jurisprudence for the doctrine of unenumerated rights, and noted that the courts had now recognised that judges could not derive rights from a superior body of law. In light of this, he said 'some degree of judicial restraint

52. See Alexander Bickel, *The Least Dangerous Branch* (Yale University Press 1962).
53. *Report of the Constitutional Review Group* (Government Publications Office 1996) 253–54. Kavanagh, 'Natural Law', 100, notes that the courts' role 'in precipitating social change has been enormous', but suggests that the relative inactivity of the Oireachtas in these areas accentuated this.
54. Hogan, 'Constitutional Interpretation', 115.
55. Richard Humphreys, 'Interpreting Natural Rights' (1993–94) 28–30 Irish Jurist 221; Gerry Whyte, 'Natural Law and the Judiciary' [1996] ILT 8; William Duncan, 'Can Natural Law Be Used in Constitutional Interpretation?' in Bernard Treacy and Gerry Whyte (eds), *Religion, Morality and Public Policy* (Dominican 1995).
56. *Re Article 26 and the Regulation of Information (Services Outside the State for Termination of Pregnancies) Bill 1995* [1995] 1 IR 1, 38–41.
57. Kavanagh, 'Natural Law', 91.
58. See Adrian Twomey, 'The Death of Natural Law' [1995] ILT 270. *Cf* Oran Doyle, 'Legal Validity: Reflections on the Irish Constitution' (2003) 25 DULJ 56; Oran Doyle, 'Legal Positivism, Natural Law, and the Constitution' (2009) 31 DULJ 206; Kavanagh, 'Natural Law'.
59. [1998] IR 321.

is called for in identifying new rights of this nature',[60] though he accepted that rights previously recognised under the doctrine would still be protected. Though a minority view in that case, he repeated his caution in *TD v Minister for Education*,[61] where it seemed to be generally accepted. Keane CJ also expressed 'the gravest doubts' about the recognition of unenumerated socio-economic rights.[62] As Doyle puts it, the doctrine 'withered'[63] with these cases, even if it was never expressly or fully overruled.

The unenumerated rights doctrine is seen to have had a positive effect; the results of the doctrine were 'generally unexceptionable',[64] and the personal rights recognised generally represented a progressive trend in Irish life. However, the suggestion that the Irish doctrine led to generally favoured outcomes does not make it legitimate if its methods were dubious.[65] Nor does it mean that such doctrines always or generally produce such outcomes; the American experience of the now reviled *Lochner* era reminds us that rights created at the whim of judiciary can just as easily be used to defend conservative social interests against hugely popular social reforms.[66]

Some might support the continuation of unenumerated rights, suggesting that judges, insulated from politics, are best equipped to defend individuals from unjust attack by the State[67]; that political minorities might be better

60. ibid 370.
61. [2001] 2 IR 259 281–82.
62. ibid 282.
63. Oran Doyle, 'Constitutional Law: Text, Cases and Materials' (Clarus Press 2008) 108.
64. ibid 108. Hogan, 'Constitutional Interpretation', 95, described the prevailing view of the doctrine as 'very positive and progressive'.
65. However, it can argued that the relatively simple process of amendment of the Irish Constitution means that any constitutional decisions not overturned by amendment are acquiesced in by the people, rendering them more legitimate. See Gerry Whyte, 'Discerning the Philosophical Foundations of the Constitutional Review Group' (1998) Contemporary Issues in Irish Law and Politics 216, 232; Conor O'Mahony, 'Constitutional Amendment and Judicial Restraint: How Restrained Should an Irish Court Be?' in Eoin Carolan (ed), *The Irish Constitution: Perspectives and Prospects* (Bloomsbury Professional 2012).
66. Named after *Lochner v New York* 198 US 45 (1905), this period of several decades saw the US Supreme Court invalidating, *inter alia* laws governing minimum wages, maximum hours, and workplace conditions on the basis that they violated an unenumerated right to economic liberty derived from the due process clause in the 14th Amendment. This frustrated many laws passed during the early years of Roosevelt's New Deal, until the Court reversed this jurisprudence in 1936. See, amongst vast literature, Soujit Choudhry, 'The Lochner Era and Comparative Constitutionalism' (2004) 2(1) ICON 1; Howard Gillman, *The Constitution Besieged: The Rise and Demise of Lochner Era Police Powers Jurisprudence* (Duke University Press 1993); Laurence Tribe, *American Constitutional Law* (2nd edn, Foundation Press, 1998) 567–86, 769–72.
67. See Gerry Whyte, *Social Inclusion and the Legal System* (IPA 2002).

treated in courts than in the political process[68]; that judges, entrusted to defend the constitutional order, are the only ones who can recognise and enforce rights that might be implicit in the values of the Constitution.[69] However, because of the concerns outlined above, these views did not prevail in the Irish courts. A new development of implied rights would, I think, have to be shown to be different enough to not fall prey to these same weaknesses.

Does Fleming Differ from the Unenumerated Rights Doctrine?

The *Fleming* development closely resembles unenumerated rights, and arguments that it does not suffer from the same flaws that beset that doctrine are not, I think, convincing.

It might be argued that the right of the person is an express constitutional right, and the High Court in *Fleming* maintained that what they were doing was recognising a facet of that right, not any implied right, thus distinguishing this development from any implied rights approach. This is a distinction without a difference. Whether one says that the word 'person' implies an unenumerated autonomy right, or says that personal autonomy of this sort is a facet of the right of the person, the effect is the same. Moreover, the High Court judgment in *Fleming* did not seem recognise a single right, but rather recognise the source of many autonomy rights. The 'facet' of the right being recognised was a general entitlement to act without State interference in any matter fundamental to 'personal welfare'.[70] Almost any autonomy claim could be given constitutional status under this right. What relates to personal welfare would be decided by judges; how their decision would be guided is unclear.

The similarity between this interpretation of the right of the person and the unenumerated rights doctrine can be seen by comparing it to Henchy J's technique of deriving unenumerated rights from the 'human personality' of the citizen. Henchy J's suggested that the Constitution gave to the citizen

> such a range of personal freedoms or immunities as are necessary to ensure his dignity and freedom as an individual in the type of society envisaged. The essence of those rights is that they inhere in the individual personality of the citizen in his capacity as a vital human component of the social, political and moral order posited by the Constitution.[71]

This approach for deriving rights does not differ significantly from the approach in *Fleming*. They are both secular methods of protecting autonomy rights; they

68. ibid; John Hart Ely, *Democracy and Distrust* (Harvard University Press 1980).
69. Hogan conceded that leaving the role of rights recognition exclusively to the Oireachtas would be a less than compelling interpretation of the constitution. Hogan, 'Constitutional Interpretation', 113.
70. *Fleming v Ireland* [2013] IEHC 2 [49].
71. *Norris v Attorney General* 71.

are both premised on the personality of the citizen being the source of these entitlements. Indeed, this passage from Henchy J was cited by the High Court in *Fleming* as representing 'the current judicial consensus on this question' of State intervention in fundamental life choices.[72]

Henchy J's method of deriving rights from the human personality of the citizen was not immune to criticisms of subjectivity. Hogan, writing as an academic, was critical of the vagaries of this test:

> [H]ow could those rights [inherent in the human personality] be objectively identified? ... It seems that this phraseology is no surer a guide to the ascertainment of these rights than is the 'Christian and democratic nature of the State'.[73]

Of course, Hogan J would be more than entitled to take a different view of Henchy J's judgment from the bench than he had taken as an academic. However, his criticism of Henchy J stands as a valid criticism of the *Fleming* development: the word 'person' in art 40.3 seems no surer a guide to determining the personal rights of citizens than Henchy J's approach.

It might further be argued that the textual basis of the right of the person distinguishes this new development from the earlier doctrine. Two points can be made in response. First, the textual link is not significant when compared to the scope of the entitlement in *Fleming*, and could not be said to limit in any way the subjectivity of judges. The word 'person' is in the Constitution, and might refer to personality as well as physical person. However, in *Fleming*, the right seemed to protect every sort of conduct that might, in the view of a judge, relate to personal welfare. This would take a single word in the text of the Constitution and define it so broadly as to lose any real textual link, and certainly lose any ability to restrain judicial discretion, which is surely the point of requiring such a link.

Secondly, the unenumerated rights doctrine was linked to the text in ways little more attenuated than this interpretation of the right of the person. The natural law had a strong basis in the text of the Constitution, and the whole doctrine stemmed from the words 'in particular' in the text of art 40.3.[74] This did not allay fears that judges, in fleshing out the content of the natural law and deriving rights from it, would simply be imposing their own views of justice. Only a link between the text of the Constitution and any *particular right or entitlement* recognised would only assuage the fears of those wary of unenumerated rights.

---

72. *Fleming v Ireland* [2013] IEHC 2 [50].
73. Hogan, 'Constitutional Interpretation', 111.
74. The Constitution suggests the existence of the natural law in art 41.1 and art 43.1. Walsh J said these articles 'emphatically reject the theory that there are no rights without laws, no rights contrary to the law and no rights anterior to the law'. *McGee v Attorney General* 310.

It might also be suggested that since the law was ultimately upheld in *Fleming*, it was not a dangerous development. However, this is of little comfort. Though the law survived the High Court's proportionality analysis in *Fleming*, the bar was a high one: the State must have a compelling justification for the limitation. There is no reason to suggest this limitations analysis would be easily satisfied and that there would be few laws in danger of invalidity. Moreover, to render *prima facie* unconstitutional every law that restricts personal autonomy is hugely significant even if many of those laws might ultimately be upheld. It would mean that any time the State wished to restrict freedom of action in any personal context, the law would be of questionable validity. The fact that the law survived in *Fleming* does not alter the reality that this was a vast expansion of personal rights, which could have significantly increased the amount of constitutional litigation. It seems to me that the objections to the old doctrine stand against the *Fleming* development, there being little to distinguish them.

Fleming in the Supreme Court

After the High Court judgment in *Fleming*, it seemed as if the right of the person might become a new unenumerated rights doctrine. However, the Supreme Court judgment in that case seems to have limited the scope for developing the right in this way. Considering Ms Fleming's claim, Denham CJ noted that she did not claim any unenumerated right, but rather a right flowing from the 'protection of life and of the person within the terms of Article 40.3. Within that context, however, the appellant invokes constitutional values of autonomy, self-determination and dignity'.[75] The Court acknowledged that the Constitution did protect a measure of individual autonomy through its protection of specific personal rights.[76] However, protection for autonomy could not be so broad that 'every law which impinges on the life of individuals is even *prima facie* inconsistent with the Constitution'.[77]

> The concept of autonomy which extends not just to an entitlement, but to a positive right to terminate life and to have assistance in so doing, would necessarily imply a very extensive area of decision [*sic*] in relation to activity which is put, at least *prima facie*, beyond regulation by the State. When it is considered that recognition of such a right implies correlative duties on the State and others to defend and vindicate that right (and which must necessarily restrict those parties' freedom of action), it is apparent that the right contended for by the appellant would sweep very far indeed. It cannot properly be said that such an extensive right or rights is fundamental to

---

75. *Fleming v Ireland* [2013] IESC 19 [110].
76. ibid [111]–[113]. It even said that Henchy J's statements in *Norris* were 'a useful structure and focus for analysis'. It is unclear to me what this approval of Henchy J was to mean.
77. ibid [110].

> the personal standing of the individual in question in the context of the social order envisaged by the Constitution.[78]

The Supreme Court judgment in *Fleming* retreated from the High Court's broader findings: the Court specifically rejected the idea that these constitutional rights created broad swaths of conduct where State restrictions on personal decision-making were *prima facie* unconstitutional. The Supreme Court did not consider the right of the person in detail, neither endorsing nor rejecting the other cases on the its meaning. It did, however, preclude the most expansive reading of the right of person suggested by the High Court in *Fleming*: very broad autonomy protections are not a facet of art 40.3 rights.

The Future of the Right of the Person

The curtailing of the right by the Supreme Court in *Fleming* seems to assuage fears that the right of the person would become something akin to the unenumerated rights doctrine. We are then left to ask whether or not the right of the person can continue to develop, and whether the case law to date – *Fleming* aside – might be endorsed by the Supreme Court. This raises a fundamental question for Irish constitutional law: can judges ever legitimately be creative and novel in their interpretation of rights? Or, after the demise of unenumerated rights, are constitutional rights essentially in stasis?

There are no clear answers, in part because this development is ongoing, and it is too early to say exactly how this right will develop. More fundamentally, the amount of judicial innovation and creativity that is legitimate or acceptable is ultimately a normative question that different people will answer in different ways. For my part, I believe that there is room for some innovation in interpreting constitutional rights, once the pitfalls that undermined the legitimacy of unenumerated rights are avoided. Therefore, some of the developments in the right of the person should be welcomed as an innovative, interesting and legitimate expounding of a forgotten piece of constitutional text. I would suggest, however, that innovative judicial enterprises such as this one should be undertaken with care, lest the legitimate role of the judiciary be exceeded.

Uses of the Right of the Person

Hogan J has invoked this right in many cases, and most of these are narrower and less consequential than the invocation of the right in *Fleming*. However, there is novelty and innovation in Hogan J's use of the right of the person, and art 40.3 more generally. It seems to focus attention on the text of the Constitution; to try to remedy violations of rights; and to bring the Constitution to bear in areas where consideration of rights has been lacking. Some of these

78. ibid [113].

trends involve more than the right of the person,[79] and may deserve detailed consideration if they persist.

Many of the invocations of the right of the person have been novel in their analysis, but not their results; we can imagine the outcomes being reached by more conventional constitutional means. Where the right protects the physical person, this could be covered by bodily integrity. The mental integrity cases, such as *Kinsella*, might have been treated as falling under the unenumerated right recognised in *Frawley*,[80] or the ECHR protection against inhuman and degrading treatment.[81] The use of the right to justify the detention of a minor in his own interests[82] is not a novel result: it resembles the older invocations of the right,[83] and could be done under other provisions of the Constitution.[84] Nor is the ordering of a blood transfusion for the child of Jehovah's Witness parents.[85] These results are not ground-breaking; the use of this long-atrophied constitutional provision to achieve them is. By reasserting the textual right of the person, Hogan J removed the need to rely on more attenuated unenumerated rights or other constitutional provisions, and focuses on the textual rights in art 40.3.

Additionally, the right of the person is a part of a larger enterprise of invoking the Constitution to better vindicate constitutional rights. The right of the person, and art 40.3 more generally, have been used to fill gaps in the remedial framework. This is focused on the idea of *vindication* – that art 40.3 demands that rights have remedies.[86] Hogan J has suggested that the common law of tort might have to be altered to protect constitutional rights such as this one.[87] Constitutional damages have been available where tort law fails to offer a remedy, even when this involved the horizontal application of the right.[88] Similarly, Hogan J has held that the right of the person and art 40.3 essentially duplicate the ECHR guarantee of an adequate remedy when rights are violated.[89] This previously underutilised right has been used to patch up cracks in the constitutional order, places where the analysis of constitutional

79. In this body of case law, Hogan J has relied on other constitutional rights in tandem with this right, including the right to life *Kinsella v Governor of Mountjoy Prison* and *FX v Clinical Director*, and good name in *Flynn v Medical Council* [2012] IEHC 477 and *II v JJ* [2012] IEHC 327.
80. *State (C) v Frawley.*
81. See *DF v Garda Commissioner.*
82. *H v HSE.*
83. *Re D and the Midland Health Board.*
84. The State's duty under art 42.5 would suffice; it was cited alongside the right of the person.
85. *Temple St v D*; see *Fitzpatrick v K* [2008] IEHC 104.
86. *S (a minor) v Minister for Justice* [2011] IEHC 31 [17].
87. *Carr v Olas* [2012] IEHC 59 [36].
88. Sullivan *v Boylan (No 2).*
89. *S (a minor) v Minister for Justice*; *cf M v Minister for Justice* [2012] IEHC 34.

rights has failed to expressly provide for something basic and fundamental, such as a redress for wrongs done. This could be a significant development; it might encourage courts to alter private law regimes, award constitutional damages, or create novel remedies for rights violations if no other remedy is adequate.

Similarly related to the notion of vindication, Hogan J has cited the right to justify and uphold elements of the legislative or administrative framework of the State. He has noted how parts of the established legal framework serve to protect the person of the citizen – that tort law,[90] criminal prosecution,[91] and administrative bodies such as the medical council[92] play a significant role in vindicating this constitutional right. These cases highlight the way in which State action, rather than forbearance from action, vindicates rights, and might suggest that the right could be used to uphold legislation, rather than strike it down.[93]

Finally, many invocations of the right of the person have been in areas where constitutional rights are perhaps less frequently considered than they ought to be. Irish courts have been more rigorous in their consideration of constitutional rights in the making of laws rather than their application. In administrative law review, the consideration of constitutional rights has, in the past, not been stringent.[94] The right of the person has been invoked in the immigration context, an area of law where failure to consider constitutional rights has led to the recent incorporation into administrative law of a form of proportionality review, to be used when rights are at stake.[95] The right has proven useful in art 40.4 applications, where breaches of constitutional rights, other than the right to liberty itself, are infrequently considered.[96] In these cases, it is the failure to

---

90. *Carr v Olas; Sullivan v Boylan (No 2)* [37]; [44].
91. *GC v DPP* [2012] IEHC 430 [27].
92. In *Flynn* [34] he noted the role of the Medical Council in vindicating the right of the person of patients and the good name of doctors by investigating alleged medical misconduct.
93. When a law *defends* rights, it is subject to less invasive constitutional review for restricting other rights; see *Tuohy v Courtney* [1994] 3 IR 1.
94. See Hilary Delany and Catherine Donnelly, 'The Irish Supreme Court Inches Toward Proportionality' [2011] PL 9, 10.
95. *Meadows v Minister for Justice* [2010] IESC 3. There is still some dispute about what the meaning and significance of *Meadows* is. See Alan DP Brady, 'Proportionality, Deference and Fundamental Rights in Irish Administrative Law: the Aftermath of *Meadows*' (2010) 32 DULJ 136; Paul Daly, 'Standards of Review in Administrative Law After *Meadows*' (2010) 32 DULJ 379.
96. In *Re Article 26 and the Emergency Powers Bill 1976*, the Supreme Court held that though the *Bill* in question was saved from constitutional invalidity by art 28, '[f]or every other purpose the Constitution may be invoked. Thus, a person detained under s. 2 of the bill may… rely on provisions of the Constitution for the purpose of construing that section and of testing the legality of what has been done in purported operation of it.' [1977] IR 159, 173. Despite this, there are no reported

respect the right of the person in the application of laws, rather than the making of them, that has primarily drawn Hogan J's attention. This has the potential to make constitutional rights relevant in areas of law where previously they have not received great attention from the courts.

The Legitimacy of this Jurisprudence

I wish to advance three arguments in support of these more limited uses of the right of the person. Of course, concerns can still be raised, but I believe these counsel restraint and caution in the development of the right rather than requiring the abandonment of the entire line of case law.

First, it is the duty of judges to defend this express constitutional right, included in one of the most important articles in the Constitution, and this demands the right be given *some* meaning. We should therefore support Hogan J's efforts to protect the physical person via this provision, removing reliance on the unenumerated right of bodily integrity, and the interpretation that protects the integrity of the mind from unjust attack as well. The treatment endured by Mr Kinsella posed a real threat to his person without causing physical harm. This might have been a violation of the right against inhuman treatment recognised in *Frawley*, but it seems plausibly to fit with the express textual right that Hogan J invoked. That is to say: these invocations of the right seem to have strong textual links, to be well-grounded in the text of art 40.3. This distinguishes them from *Fleming*.

Against this, one could argue that a vague piece of constitutional text should not be given an expansive reading if its meaning is unknown.[97] We have no information about what the right of the person means, and therefore we should not interpret it broadly. However, leaving an express constitutional right with no meaning is deeply unsatisfactory, and seems like an abdication of the judicial role.[98] To ignore constitutional language because it is difficult to interpret is to 'deny and even subvert its meaning', and to give way to an overly rigid literalism.[99]

Another version of this objection might accept that Hogan J's use of the right to protect the physical person is legitimate, but would suggest limiting the interpretation to this narrowest reading. Anything broader than this would be in principle no different to *Fleming* or the unenumerated rights doctrine, even if it were in practice not as expansively used. However, I believe both the mental and physical integrity interpretations, when not interpreted as broadly as in *Fleming*, are highly plausible, while still maintaining a strong

---

cases of a breach of constitutional rights rendering detention unlawful. *Kinsella* might realise the unfulfilled promise of this statement.

97. Robert Bork, 'Neutral Principles and Some First Amendment Problems' (1971) Indiana LJ 1.
98. Hogan, 'Constitutional Interpretation', 112–13.
99. Kavanagh, 'Quest for Legitimacy', 204, 207–8.

link to the text of the Constitution. They are not the same in principle as the unenumerated rights doctrine or the *Fleming* case, and should be supported. Desiring judicial restraint does not imply opposing any judicial creativity in interpretation.

The second argument in favour of these invocations is that there is a limit to the scope of the right once it is not understood as the High Court in *Fleming* suggested. The mental integrity of Mr Kinsella and Ms Sullivan was jeopardised by specific conduct directed against them. One can imagine other instances like this where the right might be invoked in this way, as a negative entitlement not to have one's mental or physical integrity attacked. This vastly differs from a general protection of autonomy interests that would jeopardise any law that interferes with personal decision-making, which almost resembles a positive entitlement to act however one chooses to advance one's personal welfare.[100] The right can protect mental integrity without being a sweeping protection of any conduct that might affect the human personality. If not taken as far as in *Fleming*, the scope for judicial subjectivity is limited to the determination of whether or not legislation or state action actually attacks mental integrity, which is far narrower than the discretion seen in unenumerated rights jurisprudence.[101]

Against this, it could be argued that right has been used, even in its more limited form, to justify expansive results. The *Kinsella* case, and its statements about not denying interaction with human faculties, could prove broad if attacks on mental fortitude were widely defined. Similarly, Hogan J denied immediate release to an art 40.4 applicant whose detention had been found to be unlawful in the interest of protecting the person of the applicant and members of the public.[102] Considering that art 40.4 seems to envisage immediate release of those unlawfully detained, this is significant restriction on the art 40.4 procedure. Hogan J has invoked this technique in other cases.[103]

It is also unclear how expansive the development of new remedies is. There are surely limits to what courts can do to remedy rights violations. Courts are obviously empowered to change the common law, and to award damages for breach of constitutional rights, as Hogan J has done.[104] But the novelty and breadth of this right seems to allow a judge to fill any 'gaps' in the law of tort that he or she might perceive, under the auspices of vindicating it. Similarly, to say that the guarantees of art 40.3 provide an equivalent to art 13 of the ECHR

100. The Supreme Court classified the right claimed in Fleming as 'a positive right' to terminate life with assistance. *Fleming v Ireland* [2013] IESC 19 [113].
101. See, for example, *Connolly v Governor of Wheatfield Prison* [2013] IEHC 334, where Hogan J undertook a detailed analysis of the prisoner's detention before finding his conditions insufficiently bad to violate the right of the person.
102. *FX v Clinical Director*.
103. A similar stay order was made in *Kinsella*, though the right of the person was not considered in that context.
104. *Carr* and *Sullivan (No 2)*.

seems like a desirable development, but how expansive is this? Does it suggest the restrictions courts have placed on remedial powers should be altered?[105]

As I argued above, I believe the *Kinsella* interpretation is narrow enough to be constrained, and differs in principle from the breadth of *Fleming*.[106] If it were widened, then similar concerns would arise. The validity of Hogan J's decision to delay release under the art 40.4 procedure seems to have more to do with his interpretation of art 40.4 than on his use of the right of the person: if delayed release is an unacceptable interpretation, then nothing can justify it; if it is acceptable in principle, then the right of the person seems like a relevant consideration in that determination. This technique may be an interesting development in constitutional remedies, similar to the suspended declaration of invalidity for unconstitutional legislation in Canada;[107] it is worthy of further consideration by the courts. In any event, this does not seem to be determinative of the legitimacy of the right of the person.

As to the breadth of the remedial power, there is no reason to think that Hogan J's development would alter the current equilibrium between remedies and the separation of powers. In considering this aspect of art 40.3, Hogan J has acknowledged limitations on remedies, saying they can be offered only 'so far as it is practicable to do so',[108] and has also acknowledged the limits on remedial action set in *TD*.[109] However, perhaps the limits the Irish courts have placed on remedial powers are too strict, and some expansions should be considered.[110] However, this would turn on many complex constitutional considerations, of which art 40.3 would be but one.

Finally, most of the jurisprudence to date has been focused on offering remedies for constitutional wrongs, or insisting that rights be considered in non-legislative state action. Indeed, it has even been invoked to defend elements of the legislative and administrative framework as helping to vindicate rights. After the Supreme Court limited the scope of the right in *Fleming*, there is little to

105. Limits on remedies for legislative unconstitutionality include refusal to force the Oireachtas to legislate, and refusal to invalidate a law if the unconstitutionality comes from omission. See *Somjee v Minister for Justice* [1981] ILRM 324; *Carmody v Minister for Justice* [2009] IESC 71. Remedies for unconstitutional executive action were circumscribed in *TD v Minister for Education*.
106. Again, the recent decision in *Connolly* suggests that the right is far from limitless, even in the context of solitary detention.
107. This argument was made in respect of the *Kinsella* case; Eoin Carolan, 'The Relationship between Judicial Remedies and the Separation of Powers: Collaborative Constitutionalism and the Suspended Declaration of Invalidity' (2011) 46 Irish Jurist (ns) 180.
108. *S (a minor) v Minister for Justice* [14].
109. *MEO v Minister for Justice* [2011] IEHC 545.
110. See Carolan, 'Relationship between Judicial Remedies'; David Kenny, 'The Separation of Powers and Remedies: The Legislative Power and Remedies for Unconstitutional Legislation in Comparative Perspective' in Carolan (ed), *Irish Constitution*.

suggest it jeopardises large tracts of legislation. The anti-democratic concerns that plagued the unenumerated rights doctrine seem far less acute here.

This jurisprudence does not seem to pose the same problems as the *Fleming* case did. The Supreme Court in *TD* did not preclude any new interpretation of rights, but rather urged caution in the recognition of entirely new rights. The demise of unenumerated rights does not have to mark the end of judicial innovation; this resurrection of an express constitutional right is an instance of judicial inventiveness that retains legitimacy. Some of the concerns raised here should be borne in mind when considering the legitimacy of future developments. However, I do not think they are so significant as to demand that this new development be reversed or abandoned, just that it should proceed with caution, lest it go too far.

Conclusion

Reasonable people might disagree about the right of the person, with some defending even the very broad autonomy analysis that the Supreme Court rejected in *Fleming*, and others rejecting even the narrowest applications as too much judicial invention. The Supreme Court may ultimately have to decide if the more modest uses of the right of the person, outside of the *Fleming* case, are sufficiently connected to the text and consonant with our constitutional order that they should be retained. For my part, I believe that they are. Concerns about unenumerated rights are not so strong as to preclude any broad interpretation of rights, once a link to the text of the Constitution is retained, and unfettered judicial discretion in the invalidation of laws is not invited. Otherwise, the demise of unenumerated rights has left the constitutional order so sterile that an express textual right cannot be given a plausible and limited interpretation.

It is not merely that the right of the person lacks the hallmarks of illegitimacy; the right, in a modest form, has a great deal to commend it. These invocations have a strong connection with the text of art 40.3, have helped bring the Constitution to bear in areas where it has not had great influence, have offered remedies that otherwise might be absent and have grounded important rights-protections in the constitutional text.

Moreover, this development has given new strength and vitality to art 40.3, a provision that should be at the heart of our constitutional discourse. Article 40.3 is the core of the Constitution's protection of rights. Yet, since the demise of the unenumerated rights doctrine, this clause has atrophied. Hogan J's fascinating jurisprudence seeks to return this clause to the centre of our discussion of constitutional rights. If this effort succeeds, that would be no small thing, and this could be welcomed without fear that the unenumerated rights doctrine has returned.

DAVID KENNY*

* Lecturer, Trinity College Dublin. The author would like to thank Rachael Walsh and Andrea Mulligan for comments on earlier drafts of this article.

The Right to Appropriate the Family Home – A Proposal for Reform

Introduction

Throughout the world the home is considered 'a site of major importance in people's lives'.[1] In addition to its obvious financial importance, representing the single most valuable asset owned by many couples, it may also be of deep emotional and sentimental value to its occupants. As a result, reflecting its social, cultural and financial significance, the family home often receives special legislative protection. Indeed, as Professor Fox-O'Mahony notes:

> The idea that the home ought to attract greater protection because it is a meaningful site for family life is a potent one, since... 'home' conjures up such images as personal warmth, comfort, stability and security, it carries a meaning beyond the simple notion of shelter.[2]

In Ireland, in particular, the family home is the subject of important legislative safeguards.[3] While a marriage subsists, the Family Home Protection Act 1976 places vital restrictions on the unilateral disposition of the home where it is in the sole name of one spouse.[4] Moreover, on judicial separation or divorce, the Family Law Act 1995 and the Family Law (Divorce) Act 1996 empower the

1. Lorna Fox, 'Creditors and the Concept of "Family Home": A Functional Analysis' (2005) 25(2) Leg Stud 201, 226.
2. ibid 203 (citations omitted).
3. The depth of protection afforded to the family home in other jurisdictions is often far shallower than under the Irish regime. For a discussion of the *inter vivos* protections of the family home against unilateral disposition in Ireland, British Columbia and England and Wales, see this author's article 'Protection against Unilateral Dispositions of the Family Home – An Irish Perspective' (2013) 27(3) Int'l J L P & F 399. Moreover, on death, Ireland is one of the few common law countries that operates a system of forced heirship to prevent disinheritance. When combined with the right to appropriate the family home, discussed below, this has the potential to provide considerably greater protection than is available in many common law jurisdictions such as British Columbia and England and Wales, which both operate a system of discretionary provision to protect against disinheritance.
4. See s 3 of the 1976 Act. Section 28 of the Civil Partnership and Certain Rights and Obligations of Cohabitants Act 2010 extends almost identical restrictions on the unilateral disposition of the family home to civil partners.

judiciary to effect an equitable redistribution of property between spouses[5] with special powers afforded to the courts to deal effectively with the family home.[6] However, arguably the most robust legislative protection for the Irish family home arises under the Irish succession law regime.

Pursuant to the Succession Act 1965, the protection of surviving spouses and the family home is prioritised.[7] Unlike many common law jurisdictions, a system of forced heirship protects surviving spouses against disinheritance: irrespective of whether a will exists or not, s 111 entitles a surviving spouse to a specified portion of the deceased spouse's estate known as the legal right share. Where a testator leaves a spouse and no children, the surviving spouse has a right to one-half of the entire estate. Alternatively, where the testator leaves a spouse and children, the spouse is entitled to one-third of the estate. On intestacy, s 67 provides that where an intestate dies leaving a spouse and no children, the surviving spouse is entitled to the whole estate. On the other hand, where an intestate dies leaving a spouse and children, the surviving spouse takes two-thirds of the estate.[8] Moreover, endeavouring to protect

---

5. See s 9 of the 1995 Act and s 14 of the 1996 Act.
6. See s 10 of the 1995 Act and s 15 of the 1996 Act.
7. art 43.1.2° of *Bunreacht na hÉireann* provides: 'The State… guarantees to pass no law attempting to abolish the right of private ownership or the general right to transfer, bequeath, and inherit property.' However, no constitutional impediment was considered to exist to the introduction of the Succession Act 1965 since its provisions, which afforded considerable succession rights to spouses as discussed below, were introduced in furtherance of the protection of the family and, particularly, widows pursuant to art 41. For more discussion of the rationale for the succession rights of spouses see this author's article, 'Spousal Disinheritance Protections under Irish Law: A Proposal for Reform' (2012) 41(3) Comm L W Rev 246.
   In many ways the Civil Partnership and Certain Rights and Obligations of Cohabitants Act 2010 brings the legal position of spouses and civil partners closer together with regard to succession rights. For example, s 111A of the 1965 Act as inserted by s 81 of the 2010 Act and s 67A of the 1965 Act as inserted by s 73 of the 2010 Act extend similar, though less comprehensive, rights to civil partners on testacy and intestacy, while s 56 of the 1965 Act as amended by s 70 of the 2010 Act extends the right to appropriate the home (discussed in detail below) to civil partners. However, despite appearances, 'the succession provisions in relation to civil partners also contain a number of striking departures from equality': see John Mee, 'Succession and the Civil Partnership Bill 2009' (2009) 14(4) CPLJ 86 (referring to the equivalent provisions of the Act when in Bill stage). For more discussion of the succession provisions applicable to civil partners, see John CW Wylie, *Irish Land Law* (4th edn, Tottel 2010) ch 14.
   This article refers only to the law as it applies to spouses. However, aspects of the proposal for reform advanced below may also be relevant to remedy the weaknesses inherent in the application of the provisions to civil partners.
8. The remainder will be distributed among the issue subject to s 67(4), which states that if all the issues are in equal degree of relationship to the deceased, the distribution will be in equal shares among them; if they are not, it will be *per stirpes*.

surviving, non-owning, spouses in the family home, s 56 of the Succession Act 1965 provides such spouses with the right to require the appropriation of the family home in fulfilment of the legal right share, share on intestacy or gift under the will to which they are entitled. The rationale for this protection was explained by the Supreme Court in *H v O*:

> If the house and all the lands were to be sold, it would mean that the plaintiff would be ousted from the matrimonial home where she has spent all her married life... The appropriation... will ensure that the plaintiff, who is widowed and without children, will not be condemned to the harsh fate of having to leave the dwelling and seek a new home.[9]

Although the legislature may be applauded for introducing such protection for surviving, non-owning, spouses in the family home, the current regime nevertheless harbours important weaknesses. Unfortunately, however, the shortcomings of the Succession Act 1965 have not been subject to an in-depth critique to date and, with certain notable exceptions,[10] there appears to be a level of disengagement with the 1965 Act generally among academics. Moreover, bucking the current trend across the common law world, there has been no statutory review of the legislation since its introduction.[11]

---

9. [1978] 1 IR 194, 209, 210 per Henchy J.
10. Some academics have endeavoured to critique the Act and advance proposals for reform. In particular, Shatter makes some recommendations for reform where the Succession Act 1965 and the Family Law Acts 1995 and 1996 intersect: see Alan J Shatter, *Shatter's Family Law* (4th edn, Butterworths 1997); limited measures for reform are also set out in Brian E Spierin, *The Succession Act 1965 and Related Legislation: A Commentary* (4th edn, Butterworths 2011). Elsewhere, James C Brady, *Succession Law in Ireland* (2nd edn, Butterworths 1995) provides a detailed discussion of the provisions of the Succession Act 1965.
11. By contrast, various common law jurisdictions have recently placed their respective laws of succession under the spotlight: see Law Commission for England and Wales, *Intestacy and Family Provision Claims on Death* (Law Com No 331–2011); Law Commission for England and Wales, *Intestacy and Family Provision Claims on Death: A Consultation Paper* (Consultation Paper No 191–2009); Scottish Law Commission, *Report on Succession* (Scot Law Com No 215–2009); Scottish Law Commission, *Discussion Paper on Succession* (Discussion Paper No 136–2007); British Columbia Law Institute, *Wills, Estates and Succession: A Modern Legal Framework* (BCLI Report No 45–2006); Alberta Law Reform Institute, *Reform of the Intestate Succession Act* (Report for Discussion No 16–1996); Alberta Law Reform Institute, *Reform of the Intestate Succession Act* (Report No 78–1999); New South Wales Law Reform Commission, *Uniform Succession Laws: Intestacy* (Report No 116–2007); New South Wales Law Reform Commission, *Uniform Succession Laws: Intestacy* (Issues Paper No 26–2005); New South Wales Law Reform Commission, *Uniform Succession Laws: Family Provision* (Report No 110–2005). The lack of interest shown by the Irish legislature is surprising since, as Albert Keating noted

It is argued that the provisions of the Succession Act 1965 that seek to protect surviving, non-owning, spouses in the family home following the death of the owner spouse ought in particular to be reviewed to ensure their continued effectiveness.[12] The rights conferred by the Succession Act 1965 on the surviving spouse, including the right to appropriate the family home, remain of paramount importance for many individuals. The common perception that *all* family homes are now co-owned by both spouses is simply a myth.[13] Although co-ownership of the family home has undoubtedly increased in recent years with most newly purchased properties vested in both spouses, where it is not co-owned, the consequences may now be viewed as less acceptable. As Professor Cooke observed in relation to England and Wales, this increase in co-ownership

> may… mean that the value placed on home ownership in our society is so great, that the risk of having to move is seen as correspondingly tragic, perhaps to a greater extent than it was in the early years of the twentieth century before we became a 'property-owning democracy'.[14]

This article considers the practical effect of the provisions governing the appropriation of the family home in Ireland pursuant to the Succession Act 1965. The difficulties that arise in appropriating a family home located on agricultural land are highlighted. The article investigates how these shortcomings could be effectively resolved by legislative reform. Among its proposals for reform, it argues that the introduction of a statutory right of residence in certain circumstances would ameliorate the situation for vulnerable surviving spouses.

---

in the preface to the third edition of *Keating on Probate* (3rd edn, Round Hall 2007), 'the Succession Act may have to be re-visited to take account of modern realities'.

12. Proposals for the reform of the protections against spousal disinheritance in Ireland aimed at securing the family home for surviving, non-owning, spouses were discussed by this author in 'Spousal Disinheritance Protections'.
13. See ibid, which highlights situations that may give rise to a home being solely owned. In circumstances where the home is held in a tenancy in common it is also possible serious difficulties may be encountered in the appropriation of the home assuming the deceased's interest is not left to the surviving spouse.
14. Elizabeth Cooke, 'Wives, Widows and Wicked Step-Mothers: A Brief Examination of Spousal Entitlement on Intestacy' (2009) 21(4) CFLQ 423, 433. The effect of losing a family home is often quite severe. As Fried notes in 'Grieving for a Lost Home', 'for the majority it seems quite precise to speak of their reactions as expressions of grief' as quoted in Lorna Fox, 'The Meaning of Home: A Chimerical Concept or Legal Challenge' (2002) 29 J of L and Soc 580, 601–4.

Section 56 of the Succession Act 1965: An Overview

Recognising the importance of the family home, s 56 of the Succession Act 1965 provides that, subject to certain restrictions,[15] where the estate of a deceased person includes a 'dwelling' in which, at the time of the deceased's death, the surviving spouse was ordinarily resident, the surviving spouse may require appropriation of the property in or towards satisfaction of any gift under the will, legal right share or share on intestacy to which they were entitled.[16] The term 'dwelling' is defined in s 56(14) as

> an estate or interest in a building occupied as a separate dwelling or a part so occupied, of any building and includes any garden or portion of ground attached to and usually occupied with the dwelling or otherwise required for the amenity or convenience of the dwelling.

The scope of the definition was considered in *Hamilton v Armstrong*.[17] Here, O'Hanlon J allowed the appropriation of a home and a five-acre field in satisfaction of a surviving spouse's legal right share. The plot of land was not considered a 'garden' nor used for 'amenity and convenience'. However, it did hold the septic tank and piped water for the house and, as a result, was considered 'attached' to the land.[18]

---

15. Discussed in detail below.
16. See also s 55 of the Succession Act 1965, which contains a more general power of appropriation exercisable by the personal representative.
    In relation to s 56, the limitation of the right to appropriate only to dwellings in which the surviving spouse was 'ordinarily resident' at the time of the deceased's death could cause difficulty for certain deserving claimants. If a claimant had moved out of the family home prior to the death of her husband, for instance due to domestic violence, the right to appropriate will not be open to her, even if she had previously been entitled to a half share as a tenant-in-common. If the owning spouse left his share to a third party, his successor could apply for an order for the sale of the property under s 31 of the Land and Conveyancing Law Reform Act 2009. As the non-owning spouse has no right to appropriate his successor's share of the home under s 56, it is possible that an order for sale would be granted and she would lose her right to re-occupy the family home. However, as orders pursuant to s 31 are at the discretion of the court, it is also possible that in the circumstances such an order for sale would be refused. How exactly the judiciary will exercise the discretion that they are afforded under the 2009 Act remains to be seen. To avoid such difficulties, it is submitted that the definition of a 'family home' for the purposes of the Succession Act 1965 should be amended to correspond with the definition applied under the Family Home Protection Act 1976, which defines a family home as including a dwelling in which the spouse ordinarily resided before leaving the other spouse, see s 2(1) of the Family Home Protection Act 1976.
17. [1984] ILRM 306.
18. Although the decision appears to represent good law, it has been subject to criticism for attributing 'too a wide definition to "dwelling" as defined in the Act'. See Simon

The protection afforded to surviving, non-owning, spouses is bolstered by the fact that the right to require appropriation of a home is not affected by specific devises or bequests disposing of the family home to a third party in a will but may still be invoked even if prejudicial to them.[19] Moreover, pursuant to s 56(8)(a), the personal representative cannot sell or dispose of the dwelling as long as the right under s 56 continues to be exercisable, except in circumstances where it is the only asset of the deceased. Nevertheless, where it is sold, a surviving spouse cannot rely on s 56 against the new purchaser.

The legislation also includes a number of key provisions endeavouring to ensure the practical effectiveness of right to appropriate the family home. Pursuant to s 56(4), the personal representative has a duty to notify the surviving spouse in writing of the right conferred by the section. Section 56(5)(a) then provides that the surviving spouse has six months from the receipt of notification of this right from the personal representative or one year from the first taking out of representation of the deceased's estate, whichever is the later, in which to exercise the right to require appropriation of the family home.[20]

Furthermore, where the share to which the surviving spouse is entitled is less than the value of the home they seek to appropriate, the Succession Act 1965 affords spouses three possible solutions. First, s 56(9) provides that the surviving spouse may offset the difference in value by making a payment to the estate. Second, s 56(3) provides that if there are infant children, defined as children under 21 years of age, who are entitled to a share in the deceased's estate, and the surviving spouse is a trustee for them for such shares as they are entitled to, this may be added to the surviving spouse's share on intestacy, legal right share or gift under the will in order to appropriate the home. If the deceased dies testate, making no provision for their children in their will, the children may apply under s 117 for 'proper provision' to be made for them from the estate. Such provision will then be at the discretion of the court,[21] who shall consider the application 'from the point of view of a prudent and just parent'. In particular, as Finlay CJ held in *CC v WC*, 'a positive failure in

McDonald, 'Appropriation as a Means of Satisfying the Legal Right Share?' (1999) 4(3) CPLJ 62, 67.

19. s 55(2) of the Succession Act 1965.

20. Spierin, *Succession Act 1965*, notes at 174, 'a spouse… will not be prejudiced by the failure of the personal representatives to perform their duty, and the rights will remain for so long as this duty remains unfulfilled'. In *Re Hamilton's Estate* [1984] ILRM 306, O'Hanlon J held that once a surviving spouse requires the personal representatives to appropriate the dwelling, it is immaterial that they die before the appropriation is complete.

21. Subject to the limitation that any provision for a child cannot affect the surviving spouses' legal right share, upon application by a child under s 117, where the court is of the opinion that the deceased parent has failed in their moral duty to make proper provision for them in accordance with their means, the court may order that such provision shall be made for the child out of the estate 'as the court thinks just'.

moral duty' to make 'proper provision' must be established.[22] If successful in their s 117 application, any beneficial share of an infant child, for whom the surviving spouse was appointed trustee, could be added to the surviving spouse's share to reach the value required to appropriate the home. However, the actual effect on the ownership of the family home, having exercised s 56(3), is unclear. While the Act is silent on the issue, Spierin argues that where s 56(3) is invoked:

> The spouse… will presumably… hold as trustee upon trust for himself and any infants concerned as tenants in common, in proportion to their respective contributions. The status of the spouse… as a trustee for an infant beneficiary, where the interest of the infant has been appropriated under this section, should not be overlooked in practice.[23]

By contrast, however, Brady argues:

> [S]ince the main thrust of the section is to secure the place of the surviving spouse in the family home and such infant will invariably have succession rights to the estate of the surviving spouse, it is unnecessary to give such infant a share in the family home at the time of its appropriation under section 56.[24]

The third legislative option to overcome the potential difficulty incurred where the value of the home exceeds the share the surviving spouse is entitled to receive from the estate is provided by s 56(10)(b). Pursuant to this section, a surviving spouse may apply to the court to waive the payment due to the hardship meeting the shortfall would cause. Unfortunately, however, despite the apparent utility of the section, there appears to be a lack of reported judgments arising from applications taken thereunder, resulting in higher levels of uncertainty for potential applicants. In addition to the apparent gamble involved in instigating litigation pursuant to s 56(10)(b), financial considerations may also act as a deterrent to potential applicants. Although *Elliot v Stamp* is authority for the proposition that the court will *usually* award costs to an unsuccessful litigant who challenges a will provided there was a reasonable ground for the litigation and it was conducted bona fide, this remains at the

22. [1990] 2 IR 143 at 148. For a summary of the legal principles applicable by the court in s 117 applications, see *Re ABC's Estate* [2003] 2 IR 250.
23. Spierin, Succession *Act 1965*, 169.
24. Brady, *Succession Law in Ireland*, 222. While it is submitted it is not 'invariable' that such a child will receive the benefit on the death of the surviving spouse, since in the case of testacy a child does not have a right to any provision from a parent's estate but will be compelled to apply under s 117, it is nonetheless probable that in *most* cases they will receive a share from the survivor's estate on their death. However, in the case of step-children and second families, the danger of a child being excluded from sharing in the ultimate devolution of the estate is arguably greater.

discretion of the court.[25] Despite these difficulties, however, it is submitted considerable protection may be provided by the section in an apposite case and it represents a positive addition to the Succession Act 1965.

Notwithstanding the obvious strength of s 56, two important omissions were nevertheless made in its drafting. First, no definition of 'appropriation' was included in the 1965 Act. Fortunately, this omission does not appear to have given rise to any serious difficulty or litigation and it is generally considered to refer to the act of devoting or segregating certain property for a particular purpose, person or use. Second, s 56 does not specify the appropriate valuation date of the assets of an estate subject to an appropriation. Nevertheless, this difficulty was recently resolved by the judiciary in the decision of *Strong v Holmes*.[26] Murphy J noted, 'The court must safeguard the definition which could expose surviving spouses to the vicissitudes of a fluctuating market between the date of death and the date of distribution of the estate.'[27] Holding for the plaintiff, Murphy J noted, 'The only operative and practical date for valuation is the date of distribution, since it is the only date on which the true nature and extent of half the net estate of the deceased can be determined.'[28] He concluded:

> While the... defendant is correct in saying that her legal right under section 111 of the Succession Act arises on the moment of the death of the testator, where there is right of appropriation the valuation date is at the date of the exercise of that appropriation.[29]

The most serious weaknesses in relation to the power to appropriate the family home, however, emerge in relation to the restrictions that are placed on the right. It is to these restrictions that we now turn.

---

25. [2008] IESC 10.
26. [2010] IEHC 70. See also *Estate of Denis Kennedy v Breda Kennedy* (HC 26 January 2007).
27. ibid 5.2. Murphy J also acknowledged the 'fluctuating market and, in particular... the steep decline in property values from the date of the death to the date of the proposed appropriation'. He noted such problems associated with fluctuating markets did not prevail in the 1960s when the legislation was introduced.
28. ibid 5.2. The court stated at 5.5, 'It would be arbitrary and improper to permit a beneficiary to opt for a valuation date of their beneficial share or interest in the estate, how so ever arising, on a selective basis.'
29. ibid 5.7. By contrast, the defendant had claimed that the appropriate valuation date for the legal right share was the date the legal right share vested. In support of this argument, counsel for the defendant quoted Henchy J in *H v O* [1978] 1 IR 194, who stated: 'In the general context of the Act, it must be assumed that legislative intention was that the legal right (where elected for) is to be discharged in the same manner as if one-half or one-third of the estate had been expressly given in the Will in priority over all devises and bequests.' See Albert Keating, 'The Valuation Date of an Appropriation by Personal Representatives' (2011) 16(2) CPLJ 22.

Restrictions on the Right to Appropriate the Family Home

The Succession Act 1965 places important restrictions on the right to appropriate the family home. Pursuant to s 56(6), these restrictions arise in circumstances:

> (a) where the dwelling forms part of a building, and an estate or interest in the whole building forms part of the estate; (b) where the dwelling is held with agricultural land an estate or interest in which forms part of the estate; (c) where the whole or a part of the dwelling was, at the time of the death, used as a hotel, guest house or boarding house; (d) where a part of the dwelling was, at the time of the death, used for purposes other than domestic purposes.

Section 56(5)(b) then provides that the appropriation of such family homes may only take place where the court is satisfied that the appropriation is unlikely to diminish the value of the assets of the deceased, other than the dwelling, or to make it more difficult to dispose of them in the due course of administration.[30] Unfortunately, serious difficulties have emerged from the application of these restrictions, particularly in relation to the appropriation of homes on agricultural land. Indeed, reflecting on these shortcomings, Brady suggests, 'It is arguably the case that the legislature and parliamentary draughtsmen simply failed to address the many ramifications of the legal right to require appropriation as it applies to dwellings on agricultural land.'[31] Oddly, during the second stage of the Succession Bill in the Seanad, Minister Lenihan, the then Minister for Justice, stated that s 56 would apply 'mainly' to properties in urban areas.[32] No explanation was given as to why the Minister felt this would be the case, however the prophecy has proven to be wide of the mark.

A brief analysis of the case law demonstrates the difficulties arising due to these restrictions on the appropriation of farmhouses. In *H v H* the surviving spouse applied to the court for an order under s 56 appropriating the family home in partial satisfaction of her legal right share.[33] The dwelling was located on a farm of some 113 acres. It was argued by the respondents that such an appropriation would diminish the value of the rest of the land.[34] The Supreme Court found against the applicant spouse. It held that she had failed to prove that the appropriation would not adversely affect the value of the assets other than the dwelling and would not make it more difficult to dispose of them. The court made

---

30. Although the restrictions cover other buildings or business premises also, the focus of this article is placed on the right to require appropriation of a dwelling located on agricultural land.
31. Brady, *Succession Law in Ireland*, 226.
32. Dáil Deb 14 July 1965, vol 59, col 405.
33. [1978] IR 138. For analysis of this decision, see Brady, *Succession Law in Ireland*, 224–26. The plaintiff was entitled to one-half of the estate and the appropriation of this dwelling and some personal chattels would partially fulfil this entitlement.
34. It was not suggested by the executor that the lands, or any part of them, would be required to be sold in order to ensure administration of the estate.

three key observations in relation to applications for appropriation subject to the restrictions in s 56. It held that the onus of proof rests with the applicant; the reference to assets of the deceased other than the dwelling concerns all assets, including those passing to a spouse who has exercised their legal right to one-half of the estate; and the court must be satisfied that neither the diminishment of value or increased difficulty of disposing of the assets are likely to happen.

In the immediate aftermath of the decision in *H v H*, however, the Supreme Court approved an appropriation in similar circumstances in *H v O*.[35] The estate in question comprised two 'easily identifiable and severable' plots of land.[36] One of the plots contained the dwelling house. The main beneficiary under the will sought to prevent the appropriation of the family home and desired instead that both plots would be sold as a single unit. The surviving spouse could be paid her legal right share in cash from the proceeds. The chief argument posed against appropriation was that the value of receiving one of the plots would be worth less than receiving a half share in the proceeds of a sale if the plots were sold as a single unit. Having heard evidence from land valuers, the court held the applicant spouse should receive the family home and approximately half the land with the main beneficiary under the will receiving the other plot of land.

Despite the apparent inconsistency, it is arguable that *H v O* may be distinguished from *H v H* due to the severable nature of the plots in the former case. Consequently, it appears that the actual layout of the farm could be highly influential in whether a claimant is successful in seeking an appropriation of a farmhouse. Furthermore, it is clear that irrespective of whether a sale is in fact envisioned for the property or not, if the appropriation of the home would precipitate a fall in the value of the assets of the deceased or render them more difficult to dispose of, an appropriation of the home *cannot* take place: no alternative exists. Therefore, it is submitted there are serious gaps in the protection afforded by the right of appropriation as it applies to non-owning spouses in family farmhouses and proposals for reform ought to be considered.

Appropriation of Family Homes on Agricultural Land: A Proposal for Reform

While legislative provisions specifically restricting the appropriation of dwellings on agricultural land do not appear to exist in all jurisdictions that permit appropriation of the family home,[37] Ireland is not alone in enacting such measures.[38] The appropriation of the family home could, on occasion, considerably affect the value of the farm as a whole and could certainly render

35. *H v O* [1978] 1 IR 194. This case was commenced in the High Court the same day as Kenny J gave his judgment in *H v H* [1978] IR 138.
36. *H v O*, per Henchy J.
37. For instance, British Columbia's Wills, Estates and Succession Act 2009 contains no such restriction.
38. s 2 of the Second Schedule of England's Intestate Estate's Act 1952 and s 39B(1) and sub-s (5) of Queensland's Succession Amendment Act 1997 include essentially

it more difficult to dispose of. It is submitted this could lead to a disproportionate interference with the entitlements of those who have an interest in the land, excluding the family home. It is not, therefore, recommended that all restrictions ought to be removed. Nevertheless, it is clear that an outright prohibition on the appropriation of the family home in the circumstances provided by s 56(5)(b), with no provision for any alternative arrangements, is an undoubted weakness in the legislation. Moreover, it is submitted that the need to make an application to the court in all cases where the family home is located on agricultural land represents a further shortcoming in the legislation.[39]

It is proposed that a multifaceted approach ought to be adopted to cater for the various situations where difficulties may arise, thereby avoiding, where possible, the need for court applications. A distinction may be drawn between situations where an immediate sale of the property is planned and circumstances where no such sale is envisioned. It is proposed that where an immediate sale of the property is planned, perhaps in the course of administration, and an appropriation of the family home would result in a depreciation of the value of the assets only, without rendering the land more difficult to dispose of, the surviving spouse ought to be entitled to compensate the beneficiary of the agricultural land to the value of the depreciation in order to offset the loss and thereby retain the family home.[40] However, where agricultural land is being sold immediately and the appropriation of the family home would render the land more difficult to dispose of, or where the depreciation in the value of the assets could not be offset by the surviving spouse, the appropriation of the family home ought not to be allowed.

Alternatively, where no immediate sale of the property is sought, a different solution may be adopted to provide greater protection for surviving spouses. Again, where the appropriation of the family home would diminish the value of the other assets, the surviving spouse ought to be entitled to compensate the beneficiary of the land for this loss and the appropriation of the family home ought to be allowed. Where no such offset is possible or the appropriation would render the agricultural land more difficult to dispose of, it is submitted that a statutory right of residence may to be employed to provide some protection to a surviving, non-owning, spouse. This approach would be in line with the current practice employed by many rural testators to vest ownership of the farm in a child, usually a son, subject to a right of residence in the home for the benefit of the surviving spouse.[41] Where such provisions are not in place,

---

identical restrictions on appropriation of the family home where it is located on agricultural land.

39. This is exacerbated by the considerable delays in the hearing of probate cases.
40. The possibility inherent in such a proposal is also recognised by Spierin, *Succession Act 1965*, 171.
41. The Explanatory Memorandum of the Land and Conveyancing Law Reform Act 2009 notes at 6, a right of residence is 'commonly granted to the spouse of a farmer who has left the farm to a child'.

or the farmer dies intestate, the surviving spouse is in a precarious position. However, under these proposals, the statutory right of residence could allow the agricultural land and the family home to be enjoyed by the beneficiaries subject to a right in the surviving spouse to occupy the home for the remainder of their life or for as long as they wish to live there, whether or not such a provision is included in the will.[42] The right of residence would be considered to be in full or partial satisfaction of the legal right share. In order to determine to what extent the right of residence satisfies the legal right share to which a surviving spouse is entitled, careful actuarial calculations would have to take place. If the agricultural land and the family home were subsequently sold, the surviving spouse would then be fully compensated for the loss of the right. However, the ability to avail of a right of residence would be subject to an important caveat. The surviving spouse may only benefit from a right of residence where the consent of the beneficiary is obtained.

It may be argued that the requirement to obtain the consent of the beneficiary undermines the protection proposed. Indeed, if this proposal for reform was predicated on providing a surviving spouse with a 'right' to appropriate a farmhouse where such an appropriation would diminish the value of the assets of the deceased (other than the dwelling), or make them more difficult to dispose of, as per the current restrictions in s 56(5), the inclusion of a consent requirement would certainly be problematic. However, this proposal does not intend to extend such a 'right' to spouses. Rather, it seeks to replace the existing blanket restriction that applies where the appropriation of a farmhouse would give rise to either of the eventualities enumerated in s 56(5) with a more nuanced and practical approach. It provides an *alternative* solution for non-owning spouses who wish to remain in the family home located on agricultural land while simultaneously balancing their rights with those entitled to inherit the property. Moreover, to provide otherwise could result in an intolerable situation whereby two parties would be forced to live together against their will.

The introduction of such a regime incorporating a right of residence would not be a new innovation in Irish law. Anecdotal evidence suggests that deeds of family arrangement are often availed of to provide a surviving spouse with a right of residence where such difficulties arise in appropriating the family home on

42. Although, Wylie notes that a right of residence does not confer a life interest and adds, 'At most the right seems to create a form of licence to occupy the land, though one which may bind successors in title'. See Wylie, *Irish Land Law*, 515. Section 81 of the Registration of Title Act 1964 provides that a general right of residence, or an exclusive right of residence in or on part of registered land, is to be deemed personal to the person beneficially entitled thereto and not to create an equitable estate in the land or to confer any right thereto. Nevertheless, such a right is a burden on the land protected by registration and, therefore, may affect successors in title.

agricultural land.[43] Described by Lyall as 'a right peculiar to Irish land law',[44] introducing a right of residence on a legislative basis to alleviate the difficulties caused by the appropriation of a farmhouse would build upon the current implementation of such rights in other aspects of family law. In this regard, Professor Wylie notes rights of residence are 'extremely common' in Ireland for wills and family settlements.[45] Moreover the Family Law Act 1995 and the Family Law (Divorce) Act 1996 also empower the judiciary to make an order conferring a right of residence upon judicial separation or divorce, which is regularly availed of by the courts.[46]

Prior to the introduction of the Land and Conveyancing Law Reform Act 2009 there was some 'conceptual uncertainty' regarding the legal nature of rights of residence.[47] Indeed, even since its introduction, it has been suggested that the law on this subject is 'far from clear'.[48] As Lyall notes:

> There appears to be a need in land law for a form of right which confers on the recipient, usually an elderly member of a family, a right to reside in a house for the rest of their life, or until incapacity requires other arrangements, which is personal to the recipient in the sense that he or she cannot alienate it, but which is secure against third parties. The uncertainty of the rights conferred by a right of residence in Ireland mean that it does not fulfil that requirement.[49]

In light of these difficulties, he suggests:

---

43. However, this is an informal solution currently not recognised by statute. Moreover, pursuant to these proposals, beneficiaries of the estate may well be more likely to agree to such an arrangement. By offsetting the right of residence against the legal right share, share on intestacy or gift under a will, it may incentivise the arrangement for such beneficiaries who may otherwise be reluctant to allow a surviving spouse a right of residence.
44. Andrew Lyall, *Land Law in Ireland* (3rd edn, Round Hall 2010) 525.
45. Wylie, *Irish Land Law*, 1104. See generally, Brian W Harvey, 'Irish Rights of Residence – The Anatomy of a Hermaphrodite' (1970) 21 NILQ 389.
46. See s 10(1)(a)(i) of the 1995 Act and s 15(1)(a)(i) of the 1996 Act. An analysis of the Courts Service statistics shows a constantly high level of rights of residence orders. For example, the total number of judicial separation orders granted in the Circuit Court in 2011 was 1,006 and the total number of property orders recorded was 1,212 (this apparent anomaly may be explained by the fact that more than one property order may be made in an individual case). Of these, 253 rights of residence were awarded. This equates to 20.87 per cent of all property orders made. See Court Service, 'Annual Report 2011' <www.courts.ie/Courts.ie/library3.nsf/(WebFiles)/1EAFA33B0C5E24F980257A3E0037FCC9/$FILE/Courts%20Service%20Annual%20Report%202011.pdf> accessed 5 September 2012.
47. Paul Coughlan, 'Enforcing Rights of Residence' (1993) 11 ILT 168.
48. Wylie, *Irish* Land *Law* 1104. For more on these difficulties, see 1104–11.
49. Lyall, *Land Law in Ireland*, 531–32. He explains, 'Licences… may be insecure against third parties, while life estates, if created expressly are now liable to be overreached under the Land and Conveyancing Law Reform Act 2009.'

> The legislature might... consider creating a statutory form of right which could be conferred in such cases. There is no doubt a concern that such a right should not withdraw land from the market for an unduly long time, but that could be met by restricting it in some way, perhaps by providing that it could only be conferred on recipients above a certain age.[50]

Although Lyall dodges the issue as to what age limit should be applied, and the establishment of a cut-off age would indeed be arbitrary and liable to give rise to injustice, it is clear that his proposal seeks to ensure that the home does not become unmarketable for an inordinate period of time. Despite these concerns, however, it is submitted that much of the confusion surrounding rights of residence has been removed by the Land and Conveyancing Law Reform Act 2009.[51] As a result, it is contended that the modification of the current law could confer a new lease of life on such rights.

Notwithstanding the improvement of the law in light of the 2009 Act, certain ambiguities do nevertheless remain. Lavan J recognised in *Johnston v Horace* that neither case law nor statute definitively stated whether the holder of the right of residence or the owner of the property could insist upon the right being converted into money's worth.[52] However, the court granted the plaintiff injunctions restraining the defendant from preventing her from exercising her right

50. ibid 532.
51. The Land and Conveyancing Law Reform Act 2009, in replacing the Settled Land Acts, has 'largely' resolved the problems posed where the holder of a right of residence could sell the land over the heads of other interested parties. See Wylie, *Irish Land Law*, 1106. As a result, pursuant to s 11, where the holder of a right of residence enjoys the right to the exclusion of others, a trust of the land comes into effect. The power to deal with the land will rest with trustees who are compelled to exercise them in the interests of all the persons interested in the land, not only the holder of the right of residence. Moreover, a right arising over only part of the land will not give rise to a trust: see Wylie, *Irish Land Law*, 559–60. See also the Explanatory Memorandum of the Land and Conveyancing Law Reform Act 2009, 6.
52. [1993] ILRM 594. Lavan J added at 8: 'I have no doubt but that there are circumstances in which a court could enter by agreement of the parties into a valuation of their respective interests. There are also circumstances where a court might compel such a valuation in the general interest of the administration of justice or under its equitable jurisdiction. The court in valuing the right should carry out an objective valuation independent of the alleged circumstances in which the valuation is sought.' Coughlan, 'Enforcing Rights of Residence', observes: 'Lavan J seems to have left open the question whether the owner could insist upon the sale and free the land from the right of residence. Conventional charges and annuities can be cleared off the title by tendering their capital value with the sanction of the court. It would certainly be anomalous if something which is far short of a right of ownership could hinder a person in the disposition of his land when one co-owner can force a sale on another.'

to residence.[53] Lyall notes the judgment could be indicative of 'a growing willingness to use the discretion of court… even in the case of a general right of residence, to secure the occupation of the donee'.[54] Despite this, in the recent case of *Bracken v Byrne* it was accepted that while, in general, a right of residence is enforced through the use of an injunction to prevent the land owner disregarding it, situations will arise where it is neither practical or reasonable to force parties to continue with the arrangement.[55] This is particularly so where a relationship breaks down. As a result, having regard to the landowners' ability to pay, Clarke J converted the right into a monetary value. In reaching this conclusion, he held:

> [I]n addition to satisfying the court that it has become unreasonable in all the circumstances of the case to require the beneficiary to be content with the exercise of the right, it is also necessary for the beneficiary to satisfy the court that the balance of the responsibility for that situation lies upon the owner of the right.[56]

This, it is submitted, appears to be a practical approach. As a result, it is contended that the legislation should clarify that at any point either party could choose to convert the right of residence into money's worth. Therefore, although the formulation of a statutory right of residence, which would apply where a spouse sought to exercise the right to appropriate a family home on agricultural land,[57] would need to respect the right of the owner to sell the property at any point in the future provided the spouse was compensated, it would, in the meantime, improve the position of many surviving spouses *vis-à-vis* such family homes.

---

53. The court, moreover, ordered the defendant to supply a key of the cottage and awarded £7,500 damages in recognition of the interference with the right to date.
54. Lyall, *Land Law in Ireland*, 531.
55. [2005] IEHC 180, [2006] 1 ILRM 91.
56. ibid. Clarke J awarded €236,020 as the value of the right, however, he held that rights that frequently accompany a right of residence, including rights of maintenance and support, could not be separated from the right of residence and, therefore, included them in the total sum awarded. See Wylie, *Irish Land Law*, 1107–9.
    Coughlan, 'Enforcing Rights of Residence', analysed the decision in *Johnston v Horace*, and the confusion over the right to conversion. He noted, 'it is regrettable that when the [Irish legislature] chose to legislate in this area it did not place these rights on surer footing and provide for the resolution of disputes which are very understandable given human nature… This uncertainty should be resolved by legislation covering both registered and unregistered land which would make these rights convertible into money at the election of either party and indicate how they should be valued.'
57. Or perhaps a home forming part of a building or business premises.

Conclusion

The importance attributed to, and the desire to protect, the family home in the Irish Statute Book is striking. Notwithstanding the failure of the Matrimonial Home Bill 1993 and its attempted introduction of an automatic system of equitable co-ownership of the family home,[58] considerable legislative protection for the property does nevertheless exist in Ireland.[59] In particular, pursuant to the Succession Act 1965, Ireland operates a comprehensive system of financial provision for surviving spouses, which affords special protection to the family home by virtue of s 56. As Coughlan notes, the provisions governing the appropriation of the home confer 'valuable rights on a spouse irrespective of whether the deceased dies testate or intestate'.[60] While it is important to recognise the value of these rights, it is equally important to be alert to the shortcomings of the Succession Act 1965 and potential avenues for legislative reform in order to further consolidate the protection afforded to *all* family homes in Ireland.

To this end, it is argued that the difficulties arising in relation to the appropriation of family homes on agricultural land must be addressed. After all, it is widely accepted that the restrictions included in ss 56(5) and 56(6) 'will

58. See *Re Article 26 of the Constitution & in the Matter of the Matrimonial Home Bill 1993* [1994] 1 ILRM 241. The Supreme Court unanimously found the Bill to be unconstitutional as it infringed on the authority of the family.
59. While considerable protection is afforded by the Family Home Protection Act 1976 and the Succession Act 1965, the weakest protection afforded to the home arises on marital breakdown pursuant to the Family Law Act 1995 and the Family Law (Divorce) Act 1996. Unfortunately, however, a discussion of these shortcomings is outside the scope of this paper.
60. Paul Coughlan, *Property Law* (2nd edn, Gill and Macmillan 1998) 408, referring to s 56 of the Succession Act 1965. Interestingly, the Scottish Law Commission recently rowed back on former proposals in its discussion paper that a right of appropriation be introduced in the jurisdiction on intestacy. It noted: 'The threshold sum has been set at £300,000 to ensure that in all but the most exceptional cases it will more than cover the net value of the deceased's right in the family home. Indeed, it will ensure that in the vast majority of cases the surviving spouse or civil partner will inherit the whole of the estate.' The report concluded: 'In these circumstances we have taken the view that a statutory system under which a surviving spouse or civil partner can purchase the family home and its contents would be disproportionate to the mischief that it would be designed to address. Moreover, such a scheme runs counter to the principle that intestate succession rights should not be property-specific.' See Scottish Law Commission, *Report on Succession*, 2.17–2.18. Rather than being a slight on the usefulness of the right to appropriation, this approach should be viewed in the context of the entire report, which was dominated by a desire to move away from asset specific provisions. In addition, the high threshold of the preferential share also renders the benefit on intestacy of a right to appropriation of minimal relevance in most cases. However, on testacy, it is submitted the advantages of a right to appropriation are especially missed under the Scottish proposals.

cover very many dwellings in Ireland'.[61] This article has demonstrated how such issues could be more fairly and effectively resolved by legislative reform. In addition to the inclusion of provisions allowing surviving spouses to offset any loss in value caused by an appropriation of the family home, the introduction of a statutory right of residence, providing surviving spouses the opportunity to reside in the home in situations where it would not unduly prejudice the rights of those entitled to inherit the farm, represents a simple yet effective solution to the problems presented by the current application of the 1965 Act. Moreover, the overall effect of the proposals presented here would be to reduce the need for recourse to the courts. While an application to the court could be made to determine a dispute as to whether the appropriation would diminish the value of the land or would render it more difficult to dispose of, the inclusion of these proposals would ensure more transparent and practical solutions to the difficulties posed by the appropriation of the family home on agricultural land than the current broad discretion afforded to the judiciary.

It is submitted the implementation of these proposals would fill a substantive gap in the legislation as it is currently framed and would considerably enhance the protection afforded to non-owning spouses who wish to appropriate a family home on agricultural land.

KATHRYN O'SULLIVAN*

Irish Digital Rights in Retrograde: The 'Eircom Protocol' and the Normative Framework of European Law

---

Introduction

Since 2009, voluntary and legislative graduated penalty systems or 'three-strike' laws have been recognised by policymakers[1] and the judiciary as an efficient

61. Spierin, *Succession Act 1965*, 170.

* Lecturer in Law, University of Limerick; email Kathryn.osullivan@ul.ie. The author gratefully acknowledges the helpful comments of Una Woods, University of Limerick, on an earlier draft of this paper.

1. See UK: Digital Economy Act 2010; NZ: The Copyright (Infringing File Sharing) Amendment Act 2011; France: Loi-Hadopi; South Korea: Copyright Act of 1957, as amended by Law No. 9625/2009.

means for enforcing copyright in the face of online peer-to-peer network piracy.[2] The result of corporate lobbying[3] advocating an absolutist enforcement paradigm,[4] such laws and agreements dispel the myth of internet anonymity, permitting tracking of internet protocol (IP) addresses used in the P2P network. The IP address and data concerning the infringement, eg data, time and file hash-tag, are forwarded to the ISP, who warns its customers to stop their illegal activity; failure to comply on the third warning leads to internet disconnection.[5] In Ireland, Eircom Ltd set a global precedent agreeing with EMI Records Ltd to initiate a three-strike system, the 'Eircom Protocol', on Ireland's largest internet network.[6] With IP addresses and corroborating data forwarded to Eircom by EMI agents, the consumer contract – namely clauses prohibiting infringement and a broad enforcement clause – is used to justify disconnection of users alleged to be copyright pirates. Approved by Charleton J in *EMI Records v Eircom Ltd*[7] as conforming to the Data Protection Act 1988 as amended (DPA), and judged proportionate, the learned judge later refused EMI an injunction for a similar system against UPC Ltd,[8] citing no legal basis in Irish law. Given legislation has not been forthcoming, with three-strike laws and systems increasingly recognised as disproportionate and failing to adequately protect internet subscriber fundamental rights, the question must be asked whether the Protocol accords with European law as to copyright enforcement.

EMI Records v Eircom Ltd: To each Cow its Calf, to each Book Its Copy

In *EMI Records v Eircom Ltd*, Charleton J assessed conformity of the Protocol with the DPA: although his comments speak to broader policy questions, it is significant to note it remains a private agreement rather than an injunction. A challenge by the Data Protection Commissioner (Commissioner) posed three questions for review: first, whether or not IP addresses in the hands of

2. See generally: Michael Boardman, 'Digital Copyright Protection and Graduated Response: A Global Perspective' (2010–11) 33 Loy LA Int'l & Comp L Rev 223–54; Anne-Marie Bridy, 'Graduated Response and the Turn to Private Ordering in Online Copyright' (2010) 89 Oregon Law Rev 116–32; Carole Descamps, 'Peer-to-Peer Networks and Copyright Law in France, Ireland and the UK' (2010) 17 ISLR 155; Eldar Haber 'The French Revolution 2.0: Copyright and the Three Strikes Policy' (2011) 2 Har J Sports & Ent L 297–339.
3. See Ian Hargreaves, *Digital Opportunity: A Review of Intellectual Property and Growth* <http://www.ipo.gov.uk/ipreview-finalreport.pdf> accessed 28 August 2013.
4. See Margaret Ann Wilkinson, 'Battleground Between New and Old Orders: Control Conflicts Between Copyright and Personal Data Protection' in Ysolde Gendreau (ed), *An Emerging Intellectual Property Paradigm – Perspectives from Canada* Ysolde Gendreau (Edward Elgar 2008) 227–66.
5. *EMI Records & Ors v Eircom Ltd* [2010] IEHC 108, paras 11–13.
6. Arising from settlement, ibid.
7. ibid.
8. *EMI Records [Ireland] Ltd & Ors v UPC Communications Ireland Ltd* [2010] IEHC 377.

EMI or its agent(s) constituted 'personal data' for the purposes of s 1 DPA[9]; secondly, is it within Eircom's legitimate interest to process such data;[10] and finally, whether or not the processing of such data amounted to sensitive data under s 2(b)(1) DPA.[11] Charleton J rejected all three questions, holding the inherent constitutional property dynamic of copyright takes priority, couched in the maxim 'to each cow its calf, to each book its copy'.[12] For the purposes of this analysis, the third question may be disregarded: while s 2(b)(1) DPA establishes conditions for processing of sensitive personal data including *inter alia* consent, sensitive data under the Protocol could only be construed as alleging the commission of an offence. Section 140(1) of the Copyright and Related Rights Act 2000 attaches criminality to infringement on a commercial scale; by its nature the Protocol is aimed at infringement outside the scope of criminality, eg non-commercial. The learned judge is correct in stating no issue arises in the context of the Protocol, leaving the first and second question for consideration.[13]

Are IP Addresses Personal Data under the DPA?

Addressing question one, Charleton J held that IP addresses are incapable of being defined as 'personal data' under s 1 of the DPA.[14] Section 1 defines 'personal data' as 'data relating to a living individual who is, or can be, identified either from the data or from the data in conjunction with other information that is in, or is likely to come into, the possession of the data controller'. For the purposes of the Commissioner's challenge, the section can be split into two parts, with the first dealing with the data at hand, namely the IP address, and secondly the possibility that such data could be used with other data to reveal a customer(s) identity. Charleton J was absolute in stating that EMI was not in a position to identify an individual from an IP address alone and moreover it was highly unlikely they could come within the second strand of s 1 DPA and use such IP addresses in conjunction with other data.[15] The learned judge received succour from the question put to him, which did not ask generally whether or not IP addresses are 'personal data', but rather whether or not they were such 'in the hands of EMI or its agent(s)'.[16] In turn, Charleton J had no difficulty in holding that no disclosure occurs under the Protocol where IP addresses are forwarded to Eircom, with Eircom already possessing the IP address and biographical data of its customers.

9. *EMI Records & Ors v Eircom Ltd* [2010] IEHC 108, para 18.
10. ibid para 26.
11. ibid para 36.
12. ibid para 28.
13. ibid paras 39–41.
14. ibid para 25.
15. ibid.
16. *EMI Records [Ireland] Ltd & Ors v UPC Communications Ireland Ltd* [2010] IEHC 377.

The Legitimate Interests of Eircom and Warranted Processing

Having rejected IP addresses as personal data under s 1 DPA, Charleton J asserted that even if they were, Eircom had a legitimate interest to process on three grounds: (i) as a corporate body it was expected to uphold constitutional property rights. (ii) under contract it is permitted to implement enforcement, and (iii) customer consent by virtue of the latter agreement had been obtained.[17] In considering the last two points, the learned judge relied on s 2A(1) of the DPA as amended, which provides that data shall not be processed unless (i) the data subject has given consent, or (ii) that it is necessary for, *inter alia,* the performance of a contract to which the data subject is a party, or compliance with a legal obligation to which the data controller is bound.

The Legitimacy of the Protocol: An Alternative Perspective

Article 3 of Directive 2004/48/EC[18] obliges Member States to provide for measures, procedures and remedies that are effective, proportionate and dissuasive with safeguards against abuse to enforce intellectual property under European law. Reflective of the intention of the European legislature, the import is that any measures that seek to enforce copyright must result from the national legislature, administrative bodies or courts. Outside the scope of art 3 as a private agreement and not subject to the required oversight safeguards, the question arises: Does European law preclude private agreements to enforce copyright and impose a sanction in a manner such as the Protocol?

Eircom's Legitimate Interest: Defender of Constitutional Rights or 'Mere Conduit'?

Affirming the Protocol as in Eircom's legitimate interest, Charleton J cited contractual necessity arising from prohibition and enforcement clauses within the consumer usage policy and identified Eircom as a defender of constitutional property rights.[19] With respect, ascribing such an interest or role to an ISP under private contract obscures the parameters of European law as to ISP liability and accountability in copyright enforcement.[20] Indeed, in the specific context of copyright enforcement, European law frames the interest of the ISP in terms of non-liability moving towards limited liability and accountability in strictly defined circumstances. Under the E-Commerce Directive,[21] an ISP retains

17. *EMI Records & Ors v Eircom Ltd* [2010] IEHC paras 29, 30.
18. Directive 2004/48/EC on the Enforcement of Intellectual Property Rights.
19. ibid.
20. See generally: Sophie Stalla-Bourdillon, 'Chilling ISPs... When Private Regulators Act Without Adequate Public Framework' (2010) 26(3) Computer L & Security Rev 290–97.
21. 2000/31/EC on certain legal aspects of information society services, in particular electronic commerce, in the Internal Market.

non-liability where information is either cached or stored on its network, eg via websites, where it acts expeditiously to remove such content upon notification of copyright infringement.[22] As a matter of implicit European policy, the ISP is to remain unencumbered, where possible, as to its obligations to protect copyright to promote e-commerce services and competition. To this end, art 12 identifies an ISP as a 'mere conduit' of non-liability where it does not initiate, select the receiver of, or modify a transmission in circumstances such as P2P infringement.

Yet, art 12(3) provides such status does not preclude the possibility for a court to require the ISP to 'terminate or prevent an infringement'. Moreover, art 8(3) of Directive 2001/29/EC[23] specifically requires that a rights-holder has the right at national level to apply for an injunction against an intermediary whose services are used to infringe copyright. Aside from notice and takedown procedures,[24] the legitimate interests of the ISP in terms of enforcement are therefore framed as non-liability until an injunction is sought by a rights-holder in accordance with art 12(3), giving effect to art 8(3), Directive 2001/29/EC. Moreover, the ability to impose such an injunction must be in accordance with national legal systems and, as Charleton J observed in *EMI Records Ltd & Ors v UPC Communications Ireland Ltd*,[25] such power does not exist under Irish law. While the learned judge interpreted the substantive character of the Protocol as giving effect to the contract for service, its *raison d'être* is defined outside the contract by EMI's corporate agenda. In light of art 3 of Directive 2004/48/EC requiring remedial measures and sanction to be imposed by national measures, the recognition by Charleton J of their absence under Irish law and art 12(3) of Directive 2000/31/EC specifically requiring an injunction compelling an ISP to act, is the private agreement justified? Recital 40 of Directive 2001/31/EC provides for voluntary agreements, developing 'rapid and reliable procedures for removing and disabling access to illegal information' and that ISP limited liability should not preclude the development of 'technical systems of protection and identification and of technical surveillance instruments'.

Such agreements – the only available under the Directive – are with clear reference to the procedures envisaged under art 14(3) aimed at removing or disabling access to hosted information, not *post-hoc* sanctioning. It is arguable the Protocol might be justified under Recital 40 as a 'technical system of protection', yet the Recital prescribes that the Directive should form the basis of any agreement. If such is the case, the only obligations on the ISP remain

22. ibid arts 13–14.
23. Directive 2001/29/EC on the harmonisation of certain aspects of copyright and related rights in the information society.
24. Related to arts 13–14 giving effect to non-liability for expeditiously removing cached or hosted content.
25. *EMI Records [Ireland] Ltd & Ors v UPC Communications Ireland Ltd* [2010] IEHC 377, para 131.

the expeditious removal of hosted or cached content, or under injunction, to remove or disable access to such information. Given the Protocol relates to a sanctioning function it does not appear to come within Recital 40. To this end, it is apparent that the intention of the European legislature was for ISPs to remain neutral in instances of P2P infringment, up to and including the imposition of an injunction under art 12(3). While it remains an open question whether or not the Protocol could be justified under art 12(3), it should be the case that any private agreement outside the scope of Directive 2000/31/EC should be construed as an affront to the intentions of the European legislature with dubious questions arising as to their credibility.

The Eircom Contract for Service and Consumer Consent

Blunting the Commissioner's challenge in holding IP addresses are not personal data, Charleton J held that in any event the processing would be legitimate under s 2(A)(1) DPA, providing for *inter alia* data subject consent and processing necessary for the performance of the contract.[26] In 2012, counsel for the Commissioner in *EMI Records (Ireland) Ltd & Ors v The Data Protection Commissioner & Anor*[27] argued that in light of the Protocol, the Eircom contract with its subscribers should have been altered, with the implication being that the Protocol was not operating under a valid consent per s 2(A)(1) DPA.[28] While the 2010 judgement concerning IP addresses holds, given that Charleton J legitimised the Protocol relative to the consumer contract it is worth considering whether or not the argument is correct.

Consent

The Eircom contract prohibiting copyright piracy includes an enforcement term stating: 'Eircom net reserves the right to take such action as it deems appropriate against any customer who violates any conditions of this acceptable usage policy'.[29] It is noteworthy that consumer welfarist considerations were absent from the judgment, particularly as to the broad nature of the term in question and the scope of discretionary power it vested in Eircom. Can the term be described as unfair? Directive 93/13/EEC[30] includes within its grey list terms that impose a disproportionately high sum in compensation on consumers that fail in their obligations. Given that the grey list is indicative, a term that has the same effect or is used to the same effect, eg in imposing a disproportionate

26. *EMI* Records *& Ors v Eircom Ltd* [2010] IEHC 108, paras 27–30.
27. [2012] IEHC 264. Note also, *EMI Records (Ireland) Limited & Ors v The Data Protection Commissioner* [2013] IESC 34 dealing with appeal by Data Protection Commissioner against judgement of Charleton J on technical issue concerning his finding of no reasons on notice to Eircom rather than substantive issues to the Protocol.
28. *EMI v The Data Protection Commissioner,* paras 3.7, 7.4–7.5.
29. <http://www.eircom.net/policy/> accessed 30 August 2013.
30. The Unfair Terms in Consumer Contracts Directive.

sanction such as internet disconnection, is open at the very least to suspicion as to conformity. While a fuller consideration is outside the scope of this analysis, in light of recent French reforms removing disconnections under the *Loi Hadopi* for being disproportionate, the broadness of the enforcement clause remains a concern.[31]

To this end, art 2(h) of the Data Protection Directive requires consent to be (i) freely given, (ii) specific, and (iii) an informed indication of the data subject's wishes by which the data subject signifies his/her agreement to personal data being processed. Given that the clause in question makes no mention of the fact that data processing will form any 'enforcement modality',[32] can it be said that the original consent to contract satisfies art 2(h)? The learned judge himself notes[33] that when a legislature uses different words, the canons of statutory construction indicate that different concepts are generally referenced in respect of each word. To this end, the consent *prima facie* must be more than mere assent to the contract where the processing has a specific purpose best described as tangential to the primary aspects of the contract, eg provision of service and billing. Indeed, s 2(A)(1)(a) of the DPA requires that the 'data subject has given his or her consent *to the processing*', inferring that the specific processing must be notified to the potential data subject. Consent to the processing, as required under art 2(h) and s 2(A)(1)(a) of the DPA, must surely be express and freely informed, particularly given strict requirements of the latter. Indeed, anything less would appear to contribute to what may be described as 'a normative degradation'[34] of rights that Eircom's customers should have as data subjects, had personal data been identified by the learned judge as present under the Protocol. It is respectfully submitted an express consent to the processing under the Protocol cannot be made out in accordance with European law, unless expressly notified as to the specific nature and purpose of the particular processing, whereupon a notice to the contract terms could be construed as freely given and informed.

Necessity

Charleton J was also satisfied the Protocol could be justified under s 2A(1)(b) of the DPA – necessary for the performance of a contract. The Article 29 Working Party contend[35] necessity for this purpose should be construed narrowly with a granularity to be applied to contract terms, such that while an original consent to a contract may exist, it does not necessarily satisfy the element of necessity

31. <http://legifrance.gouv.fr/affichTexte.do?cidTexte=JORFTEXT000027678782&categorieLien=id> Accessed 30 August 2013.
32. *EMI Records & Ors v Eircom Ltd* [2010] IEHC 108, para 30.
33. *EMI v Data Protection Commissioner* para 3.4.
34. See generally MJ Radin, *Boilerplate: The Fine Print, Vanishing Rights, and the Rule of Law* (Princeton University Press 2012).
35. Opinion 15/2011, 'On the Definition of Consent', WP187, 8.

as it applies to data processing. If such is the case, a fresh consent will have to be sought in line with the express consent required by art 2(h) of Directive 95/46/EC and s 2(A)(1)(a) of the DPA. Necessity of data processing under a contract for internet services may include activities incidental to the contract; the question is whether or not it extends to the imposition of a sanction that removes internet access itself. Charleton J was satisfied that it does, yet where necessity is informed by an originating consent to a contract including an overly broad enforcement term in a standard form contract, it is arguable that this is the very scenario the Article 29 Working Party were cautioning against. Notwithstanding its dubious position under European law, if the Protocol is challenged in the future as to the processing of personal data, any justification based in contract law would *prima facie* require alterations to its contractual terms. While the import of such changes may ultimately render consumer assent rather than consent, it is the minimum that should be undertaken.

IP Addresses as Personal Data

In denying IP addresses are personal data under s 1 of the DPA, Charleton J felled the Commissioner's challenge at the outset, precluding any future challenge in this regard and denying minimum accountability of the Protocol under data processing controls. The obvious question is whether or not he was correct. Under s 1 of the DPA, as amended, personal data is defined as 'data relating to a living individual who is or can be identified either from the data or from the data in conjunction with other information that is in, or is likely to come into, the possession of the data controller'. In turn, in order for data to be personal, it must identify or be capable of solely identifying the biographical data of a potential data subject. As a matter of fact the learned judge was correct in holding that IP addresses processed under the Protocol do not amount to personal data under s 1 DPA as disclosure to Eircom is of data it already holds, eg the biographical data of its customers.[36] Yet, s 1 of the DPA is far narrower than its counterpart under the Data Protection Directive, which defines personal data under art 1 as 'any information relating to an *identified or identifiable* natural person' where identification can be direct or indirect relative to a number of factors, including an identification number such as the IP address. Under art 1 the individual may already be identified when any other information relating to that individual is disclosed to a party not in possession of such information. Applying this to the Protocol, the issue is not whether or not IP addresses are personal data (they are not under the Protocol) as per the Commissioner's challenge, but rather whether the information alleging infringement constitutes 'any information relating to an identified' natural person under art 1, eg the internet subscriber.

In 2011, the ECJ declared in *Scarlet v Sabam*[37] that IP addresses are personal data under a proposed Belgian monitoring and filtering system for copyright

36. *EMI Records & Ors v Eircom Ltd* [2010] IEHC 108, para 26.
37. case C–70/10.

enforcement as they allow internet users to be precisely identified.[38] In so doing, the Court contextualised how those IP addresses were being used under the injunction in question as being part of a systemic analysis of all unlawful content sent across the internet network. If the IP address is personal data for the purposes of art 1 of Directive 95/46/EC, the logical conclusion is that information used in conjunction with the IP address must also amount to personal data as 'any information that relates to *an identified* natural person'. Indeed, the Article 29 Working Party[39] has interpreted 'relating to' under art 1 as inclusive of characteristics of behaviour or if such information is used to determine or influence the way in which that person is treated or evaluated, eg inference of wrongdoing and imposing sanction. Is there a right to privacy in such activity data if it is breaching the contract by representing actions of piracy, eg does Eircom have a right to such data per Charleton J?

Eircom uses such data to impose sanction on a customer who has limited rights of appeal that functions under a presumption of guilt, based in a corporate weighing of the balance of probabilities, namely that the IP address and data forwarded from EMI or its agent(s) is an accurate representation of subscriber infringement. In *Media CAT Ltd v Adams*,[40] Judge Birrs QC aptly noted that the acceptance of an IP address at face value as discharging the burden of proof of copyright infringement could produce skewered results for innocent subscribers where their wifi router was used without consent, or where internet connection use was sanctioned but not copyright infringement using that connection.[41] In *Durant v Financial Services Authority*,[42] the English Court of Appeal ruled that personal data should be considered akin to its effect on an individual's privacy and not linked to biographical information. Auld LJ asserted that privacy will be engaged if the data relates to the individual's 'continuum of relevance or proximity',[43] relating to an individual's private sphere. Much maligned, it remains relevant in grey areas such as the Protocol, where the IP address is used in conjunction with activity data, assessed for the imposition of sanction.

In *EMI Records & Ors v Data Protection Commissioner*,[44] Charleton J was of the opinion that any activity conducted in a P2P network did not attract a right to constitutional privacy where private communications were being used to effect a criminal activity. Yet, in all three cases before him, the learned judge was at pains to point out that nothing under the Protocol or a similar system intersects with the criminal law; rather it is a civil sanction for a civil matter.[45] As

38. ibid para 51.
39. Opinion 4/2007, 'On the Concept of Personal Data, 6–17, 9.
40. [2011] FSR 28.
41. ibid para 27–30.
42. [2004] FSR 28.
43. ibid per Auld LJ, 576.
44. *EMI v Data Protection Commissioner* para 3.4.
45. ibid para 10.0.

held by the United States Supreme Court,[46] copyright infringement is not easily equated with theft, conversion or fraud, rather it is an invasion of exclusive rights bestowed by statute, with such infringement neither wholly depriving the copyright holder of absolute control (physical or otherwise) or of the exclusive rights granted. Indeed, In *R v Cuttell*,[47] Pringle J held that even where an individual commits a criminal act, eg possession of child pornography, their privacy rights were engaged where the internet service provider (ISP) disclosed information without warrant to the police.[48] In recognising a reasonable expectation of the internet subscriber for activity conducted over a network, Pringle J held that such an expectation could be diminished by contract, eg disclosure clauses.[49]

Applying this reasoning to the Protocol, it is submitted a baseline expectation to privacy can be made out by internet users that their internet activity and IP address will not be monitored and forwarded to the sole body that may make arbitrary use of that information, eg the ISP. Indeed, contrary to the opinion of Charleton J,[50] Pringle J asserts that arguments the IP address is publicly available and no privacy arises misses the point when that data is forwarded to an ISP who can take action against the individual behind the IP address.[51] Moreover, in *Golden Eye (International) Ltd v Telefonica UK Ltd*,[52] Arnold J accepted that in ordering identity disclosure, an individual's art 7 and 8 rights under the EU Charter would be engaged.[53] Article 7 and the right to a private life is all the more engaged when an individual is wrongly accused and, if the concerns of Judge Birrs QC are well founded under the Protocol, interaction with the right to privacy becomes all the more pointed. In any event, Charleton J argues that Eircom is entitled to such information to know what its customers are doing on the network. This remains an open point – policy considerations might dictate otherwise, yet Pringle J is correct that Eircom could diminish the expectation or indeed right to privacy through contract. If, as Charleton J states, no criminal dynamic informs the Protocol, it is respectfully submitted any diminishing of a right to privacy concerning activity data would have to be shaped by the contract. Moreover, even if Eircom shaped the expectation to privacy as being limited, the fact remains that it continues to have obligations under data protection legislation, where such data is construed as personal. For the sake of argument, if Charleton J is correct and Eircom is entitled to such data, the fact remains that it obtains such data through its disclosure by a third party to Eircom. Disclosure under

46. *Dowling v United States* 473 US 207 (1985).
47. unreported, 2 October 2009 (CJ (Gen Div) (Ont)) (Ontario).
48. ibid paras 14–32.
49. *Dowling v United States* para 30.
50. *EMI Records & Ors v Eircom Ltd* [2010] IEHC 108, para 25.
51. *Dowling v United States* para 22.
52. [2013] EMLR 1.
53. ibid 47.

s 1 DPA is defined as not including disclosure as between a data controller/processor to an employee or agent for the for the purpose of the employee or agent to carry out his or her duties. Unlike biographical data, activity data is not in Eircom's possession and would constitute disclosure of personal data, if so accepted as so defined under the Data Protection Directive. Moreover, as the software company in question as data controller/processor is an agent of EMI and not an employee of Eircom, disclosure could be made out under s 1 DPA. Entitlement or not, it is *prima facie* the case that such a process would be subject to data protection controls.

Copyright Enforcement and the Need for Balance: Towards a Pluralist Paradigm?

In *Promusicae v Telefónica de España*,[54] the ECJ make clear that, although Directive 2004/48/EC requires effective measures and remedies for the enforcement of copyright, such measures must conform to the principles of Community law in general and balance must be achieved with other fundamental rights, namely under the EU Charter. In so doing, the ECJ cautioned that in interpreting European law as to the enforcement measures, due regard must be had by national legislatures and courts to the principle of proportionality.[55] In the context of online enforcement where an individual's rights ostensibly include privacy, the right to data protection, the right to communicate, freedom of expression generally and rights of due process, it is apparent the boundary of any enforcement measures are defined by the scope of such rights. Given a corporate strategy of absolutist enforcement informed three-strike laws, it is worth considering whether or not the boundary of such rights is capable of being defined as an emergent pluralist paradigm for copyright enforcement under European law.

The position of the ECJ has not changed since its decision in *Promusicae* in calling for balance between the competing rights of internet subscribers and holders of copyright, yet in *Scarlet v Sabam*[56] it established a boundary as to how far enforcement measures could be taken in the online context. The enforcement system required monitoring of all communications of every customer within the *Scarlet* network identifying copyrighted works in the process of infringement. In so doing, the system would impose a filtering mechanism on the network with active blocking of in-transit communications without an ability to filter legal and non-legal communications. Beyond finding that the system imposed prohibitive costs on the ISP in violation of art 3 of

54. case C–275/06.
55. ibid para 68.
56. *EMI Records & Ors v Eircom Ltd* [2010] IEHC 108, para 26.

Directive 2004/48 and art 16 of the EU Charter,[57] the Court held that the system could violate an individual's right to freedom of expression, eg the right to impart and receive information.[58] In *LSG v Tele2*[59] the ECJ confirmed that even where an ISP merely provides an internet connection facilitating use for infringement but exercising no control or offering other services, the ISP will be liable to injunction. As a result of *Scarlet* it would appear that injunction must accord with art 3 of Directive 2004/48/EC, be proportionate and not be prohibitively costly; significantly the Court did not preclude monitoring or indeed filtering *per se*.

In finding that the system under *Scarlet* violated art 15 of Directive 2000/31, prohibiting a general monitoring function being imposed on an ISP by national authorities, the Court executed a crafted interpretation of 'general' for the purposes of art 15. To this end, it placed emphasis on the fact *all* communications were being monitored, with no limitation in time and directed at all future infringements and works that have not yet been created.[60] Proportionality required under art 3 of Directive 2004/48/EC was clearly breached when it is considered that the system could not differentiate between lawful and unlawful transmissions and would affect all users of the network. In *EMI v Data Protection Commissioner*, Charleton J respectfully rebuked the Commissioner for construing the ECJ judgment in *Scarlet* as altering the nature of copyright enforcement under European law as prioritising fundamental rights over copyright and in turn misinterpreting the scope of the ECJ's ruling.[61] The learned judge is quite correct; a remedy continues to be required by art 3 of Directive 2004/48/EC and where necessary injunctions continue to be available under art 8(3) Directive 2001/29/EC. Although Eircom has protested[62] the Protocol is prohibitively expensive, presumably interfering with its art 16 EU Charter rights, it remains an open point arguably undermined by the fact that the monitoring is undertaken by EMI and not of the entire network by Eircom alone. To this end, the Protocol arguably does not come within a general monitoring function under art 15 of Directive 2000/31/EC if the ECJ judgment is to be construed as pertaining to monitoring of *all* communications with an active filtering mechanism intercepting communications in transit.

While the *Scarlet* decision establishes the limits of monitoring to enforce copyright under European law and the scope of ISP obligations, it also raises

57. ibid para 46.
58. ibid para 53.
59. case C–557/07.
60. *EMI Records & Ors v Eircom Ltd* [2010] IEHC 108, para 40.
61. *EMI v Data Protection Commissioner* para 8.10.
62. See <http://www.scribd.com/doc/83984628/TIF-briefing1-001> and <http://www.scribd.com/doc/83984628/TIF-briefing1-001> detailing meetings between Eircom Ltd, Minister of State Sean Sherlock and Telecommunications and Internet Federation. See also <http://irishjournalist.blogspot.ie/2012/03/eircoms-3-strikes-scheme.html> accessed 30 August 2013.

questions as to the proportionality of the Protocol (if it may be justified under private agreement) with regard to proportionality of sanction. In Charleton J's opinion the Protocol is the most proportionate means available under such monitoring systems to secure copyright holder rights while having a limited effect on internet subscriber rights.[63] Is it proportionate to disconnect an internet connection for copyright infringement? In *Scarlet*, the right to freedom of expression was clearly engaged in the blocking of communications in transit; does the same apply to disabling internet access? The learned judge argues that an internet subscriber may go to an internet café or secure another connection with a different ISP and is not unduly affected. With respect, recognising an internet subscriber may have to seek out another means to effect the same communications infers their right to communicate and impart and receive information is engaged. Admittedly, if considered as the defining interpretation of freedom of expression in this context, the ECJ's decision in *Scarlet*, eg a communication must be blocked in transit to be disproportionate, appears to have no application to the Protocol. Yet, communications in transit remain only one aspect of the right to freedom of expression. As with copyright and property rights generally, the right to freedom of expression is not absolute and subject to limitation. The UN Special Rapporteur on the promotion and protection of the right to freedom of expression and opinion argues the right to freedom of expression is linked with internet access, rooted in the internet's unique characteristics such as speed, worldwide reach and anonymity.[64] In this sense, in serving as an enabler of the right to freedom of expression, the internet is a catalyst for the application of other rights including *inter alia* those broadly defined as social and economic, such as the right to education, and civil and political rights, such as freedom of association and assembly.[65]

Moreover, he argues that any restriction must be in conformity with a three-part test.[66] First, the restriction must be provided for in law; secondly, it must pursue a legitimate interest, including the protection of rights of others; and thirdly, it must be necessary as the least restrictive means to achieve the purported purpose.[67] In 2009, the European legislature demonstrated its resolve[68] against such disconnections with the inclusion of an 'internet freedom provision' reforming the EU Telecoms Directives. Article 3(a) of

63. *EMI Records [Ireland] Ltd & Ors v UPC Communications Ireland Ltd* [2010] IEHC 377, para 37.
64. UN Human Rights Council, Report of the Special Rapporteur on the promotion and protection of the right to freedom of opinion and expression, Frank La Rue, A/HRC/17/27, 2011.
65. ibid para 22.
66. ibid para 24.
67. ibid 8, para 24.
68. See D Jančić, 'The European Political Order and Internet Piracy: Accidental or Paradigmatic Constitution-Shaping' (2010) 6 Euro Const L Rev 430–61.

Directive 2002/48/EC provides any measures aimed at restricting access to or use of services such as the internet must be appropriate, proportionate and necessary with implementation subject to appropriate procedural safeguards in accordance with European fundamental rights and Community law of effective judicial protection and due process. Moreover, measures can only be taken in respect of the presumption of innocence and privacy and must consist of a prior, fair and impartial procedure, inclusive of a right to be heard. The import being that prior to any disconnection a court hearing is necessary to sanction individual disconnections. To this end, Charleton J contends[69] the district court would be capable of dealing with imposing sanction on application of the ISP or the rights-holder, allowing also for proportionality. Yet, in applying art 3(a) of Directive 2002/48/EC to the Protocol, two issues emerge: the Irish implementing regulations post-date the Protocol,[70] and the Article is directed at the Member States rather than private entities. Notwithstanding, the Protocol remains an affront to the intention of the European legislature with an obligation for the Irish legislature to act in accordance with its obligations under art 3 of Directive 2004/48/EC in ensuring any measures to enforce copyright must be proportionate with safeguards against abuse. Private agreements circumventing the requirements of art 3(a) of Directive 2002/48/EC would appear to constitute such an abuse.

Beyond the Protocol: Emerging Trends in Strategy

In *EMI v UPC*,[71] Charleton J held that s 40(4) of the Copyright and Related Rights Act failed to transpose European law as to terminating and preventing infringements and removing and disabling access to hosted online content. In response, the European Union (Copyright and Related Rights) Regulations 2012 were enacted, giving effect to art 8(3) of Directive 2001/29/EC and permitting an injunction to be obtained against an ISP in accordance with art 14(3) of Directive 2000/31/EC. Article 14(3) provides an injunction may be secured against an intermediary to terminate or prevent an infringement and not exclude Member States from adopting procedures to remove or disable access to hosted information. As a result, EMI has secured two injunctions[72] against UPC to block and in turn disable access to the website 'PirateBay.org' to prevent infringements via the file-sharing website. Constrained by a lack of

69. *EMI Records [Ireland] Ltd & Ors v UPC Communications Ireland Ltd* [2010] IEHC 377, para 128.
70. See <http://www.comreg.ie/_fileupload/publications/ComReg1148.pdf>. Accessed 30 August 2013.
71. *EMI Records [Ireland] Ltd & Ors v UPC Communications Ireland Ltd* [2010] IEHC 377.
72. *EMI Records Ireland Ltd & Ors v UPC Communications Ireland Ltd & Ors* [2013] IEHC 274 & *EMI Records (Ireland) Ltd & Ors v UPC Communications Ireland Ltd & Ors* [2013] IEHC 204.

forthcoming legislation for an Irish three-strike law and facing a non-complicit ISP such as UPC, EMI's strategy may now rest with blocking of internet websites facilitating infringement. Yet, an asymmetrical strategy remains possible for EMI to target internet subscribers directly, namely through disclosure of identity under *Norwich Pharmacal* orders[73] and subscriber settlement rather than ligitation.

In 2005, Kelly J granted a *Norwich Pharmacal* order[74] to EMI against Eircom, with little deterrent effect, ultimately leading to the Protocol. As Charleton J notes,[75] the costs of going to court to reveal the identity of a relatively few infringers is prohibitive. Yet, recent developments in England and Wales may alter that dynamic in favour of copyright holders seeking a new deterrent strategy.[76] In *Goldeneye (International) Ltd v Telefonica UK Ltd*,[77] Arnold J sanctioned the disclosure of identities of 9,124 internet subscribers, alleged by private firms representing copyright holders to have infringed copyright. In so doing, Arnold J held that the *Norwich Pharmacal* order did not require such firms to bring proceedings against defendants but rather letters of claim seeking settlement were a legitimate means of seeking redress.[78] Although the learned judge recognised that defendants data protection and privacy rights under the EU Charter were engaged, he held the order was proportionate under art 3(2) Directive 2004/48 and it struck a fair balance, contingent on conditional safeguards being addressed under the letters of claim.[79]

Earlier doubts raised by Judge Birrs QC as to the right of such firms to act in such a manner for copyright holders, the evidentiary value of IP addresses and the effect receipt of such a letter may have on a lay defendant were effectively cast aside.[80] Arnold J was satisfied that the IP addresses and corroborating evidence presented before the court made a cogent arguable case that infringement took place at the IP address in question, with or without the subscribers knowledge, with the reality that

73. See *Norwich Pharmacal Co & Others v Customs and Excise Commissioners* [1974] AC 133.
74. *EMI Records (Ireland) Ltd & Ors v Eircom Ltd & Anor* [2005] IEHC 233.
75. *EMI Records [Ireland] Ltd & Ors v UPC Communications Ireland Ltd* [2010] IEHC 377, para 62.
76. On copyright enforcement deterrence strategy, see Robin Andrews, 'Copyright Infringement and the Internet: An Economic Analysis of Crime' (2005) *Boston University Journal of Science & Technology Law*, Vol. 11(2), pp. 256-282.
77. *Dowling v United States* para 22.
78. ibid 44–45.
79. Whereas, the original letters of claim sought a settlement of £700, the learned judge agreed with Consumer Focus that such a sum is unsupportable due to speculative invoicing and, where a subscriber admits liability, a settlement figure should be individually negotiated. ibid 48–49.
80. Opinion 4/2007, 'On the Concept of Personal Data', 6–17, 9.

most of these subscribers will have infringed copyright.[81] The decision raises the prospect of an altered strategy in Ireland, enabling deterrence to be achieved through disclosure orders and letters of claim that also give notice of further proceedings to alleged defendants. Success relies on both the ability to detect large numbers of infringers and their complicity with the letters of claim, yet as Arnold J notes, the process would be deemed necessary and proportionate in line with art 3 of Directive 2004/48/EC as copyright holders have a right to pursue such infringers under art 8 (2004/48/EC).

Indeed, in *Bonnier Audio v Perfect Communications Sweden AB*,[82] the ECJ confirmed that a copyright holder has a right to such information under art 8 of Directive 2004/48/EC, namely the biographical information of a suspected copyright pirate, in civil proceedings. In so holding, the ECJ removed doubts that such information was available to public authorities only in criminal proceedings and effectively confirmed that disclosure orders akin to *Norwich Pharmacal* orders are possible under European law dealing with copyright enforcement. The position of the Court reflects its earlier decision in *Promusicae* in which it noted that despite Directive 2002/58/EC requiring ISPs to erase and anonymise data, exceptions were permissible under art 15(1). While such exceptions are outside the scope of civil proceedings, art 15(1) includes reference to art 13(1) of Directive 95/46/EC, which provides that national legislatures may create exceptions to the need for confidential data in order to protect the rights and freedoms of others. To this end, if software is capable of detecting IP addresses in their thousands, the lack of a deterrent effect from Kelly J's disclosure order may be reversed if the strategy from revelation of identity is settlement rather than further litigation. In light of *Bonnier*, it is arguable that, with sufficient safeguards, national legislative measures could be tailored to streamline the disclosure process. From the perspective of companies such as EMI, the outcome of *Bonnier* and particularly *Golden Eye* offer the opportunity for a revised strategy for copyright enforcement. Questions surrounding proportionality and consumer welfare issues, particularly with regard to letters of claim, remain outstanding if such a strategy was pursued in the future.

Conclusion

It is beyond doubt that while the absolutist strategy employed by corporate holders of copyright has been rebuked by the European institutions, a new pluralist paradigm advancing fundamental rights to priority has failed to emerge. Rather, any consideration of fundamental rights is at best reactionary with an emerging trend that any safeguards will be considered on an

81. *Dowling v United States* 44.
82. case C–461/10.

incremental case-by-case basis. The normative framework of European law has shown itself capable of integrating both copyright enforcement and the necessary safeguards, contingent on defining the scope of rights that should apply in the online context for internet subscribers. The difficulty presented by the Protocol is it arguably represents a precedent of grounding copyright enforcement within the ISP contract for service and in turn circumventing both European policy and law as to copyright enforcement. Absent safeguards such as those directed by art 3(a) of Directive 2002/48/EC, private agreements such as the Protocol have the effect of establishing *de facto* communications and copyright enforcement policy with no apparent mandate in law.[83] From policy perspectives, regulating the scope of ISP discretion in the particular context of copyright enforcement appears necessary if agreements such as the Protocol are capable of undermining European legal norms, particularly those under art 3(1) and (2) of Directive 2004/48/EC relating to safeguards against abuse.

KEVIN T O'SULLIVAN*

State Responsibility and the Exploitation of the Oil for Food scheme: *Republic of Iraq v ABB AG et al* (2013)

Introduction

On 27 June 2008, the Republic of Iraq filed a suit in the New York Southern District Court, against 90 companies who colluded with the Hussein regime to deprive Iraqi citizens and the Iraqi State of monies directed to humanitarian purposes from the United Nations escrow account under the Oil for Food

83. See generally Timothy Wu, 'Copyright's Communication Policy' (2004) 103 Mich L Rev 278, 366.

* PhD Candidate, University College Cork. The author expresses his gratitude to the Irish Research Council for their generous funding of his doctoral studies, aspects of which inform this article, and to the anonymous reviewer for comments on an earlier draft.

scheme.[1] Among the companies listed included international giants such as BNP Paribus UK Holdings Ltd, Boston Scientific SA, Smithkline Beecham International, and Thermo King Ireland Ltd. In an elaborate system of kickbacks and surcharges, the Hussein Regime allocated oil to government-friendly corporations below the market value, for the enrichment of the corporations involved and at the expense of the Iraqi people, who were deprived of more than $7 billion from the fund destined for humanitarian goods.

On 6 February 2013, in an unusual ruling, Stein J found that Iraq did have standing to recover for injury to its proprietary interests in the United Nations escrow fund, but did not have standing to pursue quasi-sovereign interests as *parens patriae* of the Iraqi people. More interesting was the Court's reliance on, and interpretation of, the Draft Articles on the Responsibility of States for Wrongful Acts and the finding that the current government of Iraq is responsible for the illegal embezzlement of the former regime.

Key Issues

(A) The Court found that the action was justiciable because the claims represented legal rather than political questions. On this basis Iraq had standing on an alleged injury to its proprietary interests, but did not have standing *parens patriae.*

(B) The Court found that the illegal conduct of the former regime occurred pursuant to official State policy, and were therefore attributable to the current government under the laws of state responsibility.

(C) The Court dismissed Iraq's claim for relief under the Racketeer Influenced and Corrupt Organizations Act (RICO). The RICO statute did not have extraterritorial application, and therefore did not extend to claims of criminality by a foreign government defrauding a multinational organisation.

(D) Iraq could not establish a private right of action pursuant to the Foreign Corruption Practices Act as the Act did not provide for a private right of action.

(E) The Court declined the exercise of supplemental jurisdiction over common law claims, on the basis that these are barred by the *pari delicto* doctrine.

Discussion

Although the case taken by Iraq to recover the monies expropriated from the Oil for Food scheme failed, the ruling is nonetheless significant in terms of state-sponsored crime. The following discussion will broadly appraise (1) the Status of

1. *Republic of Iraq v ABB AG et al*, No 08 Civ 5951 (GEL) (SDNY) (2013) <http://www.nysd.uscourts.gov/cases/show.php?db=special&id=262> accessed 20 February 2013.

Iraq, (2) State Responsibility for the Internationally Wrongful Acts of the Hussein Regime and (3) Iraq's Proprietary Interest in the Oil for Food scheme.

Status of Iraq

Section IV of the judgment examines the relationship between the current government of Iraq and the Hussein regime.[2] The appraisal is significant in light of the controversial debate on modern *debellatio* that erupted in the aftermath of the belligerent occupation of Iraq. The traditional doctrine of *debellatio* finds that where the enemy State has annexed the territory on conquest, full sovereignty transfers to the belligerent.[3] However, Benvenisti advanced that United Nations Security Council Resolution 1483, which mandated the controversial transformative belligerent occupation of Iraq, heralded a 'modern doctrine of *debellatio*' based on the concept of popular sovereignty. This, he argued, was underscored by the creation of a 'totally new legal and political order during the period of belligerent occupation'.[4] Certainly the academic consensus on post-conflict Iraq was that the transformative belligerent occupation existed as a *sui generis* beyond the consideration of traditionally restrictive international humanitarian law on State 'conservationist' administration during occupation.[5] Notwithstanding, the question remained: what, if any, responsibility did this new legal and political order have for the actions of the former Hussein regime?

A tenuous precedent for the consideration of a 'modern doctrine of *debellatio*' derived from the post-surrender status of Germany after World War II, and the nature of administration, which ensued dogged by sweeping reforms. Significantly, after World War II, the Allies argued that the administration and institutional reforms enacted in Western Germany were not governed by the framework of Article 43 of the Hague Regulations as Germany had surrendered unconditionally. At the time, this argument splintered academic opinion,

2. No 08 Civ 5951 (GEL) (SDNY) 23.
3. Adam Roberts, 'What is Military Occupation?' (1985) *BYIL* 267; Nicholas Hansen, 'Modern Territorial Statehood' 48 <https://openaccess.leidenuniv.nl/bitstream/handle/1887/13334/NG%2BHansen%2BModern%2BTerritorial%2BStatehood%2Bfinal%2Bversion.pdf?sequence=1> accessed 16 February 2013.
4. Eyal Benvenisti, 'Water Conflicts During the Occupation of Iraq' (2003) 97 AJIL 862. This idea was expanded on by Patterson, who argued that the traditional preserve of the temporary managerial powers of the belligerent did not fit succinctly with the mandate provided under UN Resolution 1483, which envisaged a modern doctrine of *debellatio*, flanked by the contextual considerations of self-determination and modern human rights law. Melissa Patterson, 'Who's Got the Title? Or the Remnants of *Deballatio* in Post Invasion Iraq' (2006) 47(2) Harv Int't LJ.
5. Adam Roberts, 'Transformative Military Occupation: Applying the Laws of War and Human Rights' (2006) 100 AJIL 580; Nehal Bhuta, 'The Antinomies of Transformative Occupation' (2005) 16(4) EJIL; Gregory Fox, 'Transformative Occupation and the Unilateralist Impulse' (Spring 2012) 94(885) IRRC; Peter G Danchin, *The Role of International Law in Rebuilding Societies After Conflict* (Cambridge University Press 2009), 64–89.

with Von Glahn observing, 'seldom has a single and limited topic in the field of international law produced so abundant and so diverse a literature as has this particular issue'.[6] Some argued that the Article 43 framework did apply, but that there existed a 'necessity' exception, which permitted the radical overhaul of repugnant Nazi laws.[7] While the dominant argument considered that by abolishing the German government, the Allies has succeeded in destroying the German State, thereby permitting the victorious belligerents to establish sovereignty over the territory.[8] Accordingly, the German Democratic Republic and the German Federal Republic were considered as two successor states, symbolically and ideologically different to the former German Reich.[9] Although, Dumberry suggests that responsibility attributed to the German Democratic Republic for the internationally wrongful acts of the German Reich were 'driven by Cold War *realpolitik* rather than by the application of any legal principles'.[10]

---

6. Gerhrad Von Glahn, *The Occupation of Enemy Territory; A Commentary on the Law and Practice of Belligerent Occupation* (The University of Minnesota Press 1957) 274.
7. Yutaka Arai-Takahashi, 'Preoccupied with Occupation: Critical Examinations of the Historical Development of the Law of Occupation' (Spring 2012) 94(885) IRRC 66.
8. Hans Kelsen, 'The Legal Status of Germany According to the Declaration of Berlin' (1945) 39(3) AJIL 519; Hans Kelsen, 'Is a Peace Treaty with Germany Legally Possible and Politically Desirable?' (1947) 41(6) Am Pol Sci Rev 1188; See also *Ministries*, XIV TWC 690, where the Military Tribunal for Nuremberg found that owing to the unconditional surrender of Germany, the Allied occupation did not 'make a situation falling within the contemplation of the provisions of the Hague Convention applicable to belligerent occupancy'.
9. Barbara Guerin, *L'Évolution du Statut Juridique de l'Allemagne de 1945 au Traité Fondamental* (Droste 1978) 97–105; Peter E Quint, *The Imperfect Union: Constitutional Structures of German Unification* (Princeton University Press 1997) 14; David P Currie, *The* Constitution *of the Federal Republic of Germany* (The University of Chicago Press 1994) 85. See also BVerfGE 36, 1 2 BvF 1/73 *Grundlagenvertrag-decision East–West Basic Treaty* (31 July 1973), where the Federal Constitutional Court, ruling on the validity of a treaty concluded between the Federal Republic of Germany and the German Democratic Republic, considered that: 'From the political importance of the Treaty as set forth, there follows the further legal conclusion that as the basis for the new relationships *between the two German States*, there will necessarily emerge from it in the coming period a multiplicity of legal specifications of the new co-existence, *indeed togetherness, of the two States* (cf. Article 7 of the Treaty). Each of these further steps must not only be in accordance with the Treaty but also in accordance with the Basic Law. Accordingly, clarification is required right from today that everything that takes place in further legal steps based on the Treaty is not necessarily legally in order simply because the Treaty basis (the Treaty) cannot be objected to constitutionally. Accordingly, in these constitutional review proceedings, as far as can be foreseen the constitutional bounds are to be indicated that exist for the "fleshing out" of the Treaty by later agreements and accords.' Emphasis added.
10. Dumberry, 'Is a New State Responsible for Obligations Arising from Internationally Wrongful Acts Committed before its Independence in the Context of Secession?' (2005) 43 Can YB Int'l L 433. See also *Princz v FRG*, 26 F 3d 1166 (DC Cir 1994).

Any suggestion that there might exist a 'modern doctrine of *debellatio*' is significantly quenched by the traditionalist stance adopted by Stein J in *Republic of Iraq*. The Court charts the relationship between the current government and the former regime, outlining:

> The change in governments – from the Hussein Regime; to the Coalition Provisional Authority that governed subsequent to the fall of Saddam Hussein; to the contemporary Republic – did not create an entirely new state. Rather, those changes altered the leadership and government of a continuously existing state. Therefore, the Republic of Iraq is the same sovereign entity as the one controlled by the Hussein Regime. (Iraq's Mem. in Opposition to Motion to Dismiss ('Iraq's Opp.') at 9; *see* Defs.' Mem. in Support of Motion to Dismiss ('Defs.' Mem.') at 12 (same).)[11]

Regardless of notions of popular sovereignty implicit in the new legal order created in Iraq, the new government still remains responsible for the acts of government of the former, arguably illegitimate, regime. Certainly, there is no consideration of state disintegration or *debellation,* which might break or negate international responsibility for the actions of an undemocratic authoritarian regime. This was reinforced by the international recognition of the Hussein regime as the effective government, both by the United States in its international relations and the United Nations in UN SC Resolutions 661 and 986.[12] Furthermore, UN SC Resolution 1546 determined that the successors to the Coalition Provisional Authority and the Interim Government of Iraq would assume 'rights, responsibilities and obligations relating to the Oil for Food Programme that were transferred to the Authority'.[13] Different governments over time will represent the same sovereign state, which is in turn bound by its representative government.[14]

Addressing the regime change, the Court noted that the acts of the former government may redound to the sovereign:

> Changes in the government or the internal policy of a state do not as a rule affect its position in international law. A monarchy may be transformed into a republic, or a republic into a monarchy; absolute principles may be substituted for constitutional, or the reverse; but, though the government changes, the nation remains, with rights and obligations unimpaired.[15]

In terms of responsibility for the commission of fraudulent conduct over the Oil for Food programme, contrary to Security Council Resolution 986, the question

11. No 08 Civ 5951 (GEL) (SDNY) 23.
12. ibid 22.
13. ibid 32.
14. ibid 24.
15. ibid 25.

the court had to determine was whether the conduct was characterised as 'public' or 'private' in nature.

State Responsibility for Internationally Wrongful Acts of the Hussein Regime

From the context of international law, the ruling is significant in that it offers a domestic application of the Draft Articles on Responsibility of States for Internationally Wrongful Acts (2001). The ruling pivoted around an examination of art 4 of the Draft Articles, which is largely considered to be a codification of customary international law.[16] Accordingly, responsibility will be incurred for the 'internationally wrongful act of a State'.[17] The conduct of the State for the internationally wrongful act is 'attributable to the State under international law' constituting a breach by that State of an international obligation.[18] First the court needed to establish (1) whether or not the Hussein regime had committed an internationally wrongful act, (2) whether or not the conduct was attributable to the State, and if so (3) whether or not the act constituted a breach of an international obligation by the State.

Article 4 of the Draft Articles provides:

> 1. The conduct of any State organ shall be considered an act of that State under international law, whether the organ exercises legislative, executive, judicial or any other functions, whatever position it holds in the organization of the State, and whatever its character as an organ of the central Government or of a territorial unit of the State.
> 2. An organ includes any person or entity which has that status in accordance with the internal law of the State.[19]

In line with the accompanying commentaries to the Draft Articles, the Court considered whether the corruption was private in nature, or attributable to the State. According to the commentaries, 'it is irrelevant for this purpose that the person concerned may have had ulterior or improper motives or may be abusing public power'.[20] Stein J determined that the conduct of the Hussein regime was governmental and undertaken in the execution of official duties. For instance, the declaration by Hussein that the sanctions regime amounted to a form of 'economic occupation' represented 'choices made by the regime in the conduct of its foreign affairs'.[21] Moreover, Hussein ordered the government

---

16. Advisory Opinion, *Difference Relating to Immunity from Legal Process of a Special Rapporteur of the Commission on Human Rights*, ICJ Reports 1999, 62, 87, para 62.
17. Draft art 1, *Report of the International Law Commission on the Work of its Thirty-Second Session,* at 59, reprinted in [1980] 2(2) YB Int'l L Comm'n 1, 30.
18. Draft art 3(b), ibid.
19. art 4, *Draft Articles on Responsibility of States for Internationally Wrongful Acts, with Commentaries (2001), Report of the International Law Commission on the Work of its Fifty-Third Session* (United Nations 2008).
20. ibid, Commentary art 4, para 13.
21. No 08 Civ 5951 (GEL) (SDNY) 27.

agencies to effectuate the corrupt scheme of submitting false documents to the United Nations, while the Iraqi State Oil Marketing Organization (SOMO) entered into contracts with companies purchasing oil under the programme and the illicit funds were transferred to the accounts of the Central Bank of Iraq.[22]

While the Draft Articles derive the rule in art 4, commentary 13, from the general international law decisions in the *Mallén* and *Caire* cases, these cases featured abuse of governmental function, albeit on a smaller scale, but against third countries. In the *Mallén* case, the Mexican–US General Claims Commission found that an assault by an agent of the State, Deputy Constable Franco of Texas, against the Mexican consul Mallén with whom he had a personal grievance, was an act conducted in his official capacity and in the course of duty.[23] It was therefore imputable to the State. Likewise in *Caire*, the Franco-Mexican Claims Commission considered Mexico responsible when Mexican soldiers murdered a French national when he refused their attempts to extort money. There, Verjzijl famously determined that:

> for all the acts committed by its officials or organs which constitute offences from the point of view of the law of nations, whether the official or organ in question has acted within or exceeded the limits of his competence… (provided that) they must have acted at least to all appearances as competent officials or organs, or they must have used powers of methods appropriate to their official capacity.[24]

In terms of Iraq, Stein J illustrates that Iraq had already settled claims for wrongful conduct during the Hussein regime under the US–Iraq Claims Settlement Agreement, highlighting that the Iraqi State was responsible even for the illegal acts of the Hussein regime. However, a distinction can be drawn between acts of an international character incurring the responsibility of a State against a foreigner, and internationally wrongful acts, which incur responsibility against the population of the violating State, such as, for example human rights abuses. Annie Bird submits that 'traditional inter-state responsibility for breaches of international law, designed for reciprocal obligations, does not correspond exactly to the needs of the human rights regime'.[25] Although the Draft Articles refer to peremptory norms of international law, state responsibility for violations of human rights treaties from which they derive is less clear. This argument is particularly significant in light of the current case, where the net result is mass exploitation of the resources of the population, a point unfortunately missed in the course of the judgment.

Notwithstanding, the Court concluded:

---

22. ibid 28.
23. *Mallén (United Mexican States) v USA* [1927] 4 RIAA 173, Commission at 177.
24. *Caire Claim* [1929] UNRIAA, vol V (Sales No 1952, V3) 516, 575.
25. Annie Bird, 'Third State Responsibility for Human Rights Violations' (2011) 21(4) EJIL 884.

> the Complainant unmistakably alleges that the wrongful conduct of the Hussein Regime was of a governmental character, pursued for purportedly public purposes, and undertaken by the governmental authorities of Iraq. As a result, that government, however deplorable it may have been, represented Iraq and its acts, however allegedly depraved, are attributable to the sovereign.[26]

This certainly may be the case, however, there are further considerations in lieu of state responsibility that the Court failed to consider, and that arguably may have negated the wrongfulness of the conduct, namely the Chapter 5 defenses. The Draft Articles recognise conduct that may be illegal under international law, but may be justified in the following circumstances: consent, countermeasures in respect of an internationally wrongful act, *force majeure* and fortuitous event, distress, state of necessity and self-defense. Usually once the breach of international law has been established, the burden is placed on the defense to establish the defenses available.[27] This was notably absent from the case, highlighting one of the difficulties implicit in applying international norms in an *ad hoc* manner in the domestic courts.

Iraq's Proprietary Interest in the Oil for Food Scheme

Interestingly, the Court ruled that Iraq had standing to seek relief for an injury to its proprietary interests in the UN escrow accounts fund. Therefore, despite the immunities and privileges accorded to 'persons performing contractual services for the United Nations with the implementation of the Resolution' as outlined in the Memorandum of Understanding between the United Nations and Iraq, the Court found that Iraq had a proprietary interest in the fund against the contractors.[28] This was determined on the basis that the account was funded 'with the proceeds of the sale of Iraqi petroleum and petroleum products' and that Iraq 'ultimately received the balance of the UN escrow account'.[29] Similarly, these immunities were restated under Chapter VII of the Charter of the United Nations, in UN Security Council Resolution 986 (1995).[30]

Notably, the finding that Iraq has standing on the basis of a 'proprietary interest' in the Oil for Food scheme assumes significance in terms of the potential to seek relief over exploitation of the Development Fund for Iraq during the belligerent occupation of Iraq from 2003–04.[31] The Development Fund for Iraq, as the

---

26. No 08 Civ 5951 (GEL) (SDNY) 48.
27. Tom Hillier, *Sourcebook on Public International Law* (Cavendish Publishing Ltd 1998) 338.
28. S/1996/356 Memorandum of Understanding between the Secretariat of the United Nations and the Government of Iraq on the Implementation of Security Council Resolution 986 (1995) <http://daccess-dds-ny.un.org/doc/UNDOC/GEN/N96/127/71/PDF/N9612771.pdf?OpenElement> accessed 18 February 2013.
29. No 08 Civ 5951 (GEL) (SDNY) 17.
30. S/RES/986 (1995), paras 14–16.
31. S/RES/1483 (2003), para 12.

successor fund to the Oil for Food scheme, is an international fund buttressed by international privileges and immunities. However, distinct from the facts in the present case, the administering authority of the fund was the Coalition Provisional Authority, representing the military government of the United States and the United Kingdom. Similarly, the Development Fund for Iraq suffered significant depletion due to the allocation of inflated reconstruction contracts to corporations friendly to the occupation regime.[32] Potentially, the Iraqi State could now argue standing before the United States courts on the basis of a 'proprietary interest' in the Fund and the locus of the military government would override any bar precluding the examination of the case on the act of state doctrine.

Furthermore, the status of the Coalition Provisional Authority as a *de facto* governing entity under art 43 of the Hague Regulations is important in terms of attribution.[33] Although art 9 of the Draft Articles provide a basis for attributing state responsibility to the acts of the *de facto* government, the occupying belligerents are responsible for violations of international humanitarian law during occupation. Where the present case fell in terms of government attribution for the internationally wrongful act, the courts analysis centered on the *de jure* nature of the Hussein government.[34] The Coalition Provisional Authority represented a *de facto* governmental authority, and therefore any international illegal acts might not, as such, be attributable to the sovereign Iraqi state. This contention was supported by the ICJ in *Application of the Convention on the Prevention and Punishment of the Crime of Genocide (Bosnia and Herzegovina v Serbia and Montenegro)*, where the Court found that 'neither the Republika Srpska, nor the VRS, were *de jure* organs of the FRY, since none of them had the status of organ of that State under its internal law'.[35] Consonantly, responsibility for violations of the Genocide Convention was not attributable to the FRY.[36] Similarly, the

32. See SIGIR 13–003, *Development Fund for Iraq: US Army Corps of Engineers Has Missing Receiving Reports and Open Task Orders* (26 October 2012) <http://www.sigir.mil/files/audits/13-003.pdf> accessed 16 February 2013; SIGIR 10–020, *Development Fund for Iraq: Department of Defence Needs to Improve Financial and Management Controls* (27 July 2010) <http://www.sigir.mil/files/audits/10-020.pdf> accessed 16 February 2013.
33. art 43, *Convention (IV) Respecting the Laws and Customs of War on Land and its Annex: Regulations Concerning the Laws and Customs of War on Land*. The Hague, 18 October 1907. 'The authority of the legitimate power having in fact passed into the hands of the occupant, the latter shall take all the measures in his power to restore, and ensure, as far as possible, public order and safety, while respecting, unless absolutely prevented, the laws in force in the country.'
34. No 08 Civ 5951 (GEL) (SDNY) 21.
35. *Application of the Convention on the Prevention and Punishment of the Crime of Genocide (Bosnia and Herzegovina v Serbia Mongtenegro)*, judgment of 26 February 2007, para 386.
36. ibid, para 388.

ICSID arbitral tribunal considered art 4 of the Draft Articles as addressing the 'attribution of acts of so-called *de jure* organs which are empowered to act for the State within the limits of their competence'.[37]

Conclusion

It appears that, for the time being, international law is anchored neatly within the confines of protecting state power. Any indication that the occupation and transformation of Iraq might have heralded a new framework of state rebuilding in international law, focusing on the rights of the population as distinct from the state, is stymied by reference to broader international law considerations such as state responsibility. In 1998, in a scathing attack on the Draft Articles, Philip Allott argued that the Draft Articles merely preserved the self-serving interests of governments at the expense of the world population. He lamented:

> International law is trapped in the pre-revolutionary world of the eighteenth century, the world made by Vattel, the world before the American and French Revolutions, before Rousseau and Marx. The international law of the old regime is preventing the emergence of the new international society.[38]

It appears, 15 years on, not much has changed. Promises of human rights and economic self-determination are meaningless buzzwords for transitioning states. The reality is that the citizens of the world, and more particularly, the citizens of Iraq, remain deprived of the squandered monies from the sale of their natural resources.

The perpetrators are shrouded in immunity, cloaked by international laws on state responsibility designed to protect governments and human rights violating regimes who flaunt the international system for their own enrichment.

SUSAN POWER*

37. *Jan de Nul NV and Dredging International NV v Arab Republic of Egypt* (ICSID case no ARB/04/13), decision on jurisdiction of 16 June 2006, para 89.
38. Philip Allott, 'State Responsibility and the Unmaking of International Law (1998) 29(1) Harv Int'l LJ 25.

* Lecturer, Griffith College Cork.

Book Reviews

EMPLOYMENT EQUALITY LAW
by Marguerite Bolger, Claire Bruton and Cliona Kimber (Round Hall 2012)
ISBN: 978-1-85800-591-1 (lxv + 795 pp, hbk, €245)

Equality and non-discrimination play a greater role in the legal system today than ever before. No field of law has been more significantly affected by equality legislation than that of employment. Although the Employment Equality Act 1998 has now been on the statute book for almost 15 years, *Employment Equality Law*, written by three practising barristers, represents the first standalone and comprehensive treatment of the current regime. The book is comprehensive in its scope and coverage, going beyond the first and third authors' earlier work on sex discrimination to address all of the grounds of discrimination now protected under Irish law, and analysing each of the specific areas of employment law – including access to employment, pay and pensions – to which the legislation applies.

In the field of employment equality, Irish law is, to a large extent, European Union law. This is reflected in the approach adopted by the authors. In their overview of the sources of employment equality law in Chapter 2, as well as in many of the chapters that follow, EU law is quite rightly the starting point of the authors' analysis. Throughout the book, the authors make extensive reference to, and provide very strong analysis of, the evolving case law of the Court of Justice. The reception of EU law in this field in Ireland has not always been straightforward. The authors' critical discussion of the High Court decision in *Minister for Justice, Equality and Law Reform & Anor v Director of the Equality Tribunal* [2010] 2 IR 455 illustrates this well. In this case, the Court held that the Equality Tribunal could not commence a hearing that could have as its result the overruling of a statutory instrument, even if the statutory instrument were contrary to EU law. This decision has potentially far-reaching consequences for the effective implementation of EU law in Ireland. As the authors point out (at pages 32–33), it is difficult to see how the High Court could limit the Equality Tribunal's jurisdiction in this way and 'at the same time ensure compliance with Ireland's obligations pursuant to the [Framework] Directive and the relevant fundamental principles of European law which include equality on grounds of age'. It might be added that the decision is, more fundamentally, difficult to reconcile with the principle of supremacy of EU law. A decision of the Supreme Court on the point will be necessary in order to clarify the scope of the jurisdiction of statutory tribunals – such as the Equality Tribunal and the Labour Court and their successors – to apply EU law in circumstances where it may conflict with Irish law. While the book occasionally slips into pre-Lisbon terminology and numbering, this is a minor quibble. On the whole, the book places a very important and welcome focus on EU law in this field, which will be of considerable value to those working in the area. At the same time, the authors recognise that there remain some areas – for example, prohibition of discrimination on the ground of civil status – where Irish law arguably remains ahead of EU law.

In chapters 3 to 9, the book addresses the grounds of discrimination under the Employment Equality Act. In each chapter, the authors pay close attention to the now voluminous case law of the Equality Tribunal and the Labour Court under the Act. They also place emphasis on the exemptions that may be relevant to each ground. While the Irish legal system now has decades of experience in combating sex discrimination, Chapter 4 on gender and pregnancy illustrates the extent to which challenges remain and novel issues continue to arise in this area. Chapter 5, on race discrimination, recounts the manner in which the Equality Tribunal and the Labour Court have grappled with the difficulties posed by this ground of discrimination – in particular, the practical difficulty of raising a prima facie case in order to shift the burden of proof – as more and more cases have come before these bodies arising from the poor treatment by employers of workers who have come from outside Ireland. The impressive scope of this chapter is evident in the interesting analysis of the recent High Court decision in *Hussein v Labour Court* [2012] IEHC 364 on work permits and illegal contracts of employment. To their credit, the authors do not shy away from tackling the thorny issues to which the Irish legislation, and the underlying EU law, give rise, as further exemplified by the discussion of mandatory retirement ages in Chapter 8 on age discrimination.

The book then looks at the particular areas of employment law that are affected by the legislation. Once again, the discussion is situated in the context of the governing EU law. In addition to the consideration of access to employment in Chapter 10, the authors analyse in some detail the issues of equal pay and pension entitlements in chapters 11 and 13. The authors provide a clear and accessible overview of this complex terrain. In chapters 12 and 14, they explore the concepts of harassment, sexual harassment and victimisation.

Finally, in chapters 15 and 16 of the book, the authors bring their practical experience to bear on the extremely important issues of remedies and practice and procedure. While noting that there has been considerable progress and the positive potential of the alternative remedies such as equality orders and reviews under the Act, the authors conclude (at page 738) that 'Irish law clearly leaves much to be desired' in providing the effective and dissuasive remedies required by EU law. The overview of practice and procedure is useful and up-to-date, for example in its reference to the workplace relations complaint form. Of course, significant institutional changes are on the horizon, with the functions of the Equality Tribunal (and a number of the other statutory tribunals) to be transferred to the Workplace Relations Commission. Notwithstanding those changes, *Employment Equality Law* is set to become, and remain, the essential reference point on this subject in Ireland.

What distinguishes *Employment Equality Law* from many Irish legal texts is the degree to which it places its subject in context. In the opening chapter, the authors provide a brief theoretical introduction to three different models of equality. The structure of equality legislation – which is characterised by a general prohibition of discrimination in certain spheres and a patchwork of exceptions – means that these theoretical issues are rarely far from the surface in the practice of employment equality law. The authors' critical analysis of the *Portmarnock Golf Club* case provides a good illustration of this point. While that case arose under the Equal Status Acts, it is a cautionary tale for equality law more generally. However, it is not just in the opening chapter that the authors locate their subject in its broader context. Throughout the book, the authors make reference not only to comparative law and academic literature on employment equality law but also to a wide range of research on equality issues more generally. This very much enriches their treatment of the subject.

In conclusion, the authors have made a valuable contribution to Irish legal literature in providing this comprehensive and accessible overview and analysis of a complex, dynamic and increasingly important area of law. Successfully combining academic rigour and practical usefulness, the book will be appreciated by scholars, practitioners and decision-makers alike.

DAVID FENNELLY
Assistant Professor in Law, Trinity College Dublin

AN ISLAND'S LAW: A BIBLIOGRAPHICAL GUIDE TO IRELAND'S LEGAL PAST

by W N Osborough (Four Courts Press in Association with the Irish Legal History Society 2013) ISBN: 978-1-84682-416-6 (xvi + 128 pp, hbk, €35)

The most recent volume published under the auspices of the Irish Legal History Society is a bibliographical volume authored by the scholar most associated with the group. It perhaps does a disservice to the other members of the Society to single out Prof Osborough in this manner, but the tribute penned by Prof Norma Dawson makes clear that, without Osborough's tenacity, it is unlikely that the Society would exist. This volume serves as a fitting tribute to his influence for, as one turns the pages, it becomes clear the great extent to which Prof Osborough has succeeded in shaping the landscape of Irish legal history.

The work is structured as a series of three essays, with two postscripts. The earliest of the essays dates to 1986, while the most recent is from 2012. The essays are concerned with writing in Irish legal history and are subdivided into a number of different areas. The areas vary slightly from essay to essay, but this is a function of the organisation and the substantive historical areas remain similar – general narratives, constitutional history, the courts, substantive law, criminal law, the legal profession, judicial biography, courthouses, and law reporting. The area of substantive law is one that varies most substantially between the first and third essay, and is evidence of the increased work being done in this field.

The text itself demonstrates a number of different ways in which Prof Osborough's influence has been felt in the field of legal history. First, the sheer numbers of articles penned by the author on disparate issues that stud the three essays themselves demonstrates his wide-ranging interest in Irish legal history. Secondly, one notices a trend in the development of legal history; a lacuna identified by Osborough in an early survey is filled in in the intervening years (see, eg, his comments on manor courts in the first and second essays). It is rare to see the agenda set in quite so open a manner but this is primarily due to the persuasiveness of his points: there was a lacuna on manor courts that required work.

The first postscript is comprised of the essay Osborough gave when inaugurating the ILHS in 1988, while the second postscript is the tribute paid by Prof Dawson to mark his retirement from the Council of the ILHS.

The book itself is a reference work that is of the first importance to all those with an interest in Irish legal history. One mild criticism that may be levelled against the work is that it is perhaps does not fully capture the most recent work on Irish legal history. Work such as Alan Greene's historical evaluation of art 28.3.3, which appeared in the 2012 edition of the *Irish Jurist*; a similar evaluation of the constitutional protection of private property penned by Rachael Walsh, which appeared in the 2011 edition of the *Dublin University Law Journal*; and a particularly excellent article recently published by Maebh Harding on the Marriage Act (No 2) 1537 in the 2012 edition of *Legal Studies* are not referred to. It is unclear whether these articles were omitted for lack of space or because of a publication date overlap, but other volumes from 2012 do make an appearance. This criticism, if it can be characterised as such, merely calls for further editions of this invaluable bibliographical work. The erudite manner in which Osborough deals with vast swathes of legal history is particularly enlightening for those with an interest in the topic.

DONAL COFFEY
Lecturer in Law, University of Portsmouth

METHODS OF COMPARITIVE LAW

by Pier Giuseppe Monateri (Ed), (Edward Elgar Publishing 2012) ISBN: 978-1-84980-252-9 (xii + 325 pages, hbk, £115)

Within the discipline of comparative law, the turn of the millennium was characterised by a period of upheaval, rethinking and internal meta-level debate. It wasn't merely that interdisciplinary theorists and critical scholars had begun to challenge the preceding hegemony of rigorous, rule-focused study of positive private law within the discipline. In addition, the general awareness of new global perspectives and non-State legal phenomena had altered the entire agenda of legal scholarship across disciplinary borders. Comparative law certainly caught the wave, presenting itself as the truly transnational field of legal scholarship and thus the basis for legal visions of tomorrow.

Simultaneously, however, as *de facto* comparative research had become an everyday activity throughout legal scholarship, comparativists began to ask what it really meant to be a specialist in a field specifically called comparative law. Quickly, the comparative discipline had become a melting-pot of countless approaches, varying from rigorous private law functionalism to broad methods emphasising approaches such as sociology, anthropology and humanities in the context of law. While such diversity of goals was generally applauded, an inevitable concern about fragmentation emerged, suggesting that comparativists 'cannot tend to more than a dozen, and that it is better to have a few flowers bloom than a thousand wilt'.[1]

In the absence of powerful, all-encompassing approaches that could have emerged to bind the discipline together, comparativists have produced a variety of collective works and anthologies seeking not to only provide general reference, but also to chart out the general themes and topics within the discipline.[2] *Methods of Comparative Law* appears as a contribution to this literature with the specific mission of binding together the current trends of comparative methodology between its covers. As the editor Pier Giuseppe Monateri explains in the book's introduction,

> this volume aims to fill a gap in legal scholarship by structuring an intellectual project of de-familiarization from unified and framed conventions. [...] the renovation of Comparative Law feeds upon the pliable, fluid and multidimensional nature of the voices that embody it.[3]

In this spirit, the book aspires to structure its individual writings into a new, manifold narrative, beginning by rethinking the well-known canon of the discipline and then gradually opening up fresh and more recent avenues for comparative research. The celebration of the multiplicity and diversity of comparative approaches seems to resonate with the occasional references to musical polyphonies with which many students of comparative law are familiar, suggesting that the ultimate result of diversity is not cacophony but a rich composition.[4] As a background notion, *Methods of Comparative Law* seems determined to provide the reader with a general feel of progress in the field, a

1. Mathias Reimann, 'The Progress and Failure of Comparative Law in the Second Half of the Twentieth Century' (2002) 50 Am J of Comp L 697.
2. See, for example, Mathias Reimann and Reinhard Zimmermann (eds), *The Oxford Handbook of Comparative Law* (Oxford University Press 2006); Esin Örücü and David Nelken (eds), *Comparative Law: A Handbook* (Hart Publishing 2007); Mauro Bussani and Ugo Mattei (eds), *The Cambridge Compantion to Comparative Law* (Cambridge University Press 2012). For a collection of critical perspectives, see Pierre Legrand and Roderick Munday (eds), *Comparative Legal Studies: Traditions and Transitions* (Cambridge University Press 2003).
3. *Methods of Comparative Law* 1.
4. Famously Esin Örücü, *The Enigma of Comparative Law, Variations on a Theme for the Twenty-First Century* (Martinus Nijhoff Publishers 2004).

claim confirmed by many but still questionable enough to arise in comparative workshops and group discussions.

The essence of the book is therefore in the sequence and continuum of individual contributions, and the good news is that the arrangement does indeed produce a sense of combined reflection and novelty. *Methods of Comparative Law* begins by examining various purposes and intellectual underpinnings associated with the process of comparison, moves on to revisit some canonical comparative approaches and their relationship with 'scientific' assumptions and cultural relativity, plunges into deeply philosophical questions, including the ontology of law itself, and finally emerges to open seas of fresh inquiry by connecting comparative law to 'hot' topics such as international relations, global governance, and the applications of comparative law in economics. In doing so, the book manages to cover many general themes, from the formants theory to comparative law in courts and from hermeneutics to benchmarking. In other words, it does provide a little of something for everyone in the field.

Due to the broad aim of the book, the individual contributions seem to face a dual task: the reader expects them not only to contribute to their topics, but also on some level to introduce the topics to newcomers. The need for introduction and background seems evident in the earlier sections, where the topics deal with well-known issues that go back in the discipline for years or even decades. Towards the end of the book, the chapters introduce less conventional topics in comparative law, representing novelties by being incorporated into the collection. Perhaps it is due to the anthology format of the book, but the individual chapters seem to respond to these two tasks at somewhat uneven proportions.

Positively, most of the contributions do suggest and bring forth new and even surprising views and perspectives to be enjoyed by the readers. Many may make personal discoveries in the individual articles and their highlights, such as when the renowned critic Günter Frankenberg explores the 'Trento tribe' working on the Common Core of European Private Law; when Geoffrey Samuel borrows the methods of comparative theology for discussing the plausibility of one single 'truth' behind diverse legal systems; or when Jeanne Gaakeer explains from a judge's perspective how the task of translating individual and collective experiences into the technical language of law in itself constitutes a comparative endeavour. The final section of the book, considering comparative law in the context of economic performance, returns the discipline back to the issue of measuring 'better' legal approaches, but does it openly in the 21st-century language of political economy.

On the other hand, the fluid and multidimensional voices that embody *Methods of Comparative Law* remain largely compartmentalised within the individual chapters. Reflecting the overwhelming diversity of comparative approaches, the book reproduces the familiar challenge of reading comparative law as it may require extensive interdisciplinary prior knowledge for the reader to comfortably grasp the complex problems, terminologies and discourses invoked. Inevitably, when moving on from one chapter to another, the reader finds herself not only facing a new topic, but oftentimes an entire disciplinary and theoretical tradition as well. As a result, the sensation of cacophony so inherent in comparative law is not overcome.

Few of the chapters provide comprehensive introductions, not to mention 'how-to' guidance, on the particular topics and methods in question. Such aspects might be unnecessary in a collective work dedicated solely to up-to-date review of the current state of affairs in a discipline, but their absence is worth notice when the book claims to offer 'in a comprehensive and pioneering format, an accessible manual from which scholars, students and practitioners can benefit'. While the scarcity of comprehensive methodological introductions may not make the book entirely inaccessible to students and general readers, it may raise the reading threshold considerably. This would be unfortunate, because the latter chapters of the book offer precisely the sort of inspiration and incentive that many students often desperately look for in comparative law.

As a whole, *Methods of Comparative Law* represents a compilation of well-chosen articles that is worth the attention of any dedicated comparativist. The sequence of topics creates an onward-looking structure and seeks a sense of common strength by downplaying the internal discord and fragmentation of the discipline. However, the book does not quite manage to present the comprehensive and accessible manual the discipline is greatly in need of. As such, students may find parts of it confusing unless they are already familiar with the discussions touched upon by the individual chapters. Nevertheless, *Methods of Comparative Law* represents a necessary and optimistic step on a long path in the right direction.

VILLE KOMULAINEN
University of Helsinki

THE ROLE OF EMOTIONS IN CRIMINAL LAW DEFENCES: DURESS, NECESSITY AND LESSER EVILS

by Eimear Spain, (Cambridge University Press 2011) ISBN: 978-1-107-00818-2
(xvi + 306 pp, hbk, £66)

The defences of duress and necessity are said to apply where a person is compelled to commit a crime under threat of death or serious injury (duress) or to avoid terrible consequences (necessity). These defences receive only grudging recognition in appeal court judgments. The courts have tightly circumscribed duress,[1] said there is no such thing as a necessity defence,[2] and on occasion repackaged

1. *R v Howe* [1987] AC 417; *R v Hasan* [2005] 4 All ER 685.
2. *London Borough of Southwark v Williams* [1971] Ch 734, 744.

necessity scenarios as self-defence.[3] Against this background Dr Eimear Spain's monograph, *The Role of Emotions in Criminal Law Defences: Duress, Necessity and Lesser Evils* questions why some emotions are, in effect, privileged in defeating criminal liability. Why, for instance, is an intentional killing in extreme anger reducible to manslaughter (on the basis of provocation) while an intentional killing in extreme fear must remain murder (because duress is not a defence to murder)?[4]

The Role of Emotions has two main strands. A middle section, chapters 3–5, comprehensively analyses duress and necessity much in the vein of law reform reviews[5] but with the advantage of the kind of sustained research and scholarly reflection that reform project schedules typically do not allow. Spain's assessment of the history of the defences in Chapter 3 reveals their mutable nature and Chapter 4 subjects the defences' current shape to rigorous critical scrutiny, while leaving to Chapter 5 the descriptive and prescriptive analysis of the question of duress and necessity applying in murder cases.

The other strand of *The Role of Emotions* relates emotion theory and what law can learn from it. In Chapter 2 we see that 'emotion' remains a contested concept after centuries of theorising about whether it is a cognitive or physiological function or both. The modern ideas reported by Spain include the claims that emotions have a rational aspect; are occasions of thinking, not simply mechanistic human responses to stimulus; and connect with, rather than exclude, moral judgment.[6] These new views, Spain claims, are at odds with what has for centuries undergirded the law on duress and necessity, so far as they existed. *The Role of Emotions* pays much attention to cognitive appraisal theory, which says that emotions are cognitive: they are more than just feelings and sensations.[7] A person's experience of emotion – which may include physiological changes like a rise in heartbeat – is driven by cognitive appraisal, which in turn is driven by evaluation of the significance of external events in the relevant environment.[8] *The Role of Emotions* defends a moderate cognitive appraisal theory from the opposing view – emotional appraisal theory[9] – which sees emotions as free-standing, thoughtless, non-rational forces of passion.

A brilliant feature of Dr Spain's monograph is its appreciation that to understand and critically evaluate criminal law doctrines we must step outside law. Doctrinal analysis that infers rationale from case law, and then uses it to assess further case law, can only go so far. It can expose incoherency and inconsistency but it cannot, in a non-circular way, tell us whether the law is worth having in the first place. We must interrogate the so-called wisdom of the common law, which largely comes from judges in comparatively benighted times. We need to do this in light of, among

3. *Re A (conjoined twins)* [2001] 2 WLR 480, 536.
4. Spain, *The Role of Emotions*, 66–67.
5. Such as Law Reform Commission, *Consultation Paper on Duress and Necessity* (LRC CP 39–2006).
6. Spain, *The Role of Emotions*, ch 2.
7. ibid 76.
8. ibid 77–79.
9. ibid 83.

other things, neuro-scientific advances. Spain argues for overhaul and replacement with more nuanced criminal defences. She wants the defences reconstituted and her recommendations are well made; indeed *The Role of Emotions* will be an essential resource for any future project on duress and necessity, whether academic research or analysis with a view to criminal law reform or codification. From now on researchers will have to engage with Spain's well-argued recommendations that include making duress potentially available as a defence to murder, expanding the categories of threats that qualify a defendant for duress, and a proposal for a necessity-type defence available on the basis of bringing about the lesser of evils. Duress is to be understood as excusatory and the lesser evils defence as justificatory.[10]

Emotion theory is not alone in driving the book's recommendations. Consider Spain's position on the problem of deviant moral codes and the availability of defences. An example brought up years ago in critique of a purely subjectivist provocation defence was that it made the defence available for a racist who killed in a rage provoked by, as the racist saw it, the victim's effrontery in greeting the racist as an equal.[11] Spain's position is clear that the racist in this example should not succeed with a provocation defence because emotions must be reasonable in order to work in a defendant's favour.[12] (Recall that cognitive appraisal theory lets us speak of emotions as being reasonable or unreasonable.) So while the qualifying threats for duress ought to be expanded to include, say, a threat to falsely imprison, Spain does not envisage a threat to a prized possession grounding duress because, no matter how intensely felt, such fear is not reasonable.[13] Moral reasoning and evaluation – in the judgment of 'reasonable', which remains an evaluative standard even when presented, as it often is, as an empirical account of the typical person – does the argumentative work here, not the science of the emotion. Of course, the point of cognitive appraisal theory is that emotions are constituted by, and are susceptible to, moral evaluation. But whether the moral evaluation is seen as bundled with the emotion or placed separately beside it, as emotional appraisal theory would have it, makes little difference to the conclusion as to what the law should be. Even if the reimagined duress defence did not need new science to enable it, it is nevertheless undoubtedly beneficial for criminal law analysis to be clear-sighted and accurate about the psychological experiences that criminal law regulates. *The Role of Emotions* recognises that whatever cognitive science comes up with, it will still take moral argument to alter existing criminal law in its mediation between liberty and punishment.

DAVID PRENDERGAST
Lecturer, Trinity College Dublin

---

10. ibid ch 6.
11. Finbarr McAuley and J Paul McCutcheon, *Criminal Liability* (Round Hall 2000) 877, citing Jeremy Horder, *Provocation and Responsibility* (Oxford University Press 1992).
12. Spain, *The Role of Emotions*, 270.
13. ibid 273.

CORRUPTION LAW

by Imelda Higgins (Round Hall 2012) ISBN: 978-1-85800-669-7 (lxviii + 589 pp, hbk, €195)

This book is the first legal textbook to comprehensively address Irish corruption law. Indeed, as practitioners and students of this area will know, there is a marked dearth of research into many areas of corruption law in Ireland, despite its growing significance during the past two decades. This book aims to fill the lacuna that has hitherto existed in Irish corruption law scholarship.

The author, Imelda Higgins, is an experienced practitioner and lecturer in corruption law. A practising barrister, she has worked in an advisory capacity for the Tribunal of Inquiry into Certain Planning Matters and Payments and presently lectures in corruption law at Trinity College Dublin. Higgins has published widely on corruption law and regularly participates in conferences in this area.

In this outstanding book, Higgins offers a detailed account of corruption law in Ireland, while at the same time placing it in its broader theoretical and international context. The Ethics Acts 1995 and 2001, the Electoral Act 1997, and the Local Election (Disclosure of Donations and Expenditure) Act 1999 are analysed in detail for the first time, providing practitioners and students with a useful guide to this complex area of law.

Chapter 1 provides a helpful introduction to corruption law. It details various international anti-corruption efforts including by the OECD, UN, Council of Europe and EU. It also introduces the subject of corruption in Ireland, providing an overview of the various tribunals of inquiry.

Chapter 2 gives a detailed analysis of conflicts of interests and discusses them within the broader corruption framework. Higgins places emphasis on the importance of controlling conflicts of interest as an effective method of preventing corruption.

Chapter 3 deals with the important subject of political finance. The chapter provides a helpful overview of the topic, outlines relevant international instruments, and then examines domestic provisions at greater length. The Electoral Act 1997 and the Local Elections Act are examined in detail; the personal scope of these provisions, donation restrictions, electoral expenditure limits, public disclosure, exchequer funding, enforcement, and sanctions are comprehensively reviewed. Higgins provides a compelling analysis of Irish political finance law, and points out the significant deficiencies in the present regime.

Chapter 4 deals with access to information and emphasises the central role of transparency in the fight against corruption. This chapter provides a comprehensive treatment of Ireland's freedom of information laws, including a detailed analysis of the Freedom of Information Act; the author discusses the scope of its application, the right of access, grounds of refusal, active disclosure requirements (ss 15–16), correction of personal information (s 17), and the right to reasons (s 18). The Information Commissioner's role is also considered, as are the practicalities of exercising FOI rights.

Finally, there is a succinct analysis of the Official Secrets Act 1963. Higgins discusses provisions regarding the disclosure of official and confidential information, and the retention of official documents.

Chapter 5 covers bribery law in Ireland and helpfully places it within its broader international context. The chapter opens with a brief theoretical discussion of anti-bribery laws, highlighting the detrimental effect of bribery on equality, trust, morality, and democracy as well as outlining its economic consequences.

The chapter then moves on to examine the ways in which bribery may be criminalised. It discusses the merits and demerits of the improper payment model; the improper influence model; the improper conduct model; the agent principle model; and the market model. Relevant international instruments are also considered, including the OECD, Council of Europe, the UN, and the EU. The chapter then provides a detailed analysis of Irish bribery law. It starts by addressing the common law offence before analysing the statutory bribery offences, including the anti-bribery measures proposed by the Criminal Justice (Corruption) Bill 2012. Bribery offences in the UK and the US are also addressed – this is a useful discussion for Irish practitioners in light of the extensive extraterritorial reach of the British and American anti-bribery legislation. Higgins then provides a helpful overview of corporate compliance policies.

Next she addresses misconduct in public office, including the elements of the offence and sanctions. She also discusses accounting offences under international conventions and Irish law. A brief consideration of reporting offences brings this excellent chapter to a close.

Chapter 6 examines money laundering. It discusses the origins of money laundering controls, places money laundering within the corruption framework, and provides an overview of the money-laundering process. International conventions on money laundering are discussed, including the UN, OECD, and Council of Europe. The work of the Financial Action Task force and the Basel Committee are also considered, as is the broader international approach to money laundering. Finally, the chapter offers a valuable analysis of the Irish law on money laundering: it outlines the money-laundering offences, the methods of prevention and detection, and the powers of investigation.

Chapter 7 deals with asset confiscation – an important tool in the armoury of law enforcement agencies tasked with fighting corruption. The chapter commences by discussing the usefulness of asset confiscation as a weapon against corrupt activity. It outlines types of asset recovery and discusses the basis of asset confiscation. Next it considers the quantification of the proceeds of corruption, including contracts obtained through bribery, avoidance of expenses or losses, and expedition of delays. International asset-confiscation measures are succinctly discussed, followed by a detailed consideration of Irish law on asset confiscation. This analysis focuses on conviction-based confiscation, freezing orders, non-conviction based recovery, and forfeiture of instrumentalities of crime.

Chapter 8, the final chapter of this impressive book, analyses the enforcement of anti-corruption measures. It provides an overview of enforcement, including prevention measures, investigations and sanctions. International conventions, including the UN, Council of Europe, and the OECD are considered. Barriers to prosecution are analysed in some depth, including parliamentary privilege, cabinet confidentiality, whistleblower protection, and legal professional privilege.

The central role of law enforcement agencies in the fight against corruption is also examined. An Garda Síochána's functions and structure, as well as their powers of investigation, are reviewed, as are the structure, functions and powers of the Criminal Assets Bureau. Finally, there is a discussion of the role of official inquiries, including Oireachtas Committees of Inquiry, Commissions of Investigation and Tribunals of Inquiry.

This erudite and comprehensive textbook represents an invaluable contribution to scholarship on Irish corruption law. It is meticulously researched throughout, and draws extensively on international research in this area. The author's vast experience and encyclopaedic knowledge of corruption law, coupled with her succinct and lucid style, has enabled her to produce a book that no practitioner, academic, or student of Irish corruption law should be without.

MARK HARTEN
Judicial Assistant, Courts Service

EUROPEAN UNION LAW
by David Edward and Robert Lane (Edward Elgar 2013) ISBN 978-0-85793-105-4
(ccxi + 931 pp + Annexes + Index, hbk, £250)

This is an outstandingly good book by a former Scots judge of the European Court of Justice and a Senior Lecturer in Edinburgh. It is concise, clear, authoritative and extremely thorough. As well as stating the legal rules, it is practical, because it summarises how they have been implemented. There are many short, frank, objective comments. Speculation is avoided, but unresolved questions are pointed out. Short, crucial passages from judgments are given. There are many citations to national courts, not only to French, German, and British courts, but also to the courts of the 'new' Member States: in this respect it is remarkably comprehensive. There are many illuminating explanations, describing the underlying constitutional issues and controversies in various states. The book moves easily from the judgments of the European Court of Justice to the related judgments of national courts. National law and European law are integrated and explained. In short, it provides an excellent understanding of how EU law works as an organic, coherent whole. By integrating discussion of EU and national institutional issues, it is a good example of the kind of analysis that will be more and more essential in all textbooks as the EU and national legal systems become increasingly intertwined.

The book begins with a summary of the history of the EU (26 clear, concise pages). The EU structure and basic rules are set out and discussed (54 pages). Political institutions and procedures, and other bodies such as the Court of Auditors and the External Action Service, get 63 pages. The Court of Justice is dealt with in 120 pages (including a careful and detailed commentary on art 267), and the sources, nature and methods of EU law in 125 pages. The list of European Court cases cited covers over 70 pages: almost every important judgment of the Court is cited, and many judgments of national courts. What is essentially the second half of the book summarises the substantive law of the EU, including a long section (120 pages) on competition law.

The style and flavor of the book is best illustrated by a few examples. The recital in the Lisbon Preamble on democratic legitimacy is 'prosaic, almost tired'. Ratification of Lisbon involved 'bribing (not too strong a word) the Irish voters and the Czech President… by means of promises… as to future Treaty amendment'. Accession of a state to Euratom but not to the Union would be a 'constitutional/institutional Laocoön'. The various provisions on qualified majority voting are a 'labyrinth', which could not be said 'remotely to serve the simplification and efficiency in decision-making which was the primary clarion call of the Laeken Declaration'. OLAF, the anti-fraud office, which investigates among other things handling of EU funds by national authorities, 'is kept very, very busy'. The Court of Justice 'is never overtly critical of the judgment of the General Court, but, just occasionally, an Advocate General is'. As a general rule 'and perhaps a nod to national sensitivities and subsidiarity, exhaustive harmonization, never common, is falling further out of favour'. Article 352 TFEU 'is an extraordinary device to find in a federal constitution, never mind an international treaty'. (It is, however, more natural in a new kind of legal system that was always intended to change and develop, and not all the consequences of which could be foreseen.) The wider standing given by the Lisbon amendment of art 263 may be 'a poisoned chalice' because of the rule that a party that had standing but failed to use it may not subsequently challenge the act in question in a national court.

Formal legal rules are usefully supplemented by information, eg on the background to the few cases in which one Member State has brought another before the Court (page 193), statistics of cases brought by the Commission (page 204), and requests for preliminary rulings from different Member States (pages 275–77), and on the duration of various cases (page 184). Four of the ten judges appointed on the 2004 accessions had previously been judges in the Court of Human Rights, and that may have encouraged the Court of Justice to refer more often to Strasbourg case law. These examples illustrate the practical approach of the whole book: it explains how the legal system works.

Throughout, a very large number of judgments and other official documents are referred to. There are useful explanations of terminology in various languages. Articles in law journals are cited very selectively, but many issues that have been the subject of controversy are referred to and, in most cases, resolved briefly and clearly. The legal consequences of the dismemberment of a Member State are discussed carefully (pages 80–84), concluding that 'to allow one part of a dissolving Member State, to the exclusion of another, to succeed to its membership would be to deprive the other part(s) of acquired rights and their populations of citizenship rights'. This is contrary to the view, unduly based on public international law and not sufficiently on EU law, adopted by the UK government in connection with Scottish independence. The questions of direct effect and primacy (pages 293–307) and the less important but more complex questions of the 'exception of illegality' (pages 237–38) are explained with clarity, carefully avoiding overstatement and over-simplification. The constitutional issues in the UK, Germany and the Czech Republic are explained in a way that brings out the parallels between them. The main problems concerning directives are concisely analysed (pages 342–56) and the four rules that reduce the anomalies resulting from the absence of 'horizontal' direct effects (obligations for private parties) are explained: interpretation of national law where possible so as to comply (*Marleasing*), control mechanisms for national measures (*CIA Securities*), *Francovich* damages, and the direct effect of certain General Principles. This last rule, articulated in *Kücükdeveci* and perhaps illustrated in *Agonese*, says that a general principle may be linked to a directive and may create obligations for private parties even though the directive itself would not. As the authors say, 'This is new, and faces formidable logical and practical obstacles. These rules… are still evolving and their full implications are not yet known.' In another important comment on future implications, the authors say that the Court has not yet built upon the *Eurocoton* judgment that mere inaction when there is a duty to act can constitute a refusal that can be challenged under art 263.

The section on General Principles (42 pages) is particularly useful. This section includes fundamental rights and their sources in the constitutional laws of Member States, the European Convention on Human Rights and the Charter. The most important rights are to effective judicial protection and a fair hearing, respect for human life and dignity, and respect for family life (furthest developed in connection with expulsion of family members, Union citizenship, and judicial cooperation in matrimonial cases). 'Constitutional' rights include the right to equal treatment, the principle of legal certainty (which gets a fuller discussion than proportionality), and procedural rights. (The test of proportionality under EU law is now the subject of a substantial difference of opinion between the English Court of Appeal and the Inner House of the Court of Session, in two cases brought by *Sinclair Collis*).

This book is about law, not politics. But it would have been useful to explain why the Commission has the exclusive right to propose EU measures (the 'Community Method'). The Commission's responsibility is to make proposals that reconcile, as far as possible, the interests of any minority and those of the majority. Its proposals may be adopted by qualified majority, but they may be amended only by unanimity. This is a safeguard for minority interests, to make majority voting acceptable, which is not sufficiently understood. It explains why the Commission is intentionally technocratic, and it means that the European

Parliament has no right to initiate legislation, something that MEPs resent, and profess not to understand.

One of the most important changes made by the Lisbon Treaties lies in art 255 TFEU, which set up a committee to assess nominees for judgeships in Luxembourg. This is mentioned, but its importance is not stressed. This committee has already advised against seven nominees, and is providing valuable pressure on Member States to nominate only well-qualified candidates. A similar committee is needed for the Court of Human Rights.

The second half of the book summarises the substantive law of the EU. Inevitably, it is more descriptive, although there are shrewd and practical comments. A great deal of information is compressed, very clearly, into a relatively short space. Some of the complications resulting from differences between the citizenship laws of Member States are explained. The obligations of private parties resulting, directly and indirectly, from Treaty rules on free movement of goods are becoming more extensive. Unresolved problems are mentioned: how far non-discrimination principles bind private parties (*Angonese*, *Mangold*, *Kücükdevici*) and the implications of Union citizenship as indicated by the Court in *Grzelczyk* and stressed by Advocate General Sharpston in *Ruiz Zambrano*. Some of the complexities of 'mixed' agreements are outlined, including those caused by the duty of sincere cooperation under art 4(3) TEU, the great importance of which is stressed in other contexts in the section on enforcement of Union rights. The discussion of freedom to provide and to receive services is particularly clear. It is said, rightly, that the Services Directive 'will doubtless become a focus of spirited litigation'. All these comments are useful. But, while the first half of the book is a first-class analysis of the constitutional structure of the EU, for completeness the second half would need to be read in conjunction with specialised works. For example, approximately 15 clear but brief pages outline the law on abuse of dominance under art 102: in comparison, this is now the subject of all of an excellent book by O'Donoghue, *The Law and Economics of Article 102 EU*, in 18 chapters and hundreds of pages.

The authors are willing to express forceful opinions. Only two seem a little unfair. First, it is said that art 2(2) TFEU on the concurrent jurisdiction of the EU and Member States is 'trite'. But it is basic in anything resembling a confederal system, and it is surely valuable to have it said clearly. Before the Lisbon Treaty, there were demands for a Treaty statement on national and Union competences. Secondly, it is twice noted that although the Court may review an EU measure designed to give effect to international Treaty obligations, it does not review their validity under international law (which of course is correct). But it is said that the Court does not extend the courtesy to allowing Member States' constitutional rules to override EU law. This is confusing (the situations are surely different: Member States are bound by the Treaty but the international community is not), and it is necessary for any effective legal system that the laws of constituent members should not prevail over the common rules in the sphere in which those rules legitimately apply.

The authors have succeeded in saying new and important things, concisely and clearly, about a legal system of which one might think there was little new to say. This is an important book, as well as a useful, interesting and well-written one. As Advocate General Sharpston says in the foreword: 'it is very rare to find a book on EU law that manages to combine such deep scholarship, accurate insider knowledge and truly comprehensive coverage with readability. This is a learned text that wears its learning lightly.'

JOHN TEMPLE LANG
Cleary Gottlieb Steen & Hamilton LLP, Brussels

RELIGION, LAW AND THE IRISH STATE
by Eoin Daly (Clarus Press 2012) ISBN: 978-1-905536-49-8 (xxxii + 464 pp, pbk, €80)

Eoin Daly has written an interesting and richly theoretically-informed account of the relationship between religion, law and the Irish State. He gives a detailed account of the norms that characterize the Irish approach to the relationship between religion and law and places these norms in a comparative context. His book provides a well-argued critique of the failure of Irish judges and legislators to adequately articulate or develop the key principles that appear to underpin the approach of the Irish State to this increasingly controversial issue.

This work consists of an introduction along with chapters on religion in the constitutional order, religious freedom, equality and discrimination, two chapters on the patronage system in the educational field, separation of church and state, denominational autonomy and finally, blasphemy. Curiously, there is neither a concluding chapter nor a bibliography. A key theme of the book is that 'the constitutional framework has not provided sufficiently robust protection against the risk of domination of citizens' choices, arising from dangerous alliances of civil and religious power and from any arrogation of civil competence to legislate for religious ends and purposes' (14). The author sees this as arising from the text of the Constitution itself but also from the 'implausibly narrow and conservative interpretation' accorded to the provisions relevant to religion by the judiciary. (14).

The introduction and chapter on the Constitution provide a fascinating account of the evolving role of religion in the constitutional order. Daly notes how the close relationship between the State and the Catholic church and the overwhelming influence of that church over law and society in the early decades of the State never resulted in formal establishment. The Constitution gave, he notes, 'a remarkably inadequate account of the relationship between the State and religion' (8). Indeed he convincingly argues that 'the political and social influence of the hierarchy was such that it needed no formal powers to exert domination in the political and social spheres' (8). Daly is certainly correct in his conclusion that in Ireland 'the constitutional separation of civil and religious authority has been incapable of securing the liberal aims that have historically underpinned this model, in particular the aims of privacy, personal autonomy and freedom of choice in religious matters' (9). However, I would add that 'the dog that doesn't bark' is often as important as the dog that barks and the failure to enshrine the Catholic Church's informal power in the Constitution was ultimately quite important as it ensured that the Constitution did not serve so as to obstruct the liberalizing project which radically changed the role and influence of religion on Irish law and society from the 1960s onwards.

The chapter on the Constitution is the richest in the book and shows in an extremely enlightening manner the tension between different elements of the 1937 Constitution; namely the 'Republican element where sovereignty is with the people and recognition of God and religion as a higher source of authority' (23). Daly notes how religion was, unsurprisingly, part of the 'interpretative fabric' of the Constitution but in a way which, as was shown in the striking down of the ban on the manufacture or importation of contraceptives in *McGee v Attorney General*,[1] sometimes went against Catholic teaching.

Daly also rightly notes how constitutional interpretation has not been immune from the secularization of Irish society to the extent that 'the use of religion as a background moral framework for constitutional interpretation has all but disappeared' (49). He notes however that there is 'little sense of what might replace it' (50) and is critical of the failure of Irish judges to 'locate an alternative principled basis for constitutional adjudication which conceives of the constitutional provisions as expressing a deeper scheme of political-moral principle [...] yet which is addressed to the political structure of society alone rather than controversial comprehensive theories of the good on which citizens are deeply and permanently divided' (40). This criticism is echoed in the chapter on religious freedom which Daly notes has been interpreted by the courts in a 'markedly ad hoc' manner (82). Whether positive accommodation of religion is required or merely permitted by the Constitution has, he notes, been left unclear by decisions of the Supreme Court. In an interesting discussion on the failure to exempt civil registrars from the duty to register civil partnerships, Daly argues that the failure to grant such an exemption 'cannot have been 'the rights of others' as there would be no material disadvantage [once individuals seeking to register partnerships were not denied the relevant service]' (127). Interestingly this is a conclusion that is directly contrary to the conclusion of the European Court of Human Rights in *Eweida and Others v United Kingdom*[2] that measures that aim to prevent the harm to dignity in discriminatory acts can be seen as protecting the rights of others, even in the absence of service deprivation.

Chapter 3 focuses on the relationship between equality, discrimination and religious freedom. Daly notes the tension between these norms and the 'remarkable extent' to which 'this claimed interest in religious freedom invariably

1. [1974] IR 1.
2. [2013] ECHR 37.

receives priority in both legislation and case law over the competing claim to non-discrimination' (133). This is the case, he notes, even when the relevant religious body is providing public services or is in receipt of public funds to provide such services. In the area of employment he notes the 'clearly excessive' exemptions for religious employers in the Employment Equality Act while in the context of religious schools he notes how exemptions allowing religious schools to discriminate in the recruitment of pupils has meant that the prohibition of religious discrimination in this area has been 'denuded of force' in the light of the preponderance of religious schools. (143). Although the current system forces many to feign religious belief in order to access state-funded schooling, jurisprudence and policy in this area have been, Daly notes, 'curiously devoid of any reflection on how religious discrimination might, rather than representing the exercise of religious freedom by denominational institutions, actually undermine the religious freedom of those against whom it is practiced' (149).

Chapters 4 and 5 analyse religious freedom under the 'patronage model' under which public education is largely devolved to religious institutions. He shows how the current system was initially justified on the basis of 'the intrinsic good of religion and triumphalist Catholicism' but is now justified by defenders on grounds of choice (245). Daly very effectively demolishes such choice arguments. He shows both how the neoliberal philosophy of school choice is inconsistent with the 'nationalist and communitarian norms of the Constitution' and that the current system fails to provide choice in any event as there is no mechanism to actually link patron recognition and parental choice and parental choice rights are subject to demographic factors (245-7). He is very critical of the Supreme Court decision in the *School Chaplains* case where the Court allowed a textually-unfounded right to religious education to qualify the negative right to be free of indoctrination (222) and notes the degree to which a patronage model ignores heterogeneity within religious groups and may empower powerful orthodox strands within minority religions to a dangerous degree (283).

Chapter 6 deals with the issue of separation of church and state. Daly is highly critical of the very limited jurisprudence in this area which he argues has 'focused on the literal and technical meaning of the term "endow" in Article 44.2.2 [….] and had largely overlooked the deeper lattice of constitutional values and purposes […] which might guide a broader and more contextual approach to its interpretation' (319). He contrasts the Irish case law with the much richer French and American jurisprudence in this area and notes the failure of the Supreme Court to read the non-endowment clause in the light of Ireland's history of sectarian strife and the role such strife played in the reasons for non-establishment (348). In a similar vein, chapter 7 focuses on legislative intervention in the religious function. Daly is very critical of the ruling in *McNally v Ireland*[3] upholding the imposition of criminal sanctions for the selling of fraudulent Mass cards. Again, he compares Irish jurisprudence in

3. [2009] ICHE 573.

this area to French and US case law. The final chapter deals with the issue of blasphemy. Daly notes the refusal of the Supreme Court to give a definition of the constitutional offence of blasphemy in the Corway case, seeing it as part of the secularizing trend in constitutional interpretation noted in chapter 1. This has extended to making the secular legitimation of hurt feelings the rationale for the 2010 legislative codification of the offence.

This book is an outstanding contribution to Irish legal scholarship. It provides an in-depth analysis of the major decisions of the Irish courts and the major legislative interventions in the area of religion and law. Most importantly it places this case law and legislation in a broader theoretical and comparative context. His book is accordingly the perfect antidote to what the author rightly identifies as the sometimes narrow, literal and theoretically-underdeveloped approach of the Irish judges and legislators in this increasingly controversial area. As Keynes so perceptively argued: 'The ideas of economists and political philosophers, both when they are right and when they are wrong, are more powerful than is commonly understood. Indeed, the world is ruled by little else. Practical men, who believe themselves to be quite exempt from any intellectual influence, are usually the slaves of some defunct economist.'[4] The interpretation of law and particularly constitutional law, cannot merely be a question of 'common-sense'. Perhaps the formation of the new Court of Appeal will allow the Supreme Court more scope to fulfill Daly's wish that constitutional interpretation may reflect a greater sense of what he calls 'a deeper scheme of political-moral principle' underlying the Constitution.

To draw general principles from the limited range of cases and legislation that exists in this area is a difficult task. In these circumstances, it is perhaps inevitable that a degree of repetition creeps in. It may have been advisable to reduce the two and a half chapters dedicated to discussion of the patronage model in the education system somewhat. The absence of a concluding chapter was regrettable as Daly has very insightful things to say as is shown by the very compelling analysis of in the first two chapters of the book where he ties trends in constitutional adjudication together in an extremely compelling and engaging manner.

Overall, this is an excellent piece of work. Its analysis is rich and sophisticated and it forms a major contribution to our understanding of the approach of the Irish State in this increasingly important area.

RONAN MCCREA
Senior Lecturer, University College London

4. J Maynard Keynes, *The General Theory of Employment, Interest and Money* (Palgrave Macmillan, 1936) Book 6, Chapter 24, Section 2, 376.